DISPLAY SYSTEMS

DISPLAY SYSTEMS
Design and Applications

Edited by

Lindsay W. MacDonald,
Cheltenham and Gloucester College of Higher Education, UK,

and

Anthony C. Lowe,
IBM TJ Watson Research Centre, USA

Published in Association with the *Society for Information Display*

JOHN WILEY & SONS
Chichester • New York • Weinheim • Brisbane • Singapore • Toronto

Other Wiley Editorial Offices

John Wiley & Sons, Inc., 605 Third Avenue,
New York, NY 10158-0012, USA

Jacaranda Wiley Ltd, 33 Park Road, Milton,
Queensland 4064, Australia

John Wiley & Sons (Canada) Ltd, 22 Worcester Road,
Rexdale, Ontario M9W 1L1, Canada

John Wiley & Sons (Asia) Pte Ltd, 2 Clementi Loop #02-01,
Jin Xing Distripark, Singapore 0512

Designations used by companies to distinguish their products are often claimed as tradmarks. In all instances where John Wiley & Sons is aware of a claim, the product names appear in Initial Capital or all Capital letters. Readers, however, should contact the appropriate companies for more complete information regarding trademarks and registration.

British Library Cataloguing in Publication Data

A catalogue record for this book is available from the British Library

ISBN 0 471 95870 0

Typeset in 10/12pt Times by Laser Words, Chennai, India
Printed and bound in Great Britain by Bookcraft (Bath) Ltd
This book is printed on acid-free paper responsibly manufactured from sustainable forestation, for which at least two trees are planted for each one used for paper production.

Contents

17 Techniques for high-quality, low-cost, colour measurement of CRTs   **329**
Tom Lianza

Colour plates

About the editors

Lindsay MacDonald is Professor of Multimedia Systems at the Cheltenham and Gloucester College of Higher Education in Cheltenham, UK, where he is Head of the Centre for Research in Applied Multimedia (CREAM). His research interests are in digital colour image processing and the usability assessment of multimedia systems. He is also Managing Director of MacColour Ltd, a specialist consultancy in multimedia imaging.

Originally from Australia, Lindsay worked for 18 years for Crosfield Electronics Ltd, the UK's leading manufacturer of professional graphic arts systems. There he was responsible for the design of application software, image processing algorithms and human–computer interfaces for a series of high performance electronic pre-press systems, resulting in over 20 patents for inventions in related fields. He led teams at Crosfield in the development and introduction of two digital cameras, a display colour calibration device and colour management software products. He also managed Crosfield's involvement in three collaborative research projects in colour modelling, image processing and the reproduction of fine art paintings.

Lindsay MacDonald is a Fellow of both the British Computer Society (BCS) and the Institution of Electrical Engineers (IEE), and a Member of the Society for Information Display (SID). He was the co-author of *Computer Generated Color* and co-editor of *Interacting with Virtual Environments*, both published in 1994 by John Wiley & Sons.

Tony Lowe is a Senior Scientist, Program Manager of Advanced Display Technology with the IBM Personal Computer Company in Greenock Scotland, and a member of the IBM Academy of Technology. He received the degrees of B.Sc. (Hons) in chemistry and Ph.D. in interfacial thermodynamics from the University of Southampton. After a postdoctoral fellowship at the University of Victoria, British Columbia, he joined IBM in the UK.

His scientific and managerial career has involved several technical areas, foremost among which has been display technology, from basic research to product development, in which field he has numerous publications and patents. His work in displays has resulted in his twice being assigned into IBM Research Division in the USA. He has recently returned from the most recent of these assignments where, from 1994 to 1996, he initiated and managed a reflective flat panel display research project at the TJ Watson Research Center in New York.

A long standing member of the Society for Information Display, Tony has been active in promoting the extension SID's membership and technical activities within Europe and Asia, where he was responsible for the formation of several new chapters of the society. Following a reorganisation of SID's Executive and geographical structure he was, from 1992 to 1994, the first SID Regional Vice-President for Europe. At the time of publication of this volume he is SID President Elect. He is a member of the International Liquid Crystal Society.

Contributors

Mr Andrew Baird
Human Applications
139 Ashby Road
Loughborough, Leics. LE11 3AD
UK

Dr Timothy Bardsley
Imaging and Displays Research Group
Department of Computer Science
De Montfort University
The Gateway
Leicester LE1 9BH
UK

Prof. Dick Bosman
Gronause Straat 34
7533 BN Enschede
The Netherlands

Dr Jean-Pierre Budin
Institut d'Electronique Fondamentale
Université Paris Sud, Bât. 220
91405 Orsay
France

Mr Patrick Candry
Barco N.V. Projection Systems
Noordlaan 5
Industriezone
B-8520 Kuurne
Belgium

Mr Richard Chimera
Department of Computer Science
University of Maryland
College Park, MD 20742
USA

Dr Jean Glasser
DRI/SI Groupement Composants
France Télécom
6 Place d'Alleray
75505 Paris Cédex 05
France

Mr Andrew Hanson
Division of Quantum Metrology
National Physical Laboratory
Teddington, Middx. TW11 OLW
UK

Mr Nigel Heaton
Human Applications
139 Ashby Road
Loughborough, Leics. LE11 3AD
UK

Dr Richard Holmes
Design Director
Virtuality Entertainment Ltd
3 Oswin Road
Brailsford Industrial Park
Leicester LE3 1HR
UK

Mr Ninad Jog
Department of Computer Science
University of Maryland
College Park, MD 20742
USA

Mr Tom Lianza
Technical Director
Sequel Imaging Inc.
25 Nashua Road

Londonderry, NH 03053
USA

Dr Anthony C. Lowe
IBM TJ Watson Research Center
Route 134 (10-106)
Yorktown Heights, NY 10598
USA

Prof. Ernst Lüder
Institut für Netzwerk- und Systemtheorie
Universität Stuttgart
Pfaffenwaldring 47
70550 Stuttgart 80
Germany

Prof. Lindsay W. MacDonald
Centre for Research in Applied Multimedia
Cheltenham and Gloucester College of
Higher Education
Broadlands, The Park
Cheltenham, Glos. GL50 2QF
UK

Dr Carl Machover
Machover Associates Corporation
152A Longview Avenue
White Plains, NY 10605
USA

Mr Jim McKenzie
Human Applications
139 Ashby Road
Loughborough, Leics. LE11 3AD
UK

Dr Alan Mosley
GEC Hirst Research Centre
Elstree Way
Borehamwood, Herts. WD6 1RX
UK

Mr Amboise Parker
SAGEM
Centre de Pontoise
Chaussée Jules César
95520 Osny
France

Dr David W. Parker
Philips Research Laboratories
Cross Oak Lane
Redhill, Surrey RH1 5HA
UK

Dr Philip K. Robertson
CSIRO Division of Information Technology

GPO Box 664
Canberra, ACT 2601
Australia

Mr Ludwig Selhuber
SAGEM
Centre de Pontoise
Chaussée Jules César
95520 Osny
France

Dr Ian Sexton
Imaging and Displays Research Group
Department of Computer Science
De Montfort University
The Gateway
Leicester LE1 9BH
UK

Prof. Ben Shneiderman
Director of Human–Computer Interaction
Laboratory
Department of Computer Science
University of Maryland
College Park, MD 20742
USA

Dr Louis D. Silverstein
VCD Sciences Inc.
9695 East Yucca Street
Scottsdale, AZ 85260
USA

Mr A.A. Seyno Sluyterman
Philips Display Components
Building RAF2, P.O. Box 218
5600 MD Eindhoven
The Netherlands

Mr Ren Stimart
General Electric Information Service
401 N. Washington Street
Rockville, MD 20850
USA

Mr David White
General Electric Information Service
401 N. Washington Street
Rockville, MD 20850
USA

Preface

Display technology and (just as importantly) display systems have been subject to rapid development over the past few years. This development has been substantially enabled by the advances in performance and simultaneous reduction in the cost/performance ratio of computer systems. So rapid has been the rate of this development that users are increasingly expecting, and can increasingly afford, almost unlimited resolution and performance from display systems.

Such customer expectations create additional challenges for the display systems engineer and for the designer of any product that uses a display system. What performance is possible? What are the limits? What is permissible or not in terms of standards requirements and legislation? What are the trade-offs between cost, size, resolution, image quality, weight, power consumption, etc.? Which new display technologies are becoming available that might be more appropriate for the application?

For any display-based product to be successful, the needs of the application must be properly matched to the capabilities of the display system. This match can only be made in the context of the whole product design and development process. It must start with the analysis of market requirements, including an understanding of the tasks and needs of the users. It must figure in the prototyping and refining of the user interface and transaction dialogues. And it must be central to the integration of the display with the computer platform hardware and operating system software.

Seamless matching of the display to the application requires an understanding of system design from many perspectives, and brings to bear multidisciplinary skills in hardware, software, human factors, imaging, usability assessment and many other fields. The continuing development of display technology is just as much driven by the needs of new applications (in multimedia and virtual reality, for example) as the applications are shaped to exploit the capabilities of displays.

Recognizing these issues and realizing the need to create a forum where representatives of the wide range of disciplines encompassed by this subject could meet and interact, the European Region of the Society for Information Display (SID) organised an international two-day conference, 'Getting the Best from State-of-the-Art Display Systems', at the National Gallery, London, in February 1995. This event brought together a number of the leading experts from around the world and succeeded in placing the closer integration of display capabilities with application needs on the agenda for leading display system developers.

The objective of this volume is to extend the discussion to a wider audience. It contains a majority of the papers presented at the London conference, the authors of which are all recognised experts in their fields. Following the conference, all the papers were sent for external review by at least one independent reviewer, and, in addition to the requested revisions, many of the papers have also been greatly expanded and their references updated. Our intention has been to present as complete a coverage of the subject as possible within the obvious constraints of space and time to publication, since this is a rapidly developing field.

The book is divided into three sections. The first deals with the requirements for display systems and what drives them. The second section deals with display technology — what it can deliver today, the constraints and limitations on future development, and some predictions of future trends. The third section deals with display characterisation, highlighting the influence of display technology on characterisation methods. It also deals with the ergonomic requirements for display systems with some emphasis on how these are influenced by increasingly comprehensive standards and, more recently, by legislation.

Thus we have sought to provide sufficient breadth and depth on the subject of Display Systems to make this book useful to professionals across all the wide range of disciplines this subject embraces. We are pleased to offer this as the first in a series of SID books on display engineering, and we gratefully acknowledge the strong support that SID has provided throughout.

Finally, this preface would be incomplete without acknowledgment to our wives Jean and Sandra, whom we thank for their forbearance and unwavering support over these past months.

Tony Lowe
Lindsay MacDonald

Abbreviations

AC	Alternating Current
ADB	Apple Desktop Bus
ADC	Analogue to Digital Converter
AM	Active Matrix
ANSI	American National Standards Institute
API	Application Program Interface
ARPA	Advanced Research Projects Agency
ASTM	American Society for Testing and Materials
ATC	Air Traffic Control
BS	British Standard
CAD	Computer Aided Design
CAE	Computer Aided Engineering
CAM	Computer Aided Manufacturing
CAT	Computer Assisted Tomography
CCD	Charge Coupled Device
CCIR	Consultative Committee for International Radio
CD-ROM	Compact Disk–Read Only Memory
CIE	Commission Internationale de lÉclairage
CMD	Colour Matrix Display
CMF	Colour Matching Function
CR	Contrast Ratio
CRT	Cathode Ray Tube
CVD	Capacitive Voltage Discharge
DAC	Digital to Analogue Converter
DC	Direct Current
DIN	Deutsche Industrie Normen
DIS	Draft International Standard
DMD	Digital Micro-mirror Device
DOS	Disk Operating System
DSE	Display Screen Equipment
DTP	Desk Top Publishing
EBU	European Broadcasting Union
EC	European Commission
EEC	European Economic Community (now the European Union)
EFL	Equivalent Focal Length

EIA	Electronic Industries Association
ELD	Electro-Luminescent Display
FAA	Federal Aviation Authority
FED	Field Emission Display
FLCD	Ferroelectric Liquid Crystal Display
FOV	Field Of View
FPD	Flat Panel Display
GIS	Geographical Information Systems
GUI	Graphic User Interface
HCI	Human-Computer Interface or Human-Computer Interaction
HDD	Head-Down Display
HDTV	High Definition Television
HMD	Helmet-Mounted Display or Head-Mounted Display
HSE	Health and Safety Executive
HUD	Head-Up Display
HVS	Human Visual System
IC	Integrated Circuit
ICC	International Colour Consortium (also known as InterColor)
IDRC	International Display Research Conference
IEC	International Electrotechnical Commission
IR	Infra-Red
ISO	International Standards Organization
IT	Information Technology
ITO	Indium Tin Oxide
IVR	Immersive Virtual Reality
JND	Just Noticeable Difference
LAN	Local Area Network
LCD	Liquid Crystal Display
LED	Light Emitting Diode
LSF	Line-Spread Function
LUT	Look-Up Table
MFD	Microtip Fluorescent Display
MIM	Metal–Insulator–Metal
MPRII	Swedish National Board for Measurement and Testing (the abbreviation comes from the board's initials in Swedish)
MRF	Markov Random Fields
MTBF	Mean Time Between Failures
MTF	Modulation Transfer Function
NA	Numerical Aperture
NASA	National Aeronautics and Space Administration
NHK	Nippon Hoso Kyokai (Japanese National Television Corporation)
NMS	National Measurement System (in the UK)
NPL	National Physical Laboratory
OSF	Open Software Foundation
PC	Personal Computer
PDP	Plasma Display Panel

PM	Passive Matrix
PSF	Point-Spread Function
PST	Primary, Secondary, Tertiary
QFD	Quality Function Deployment
R&D	Research and Development
RGB	Red, Green, Blue
RSI	Repetitive Strain Injury
SID	Society for Information Display
SPD	Spectral Power Distribution
STN	Super-Twisted Nematic
TFEL	Thin Film Electro-Luminescent
TFT	Thin Film Transistor
TQM	Total Quality Management
TV	Television
UK	United Kingdom
UV	Ultra-Violet
VDT	Visual Display Terminal
VDU	Visual Display Unit
VDS	Visual Display System
VESA	Video Electronics Standards Association
VFD	Vacuum Fluorescent Display
VGA	Video Graphics Architecture
ViDEOS	Video Display Engineering and Optimatization System
VOC	Voice Of the Customer
VR	Virtual Reality
VRD	Virtual Retinal Display
WRULD	Work Related Upper Limb Disorder

PART 1

Applications

What drives the requirements for displays?

Contents

How applications have driven display requirements

Carl Machover

1.1 INTRODUCTION

Throughout the history of information displays and computer graphics, application requirements have always been a driving factor on the design of displays. Back in 1972 the author wrote an article for the *SID Journal* entitled 'Interactive CRT terminal selection' in which he described a systematic method for evaluating various terminal types in terms of the application requirements. The recommended procedure was:

A   The various types of commercially available terminals are categorised.
B   Relevant performance characteristics are listed.
C   A numeric value is assigned to each of these characteristics for each of the terminal categories.

When that article was written the application requirements generally far exceeded the capability of the available display technology and it was critical to get the best fit between the application and the available displays. Today display technology generally is not the limiting factor, but it still remains important to compare display requirements against application requirements to get the 'best fit'. This chapter addresses some of the issues involved.

Broadly, the applications for computer graphic displays can be categorised as industrial/commercial, military and consumer, representing about 72 percent, 18 percent and 10

Table 1.1 Worldwide forecasts for commercial and industrial computer graphics applications, 1995–2000

Application	1995	($bn)	2000	($bn)
CAD/CAM	$11.9	27%	$15.2	18%
Art/animation	$ 3.4	8%	$ 7.4	9%
Multimedia/presentation[a]	$14.7	34%	$29.5	36%
Real-time simulation	$ 0.7	2%	$ 1.3	2%
Scientific visualisation	$ 2.9	7%	$ 6.5	8%
Graphic arts	$ 4.0	9%	$11.2	14%
Virtual reality	$ 0.4	1%	$ 2.1	3%
Other	$ 5.3	12%	$ 8.7	10%
Total	$43.3		$81.9	

[a]Includes desktop video.
Source: Machover Associates Corp., © 1995.

percent respectively of the estimated $60 billion worldwide market in 1995. Table 1.1 lists some specific industrial/commercial applications and their estimated revenues in 1995 and 2000. Computer graphics has certainly moved from being 'a cure for no known disease' in the early 1960s to being 'a cure for every known disease' in the mid-1990s!

History suggests, however, that display applications were not broadly implemented until the displays provided the kind of performance characteristics that the user of the application found necessary. Tektronix Inc. has characterised the customer environment as having four types of users — *innovative, early adopter, late adopter* and *conservative*. While the innovator is anxious to try new, emerging technologies and is willing to tolerate performance that may not be ideal, the rest of the user community, which represents the bulk of the market, is much less tolerant of inadequate performance.

This chapter presents a review of the principal applications for displays and their salient characteristics, followed by a discussion of the most important display parameters that are influenced by applications, including resolution, addressability, brightness, colour, flicker/image motion, field of view, display size, health and safety, and price/performance.

1.2 APPLICATIONS OF DISPLAYS

Computer-Aided Design (CAD) can be the most demanding application for computer generated electronic displays, often requiring flicker-free images in colour at high resolution with fast response and medium to large screen size. Initially it accounted for the majority of computer graphics applications and the display requirements were among the most severe. The stringency of the requirements has not diminished over the years, but there are now numerous other applications that call for equal or greater stringency in terms of resolution, colour and display quality in general. Thus, the most popular technology for systems designed to meet CAD requirements has been the CRT, which still remains the best display device for attaining the highest visual quality, not only for the rendered image but also for the complex graphic user interface (Figure 1.1 — Colour Plate 1). Flat panel displays are starting to compete with CRTs, however, in particular the active matrix

LCDs, so that the time is perhaps not too distant when FPDs may be used for CAD on desktop workstations as well as on laptop computers.

Computer-Aided Engineering (CAE) is probably the oldest example of the use of computers to aid the development and design of electrical and mechanical products. Initially the display function was restricted to the generation of graphs and tables on plotters, but modern applications go far beyond this limited form of presentation and use the full capabilities of computer generated display systems. Examples of outputs include schematics, wiring diagrams, mechanical drawings and other engineering-related visualisations. These require a display with the full range of resolution, colour and image quality so that CRTs have always been preferred, although FPDs are beginning to meet those needs.

Computer-Aided Manufacturing (CAM) is a companion to CAD and is frequently presented as CAD/CAM as though the two were inseparable. In actuality they are independent applications, with CAM the less demanding. This does not mean that CAM requirements for electronic display performance are minimal, nor that simple alphanumeric displays are adequate. Indeed, the trend is towards more elaborate displays as manufacturing becomes more automated and introduces a need for more information on the factory floor in order to monitor performance adequately. Ruggedness and resistance to dust and chemicals impose additional requirements on the display packaging, and touch panels are often used over the display screen for finger selection of menu items.

Desktop Publishing (DTP) is a broad classification that may include a wide variety of actual applications such as books, magazines, catalogues and brochures. As a result, the actual requirements are quite varied, depending on the quality and type of results expected. Desktop publishing may be described as the set of operations needed to bring together text, graphics, images and design into a final form ready for printing. For example, in the case of a simple in-house publication, the system may be relatively minimal and the display requirements equally minimal, whereas when the final product is a professional design and layout for a fashion magazine, the display requirements are correspondingly severe. Desktop publishing is taking over many of the publishing operations that used to be served by expensive 'high end' pre-press systems, and the total potential of the application remains large. The display requirements for DTP are those of desktop computers; indeed it can be argued that the displays of desktop computers have evolved in order to support DTP applications, with their reliance on legible text, good quality colour image and versatile graphic user interfaces (GUIs).

Graphic Arts industry has seen a revolution in the past 15 years, with the graphic artist's drawing board and airbrush being rapidly replaced by computer-based tools. Software packages now permit the artist to duplicate the effects of drawing or spraying on a textured surface, driven by input devices such as the pressure-sensitive stylus that can be used like a pencil, crayon or brush. Photo-retouching of digital images has replaced the old etching and dyeing of photographic film. The cut-and-paste operations of page layout are now performed routinely in the West by software packages on desktop computers (although in the Far East labour rates are still low enough that the traditional methods remain viable). These applications require large full-colour displays with high resolution and CRTs are still the only option. A unique requirement of the graphic arts applications is the need to match the displayed colour with that produced by the printing process for true 'what you see is what you get' (WYSIWYG) soft-proofing.

Electronic Games are particularly intriguing because they may use either very simple or highly complex graphics. The inexpensive battery operated hand-held models all use flat panel displays based on LCDs and provide rather minimal graphics. The large high-quality units in arcades have complex graphics capabilities and are still based primarily on CRTs. Sophisticated games are increasingly being developed for PCs, taking advantage of the good quality desktop display capabilities. As FPDs become cheaper and more capable of high quality colour graphics, they should begin to replace CRTs because of their advantages of portability and low power consumption. As the use of CD-ROM based games grows, the need for inexpensive, real-time, photorealistic presentations will become dominant.

Mapping is the more common activity, but geographic information systems (GIS) is the more inclusive designation, which can refer to the generation of all types of map-like images. These maps can be quite complex, with multiple colours, although for traditional cartographic maps four or five colours suffice. The resolution requirements can be very high because of the combination of large size and fine detail present in many maps, and CRTs are the preferred technology. Some emerging mobile GIS applications, such as automobile and maritime navigation aids, use the FPD very effectively in a small panel-mounted unit in the cabin of the vehicle.

Medical is a rather broad category containing many different sources of images that need to be presented in electronic form. Examples are the various types of medical images such as X-rays, CAT scans and MRI scans. These can be very dense data sets, requiring high resolution capabilities with colour as a useful adjunct for labelling or the identification of structures, although the original images may be monochromatic. Increasingly, medical applications involve three-dimensional imagery, using voxel rather than pixel data and solid modelling and surface rendering techniques rather than two-dimensional transformations. Although high resolution displays with a wide grey scale capability are generally required, the actual image resolution is frequently determined by the resolution of the scanning device.

Military applications were most advanced prior to the cessation of the Cold War, and supported the majority of research and development activity in electronic displays. The military market comprises a wide range of applications, mirroring the full range of civilian applications but frequently requiring higher performance and more rugged packaging for use in military vehicles and in battle conditions. Avionics displays are categorised as head-down (HDD) or head-up (HUD) or helmet-mounted (HMD). The HUD versions are generally more advanced, with the addition of holographic techniques to generate 3D images, and these are finding new applications in the automotive market. Other military applications for displays are in control and monitoring systems for radar, missiles, vehicle navigation, etc. General information systems in the C^3I category (command, control, communication and intelligence) also find many applications for displays.

Multimedia is a difficult application to classify, as it actually consists of a number of separate applications collected under a single designation. For example, a multimedia installation may be used for animation, art, 3D modelling, presentations or video editing, to name but a few of the possible applications. All of these also exist in their own right with their own display requirements, so the multimedia display requirements should ideally span the full range. This can lead to compromises in design and selection of the display system, in trying to cater for both text/graphics and photorealistic imagery *and* for both static and dynamic images. As a result, the multimedia display specification will be quite demanding and it may prove more economical to satisfy only the more important requirements. This could lead to a system with fewer capabilities than might be possible if best all-round performance were achieved, but the lower cost should compensate for this reduction in performance. While CRTs continue to dominate the workstation, desktop and kiosk operating environments, the addition of CD-ROM players in portable laptop computers is growing, driving the demand for colour FPDs capable of producing dynamic, full-colour pictures.

Presentations require high display performance to achieve the maximum effect, but are sometimes satisfactory with only moderate image quality. The actual requirements depend on the specific context of the presentation, related to audience expectations, information content and type of auditorium. Video and computer-generated images are beginning to displace projected 35 mm slides, although the latter offer far higher image quality in terms of grey scale range, colour rendering and spatial resolution. A full function video presentation requires a high resolution full-colour projection display, of either CRT or light-valve technology, whereas satisfactory still image presentations may be achieved with LCD panels placed on a conventional overhead projector.

Process Control involves both control and monitoring. Although these are somewhat separate functions, their specifications are sufficiently similar that they may usually be combined. The displays provide information on the state of industrial systems for products such as chemicals, pharmaceuticals and manufactured items. Also they may be employed on-line in the distribution of electricity, gas or water supplies. The display system must be able to show the system state and associated information in a variety of forms. Text and graphics tend to be most common, although live video displays are important for surveillance and site monitoring. CRTs have been used extensively, often with several screens combined in a large console for complex installations, supplemented by groups of numeric and alphanumeric display devices. FPDs are becoming more common, especially for large board displays. Because the displays are usually sited in purpose-built rooms, good control over ambient lighting can usually be achieved, unlike in most office and domestic situations.

Simulation applications range from moderately simple representations of product movement on the factory floor to full scale flight simulators. The former provide a cost-effective tool for exploring manufacturing processes, whereas the latter can create extraordinary realism for training pilots and other aircrew. Simple manufacturing simulation can be accomplished on personal computers of moderate performance and limited colour capability, while flight simulators are custom built, cost millions, and push display requirements for size, colour and dynamic capability to the limit (Figure 1.2 — Colour Plate 2). In some cases special calligraphic display devices have been constructed, which produce both raster and vector imagery in a single unit for optimum performance. Probably no other display application family has a wider price and performance range.

Television is the most prevalent application for display systems, with the billions of TV sets far exceeding the number of displays used for all other applications except personal computers. It is estimated that worldwide there about two TV sets for every PC, although the value of the television market does not exceed the totality of all other display markets because of the much lower cost of individual TV sets. CRTs remain the leading technology in television displays, despite their bulk and high power consumption, because of their large screen size, high brightness and relatively low cost. With the advent of HDTV, however, the demand for even larger (in excess of 36" diagonal) screen sizes has led to an increasing emphasis on improving the performance of FPDs or on finding novel ways of constructing projection TV systems.

Transportation applications use electronic displays primarily as a means of conveying status information, such as the times of arrivals and departures. The prime examples are the large board displays and multiple monitor installations found in airports, train termini and bus stations. The large board displays are usually of the electromagnetic type, operating segmented or dot-matrix characters, though large format billboard style FPDs are now developed to the point where they could begin to make inroads; the monitors are standard CRTs with large fonts. The primary application requirements are legibility and reliability. One interesting new transportation application is the use of in-vehicle entertainment displays. Projection television has been used for some time in aircraft, but recently individual colour FPDs have been fitted on seat backs, providing each passenger with an individual choice of programme. Backlit LCDs are well suited to this application because they are thin, and the fixed viewing angle and relative closeness of the viewer make a small screen size acceptable.

Virtual Reality (VR) is a new and exciting application whose principal uses are in entertainment, training, simulation, CAD, scientific visualisation and architecture. It is difficult to establish exactly what the display requirements might be until more experience is available. However, it does appear that this may be one of the most demanding display applications and will require the highest performance characteristics to be successful. Generally full 'immersion' requires the use of a helmet-mounted display (HMD), although some room immersion techniques are being investigated. Small CRTs (with screen sizes of around 1" diagonal) have been most successful in creating convincing display imagery in HMDs, but FPDs have the advantages of ease of construction, low weight and no high voltages. The most pressing issue in VR is that affordable HMDs have image quality so poor as to be almost unacceptable, and the HMDs with generally acceptable image quality are currently very expensive.

1.3 RESOLUTION AND ADDRESSABILITY

Resolution, which is related to CRT spot size or graphics pixel size, is associated with the physical properties of the display device. Addressability (often given in the same terms as resolution — i.e. as dots per inch) is related to the circuitry driving the display. For discrete display devices like LEDs and LCDs, resolution and addressability are essentially the same. However, for analogue devices like the CRT, resolution and addressability are not necessarily the same.

It could be argued fairly persuasively that word processing in Japan required the development of high resolution CRTs. The normal alphabetic upper-case character in the US could be fairly well identified with a resolvable 5×7 dot format. By increasing the matrix to 7×9 dots, one could achieve a good range of upper and lower case characters together with punctuation marks. However, the consensus seems to be that in order to clearly see the Japanese character sets one required a 16×16 dot matrix, as shown in Figure 1.3. This twofold to threefold increase in resolution requirement drove, in my judgement, the Japanese development of higher resolution CRTs with smaller spot sizes giving better screen resolution.

Some of the early photo-typesetting systems demanded extraordinarily high resolution requirements. When considering the printing requirements for a character, it was not unusual to expect 300, 600 or 1000 lines per inch. The need for display resolution that could generate imagery of a quality virtually indistinguishable from printed pages, led to the development of monochromatic displays in the 3000–5000 line resolution range. This was achieved by using very fine grain phosphors without a shadow mask, written by a tiny spot driven at very high speeds.

Earlier techniques for eliminating 'staircases' on curves and sloping lines and edges, known as anti-aliasing, were satisfactory in those applications that needed improved character legibility or improved quality of graphics to overcome the lack of display resolution (Figure 1.4). However, where the actual data were critical, the user would not accept any of the image smoothing techniques. For example, in medical applications the user community was most distrustful of any processes that altered the raw data. The feeling was that the raw data contained significant information that could be obscured if anything was done with the pixel processing. Therefore, until the images could be shown with appropriate

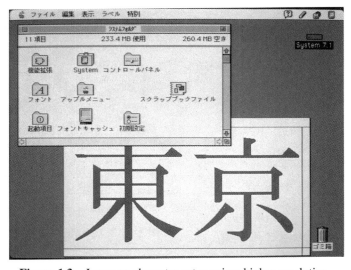

Figure 1.3 Japanese character set requires higher resolution

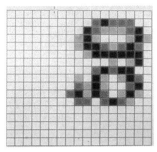

Figure 1.4 Anti-aliased character formation

resolution for the raw data, and not requiring some kind of picture enhancement, the potential for displays to be used in medical imaging applications was low.

When we look into the application requirements for Virtual Reality it has been pointed out that the typical LCD display used in low-cost Virtual Reality helmets makes an individual legally blind. The definition of legal blindness is 20/200 vision and most commonly used LCDs are equivalent to about 20/210 vision. The LCD is an attractive element of a helmet-mounted display (HMD) because the user perceives no danger from radiating voltages. It would certainly be feasible to build a helmet-mounted display in which the imagery were supplied from high resolution cathode ray tubes — the kind that are used in data recording. Although military HMDs often use small CRTs (Figure 1.5), there is a well-founded belief that the commercial user would be very uncomfortable with some kind of high voltage source in close proximity to the eyes and head. It is possible to create an effect by using fibre-optic piping from a remotely located CRT, but such a solution is cumbersome and expensive.

In general the best solution for HMDs is to use relatively high resolution flat panel displays with an adequate field of view (see Chapter 5). While it is not certain that even

Figure 1.5 Military head mounted display

if these relatively high resolution, low cost helmet-mounted displays became universally available, the casual user would still be comfortable with a helmet environment, it is almost certain that there is no chance of success for a wide usage of the helmet-mounted display unless those become available. There may be specific areas where lower quality displays will be tolerated. For example, there is a prestige factor involved in using these displays as part of a Virtual Reality game. But to believe that these lower resolution helmet-mounted displays will become as pervasive as the graphic display terminals we see everywhere seems to be naive.

1.4 BRIGHTNESS AND COLOUR

In aircraft applications, CRTs could not be used in conventional cockpits until they had sufficient contrast and brightness to be visible in the presence of high ambient light, and were sufficiently rugged to withstand aircraft shock and vibration. The 'glass cockpit' became possible only when the CRTs offered sufficiently high resolution that the glass panel instruments were virtually indistinguishable from their electromechanical counter-parts (see Figure 1.2 — Colour Plate 2). This also required that rotating lines to represent pointers and artificial horizons could move without appearing to 'wiggle', which implied higher resolution than one might normally expect from a conventional raster display. As a matter of fact, the need for this kind of performance led to the combination raster/vector units or the use of line-smoothing techniques such as anti-aliasing.

Various artistic and graphic arts applications were fairly dormant until the computer graphics sub-systems driving CRTs began to deliver a broad range colour. Today we take for granted the 16 million colour combinations produced by 8 bits each in the red, green and blue channels, but early colour CRTs were much more limited in range and were simply not suitable for typical graphic arts and fine arts applications. While the storage tube could easily be used to generate a series of monochrome 'negatives' that could be used for colour print separations, the desirability of being able to view a full colour image became extraordinarily important as the CRT began to be used in more sophisticated graphic arts applications, particularly in the pre-press area. Early users encountered significant problems because the colours seen on the CRT often did not match what was reproduced on hard copy and did not match the conventional printing ink colours. It became necessary to create a correlation between what was shown on the CRT and what became printable.

There is no doubt that users' interest in colour for most applications was one of the driving factors for the development of raster displays. Once the cost per bit of display memory became inexpensive enough to store complex, high resolution colour images, non-raster CRT displays essentially became obsolete. Because users generally preferred to see colour on screen, colour raster displays quickly became the *de facto* standard once there was no longer a need to justify a significantly higher cost for colour.

With the growing popularity of various flat panel displays, the issue of broad colour range has again become important. LEDs, electroluminescent and plasma displays continue to have restricted colour capability and are therefore effectively excluded from applications such as graphic arts, which require 'millions' of colours with high quality rendering.

One of the other issues that we explore from time to time is the question of colour blindness as related to gender. Conventional data suggest that males have about ten times the incidence of colour blindness as females. This suggests that in applications where critical decisions are to be made based on colour discrimination, redundant 'clues' such as changes in size, orientation, texture or shape need to be used to supplement colour clues.

1.5   FLICKER AND IMAGE MOTION

In the early development of CRTs, when stroke-writing systems were most common, the user faced a trade-off between data content, flicker rate and phosphor decay. In principle, one could get away with lower refresh rates by using longer persistence phosphors. However, in those applications in which there was dynamic motion associated with the display, the longer persistence phosphors caused undesirable smearing. Since the desired high refresh rates required very expensive electronic circuitry in both the graphics controller and the display monitor, lower frequency displays were commonly employed. This led to very noticeable image flicker and the associated worries about the physiological effects associated with flicker. The lore of the 1960s was that it was possible to induce a catatonic state in a user by forcing him or her to look at a display rate in the 10–12 frames per second range.

It is important to distinguish between 'refresh rate' and 'movement rate'. Applications in which a low refresh rate might result in unacceptable flicker can often tolerate low 'movement' rates to create the illusion of continuous motion. For example, some game and simulation applications that use animated images may redraw the image at 30–60 frames per second, but only change the image position 6–10 times per second (perhaps because the image is so complex that the processor creating each new view requires 0.1–0.2 seconds to calculate the new view). Generally, image animation at 10 changes per second or faster is perceived as continuous motion. Refresh rate is often determined by the display hardware, whereas animation rate is often determined by the display computer.

Today display flicker is much less of an issue because very high frame rates can be achieved in raster displays. However, a smoothly moving graphic image has become more difficult to achieve because the more sophisticated user of today demands a much more realistic image. While this is not necessarily a CRT function, it certainly is a function of the driving electronics. When one tries to show a realistic image moving in real-time at flicker-free refresh rates, the display processing requirements are enormous. For example, a flight simulator of the kind Evans and Sutherland and others have become famous for, offers the best example of what is currently available in photorealistic, real-time imagery. Yet the quality of that imagery, compared to what one would see when looking out of the window of a real airplane, suggests that one still needs to have display processors that are two to three orders of magnitude faster.

To support stereo-viewing and applications where the eyes are presented with alternate views, refresh rate requirements had to increase by at least a factor of two in order to reduce or eliminate flicker. Today, it is quite common to work with displays that have refresh rates of 70–120 frames per second.

1.6   FIELD OF VIEW AND DISPLAY SIZE

One other issue that we are only beginning to study, especially with Virtual Reality, is the impact of field of view. Simplistically, the VR environment requires total immersion.

However, in practice it appears that as long as the field of view covered by the display is of the order of 150–200 degrees, the user gets the feeling of being totally immersed. In fact, some of the current technology puts the user 'inside a cave', totally surrounded by display technology, following on from the configurations used in flight simulators.

Early computer-aided design (CAD) applications were inhibited because of the relatively small size of inexpensive displays. It was really a price versus size trade-off. The original storage tube displays (once we got past the 5″ units) were about 11″ diagonal, a good example in the mid-1970s being the Tektronix 4010. The fact that the displays were inexpensive and could store complex imagery with good resolution and addressability made them very attractive for CAD applications. However, the small physical size of the display surface, the absence of colour capability and the relative lack of dynamic capability acted as inhibiting factors.

When Tektronix began to offer larger screen units (19″ diagonal) the use of the small screen-size workstations practically disappeared and the use of the CAD systems grew impressively. Early on, in fact, there was concern that unless the industry could supply a CRT display screen the same size as a drafting table, it was unlikely that people would use CAD. One of the early specifications for a highly interactive CAD system that was developed by Ford, asked that the CRT be flat-faced, be about 20″ in diameter, with an addressability of 4000 × 4000. The expectation was that the user would want to deal with the drawing in the same way they had in the past on the drafting table, i.e. that the draftsperson would lean down against the edge of the table (tube) and sight along the lines to see how smooth they were.

Eventually the typical drafting system workstations featured displays in the range 14″ to 21″. As time progressed, a larger diagonal display became available (typically about 27″), but its relative cost, and the fact that the operators were sitting rather close to the systems, seemed to limit the use of these larger CRTs. The mapping and geographical information systems (GIS) parts of the CAD industry did tend to use larger displays, and for these the 27″ CRT became fairly standard.

There was also periodic interest in a projection system which would back-project an image onto a drafting sized table, or use a flat panel display of drafting table size. Although a few of these devices were built to satisfy the CAD environment, they were not widely used. Also, graphic user interface technology had developed to provide features such as views in multiple windows, zoom and scroll, and grid positioning, so that there was no longer an expectation or need for an exact image correspondence between the screen and the old paper-based drawings (see Chapter 3).

Another way in which imaging applications drove display requirements was that several vendors found a competitive advantage to mounting dual displays within a console. This was commonplace in large expensive systems through the 1970s and 1980s in various fields, including scientific image processing, medical imaging, packaging design and graphic arts publishing systems. Typically one screen would be used for the colour image while the other(s) would display text and graphics information. Again, these configurations were made redundant by the availability of powerful window management systems such as *X Windows* on standard computer platforms, together with graphic user interface toolkits.

Larger displays did find an application in group design meetings. One interesting sidelight of the introduction of very large screen displays came out of early FAA attempts to provide group displays for their air traffic control (ATC) operators. In evolving from the classic 'croupier' horizontal table-top screen display, in which shrimp boats were moved along the face of a CRT, to the later generation of fully electronic displays, there was an interest in exploring the possibility of providing a room-sized display for a group of controllers. The anecdote goes that the controllers would be sitting in front of the group displays and individuals would periodically leave their seats to go up and readjust the brightness or contrast of the display, go back to their seat and then someone else would get up and do the same thing. They had apparently worked with individual displays for so long that they could not easily arrive at a common presentation characteristic.

Certainly, display size is also dictated by the normal viewing distances. For example, individual desktop workstations are typically viewed from about arm's length, about 18–24 inches, whereas television displays are typically viewed from a distance of three to five times the image height.

1.7 OTHER FACTORS

Health and safety concerns now drive designers to reduce low frequency and high frequency radiation. Once the CRT began to find wider applications among the non-technical user community, all sorts of ills were blamed on it — the effects of flicker, high frequency and low frequency radiation led to a series of 'horror stories' a decade or so ago about how CRTs could give rise to cataracts and interfere with pregnancy. CRTs used in that environment drove much of the consciousness regarding health and safety.

Although price/performance ratio is not usually considered a technical characteristic, an appropriate price needs to be coupled with the technical characteristics of a display. One of the factors that has accelerated the use of computer graphics in a wide variety of desktop applications is that we have reached points at which both the performance and the price are generally acceptable. Today we have new applications such as Virtual Reality, where the price/performance ratio is marginal at best.

For some applications physical limitations also have had an impact on CRT design. As we began to put CRTs into some consumer products in which depth limitations were severe, we began to have more and more interest in flat panel display technology. Today the most visible flat panel display is based on the use of liquid crystal technology. But several years ago when Buick decided to put an active display in their cars, they ended up using a CRT rather than a flat panel display. The reasons for that decision were fairly complex, but the price/performance of the CRT over the liquid crystal display certainly had a significant effect. The greater resistance of the CRT to environmental conditions was important, and also the fact that the CRT was 'self-illuminated'.

Power, weight, life and volume are among the other parameters that are driven by application requirements.

1.8 CONCLUSION

On balance, the development of technology over the last three decades has reached the point where there are very few application situations in which the user is asked to make significant compromises. The cost of the technology has gone down dramatically, while the performance has increased significantly, leading to the cliché that if the automobile industry had experienced the same changes in price/performance ratio one would be able to buy a Rolls-Royce for a dollar and get a million miles to the gallon. Of course the caveat that goes with this is that in the old days you needed to be one inch high and you had to be prepared for the system to break down every half-hour.

With the exception of stereo-viewing, Virtual Reality and wall-size flat TVs, there are virtually no applications that are not adequately served by today's display technologies. In the stereo-viewing and VR environments, a number of display and associated hardware factors will need to be improved if the applications are to realise their full potential. The 'unsolved' problems associated with computer graphics and virtual reality include the following issues:

- HMDs: improve the resolution and field of view; present performance leaves the user legally blind!
- Improve user mobility, eliminate tethering, increase operating volume.
- Improve and develop autostereoscopic and other non-HMD stereo-viewing techniques.
- Improve user interaction techniques including haptic and force-feedback devices.
- Investigate desirability of 'VR chips' analogous to 'multimedia chips'.

About a century ago, the United States was encouraged to close its Patent Office because, so the argument went, everything had already been invented. Fortunately, the responsible parties were not so sanguine and the Office continues in operation. Similarly, we sometimes hear in computer graphics that 'all the interesting problems have been solved ... the rest is detail!'. It seems to me that quite the opposite is true. Many interesting, in fact critical, problems still need to be addressed. System problems such as true cross-platform independence, hardware problems such as non-invasive stereo and VR displays, and software problems such as true user friendliness, are all crying out for imaginative solutions. Even the president of IBM, Louis V. Gerstner Jr., said at a press conference recently that there continues to be a need for hardware and software that allow different systems to share data easily.

Important research issues that still need to be addressed by the visualisation community were well covered in the March 1994 issue of IEEE *Computer Graphics and Applications*. Areas that demand solutions or further research include multimedia standards, intelligent TVs, voice input, large screen flat panel displays, eye-trackers, potential and actual physiological problems connected with VR, visualisation application modules with sense feedback, real-time photorealism with low cost resources, multimedia expert or template authoring systems, low-cost motion platforms, lossless real-time image compression, tactile I/O devices, and parallel processing software. The future looks unlikely to be dull!

BIBLIOGRAPHY

Brown, J.R., Earnshaw, R., Jern, M. and Vince, J. (1995), *Visualisation: Using Computer Graphics to Explore Data and Present Information*, John Wiley & Sons, New York.
Durlach, N. and Mavor, A.S. (eds) (1995), *Virtual Reality: Scientific and Technological Changes*, National Academy Press, Washington, DC.

Earnshaw, R.A. and Vince, J.A. (eds) (1995), *Multimedia Systems and Applications*, Academic Press, San Diego, CA.

Gold, L. (1995), What will the future hold for process control? *Managing Automation*, March.

Jarett, I.M. (1993), *Financial Reporting Using Computer Graphics*, John Wiley & Sons, New York.

Kaufman, A. (1991), *Volume Visualisation*, IEEE Computer Society Press, Los Alamitos, CA.

Keller, P.R. and Keller, M.M. (1993), *Visual Cues: Practical Data Visualisation*, IEEE Computer Society Press, Los Alamitos, CA.

Labuz, R. (1993), *The Computer in Graphic Design: From Technology to Style*, Van Nostrand Reinhold, New York.

Laurel, B. (1990), *The Art of Human–Computer Interface Design*, Addison-Wesley, Reading, MA.

MacDonald, L. and Vince, J. (eds) (1994) Interacting with Virtual Environments, John Wiley & Sons, Chichester, UK.

Machover, C. (1994), Four decades of computer graphics, *IEEE Computer Graphics and Applications*, November.

Nielson, G.M. and Shriver, B.D. (eds) (1990), *Visualisation in Scientific Computing*, IEEE Computer Society Press, Los Alamitos, CA.

Sherr, S. (1993), *Electronic Displays*, 2nd Edition, John Wiley & Sons, New York.

Tannas, L.E. Jr. (1985), *Flat-Panel Displays and CRTs*, Van Nostrand Reinhold, New York.

2

Display requirements for desktop electronic imaging

Lindsay MacDonald

2.1 INTRODUCTION

Displays are of central importance to desktop imaging systems. Indeed the display is in a real sense the user's window into the system and provides the principal means of visual representation of the system's state, behaviour and control points, so it must have the proper affordances for interaction and the graphic user interface. In imaging applications the display furnishes the medium through which the image is presented to the user for manipulation and verification, so it must portray images with high fidelity. People who work with desktop applications may spend more time looking at the display screen than at anything else in the office, so the display must be comfortable to use, minimising fatigue and maximising productivity.

In the 1970s and 1980s system manufacturers frequently integrated display monitors with other system components to provide a complete packaged solution for a specific imaging application. The display itself could therefore be closely specified and tested for optimum performance before delivery to the customer. Because the display characteristics were known precisely, the visual presentation could be optimised, often in special housings. Custom design allowed the graphics controller, system software and user interface to be ideally matched to both the capabilities of the display and the requirements of the application. Such systems delivered good performance and high image quality for the application for which they were designed, but were very expensive and suffered from

Display Systems, Edited by L.W. MacDonald and A.C. Lowe. © 1997 John Wiley & Sons Ltd.

closed architectures, making them difficult to connect to peripherals or software packages not supported by the manufacturer.

The situation has changed in recent years as a result of the relentless evolution of graphics controller technology. Over the past 20 years CRT monitors have not changed much in terms of their basic technology, though they have become cheaper, more reliable and available in a variety of convenient sizes for desktop use. What has changed radically is the cost and size of the frame store needed to drive a monitor with a high-quality 24-bit colour image. In 1975 a 512×512 pixel 24-bit frame store occupied about 3 cubic feet, was mounted in a 19-inch rack, refreshed the monitor at 50 Hz (interlaced) and required a major investment with a cost approaching $100 000. Today it fits on a postcard sized plug-in card, has over double the resolution (typically 1280×1024 pixels at 75 Hz non-interlaced) and costs about $2000. A simple palette-mapped 8-bit frame store is now included as standard equipment on the motherboard of most personal computers, so that colour displays have become almost ubiquitous on the desktop.

The advent of the graphic user interface (GUI) has had important consequences for display usage. By mixing images with text and graphics, system software developers make greater demands on the display to support movement of images and high levels of interactivity, whilst not diminishing the need for clear, sharp presentation of fine detail when the image is static. Positive presentation (black text on a white page) combined with higher luminance levels to allow the displays to be used in ordinary office conditions have forced ever higher refresh rates and non-interlace raster scan patterns to reduce flicker perception.

The rise in power and graphical capabilities of standard desktop computer platforms, such as the PC and Macintosh, has now made it uneconomical for vendors of imaging systems to develop their own display controllers and integrate carefully-specified display monitors into complete systems. Vendors now accept that the end user can purchase a standard computer platform plus a range of peripherals, including the display, and 'plug and play' them together with relative ease. Under these circumstances it has become difficult, if not impossible, to control the quality of the displayed image directly. One must rely on the display manufacturers themselves to respond to market pressures and customer needs by improving the specification of display monitors, and supplement these with instruments and procedures that customers can use (if they are sufficiently motivated) to calibrate their displays to the optimum operating state.

2.2 QUALITY IN PRODUCT DESIGN

2.2.1 Quality Function Deployment

In recent years quality has become a central issue in product design and development. Spurred by the obvious successes of Japanese companies in manufacturing cars and electronic goods for the world market, companies in Europe and the USA have been closely examining how to raise quality levels. At the heart of Total Quality Management (TQM) are two simple aims: how to make things right first time and how to manage continual improvement. The tangible benefits to the customer are that he or she gets something that does the right task, works properly and is pleasing to use. The benefits for the supplier are the reduction in warranty claims and service failures, and minimised waste in manufacturing due to the reworking of defective components or designs (Cullen & Hollingum, 1989). To be effective TQM must be adopted as part of the corporate culture at all levels from the Chief Executive downward, and must be built into all processes of the business. To use TQM effectively in systems engineering a paradigm shift has to take place in the attitudes and approach of people throughout the organisation, by encouraging multi-disciplinary contributions and team building (Kasser, 1995).

Quality Function Deployment (QFD) is an integral part of the TQM philosophy. QFD provides a systematic means of ensuring that customer or marketplace demands (requirements, needs and wants) are accurately translated into relevant technical requirements. It allows the consumers' demands to be converted into 'quality characteristics' by systematically exploring and deploying relationships between market demands and product characteristics. This deployment may affect all functions of any organisation responsible for delivering quality goods and services to the end user. Sullivan (1986) observes that in Japanese companies the customer's voice drives all activities, whereas in the US it is frequently the executive's voice or the engineer's voice that prevails. Japanese companies, moreover, tend to concentrate on what the customer likes, whereas US companies pay more attention to what the customer doesn't like. The result of this different cultural approach is that the Japanese put more effort into designing in quality at the product development stage, whereas US companies put a greater emphasis on problem solving.

Zairi (1993) identifies four key aspects of QFD:

- QFD embraces *all* the customer needs known at the time.
- It emphasises *positive* aspects of quality in determining the best deal for the customer.
- It focuses on the *process* by working through the customer–supplier chain.
- It brings about a new *culture* and new methods of delivery to the end customer.

QFD therefore represents a critical shift in the strategy for quality control from manufacturing processes, where the emphasis is on minimising variance, to product development processes. The benefits accruing from this shift have been widely documented, particularly in the design of user interfaces where user participation at all stages helps to keep the project focused on real user needs (Grossman *et al.*, 1992). Cross-functional design teams including marketing and field personnel, as well as actual customer representatives, produce clearer requirement definitions and design specifications (Hutchings & Knox, 1995). The effectiveness, or 'task-fit' as ergonomists call it, of an administrative system is enhanced through the participation of user representatives in the concept development stages, and many techniques are available to improve the level of shared understanding in meetings (O'Brien, 1991).

2.2.2 Voice of the customer

In a QFD-focused company all operations of the organisation are driven by the 'voice of the customer'. QFD starts with a list of objectives, known as the <u>whats</u> of the project, which are initially rather general and vague and difficult to implement directly. QFD assists in the further detailed definition and quantification of the customer objectives, and their translation into the <u>hows</u> of the product design. Initially many customer wants will not be verbalised by the consumer, for example the performance of 'hidden' components such as the internal circuitry of a display monitor. In addition, many products should exhibit features which, although not strictly necessary, add pleasant surprises or a feeling of excitement to their use. Examples would be an electric sunroof on a car or a remote control on a television set. The key to successful product design is to gather and classify correctly all the customer requirements, especially the unspoken, or 'implicit', ones.

An influential model of quality relating the voice of the customer to product quality was introduced by Kano. In a classic paper (Kano *et al.*, 1982) he proposed two dimensions for customer requirements, as shown in Figure 2.1. One dimension is the degree of customer satisfaction (vertical axis); the second is the degree of achievement or 'physical fulfilment' as he puts it (horizontal axis). Traditional market analysis methods failed to distinguish these, lumping them instead into a unidimensional quality scale resulting in satisfaction when fulfilled and dissatisfaction when not fulfilled (the line at 45° in Figure 2.1). By applying this analysis of the voice of the customer *prospectively* to product features, Kano was able to show that products could be designed much more effectively to meet consumer needs. He subsequently developed a theory of Quality Creation, which he

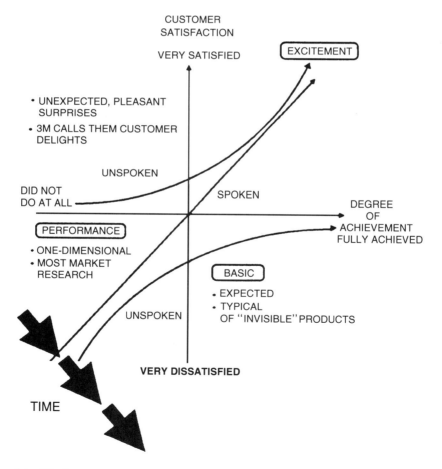

Figure 2.1 The Kano model of quality (reproduced by courtesy of American Supplier Institute)

defines as 'a company-wide systematic activity, which works for originating products with functionality, performance and operability that we haven't seen before' (Kano, 1987).

The process for capturing the voice of the customer (VOC) has a well-defined sequence of collecting the data, organising and interpreting it, and then deploying the resulting information in the following design process. The VOC process necessarily defines requirements in a 'slice of time', and key customer requirements must periodically be re-evaluated to determine whether their importance has changed. Methods have been proposed to extend VOC into the future, thereby improving a company's ability to produce products that will remain competitive for longer (Shillito, 1995).

One effective method of getting potential customers to focus their minds on the relative importance of the attributes of a product is to put a monetary value on them. In blunt terms the value of a consumer item is proportional to how much money someone is prepared to pay for it. It is important when considering industrial or office equipment such as displays, which might often be purchased on a corporate budget, to ask the customer how much he or she would be prepared to spend *personally* on the feature. This approach is similar to the technique of contingent valuation, which analyses the value of a transaction in terms of the good (product or service), the value measure (payment) and social context (or marketplace). Goods are characterised as bundles of attributes, representing outcomes of accepting the transaction that might be valued either positively or negatively or might not affect its value at all (Fischhoff & Furby, 1988). Contingent valuation can even be applied to public goods to determine how much people are willing to pay for something from which they may derive no personal consumption benefits, such as the protection of animal species on another continent. It has been established that willingness to pay is well correlated with other methods of rating the importance that people attach to issues, though it is not clear how the scale of hypothetical dollars relates to other measures of the intensity of attitudes (Kahneman *et al.*, 1993).

2.3 GATHERING USER REQUIREMENTS FOR DISPLAYS

As part of the Crosfield Electronics product development programme for colour management systems, a QFD study was undertaken of users' expectations of desktop displays. The objective was to determine which characteristics of displays were rated most important, in order to identify those areas in which value might best be added to the standard colour monitors and operating software provided by workstation vendors. The emphasis was to be on 'front of screen' requirements, as perceived by purchasers and users of displays, rather than the 'back of screen' technical view of engineers and software developers. The exercise was highly successful, because in addition to yielding clear indicators for adding value to displays, it produced a classification of the quality attributes of displays and their priority ranking by professional users.

2.3.1 Focus Group of experts

The first stage of the study was to construct a comprehensive list of display characteristics, which the users would subsequently be asked to rate in importance. The method chosen was to convene a Focus Group of six expert display users from within the company, all of whom had extensive experience both as users of desktop systems and as developers of desktop publishing applications. The group met for a two-hour structured brainstorming session, and were given the following brief:

> 'What are your opinions and comments on the specification and characteristics of the ideal colour display for desktop imaging systems, to suit your requirements now and in the future? Consider such applications as publishing, multimedia, scientific visualisation and computer-aided design but *exclude* monochrome displays, portable and public information displays and non-imaging applications.'

The session was conducted in two parts. In the first part, as a warm-up and group consolidation exercise for about 20 minutes, the participants were asked to describe all the problems they encountered with current displays. In the second part, they were asked to define the characteristics of the ideal display, guided by the author as moderator who led the discussion through a series of categories, including image quality, functionality, viewing characteristics, ergonomics, reliability, cost/performance trade-offs, installation and vendor support. All points were captured in writing on a flipchart, the successive sheets of which were stuck around the walls of the meeting room so that they were visible to all participants.

The information gleaned from the Focus Group fell into three distinct levels, denoted Primary, Secondary and Tertiary. The moderator's job was to draw out the user needs at the correct level, working from the general (Primary) down to the specific (Tertiary):

Primary   Broad statements containing little specific information, such as:

> 'It should have high image quality',
> 'It should be easy to use',
> 'It should be well designed', etc.

Secondary   Subdivisions of the primary requirement classes, into statements about particular scenarios or aspects of the requirement. For example, the primary requirement 'The image should not contain any defects' could be broken down into the secondary requirements:

> 'The image quality should be uniform throughout the screen area',
> 'There should be no spatial problems',
> 'The image should remain stable over a period of time', etc.

Tertiary   Tertiary requirements provide the lowest level of detail, giving the specific characteristics that are desired. For example, the secondary requirement 'It should be easy to install' could comprise the tertiaries:

> 'It should be ready to go out of the box',
> 'There should be no configuration switches to set up',
> 'It should be easy to connect to the host computer', etc.

2.3.2   Constructing a PST tree

The PST tree is a structured chart containing all the user requirements at Primary, Secondary and Tertiary levels, in the form of a family tree. These three levels allow the product to be scoped more effectively during the subsequent design phases. The Tertiary level contains specific requirements (<u>whats</u>) which can be assigned measurable design characteristics (<u>hows</u>). The Secondary level identifies complete subsystems, or groups of related tertiaries, that need to be integrated into the product design. The Primary level defines the overall characteristics of the product, which can be considered as its primary selling features.

The process of sorting all the requirements was carried out by a cross-functional team, containing representatives of all the departments involved in developing and supporting a successful product, namely R&D, manufacturing, service, marketing and finance. Cross-functional discussion allowed each member of the team to understand more clearly the real requirements of the user and also to identify those requirements related to his or her own area of the business, such as training, documentation, tooling, etc.

Each display attribute arising from the Focus Group was written onto a yellow Post-it note, being careful to preserve the 'voice of the user' as well as the essence of the requirement. In all there were about 200 separate notes, and these were stuck onto a large wall where they could all be viewed simultaneously. Initially placed at random, the team exercise was to sort them into related groups, first establishing loose relationships between the requirements, then successively refining the classifications, removing duplicates and creating primary and secondary headings where necessary to produce the best PST structure. The rule of thumb followed for the tree was to have approximately three Secondaries for each Primary, and five Tertiaries for each Secondary, i.e. P:S:T = 1:3:5.

2.3.3 Analysis of the PST tree for displays

The final PST tree of display requirements is set out in Appendix A. It contains 12 Primaries, 38 Secondaries and 181 Tertiaries. The first four Primaries cover the visual and image quality aspects of the display:

- Good for a wide range of desktop imaging applications
- High image quality
- Image free from defects
- Well-controlled colour

The next three Primaries deal with the physical viewing and usability characteristics:

- Optimal physical screen characteristics
- Full set of control facilities
- Easy to use

The last five Primaries cover all the product design, installation and support issues:

- Good design and engineering
- Convenient installation and setup
- No environmental problems
- Competitive price/performance ratio
- Full range of support services

Each of these three groups of Primary requirements contains about the same number of Tertiaries, indicating that the users' articulated needs spanned a wide range of aspects, not just the appearance of the image on the display screen.

Although the inputs to the process were derived primarily from the experts' familiarity with CRT monitors, some of the specific requirements (Tertiaries) go well beyond the capabilities of any normal CRT monitor. Under the Secondary 'Wide range of viewing positions', for example, appear not only the conventional swivel and tilt adjustments but also the ability to fold the display down to work horizontally on the work surface and even to have a display light and flexible enough to be handled like a sheet of paper. Under 'Compact size cabinet' are not only a small footprint on the desktop, but also the ability to fold the display away when not in use or to hang it on the wall. Under 'Attractive product styling' it was suggested that the display should be 'transparent', in the sense that its cabinet and surround should be so minimal that they would disappear, leaving only the image on a flat substrate. None of these Secondary requirements was rated very highly in the subsequent EASI analysis, however, suggesting that such futuristic flat panel displays are not of great concern to the users of existing desktop workstations.

2.4 EASI ANALYSIS

2.4.1 The EASI groups

The user requirements set out in the PST tree in Appendix A represent a 'wish list' of all the characteristics that users would like to see in a desktop display. In practice some of these are more important to users than others, with some being seen as mandatory while others are merely attractive but non-essential features. The second stage of the study was therefore aimed at harnessing the voice of the customer to establish a priority ordering of the requirements, separating out the necessary from the unnecessary, so that Crosfield development resources could be applied to the most appropriate product attributes.

Each Secondary requirement of the PST tree was to be classified into one of four groups, called *Expressed, Attractive, Scrap* and *Implicit*, and known collectively as the EASI groups.

The *Expressed* group contains requirements that users have explicitly requested because they are characteristics of the product necessary for their application or work practices. Significant effort should be applied to providing or improving this group of Secondaries in the product. The Expressed group ranks second in importance after the Implicit group.

The *Attractive* group contains product features and facilities which the majority of users consider could be useful, valuable or interesting in some way, but not really essential. Novelty features also fall into this group–users might consider purchasing these features if they were available, but could do without them. Marketing consideration should be given to providing some or all of these Secondaries, as they are likely to be the features that will differentiate the product from competitors. The Attractive group ranks third in importance after the Implicit and Expressed groups.

The *Scrap* group contains characteristics that users consider largely unnecessary. They do not need them and probably would not be interested in purchasing them even if they were available. Development effort should not be wasted on Secondaries in this group.

The *Implicit* group contains characteristics that are needed to meet the expectations of the majority of users of the product. Without these facilities it is highly likely that the product will not be successful. Typical examples of requirements that usually fall into this group are high reliability, excellent quality and good service. Maximum effort should be applied to providing or improving the Secondaries in this group, which has the highest priority ranking of all four groups.

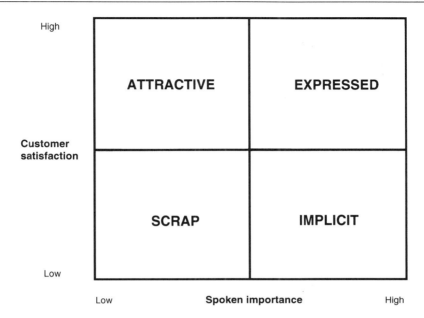

Figure 2.2   Classifying product requirements in terms of their spoken importance and customer satisfaction

These four groups may be visualised in terms of a matrix (Figure 2.2) derived from Figure 2.1 in which the axes are the spoken importance and customer satisfaction of the requirements. An Expressed requirement is high in both respects, meaning that customers say that the requirement is important and in fact satisfaction rises when they get it and declines when they do not. An Attractive requirement is one which customers may say is not necessarily important, but which when they do experience it produces a dramatic rise in satisfaction. An Implicit requirement is one which customers will always say is important (such as having good brakes in a car), but which has no appreciable impact on satisfaction with the product (Robertshaw, 1995).

2.4.2   The Quality Game

To provide a structured but simple method of classifying the Secondary requirements into the four EASI groups, we played the Quality Game with a series of users. This procedure was developed several years ago at Crosfield and has been tested extensively to ensure that it gives an accurate indicator of the importance that users attach to each characteristic (Jeffries, 1991).

The Quality Game takes the form of a card game, and takes about 20 minutes to play with each user. It is divided into two phases, corresponding to the two axes of Figure 2.2: the 'excitement' phase establishes the level of enthusiasm or expectation of the user with regard to each Secondary requirement, correlated with the degree of customer satisfaction; the 'disappointment' phase determines the level of disappointment experienced by the user if the Secondary requirements is not provided, correlated with the spoken importance. At the end of the game all the Secondary requirements will have been distributed into the four EASI groups.

To prepare for the Quality Game each of the 38 Secondary requirements from the PST tree was written onto a white card of approximately postcard size (5 by 3 inches). Additionally, two Category Cards were produced on yellow card at a larger size (10 by 8 inches). Category Card 1 has the wording 'Would you be HAPPY or INDIFFERENT if you WERE provided with a display with/that . . .?' and was used in Phase 1 of the Quality Game. Category Card 2 has the wording 'Would you be *UN*HAPPY or INDIFFERENT if you were NOT provided with a display with/that . . .?' and was used in Phase 2 of the Game.

The Quality Game was played with each user individually in a quiet room free from disturbance or interruption, as shown in Figure 2.3. The player sat at a table with sufficient space to lay out the cards with the moderator at one side to direct the game and provide any explanations. To set the scene the moderator briefed the player as follows:

> 'Imagine that you are about to spend your own money on purchasing a display for use at home or in your private company for electronic colour imaging applications such as desktop publishing or multimedia or scientific visualisation. Each card has one feature of a display. Please answer the question on the yellow card and place each white card on one side or the other. Choose HAPPY only if you would definitely be happy with this feature; choose INDIFFERENT if you're not sure or don't care.'

In Phase 1 of the Quality frame, the excitement phase, the Category Card 1 was placed on the table with the text facing the player. The player then took each Secondary Card in turn and read the wording of the Category Card, adding the text of the Secondary at the end of the question, for example, 'Would you be happy or indifferent if you were provided with a display that conforms to all relevant standards?'. He or she then placed the Secondary Card in one of two stacks, to the left if happy with the attribute, or to the right if indifferent. Figure 2.4 shows the flow of Phase 1.

In Phase 2 of the Quality Game, the disappointment phase, each of the two stacks of Secondary Cards resulting from Phase 1 was further subdivided into two stacks. To

Figure 2.3   The Quality Game in progress, with the author as moderator briefing a subject

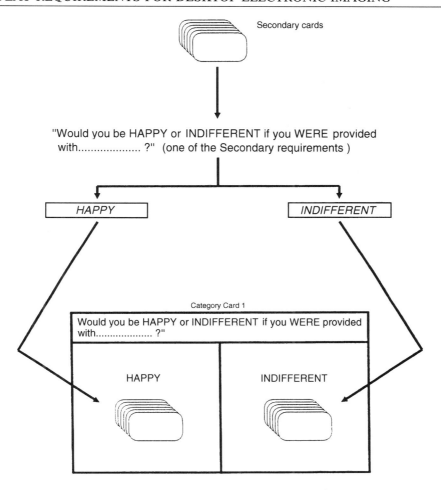

Figure 2.4   Phase 1 of the Quality Game — The Excitement Phase

begin Phase 2 the 'Indifferent' stack from Phase 1 was set aside and the large Category Card 1 swapped for Category Card 2. The player then took each Secondary Card in turn from the 'Happy' stack and read the wording of the Category Card, adding the text of the Secondary Card at the end of the question, for example, 'Would you be *un*happy or indifferent if you were *not* provided with a display that stays clean and new-looking?'. The moderator explained that the question could be paraphrased as "Would you really care if your display did not have this attribute–yes or no?'. The player then placed each Secondary Card in one of two stacks, to the left if unhappy about the absence of the attribute, or to the right if indifferent. Finally the procedure was repeated with the same question for the other stack, the 'Indifferent' cards from Phase 1.

The four resulting stacks of cards correspond to the four EASI categories. The *Expressed* (E) category contains those attributes that the player would be happy to have and unhappy not to have, i.e. for which he expresses a definite interest. The *Attractive*

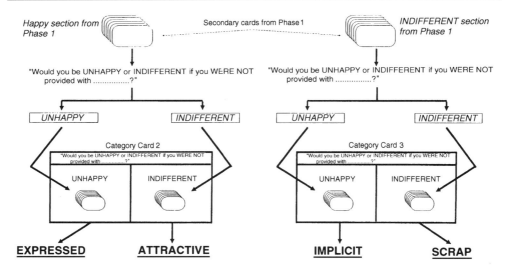

Figure 2.5   Phase 2 of the Quality Game — the Disappointment Phase

(A) category contains attributes the player would be happy to have but wouldn't care if he didn't have them. The *Implicit* (I) category contains attributes he wouldn't ask for but would miss if they weren't incorporated. The *Scrap* (S) category contains attributes about which the player is completely indifferent, i.e. he doesn't care one way or the other. Figure 2.5 shows the flow of Phase 2.

Because preliminary experiments showed that the great majority of requirements were classified as *Expressed*, an additional phase was added to the Quality Game in an attempt to separate out those requirements perceived to be essential. After the completion of Phase 2, the stack of cards corresponding to *Expressed* was placed again in front of the player with a third Category Card putting the question: 'Is this feature *absolutely essential*? Even though the feature may be unexciting, the product would be a failure if it did NOT include this feature.' The player then placed each Secondary Card in one of two stacks, to the left if yes (essential), or to the right if not. The resulting essential requirements were denoted *Explicit* (X), whilst the others remained as *Expressed* (E).

2.4.3   Analysis of EASI results

The Quality Game was played with 40 subjects, covering a wide variety of users and application interests. The first group of 20 subjects (Group 1) consisted of Crosfield employees, drawn from the R&D, Marketing and Photographic Quality departments. Their views are representative of desktop display requirements for the professional graphic arts industry. The second group of 20 subjects (Group 2) consisted of users from a wide range of industries, including photographers, earth sciences, medical systems, computer equipment suppliers and academia. The EASI classifications for each of the 38 Secondaries are tabulated for the two groups in Appendix B, with the results of each player shown as one column of letters. Frequencies of the EASI scores for each Secondary are given as row totals.

Table 2.1   Assessment of importance of Secondary requirements

Secondary Requirement	I	X	E	A	S	Class	Score	Rank
Essential								
1 Good for text and graphics	1	37	2	–	–	X	119	1
6 Good image sharpness	1	36	2	1	–	X	117	2
7 Image quality uniform over screen	–	36	4	–	–	X	116	3
5 Good colour characteristics	–	35	5	–	–	X	115	4
27 Very high reliability	–	35	4	1	–	X	114	5
4 Good tonal characteristics	–	30	6	4	–	X	106	6
8 No spatial artifacts	–	29	8	3	–	X	106	7
35 Good value for money	2	27	6	5	–	X	106	8
22 Causes no discomfort to user	–	30	7	1	2	X	105	9
10 Predictable colour	1	29	5	4	1	X	105	10
9 Image stable over time	–	29	7	4	–	X	105	11
Highly desirable								
11 Good calibration facilities	3	24	7	3	3	X	101	12
36 Good support from vendor	4	21	8	6	1	X	101	13
16 Image viewing controls	1	24	11	1	3	XE	99	14
2 Good for soft-proofing of images	1	26	5	4	4	X	96	15
3 Good for general interactive display	1	23	8	7	1	X	96	16
28 Conforms to all relevant standards	7	18	5	4	6	X	96	17
12 Good viewing characteristics	3	20	7	7	3	X	93	18
20 Easy to operate the controls	5	13	13	5	4	XE	90	19
38 Good documentation	7	12	4	11	6	XA	83	20
30 Good cables and connectors	8	9	7	8	8	XI	81	21
Desirable								
31 Multiple configuration options	6	9	8	12	5	A	79	22
21 Requires little skill to operate	4	10	10	11	5	AXE	77	23
32 No special environment necessary	2	15	8	7	8	X	76	24
33 Minimal impact on office envt.	3	11	11	9	6	XE	76	25
13 Large display area	1	13	10	9	7	XE	72	26
17 Operating state controls	5	10	8	4	13	SE	70	27
29 Easy to install	3	10	7	13	7	AX	69	28
37 Effective diagnostics	4	9	5	10	12	SA	63	29
34 Environmentally friendly	3	9	5	13	10	AS	62	30
Unimportant								
18 Wide range of viewing positions	3	7	9	10	11	SA	61	31
19 Ergonomically designed controls	3	7	6	10	14	SA	55	32
14 Flat rectangular screen	5	4	7	9	15	S	55	33
25 Attractive product styling	3	5	3	14	15	SA	47	34
26 Stays clean and new-looking	3	2	6	15	14	AS	45	35
24 Compact size cabinet	1	1	5	16	17	SA	33	36
23 Good portability	4	1	3	6	26	S	31	37
15 Minimal screen surround	1	–	1	10	28	SA	16	38
Totals	99	666	243	257	255			

The collective classification for each Secondary requirement was determined in each group by arranging the five category scores in descending order and omitting any categories that received less than 5 out of 20. Thus Secondary 23 ('Good portability'), which in Group 2 received scores I 1, X 1, E 2, A 3, S 13, was classified as S. In some cases, where the scores were widely distributed, the overall classification included two or even three of the categories. Thus Secondary 18 ('Wide range of viewing positions'), which in Group 1 received scores I 0, X 2, E 7, A 6, S 5, was classified as EAS. The overall classifications were obtained by adding the scores of the two groups to give the results shown in Table 2.1.

To obtain a measure of their relative importance, a score was computed for each Secondary using the weighting factors I = 4, X = 3, E = 2, A = 1, S = 0 and the Secondaries were then ranked according to this score as shown in the columns on the right in Appendix B.

2.5   RESULTS OF THE STUDY

It can be seen from Appendix B that the majority of all user selections, some 60 percent of the total, fell into the *Expressed* category at the end of Phase 2 of the Quality Game, which the additional question divided into 44 percent *Explicit* and 16 percent *Expressed*. It is not surprising, therefore, that for 31 out of the 38 Secondaries the combined category scored highest. This provides an affirmation of the perceived importance of the Secondaries in the PST tree derived from the process of gathering and sorting requirements: users believe that most of them really are important.

The other three EASI categories, *Attractive*, *Scrap* and *Implicit*, received 17 percent, 17 percent and 6 percent of the selections respectively. Nine of the Secondaries received the highest number of selections as *Scrap* and only five as *Attractive*. None was classified primarily as *Implicit*. This indicates a possible weakness in the way the Quality Game was played, in that a reasonable number of the players found it difficult during Phase 2 to separate the Secondary Cards they had classed as Indifferent in Phase 1. Possible improvements include stronger direction by the moderator to choose Happy in Phase 1 only if absolutely positively happy, or reversing the order of the two phases by making the Category 2 selection first.

Some differences are evident between Groups 1 and 2. For the overall scores Group 1 had more *Implicit* whereas Group 2 had more *Explicit* classifications, suggesting that the professional graphic arts users are perhaps more inclined to take good quality displays for granted. Rankings for individual Secondaries are similar in most cases, though there are a few significant differences, again suggesting that the graphic arts users are more preoccupied with the control of colour on the display, whereas other users are more concerned with general usability issues:

Group 1 rated higher	Group 2 rated higher
2 Good for soft-proofing of images	18 Wide range of viewing positions
3 Good for general interactive display	20 Easy to operate the controls
11 Good calibration facilities	24 Compact size cabinet
12 Good viewing characteristics	29 Easy to install

The results of Appendix B are summarised in Table 2.1, with the Secondaries rearranged by rank based on their computed scores. Based on their EASI class and rank, they have been divided into four groups. In the highest ranking group, denoted Essential, all but three of the Secondaries come from the first four Primaries, which cover the visual and image quality aspects of the display. The other three relate to high reliability, value for

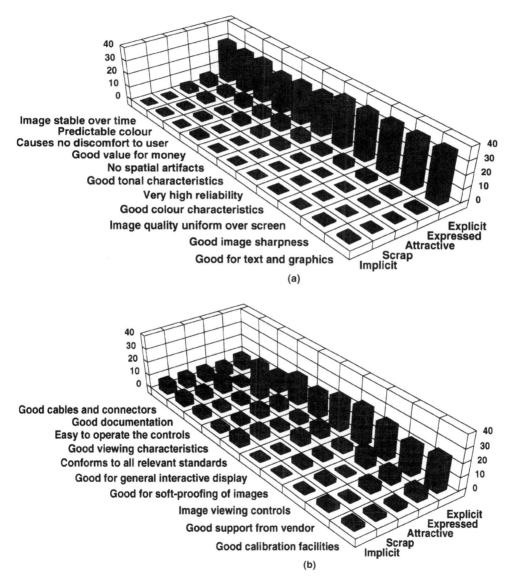

Figure 2.6 Four classes of display requirements: (a) essential requirements have high Explicit ratings; (b) highly desirable requirements combine Explicit and Implicit; (c) desirable requirements score well as Attractive; (d) unimportant requirements have high Scrap ratings

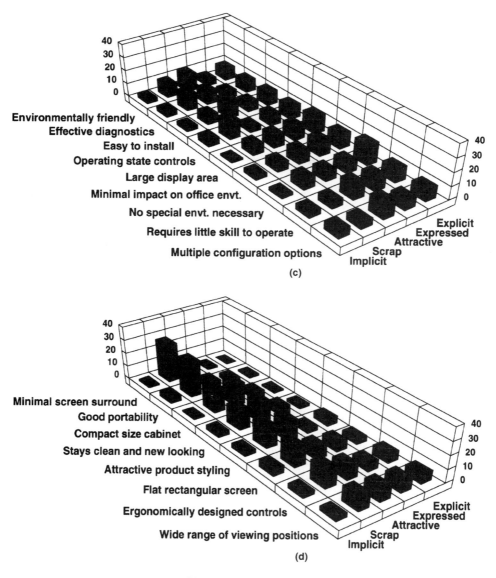

Figure 2.6 *(continued)*

money and user comfort. The principal function of a display must be to deliver a high quality image.

The second ranking group, denoted Highly Desirable, includes Secondaries from across a wide range of Primaries. High *Implicit* ratings are achieved for conformance to standards, documentation and good cables and connectors. It is worth noting that at the head of this group is 'Good calibration facilities', which indicates an opportunity to add value to the monitor. Two usability characteristics appear in this group, but ease of use was not very highly rated overall. As one of the users said, 'Most of the time you just want to look at a display without having to fiddle with its controls.'

The third ranking group, denoted Desirable, contains mainly Secondaries that received high *Attractive* ratings, though some show mixtures of *Expressed* and *Scrap*. They are mostly related to usability issues and the operating environment, and it is instructive to note that 'No special environment necessary' ranks significantly higher than 'Environmentally friendly'. Opinion was rather divided on 'Operating state controls' and 'Effective diagnostics', with some users stressing their importance whereas others were quite indifferent. The two features that are prominent by their high *Attractive* scores are 'Multiple configuration options' and 'Easy to install'.

The lowest ranking group, denoted Unimportant, is possibly the most instructive because it contains the Secondaries that the majority of users felt were of little or no value and therefore classified as *Scrap*. These include external product styling and some ergonomic features. Lowest on the list are the characteristics of the display cabinet, including its weight, volume and bezel dimensions. Clearly users care much more about the visual characteristics of a desktop display than the package in which it is housed.

Figure 2.6 shows the four groups of Table 2.1 in graphical form, indicating clearly the change in balance of classifications from *Explicit* for the highest rated features to *Scrap* for the lowest rated. In the middle are features that are not well classified because users were not sure or differed in opinion, resulting in a spread of classes.

2.6 CONCLUSIONS

The study was successful in gathering a comprehensive set of user requirements for desktop displays for electronic imaging applications, as part of an engineering product development programme utilising QFD methods. The PST tree in Appendix A gives a structured presentation of all aspects of displays that were found to be of interest to users. The EASI classification of the Secondary requirements from the PST tree indicated clearly, moreover, the relative priorities that users attach to the different product features of displays.

The Quality Game was shown to be a valuable technique for determining the EASI classifications of a set of product requirements. It can be administered with a minimum of preparatory work or training, is quickly performed and enjoyed by the players (who might otherwise be known as experimental subjects), and yields meaningful results that can readily be used to guide the effective assignment of product development resources. The Quality Game has a place amongst QFD tools for capturing the voice of the customer.

This study was performed when the author was employed as Principal Consultant at Crosfield Electronics Ltd. Thanks are due to Malcolm Shaw and Sinclair Morgan at Crosfield for their advice on the methodology and procedures employed, and to colleagues who participated in the Focus Group. Thanks also to the 40 professional users who gave their time in playing the Quality Game.

REFERENCES

Cullen, J. and Hollingum, J. (1989), *Implementing Total Quality*, IFS Publications, Bedford, UK.
Fischhoff, B. and Furby, L. (1988), Measuring values: a conceptual framework for interpreting transactions with special reference to contingent valuation of visibility, *J. Risk and Uncertainty*, **1**, 147–184.

Grossman, S., Lynch G. and Stempski, M. (1992), Team approach improves user interfaces for instruments, *EDN*, 4 June, 29–134.

Hutchings, A.F. and Knox, S.T. (1995), Creating products customers demand, *Comm. ACM*, **38**(5), 72–80.

Jeffries, G. (1991), *EASI Groups and the Quality Game Explained*, Technical Note, Crosfield Electronics Ltd, Hemel Hempstead, UK.

Kahneman, D., Ritov, I., Jacowitz, K., and Grant, P. (1993), Stated willingness to pay for public goods, *Psychological Science*, **4**, 310–315.

Kano, N. (1987), TQC as Total Quality Creation, *Proc. Int. Conf. on Quality Control*, Tokyo, 143–148.

Kano, N., Seraku, N., Takahashi, F. and Tsuji, S. (1982), Attractive quality and must-be quality, *Proc. 12th Annual Meeting of the Japanese Society for Quality Control*.

Kasser, J. (1995), *Applying Total Quality Management to Systems Engineering*, Artech House, Norwood, MA.

O'Brien, D. (1991), *User-oriented, Structured-thinking Procedures for the Concept Stage of System Design*, Technical Note, Home Office, London.

Robertshaw, W.G. (1995), Using an objective sales point measure to incorporate elements of Kano Model into QFD, *Proc. 7th Symp. on Quality Function Deployment*, Novi, MI.

Shillito, M.L. (1995), VOC with a future dimension, *Proc. 7th Symp. on Quality Function Deployment*, Novi, MI.

Sullivan, L.P. (1986), Quality function deployment, *Quality Progress*, American Society for Quality Control, June.

Zairi, M. (19930), *Quality Function Deployment: A Modern Competitive Tool*, TQM Practitioner Series, Technical Communications Ltd, Letchworth, UK.

APPENDIX A

PST tree of requirements for desktop displays

Good for a wide range of desktop imaging applications
1   Good for text and graphics
   Easy to read fine text
   Good display of graphics
   Good display of fine lines (horizontal and vertical)
   Good display of photo-realistic images

2   Good for soft-proofing of images
   High quality image rendition
   Accurate soft proof prediction
   WYSIWYG colour
   Good reproduction of white paper
   Simulate gloss/matt finish

3   Good for general interactive display purposes
   Suitable for other applications besides DTP
   Good for interactive operations (GUI)
   Responsive to a moving image
   Good image quality in wide range of viewing conditions

High image quality
4   Good tonal characteristics
   Bright clear image
   High contrast range
   Dark blacks

Tonal range same as print
Good rendering of mid-tones
No tone jumps (contouring)

5   Good colour characteristics
Accurate colour rendition
Good colour saturation for all hues
Very pure primary colours
Wide colour gamut
Shows all printable colours

6   Good image sharpness
Sharp crisp images
Good fine detail
High resolution (pixels/mm)
Same resolution as printed page

Image free from defects
7   Image quality uniform throughout screen area
Image not distorted
Luminance same at sides and corners as at centre
No colour purity errors
No sharpness/focus changes

8   No spatial artifacts
No 'jaggies' on lines
No moiré or patterning
Microstructure of display not visible
No colour convergence errors
No visible 'noise' on image
No motion 'drag'

9   Image stable over time
Luminance and colour do not drift
Image geometry and focus do not drift
Long time between recalibrations
No visible image movement
Fine detail does not 'twitch'
Does not flicker
Stabilises quickly after power-on

Well-controlled colour
10   Predictable colour
No visible difference in primaries (phosphors) from standard
Good match between any two monitors of the same model
Can resolve just noticeable colour differences
Patch colour is not affected by rest of display

11   Good calibration facilities
Control software on host computer to define calibration state
Built-in calibration sensor
Automatic calibration to defined calibration state
Accurate tracking of colour temperature throughout grey scale
Fast to calibrate

12   Good viewing characteristics
View from any angle
Minimal/no reflections from screen

Cabinet colour does not affect appearance of displayed image
Optional/adjustable viewing hood
Use in normal office lighting
Compensates for ambient light level and colour

Optimal physical screen characteristics

13 Large display area

Display an A3 image at true size
Maximum usable screen area (low wastage at edges)
Large enough to include a border around image
Choice of screen sizes

14 Flat rectangular screen

Minimal/no curvature on either axis
Straight sides to screen
Square corners on screen

15 Minimal screen surround

Small width of fascia panel
Minimal depth of fascia panel
Multiple units can be butted together into an array

Full set of control facilities

16 Image viewing controls

Brightness control
Contrast control
Luminance level control
White point control

17 Operating state controls

On-off switch
Degauss button
Convergence control
Range of user-selectable modes
Controls adjustable through host computer interface
Power-on indicator

18 Wide range of viewing positions

Swivel and tilt adjustments
Rotate through 90° degrees for portrait format
Possible to mount horizontally on work surface
Handle like a paper proof

Easy to use

19 Ergonomically designed controls

Simple switch on–off procedure
Controls easily accessible on front panel
Controls cannot be disturbed accidentally
Clear legends on controls and connectors
All controls are at operator's fingertips
Easy to adjust display viewing position

20 Easy to operate the controls

Simple controls
Easy to identify controls
Easy to reset controls to a known state
Easy to make control adjustments
Easy to calibrate

21 **Requires little or no skill to operate**
    Consistent results from different operators
    On-screen menus for control adjustments
    Voice-activated controls
    Easy to identify manufacturer and model
    No special training required

22 **Causes no discomfort to user**
    Minimal/no glare from screen
    No harmful radiation
    No static build-up on screen
    Not hazardous to use
    Does not cause fatigue
    Does not cause nausea

23 **Portable**
    Light weight
    Easy to move around desktop
    Incorporates grips for lifting
    Easy to carry

24 **Compact size cabinet**
    Fits on desktop
    Small desk footprint
    Shallow cabinet (front to back)
    Folds away when not in use
    Hang on the wall

Good design and engineering

25 **Attractive product styling**
    Looks reflect product value
    Designed in sympathy with desktop products
    Should look 'hi tech'
    Should look exciting
    Should be 'transparent' (cabinet disappears)
    Looks robust and well made

26 **Stays clean and new-looking**
    Strong packaging prevents damage in transit
    Cabinet resists scuffing and external wear
    Resists spills of liquids
    Easy to clean
    Screen surface resists damage
    Does not show fingerprints on screen

27 **Very reliable**
    Long lifetime (MTBF >5 years)
    Doesn't break down
    Doesn't exhibit intermittent faults
    All units manufactured to same high quality
    No routine servicing required
    Screen saver to protect phosphors

28 **Conforms to all relevant standards**
    Complies with all ergonomic standards
    Complies with all safety standards
    Complies with all EMC standards
    Standard input signals
    Supplied with InterColour profile

Convenient installation and setup

29 Easy to install
> Ready to go out of box
> Easy to connect
> No configuration switches to set up
> Fast to install

30 Good cables and connectors
> Supplied with all necessary cables and adaptors
> Cables are of adequate length for workstation
> Effective and reliable video connectors
> Easy to chain additional monitors

31 Multiple configuration options
> Works on any mains voltage and frequency
> Connect to any host computer
> Driver software auto-configures for variety of graphics cards
> Can be set up independent of host computer

No environmental problems

32 No special environment necessary
> Operates in normal office environment
> Not affected by changes in temperature
> Not affected by external magnetic fields
> Not affected by minor knocks and bumps

33 Minimal impact on office environment
> Low noise level
> No distracting noises
> Low heat output
> No static discharge
> Does not vibrate
> Does not cause interference with other equipment

34 Environmentally friendly
> Low power consumption
> Minimal power consumed when not in use
> No toxic materials for end-of-life disposal

Competitive price/performance ratio

35 Good value for money
> Costs no more than competitors
> Low cost of ownership
> Cheap to run
> No consumables
> Upgradable with new technologies

Full range of support services

36 Good support from vendor
> Comes with a lifetime guarantee
> Fast support when needed
> Telephone support from vendor (help-line)
> Local support office
> Stable supplier organisation

37 Effective diagnostics
> Built-in range of test patterns
> Built-in warning systems
> Built-in diagnostics

   Fault diagnosis from host computer
   Short down-time periods (MTTR <2 hours)

38 Good documentation
   Comprehensive documentation
   Well-illustrated documentation
   Understandable operator manual

APPENDIX B

Results of EASI classification of secondaries

(Tabulated on pages 40–41)

EASI Results for Desktop Display Requirements – Group 1

	Requirement	I	X	E	A	S	Class	Score	Rank
1	Good for text and graphics	–	19	1	–	–	X	59	1
2	Good for soft-proofing of images	1	13	4	2	–	X	53	6
3	Good for gen. interactive display	1	12	5	2	–	XE	52	7
4	Good tonal characteristics	–	14	4	2	–	X	52	7
5	Good colour characteristics	–	16	4	–	–	X	56	4
6	Good image sharpness	–	18	3	–	–	X	58	2
7	Image quality uniform over screen	–	17	3	–	–	X	57	3
8	No spatial artifacts	–	12	7	1	–	XE	51	8
9	Image stable over time	–	13	4	3	–	X	50	9
10	Predictable colour	1	12	5	2	–	XE	52	7
11	Good calibration facilities	3	9	7	1	1	XE	54	5
12	Good viewing characteristics	2	10	5	2	1	XE	50	9
13	Large display area	1	6	6	4	3	XE	38	17
14	Flat rectangular screen	3	1	4	5	7	SA	28	21
15	Minimal screen surround	1	–	–	7	12	SA	11	29
16	Image viewing controls	1	9	8	1	1	XE	48	11
17	Operating state controls	4	4	6	1	5	ES	41	15
18	Wide range of viewing positions	1	2	7	6	5	EAS	26	24
19	Ergonomically designed controls	–	3	7	6	7	SA	27	23
20	Easy to operate the controls	2	5	5	6	3	EX	43	13
21	Requires little skill to operate	3	7	7	2	2	XA	41	15
22	Causes no discomfort to user	2	7	3	6	1	XE	52	7
23	Good portability	3	–	5	–	13	S	17	27
24	Compact size cabinet	1	–	1	6	12	SA	12	28
25	Attractive product styling	2	3	1	5	9	SA	24	25
26	Stays clean and new-looking	2	–	3	9	6	AS	23	26
27	Very high reliability	–	18	1	1	–	X	57	3
28	Conforms to all relevant standards	5	4	4	4	3	I	44	12
29	Easy to install	1	4	3	7	5	AS	29	20
30	Good cables and connectors	5	3	4	4	4	I	41	15
31	Multiple configuration options	3	3	3	6	2	EA	39	16
32	No special environment necessary	–	8	6	3	5	XS	37	18
33	Minimal impact on office envt.	2	5	5	3	4	XE	37	18
34	Environmentally friendly	1	4	3	7	5	AS	29	19
35	Good value for money	1	14	2	3	–	X	53	6
36	Good support from vendor	3	8	5	3	1	XE	49	10
37	Effective diagnostics	3	2	2	4	8	S	28	21
38	Good documentation	5	4	3	6	3	AI	42	14
	TOTALS	63	296	146	128	127			

EASI Results for Desktop Display Requirements – Group 2

#	Requirement	I	X	E	A	S	Class	Score	Rank
1	Good for text and graphics	1	18	1	–	–	X	60	1
2	Good for soft-proofing of images	–	13	1	2	4	X	43	11
3	Good for gen. interactive display	–	11	3	5	1	XA	44	10
4	Good tonal characteristics	–	16	2	2	–	X	54	5
5	Good colour characteristics	–	19	1	–	–	X	59	2
6	Good image sharpness	1	18	–	1	–	X	59	2
7	Image quality uniform over screen	–	19	1	–	–	X	59	2
8	No spatial artifacts	–	17	1	2	–	X	55	4
9	Image stable over time	–	16	3	1	–	X	55	4
10	Predictable colour	–	17	–	2	1	X	53	6
11	Good calibration facilities	–	15	–	2	3	X	47	9
12	Good viewing characteristics	1	10	2	5	2	XA	43	11
13	Large display area	–	7	4	5	4	XA	34	17
14	Flat rectangular screen	2	3	3	4	8	S	27	21
15	Minimal screen surround	–	–	1	3	16	S	5	26
16	Image viewing controls	–	15	3	–	2	X	51	8
17	Operating stage controls	1	6	2	3	8	SX	29	19
18	Wide range of viewing positions	3	5	2	4	6	SX	35	16
19	Ergonomically designed controls	1	4	4	4	7	S	28	20
20	Easy to operate the controls	2	8	6	3	1	XE	47	9
21	Requires little skill to operate	2	3	7	5	3	EA	36	15
22	Causes no discomfort to user	–	16	2	1	1	X	53	6
23	Good portability	1	1	2	3	13	S	14	25
24	Compact size cabinet	–	1	4	10	5	AS	21	24
25	Attractive product styling	1	2	3	9	6	AS	23	22
26	stays clean and new-looking	1	2	3	6	8	SA	22	23
27	very high reliability	–	17	3	–	–	X	57	3
28	Conforms to all relevant standards	2	14	1	–	3	X	52	7
29	easy to install	2	6	4	6	2	XA	40	13
30	Good cables and connectors	3	6	3	4	4	X	40	13
31	Multiple configuration options	3	6	3	6	3	XA	40	13
32	No special environment necessary	1	7	5	4	3	XE	39	14
33	Minimal impact on office envt.	1	6	6	5	2	XE	39	14
34	environmentally friendly	2	5	2	6	5	AXS	33	18
35	Good value for money	1	13	4	2	–	X	53	6
36	Good support from vendor	1	13	3	3	–	X	52	7
37	effective diagnostics	1	7	2	6	4	XA	35	16
38	Good documentation	2	8	2	5	3	XA	41	12
	TOTALS	36	370	97	129	128			

(Table also includes an "Individual Classification" matrix of per-respondent X/S/A/E/I ratings for each requirement.)

3

Application requirements and the evolution of displays

Philip Robertson

3.1 INTRODUCTION

Advanced applications, such as geological modelling and geophysical exploration, push computational and display technologies to their limits. This applies not only to hardware performance but also to the software and system support. Significantly, available display and computational capabilities are often not utilised effectively because of poor linkage to the working environment of application specialists, who currently spend much effort struggling with computational tools and associated displays of data. Graphical interfaces can provide easier access to these computational functionalities, but seldom map the functionalities effectively into the working 'paradigm' of an application specialist.

This situation is illustrated in Figure 3.1. The increasingly high performance tools of the 1980s still require applications specialists to spend time on side issues such as data format interchange, explicit functionality descriptions, and other tedious tasks that distract from the main task of high value work in the application domain. The ideal environment, illustrated by the utopia of the 2000s on the right-hand side of the figure, allows a specialist to interact with the data, on a large format, scale-accurate 3D display with appropriate support for visualisation, accessing networked data sets and querying or formulating hypotheses in domain-specific terms. Such capabilities require intelligent support, and the capacity to map from domain-specific requirements or constraints to domain-independent or generic computational functionalities.

Display Systems, Edited by L.W. MacDonald and A.C. Lowe. © 1997 John Wiley & Sons Ltd.

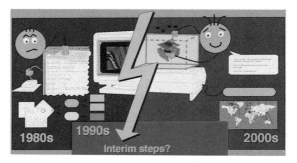

Figure 3.1 Schematic representation of environments of the 1980s, requiring extensive use of computational tools and systems, and projected environments of the 2000s, offering intelligent support for domain-specific functions

The concept of interactive visualisation is core to achieving such a capability. Visualisation implies the building of a mental model linking the display with its context. This leads to consideration not only of the perceived display, but also of its interpretation, which depends on the mental model or internal representation that the user has built, which in turn depends on the context and environment of use. Considering the needs for interactive visualisation thus helps to focus on the broader needs for developing application-sensitive working environments. In fact visualisation systems are increasingly evolving to meet the needs of advanced applications, and are starting to include perceptual control over display variables.

This prompts a closer look at the evolution of visualisation systems, and the types of capability that have emerged, or might be expected to emerge. Three major advances in capabilities stand out, as illustrated in Figure 3.2:

- Geometric transformations: the capability to perform spatial transformations on screen-sized data sets, ideally at interactive rates.
- Perceptual addressing: the capability to specify and control display parameters such as colour in perceptual terms, with associated modelling of display devices to ensure accurate realisation.
- Guidance for design of visualisations: the capability to incorporate intelligence aimed at helping a user decide what visualisation technique and tools to use for a specified

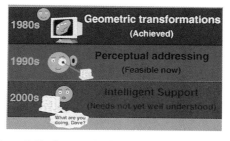

Figure 3.2 The evolution of display capability for geometric transformations during the 1980s, the potential for perceptual control in the 1990s and the end target of intelligent support in the 2000s

task, and, more generally, in allowing the user to work in terms relevant to an application environment.

Of these three needs, only the first has been effectively addressed to date as part of display capability. Early systems provided geometrical transformation capabilities increasingly embedded as part of display functionality, both as polygon transformation pipelines with associated scan-conversion support, and as image transformation for geometrical warping in specialised image processing systems used for remote sensing applications. Even so, performance is still not sufficient for real modelling or simulation tasks.

Perceptual colour addressing has been accessible in a small number of application systems for some years but has not been supported by display functionality, and thus not performed at interactive rates for screen-sized images. Although systems have provided hardware support for simplified perceptual addressing in device-dependent terms, perceptual addressing in device-independent terms has not been supported. Yet the requirements for perceptual colour control are now fairly well understood.

The requirements for increased intelligence in visualisation systems, however, are far from being well understood at present; they are really only just being considered at a generic level (Robertson & De Ferrari, 1994). Thus whilst the future path for visualisation systems clearly hinges around exploiting intelligent systems, possible architectures and implications for display designs are still being worked out. How then do we move towards such a target capability, elicit the system requirements to make it possible, and map these requirements onto the underlying display and computational architectures and technologies? The problem is significant — we need to understand what types of system architectures are required for intelligent support to be able to design suitable supporting display and computational systems, in the same way that understanding of the needs for graphical user interfaces and graphics modelling led to architectures and technologies for display design in the 1980s.

In this chapter we review and explore at a general level the needs of advanced applications, the types of intelligent support required, and display issues and their dependence on these required functionalities. We then propose a specific interim step towards improved display design — that of achieving perceptual control over visualisation parameters — as a viable path towards a more fully intelligence-supported environment. Such perceptual control generates explicit requirements for display technologies, and can also specify a framework for applying intelligent support (Robertson & Hutchins, 1995). Figure 3.2 illustrates the context of such a focus, recognising the evolution of display capability for geometric transformations during the 1980s through the potential for perceptual control in the 1990s to the end target of intelligent support in the 2000s. Section 3.2 explores in more detail the requirements for interactive visualisation in advanced applications. Approaches to perceptual control are then described in Section 3.3, and system and hardware requirements are derived from these approaches. The broader potential to draw on this approach is summarised in the final section.

3.2   THE NEEDS OF ADVANCED APPLICATIONS

Interactive visualisation in advanced applications can take several forms: adjusting viewing parameters (such as the angle of view), adjusting representation parameters (for example, whether a variable is represented spatially, by colour or by time variation), or adjusting modelling parameters (such as the physically significant inputs to a model). These forms of interaction can be separated conceptually, even if in practice they are concatenated in, for example, a graphics pipeline. Interacting with modelling parameters is generally the most demanding, but is also critical to support hypothesis testing or model exploration. Requirements are considered here in terms of the computational performance needed, the desired working context or paradigm and its architectural implications, and the kind of display hardware support that would be ideal.

3.2.1   Achieving interaction — performance requirements

At the hardware level, current computational technologies are several orders of magnitude too low in performance to allow application specialists such as geoscientists to interact with significant parameters of their models for realistic data sets. Computation requirements may be of the order of teraflops (10^{12} floating-point operations per second) for seismic or geological modelling, for example.

Interaction can range from straightforward pointing or selection, through manipulation and adjustment, to coordinated and highly complex operations. Pointing and selection are well handled by current technologies. Manipulation is much less well handled, however, because of the lack of good input metaphors and supporting devices, although data gloves and similar 3D control devices are helping in this area. Even changing the geometrical viewpoint, often the easiest way to resolve ambiguities, generally requires experience with the system being used and often has constraints that are difficult to predict in advance (Felger & Schroder, 1992). This immediately contravenes a core tenet of manipulation in the real world: that we can perform it intuitively or pre-attentively and allow our attentive resources to be concentrated on observing and interpreting the results. With existing computing systems a significant part of the manipulation task requires our attentive mechanisms — working out how to perform the required manipulation with the tools provided — thus distracting from observing and interpreting the result. The more successful interfaces for viewpoint manipulation are those that map the interaction devices to the controls of a meaningful real-world metaphor.

Interacting with model parameters — that is, parameters significant to the process being investigated — can be a powerful way of building an understanding of model scope and constraints. The direct feedback of the effects of adjusting a model parameter can provide information about non-linearities or other types of behaviour that may be very difficult to determine from static views of the results of a particular set of parameter values. A simple example is the detection of instabilities between otherwise stable regions, where it is a matter of chance whether static samples would detect such instabilities. Interacting with model parameters also enables the testing of hypotheses ('what-if' scenarios), and the guiding of parameter selection, e.g. for damping, on the basis of viewing the result. This process is often known as computational steering.

Current technologies offer immersion or 'virtual reality' possibilities, the basis of which is that the user is immersed within the data and can therefore draw on a broader and perhaps richer set of senses (Breen *et al.*, 1992). Immersion has drawbacks such as making it difficult to work simultaneously with other materials such as paper charts, telephones, and books or reports. Virtual functionalities pose additional problems if the previous physical methods of clarification, such as lifting up a map sheet, cannot be realised to provide similar capability, for example to resolve ambiguities, in a metaphoric software version. While alternative capabilities could be provided, the need to stay within, or at least to evolve from, the specialist's working paradigm remains critical.

Such virtual functionalities necessitate richer tools for data integration and display, and also for systematic methods of performing such integration under computational control. The technologies to create them are at present immature but some of the key features can be realised effectively without requiring immersion. An example is user-position-responsive viewing, where the user's head position influences the view presented, allowing effective depth disambiguation, a much more effective 3D cue than stereo display (Dickinson & Jern, 1994).

These functionalities all require the mapping of model parameters to interaction modes, so that the model, representation and display computations must be performed within the interaction latency time. For small problems, model computation might be of the order of Mflops (10^6 floating-point operations per second), but for models of any reasonable complexity, Gflops (10^9 floating point operations per second) are likely to be needed. Even this computational power is typical only for screen-sized image data. Although processor performance increases steadily, achieving the increase in performance needed for interactive modelling will require multiple, or very likely massively parallel, processors. Whether such computational capabilities can be built into the display, as with polygon pipeline processors in current technologies, will depend on whether sufficiently generalised forms of the computation can be found. Massively parallel pixel-oriented processors may offer adequate performance if generalised classes of algorithms can be exploited for the modelling.

In fact limitations in screen technologies have allowed, fortuitously, a constraint that has remained nearly constant for over a decade. Because larger images cannot be displayed, the problem size has often been reduced to that required only for the display resolution. Although not all problems can be so reduced, the constraint did open a window of opportunity for highly optimised graphics workstations relying on multiple polygon pipeline architectures to achieve the required performance. In general polygon-based algorithms do not scale linearly with data size — scaleable performance needs algorithms that scale linearly with data size and with the number of processors introduced.

These very high performance requirements are thus most likely to be met by parallel processors using pixel-based algorithms (Vezina *et al.*, 1992a,b), which have the additional benefit that they can maintain sampling information, often critical for sensed data from which deductions are being drawn. Because polygon algorithms introduce artifacts (polygon edges), which must then be removed by anti-aliasing methods to avoid their impact on the display or on subsequent modelling stages, it can be very difficult to maintain and represent accurate original sampling information (Greenberg, 1991). It should also be recognised that interactive visualisation is probably only going to be helpful when integrated within standard working tools, which can pose performance demands outside the scope of those tools. Improved systems design is thus necessary (Treinish *et al.*, 1992; Ribarsky *et al.*, 1992; Abel *et al.*, 1993.

If the performance for interactive visualisation can be achieved, there may be significant benefits from exploiting manipulation and model parameter adjustment. One example is in exploring the solution space of a multi-parameter model or simulation. A complex problem may have many possible solutions from different combinations of parameters, and being able to scan through different parameter combinations interactively can be important in avoiding, for example, local extrema. The ability to adjust more than one parameter simultaneously, again something we become very adept at in the real world, can make a substantial difference in exploring the nature of a problem and its potential solutions. This begins to draw on the more sophisticated skills of a human specialist, and thus starts to enable human expertise to be applied to the problem.

Equally powerful is the potential to exploit interactive forward modelling, and observation of its results, to help solve inverse modelling problems. This can be by comparison with expected results or with measured data. In each case the specialist is effectively drawn into the process of hypothesising and refining, and in so doing is utilising experience and learning capacity. Such a process is effectively taking advantage of the specialist's expertise (Robertson, 1993).

Humans have an ability to recognise structure or patterns in time-varying imagery that may not be evident in static images. Increasing the ability to correlate such patterns with interactively adjusted parameters should more effectively enable analysis skills such as detecting artifacts and surmising their cause, or more clearly distinguishing artifacts from real characteristics. For example, interactively adjusting filtering parameters applied to sensed data can highlight ringing or other filter characteristics, and distinguish these from data characteristics, if parameters such as filter damping, width, and type can be changed. Again, the specialist's understanding of the impact of different filters can be both enabled and increased.

3.2.2   Working context or 'paradigm' — generic architecture requirements

The visualisation itself, and interaction with its parameters, are just part of the overall interface requirements. The interface must also be able to support a user-centred approach to tackling the problems or needs in any particular application domain. In other words, computing systems should support the normal working environment of application specialists, allow them to work on problems in a manner consistent with this environment, and make the underlying tools or technologies transparent to their use. Existing computing environments do not currently achieve this.

Current computing environments for the most part promote a paradigm of use that is many steps away from the natural or preferred paradigm. Most specialists work in an environment that can best be described as a 'computational systems and tools' paradigm. That is, they struggle with tools, systems, networks, incompatibilities, different data formats, primitive data-flow representations of their processes, minimal automatic documenting and logging of operations they perform on their data, minimal back-track or 'undo' capability, minimal capture of the algorithm just applied to the data, and even often minimal support for preserving data integrity — hand-recorded log books are still crucial.

Even if data integrity is slightly better preserved, under a 'database update' paradigm, database languages are not sufficient for describing complex modelling or comparison operations. And this is still not a working context that is easy or natural for an application specialist. A 'visualisation-centred' paradigm, based on the recognition that pictures often provide the most effective and influential form of communication, in both static and dynamic forms, or even in 'hot-spot' enquiry mode sympathetic to an object-oriented software approach, can be an improvement.

But this is still several steps away from a true 'working-application environment' paradigm. One step closer might be a 'document or report' paradigm, where the main deliverable is a document or report for policy advice, or for giving a critical analysis. An interface that supports such a document as its main component, and where visualisations and other information provide linked access to data and models transparently, can get close to a 'working-application environment' paradigm. In the end, the actual working environment of application specialists needs to be reflected in both the interface and the set of expectations behind its use. This general need for interaction paradigms to evolve from being system-focused to being user-focused is illustrated in Figure 3.3. Achieving such paradigms requires the representation and application of knowledge about the domain and about users' needs for that domain, and an awareness of the tasks to be undertaken. Current trials in this area are focused on knowledge engineering — exploiting knowledge representation within a framework sufficiently formalised to capture and maintain the relevant information.

A key component is user modelling: that is, modelling and supporting user needs and behaviour patterns, and adaptability to the evolving needs of users. This focuses on the distinction between user-oriented approaches and systems-oriented approaches. Existing software systems, including user interface management systems, focus on system functionalities, and what the user needs to do to access them. What is required is the opposite: to concentrate on user needs and wishes, and what the system needs to do to meet those needs and wishes.

This leads to the central concept of developing appropriate interaction paradigms, which can form the basis for designing the interaction the user will perform, and the visualisations on which it will be performed, for a complex series of tasks associated with any given application (Carroll, 1991; Treu, 1992; Nardi & Zarmer, 1993). An interaction paradigm can be viewed as a high-level metaphor, embracing groupings of individual metaphors each of which may only be independently sustainable in a limited context within a broad framework that allows the expectations for interaction to be predicted. Such a paradigm should evolve from modelling the user expectations of the system, based on task analysis.

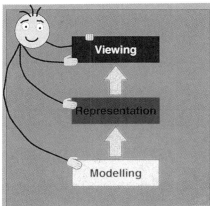

Figure 3.3 Interaction paradigms for visualisation must evolve from being system-focused to being user-focused

This general problem, of bridging between application working paradigms and computational paradigms, is probably the most critical factor limiting the effective use of existing technologies by applications specialists (Treu, 1992). For example, geologists like to manipulate 'faults' and preserve 'contacts' while hypothesising geological structure, but computational toolkits offer lines, polygons, and other graphical primitives or modelled objects; it is a non-trivial task to build application-context sensitive graphical editors (Lin *et al.*, 1995). This is one example of the need to incorporate intelligence in a display capability. Another is providing adaptive behaviour, and formalising the mechanism for learning a user's preferences, capabilities, and task context. If this type of gap can be bridged, and tools that meet the specialist's need can be realised, we will have a stronger basis for determining the highest priority requirements at a hardware level for displays and other computational facilities.

Some work in developing context-sensitive interactive editors has arisen from diagrammatic user interfaces, which have emerged in response to the need to apply specific constraints to diagram layout tasks. This work has provided generic user-interfaces, in recent times exploiting object-oriented approaches to simplify the mapping of real models to computational structures, within which domain-specific constraints can be applied. This type of approach is significant because it provides a method of incorporating domain-specific intelligence, such as the earlier-mentioned preservation of geological features, in a generic interface.

Underpinning such systems is the ability to map from domain-specific data models to generic computational geometry models, and thus to graphics primitives that can be realised in hardware for efficient display. If the requirements for intelligent support for application environments are to be met effectively, this type of mapping from domain-dependent to generic functionality, and hence to the requirements for specific hardware or fast software support, must be achieved. The capacity of display systems to achieve better than incremental performance increase on such problems will depend on finding elegant and generic mappings of this type, in the same way that hardware to perform core operations for graphical user interface management, such as bit-blit, provided such a performance boost to displays in the early to mid-1980s.

3.2.3   Display surface — GUI and geometry requirements

For most serious applications, current displays are simply not big enough. A typical geoscientist's office has map-sheet sized light tables covered in plans, overlays, interpretation sheets and other working charts. A similar size of flat-panel, providing a scale-accurate electronic version of a light table and associated digitising capability, would be a boon to geoscientists if it allowed direct input of interpretation plots, rescaling of charts and images to standard formats, and display of combinations of map sheets as required. Scaling requirements are demanding — geoscientists work over a large range of scales, and quantised scale mappings could cause problems.

Integration of different input and output modalities at different scales is a non-trivial problem. The added requirement of integrating information handling with advanced visualisation poses a significant HCI problem that is not easily addressed by user-interface tools or simple metaphors. User-interface design for small screens has given rise to few satisfactory interfaces that integrate complex functionalities. Extensions of simple 'metaphor' concepts to produce working 'paradigms' are few because the problem is difficult. This suggests an even greater problem for a screen that must be operable at small and large scales, at detailed and overview levels, and utilising both computer and manual methods.

There is thus a paradigm difference between the light table cum digitising tablet as used by geoscientists, and the graphics workstation environment. The Former assumes a scale-invariant, transparent or translucent overlay, with an implicit data fusion approach, and direct interaction constrained by the spatial resolution of the interaction instrument. Current workstation technologies, on the other hand, are based on a scale-varying combination of desktop and tool-based paradigms, with an underlying data flow approach, and direct interaction constrained by the spatial resolution of the display. Previous efforts to integrate such different paradigms have not been very successful, limiting the functionalities and often the uptake of new technologies. This is because the functionalities have developed independently, and one paradigm of use can effectively disrupt another, leaving the user in a confused and ineffective state.

Limits to human context switching capability, and the amounts and kinds of information that must be temporarily stored and retrieved mentally to allow a paradigm switch, often preclude the effective use of different paradigms. Recent research in HCI and cognitive science has focused attention on the problem of developing effective paradigms, and supporting metaphors, for work environments that support varying functionalities. Research on perceptual cues for context switching, intuitive induction of such cues, and effectiveness of induced switching, is also relevant. An example of this problem is the lack of integration of electronic whiteboards with computer-based word-processing and drawing capabilities, significantly limiting the whiteboard as an integrated work environment. An electronic light table thus does not just pose a simple problem of component interfacing, often misleadingly termed integration; it would be unlikely to perform its required role if developed using that approach. Similar capabilities are being explored in environments such as medical applications. Although large formats and immersion techniques are being used, resolution is low at present (Tani *et al.*, 1994).

Not all such needs have to be met with hardware solutions. For example, geoscientists are increasingly using workstations for display and interpretation, exploiting zoom and other functionalities to redress the problem of the display being too small. And distortion oriented interfaces offer metaphors for interaction that can help overcome continuity problems. But such tools are often not well designed to suit the working environment of, for example, a geologist or geophysicist; in general the required application functionalities may be difficult to achieve with the available tools by a computational non-expert.

3.2.4   Overall implications of application requirements

The implication of the above issues for display design is that performance on current modelling and viewing tasks is only one aspect influencing the design of display hardware and software support. Work is needed on exploring usage patterns, and their architectural implications, before capabilities can be realised in hardware, even though it appears that the needs are clear. For example, an agent-based architecture could allow 'plug-in modules' to enhance display adaptability. Modules might access different knowledge bases for data or device characteristics and hence influence computational operations such as sampling or device modelling. Required functionalities could thus be limited to multiple and interchangeable generic sets, from which domain-specific higher level operations could be constructed.

This section has explored the needs of advanced applications, and discussed the general implications and issues that should influence the future evolution of displays. The subsequent sections of this chapter deal with improvements that could be made to displays now, based on current understanding of generic functionality requirements, for providing perceptual addressing of display parameters.

3.3   DISPLAY SUPPORT FOR PERCEPTUAL COLOUR ADDRESSING

This section discusses the display design implications of perceptual addressing, using the example of mapping application data into perceptual colour gamuts to show how requirements of a display can be determined. The generic form of the technology provides the necessary specification for display capability. Specifically, the application requirement is to be able to map data variables into perceptually defined colour sequences, defined in terms of perceptual attributes of colour and realised within a perceptual colour space. To achieve this requires a user-interface that allows the specialist to choose colour sequences, realisable on the chosen display device, within constraints determined by perceptual rationales. Achieving this reliably and reproducibly requires accurate device modelling and colour transformation, and also the ability to incorporate additional information about lighting and viewing conditions.

This example, of how an advanced application or set of applications can be reduced to a generic set of requirements which then drive display system requirements, can be applied more broadly. Several other examples covering perceptual sound control and perceptual texture control are given and their implications for emerging display technology are explored.

3.3.1   Requirements for perceptual colour control

Although perceptual colour spaces have been used for over 15 years in advanced applications (e.g. Meyer & Greenberg, 1980), it is only recently that colour management systems have been effectively embedded within computational systems. The basic premise underlying the need for perceptually based colour management systems is that interpretation and thus comprehension will be improved if colour can be specified and controlled in perceptually meaningful terms, and if perceived colour differences can be directly related to variations in data values. This need is even more evident with interaction; effective adjustment of colour choices depends on relating the perception of change to the controls in a predictable manner, which in turn means that the controls must be perceptually 'linearised'. Figure 3.4 (Colour Plate 3) shows an example of a colour sequence specified directly in device RGB coordinates (left), and in perceptually uniform coordinates (right), showing the smoother colour gradations resulting from the perceptually specified sequence.

Perceptual colour spaces offer a framework for specifying colour in terms of its perceptual attributes hue, saturation and lightness, thereby allowing mappings of data into colour to be defined in these terms. Perceptual attributes are realised within a colour order system or colour space whose metric reflects the perceived size of colour differences. Several perceptual spaces are widely used, the most common of which are the CIELAB space, suitable for reflective viewing conditions, and the CIELUV space, suitable for emissive displays (CIE, 1978).

Mapping data into a perceptual colour space requires awareness of the perceptual colour gamut of the chosen target device (Robertson, 1988), because different devices have different colour gamuts. While device dependent colour specifications such as red, green, blue addressing methods are convenient for specifying colours in hardware controls, the dependence of these addressing methods on the display characteristics means that problems of colour reproduction arise. Device-independent colour control requires device-independent colour specification, within which device characteristics such as the gamut extent can then be represented.

Characterising a display in device-independent perceptual terms requires knowledge of the relationship between input signals and output colours in device-independent terms (usually in terms of CIE coordinates: see Chapter 17). Such relationships may arise from modelling the device behaviour in physical terms, or may arise from empirical measurements, possibly incorporating numerical modelling. Most colour management systems now use look-up tables, or look-up tables in conjunction with interpolation, to perform the transformations between device and perceptual coordinates. The look-up tables must be three-dimensional because displays are in general not only non-linear, but also non-additive, in a perceptual sense. Resolution requirements can necessitate very large look-up table sizes, so that a compromise between look-up table memory and computational interpolation is generally made for colour rendering that is both accurate and efficient.

3.3.2   Perceptual colour gamut representations

Figure 3.5 (Colour Plate 4) shows a graphical representation of the perceptual colour gamut of a CRT display, using 3D wire-frame and 2D cross-sections through the gamut. The vertical axis is the lightness axis, the radial axis colour saturation, and the hue varies with the angle around the lightness axis. Cross-sections of constant (opposing) hue containing the lightness axis, and of constant lightness are shown. Figure 3.6 shows interactive tools for defining data mappings into the gamut, schematics encapsulating the chosen mappings to help interpretation, and the resulting image. Such a representation, used as an interactive interface for mapping data into colour, provides the additional benefit of encouraging implicit learning; the user develops an understanding of different display capabilities in terms of their perceptual colour gamuts (Robertson *et al.*, 1994). The gamut boundary in the representation depends on the particular display, and hence determines scaling and other factors that must be applied to chosen data mappings. These tools have been developed for geoscience applications where colour is used both for categorical coding, and also for graded interpretation purposes (Robertson & O'Callaghan, 1988).

The upper left and right images in Figure 3.7 (Colour Plate 5) show cross-sections through colour monitor and laser printer (CLC500) gamuts respectively, illustrating the substantial differences between the devices. These display gamut representations show clearly why gamut mapping, the process of mapping data from the gamut of one display to that of another with different characteristics, is a non-trivial problem whose solution

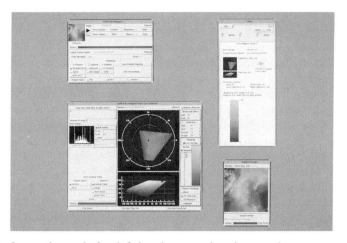

Figure 3.6 Interactive tools for defining data mappings into a colour gamut, schematics encapsulating the chosen mappings to help interpretation, and the resulting image. Upper left: overall control panel and 'interactive feedback' image. Lower left: interactively defining a 1D colour sequence for the variable with histogram shown. Upper right: encapsulation of mappings performed for data history. Lower right: result of applying the chosen mapping to the data.

may well be application dependent. Therefore flexible, task-dependent strategies for gamut mapping are necessary, as are flexible approaches to handling data points that fall outside the gamut in a particular specified mapping. The lower left image of a hypothetical geological structure shows out-of-gamut points for the defined mapping highlighted in pink. These out-of-gamut points have been returned to the gamut along a line of constant lightness (lower centre image), and along a line to the mid-point of the grey axis (lower right image). The appropriate return-to-gamut strategy depends on both the application and the interpretation task.

Perceptual control also implies that enhancement can be performed interactively in perceptual terms, for example by simply adjusting the end points of the arrows representing data mappings in the gamut. Figure 3.8 (Colour Plate 6) shows the results of applying chromatic expansion on a delineated region of an image, based on a 'spectral magnifying glass' approach (Juday, 1981).

3.3.3 Implications for display design — perceptual colour control

Colour mapping tools are most effective when interactive, allowing a user to adjust the chosen mappings, within specific constraints if appropriate, and observe the corresponding changes that result. This implies that colour coordinate conversions must be performed for image sizes up to a full screen at frame refresh rates, or at least at rates sufficient to support effective interaction.

Various schemes have been developed to reduce the costs of performing 3D interpolation. Despite this, even efficient software realisations on high performance workstations need to gain two to three orders of magnitude in performance to reach interactive rates. Hardware support on dedicated hard-copy devices can increase performance for device throughput, but there remains a clear need for frame-rate colour space transformations on standard workstations. The requirement is well defined, the domain and range of the mappings are constrained to physical device capabilities and so are limited, and the resolution requirements and sensitivities are also linked to either device capabilities or known visual system limitations. There is thus no reason in principle why displays should not have specially designed hardware support for this capability. An example is the recently developed *Chameleon* accelerator (Van de Cappelle & Plettinck, 1995). An additional capability required is to be able to substitute in-gamut colours for data points that have been mapped outside the device gamut. Various computational schemes can be used for this, including again a combination of computation and table look-up. Because various return-to-gamut strategies may be required, a generic form of solution is needed.

Perceived colour depends on ambient conditions. Displays should have built-in sensors that detect the spectral distribution of ambient conditions and compensate the colour gamut representation and mapping operations accordingly. Similarly, if adjustment of the display control knobs is allowed, built-in compensation to the displayed gamut should be feasible. The user should be aware that the colour gamut of the display has changed as a result either of the adjustment or of the ambient viewing conditions. Self-calibrating displays are most desirable, though an external calibrating device and associated adjustment capability can give very good results (see Chapter 18).

3.4 PERCEPTUAL SOUND CONTROL

Perceptual colour spaces have received more treatment than other perceptual spaces, but as multimedia capabilities become more commonplace, and systematic approaches to data representation and interpretation gradually take over from *ad hoc* approaches, there will be a growing need for similar perceptual spaces to cover other areas of perception. Eventually, as immersive environments evolve, there will be a need to integrate such perceptual spaces to cover combined perceptual control across colour, sound, texture, and perhaps other sensations.

Figure 3.9 (Colour Plate 7) shows a spatial representation of the three-dimensional gamut of a perceptually linearised sound space built around timbre, brightness and pitch attributes of sound (Barrass, 1994a,b), illustrated in wire frame. The vertical axis represents increasing pitch, using a Western diatonic scale. Brightness, effectively the degree of harmonic content, increases on a scale from dull at the central pitch axis to bright on the perimeter, in a manner comparable with colour saturation in a perceptual colour space. Timbre, derived from the tonal qualities of different instruments, varies around the pitch axis.

Such a space clearly does not span all perceptions of sound, just as perceptual colour spaces do not span all perceptions of colour, and colour displays do not cover the full human visual colour gamut, but it nevertheless offers a framework for systematic control and interpretation of a limited set of sounds for data representation and interpretation tasks. The shape of the gamut is determined by the set of sounds used to construct the space; the bulge at mid-pitch levels arises from the limitations placed on interpolation between samples. Denser sampling of the original instrument space would fill out this bulge. In fact the approach allows for different sets of spaces based on different timbre characteristics, effectively adding a categorical fourth dimension to the space.

Just as in the colour gamut case described earlier, sound sequences can be chosen to represent data variables by specifying paths in the perceptual sound space. Figure 3.10 (Colour Plate 8) shows a bivariate sound representation, in which two variables are mapped to a combination of sound attributes as shown by the blue arrows. Each arrow represents the mapping of a variable into sound attributes, defined by the path of the arrow through the perceptual sound space. Thus similar values in both variables will result in dull sounds (sounds from along the pitch axis), whereas different values in each variable will result in sounds that are brighter; the timbre will determine which is the dominant variable. This type of mapping is suited for investigating correlations between variables: positive correlation is represented by pitch, and negative correlation by brightness of the sound.

The perceptual sound space illustrated in Plates 7 and 8 is derived from psychoacoustic data and a recent history of developing concise sets of descriptors for sound (Grey, 1975; Bregman, 1990). The timbre data are taken from a set of musical instruments, and being a categorical attribute like colour hue, can be represented in a timbre circle. Pitch, an ordinal attribute of isolated sounds, is represented on a vertical axis, and brightness, also an ordinal attribute, is represented as a radial axis. This space is currently being explored for navigation support through complex information spaces (Barrass & Robertson, 1995). Multidimensional scaling and sequential streaming were used to linearise the axes. The CSOUND software is used to synthesise the composite sound sequences (Vercoe, 1991).

Systematic, as opposed to *ad hoc*, use of sound has yet to be widely exploited. Likely applications are for matching tasks that are difficult to perform using colour, and context generation tasks such as navigating through large information spaces, when visual attention may be fully occupied with content examination.

From a display point of view, the key issue is that a systematic approach to the use of sound by constructing a perceptual space provides a basis for a generic capability for which hardware support can be provided. Although it is too early to be specific about exactly what support is required, a capability for synthesis, for example specified by the CSOUND software functionality, would allow sound generation at interactive rates. Such a computational capability goes beyond the requirements for the specific sound space described above, allowing for evolution of perceptual sound control without necessarily requiring new sound generation capability. Not only sound synthesis but also mixing capabilities, multiple asynchronous channels, and full 16-bit 44 kHz sampling are needed. A sophisticated workstation, such as the IRCAM (Lindemann, 1991), could support not only the perceptual sound space and systematic use of sound described above, but also multiple sequencing and other complex mappings from data to sound to support interpretation and navigation.

3.5 PERCEPTUAL TEXTURE CONTROL

There is a long history of psychophysical studies on texture that attempt to find cardinal attributes of texture perception and hence description. Many have focused on second-order statistics (dipole characteristics) as best representing the salient perceptual characteristics. Computational generation of textures can be used to convey specific information, for example supporting colour in complex multi-layer information displays, as discussed earlier, to help disambiguate or enrich the information. An example is in volume visualisation, where translucent surfaces can be difficult to distinguish, particularly when viewed or examined statically. Using different textures for the surfaces offers a continuity cue to help disambiguation. Similarly texture can help to retrieve surface information obscured because of reflective highlights. Coding by texture is also a widely used facility in iconic representations (largely from prepared samples), though not yet widely exploited in image representations because of the complexity of controlling the required texture variation.

This raises the problem of developing a good computational method for controlling textures in perceptual terms. Markov Random Fields (MRF) provide a powerful computational method of generating textures in a systematic manner (Yuan & Rao, 1993), but do not have obvious perceptually linearised parameters. As with colour and sound, perceptual texture spaces need not span all perceptions of texture; rather they need to cover a sufficient range of texture perception to be of value in systematic representation and interpretation tasks. And again, computational methods of generating texture may well be applicable outside the domain of the specific perceptual spaces they initially serve, allowing for extension or refinement as understanding emerges of the perceptual space requirements and capabilities.

Grey-level dependence (co-occurrence) matrices have been shown to provide a perceptually meaningful representation of texture (Berry & Goutsias, 1991). Figure 3.11 shows a set of textures generated using a MRF model that is mathematically linked to the grey-level dependence matrices, thereby providing perceptual control (Li & Robertson, 1993). The figure illustrates the variation of two perceptually linearised second-order MRF parameters varying in regular increments along horizontal and vertical directions. The figure shows that the intermediate texture tiles appear to be approximately halfway between their neighbours, supporting the hypothesis that the controls for the texture generator are perceptually linearised. The data used to calibrate the model are taken from texture perception literature, and the model establishes the relationship between grey-level dependencies and second-order MRF parameters. The perceptual space is established by constraining the MRF parameter range to a neighbourhood within which a Euclidean metric holds.

The key factor for display design is that if a computational MRF generation model capability is provided, with the linearised second-order parameters as input parameters, this then gives the capacity to generate textures under perceptual control. This work is in its early stages, but is indicative of the type of capability that will be required, and could be provided by special purpose hardware in displays.

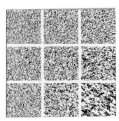

Figure 3.11   Texture tiles generated from an approximately uniform MRF texture generator. Horizontal and vertical perceptually linearised parameters increase by regular intervals. Uniformity is reflected in the observation that a texture between any other two looks roughly like a midpoint interpolation

3.6 SUMMARY AND BROADER ISSUES

It is realistic to expect displays to incorporate new functionalities when the generic requirements across a range of applications have emerged, with associated formalised models of functionality and interface standards. Thus geometric transformations have become part of display capability in both desktop systems and advanced graphics and imaging architectures, paralleled by software facilities such as X-windows and 3D graphics libraries. The move towards intelligent support and improved user-friendly environments for advanced applications will have significant impact on future display designs, both in terms of computational and display architectures, and in terms of specialised support for realising generic components of such architectures. Although it is too early to predict the generic requirements for such systems, an interim step in bridging the link between humans and technology is to provide perceptual control over display parameters.

Perceptual colour spaces offer an example of a generic framework for perceptual colour control. Their interactive and thus effective use depends on providing supporting colour transformations and associated operations at frame refresh rates. Models of functionality and interface standards are now well established. Digital pre-press has been the major drive for this capability, even though advanced applications were exploiting it many years earlier. The use of other display parameters, such as sound or texture, under perceptual control is at an early stage but models of generic requirements are nevertheless emerging.

The core requirement for colour space transformations is for non-linear 3D transformation. Currently the most efficient approaches to this are based on interpolated look-up tables which can provide a degree of accuracy sufficient for display and human visual characteristics. In fact a generalised 3D look-up table and interpolation capability would be of benefit for other non-linear multi-dimensional transformation or mapping tasks with constrained domains and ranges. For example frame-rate geometric transformation, with appropriate addressing and throughout mechanisms, could also be used for non-linear spatial warping and distortion requirements, such as magnifying glass functions, distorted work surfaces, or multi-spectral registration of satellite images.

Despite the scope for distortion oriented techniques to compensate for limited screen sizes, there remains an urgent need for the development of large, flat, scale-accurate screens with integrated display, computation, digitising and analysis capabilities. For example, integration with historical data in the form of map sheets, with hard-copy products, and with hand-drawn interpretation will remain an essential part of the geoscientist's working environment. 3D spatial and spectral transformations form a critical functionality requirement of such displays. The 3D equivalent of such a display, possibly through an immersive environment, would require the same capabilities. Interactive display update rates are vital; even though increasingly supported by intelligent methods, 'live' interpretation will remain a cornerstone of the skilled specialist.

ACKNOWLEDGEMENTS

The requirements discussed in this chapter arise from discussions with colleagues in the Visualisation Systems Program of the CSIRO Division of Information Technology, which has over 15 years' experience in developing visualisation systems for advanced geoscience applications with state-of-the-art displays and computational systems. Colleagues in the

CSIRO Division of Exploration and Mining, together with industrial collaborators, have focused requirements for the large flat-panel electronic light table and other applications. The perceptual space images were developed by Matthew Hutchins, Stephen Barrass and Ron Li, arising from their research into the use of perceptual spaces in visualisation. Particular thanks are due to Matthew Hutchins for review and assistance in preparation. Data used in examples were provided by colleagues in the CSIRO Divisions of Exploration and Mining and Wildlife and Ecology.

REFERENCES

Barrass, S. (1994a), A naturally ordered geometric model of sound inspired by colour theory, *Proc. Synaesthetica'94*, Australian Centre for the Arts and Technology, Canberra, July.

Barrass, S. (1994b), A perceptual framework for the auditory display of scientific data, *Proc. ICAD'94*, Santa Fe, November.

Barrass, S. and Robertson, P.K. (1995), Navigating with sound using a perceptually linearised sound space, *Proc. SPIE Conf. on Visual Data Exploration and Analysis II*, San Jose, February, Vol. 2410, 313–322.

Berry, J.R. and Goutsias (1991), A comparative study of matrix measures for maximum likelihood texture classification, *IEEE Trans. Sys. Man Cyb.*, **21** (1), 252–261.

Breen, P.T., Grinstein, G.G., Mizell, D.W., Satava, R.M., Smith, B., Stevens, M.M. and Zeltzer, D. (1992), Real virtual environment applications — now, *Proc., IEEE Visualisation'92*, Boston, MA, 375–379.

Bregman, A.S. (1990), *Auditory Scene Analysis: The Perceptual Organisation of Sound*, MIT Press, Cambridge, MA.

Carroll, J. (ed.) (1991), *Designing Interaction*, Cambridge University Press, New York.

CIE (1978), *Recommendations on Uniform Colour Spaces: Color Difference Equations, Psychometric Colour Terms*, Publication No. 15 (E-1.3.1)/TC-1.3, Supplement No. 2, CIE, Paris.

Dickinson, R.R. and Jern, M. (1994), A unified approach to interface design for data visualisation using desktop and immersion virtual environments, *Proc. CGI'94*, Melbourne, September.

Felger, W. and Schroder, F. (1992), The visualisation input pipeline — enabling semantic interaction in scientific visualisation, *Proc. Eurographics'92, Computer Graphics Forum*, **11**(3).

Greenberg, D. (1991), More accurate simulations at faster rates, *IEEE Computer Graphics and Applications*, **11**(1), 23–29.

Grey, J.M. (1975), *Exploration of Musical Timbre*, PhD Thesis, CCRMA Dept. of Music, Stanford University, Report No. STAN-M-2.

Juday, R. (1981), The magnifying glass: a feature space local expansion for visual analysis, *Proc. Int. Geoscience and Rem. Sens. Symp.*, IEEE, New York.

Li, R. and Robertson, P.K. (1993), Towards perceptual control of Markov random field textures, *IFIP Workshop on Perceptual Issues in Visualisation*, San Jose, October.

Lin, T., Ward, M.O., Power, W. and Landy, D. (1995), Providing a user friendly visual environment for creating geological block models, *Proc. Int. APCOM XXV* (Applications of Computers and Operations Research in the Minerals Industries), *AusIMM Bulletin*, July.

Lindemann, E. (1991), The architecture of the IRCAM musical workstation, *Computer Music Journal*, **15**(3), 41–49.

Meyer, G.W. and Greenberg, D.P. (1980), Perceptual colour spaces for computer graphics, *ACM Computer Graphics (Siggraph)*, **14**, 254–261.

Nardi, B.A. and Zarmer, C.L. (1993), Beyond models and metaphors: visual formalisms in user-interface design, *J. Visual Languages and Computing*, **4**, 5–33.

Ribarsky, W., Brown, B., Myerson, T., Feldmann, R., Smith, S. and Treinish, L. (1992), Object-oriented, dataflow visualisation systems — a paradigm shift?, *IEEE Visualisation'92, Proc.*, 384–388.

Robertson, P.K. (1988), Visualising colour gamuts: a user-interface for the effective use of perceptual colour spaces in data displays, *IEEE Computer Graphics & Applications*, **8**(5), 50–64.

Robertson, P.K. (1993), Interactive visualisation, *Australian Pattern Recognition Society DICTA '93 Proc.*, Sydney, 27–34.

Robertson, P.K. and De Ferrari, L. (1994), Systematic approaches to visualisation: is a reference model needed?, *Proc. ONR Workshop on Data Visualisation*, Darmstadt, 1993, published in *Scientific Visualisation: Advances and Challenges*, Academic Press, 287–305.

Robertson, P.K. and Hutchins, M. (1995), Guided colour representation using perceptual colour spaces, *SPIE Symp. on Electronic Imaging Science and Technology: Human Vision, Visual Processing and Digital Display VI*, San Jose, 5–10 Feb., Vol. 2411, 44–50.

Robertson, P.K. and O'Callaghan, J.F. (1988), The application of perceptual colour spaces to the display of remotely sensed imagery, *IEEE Trans. Geoscience and Remote Sensing*, **26**(1), 49–59.

Robertson, P.K., Hutchins, M., Stevenson, D.R., Barrass, S., Gunn, C. and Smith, D. (1994), Mapping data into colour gamuts — using interaction to increase usability and reduce complexity, *Computer & Graphics*, **18**(5), 653–665.

Tani, M., Horita, M., Yamaashi, K. and Tanikoshi, K. (1994), Courtyard: integrating shared overview on a large screen and per-user detail on individual screens, *Proc. CHI'94, Human Factors in Computing Systems*, Boston, MA, 44–50.

Treinish L.A., Butler D.M. Senoy H., Greinstein G.G. and Bryson S.T., (1992), Grand Challenge problems in visualisation software, *IEEE Visualisation'92 Proc.*, 366–371.

Treu, S. (1992), Interface structures: conceptual, logical, and physical patterns applicable to human–computer interaction, *Int. J. Man–Machine Studies*, **37**, 565–593.

Van de Cappelle, J.-P.R. and Plettinck, L.C. (1995), Usage of the Chameleon accelerator for colour transformations, *Proc. SPIE Symp. on Electronic Imaging Science and Technology: Device-Independent Colour Imaging II*, San Jose, 5–10 Feb., Vol. 2414, 188–191.

Vercoe, B. (1991), *CSOUND, A Manual for the Audio Processing System and Supporting Programs*, MIT Media Laboratory, Cambridge, MA.

Vézina, G. and Robertson, P.K. (1992), Data-parallel visualisation using multi-dimensional transformations, *Proc., IEEE Frontiers'92: Frontiers of Massively Parallel Computation*, 230–239.

Yuan, J. and Rao, T.S. (1993), Spectral estimation for random fields with applications to Markov modelling and texture classification, in R. Chappella and A. Jain (eds), *Markov Random Fields: Theory and Application*, Academic Press, 179–209.

Head-mounted display technology in Virtual Reality systems

Richard Holmes

4.1 INTRODUCTION

Immersive Virtual Reality (IVR) is a technology that enables users to 'enter into' and participate in computer generated 3D environments. Quite unlike conventional 2D displays, the tracked headsets make the experience omnipresent. They actually place the user into the computer generated world. The perceived fidelity of the system is dependent on the quality of the interface technologies and the seamless level of engineering integration.

Head-mounted displays (HMDs) constitute a core enabling technology for IVR, and the rapid advance of active matrix LCDs and other display devices will be one of the keys to the development of IVR into a powerful computer interface for the 21st century.

Virtual Reality (VR) is a rapidly developing, evolutionary computer technology with an indeterminate number of new applications, which is being driven forward even faster than many experts thought possible. It has fragmented into two groups, Desktop VR using a display monitor for CAD type applications and Immersive VR (IVR) using HMDs as the primary interface.

The following definitions of Virtual Reality are given as a reference, for the terminology seems to be in a permanent state of metamorphosis. These are summarised in Figure 4.1.

True VR is mathematically constructed, three-dimensional computer generated imagery, constituting geometry models and surrounding environment, with all of which

Display Systems, Edited by L.W. MacDonald and A.C. Lowe. © 1997 John Wiley & Sons Ltd.

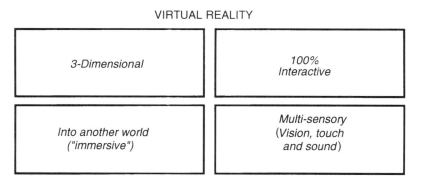

Figure 4.1 Elements of VR

the user can interact in real time (at 10 frames per second or faster). True VR can easily be confused with 'stop frame' filmed computer imagery which uses highly rendered computer graphics that are captured, image by image, on video to make it appear real time, often very convincingly, as in the film *Jurassic Park*.

Immersive VR involves the additional monitoring of body movement via head-mounted display devices that update the graphics presented to the user depending on where he or she looks, enabling intuitive participation with, and within, the virtual world. Additional tracked peripheral devices permit virtual navigation and pick-and-place manipulation of virtual objects, typically using data gloves, space joysticks or 3D tracker balls. This yields the third key element in true VR, that it is 100 percent interactive.

Additional sensory devices, such as body suits and goniometers, allow accurate real time replication of the human user's movements by his virtual character. More than anything else, IVR offers an opportunity to experience an alternative omnipresent world, entirely of man's own creation. This world is presented to the human user at a multi-sensory level using vision and sound as a minimum. At a higher level it can also include touch, orientation and olfactory senses, giving the final qualification of true VR.

We are now seeing entertainment applications pioneer and exploit the early experimental military and space sponsored initiatives (NASA, Wright Patterson USAF Airbase, BAe). Entertainment systems allow people to rent this expensive equipment for a typical cost, in 1995, of $1 per minute. They also allow maximum exploitation of the application software, in this instance expensive VR games, and hence are the first real commercial applications. Colour Plates 9 and 10 (Figures 4.2 and 4.3) show an HMD in use and a typical scene in an immersive entertainment application.

We are also seeing spinoff markets develop from entertainment, such as corporate promotion, using the same hardware with custom application software targeted at the general public. We are about to see the education market take off via multimedia and on to VR. Students will make use of the combined power of vision and sound as a replacement for text and will discover that it is fun, and offers a new powerful educational tool. Business will use VR as new applications are developed for design, training and communications.

As the costs of systems tumble and personal ownership of VR systems becomes viable, as it has for the PC market in the 1990s, so vast new potential will appear in communications, 'edutainment', retailing and the myriad of applications that the information superhighway is now claiming to support.

It is the intention of this chapter to review immersive display requirements, a small but critical core VR technology. It presents an analysis of what IVR demands from display technology and where the limitations inhibit performance, and gives ideas for making improvements.

4.2 OVERVIEW OF VR DISPLAY REQUIREMENTS

In order to understand the limitations and demands of today's IVR display technology, we should start by answering two key questions:

Q. What are we trying to achieve with an immersive VR system?

A. The ultimate goal of immersive Virtual Reality is to use the human's highly developed sensory perception of the real world to interact with computer generated media, and apply this deception to simulate new worlds and objects. These sophisticated real time sensory interfaces encompass vision, audio, tactile, olfactory and motion. For the purposes of this discourse we will concentrate on the vision related goals and associated display technology.

Q. What does an IVR head-mounted display (HMD) system offer that a conventional high resolution workstation monitor cannot?

A. (1) An omnipresent viewing capability, provided by virtue of the visually coupled head tracking system, fundamental to true IVR.

(2) Wide binocular field of view giving a greater feeling of immersion, akin to the effect of an Omnimax projection theatre or multi-monitor cockpit array.

(3) Stereoscopic 3D viewing capabilities without any positional limitations in the world, and the full range of depth cues such as stereopsis. This is essential when dealing with more complex images and interactions, such as the docking procedure that a molecular chemist may encounter when modelling structures, or the network of pipes found on the periphery of a jet engine.

It is the combination of these three factors that makes even the relatively low fidelity of today's IVR systems so compelling and will continue to drive IVR HMD devices through rapid development and market growth.

Although IVR HMD based systems hold great promise for the future, their display quality is still primitive when compared with the potential acuity of the human visual system. In VR today we live in a low-resolution pixellated world.

It is estimated that to approximate reality we would need a display capable of depicting a spatial resolution of around 4800 (H) by 3800 (V) or 18.24 million pixels (McKenna & Zeltzer, 1992) to equal the eye's foveal resolution (quite apart from peripheral vision). The highest resolution off-the-shelf liquid crystal display (LCD) today can offer only 1068 (H) by 480 (V) or 512 880 pixels (Sony LCD Product information), so we still have great scope for progress, and achieving a 35 × resolution improvement presents a considerable technical challenge to the display industry.

4.3 REVIEW OF HMD OPTIONS

4.3.1 Cathode ray tubes

CRT technology possesses a number of key disadvantages for the HMD designer. It generates a magnetic field (which can corrupt the sensitive magnetic position-tracking sensors). It emits heat close to the user's head which is undesirable in a HMD. CRTs usually occupy a comparatively large space envelope when compared to flat panel displays (see Figure 4.4). Weight has to date been the single largest disadvantage whenever a high resolution colour CRT display has been identified for use in a HMD. Mass in an HMD interferes with freedom of head movement and creates problems in ensuring sufficient levels of comfort for users.

CRTs also suffer from a number of specific potential health and safety hazards which do not apply to most flat panel displays:

- High voltages are needed to drive the focus and scan coils, clearly not desirable for a device in such intimate contact with the human head as HMD. This can of course be resolved by double insulation techniques but only with additional cost and weight.
- The flicker inherently generated by the CRT raster system can be an undesirable side effect of the technology, which leads to the need for high frequency, high performance CRTs for HMD applications, all at extra cost.

Figure 4.4 CRT-based HMD (courtesy of CAE Electronics Ltd)

- X-radiation is the other well-documented hazard, now well defined and controlled, with low emission screens becoming the norm. For conventional display requirements in the workplace, EC directive 90/270 (Chapter 21) sets out the minimum safety requirements.

When all the above factors are taken into consideration, even the impressive super high resolution 1000 line per inch LCD shutter CRT systems are only suitable for specialist high end applications in VR because of their cost and complexity.

CRTs have been striving towards the 'flatter squarer' viewing screen. The spherical curvature needed for the raster scan can create HMD optical field curvature problems for high power optics with very shallow depths of field. (The Visette 2 optics described below have a depth of field of only 0.5 mm and a flat display is essential for this design.)

Today's highly developed CRTs are superior in resolution, speed and price performance to flat panel devices. LCDs do, however, appear increasingly competitive in the sub 2″ display size, driven by the large market for camcorder viewfinder applications and future TV projection systems.

4.3.2   Flat panel displays

Flat panel technologies will ultimately be the main beneficiaries of the coming accelerated growth in applications of display technologies. The new 'vertical' market will be driven by the digital imaging revolution and the advent of digital satellite television, the digital video compact disk and multi-media telecommunication convergence.

This paradigm shift from analogue to digital is wholly commensurate with flat panel technology and will create fantastic new product opportunities in the developing Digital Photonics industry. IVR will ultimately be a key sector of the digital imaging industry and will probably necessitate displays from more than one type of technology.

For today's HMD designers, who wish to design practical affordable products that are both lightweight and compact, AM-TFT LCDs have strong advantages when compared with CRTs and other flat panel display (FPD) technologies. The high temperature poly-silicon devices, in particular, offer low power consumption, lightweight flicker-free images, thin profiles, low voltage operation, high contrast ratios, full colour and a large dynamic range of screen luminance.

The dominance of LCDs is expected to change, however, as niche display technologies are accepted into the HMD market. These displays may be differentiated in various ways, such as by very low cost or high performance (at a price) or by technical features such as bistability, but the HMD market is already starting to fragment into application specific sectors and will welcome more diversity in display product features. To try to predict which new display technology will become dominant in the near future is a pointless exercise. There are so many exciting display technologies with great future potential and each one will find its niche or quietly disappear due to lack of commercial viability.

FLCD technology (as being developed by the Sharp Corporation) has the bistable non-volatile capability to store pictures even when the power is off (Hewson, 1994). This will allow a number of interesting applications such as passive calibration of displays, and will be useful for 3D viewing of still stereo images.

It is most likely that display technologies will be driven into niche product sectors based on a size and price/performance formula. Plasma Displays (PDs), Vacuum Fluorescent

Displays (VFDs) and Field Emission Displays (FEDs) may all prove to be suitable for large wall displays. By contrast, Light Emitting Diode (LED), Ferroelectric Crystal Displays (FECDs) and Electroluminescent Displays (ELDs) will probably dominate the smaller portable display market along with the LCD family of technologies. This latter sector will provide new product opportunities to the HMD designer and enable the development of improved personal display devices.

4.3.3 Advanced alternative display technologies

Outside the realm of FPD technology, IVR is already looking to devices such as Texas Instruments' Digital Micromirror Device (DMD) (see Figure 4.5) and the Virtual Retinal Display (VRD), a development under way at the Human Interface Technology (HIT) Laboratory at the University of Washington, Seattle, to deliver potentially high resolution systems for advanced applications.

The Digital Micromirror Device has been developed as a display system offering superior performance in resolution, brightness, contrast, response time and colour fidelity compared to other display technologies. This revolutionary display concept uses a matrix of highly reflective mechanical micromirrors, each 16 μm square, fabricated over a standard SRAM chip. In operation the mirrors are tilted about the hinge at either +10° (on) or −10° (off) or they are parked flat when the display is deactivated.

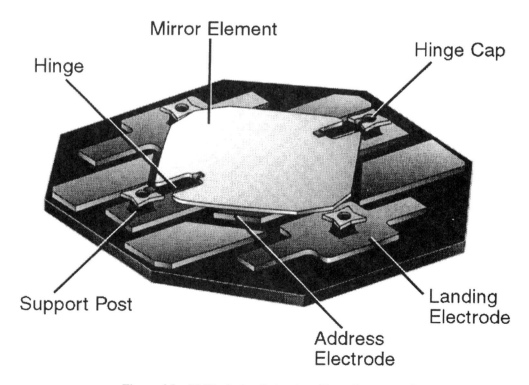

Figure 4.5 DMD pixel cell structure (Texas Instruments)

The Texas Instruments demonstration system has an array of micromirrors on a 17 μm pitch (centre to centre) 768H × 576V (442 368 pixels). It is being used as a large screen projection display device. Light from the illumination source is reflected through the optics to create a pixel image on a screen, while redundant light is reflected off to a dark trap. Texas Instruments are currently attempting to scale up this technology to HD resolution (2048 × 1152 pixels) which presents new challenges in the chip lithography and fabrication process (Younse & Monk, n.d.).

The VRD is another device that could generate a quantum leap in HMD performance. Instead of wearing a large electro-optical system on the head, the user will place a pair of spectacles with a 'domino' sized display generator for each eye attached to the frame. The image is then projected directly onto the eye's retina via four subsystems. Projection optics focus a photon generator (laser) which is turned on and off by a modulator (to generate pixels). A scanner then controls the position of the photon pixels in the X and Y axes to generate a potentially wide field of view on the retina.

The difficult key technical problems to solve are the provision of full colour from the laser source and the extremely precise beam control needed to effect the device. The beam controller must be prevented from locking accidentally whilst the collimated light is on the retina, or permanent eye damage may be caused. These are the technical challenges that currently face Thomas Furness and Joels Kollin, who along with the rest of the Seattle HIT lab team continue to develop the VRD (Microvision Inc., 1994). These new technologies offer great promise but still need further considerable development for advanced commercial HMD applications, let alone any consumer products.

Other technologies of interest include Reflection Technology's Vibrating Mirror LED system, as used in its own 'Private Eye' product and recently released in the Nintendo 'Virtual Boy' 3D game viewer. This technology is currently limited to a monochromatic red on black background and as such has limited performance for complex graphics applications until a colour system can be developed (Wells, 1991).

4.4 HUMAN FACTORS OF HEAD-MOUNTED DISPLAYS

With HMD systems, human factors are a key consideration and the issues are wide ranging. Many display-related issues are also optics-related, such as vision accommodation and convergence (when considering 3D simulations). Of principal concern to the HMD designer are the side effects that can be generated in IVR applications by poorly designed or incorrectly set up equipment.

4.4.1 Photosensitive epilepsy

One person in 200, typically, will suffer from 'active epilepsy' and about one person in 20 may experience a single seizure in isolation (David Lewis Centre for Epilepsy). People who have repeated spontaneous seizures are described as epileptic. Seizures may also be triggered in epileptics by internal and external factors, i.e. unusual fatigue, hormonal changes, emotional upsets, etc. It should be noted that the condition is particularly common in young children, the majority of whom will grow out of it by the time they become adults. Flicker, certain types of graphic depictions and display spatial frequencies can then be a trigger for those with photosensitive epilepsy. Prior to the development of video games, those with photosensitive epilepsy amounted to an estimated 1 in 4000 of the population (Binnie & Jeavons, 1992), a smaller subgroup of the full epileptic condition. The critical frequency range to avoid is 7–30 Hz (Binnie & Jeavons, 1992). This frequency range should also be avoided in the specification of a backlight. LCDs themselves, not being raster devices, are not flicker generators.

In general, displays should avoid certain types of graphic depictions:

(1) Avoid close vertical and horizontal stripes with spatial frequency in the range 1–8 cycles per degree (W Industries Ltd, 1994) in display software to avoid disturbing users with heightened pattern sensitivity. Such stripes may provoke discomfort, eyestrain, headaches and very rarely epileptic seizures.
(2) Avoid sudden bright or highly contrasting flashes, certainly on a repeating basis.
(3) Avoid 'moiré fringe' or pattern interference effects.
(4) Avoid any visibility of the display pixels where their spatial frequency is close to the maximal sensitivity of the human visual system.

4.4.2 Accommodation and convergence disassociation

When the human visual system views the world through two forward facing eyes, spaced between 40 mm and 75 mm, it sees a stereo image. Stereo enhances our ability to interpret depth in a 3D world, which is important but not critical in everyday activity. (Many people get through life with one eye and train themselves to cope with a monocular view of the world using the range of depth cues available for monocular vision, such as motion parallax, interposition and perspective.)

In IVR we have a choice. It is possible to provide an identical image to each eye from a single image generator. Alternatively, two different images can be provided by using two image generators, each drawing the world from a different perspective, allowing the addition of stereopsis as a depth cue.

Herein lies the complication. In the real 3D world the involuntary actions of convergence (eyes rotate tracking inwards onto the object in view at its position in the overall depth of field) and accommodation (focusing onto that object, ranging from close focus to infinity focus) are intimately associated.

With flat panel displays and conventional optics this action becomes disassociated because all the 3D imagery is actually presented on a 2D panel with no true depth of field and the eye is simultaneously capable of focusing on near and far objects. This is now known to generate a degree of confusion to the visual system and some consequent physiological strain, primarily with stereo systems (Mon-Williams *et al.*, 1993).

It should be noted that for VR to generate a binocular disparity enabling stereopsis, two separate image generators are required, one for each eye. This means that stereo systems will be restricted, for some time, to professional applications.

4.4.3 Motion sickness

Motion sickness in IVR is very similar to the motion sickness that conventional screen-based computer simulators with multi-axis motion are known to generate. Simulator sickness is not new, having been reported in 1957 when the first flight simulators were developed. The symptoms are very similar to those of common motion sickness, i.e.

nausea and disorientation. The most recent research indicates that motion sickness could be the result of an incompatibility between the signals received by our various spatial senses, in particular the visual and vestibular apparatus.

As IVR uses the ear's semi-circular canal (balance organ) as part of the human interaction, it is not surprising that so called simulator sickness can be induced. Like all human factors problems, every person can react differently and some people are far more sensitive to common motion sickness than others. Studies indicate that people susceptible to motion sickness are also the most likely to experience simulator sickness.

The body is capable of adapting over a period of time to changes in its environment (sailors adapt to ship motion), but with IVR there is no time to adapt because the user is instantly immersed in a virtual world. If that world introduces a different set of physical parameters to the user's frame of reference then motion sickness can be induced. The problem seems to be that virtual world information received by the visual system may not always correspond with the signals from the real world reaching the vestibular system. For example, while performing a virtual flight, the eyes may be getting information that implies that the user is soaring in the sky, but the vestibular system does not detect any such movement of the body (Howarth, 1994).

Simulator sickness symptoms lasting up to one hour after immersion have been reported. Yet some reports indicate that the sickness drops off significantly after several immersions. Other factors such as display update lag and display fields of view larger than 50° have also been found to influence simulator sickness (Howarth, 1994). It is possible to reduce the occurrence of simulator sickness by developing systems that allow more compatibility between the different signals received by our spatial senses. For example, seating users or standing them on treadmills during VR immersion may reduce the symptoms.

An important cause of negative effects in IVR is disassociation between actions and sensory information, commonly referred to as system lag. This is generally created by poor system integration or technology limitations. The most common system weakness has been in tracking systems of which there are various technologies. Current tracker systems generally lag by less than 30 ms (over 30 updates per second) and can achieve 10 ms (100 updates per second) with infra-red tracking. At these update rates no simulation sickness will result from the tracking system.

The human visual system can also react badly to poorly controlled or low fidelity image effects. These are caused not by the display but by system interactions which manifest themselves as imaging problems:

(1) Distortion of the virtual world, which can be induced by magnetic field effects or software rendering limitations.

(2) Uncontrolled motion of the virtual world (jitter and swimming effects), both of which can be generated by faulty or badly set up tracking systems.

(3) Navigational disorientation can occur if the navigation technique used in the virtual environment does not result in the desired control of movement.

4.4.4 Image quality

As image quality improves through better displays and higher levels of graphics performance it would be logical to assume that visual problems would also reduce. Expert opinion (Mon-Williams *et al.*, 1993), however, dictates that it is far more likely to increase the negative effects of accommodation and convergence. The side effects of induced prism, focal error and the conflict between accommodation and convergence will become exaggerated. This can be explained by the fact that with a poor quality image the precision of accommodation is not so critical, but as the image quality improves, so will the demands on the accommodation and convergence systems (Howarth, 1994).

Resolution is only one factor in a list of desirable image quality improvements. Offering higher levels of colour, contrast, brightness and clarity will have a significant effect on the ability of the human user to behave more intuitively in IVR.

4.4.5   Colour

Colour is critically important as it expands the information bandwidth available to the human viewer, significantly increasing visual comprehension over black and white imagery. Colour setup and balance in an HMD system is important, particularly for dual-display stereoscopic devices, and quality controls need to be imposed on the consistency of colour and luminance in both displays to avoid binocular rivalry effects.

The three perceptual dimensions of colour sensation are hue, saturation and brightness. Hue is determined by the dominant wavelength of the light reaching the eye. Saturation relates to the purity of a colour or the amount of white light mixed with the hue. Both the spectral power distribution of the backlight and the spectral transmittance characteristics of the colour filters are important in determining the maximum saturation that can be achieved at each hue and level of brightness.

When we perceive our surrounding environment, the colour of each object within our gaze is determined by a complex set of factors including the colour of the object itself, the intensity of light falling onto its surface, the wavelength of that light and also the influence of any light reflected from surrounding colours (radiosity). Excessive brightness can also make a colour appear to shift in hue.

The key colour-related issue for displays today is that the human visual system is capable of detecting many colours outside the gamut of the trichromatic display device. This issue is quite separate from the number of colours that can be produced by the image generator. Much effort is being devoted to expanding display colour gamut, either by increasing the purity of the primaries (phosphors or filters) or by adding further primaries (e.g. including a yellow primary with the usual red, green and blue to produce a tetra-chromatic display), as described in Chapter 9. Display technology will always be under pressure to improve its colour performance.

4.4.6   Brightness

Brightness is related to the rate of transfer of luminous energy and, when the white point is correctly set, should not bias the colour saturation of the display. The ambient light level variation is restricted by design of HMDs in general. The variation relates to light which enters the area between the face and the lens and is controlled by the design of the HMD face mask. Area brightness levels for HMD displays can be kept lower than for exposed 'open view' devices. For dual display systems, however, it is important to match the left and right display brightness, otherwise the eyes' pupils accommodate differentially to brightness variations, resulting after removal of the HMD in temporary visual impairment in the eye with the more dilated pupil (through dark adaptation).

In general, brightness range requirements for HMD screens are lower than those for many other display applications, particularly where displays are mobile, such as camcorder monitors which are expected to be viewed in sunlight.

4.4.7   Contrast

Contrast, defined as the ratio between the black and white levels of a display, has improved markedly in recent high density LCDs, reaching typically 200:1, but 300:1 has been attained (Wei Wu, 1994). This is helpful not only for the visual comfort of the user but also because the capacity of the human eye to detect luminance differences of objects is increased. As the level of illumination increases, a higher contrast ratio increases the visual acuity of the user with respect to separation of the foreground objects from background scenes, thereby enhancing depth perception (Microvision Inc., 1994). The greater the difference in luminance the steeper the contrast gradient and hence the better the perception of objects. In particular, very small objects and details become clearer at high luminance levels.

Current display and computing technology cannot yet deliver a faithful simulation of all the subtle tonal effects of real world scenes. One reason is that the light valves used to modulate the backlight on today's display technology are too crude for high fidelity imaging, because they deliver too few grey levels resulting in tonal contouring. Also most display technologies are susceptible to ambient light, reducing the maximum image density achievable.

With movement in the virtual world, improving the contrast between moving objects and a stationary background makes the perception of that movement much clearer and more obvious (Vernon, 1971). This is a key requirement for effective simulation.

4.5   TECHNICAL ISSUES IN HEAD-MOUNTED DISPLAYS

4.5.1   Backlights

With flat panel devices that are not self-luminescent, such as LCDs, backlights are an important factor in the display performance. Recent developments have led to flat cold cathode backlight panels, which offer an effective alternative to the previous solution, a miniature fluorescent tube and reflector which had to be matched to a specially graded diffuser, to provide even brightness over the area of the display. By comparison the flat panel cold cathode makes the HMD designer's task simpler, but these devices are still expensive relative to the display, and they add weight and heat to the system. Photopolymer technology is now able to deliver near-white electroluminescent panels that may eventually provide a low cost alternative to the cold cathode panel (Seikosha Co. Ltd).

Brightness enhancement films also offer real performance benefits. As part of the system they can increase the efficiency of the lamp and improve the purity of the white light by collimating forward-directed light and reflecting back scattered light.

4.5.2 Resolution

Resolution is typically defined by the number of pixels that can be displayed in the horizontal and vertical directions for a given size of display. It can also be measured in terms of the number of pixels per degree of view, through the combination of pixel x and y dimensions and the visual angle the pixel subtends from the viewing point.

Pixellation is the term most frequently used to describe the appearance of low resolution displays. The level of pixellation is a critical factor in the quality assessment of a HMD. At today's level of product resolution, the preferred solution is to apply a diffuser, typically using microlens filters to magnify and overlap the pixel colour groups. The effect prevents the eye's acuity from seeing the pixel structures instead of the displayed image, but has the disadvantage of presenting a softer focus style of display.

One of the most effective types of depixellation filter is the Microsharp technology (Johnson, 1993) which uses photopolymers exposed to light in such a way as to create graded refractive index lenses of sub-micro dimensions (Figure 4.6(a)). These, when placed close to the LCD image, are very effective at removing the pixel structure from the pixellated image by allowing the light only through the micro lenses. They can be incorporated into the panel, permitting closer proximity to the focal plane and a matched integration with the pixel spatial layout (Figure 4.6(b)).

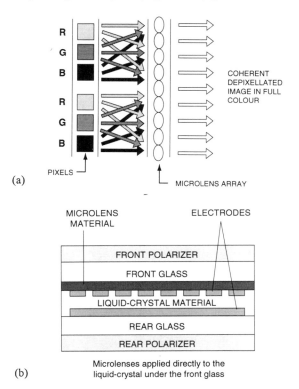

Figure 4.6   (a) Operation of the microlens depixellation system; (b) Position of the microlens depixellator in the LCD sandwich.

Head-mounted displays for VR applications should not be considered as direct viewing devices, because optics of one design or another are necessary to enable infinity viewing. The highest levels of resolution are nevertheless demanded, as the display forms the entire field of visual information for the user. The closest market comparison to the VR display application is the growing projection display market sector (see Chapter 14). Here displays already in production are setting new standards of micro-miniaturisation. The small quartz substrate LCDs used for this market are approaching the complexity of the PAL HDTV specification (1920 colour pixels per line with 1125 lines, giving 2.16 million pixels). Sharp Corporation have demonstrated a prototype 1.31 million pixel LCD panel (Tannas, 1994).

Thus IVR displays are resolution intensive, and lens systems used with them are often of high magnifications in order to offer the wider Field of View (FOV). For example the Visette 2000 optics shown in Figures 4.13 and 4.14 were custom designed for the 1.3″ diagonal LCD panel size and offer a FOV of 60° horizontal by 46.8° vertical with a magnification of almost 10.5. Now that LCDs can produce pixel densities approaching 1 million per square inch (Wei Wu, 1994), the associated pixellation problems are diminishing. Displays still face a formidable challenge in satisfying the human eye, which at its absolute peak performance can detect detail resolutions down to 10 seconds of arc. Human subjects can typically perceive a target as small as 1′ 30″ of arc for 50 percent of the viewing time (Rolfe & Staples, 1989).

4.5.3 Transmittance

Backlit LCDs have an energy, weight and cost penalty that designers currently have to accept. Optical transmission efficiencies of LCDs have in the past been very low, down to around 4 percent, although the latest generation are now closer to 6 percent. With two polarisers needed and the traditionally low aperture ratio of the light valve system, high levels of source luminance have therefore been required from backlight components, contributing to significant heat buildup in the HMD.

The efficiency of the backlight needs to be high, because the LCD system has two limiters on efficient light utilisation, namely transmittance and aperture ratio. Transmittance is defined as the percentage of light that is actually emitted from the viewing side of the display relative to the light incident on the back side of the display from the backlight system.

The aperture of the LCD is the actual area designed to allow light passage and therefore the effective image forming part of the display. The aperture ratio is the area of the aperture relative to the area of the complete light valve, including the opaque masks and tracks carrying control signals to the operating transistors. Micro-miniaturisation of tracks and transistor technology is allowing considerable improvements to be achieved in aperture ratios, with the latest products offering around 60 percent compared with 25–40 percent on previous generations (Wei Wu, 1994).

For cold cathode fluorescent backlights, the inverter is also prone to emit its own electromagnetic radiation and shielding is needed to maintain compliance with EMC regulations. The lifetime of the backlight, typically only 10 000 hours, often dictates the usable lifetime of the HMD system.

The HMD designer's goal for the future will be that, ideally, backlighting will be eliminated for FPDs, because low transmittances limit efficiency and complicate the design

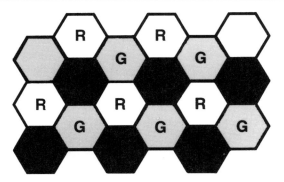

Figure 4.7   Hexagonal pixel arrangement

of display devices and as such add cost for VR applications. Emissive display devices will ultimately prove to be the preferred HMD technology, because they will eliminate the complication of backlighting.

4.5.4   Pixel shape

The production engineering of pixel layouts using current manufacturing technology means that pixels are typically square or rectangular. It may be possible in the future to create more effective displays by grouping hexagonal pixel shapes in nestled arrangements, as shown in Figure 4.7, rather than the current stacked row arrangements. This will have the advantage of closer grouping of the RGB elements, giving a sharper colour delivery.

4.5.5   Screen aspect ratio

The issue of aspect ratio is interesting. Here the HMD designer must balance the horizontal and vertical field of view (FOV) against the optical challenges of field curvature, optical aberrations and vignetting of the image. The most significant mismatch is that lens systems work at their best when they are circular, so ideally a display should be square, but most displays are currently rectangular.

The eye's binocular visual capability is determined by its FOV, with constraints imposed by facial geometry and eye physiology (Figure 4.8). Hence one might suppose that display imagery in a HMD need not be bound by the rectangular windows imposed by convention in today's display industry. In IVR, if the user needs to view imagery beyond the viewing frame of the display, he intuitively turns his head.

Human vision is naturally capable of good focus over the FOV by rotation of the eye in its socket, and if we need greater range we move our heads. IVR currently doesn't really use eye rotation because display system FOVs are not yet wide enough. We rely on head movement to scan, albeit somewhat mechanically, the virtual environment.

In IVR the motivation to achieve wide FOVs, in particular wide horizontal FOVs, requires the human sensory system to operate normally. Our current level of development in HMDs in effect puts blinkers on users, preventing them from detecting peripheral onset cues that would trigger head and eye rotation to intercept the object or activity of interest. In some instances these cues can come from alternative senses with 3D sound

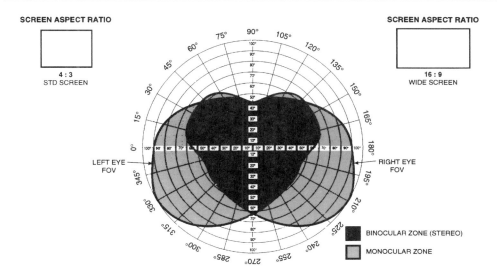

Figure 4.8 Typical human binocular visual field (USAF, 1958)

generated by binaural sound placement systems but these are reinforcements of visual information.

In practice the display formats currently available, with aspect ratios of 4:3 and 16:9, are both useful depending on the detail of the application, with the ideal being somewhere between the two sizes to balance the horizontal and vertical FOV demands with requirements for partial overlap needed in stereo HMDs.

In IVR stereo systems, if the overlap is reduced from 100 percent down to 50 percent we can increase the apparent horizontal field of view by 33 percent by providing a central 1/3 overlap and left and right monoscopic display areas. This arrangement lends itself to the 16:9 format, and several interesting display factors need to be considered.

Where the two disparate displays are expected to fuse to give a seamless image, an apparent joint line is created. This is known as luning (Kalawsky, 1993). The superposition of the edge band of one eye's view onto the continuous image of the other results in a dark band appearing over the image when the views of both eyes are combined. This is an artifact of the display, i.e. a perceptual interpretation of something that doesn't in fact exist (see Figures 4.9(a) and (b)).

Where displays have an image edge that finishes inside the display frame, the HMD designer needs to apply a separate occlusion mask, ensuring no extraneous backlighting is allowed to stray into this critical peripheral image zone and that the viewed image is totally dominant over a redundant image in the other eye. Luning is a complex perceptual issue to resolve.

4.5.6 Display size

Useful display panel sizes for HMD applications are in the range 0.5″ to 3.5″ diameter. The preferred size range is 1″ to 2″. Below 0.5″ panels are too small and the advantage of weight and size reduction in the display and backlight is negated by the

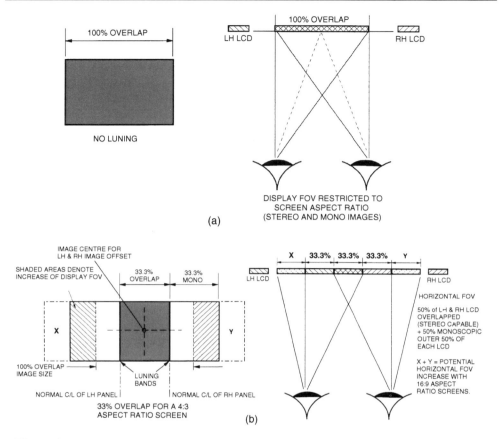

Figure 4.9 (a) Simple 100 percent overlap arrangement; (b) typical variable overlap display

significantly increased optical power and complexity needed to provide the field of view. The larger screens currently have the disadvantages of weight and bulk, which need to be accommodated within the tight space envelope constraints of a usable HMD.

By their very nature, HMDs are handled a great deal and will be frequently dropped and subject to knocks. The larger panels need greater protection to minimise g-shock and the possibility of screen dislocation relative to the optics.

Flat cold cathode backlight panels, which currently provide the optimum consistent overall area quality of backlighting, become increasingly heavier and expensive above the 2″ size. Cold cathode tubes with diffusers are preferable for larger screens.

One final aspect of display panel size is the physical separation of the human eyes. The 50th percentile adult male inter-pupillary distance (IPD) is around 63 mm. For viewing binocular display devices, where displays are positioned in front of the eyes behind the eyepiece optics, this is a definitive parameter (Figure 4.10).

The Visette 1000 (Figure 4.11) was Virtuality's (or W Industries Ltd, as it was then) first commercial HMD designed in 1989, of which about 400 were produced. This device

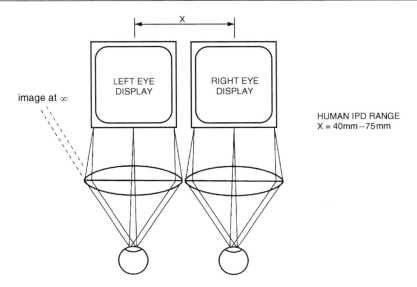

Figure 4.10 Typical binocular HMD with front mounted displays X is the inter-pupillary distance (IPD)

used two of the 3″ sized displays that were most commonly available for direct view applications in video related markets.

This HMD had a resolution of 121 108 (621 horizontal × 195 vertical) pixels and was offered as a true stereo system with two supporting graphics cards, each providing its own independent viewpoint of the virtual world. The LCDs were arranged as a Wheatstone stereoscope (Figure 4.12) to resolve the problem of forward positioned mass and the balance issues associated with displays of this size.

The main problem with the Visette 1000 was its mass (3 kg) which resulted from two 3″ LCDs with their associated backlight systems, optics, driving electronics, headphones plus all the packaging and engineering needed to contain these systems and allow them to fit comfortably on the heads of 95 percent of the world's adult population. The unit was nevertheless used in entertainment, educational and research applications and proved to be a very successful pioneering design, still in use today.

By comparison the newer Visette 2000 (Figure 4.13) uses two 1.3″ Epson panels which move with the motorised inter-pupillary system through the range 58 mm to 70 mm (Figure 4.14). This design is based on the conviction that display panel sizes in the range 1″ to 1.5″ are needed for optimum balance of the trade-offs discussed.

The Visette 2000 is Virtuality's second generation HMD which was developed using experience of the market, ergonomic and engineering knowledge gained from the manufacture of the Visette 1000 series systems. Because it is lighter, more comfortable, and easier to handle, don and doff, the Visette 2000 series still represents the state of the art in HMD price performance and is used for entertainment, product promotion and commercial applications as part of Virtuality/IBM's VR development programme. Eighteen months after its launch, over 1000 units have been manufactured.

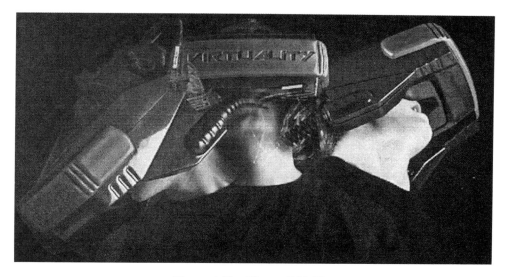

Figure 4.11 Visette 1000 HMD

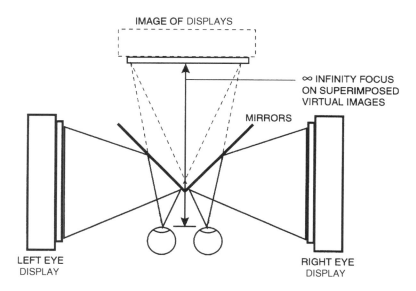

Figure 4.12 Wheatstone stereoscopic arrangement in Visette 1000 series

The Visette 2000 HMD design employs two Epson 1.3″ (33 mm diagonal) full colour LCD displays with integral depixellators (to compensate the delta pixel arrangement) and advanced custom designed three-element aspheric optics. Each LCD panel consists of a polysilicon thin-film-transistor active matrix on a quartz substrate, with a PAL resolution of 756 (H) by 244 (V) pixels, giving a total of 184 464 pixels. The panel has a pixel pitch of 0.035×0.083 mm, a contrast ratio of 100:1 and an aperture ratio of 32 percent.

Figure 4.13 Visette 2000 HMD

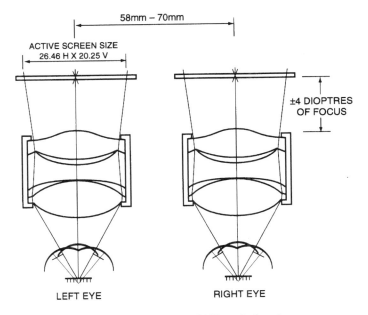

Figure 4.14 Visette 2000 optical path

4.5.7 Viewing angle

Television and display monitors need wide viewing angles to be practical in everyday use by individuals and groups of users. HMD systems, in contrast, are intimate personal products. As the HMD is secured to the user's head in a way that inhibits angular display movements relative to the head, one could assume that wide viewing angles are not required. In fact for some applications, typically those using eyepiece optics, it is not a critical factor. However, IVR is constantly pushing the boundary of display technology and is always seeking to 'squeeze more from less'.

With pupil projection optics, a wide viewing angle is important. This is because radical optical designs are needed to extend the boundary viewing angles, in order to deliver a wide field of view and high magnifications with good contrast ratios over the entire FOV.

When using smaller 0.7″ and 0.55″ LCDs the viewing angle needed by the relay lens (which generates the aerial image) can become extreme, resulting in a partial loss of contrast and apparent brightness variations. Iso-contrast polar plots are available from manufacturers for each display product and provide a useful guide to its unique contrast and viewing angle characteristics. Displays ideally need to offer a symmetrical viewing angle, something LCDs don't readily achieve. This can also be a design limitation for the HMD designer, where binocular magnifier systems using one LCD can result in contrast disparities between the left and right optics.

4.5.8 Screen refresh rate

In order to achieve smooth animated movement of the virtual world, the screen update rate has to match the screen refresh rate. In PAL television, the screen is refreshed at 25 frames per second, doubled by interlace scanning to 50 fields per second. For the best visual perception, the geometry calculations and rendering to screen should match or exceed this rate. In practice, a screen update rate down to 12 Hz is usable. Below 12 Hz the screen update (and the sensation of motion) starts to look discontinuous and the user no longer perceives an interactive environment.

Screen update rate also has an implication with regard to lag. A 12.5 Hz screen update rate induces 40 ms of lag into the system. This could be in addition to the lag induced by the tracking system. Ideally all these factors would be synchronised to achieve the most seamless presentation possible for maximum interactivity. However, any lag in VR is a specification penalty and as tracking system performances improve and reduce their lag (Virtuality's V-Trak infra-red system has only 10 ms of lag) so pressure will intensify on the display technology to improve the response times of its panel. Currently the LCDs used in the Visette 2000 exhibit a response time of 40 ms at 25°C operation.

4.5.9 Video format

Display format is intrinsically linked to resolution and is governed by the image generator as well as the display design. Diverse worldwide TV transmission standards have produced a range of TV systems that are mutually incompatible, with NTSC, PAL, SECAM and HDTV all varying in frequency and line composition. Computer screens offer their own standards, originally based around the need for text legibility and resolution standards for graphics, CGA, VGA, SVGA, XGA and EWS.

All these factors conspire to make the HMD and IVR system designer's task more complex in the choice of display, one constant problem being the need to interface with various types of external reference monitors, in addition to supporting the HMD displays. A VGA screen for computer code inspection may also be needed.

The future digital revolution will eventually allow the introduction of a worldwide compatible standard for TV, video and computer display to reduce costs and complexity for manufacturers and users worldwide. This opportunity for standardisation will need to consider the rapid advances in display performance and permit an evolving upgrade path.

4.5.10 Screen geometry

As previously discussed, LCDs have the advantage of being 'flat panels' whereas CRTs have traditionally needed the display screen to be compound curved. When using high magnification optical systems, the challenge is to achieve the design magnification but with minimum levels of fields curvature and chromatic aberration.

Future systems for a highly developed IVR market may be manufactured with a 'display screen geometry' perfectly matched to and compensated for the associated optical system. Then the optical and display designer, whose tasks are both challenging and complex, will be able to achieve a significant increase in viewing fidelity and cost reductions. Reducing all the trade-offs and compromises forced upon optical designs by curves that go the wrong way or flat surfaces that are difficult to project optically over very wide FOVs, is a systems integration issue which future display designers will need to consider.

4.6 CONCLUSION

HMDs for IVR arguably constitute one of the most complex yet effective interfaces between man and machine yet devised. It is therefore not surprising that they have attracted such attention in the media. Human factor research on early HMD systems and their related technology has created a plethora of press speculation on the dangers of VR. These journalistic analyses must be viewed as of historic interest only, in the context of what is a very fast moving industry. Many of the criticisms are valid for poorly designed and manufactured electro-optical systems, but the business is wholly dependent on the user's experience of VR being positive. If VR engineers fail to deliver the quality of design needed to resolve these human factor issues then so will their industry.

In the longer term as new panel technologies emerge, it may become possible to integrate other useful features such as eye tracking sensors into the screen itself. This would permit the depth of focus of the displayed image to be adjusted automatically as the eye moved around the screen, viewing objects at different depths in the image to suit the eye's region of interest. This would mimic the human's visual interaction with the real 3D world far more accurately when using a flat display device and would have significant benefits for the issue of eyestrain due to the decoupling between convergence and accommodation that occurs with stereoscopic 3D simulations on FPDs. Eye tracking of this type would allow the system to adapt automatically to the task being performed by the user in the virtual world and would potentially allow highly detailed command and control, via menu selection, from within the immersive virtual environment.

This chapter has examined a range of display related topics. In 1995, I have no doubt that the technology most suited to the demands of the HMD engineer is the polysilicon TFT with its rapidly improving resolution and colour quality. Disadvantages of TFT display technology are the panel's slow refresh rate and its manufacturing complexity (and hence high selling price) and this will no doubt define the battlefield for mass market, low cost, consumer IVR displays. There will always be specialist VR applications in commerce and science, where the HMD represents the 'bottleneck' sensory interface, connected to very expensive image generation systems. These systems (and we will be using many of them in the near future) will demand the highest levels of image quality from displays but only at significant cost.

REFERENCES

Binnie, C.D. and Jeavons, P.M. (1992), Photosensitivity epilepsy, in J. Roger, C. Dravet, M. Bureau, F.E. Dreifuss, A. Perret and P. Wolf (eds), *Epileptic Syndromes in Infancy, Childhood and Adolescence*, 2nd Edition, John Libbey, London and Paris, 299–305

David Lewis Centre for Epilepsy, Mill Lane, Warford, Alderley Edge, Cheshire, UK.

Hewson, D, (1994), Innovations and technology, *Sunday Times*, 4 December.

Howarth, P.A. (1994), *Virtual Reality: an occupational health hazard of the future*, conference paper presented at RCN Occupational Nurses Forum, Glasgow, 'Working for Health' 22 April 1994.

Johnson, W. (1993), Microsharp, *SID Conference EID 93*, 7 October.

Kalawsky, R.S. (1993), *The Science of Virtual Reality and Virtual Environments*, 53, Addison-Wesley, UK.

McKenna, M. and Zeltzer, D. (1992), Three-dimensional visual display system for virtual environments *Presence*, **1**(4).

Microvision Inc., Private memorandum, 18 March 1994.

Mon-Williams, M., Wann, J.P. and Rushton, S. (1993), Binocular vision in a virtual world — visual deficits following the wearing of an HMD, *Ophthalmic & Physiological Optics*, **13**(4), 387–191.

Rolfe, J.M and Staples, K. (1989), *Visual Systems in Flight Simulation*, Cambridge University Press, Cambridge, UK.

Seikosha Co. Ltd, Ultra Thin EL Sheet.

Sony LCD product information — 1.35″ HDTV model LCK007.

Tennas, L.E. Jr. (1994), Flat panel-display technologies in Japan, *Info. Display*, **2**, 12–20.

USAF Wright Patterson Air Force Base (1958), *Vision in Military Aviation*.

Vernon, M.D. (1971), *The Psychology of Perception*, Pelican Books.

W Industries Ltd (1994), *VR Simulator Product Safety*, Arnold Wilkins Evaluation, 4 October.

Wei Wu, I. (1994), High definition display and technology trend in TFT LCD's, *SID Journal*, **2**(1).

Wells, B.A. (1991), *Head Mounted Displays for Miniature Video Display System*, US Patent Number 5,003,300, 26 March.

Younse, J. and Monk, D. *The Digital Micromirror Device (DMD) and its Transition to HDTV*, Texas Instruments.

5

Evaluating the spatial and textual style of displays

**Ben Shneiderman, Richard Chimera, Ninad Jog,
Ren Stimart and David White**

5.1 INTRODUCTION

Designing a user interface is a complex process (Hix & Hartson, 1993; Shneiderman, 1992). It begins with analysis of the users and their tasks, goes through creative stages in which key screens are designed and reviewed, and proceeds with detailed design of hundreds or thousands of screens, dialogue boxes, form fill-in layouts, output formats, visual information presentation, help screens, tutorials, etc. Usability testing can begin early and be repeated with larger groups of users as the design becomes more stabilised and complete. The development process has been sped up in remarkable ways by the presence of user interface management systems and powerful development tools. It is now possible to build running systems of elaborate design in weeks and make refinements in hours.

Although powerful tools enable designers to create excellent systems rapidly, designers can still produce poor designs. Commercial pressures are forcing many novice designers to turn out larger, more numerous systems at a more rapid pace, so concerns about software quality are greater than ever. Furthermore, when several designers contribute to a large project coordination is needed to prevent unnecessary diversity. Quality control and acceptance testing procedures are being introduced in many organisations but system auditors are often at a loss to specify evaluation methods, criteria and norms.

Display Systems, Edited by L.W. MacDonald and A.C. Lowe. © 1997 John Wiley & Sons Ltd.

The most popular and effective methods appear to be usability testing and expert reviews. The dramatic expansion of usability testing has helped to improve designs, because designers are forced to work to a clear schedule and feedback from structured testing has proven to be powerful in revealing flaws early. Unfortunately, usability testing generally cannot reveal what levels of user performance will be achieved after months of usage. Moreover it is usually not possible for participants in a usability laboratory test procedure to exercise every dialogue box. This problem of 'coverage', a term borrowed from software testing, becomes increasingly important as systems grow in complexity and size. By contrast, expert reviews can be effective in coping with the coverage problem by diligent examination of each dialogue box, but the reviewers may differ in their opinions and can hardly be expected to notice all differences, omissions and flaws when there are hundreds or even thousands of dialogue boxes. A further problem with usability testing and expert reviews is that they are relatively costly and time consuming, when compared with automated evaluations and interface metrics.

The criteria for excellent graphic user interface (GUI) design are still emerging from creative graphics designers and from the results of empirical studies. Guidelines documents from Apple (1992), IBM (1991), Microsoft (1995) and others are a first step, but many GUI design issues are not addressed by these already voluminous books (Brown, 1988; Galitz 1989; Marcus, 1992). While there will always be room for innovative designs, there is a growing need for methods that enable ordinary software application designers to create effective systems reliably, on-time and on-budget.

The development of graphical user interfaces can be greatly facilitated with software tools such as *Visual Basic*, *Reality* or *PowerBuilder* (Microsoft Corp.), and with more complex cross-platform development systems such as *Galaxy* (Visix Corp.), *XVT* (XVT Corp.) and *Open Interface* (Neuron Data). Such tools can facilitate standardisation across platforms and provide the software infrastructure for new evaluation tools. Software tools to assist designers are being implemented by practitioners for their products while researchers have begun to develop some exploratory systems that help automate the design process (Kim & Foley, 1993; Sears, 1994).

We have used *Galaxy* to create a lively visual information-seeking environment called *FilmFinder* (Ahlberg & Shneiderman, 1994), which tries to overcome search problems by applying dynamic queries with a star field display and tight coupling among components. Dynamic queries are supported by means of a double-box range selector to specify the film length in minutes, together with radio buttons for ratings (G, PG, PG-13, R), large colour-coded buttons for film categories (drama, action, comedy, etc.), and novel 'alpha-slider' interactive widgets for film titles, actors, actresses and directors, as shown in Figure 5.1.

The query result in *FilmFinder* is continuously represented in a 'star-field' display (Figure 5.2 — Colour Plate 11), which places the films in a two-dimensional space with dimensions of year of production (X axis) and popularity (Y axis). The user can zoom into a selected region of the time–popularity space (Figure 5.3 — Colour Plate 12), causing the coloured spots representing films to grow larger and giving the impression of flying in closer to the films. The labels on the axes are also automatically updated as zooming occurs. To obtain more information about a particular element of the query results the user can click on that element, resulting in the display of an information card (Figure 5.4 — Colour Plate 13) showing attributes such as actors, actresses, director and language. Whereas in a traditional retrieval system users would have to start a new query

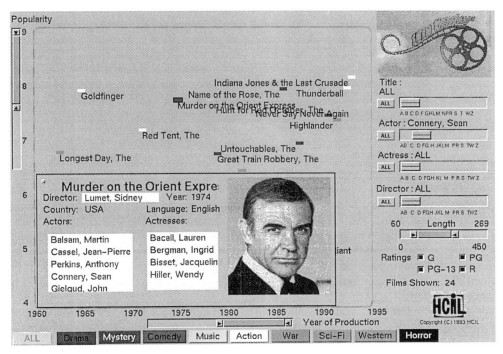

Figure 5.1   Graphic user interface for FilmFinder showing results of a query

to obtain more information, in *FilmFinder* users can select highlighted attributes on the information card and thereby set the value of the corresponding alpha-slider directly to the value of that attribute. This forms the starting point for the next query and thus allows graceful and rapid exploration with no fear of error messages.

5.2   GUI DESIGN METRICS

While automated layout holds promise for standardised GUI design situations, in more complex situations simple automated evaluations can provide feedback to designers, even at early stages of development. Many of the guidelines documents include recommendations about appropriate numbers of menu items, colours, widgets, etc. Sometimes there is experimental support for these recommendations but often they are based on only subjective judgements and thoughtful analyses. Streveler and Wasserman (1987) proposed novel visual metrics such as symmetry, balance, percentage of screen used and average distance between groups of items, but they did not apply or test these notions.

Tullis (1988a,b) carried these ideas further and implemented a system for evaluating the visual displays from character based interfaces only. He implemented metrics for overall and local density (based on the number of characters filled), grouping (number of groups and their sizes), and layout complexity (vertical and horizontal alignment). His metrics were partially validated in a useful series of studies and his tool was widely distributed. The subsequent transition to graphic user interfaces with multiple font sizes, three-dimensional widgets, etc. has meant that new analyses and metrics have become necessary.

The availability of more graphic design features has raised interest in spatial properties such as balance, symmetry, regularity, alignment, proportion, horizontality, simplicity, economy, neutrality, unity, grouping, predictability, sequentiality, etc. These and a dozen more were identified and discussed in the context of both traditional and multimedia layouts (Vanderdonckt & Gillo, 1994). The properties were intended to serve as a basis for an automatic placement tool (Bodart *et al.*, 1994), but specific metrics and acceptable ranges were not tested. Other efforts at automatic layout may lead to useful tools for some situations (Feiner, 1988; Kim & Foley, 1993; Byrne *et al.*, 1994), but there is very little experience to date with substantial commercial applications.

Aesthetically pleasing layouts are important, but the layouts should also match the sequence and frequency of the user's tasks. The term 'layout appropriateness' (Sears, 1993, 1994) was chosen to convey the correspondence between layout and task. Layout appropriateness requires more inputs concerning usage patterns, but it is far more powerful in providing reliable evaluations and can even be used to generate layouts that would be optimal with respect to a specific metric, such as the distance traversed. Early testing has demonstrated its effectiveness in analyzing simple dialogue boxes and complex control panels from NASA applications.

These preliminary efforts have all been helpful in identifying potential metrics and evaluation tools that could be used in the context of modern software construction tools for generating graphic user interfaces. We sought to take these ideas from the laboratory into field testing and to develop tools for professional software developers working for General Electric Information Systems.

5.3   DIALOGUE EVALUATION METHODS

Our research expanded from single screen analyses, towards evaluation spanning the dozens or even hundreds of dialogue boxes found in many user interfaces. We focused on consistency across screens and on feedback to designers to guide them to issues that might require further analysis. In earlier work (Chimera & Shneiderman, 1993) we demonstrated that consistency in colour, terminology, layout, instructions, etc. does make a difference to users' perceptions, performance and subjective satisfaction. While consistency is a complex concept and sometimes violations are appropriate, some aspects of consistency checking are indeed candidates for automation. It would seem appropriate for designers to preserve spatial properties such as position of similar items, size or aspect ratios of related dialogue boxes, minimal wasted space, consistent margins, and aligned, balanced layouts.

Visual properties of text such as colour, fonts, font sizes, font styles and justification of labels would similarly be more acceptable if they were used consistently. Finally terminological consistency, standard spelling, abbreviation and capitalisation all seem to be important in simplifying an interface for novice and expert users, whether they be first-time, intermittent or frequent users.

Our goal was to give designers rapid feedback as they developed their designs and steer them to examine certain screens in detail to see if there was a need for improvements. We wanted to provide a kind of medical laboratory report (like a blood test) for a set of dialogue boxes that would reveal potential anomalies but not prescribe cures. To do this we used the descriptions of dialogue boxes generated by tools such as *Visual Basic* and we developed a canonical format for dialogue box descriptions as the input to our evaluation programs. Other development tools produced different descriptive outputs, but we assumed that a knowledgeable developer could write a conversion program to put the information into the canonical format.

We developed two reports. The first is a dialogue box summary table that gives a compact overview of spatial and visual properties. The second report, a concordance, is built by extracting all the words that appear in every dialogue box and sorting them into one file with references to their occurrences.

5.3.1   Dialogue box summary table

The dialogue box summary table is intended to provide designers with a compact overview of the dozens or hundreds of dialogue boxes generated by the single or multiple GUI designers in a project. Each row represents a single dialogue box and each column represents a single metric. Typical use would be to scan down the column looking for extreme values, spotting inconsistencies and understanding patterns within the design.

The order of the rows was initially alphabetical and the dialogue box summary table was printed on paper, but other orderings based on functional groupings of dialogue boxes (so that all the dialogue boxes related to, say, installation or printing might be seen as a group) might also be useful. Viewing and analyzing the dialogue box summary table within an electronic spread sheet would be logical. The order of the columns was less clear to us and we simply appended new columns as the software was created. A compact presentation which squeezed as many columns as possible across a wide printout was seen as advantageous.

The choice of the metrics was our most critical issue. The groups at the University of Maryland and General Electric brainstormed independently for a week, consulting with colleagues and generating two lists with approximately 40 proposed metrics each. Specific items were grouped into categories such as consistency, spatial layout, alignment, clustering, cluttering, colour usage, fonts, attention getting, etc. The two lists had many similar items and categories so we were encouraged. A second independent brainstorming session chose an ordered list of metrics for implementation. Highly ranked items were those we expected to have high payoff and be easy to implement.

The implementation, written in C++, revealed problems in obtaining the required values in a complete and consistent manner. Definitions of the metrics were therefore revised, special conditions were handled and bugs were resolved one by one as the columns emerged. The current columns are explained below and a portion of the dialogue box summary table is shown in Table 5.1.

Dialogue Name: Name of the file in which dialogue is contained.

Aspect Ratio: The ratio of the height of a dialogue to its width. Values in the range 0.3 through 1.7 are desirable.

Widget Totals: Counts of all the widgets and the top-level widgets. Increasing difference between all and top-level counts indicates greater nesting of widgets, such as buttons inside containers.

Table 5.1 Analysis of dialogue boxes

No.	Dialogue Name	Aspect Ratio (H/W)	WIDGET TOTALS All	Top-Level	Non-Widget Area (%)	Widget Density widget/area	MARGINS (pixels) Left	Right	Top	Bottom	Gridness X	Y	Balances- Area Ratios Horiz (L/R)	Vert Ratios (T/B)	Distinct Type-faces
1	aboutedi.cft	0.49	6	5	74.4	76	64	30	8	6	1.0	1.0	1.0	0.7	1
2	actlog.cft	0.67	16	14	-0.0	60	0	6	0	-241	2.0	1.4	1.1	0.4	1
3	addexp.cft	0.43	3	2	46.0	38	8	33	8	17	1.0	1.0	1.1	3.2	1
4	addfamdf.cft	0.77	25	13	28.3	74	8	26	8	4	1.3	2.6	1.0	0.7	1
5	addr.cft	0.73	47	8	23.9	36	8	26	8	4	1.1	2.7	1.1	0.9	1
6	addrbk.cft	0.84	45	29	15.5	177	0	13	0	6	1.7	2.2	1.1	0.8	1
7	addsec.cft	0.50	7	6	32.9	84	8	23	8	9	1.2	2.0	1.5	0.8	1
8	addseg.cft	0.63	7	6	42.4	103	16	23	8	12	1.0	2.0	1.4	0.6	1
9	addstand.cft	0.41	3	2	60.9	44	24	38	24	12	1.0	1.0	1.0	2.1	1
10	admpwd.cft	0.70	14	6	31.9	63	16	21	8	5	1.0	2.0	1.0	0.7	1
11	adrmsg.cft	0.74	28	14	23.2	61	8	21	8	7	1.4	2.3	1.0	0.5	1
12	adrmsg2.cft	0.74	28	14	23.0	61	8	21	8	6	1.4	2.3	1.0	0.5	1
13	adrmsg3.cft	0.76	28	14	24.7	60	8	13	8	7	1.4	2.3	1.0	0.5	1
14	advsched.cft	0.82	4	3	35.6	42	16	23	16	13	1.0	1.5	1.0	1.3	1
15	afile2.cft	0.66	4	3	47.7	57	16	33	8	13	1.0	1.5	1.0	1.6	1
16	alert1.cft	0.47	5	4	42.4	129	8	18	8	4	1.0	1.3	1.0	1.5	1
17	archive.cft	0.57	23	14	44.6	86	8	33	8	26	1.6	1.8	0.9	0.6	1
18	archok.cft	0.60	13	12	48.8	130	8	11	8	6	1.5	3.0	1.1	1.1	1
19	asgnfam.cft	0.49	12	11	50.8	82	16	7	8	3	1.2	2.2	1.0	0.4	1
20	autoff.cft	0.42	10	9	38.7	87	16	23	8	4	1.1	3.0	1.2	0.8	1
21	autofile.cft	0.39	10	5	34.1	74	16	31	16	4	1.2	1.7	1.3	0.7	1
22	autoupd.cft	0.37	8	5	52.6	89	16	26	8	4	1.0	1.7	1.1	1.1	1

Table 5.1 *continued*

23 backnow.cft	0.49	12	11	56.4	102	24	24	8	14	1.4	2.8	0.8	1.0	1
24 btmail.cft	0.48	3	2	50.3	109	8	20	8	10	1.0	1.0	1.0	3.1	1
25 buildcl.cft	0.58	4	3	38.8	56	8	18	8	11	1.0	1.5	1.0	1.7	1
26 cc.cft	0.44	3	2	76.5	76	32	49	16	15	1.0	1.0	1.1	1.4	1
27 chgstat.cft	0.43	3	2	47.6	87	8	20	8	7	1.0	1.0	0.9	2.9	1
28 ckdoc.cft	0.55	3	2	47.9	47	8	31	8	12	1.0	1.0	1.0	3.5	1
29 conhost.cft	0.47	3	2	46.7	55	8	13	8	14	1.0	1.0	0.9	3.8	1
30 connect.cft	0.61	17	16	49.7	142	16	31	16	2	1.8	1.8	0.6	1.9	1
31 contacts.cft	0.73	105	13	-358.8	47	8	12	8	-1403	1.6	1.9	1.3	0.3	1234
32 create.cft	0.71	92	12	0.2	44	0	14	0	9	4.0	1.3	1.0	0.9	1
33 dbback.cft	0.37	14	5	45.2	65	16	29	16	11	1.0	1.7	1.1	0.8	1
34 dearch.cft	0.53	15	14	48.6	119	8	11	8	5	1.8	3.5	1.3	0.8	1
35 dearch2.cft	0.59	10	9	41.1	68	24	26	0	16	1.1	4.5	1.5	1.2	1
36 dearchok.cft	0.63	10	9	35.2	63	16	26	8	12	1.0	4.5	1.6	1.0	1
37 delconf.cft	0.41	6	5	63.2	118	16	14	16	7	1.7	1.0	0.9	2.7	1
38 dociduti.cft	0.69	29	3	23.8	14	16	28	16	16	1.5	1.5	1.3	1.0	1
...														
Maximum	1.00	170	31	97.5	271	80	56	24	27	4.4	4.5	6.2	8.6	
Minimum	0.32	3	2	0.0	14	0	0	0	0	1.0	1.0	0.3	0.0	
Average	0.60	17	8	35.3	86	11	19	7	7	1.6	1.7	1.1	1.4	

1 = MS Sans Serif 8.25 Bold
2 = MS Sans Serif 8.25
3 = MS Sans Serif 9.75 Bold Italic
4 = MS Sans Serif 8.25 Bold Italic
5 = Arial 8.25 Bold
6 = MS Sans Serif 18 Bold
7 = MS Sans Serif 9.75 Bold

Non-Widget Area: The ratio of the non-widget area to the total area of the dialogue, expressed as a percentage. Values closer to 100 indicate high utilisation, whereas low values (<30) indicate possibilities for redesign.

Widget Density: The number of top-level widgets divided by the total area of the dialogue (multiplied by 100 000 to normalise it). High values indicate that a comparatively large number of widgets is present in a small area. Widget density is a measure of the 'crowding' of widgets in the dialogue.

Margins: The number of pixels between the dialogue box border and the closest widget. The left, right, top and bottom margins should all be approximately equal to each other in a dialogue, and should also be the same across different dialogues. Dialogues that contain widgets extending beyond the dialogue's bounds (such as lists) give rise to negative figures for the bottom margins.

Griddedness: The ratio of the total number of widgets in a dialogue to the number of distinct x or y positions that the widgets have. This gives rise to distinct x-axis and y-axis measures for griddedness. If all the widgets in a dialogue have different values for the x-coordinate of their positions, the x-griddedness will be 1. A number greater than 1 is evidence of grouping. If the x-griddedness is greater than the y-griddedness in a single dialogue, it indicates that widgets are stacked into columns rather than rows.

Area Balances: A measure of how evenly widgets are spread out over the dialogue box. There are two measures: a horizontal balance, which is the ratio of the total widget area in the left half of the dialogue to the total widget area in the right half; and the vertical balance, which is the ratio of the total widget area in the top half of the dialogue to the total widget area in the bottom half. Dialogues in which all widgets are vertically centred, or in which all widgets are symmetrical about the vertical centre-line, have a horizontal balance of 1 (Left Area = Right Area). In general we expect both horizontal and vertical balance to be greater than 1 because many dialogues typically consist of large-size widgets in the left and top halves, and smaller widgets (such as buttons) at the right and bottom.

Distinct Typefaces: Typeface consists of a font, font-size, bold and italics information. Each distinct typeface in all the dialogue boxes is randomly assigned an integer index value and is described in detail at the end of the table. For each dialogue box all the integers representing distinct typefaces are listed so that any typeface inconsistencies can be easily spotted locally within each dialogue box and globally among all the dialogue boxes. The recommended guideline is that a distinct typeface should be used for all the dialogue boxes. Occurrence of too many typefaces within a dialogue box is generally undesirable.

Distinct Colours: (This column is not shown in Table 5.1 because of lack of space.) All the distinct background colours in a dialogue box are displayed. Each distinct colour in all the dialogue boxes has been randomly assigned an integer index value for display and comparison convenience and is described in detail at the end of the table. The purpose of this metric is to check whether all the dialogue boxes have the same background colours. Multiple background colours in a dialogue box may indicate inconsistency.

Table 5.1 reveals some interesting anomalies that led to reconsideration of proto-type GUI designs. The user interface of the application under test had about 140 dialogue boxes and was a well-reviewed and polished design. Very few obvious bugs appeared but many interesting questions were raised as we reviewed the detailed analysis. For example the varying aspect ratios were a surprise and irregular margins were a sign of lack of coordination. The griddedness values did lead to some review of layouts, but we are not yet sure how to refine this measure. The balance ratios were effective in finding non-standard layouts. The unusual variety in typefaces in `contacts.cft` was a surprise and it turned out to be the work of a single designer who had created other dialogue boxes of the application with his distinctive style. Similar surprises occurred in the distinct typefaces and colours columns.

Minimum, maximum and average values were computed for the metrics. Dialogue boxes with extreme values should be examined as candidates for redesign.

A second part of the dialogue box summary table (shown in Table 5.2) gives information on frequently used buttons: OK, Cancel, Help and Close. The columns enabled us to spot the highly inconsistent sizes and relative placement of these buttons in this application.

Presence of OK and Cancel Buttons: If a dialogue has OK or Cancel buttons, their height and width in pixels and printed. The intention is that they should have the same sizes, and designers can verify the presence of these fundamental controls.

OK and Cancel Button Relative Positions: For dialogues that have both OK and Cancel buttons, this metric indicates their relative positions. If the Cancel button is to the right of the OK button, the offset in pixels is printed as $x +$ offset. Similarly if it is below the OK button, it is printed as $y +$ offset.

Help and Close Button Sizes: If a dialogue has Help or Close buttons, their height and width in pixels are printed. The size of the buttons should be consistent.

A string concordance was generated to list all occurrences of words that appear in labels, buttons, menus, user messages, etc. throughout the user interface in a canonical format.

Table 5.2   Button usage information

No.	Dialogue Box Name	OK Button (height,	Cancel Button width)	Relative Position	Help Button (height,	Close Button width)
1	aboutedi.cft	25,89				
2	actlog.cft					25,123
3	addexp.cft	25,97				
4	addfamdf.cft	25,73	25,73	$y + 7$	25,73	
5	addr.cft	25,81	25,81	$y + 7$	25,81	
6	addrbk.cft					25,89
7	addsec.cft	25,73	25,73	$y + 7$	25,73	
8	addseg.cft	25,73	25,73	$y + 7$	25,73	
9	addstand.cft	25,89				
10	admpwd.cft	25,65	25,65	$y + 7$	25,65	
11	adrmsg.cft	25,57	25,57	$y + 7$	25,57	
12	adrmsg2.cft	25,57	25,57	$y + 7$	25,57	
13	adrmsg3.cft	25,57	25,57	$y + 7$	25,57	
14	advsched.cft	25,97				
15	afile2.cft	25,65				
16	alert1.cft	25,97				
17	archive.cft	25,73	25,73	$x + 23$	25,73	

Table 5.3   Frequencies of occurrence of related words

Message		18		
	addr.cft		addr.cft	dociduti.cft
	docsearc.cft		docsearc.cft	docsearc.cft
	docsort.cft		docsort.cft	famdef.cft
	ffadd.cft		in.cft	moreinfo.cft
	moreinfo.cft		moreinfo.cft	moreinfo.cft
	profile.cft		profile-cft	profile.cft
Message:		2		
	profile.cft		remfam.cft	
MessageIDs		1		
	dociduti.cft			
Messages		4		
	archive.cft		autofile.cft	autofile.cft
	profile.cft			
	messages	1		
	dibback.cft			
msgs		1		
	dbback.cft			

Designers can use the concordance to identify many aspects of (in)appropriate word use such as spelling, case consistency, passive/active voice, noun/verb choice, etc.

There is a short format and a long format of the string concordance. Both formats create a file as an ASCII table with multiple columns, in which the first column gives the individual words sorted in alphabetical order. Occurrences in different case are preserved as unique occurrences of words, and are listed sequentially in the sorted list so that conflicting usage of upper and lower case is clearly pointed out. The normal alphabetical sorting order is a ... zA ... Z, but this would separate occurrences of 'find' from 'Find' or 'FIND' and so our program sorts words as aAbB ... zZ.

The short format lists each word and the number of times it appears. The long format identifies the files in which the word appears (see Table 5.3). Thus the word 'Message' appears 18 times in the files whose names follow it, 'Message:' appears twice, and further down the list 'messages' (uncapitalised) appears once and 'msgs' appears once. These variant forms may be acceptable, but they may also indicate spelling errors or inconsistencies in design that should be reconsidered.

5.4   TESTING OUR METHODS

Our testing included applying the metrics to a prototype application, reviewing the results for concept validity, and gathering reactions from developers. The prototype with 140 highly varied dialogue boxes was a GE Information Services' Electronic Data Interchange application. The user interface was written in Microsoft *Visual Basic*, independent of our efforts to create metrics to evaluate the spatial and textual aspects of displays. The prototype simulated typical actions to show what the user would see. It served as a portion of the functional specification to which the final product was designed. It was also used in an early usability test to confirm the design concepts.

A translator was written to convert *Visual Basic*.FRM files into the canonical format for input to the evaluation program. Screen shots were also taken of all dialogue boxes in the prototype and these were printed. Output from the metric evaluation program was scanned for patterns and anomalies that were compared with the screen printouts. Several iterations of generating output, comparing screen printouts and reworking the program took place until a stable and accurate set of metrics emerged. These metrics were then shown to the software developers and quality assurance staff at GE Information Services for preliminary feedback.

A series of three controlled experimental studies with 20 professional subjects was conducted to determine the impact of inconsistent colour, position and size of buttons. With 30 percent of the button occurrences being inconsistent with the standard style, subjects showed statistically significant changes in performance speed and subjective satisfaction. In each case there was a slow-down of approximately 5 percent with the inconsistent versions, providing support for our belief that it is valuable to ensure visual consistency.

5.5   CONCLUSIONS

As the complexity of GUIs increases, software developers are finding that they need more help in the analysis and testing of their designs. Quality assurance is also finding increasing difficulty in adequate testing of all aspects of current user interfaces. Initial feedback on the metric evaluation program from these groups at GE Information Services indicates a definite perceived value in such tools. While the feedback was positive on the concept and initial output, several issues and suggestions were raised. In its current format, the output needs to be scanned visually for anomalies and patterns and there is a desire to have these highlighted automatically by the tool.

For developers:

- Prescriptive directions on how to correct the interface problems. In some cases it is obvious what to do, such as when there are multiple usages of capitals and lower case for the 'Cancel' button, or different fonts and button sizes. Easier still would be a message advising use of a particular font with a capitalisation rule wherever encountered. Guidance for more difficult cases like widget density or gridedness has yet to be formulated.
- An interactive tool that displays the problems as they are encountered. This may exceed the processing speeds of most current PCs, but intuitively it would seem preferable to identify each problem on-line rather than consigning it to a printout for later analysis.
- A tool that is usable in all standard development environments. The developer using C++ or new cross-platform development tools will want the same capability that we have demonstrated with Microsoft *Visual Basic*. This supports the canonical format approach and implies a need to have a translator from whichever environment is in use.

For Quality Assurance staff:

- A summative tool that checks across the entire application and reports back on problem areas.

- An indicator of the severity of the problem. While any item uncovered as an issue is probably worth trying to resolve, QA staff tend to be worried more about items that could have a significant impact on users.
- A check for consistency of wording and layout, which with increasing GUI complexity is becoming very difficult to do manually. There are so many different aspects to examine that it is often a challenge just to make sure that every dialogue box has been checked. Ideally the evaluation tool should validate the software against the design specification.

There are many other possible measures that were not attempted in this first effort. We know from this initial exploration that we are touching only the tip of the proverbial iceberg for aspects of displays that could be evaluated automatically. Where it is practical, assessment against industry standards should be undertaken. We need to expand the number of metrics to get better measures of usage consistency and to assess conformity to an organisation's 'look and feel' guidelines for their products.

Perhaps the hardest aspect of future refinement of the evaluation tools will be to define the 'goodness' measures for the metric values, for the benefit of those not schooled in human factors. In many cases it may be acceptable if there is not a clear recommendation supported by research. Educated judgements will often suffice to provide *ad hoc* rules for development and to achieve the necessary consistency across applications.

The next steps are underway to develop a computer-based tool that provides some of the analysis that developers would like to use the metrics thus far established. Figure 5.5 shows a sample layout.

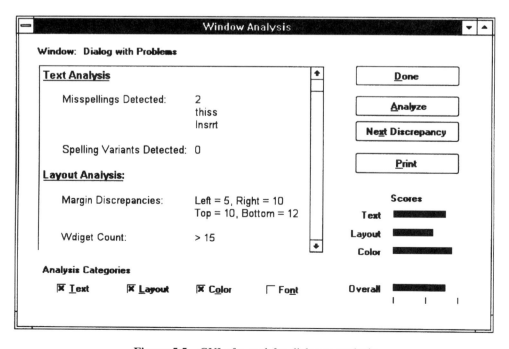

Figure 5.5   GUI of a tool for dialogue analysis

The tool will allow developers and quality assurance specialists to view on-line summative metrics for multiple dialogue boxes and metrics for individual dialogue boxes, all with highlighting of anomalies. They would receive feedback for the current dialogue box by pressing the 'Analyze' button. Once the dialogue box has been analyzed the evaluators could walk through each set of discrepancies or review the scores for that dialogue box.

Our first attempts led to lengthy outputs of uncertain merit, but as we refined our choices of metrics the outputs became more provocative and productive. New ideas flowed more easily and new metrics, output formats and theories of automated evaluation emerged. We are still in the initial phases, but we see that there is real potential for these evaluation tools because they are quick and simple to apply and they reveal interesting properties of complex GUI designs.

ACKNOWLEDGEMENTS

We appreciate the support for this project from GE Information Services and the Maryland Industrial Partnerships programme. We are grateful for comments on the draft from Vic Basili, Catherine Plaisant and Anne Rose, and for programming assistance from Rohit Mahajan.

REFERENCES

Ahlberg, C. and Shneiderman, B. (1994), Visual information seeking: tight coupling of dynamic query filters with star field displays, *Proc. ACM CHI'94 Conf.*, 313–317 + colour plates.

Apple Computer, Inc. (1992), *Macintosh Human Interface Guidelines*, Addison-Wesley, Reading, MA.

Bodart, F., Hennebert, A.-M., Leheureux, J.-M. and Vanderdonckt, J. (1994), Towards a dynamic strategy for computer-aided visual placement, in T. Catarci, M. Costabile, S. Levialdi and G. Santucci, (eds.), *Proc. Advanced Visual Interfaces Conf.'94*, ACM Press, New York, 78–87.

Brown, C.M. (1988), *Human–Computer Interface Design Guidelines*, Ablex, Norwood, NJ.

Byrne, M., Wood, S., Sukaviriya, P., Foley, J. and Kieras, D. (1994), Automating interface evaluation, *Proc. ACM CHI'94*, New York, 232–237.

Chimera, R. and Shneiderman, B. (1993), User interface consistency: an evaluation of original and revised interfaces for a videodisk library, in B. Shneiderman (ed.), *Sparks of Innovation in Human–Computer Interaction*, Ablex, Norwood, NJ, 259–271.

Feiner, S. (1988), A grid-based approach to automating display layout, *Proc. Graphics Interface'88*, 192–197.

Galitz, W.O. (1989), *Handbook of Screen Format Design*, 3rd Edition, Q.E.D. Information Sciences, Wellesley, MA.

Hix, D. and Hartson, H.R. (1993), *Developing User Interfaces*: *Ensuring Usability Through Product and Process*, John Wiley & Sons, New York.

IBM (1991), *Systems Application Architecture: Common User Access, Advanced Interface Design Reference*, IBM Document SC34-4290-00, Cary, NC.

Kim, W. and Foley, J. (1993), Providing high-level control and expert assistance in the user interface presentation design, *Proc. CHI'93*, ACM, New York, 430–437.

Marcus, A. (1992), *Graphic Design for Electronic Documents and User Interfaces*, ACM Press, New York.

Microsoft (1995), *The Windows Interface Gwolelines for Software Design*, Microsoft Press, Redmond, WA.

Sears, A. (1993), Layout appropriateness: a metric for evaluating user interface widget layouts, *IEEE Trans. Software Engineering*, **19**(7), 707–719.

Sears, A. (1994), *Using automated metrics to design and evaluate user interfaces*, DePaul University Dept. of Computer Science Technical Report #94-002, Chicago, IL.

Shneiderman, B. (1992), *Designing the User Interface: Strategies for Effective Human–Computer Interaction*, 2nd Edition, Addison-Wesley, Reading, MA.

Streveler, D. and Wasserman, A. (1987), Quantitative measures of the spatial properties of screen designs, *Proc. INTERACT'87*, Elseiver, Amsterdam, 125–133.

Tullis, T.S. (1988a), Screen design, in M. Helander, (ed.), *Handbook of Human–Computer Interaction*, Elsevier, Amsterdam, 377–411.

Tullis, T.S. (1988b), A system for evaluating screen formats: research and application, in Hartson, H.R and Hix, *Advances in Human-Computer Interaction*, Vol. 2, Ablex, Norwood, NJ, 214–286.

Vanderdonckt, J. and Gillo, X. (1994), Visual techniques for traditional and multimedia layouts, in T. Catarci, M. Costabile, S. Levialdi, and G. Santucci, (eds.), *Proc. Advanced Visual Interfaces Conference'94*, ACM Press, New York, 95–104.

Estimation of the visibility of small image features on a VDU

Dick Bosman

6.1 INTRODUCTION

Neither the global technical specifications alone nor classic ergonomic considerations in the design phase of the display are sufficient to assess the legibility of text on VDUs. Ergonomic evaluations of completed prototypes, using questionnaires and many subjects, must be used to assess whether modifications to the design parameters are required, and to obtain data on the optimum multilevel driving signals. Such tests are costly and it would be advantageous if, at the beginning of the design, the visual appearance of the display could be modelled and subjected to a quality rating by an agreed 'standard observer', a vision model, available in software.

Human operator response is characterised by 'uncertainty', which can be described as the inability to make a positive identification given a limited time for observation. In vision, this is due partly to cognitive effects, and partly to ambiguous stimulation in the brightness (B) domain (perception of luminance takes time). The legibility of text depends on many factors in the domains of layout and font, display parameters and the task at hand (see Table 6.1; factors discussed in this paper are marked ($\sqrt{}$) in the table). Together these factors define an n-dimensional space where, ideally, all the individual symbols are separated from each other by a uniform distance. To avoid confusion, each of these factors must be 'distinctly' perceived, especially in the practical cases where some font members

Display Systems, Edited by L.W. MacDonald and A.C. Lowe. © 1997 John Wiley & Sons Ltd.

Table 6.1   Some legibility factors

Symbol height	√
Stroke width/pixel size to symbol height ratio	√
Spatial pixel distribution (font)	√
Symbol width to height ratio	
Symbol spacing	
Size of the alphabet, redundancy in syllabes	
Line spacing	
Layout	
Luminance L	√
Luminance contrast C	√
Colour contrast	√
Observation time	
Quantisation	√
Active area and brightness ripple	√
Line jumping due to interlace (twinkle)	
Reflections	
Blur	√
Flicker	
Noise	
Shading	
Task dependent factors	

share certain features while other features, which are member specific, force separation in spite of commonalities.

An operational measure of legibility can be defined as the probability with which characters, or clusters of characters, will be recognised within a fixed time period. Legibility is attributable to a combination of visual processing on the one hand and cognitive effort on the other. So little is known of the latter process that it is impossible to define a 'standard legibility observer'. The display engineer must therefore operate on the next best metric: the requirement that the threshold of seeing important local features of members of the fonts in question must be exceeded. To ascertain legibility, one must understand the factors determining visibility.

Several visibility models have been developed, e.g. those of Bosman (1989a), Guth (1991) and ViDEOS (1994). Their outputs predict which symbol features produce good visibility i.e., a sufficient change in local brightness, in one fixation ($\approx$0.2 s), to be detected with high probability (e.g. >99 percent). See also Chapter 7.

This is true for both the 'written' features of a character and for the 'empty' or 'non-written' spaces in between. Difficulties are encountered in the estimation of probabilities in the range denoted by uncertainty, and in the following only the '>99 percent' threshold is considered for the discrimination of local features and the analysis of their relations to, e.g., character height, stroke width, contrast, active area and blur and colour. It will be shown that many effects can be measured or explained by image processing methods.

6.2 RESPONSE TO SYMBOL STRUCTURE

6.2.1 Analysis in the opto-spatial distance domain

Relevant structural details of symbols on the display face are characterised by the distance coordinates (x, y) coupled to the metrical variable luminance, $L(x, y)$. Actually the brain reacts to photon density and observation time (i.e., to the number of photons received per receptor in the retina) which evoke the brightness sensation, $B(x, y)$. Stimulation is a stronger function of pupil size than would be expected from pupil area alone, but in the following this effect is ignored and we assume a 'standard observer' with a pupil of area $A_0 = 4.5$ mm^2.

Many font members have very local features of the order of one minute of arc ($1'$). Such fine detail (e.g., one pixel, Figure 6.1(a)) must be perceived, despite the fact that it is smeared out by the eye optics' point spread function (PSF), $P_r(x, y)$, due to pupil diffraction, by lens errors and by scatter (Figure 6.1(b)) (Westheimer & Campbell, 1962; Gubisch, 1967). One ray of light, with a certain photon density, is spread out, thereby decreasing the individual receptor 'photon catch'. PSF response occurs for every single ray in the light distribution and the resulting illuminance distribution, $E_r(x, y)$, at the retina is the convolution of $P_r(x, y)$ with $L_s(x, y)$:

$$E_r(x, y) = P_r(x, y) * L_s(x, y) \qquad \text{(lux)} \qquad 6.1$$

One major effect is that the area A_1 of $L_s(x, y)$ and the *effective area* A_2 of $P_r(x, y)$ add in $E_r(x, y) : A_3 = A_1 + A_2$. Blurring of edges and small features occurs.

Note that the cylinder is a convenient zero-order approximation of complicated PSF distributions such as Gaussian. It has the same average linear and power gain as the PSF, determined by its so-called effective area A and height G. For instance, the circular 3D normal distribution of normalised height $= 1$ and standard deviation σ has an effective area of $A = \pi.(2\sigma)^2$ and a gain of $G = 0.5$. Because of the wide skirt of the eye PSF, its effective area is large (about 1500 μm^2 for the normalised pupil of diameter $\phi = 2.4$ mm), yielding a σ of the approximating Gauss function of about 11 μm or $2.2'$.

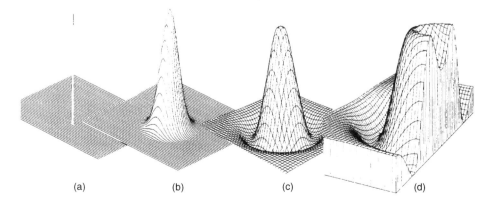

Figure 6.1 (a) Point source; (b) PSF (x, y) of the eye optics; (c) total eye PSF including neural enhancement; (d) response to a $3.6'$ disc

Example 1:

Area addition provides a useful estimate of the impact of technical requirements. The ANSI standard for Human Factors Engineering of Visual Display Terminal Workstations states that the minimum permissible fill factor, FF, in flat panel displays is 30 percent, with a preferred value of 75 percent. With pixel pitch $p = 2'$ and a 'standard' eye PSF (Figure 6.1(b)) with $\sigma = 2.2'$, the 30 percent fill factor results in a modified PSF with $\sigma' = 2.22'$ solid angle; for FF = 75 percent $\sigma' = 2.25'$.

Since spreading does not alter the number of photons involved (except for extra reflections and absorptions, which, to first order, can be ignored) the average illuminance at the receptor layer reduces by:

$$\bar{g} = A_1/(A_1 + A_2) \qquad\qquad 6.2$$

When the target is a disc of constant luminance, the response, $E_r(x, y)$, is a bulge, the height of which increases with the area of the disc until it becomes mostly flat-topped. The observation that the visibility of small radiant targets is proportional to area target has been confirmed by many researchers.

Example 2:

The area projected at the retina by one single disc of diameter d arc minutes is approximately equal to $20d^2$ μm^2. At a viewing distance of 470 mm, the retinal illuminance from a $2'$ disc (e.g., the 0.28 mm spot of a CRT) has an effective area of $80 + 1500$ μm^2. The attenuation of photon density is: $\bar{g} = A_1/(A_1 + A_2) = 80/1580 \approx 0.05$! If the pixel size is reduced to 40 μm, or $0.33'$, a value typical of a high quality printer pixel, the attenuation, $\bar{g}$, reduces to ≈ 0.0014, so $36 \times$ more luminance is required for the same pixel visibility as for a 0.28 mm pixel! These small pixels are almost point sources. Their photon flux also increases with target area at constant luminance.

Post-retinal contrast enhancement, or lateral inhibition, is also a PSF, $P_n(x, y)$, acting on the signals, $f\{E_r(x, y)\}$, from the receptors. The brightness distribution, $B(x, y)$, becomes:

$$B(x, y) = P_n(x, y) * f\{E_r(x, y)\} \qquad\qquad 6.3$$

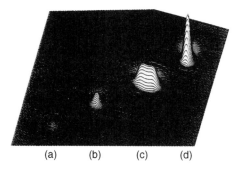

(a)   (b)   (c)   (d)

Figure 6.2   Response of total eye PSF for targets of different areas: (a) one point; (b) a line of five points; (c) a 'long' line; (d) an area of 5×5 points

$P_n(x, y)$ alters the receptor response, to form the total eye PSF (Figure 6.1(a)–(c)) (Blommaert & Roufs, 1981). $P_n(x, y)$ is not invariant as it depends on opto-spatial structure and on the detection of signals embedded in noise of both luminous and neural origin. $B(x, y)$ depends both on viewing conditions and on the image luminance distribution itself, as will be seen by comparing the total PSFs of a point source and a 3.6′ disc (Figure 6.1(c) and (d)).

The capability of lateral inhibition to emphasise edge contrast is limited and cannot fully restore the original image. Contrast perception still decreases with target size and fine symbol detail as depicted in Figure 6.2(a)–(d). The brightness, B, i.e., the perceived

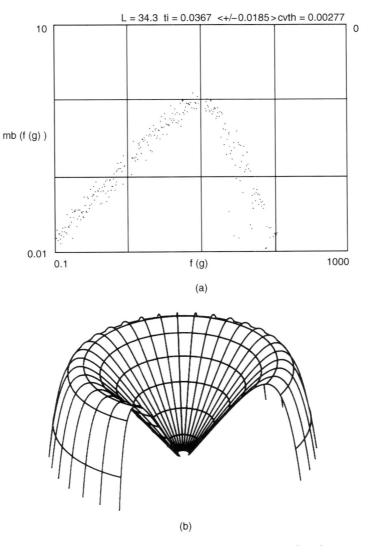

(a)

(b)

Figure 6.3 (a) 2D and (b) 3D modulation transfer functions

luminance, of details of font members varies with line length and width and with positive and negative contrast.

From the above arguments it is reasonable to conclude that the quality of perception cannot be inferred solely from large area photometric notions such as luminance and contrast. Factors involving the structure of the symbols and the form of the pixels must also be considered.

6.2.2 Analysis in the opto-spatial frequency domain

Analysis in the spatial frequency domain, assuming a strictly linear vision system, was popular in the past because the convolutions in the spatial distance domain change into multiplications, which are easier to handle without the aid of computers. The total eye response is then estimated by presenting to test subjects rasters of variable contrast which are periodic in one direction and usually of very large size in the other (Campbell *et al.*, 1978). This fact led to the introduction of the well-known 2D modulation transfer function (MTF), which peaks at 3 to 4 cycles per degree and falls almost to zero at about 60 cycles per degree (Figure 6.3(a)).

However, members of families of fonts have little periodicity. Their spatial frequency content is smeared in clusters over the entire spatial frequency plane, necessitating the use of the 3D MTF shown in Figure 6.3(b). The function shown is circular, typifying a non-astigmatic eye. The method used to obtain the visual response is to (i) transform the spatial distance distribution (2D bi-level or 3D grey level) of every symbol to the frequency domain obtaining both the magnitude and phase distributions, (ii) multiply the magnitude distribution with the 3D MTF (which has zero spatial phase shift because the circular MTF is an even function), and (iii) make the inverse transformation; see Figure 6.4 (Ginsburg, 1977).

Consider circular rings of equal width taken from the the 3D MTF of Figure 6.3. Those at greater distance from the origin (i.e. at high frequencies) have more volume (bandpass gain) than those near the origin (low frequencies) because of their larger circumference.

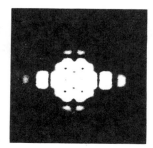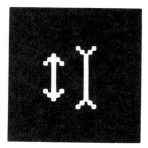

Figure 6.4 Visual response obtained through multiplication by the MTF of the frequency transform of a symbol and subsequent inverse transformation to the spatial domain

The 2D representation MTF, which is equivalent to the cross-section, is too pessimistic in this respect. The spatial high frequency response is not as bad as the 2D MTF predicts, provided the high frequency content of the symbol is distributed sufficiently densely in every direction across the spatial frequency plane. This is a severe limitation of MTFA (based on the 2D MTF) as a measure of display quality.

6.3 COMFORTABLY SEEING DETAIL

6.3.1 Visibility in terms of just noticeable differences (JNDs)

For every display technology (CRT, LCD, EL etc.), the models of the screens of displays operate in the spatial luminance/distance domain by calculating the luminance distribution at the display face of a given displayed pattern. Therefore it is reasonable to have an eye model (a kind of standard visibility observer) also operating in that domain. Nowadays the frequency-domain method of analysis no longer is the most convenient, since digital computers make simple the necessary convolutions of symbol spatial structure with spatial eye characteristics. Moreover, being unconstrained by transform conditions, spatial distance domain eye models can accommodate many kinds of dependencies and non-linearities in the calculation of the brightness, B, and this has already been incorporated into some models.

The unit of JND is that change of brightness for which the probability of detection is 50 percent. Visibility is defined here as the factor which describes by how much, in one fixation, the magnitude, n, of a local brightness change $\Delta B = n.\Delta B_{th}$ exceeds the 'just noticeable difference' threshold, ΔB_{th}, in terms of the probability of detection, P_{do}, where $\Delta B_{th} = 1$ JND.

The constraint of one fixation (≈ 0.2 s integration time) refers to the fact that the 'photon catch per receptor' is the determining factor, not just the luminance (Bosman, 1989a). This explains the constants in expression 6.4 below. *If* the probability of detection as a function of the number, n, of JNDs obeys an error function (which we assume to be true further on in this chapter) *then*, at $n = 3$, $P \approx 0.957$. However, Carel (1965) found that such meagre imagery looks ghostly; and most ergonomic researchers prefer n to be at least 7.

An early model of visual processing (Bakker & Bosman, 1988) is used to calculate iso-brightness contours of characters from their luminance distributions perceived in one fixation period. This maps the luminance distribution into a brightness pattern and includes comparators to detect the iso-brightness contours. Examples are depicted below in Figure 6.7.

Many JND experiments have been made. In view of the circular symmetry of the eye PSF it seems reasonable to use data obtained on circular targets (Blackwell, 1946). Under conditions for which Weber's law holds, Blackwell found, for discs with diameter $> 1°$, that over a large range of display background luminance the visual threshold contrast is constant: $C_{vth} = \Delta L_{th}/L = 0.0027$. The main cause of this effect is image-independent neural noise. For disc sizes similar to point sources, the point spreading is largely determined by the eye PSF, but in the size range $1' < \Delta x < 10'$ contrast sensitivity CS ($= 1$ JND) decreases in inverse proportion to the area, $(\Delta x)^2$, as was shown in expression 6.2. Moreover, at lower luminance, CS strongly depends on luminance because of the effect of luminous Poisson-type noise. From physics one can deduce that, for the condition of invariant detector efficiency, this noise is proportional to $A_0.L^{0.5}$ Troland. The variances of luminous and neural noise add and the average threshold visual contrast C_{vth} is given by expression 6.4, which is valid for targets of size Δx, where $0.15 < \Delta x < 1.5$ mm:

$$\overline{C}_{vth} = \frac{0.0027}{\overline{g}} \left(\frac{90}{\overline{g}LA_0} + 1 \right)^{0.5} \qquad 6.4$$

Example 3:

Assume a background luminance, $L_b = 90$ nit. At the standard viewing distance of 470 mm, the retinal projection of a disc which has a size $\Delta x = 1$ mm at the screen is 1027 μm. $\overline{g} \approx 0.41$ and $C \approx 0.0083$. Poisson noise is less than neural noise. At the 1 JND threshold ($n = 1$), the foreground luminance, $L_s = 90.7$ nit. At $n = 7$, $L_s = 95.2$ nit. For the 0.28 mm, $2'$ target in Example 1, $\overline{g} = 0.05$, and the Poisson noise already dominates neural noise by a factor 4.4. $\overline{C}_{vth} \approx 0.13$, so at $n = 1$, $L_s \approx 102$ nit and at $n = 7$, $L_s = 170$ nit.

At this stage it is in order to make the JND operational in the engineering sense by constructing an interval scale of B so that we can assign numbers to ΔB like we do to luminance and distances x and y. The brightness distribution was given in expression 6.3:

$$B(x, y) = P_n(x, y) * f\{E_r(x, y)\} \qquad 6.5a$$

To establish the unit interval of 1 JND on the linear B-scale, we use the condition of large area response (flat top, the effects of $P_r(x, y)$ and $P_n(x, y)$ have vanished). Threshold contrast is thus described by the large area $C_{vth} = \Delta L_{th}/L$ at $\Delta B_{th} = 1$ JND. Assuming that $\Delta B/\Delta L \approx \partial B/\partial L$ is universally valid for the relation $B = f\{L(x, y)\}$ and integrating, one obtains:

$$B \approx 370 \ln K.L \qquad \text{(JND)} \qquad 6.5b$$

(This is a simplification, as the noise factors have been left out.) Recalling the spatial distribution relations in 6.3, expression 6.5b can be written:

$$B(x, y) \approx 370 P_n(x, y) * \ln K.P_r(x, y) * L(x, y) \qquad \text{(JND)} \qquad 6.5c$$

But since our interest is in an interval scale we note that, with $L_s(x, y)$ and L_b the (uniform) background luminance:

$$B_s(x, y) - B_b(x, y) \approx 370 P_n(x, y) * \ln \left(\frac{P_r(x, y) * L_s(x, y)}{L_b} \right) \qquad \text{(JND)} \qquad 6.6$$

$$\Delta B_{sb}(x, y) \approx 370 P_n(x, y) * \ln\{P_r(x, y) * C_{rs}(x, y)\} \qquad \text{(JND)}$$

where $C_{rs}(x, y)$ is the contrast *ratio*, $L_s(x, y)/L_b$. For a symbol instead of the large area value, $C_v = \Delta L/L = (L_s - L_b)/L_b$.

Note that Expression 6.6 describes the situation for achromic (black and white) displays. Recent research (Spenkelink, 1994) has demonstrated that, given adequate luminance contrast, additional colour contrast hardly improves legibility.

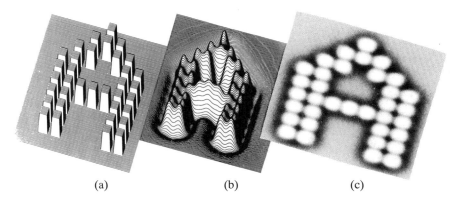

| (a) | (b) | (c) |

Figure 6.5 Symbol processing by an engineering model of vision: (a) luminance profile; (b) 3D brightness profile; (c) grey level brightness image

The eye/brain system adjusts itself to the level of B_b, shifting the apparent brightness interval scale to become a ratio scale with its zero at the background brightness. Thus, in the example of Figure 6.5(b), the peak level B_p of the brightness distribution, $B_s(x, y)$, is equal to 250 JNDs. The trough in the modulation B_t depends on the extent of merging of the eye PSF and of image enhancement.

In Figure 6.5, examples are depicted of:

(a) the 3D luminance distribution of a character 2.5 mm high, driven at a foreground luminance of 200 nit and a background luminance of 100 nit, with a resolution of 3.6 pixels/mm and an active area of 67 percent;

(b) the same character viewed at a distance of 470 mm (a pixel diameter of 2′) after being processed by the model (the brightness contrast ratio = 250 JNDs);

(c) the luminous brightness response of (b).

Note the apparent size difference of pixels and spatial shifting due to lateral inhibition.

Visibility (for bilevel imagery) was defined as the probability P_d of detecting symbol details in one fixation, and not as the number of JNDs available. We now introduce the error function to equation 6.6 and adjust the constant such that $P_{dsb} = 0.5$ for $C_{rs} = 1.0027$:

$$v = P_{dbs}(x, y) \approx \mathrm{erf}[177P_n(x, y) * \ln\{P_r(x, y) * C_{rs}(x, y)\}] \qquad 6.7$$

This function is graphically depicted in Figure 6.6, which shows the visibility, $v = 0.957$ at $\Delta B = 3$ JND. For $\Delta B > 7$ JND, $v > 0.999$.

6.3.2 Average brightness resulting from local modulation within the symbol

At a display resolution of 3.6 pixels/mm (a pixel size of 2′) it is seen from the brightness distribution of Figure 6.5(b) and (c), that the responses of adjoining pixels in the oblique bars merge less than those of pixels in rows and columns. The oblique brightness

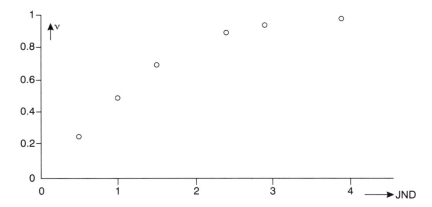

Figure 6.6   Visibility factor against number of unit brightness intervals

modulation presumably gives a weaker impression because the average brightness B_{av} is reduced. In addition, spatial modulation of the width of lines occurs, as depicted in Figure 6.7(b) and (c), which show iso-brightness contours at constant JND levels and include the enhancement described by expression 6.3. In Figure 6.7(c), three contours are depicted of the 7×9 symbol 'A' in EL technology with a pixel size of $2'$ and a luminance, L_b, of 100 nit, at the levels of 1 (outer dashed line), 3 (inner dashed line) and 7 (solid line) JNDs. Large area contrast ratio $C_{rs} = 1.4 \rightarrow B_p = 60$ JND.

The iso-brightness contours calculated from measured images of two early display realisations are shown in Figure 6.8(a) (H-P LCD) and (b) (Planar EL). The separation gaps are visible in the symbol itself in the EL display, but only in the background in the LCD. Background modulation, since it stimulates a large area of the retina, has the danger of 'masking' the line and column frequencies in the displayed symbols.

Our model uses circularly symmetrical invariant PSFs including the PSF for lateral inhibition. As experimental evidence suggests that the eye–brain system adjusts its receptive fields (PSFs of locally pooled receptors and associated neurons) to elongate and

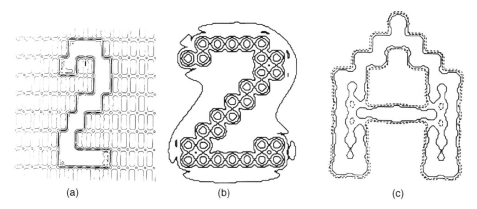

(a)   (b)   (c)

Figure 6.7   Iso-brightness contours (see text)

Table 6.2

Actual modulation index (%)	B_{av} (JND)	v
100	3.5	0.982
67	4.2	0.995
30	5.4	0.997
0	7.0	0.999

align with line directions, our model data are pessimistic but, in our opinion, still provide usable estimates. By the same argument, the brightness ripple (or modulation) in line pieces must be determined along the cross-section through the peaks and not by the use of volume ratios. For symmetrical ripples, $B_{av} = B_p/(1 + m)$, so that the visibility of a stroke reduces as shown in Table 6.2, which was calculated for $B_p = 7$ JND.

At a display resolution of $2'$ per pixel (as in Examples 1 and 2), the optical attenuation factor for one isolated pixel (e.g., as in the oblique bars in Figure 6.5(b)) was calculated at 0.05.

The enhancement by lateral inhibition becomes less important if the condition of 'sufficient' brightness is satisfied. Then one obtains worst-case estimates by ignoring it. From Table 6.2, for a visibility for isolated pixels of 0.999 ($\equiv 7$ [JND]), the required large area contrast ratio (from equation 6.6) is given by:

$$C_{rsb} = (0.05)^{-1}.\{\exp(7/370) - 1\} + 1 = 1.38 \qquad 6.8$$

$C_{rsb} = 1.38$ is equivalent to a brightness step, ΔB, of 120 JND. This contrast ratio is valid for conditions where Weber's law holds, but is not sufficient for extreme luminous conditions such as 'wash-out'. We may conclude that, for the unaided, young, healthy eye, viewing a display with $2'$ pixels, the visibility of isolated pixels and 100 percent modulated, one-pixel-wide lines is assured at a contrast ratio of 1.4.

Klein and Carney (1990) argue that, from the viewpoint of resolution, the pixel size should be $0.33'$ or better. Then merging of PSFs yields only a very small modulation; with PSF peak response $\geqslant 7$ JND, the contrast ratio requirement for the same luminance and visibility increases to a value $C_{rsb} = 15$. In practice, single pixel line widths at this resolution will not be used, and doubling the line width to two pixels reduces the contrast requirement to $C_{rsb} \approx 4$.

There are also factors relating to 'visual fatigue' and, of course, the age of the subject, which will necessitate the use of higher contrast ratios than those calculated above for prolonged periods of display use. For example, at age 60, the average static visual acuity drops by a factor of 0.7. This means that the effective area of the eye PSF increases by a factor of about 2. Attenuation (equation 6.2) increases by the same amount, doubling the required minimum contrast for this effect alone. The reason why older people in particular tend to operate emissive displays at higher luminances can be traced to the desire to ascertain the visibility of very small features.

6.3.3   Effects of stroke width and character height

The discomfort of quantisation and the associated brightness ripple (modulation) of the character is a combined effect of visibility and cognitive factors, which are inseparable and therefore must be considered together. Many experiments, e.g. Shurtleff (1974) and Watson (1989), were devoted to the assessment of the quality of quantised fonts. Early publications lack generality as they reflect the state of the art in the display technology of their epoch.

Spatial resolution, measured as a solid angle, is often not explicitly varied and usually only one character height is specified in the experiment. The results have in common that for (familiar) fonts, the legibility as a function of quantisation shows an exponential trend from coarse to fine, a result that is intuitively acceptable.

Generally, if a stroke is very thin, the visibility of the stroke is low. Conversely, if character height and font, in combination with the stroke width, leaves little room for intrasymbol spaces, the PSFs merge, reducing the local contrast of these spaces and thus their visibility. Consequently one may expect that visibility of character features, as a function of the stroke width, peaks at a certain width interval.

A vision model calculates the brightness distribution across the character matrix, thus transforming its result into the symbol feature visibility matrix. The distribution over this matrix depends strongly on the character in question. As there exists large variance within the total alphanumerical alphabet, this then must also be the case with 'legibility'.

Insight into the modelling process is obtained by approximating the eye PSF with a Gaussian distribution, even though its skirt is not wide enough (Gubisch, 1967). The cross-section of the line results from convolving the uniform stroke luminance distribution with this PSF. For thick strokes, the line edge becomes S shaped, and is approximated by an error function.

When two edges overlap in reverse contrast, as shown in Figure 6.8(a), for the overlap region to be visible requires that the brightness difference, $(B_p - B_t) > 7$ JND. For light emitting displays, technologies exist which have adequately high luminance to provide very thin lines at good brightness, e.g., light emitting diodes. Figure 6.8(b) shows why the visibility of very small gaps in LED arrays is high. Figure 6.8(b) is derived from Figure 6.8(a) for the threshold separation $\Delta B = 7$ JND.

Consequently, from the requirement of visibility alone, character height can be quite small. At high luminance and contrast, the young healthy eye should see every feature of

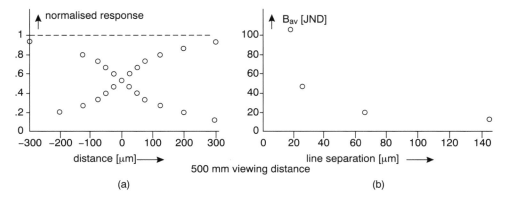

Figure 6.8 (a) Overlapping eye responses for two just touching lines; (b) required brightness of radiant lines for noticeable separation

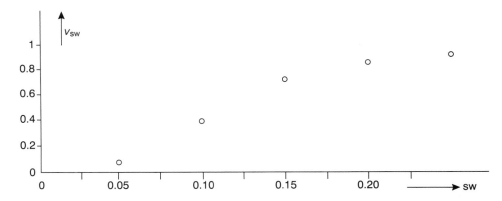

Figure 6.9   Visibility v vs stroke width, sw (in mm), at a viewing distance of 470 mm

familiar fonts in radiant thin strokes, at character heights down to 0.7 mm at a viewing distance of 470 mm (an angle of substense of 5′ at the eye). However, the requirement for recognition as well as visibility has a drastic effect as was shown by Osga (1984), who concluded that the character must be greater than or equal to about 12′ and must be even larger than this for thicker strokes.

For positive contrast, the same arguments lead to different conclusions. The brightness of the screen background and surround can be matched, to reduce user fatigue. At higher background luminances the eye PSF is narrower and this allows sharper vision under favourable contrast/size conditions. However, strong merging of the PSFs takes place for very thin strokes. Because, at a constant ratio of stroke width to symbol height, the stroke width shrinks proportionally to character height and viewing distance, the contrast of the whole symbol suffers, and not just the contrast of certain features, as is the case with negative contrast.

If we assume ample background brightness and apply the data from Figure 6.6, the effect is depicted in Figure 6.9, and is consistent with Reger *et al.* (1989) for 9 × 12 matrix blocks or larger. At very small angular character height, i.e. small pixel size, the smaller intra-symbol spaces, e.g. within the 'a' and 'e' characters, which have a dimension < 2′ also suffer contrast reduction. This causes a sharper reduction of legibility than for other characers which have larger minimum feature dimensions. The same thing happens when stroke width increases at constant character height, implying that the curve of Figure 6.9 should mirror at thicker stroke widths.

6.4   EFFECT OF BLUR

Little is known about the effects of blur on visibility as defined here in the distance domain. Instead, measurements are made mostly in the frequency domain because the limitation in resolution of the eye is often given in terms of the Modulation Transfer Function, MTF (Carlson & Cohen, 1980). Moreover, MTF is also the function predominantly used for assessment of the quality of 'natural' images (Barten, 1987; Snyder, 1973).

Yet, the requirements for image quality are different for, e.g., natural imagery and text, since a greater impression of edge sharpness is required for the latter (see discussions in Sherr (1993), Chapter 1). Blur in the optical path is caused by extra point spreading in addition to the PSF responses already discussed in Section 2.1. Blurring of the image stored in computer memory is sometimes done on purpose, but in the optical path it mostly occurs as a by-product of some other desired action. The appearance of the blur depends on the volume and the shape of the blur point spread function, PSF_{bl}.

Blur mainly influences the grey level gradients of edges and lines in the image. The contrast ratio is affected only for lines which are thin compared to the standard deviation of PSF_{bl}. Blur is most visible at abrupt changes of direction of edges and lines. It also narrows intra-symbol spacing, which should be avoided.

In the optical path between the front of the display and the eye, a spatially invariant PSF_{bl} can exist, which is caused by the layers coated on to the front of the screen. A circularly shaped PSF_{bl} results, e.g., from a matt finish or from special anti-reflection coatings. Increasing the distance between the image-generating layer and the point spreading surface layer results in a larger effective area, A_{bl}, of PSF_{bl} and reduced contrast of image detail. A wide range of optical interpolation and stereo mixing filters exists, especially for grid-like imagery such as text. These have dedicated, non-circularly symmetric PSF_{bl}s, which are, nevertheless, continuous. The additional grey levels which result alongside lines and hard edges are also continuous and do not cause extra contrast or colour contouring, provided the metrical resolution is sufficiently high, i.e., in a digitally addressed display that the number of grey level bits is sufficient.

Hamerly and Dvorak (1981) made the interesting finding that, for normal 10 point print, edge gradient softening of up to $\sim 0.4'$ creates the impression of bolder but 'sharp' edges, rather than noticeable blur, i.e. visibility of the gradient, for the range of contrast between 0.1 and 0.9, at a maximum luminance of about 90 nit. However, it should be noted that neither visibility nor legibility were the objective of their research, but rather the limits of faithfulness in the perception of copied text. They obtained similar results for lines with a stroke width of 343 μm (i.e., 2.5' at 470 mm viewing distance). From Figure 6.9, we can infer that the visibility should hardly change at such stroke widths. Their experiments gave no data at the smaller stroke widths which are possible with today's high quality displays, but one thing is certain: at 12 pixels/mm, very little blur can be allowed. Anti-reflection layers must be very thin and situated close to the image-generating layer; σ of PSF_{bl} must be less than ~ 50 μm, a figure supported by Klein and Carney (1990).

Example 4:

Assume an anti-reflection layer also causes 10 percent diffusion. According to Bosman (1989b), page 22, the distance between it and the image generating layer must be about 0.6 mm or less.

Blur can actually improve perception. The apparent thickening effect can be used to advantage to modulate the perceived stroke width as required in high quality fonts (Ginsburg, 1977; Naiman & Farrell, 1989). For invariant, circularly symmetrical blur PSFs, which are image independent, the turning point in resolution can be expected at about 2' per pixel, including the interpixel gap, which corresponds to a spatial frequency of 30 cycles/degree. The pixel pitch is 0.27 mm at 470 mm viewing distance, which means that, in really high resolution displays, e.g., 600 dots/inch, character strokes up to six pixels wide are allowed, giving considerable freedom to design high-quality fonts.

At higher resolutions and in applications with high font quality requirements, simple invariant blurring operations are not satisfactory. Correlations between the grey levels of display pixels in characters are image-dependent and must be individually defined for each symbol matrix. Such 'blur' operations, are nonlinear and can be determined either with the aid of the calculated spatial brightness distribution, or by interactive experiments.

6.5 EFFECT OF ACTIVE AREA OF THE DISPLAY ELEMENT ON LOCAL BRIGHTNESS MODULATION

Solid state displays have separation gaps between the pixels; TFT addressed displays must also accommodate the area of the TFT within the boundaries of the pixel. Thus the fill factor, FF, or the ratio of the active area to the total area of the pixel, is less than 1. For relatively large pixel sizes, although the ratio may approach 0.85, visibility of the alternating active (radiating) and dark (non-radiating) patches is high; so substantial modulation occurs.

From the foregoing it is obvious that, for line and column pitch $p \geqslant 2'$, the resulting brightness modulation varies greatly with pixel size and interpixel gap width. For pitch $p < 2'$, the pixel becomes a point source, the eye PSF standard deviation, σ, dominates and strong merging takes place. The extent of merging is slightly dependent on the adaptation state of the eye.

Figure 6.10 shows how the modulation index, m, may depend on the ratio p/σ, as a function of the fill factor, FF. Note that at $p < 2'$ the modulation becomes very small.

Example 5:

The merging effect. The ANSI standard mentioned in Example 1, at small pixel pitch, $p < 2'$, yields almost identical composite pixel areas, so that in the range $0.3 < \text{FF} < 0.75$,

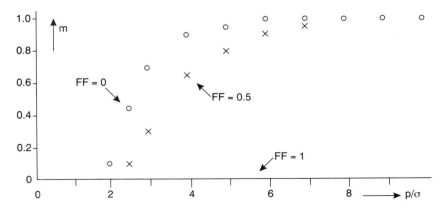

Figure 6.10 Combined effect of pitch, active area and eye PSF on brightness modulation

the modulation, m, is comparable and small. The modulation ripple is still observable, but it is most visible in the diagonal direction where the interpixel pitch is greatest. It follows that the ANSI requirement is realistic.

It is not yet possible to predict how objectionable spatial modulation of the entire image or local of parts of the image may become during prolonged VDU use. One should be able to quantify this effect in terms of permissible JNDs. To calculate modulation depths, it will be necessary to use a vision model. By the same means it will be possible to design in the reduction of orientation dependent, unwanted modulation, by using grey level blurring techniques.

6.6 EFFECT OF COLOUR

The display designer needs to be able to predict the appearance of specified imagery on a display. Unfortunately, whilst colour theory provides a very usable model, it does not necessarily predict what we see in local detail. For instance, the high sensitivity of the visual system for colour changes is measured using relatively large uniform patches, but small patches, which are more typical of the detail seen on a display, seem to have different colour from their large counterparts. Design engineers experience similar large/small area problems with achromic contrast perception predicted by the vision model. At present, there really is no existing model that integrates both luminance and colour contrast which is both validated and widely accepted.

It is well known that three spectral primaries suffice for naming all physically realisable colours in the luminance range possible over the colour interval 380–760 nm. Since the neutral, or achromatic range grey/white is composed of their weighted sum, only two of the three can be chosen independently. Their chromaticity coordinates at given luminance, the third coordinate, lie in 2D planes which are defined on perpendicular axes. The luminous stimulus can be monochromatic (i.e. of small spectral bandwidth) or of a multispectral variety (with more than one monochromatic or wideband spectral source possibly giving the same colour sensation). The corresponding chromaticity coordinates form vectors and are bounded by the line of spectrally pure colours. The angle of vectors from the achromatic point to the spectral locus is representative of 'hue', and the relative distance of 'saturation'. The JND vectors describe roughly elliptical trajectories. The absolute sensitivity of the eye is a strong function of wavelength, peaking, for stimuli of small bandwidth, in the yellow-green at 555 nm. Colour contrast sensitivity is comparable to achromatic, ranging between 100 and 300, which means that differences in wavelength, $\Delta\lambda$, can be identified between monochromatic sources of 1 nm in the red and 4 nm in the blue. In display technology there are hardly any monochromatic sources, so colour discrimination is less than the above predictions for monochromatic stimuli.

If any of the three types of cones providing colour selectivity are stimulated by very high, blinding, photon density of any spectral distribution, all three types of receptors fire and colour washout occurs. So at very high luminance, there are no real colour coordinates and the visual experience seems white. An absence of photons (complete darkness) requires only one point for its representation. From completely black to blinding intensity, the achromatic line (the main subject of this Chapter) connects the achromatic points in each colour plane.

The point which the reader is asked to remember in particular from this discussion is that, for small details, it is difficult to predict the combined effect of luminance contrast and colour contrast. It is still debated whether the two types of contrast add algebraically or in RMS fashion and whether, and under what conditions, there is enhancement like grey level lateral inhibition.

In our achromatic or single channel model, the $P_n(x, y)$ of expression 6.3 responsible for lateral inhibition is made up of two branches which operate on the retinal signal in spatially different ways (Bosman, 1989a, pp. 72–73). The retinal output is denoted by $f_1\{E_r(x, y)\}$. A slender PSF, $P_f(x, y)$, operates on this signal in the 'foreground' branch, and a rather wide PSF, $P_b(x, y)$ operates in the 'background'. The signals from the two PSFs each undergo a further metrical operation f_2, common to every pixel, to account for, e.g., neural noise and additional non-linearity. The end result, or brightness B, is obtained by subtracting the background branch signal $f_2.P_b(x, y) * f_1\{E_r(x, y)\}$ from the foreground branch signal $f_2.P_f(x, y)^* f_1\{E_r(x, y)\}$, a method known in image processing as 'enhancement by unsharp masking'. The wide skirt of the background branch $PSF_b(x, y)$ causes the troughs in the responses depicted in Figures 6.1 and 6.2. We shall now consider how this type of process, which is responsible for achromatic contrast enhancement, increases the visibility of colour contrast.

Extension of the model to colour requires tripling of the foreground branches because there are three types of wavelength dependent receptors: Long, Medium and Short wavelength. For practical reasons we used Red, Green and Blue primaries in the computer model, although, for complete accuracy, different stimuli are required (Hekstra, 1994).

We have reason to assume that at least two and probably three colour channels have one multispectral background in common: the background pattern used for enhancement is determined by the total of weighted firings of every cone and rod within reach of the centrally located foreground receptor, i.e. the subtractive background is the sum of local photon energy distributions. The channel luminances associated with the colours

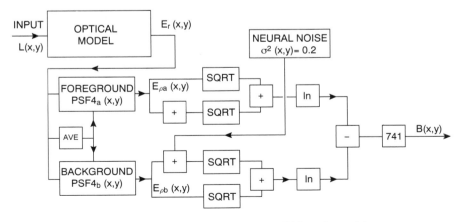

Figure 6.11   Vision model to calculate visibility of actual images

have spatially dependent effects in the calculation of brightness. Stimulation by several primaries having the same luminances yields a sum-background PSF which is deeper and wider than each PSF would yield separately. This deepens and widens the trough in the brightness point response, thus yielding local multispectral edge information between differently coloured patches which is not available in the luminance distribution proper of the input image.

The result is that, unlike in achromatic or monochromatic images, Mach bands occur at the edges of patches having colours of the same luminance but different hue. These Mach bands are rather wide, and improve the edge contrast by a factor between 1.2 and 2. Thus colour images provide higher contrasts in image structure, i.e. somewhat better visibility, than do achromatic or monochromatic images. This was already known from qualitative psychophysical measurements but quantitative effects as functions of size and area of the image detail need to be determined by computer simulation using the accepted eye model. This will also allow some effects of colour induction to be investigated.

Although numerous ergonomic measurements made under usual office conditions (Spenkelink, 1994) indicate that addition of colour seems mostly of cosmetic value, for other conditions, e.g. military, industrial and traffic (road, marine, air), the use of colour may prove to be vital in critical situations.

6.7 CONCLUDING REMARKS

Faithful transmission of imagery to the brain depends on providing sufficiently dense photon distributions at the retina of the eye; the 'photon catch' per receptor is the actual variable that produces the sensation of brightness. It is shown that the strong spreading or smearing in the optical part of the eye particularly attenuates the small detail patches in the image. This contrast sensation is partly corrected by smart lateral inhibition, also located in the early vision system, but this process cannot restore lost luminous energies.

Considering the optical 2D resolving power of the eye–brain system, the required display resolution need not be higher than 20 pixels/mm. At present, the peak luminous flux required reliably to see a single pixel 50 μm wide and high under adverse conditions is very high, but not unrealistically so, providing the display technology can deliver high peak luminance (as is the case for the CRT, but not for LCDs), provided the frequency of occurrence of such pixels is low. Moreover, by means of image preprocessing, these luminance requirements can be somewhat reduced.

The complex operations involved in visually absorbing a text shown on the screen of a given type of display — displayed in structurally complicated symbols in both luminous levels and colours — cannot be easily taken into consideration by the display designer. Nor can the total end result, as it appears on the screen, be visualised without CAD. The use of image processing for the estimation of visibility (the probability of seeing symbol detail in a given fixation time) is indispensable.

Therefore, more work on vision modelling (particularly including the use of colour) and on creating worldwide acceptance of such models is necessary. In this field, standards have the function more of protecting both the designer and the user rather than of enabling the design of improved displays, which requires the application of improved vision models.

REFERENCES

Bakker, W.H. and Bosman, D. (1988), Engineering how we see a display, *Digest Int. Symp. SID*, **XIX**, 439–444.

Barten, P.G.J. (1987), The SQRI method; a new method for the evaluation of visible resolution on a display, *Digest Int. Symp. SID*, **XVIII**, 254–259.

Blackwell, H.R. (1946), Contrast thresholds of the human eye, *J. Opt. Soc. Amer.*, **36**(11), 624–643.

Blommaert, F.J.J. and Roufs, J. (1981), Fovial Point Spread Function as a Determinant for Detail Vision, *Vision Research*, **21**, 1223.

Bosman, D. (1989a), An engineering view on the visual system–technology interface, in D. Bosman (ed.), *Display Engineering*, North Holland, Amsterdam, 60–74.

Bosman, D. (1989b), Image characterisation and formation, in D. Bosman (ed.), *Display Engineering*, North Holland, Amsterdam, 22.

Campbell, F.W., Howell, E.R. and Johnstone, J.R. (1978), A comparison of threshold and suprathreshold appearance of gratings with components in the low and high spatial frequency range, *J. Physiol.*, **284**, 193–201.

Carel, W.L. (1965), *Pictorial displays for flight*. Report Office of Naval Research, NTIS-AD 637669.

Carlson, C.R. and Cohen, R.W. (1980), A simple psychophysical model for predicting the visibility of displayed information, *Digest Int. Symp. SID* **XI**, 233–238.

Ginsburg, A.P. (1977), Visual information processing based on spatial filters contained by biological data, PhD Dissertation, Cambridge University, UK.

Gubisch, R.W. (1967), Optical performance of the human eye, *J. Opt. Soc. Amer.*, **57**(3), 407–415.

Guth, S.L. (1991), Model for colour vision and light adaptation, *J. Opt. Soc. Amer. A*, **8**(6), 976–993.

Hamerly, J.R. and Dvorak, C.A. (1981), Detection and discrimination of blur in edges and lines, *J. Opt. Soc. Amer.*, **71**(4), 448–452.

Hekstra, R.A. (1994), Design and implementation of a model of, and simulation of, human early colour vision, M.Sc. Thesis 003M94, Control Engineering and Computers Systems Group, Faculty of Electrical Engineering, University of Twente, Enschede, The Netherlands.

Klein, S.A. and Carney, T. (1990), How many bits are needed for the perfect display? *Digest Int. Symp. SID*, **XX**.

Naiman, A. and Farrell, J. (1989), Modelling the display and perception of grayscale characters, *Digest Int. Symp. SID*, **XIX**, 424–427.

Osga, G.A. (1984), Legibility study of a tactical graphics language for high resolution monochrome display, *Digest Int. Symp. SID*, **XV**, 287–290.

Reger, J.J., Snyder, H.L. and Farley, W.F. (1989), Legibility of emissive and non-emissive flat-panel displays under fluorescent and daylight illumination, *Digest Int. Symp. SID*, **XX**, 364–367.

Sherr, S. (1993), *Electronic Displays*, John Wiley & Sons, New York.

Shurtleff, D.A. (1974), Legibility research, *Proc. SID*, **15**(2), 41–51.

Snyder, H.L. (1973), Image quality and observer performance, in L.M. Biberman (ed.), *Perception of Displayed Information*, Plenum Press, New York, 97.

Spenkelink, G.P.J. (1994), Visual Display Units, the perception of image quality, PhD Dissertation, University of Twente, The Netherlands.

ViDEOS (1994), ViDEOS video display engineering and optimisation system, *Digest Int. Symp. SID*, **XXV**, 197–200.

Watson, A.B. (1989), Modelling character legibility, *Digest Int. Symp. SID*, **XX**, 360–363.

Westheimer, G. and Campbell, F.W. (1962), Light distribution in the image formed by the living human eye, *J. Opt. Soc. Amer.*, **52**, 1040–1045.

Colour matrix displays: a paradigm shift for the future of electronic colour imaging

Louis Silverstein

7.1 INTRODUCTION

Colour is a pervasive feature of our environment as well as a natural and vital part of our everyday visual experience. It is thus not surprising that for most visual tasks monochromatic images tend to be unsatisfying. These facts have stimulated the seemingly relentless quest for colour in synthetic images. In the past decade, we have witnessed a tremendous proliferation both in the use of colour in synthetic images and in the enabling technologies for colour reproduction.

Electronic colour displays have become a part of everyday life. From television receivers to computer monitors to automobile dashboards and even aircraft cockpit instruments, the ubiquitous colour cathode ray tube (CRT) has introduced modern colour technology into our lives. With the advent of the shadowmask colour CRT in 1950 and the widespread introduction of colour television in the late 1950s and 1960s, colour display technology achieved important status. Colour television continued to evolve and with it came heightened interest in other applications for electronic colour imaging. However, despite the popularity and relative maturity of colour television, most information display and graphics imaging applications were constrained to monochromatic display devices until the middle to late 1970s. The widespread use of colour displays awaited the ready availability of computers and particularly the astonishingly rapid developments in microprocessors and personal computers which began in the late 1970s and early 1980s.

Display Systems, Edited by L.W. MacDonald and A.C. Lowe. © 1997 John Wiley & Sons Ltd.

Obviously, it was computer technology which provided the necessary processing power to enable colour images to be generated and stored efficiently, but perhaps more importantly computers provided the means to effectively encode, manipulate and control colour in electronic display systems. From this starting point for contemporary colour imaging, and in only a scant 15 years, we have witnessed almost exponential growth in both the technology and application of colour.

When most of us think of colour television or colour computer monitors, we think of the shadowmask CRT. Indeed, the venerable CRT has almost totally dominated the display market for the past 45 years despite repeated claims of its imminent demise. The colour CRT is a remarkably robust device and, from the standpoint of colour image generation, it is the benchmark against which all other colour display technologies must be judged. The shadowmask CRT is capable of high image resolution, a large colour gamut, intrinsically high grey scale capability, good temporal dynamics, a wide and symmetric viewing angle, and quite satisfactory image luminance and contrast in most operating environments. Moreover, the CRT is inherently dimmable over a wide dynamic range and is relatively unaffected by ambient temperature. On the negative side, the colour CRT is large and heavy, power consumption and operating voltage are high, and vibration endurance is low. Detrimental imaging characteristics include poor ambient contrast due to diffuse reflection from the phosphor surface, a propensity towards flicker, geometric distortion and a correlation between spot size and image luminance. Thus, while the CRT is an excellent colour imaging device with many positive attributes, the negative characteristics of the CRT are significant and have provided the initiative for the continuing quest for a high-quality, full-colour visual display which overcomes the size and performance limitations of the CRT.

Table 7.1 shows a comparison of the major display technologies currently capable of generating full-colour imagery. The information in this table reflects current technology trends and is intended to provide a general summary of the capabilities and limitations of the various display technologies in their full-colour form. The first four technologies are of the emissive type of display: the shadowmask CRT; the plasma display panel (PDP; both DC and AC); the thin-film electroluminescent display (TFEL; both DC and AC); and the vacuum fluorescent display (VFD). The last two technologies are illustrative of the principle class of non-emissive display: the super-twisted nematic liquid crystal display (STN-LCD;) and the active-matrix liquid crystal display (AM-LCD), which is typically of the twisted-nematic (TN) type. Note that asterisks in Table 7.1 indicate a feature or capability which is currently only available in laboratory or prototype form and that shading denotes a feature or attribute which is a limitation of the technology.

All of the above technologies, with the exception of the CRT, may be considered colour matrix displays (CMDs). The defining characteristics of the CMD are a discrete two-dimensional spatial sampling structure, direct addressability of individual image-forming elements, and an imaging structure which is fixed by the physical geometry of the device. These attributes, along with advances in fabrication processes, contribute degrees of freedom for display design and enable both the imaging characteristics and form factor of CMDs to be tailored to specific applications. However, inspection of Table 7.1 reveals significant differences in the visual parameters of the various CMD technologies. Among the currently available full-colour CMD candidates are TFEL displays, PDPs and, of course, the now omnipresent LCD. Other CMD technologies, such as the field-emitter

Table 7.1

DISPLAY ATTRIBUTES	CRT	PLASMA DC/AC	ELECTRO-LUMINESCENT DC/AC	VFD	STN/LCD	AM/LCD
DISPLAY VISUAL PARAMETERS						
Pixel Density	High	High	High	Medium	Medium	High
Screen Resolution	High	Med/High	Medium	Medium	Medium	High
Raster Distortion	Yes	No	No	No	No	No
Flicker Propensity	High	Med/Low	Med-High	High	Low	Low
Luminance	High	Medium	Medium	Medium	Medium	High
Dimming Range	High	Medium	Medium	Medium	Medium	High
Contrast	Medium	Low/Med	Med/High	Medium	Medium	High
Gray Shades (Intrinsic)	High	Medium	Medium	Medium	Low	High
Viewing Angle	High	High	High	High	Low	Medium
Ambient Contrast	Low	Medium	Low/High	Low	Medium	High
Colour Capability	High	Med/High*	Med/High*	Medium	Medium	High
Screen Update Time	Fast	Fast	Fast	Fast	Slow	Fast
DISPLAY SYSTEM PARAMETERS						
Power	High	High	Medium	High	Low	Low
Temperature Range	Wide	Med/Wide	Wide	Wide	Narrow	Narrow
MTBF	High	Medium	Medium	High	High	High
RFI Emanations	High	Medium	Medium	Medium	Low	Low
Vibration Endurance	Low	Medium	Medium	Medium	High	High
Volume	High	Low	Low	Low	Low	Low
Weight	High	Medium	Low	Medium	Low	Low

display (FED), loom on the horizon. For the present, LCDs are the leading candidate technology for the next generation of high-performance colour workstations. Colour LCD technology has been maturing at a rapid pace along with major improvements in display performance. This is at least in part due to large research and development expenditures focused on bringing high-performance colour LCD technology to market. Moreover, LCDs offer the extraordinary design flexibility of a light-valve based device, while exhibiting the desirable characteristics of relatively low volume, weight and power consumption. With proper optimisation of optical and electronic components, LCDs are now capable of colour imaging performance equal to or exceeding that of the shadowmask colour CRT (Silverstein & Fiske, 1993).

Along with increased degrees of freedom for specifying the visual parameters of CMDs and the ability to optimise them for specific display applications came the burden of supporting CMD design decisions with empirical and analytical data. Moreover, the need for an improved understanding of the relations between display visual parameters and the quality of images generated by these new display devices became apparent. It was fortuitous, then, that advances in imaging science, applied vision and human factors had already paved the way and provided many of the tools and methods which would be needed to harness the potential of fully digital colour displays. For the remainder of this paper, the author will describe some of the trends and developments in the evolution of CMD imaging analysis and optimisation.

7.2 EMPIRICAL STUDIES OF CMD IMAGE QUALITY

The first high-resolution CMDs to appear in significant numbers were the miniature AM-LCD colour televisions which became popular in the early to mid-1980s. While these first devices were impressive from the standpoint of technical and manufacturing achievements, they suffered from poor image quality and a rather limited market. However, they did signal the emergence of CMD technology and pointed the way for future information display applications of AM-LCDs. In the early 1980s AM-LCD technology captured the attention of the avionics display community. First and second generation colour CRTs had already been successfully deployed in both military and commercial cockpits, and the potential of colour LCDs to reduce the volume, weight and power of avionics displays provided the initiative for active research and development programmes targeted for the next generation of cockpit instrumentation. In addition, the luminance and ambient contrast limitations of colour CRTs were problematic in the avionics environment and LCDs offered performance improvements in these critical display visual parameters (Silverstein & Merrifield, 1985).

The use of AM-LCDs for aircraft instruments marked an initial, critical information display application for CMD technology. This application required the rendering of colour line graphics, alphanumerics and non-shaded background fills. Figure 7.1 shows an early avionics AM-LCD prototype. The inset of Figure 7.1 provides a magnified view of the imaging surface of the display and reveals the mosaic of colour filters, addressing lines and thin-film transistors. Initial attempts to produce even simple graphical images on early AM-LCDs yielded disappointing results. The relatively low pixel densities, lack of grey scale capability and fixed colour mosaic patterns of these early displays produced graphical images with significant spatial distortion (e.g. jaggies and positional errors) and chromatic artifacts (e.g. colour fringes and colour banding). It quickly became apparent that there was much that was not known about this new technology and the implications of generating colour images with a discrete, two-dimensional display surface. Basic psychophysical data on the perceptual effects of many CMD characteristics were lacking. These included characteristics of individual imaging elements (e.g., pixel shape and size), the geometrical mosaic of primary colour elements, the density of the sampling matrix, algorithms for pixel addressing, and grey scale functions. Many of these parameters had a significant impact on the cost of CMD-based display systems, and it became essential to establish the perceptual limits of these parameters for the types of graphical images used in avionics and many other information display applications. Moreover, imaging system features which were taken for granted with colour CRTs, such as the band-limiting or spatial filtering operation of the Gaussian electron beam, were lacking in CMDs and their absence contributed to the poor colour image rendering capabilities of these early displays.

In order to address many of these issues, a programme of empirical research on CMD image quality was established (Silverstein *et al.*, 1990) which led to the development of a CMD image simulation system to generate and control the presentation of test

Figure 7.1 An early avionics AM-LCD prototype. The inset shows magnified detail of the imaging surface of the display

images. This system consisted of a high-quality colour CRT monitor, a binocular optical system and a high-performance colour graphics workstation. The hardware components of the CMD image simulation system are illustrated in Figure 7.2. The system software allowed the generation of up to four simultaneously presented simulated CMD images with any combination of visual parameters (e.g. colour pixel mosaic, pixel density, pixel shape, addressing algorithm, etc.) within independently controllable windows on the CRT monitor. The optical system enabled a binocular, minified virtual image of the image presented on the CRT to be relayed to the observer. The magnification, virtual image distance and binocular disparity of the optical system could be set to correspond to a broad range of design viewing distances and visual spatial frequencies. The CMD simulation system enabled us to conduct psychophysical experiments in an efficient manner without the need to develop prototype CMDs and permitted the simulation of CMD parameters which were beyond the current state-of-the-art. A variety of psychophysical methods were used, including magnitude estimation, rank order procedures, and multi-alternative forced-choice techniques. The focus of this work was on the degree to which two types of perceptual distortions, spatial and chromatic, were manifest in CMD test images with varying design parameters and the manner in which these two types of distortions combined to determine overall CMD image quality.

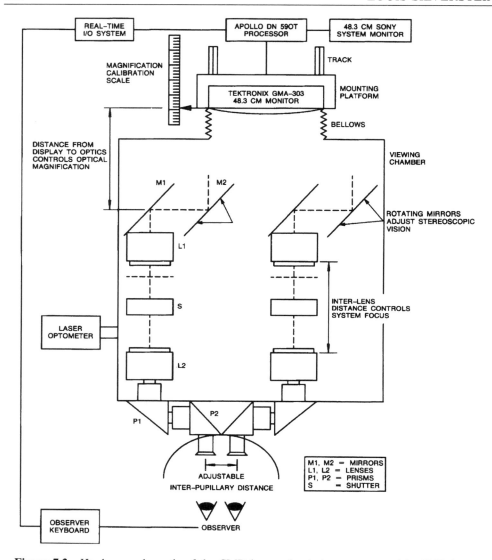

Figure 7.2 Hardware schematic of the CMD image simulation system used in CMD image quality experiments

The initial experiments concentrated on colour pixel mosaics and pixel density for binary CMDs (i.e., only two possible luminance states). These studies revealed that an RGBG quad pixel mosaic (i.e., a four-element, full-colour pixel with redundant, diagonally-opposed, half-intensity G elements) provided better overall image quality than either RGB stripe mosaics (vertical, horizontal or diagonal) or an RGB triad mosaic reminiscent of the delta pattern common to many colour CRTs. The pixel mosaic results were similar to those obtained in psychophysical experiments reported by Rogowitz (1988), and Barten (1993) subsequently provided analytical verification of these findings using the square-root integral (SQRI) image quality metric. Theoretical analyses of the sampling structures of LCD pixel mosaics have offered further elucidation of the findings from empirical and image-quality modelling studies (Ruelberg & Zander, 1993).

Additional findings from these early experiments revealed that spatial image quality was the principal determinant of overall CMD image quality and that spatial distortions were perceptible in binary CMD images even at very high pixel densities. These results were consistent with known characteristics of the human visual system (HVS): the higher sensitivity to spatial rather than chromatic distortion reflected the higher spatial resolution of the luminance versus chromatic channels of vision; and the persistence of perceptible spatial distortions with binary CMD images resulted from spatial hyperacuity for the jagged, aliased lines produced with only two luminance states (Silverstein *et al.*, 1990). It was apparent that in order to produce high-quality graphical images on a CMD it would be necessary to incorporate a band-limiting or anti-aliasing spatial filter into the CMD system via the use of additional grey levels.

Subsequent experiments from the above programme and others (e.g., Jacobsen, 1990) indicated that a Gaussian band-limiting or line-spread function (LSF) provided superior anti-aliasing performance to other candidate functions (trapezoidal, triangular, rectangular or sine^2) and that a linear luminance ramp for assigning grey levels to the quantised LSF was superior to either logarithmic or power function ramps. Given the cost of display drivers for implementing grey levels in a CMD, it was important to determine the minimum number of bits of grey scale which yielded asymptotic imaging performance for graphics images. Moreover, the combined effects of pixel mosaic, pixel density and number of grey levels appeared to be the primary determinants of CMD image quality. Figure 7.3 shows the composite results from several experiments which illustrate the relations between these parameters and CMD image quality (Silverstein *et al.*, 1990).

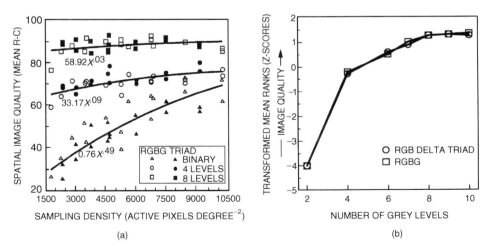

Figure 7.3 (a) Effects of pixel sampling density, pixel mosaic and number of grey levels on CMD spatial image quality. The data and curves for eight grey levels have been shifted upward by 10 units for clarity. The solid lines and equations for each set of data represent the least-squares best fit of a power function to the data within each grey level category. (b) Effects of number of grey levels on overall CMD image quality

Several important findings are revealed in Figure 7.3(a). First, spatial image quality for binary CMDs tends to be higher for the RGBG than for the RGB delta triad pixel mosaic at comparable levels of pixel sampling density. Second, spatial image quality for binary displays does not approach an asymptote across the range of pixel sampling densities tested. Third, sampling density and number of grey levels interact, such that the slope of the function relating sampling density to spatial image quality decreases with increasing grey levels. Thus, sampling density is the primary determinant of spatial quality for binary CMD images and, as would be predicted from sampling theory, has a reduced effect when the image is band limited via the use of grey scale. Fourth, since the effects of pixel mosaic are generally attributable to the sampling density of pixels for each mosaic, the relation between pixel mosaic and spatial image quality is accordingly reduced with increases in the number of grey levels. Finally, the vertical offsets between the three grey level functions reveal large differences in effective imaging performance between two and four grey levels and only a minimal improvement in spatial image quality between four and eight grey levels. Figure 7.3(b) shows the relation between overall image quality and the number of grey levels, revealing that asymptotic imaging performance for graphic images is reached at three bits or eight grey levels. The grey scale asymptote for line graphics and alphanumerics has been replicated in other experiments and contexts (Cushman & Miller, 1988; Jacobsen, 1990; Naiman & Makous, 1991; Rogowitz, 1988) and has also been successfully modelled using the SQRI image-quality metric (Barten, 1993).

Empirical investigations of CMD image quality were successful in determining the display visual parameters required for early, graphical applications of CMD technology. However, the evolution of CMD technology has expanded the range of applications to include more complex graphical presentations incorporating continuous shading as well as static and dynamic video imaging. The technology has now infiltrated many industrial and military display systems and has become an enabling technology for colour notebook computers. Penetration of the high-performance colour workstation market is just beginning as 24-bit colour AM-LCDs are now being introduced into the marketplace (Conner, 1994) and large, full-colour PDPs and TFEL displays emerge in prototype form (Birk, 1994). This burgeoning range of CMD systems and applications has resulted in a parameter space which is too large to negotiate through the use of empirical methods alone. Clearly, a more analytical, model-based approach to the selection and optimisation of CMD design parameters is required.

7.3 DISPLAY MODELLING AND OPTIMISATION

Visual display design has long been recognised as a difficult, multidisciplinary exercise. As illustrated in Figure 7.4, effective colour display system design requires the integration of information from a diverse pool of both technical and non-technical disciplines. The complexity of display design has for years motivated the development of analytical methods and tools for relating display parameters to the visibility of displayed information and the quality of displayed images. Thus, the modelling of display and image quality has a significant and varied history with its roots in the analysis of television systems and monochrome, raster-scanned CRTs (Biberman, 1973). Perhaps the best known and most widely used metrics for display and image quality are the modulation transfer function area (MTFA) introduced by Snyder and his colleagues (Snyder, 1973), the Carlson and Cohen

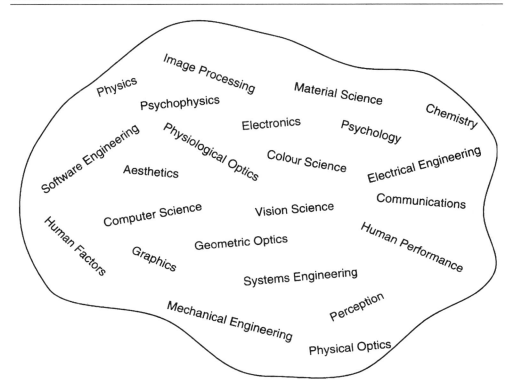

Figure 7.4 Pool of technical and non-technical disciplines involved in effective colour display system design

(1980) contrast just-noticeable difference (JND) model and the SQRI metric of Barten (Barten, 1990, 1993). While each of these metrics has achieved considerable success in predicting image quality within a limited domain, primarily for monochrome imagery displayed on raster-scanned CRTs, they are all based on non-mechanistic descriptions of human contrast sensitivity and therefore lack generality. Moreover, none of these quality metrics has been incorporated into a comprehensive system for visual display design and optimisation. Rapid advances in display and processor technology, image processing and computer graphics have created the need for a much more sophisticated and integrated suite of design tools for today's diversity of visual displays and display applications.

In anticipation of the many complex display system design problems engendered by emerging new display technologies, the US Advanced Research Projects Agency (ARPA) initiated a comprehensive programme for display modelling and optimisation in the latter half of 1991. This programme, which is administered by the National Aeronautics and Space Administration's (NASA) Ames Research Center, is entitled the Video Display Engineering and Optimisation System (ViDEOS).

The overall goal of ViDEOS is the development of a comprehensive, rigorous, and integrated display system design tool based upon functional criteria derived from human visual processing. The tool is conceptualised as both an analytical and educational aid for designers/developers of advanced display systems, enabling alternative design concepts and tradeoffs to be rapidly investigated, prototyped and displayed as an image simulation, and analyzed at a multiplicity of levels ranging from variations in basic display visual parameters (e.g., resolution, contrast, chromaticity etc.) to a full estimate of imaging characteristics as processed by an integral visual processing module. ViDEOS consists of a number of separate but integrable software components configured in a modular and extensible architecture. These include device-dependent design modules and device-independent modules for image and display transformations, image simulation and visual processing (Larimer *et al.*, 1994). A conceptual schematic of ViDEOS is illustrated in Figure 7.5.

Most of the ViDEOS modules, whether device-specific design modules or device-independent visual processing modules, may be sub-classified according to one of three separate but mutually interactive domains: the colour/intensity domain, the spatial domain, and the temporal domain. Device-specific modules in the colour/intensity domain estimate the spectral power distribution (SPD) of a device and/or its features as a function of device and viewing parameters. CIE tristimulus values (X, Y, Z) and contrast (C) are computed from the final pixel SPDs. The corresponding visual processing module in this domain provides higher-level transformations which estimate visual functions such as perceived brightness, grey scale functions, and perceptual colour difference estimators. The output of the modules in this domain feed forward to provide input to modules in the spatial and temporal domains.

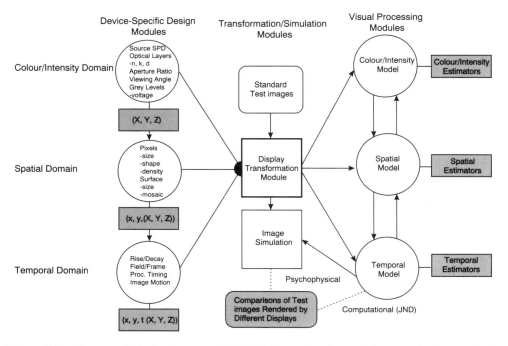

Figure 7.5 Conceptual block diagram of ViDEOS illustrating the modular organisation and both device-dependent and device-independent components

In the spatial domain, device-specific design modules define the spatial distribution of light across the display surface $(x, y, (X, Y, Z))$ given the outputs of prior processing of colour/intensity modules, a description of the pixel characteristics of the imaging device (e.g. pixel sampling density, colour pixel mosaic, pixel shape, point spread function of components or integral addressing algorithms), and the mapping of the test image to the device imaging structure. At this point, the fundamental spatial characteristics of the candidate display system, i.e. the system modulation transfer function (MTF), may be obtained and utilised by the designer as an indicator of the spatial resolution capabilities of the system. Device-independent visual processing modules then utilise the transformed spatial definition to decompose the processed display image into a set of spatial frequency channels, apply appropriately 'tuned and oriented' spatial filter functions and scale factors (including functions to account for known spatio-chromatic dependencies), and provide estimators of the 'visual effects' of spatial display parameters on the test image (Lubin, 1993). Summary metrics are provided in the form of visible difference predictors between test images rendered using different display configurations and include both local point-by-point maps of just-noticeable differences (JNDs) and weighted global JND estimates. The ViDEOS visual processing module has been shown to provide accurate predictors of basic visual functions such as contrast detection and discrimination, edge sharpness discrimination and the discrimination of simple alphanumeric letter forms (Lubin, 1993). In addition, the module has been used successfully to investigate the design tradeoffs between spatial resolution and grey-scale quantisation in sampled display images (Gille *et al.*, 1994a,b) and the visual effects of the aperture ratio and black matrix structure in matrix displays (Larimer *et al.*, 1995).

An analogous structure and set of operations occur for temporal domain modules, although the basic data set is now $(x, y, t, (X, Y, Z))$, where t corresponds to the time-varying response of the system. Display-specific design modules in the time domain utilise information from the designer regarding pixel rise/decay times, field/frame rates of the system, type of interlacing scheme, and other timing constraints inherent to the display processor. Temporal domain visual processing modules operate on the temporal descriptions of the display system, as well as spatial domain visual estimators, to apply appropriately 'tuned' temporal filters and account for known spatio-temporal dependencies. ViDEOS outputs at this level provide estimators of the 'visual effects' of temporal display parameters, which include perceptibility of flicker and fidelity of time-sampled moving images. Within the timing constraints of the video subsystem of the ViDEOS host computer, the manifestations of temporal parameters of the candidate visual display system may be presented directly to the display system designer via the integral image simulation module.

The transformation and simulation modules accomplish the mapping of data from the device-dependent design modules to appropriately resampled and tiled representations of test images as rendered by candidate displays with particular configurations. A highly flexible tiling algorithm has been developed and incorporated into ViDEOS to subserve this function (Samadani *et al.*, 1994). The rendered test images are scaled for the design viewing distance and converted into an appropriately filtered 'retinal image representation', which may then be displayed via the ViDEOS simulation module for examination or use in psychophysical evaluations and/or passed to the visual processing modules for computational estimation of visible differences.

Currently, the most highly evolved device-dependent module in ViDEOS is LCD Tool, which is a comprehensive module for the design of LCDs. There are two principal computational elements within LCD Tool. The first subdivides the LC layer and utilises numerical methods for fluid dynamics to find the local molecular orientation of LC molecules (i.e., the director configuration) within each layer subdivision as a function of LC material parameters, cell geometry, and applied electric or magnetic fields (Berreman, 1983). The second element employs a 4×4 propagation-matrix approach to compute the optical transmission and reflection for multi-layered LCD optical structures as a function of optical layer characteristics, wavelength, and the angle of incidence and polarisation state of incoming light (Berreman, 1972, 1973). The 4×4 matrix approach is an exact solution for calculating the optical propagation of monochromatic plane waves through layered media and completely accounts for all transmission, reflection and interference effects. Figure 7.6 illustrates the major optical components of a typical colour AM-LCD and their spectral tuning characteristics.

The accuracy of colorimetric and photometric modelling of LCDs has recently been evaluated using the ViDEOS LCD Tool module and specially prepared LCD test cells (Fiske & Silverstein, 1994). The results showed that the effective chromaticity, luminance and contrast of LCDs can be modelled accurately across grey levels and viewing angle. In addition, the LCD Tool module has been used to model the colorimetric and photometric performance of an optimised AM-LCD with eight linear voltage-controlled grey levels

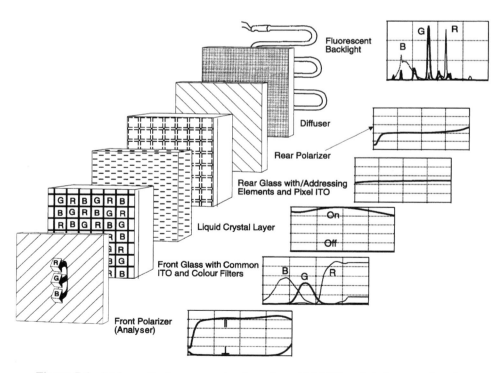

Figure 7.6   Major optical components of a colour AM-LCD and their spectral tuning characteristics

operated in the normally white mode (Silverstein & Fiske, 1993). The optical components of the model LCD were all available materials, and the hot-cathode fluorescent illumination source, thin-film colour filters, and LC cell parameters were all optimised to achieve maximum colour saturation and contrast. The model display utilised a RGBG quad mosaic of colour filters in part to reduce the impact of spectral contamination caused by the side bands of the G phosphor emissions spreading into the spectral passbands of the R and B colour filters. For a given display white point, the reduction in spectral contamination is achieved by attenuating the G phosphor emissions while simultaneously increasing the G pixel area by the same proportion.

The calculated pixel element chromaticity coordinates of the R, G, B primaries of the model LCD as a function of grey levels are presented in Figure 7.7(a), which reveals that the chromaticity of R and G pixels is relatively stable across grey levels while the B primary exhibits increasing saturation as display luminance is decreased from 100 percent to 1 percent of peak display luminance. These variations in chromaticity may be attributed to the changing shape of the LC cell spectral transmission function. The final illustration, Figure 7.7(b), plots the space-average chromaticity coordinates of the model LCD for the R, G and B primaries, the display white point, and the display background or off-state as a function of grey levels. For reference, also plotted on this figure are the primary chromaticity coordinates of a high-performance colour CRT monitor for values of 1 percent and 100 percent of its peak luminance.

While the pixel element chromaticity coordinates reflect only the SPDs from individual pixels, the space-average coordinates include the additional contributions of the 'leakage' or non-zero off-states of unaddressed pixels. The proportional contributions of these 'leakage' effects increase as the grey levels decrease for both the model LCD and the CRT. The space-average chromaticity coordinates are representative of the effective colour visual stimulus and thus are more closely correlated with the actual appearance of display colours. Examination of Figure 7.7(b) reveals two important findings. First, the colour gamut of the model LCD significantly exceeds that of the high-performance colour CRT monitor. Second, the colour tracking of the model LCD across grey levels ranging from 1 percent to 100 percent of peak display luminance is equivalent to or better than that of the colour CRT. Both of these characteristics are vital for colour-critical display applications capable of supporting vertical colour rendering and the transportability of colour across imaging media. Recent technology demonstrations have unveiled a similarly optimised prototype colour LCD with addressable resolution of up to 1536×1024 full-colour pixels, advanced colour synthesis techniques, and remarkable colour and image fidelity (Martin *et al.*, 1993).

7.4 THE FUTURE OF ELECTRONIC COLOUR DISPLAYS

Evolutionary trends in colour display technology, leading from CRTs to today's current generation of high-performance CMDs, have produced a paradigm shift for the future of electronic colour displays and colour imaging. The flexibility inherent to CMD technology offers the opportunity for significant advances in colour display performance as well as the integration of colour imaging into a much broader range of applications and operating

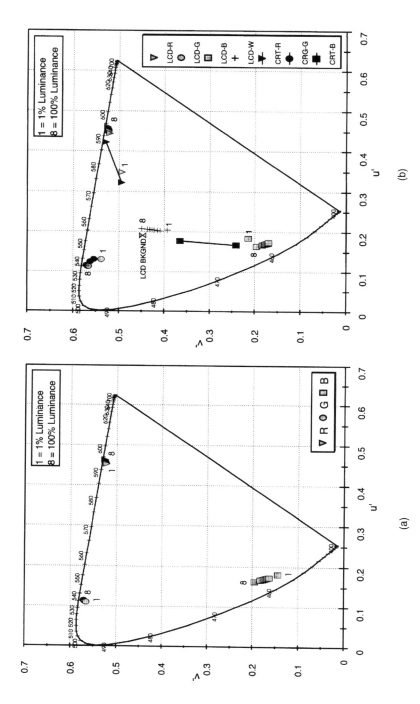

Figure 7.7 (a) Pixel chromaticity coordinates of the model colour LCD as a function of grey level. (b) Space-average chromaticity coordinates, white point and background of the model LCD and a reference colour CRT as a function of grey level

environments. The colour LCD screens which are now commonplace in battery-operated notebook computers offer a strong testimonial for these claims. The future promises displays with higher resolution, enhanced colour and luminance, and with a broader range of screen sizes and configurations than were thought possible even a few years ago. While colour LCD technology continues to dominate the CMD landscape, advances in colour PDPs for very large format displays and improvements in the luminance and contrast of colour TFEL devices have been recently evident. Emerging new technologies such as colour FEDs continue to be a focus of research and development efforts, and a myriad of new materials and optical system designs have led to innovative applications for projections and head-mounted colour display systems.

Taking full advantage of the opportunities afforded by CMD technology, however, requires the development of improved analytical and empirical methods for the visual display design process. We are currently at a threshold where display technologists, imaging scientists and vision scientists have evolved a common understanding and frame of reference for the imaging process. From here, the future of electronic colour imaging is as much dependent on the integration of knowledge from these disciplines as on the rapid innovations in colour display technology.

ACKNOWLEDGEMENTS

The author would like to thank the many colleagues who contributed to various facets of the work described in this chapter. For the work on CMD image simulation and empirical studies of CMD image quality, the support of Honeywell Inc. and the contributions of Dr Yei-Yu Yeh, Dr John Krantz, Dr Frank Gomer and Robert Monty are gratefully acknowledged. The work on ViDEOS and liquid crystal optical modelling were generously supported by ARPA and the NASA Ames Research Center, where the efforts of Dr James Larimer, Dr Dwight Berreman and Dr Ramin Samadani cannot be overemphasised. Finally, the work on colorimetric and photometric modelling of colour LCDs was supported by the Xerox Palo Alto Research Center, where the author is especially grateful to Dr Thomas Fiske for his many technical contributions and to Dr Malcolm Thompson for his unwavering support.

REFERENCES

Barten, P.G.J. (1990), Evaluation of subjective image quality with the square-root integral method, *J. Opt. Soc. Amer. A*, **7**, 2024–2031.

Barten, P.G.J. (1993), Effects of quantisation and pixel structure on the image quality of colour matrix displays, *J. Soc. Inf. Disp.*, **1**, 147–153.

Berreman, D.W. (1972), Optics in stratified and anisotropic media, *J. Opt. Soc. Amer.*, **62**, 502–510.

Berreman, D.W. (1973), Optics in smoothly varying anisotropic planar structures: application to liquid-crystal twist cells, *J. Opt. Soc. Amer.*, **63**, 1374–1380.

Berreman, D.W. (1983), Numerical modelling of twisted nematic devices, *Phil. Trans. Roy. Soc. Lond.*, **309**, 203–216.

Biberman, L.M. (1973), *Perception of Displayed Information*, Plenum Press, New York.

Birk, J.D. (1994), Emissives get brighter — with colours, *Information Display*, **10**(12), 20–22.

Carlson, C.R. and Cohen, R. (1980), A simple psychophysical model for predicting the visibility of displayed information, *Proc. Soc. Inf. Disp.*, **21**, 229–245.

Conner, A.R. (1994), Active matrix, passive matrix ... or something in between?, *Information Display*, **10**(12), 16–19.

Cushman, W.H. and Miller, R.L. (1988), Resolution and grey-scale requirements for the display of legible alphanumeric characters, *SID Digest of Technical Papers*, 432–434.

Fiske, T.G. and Silverstein, L.D. (1994), Modelling and optimisation of colour gamut and colour tracking in high-performance AMLCDs, *SID Digest of Technical Papers*, 329–332.

Gille, J., Martin, R. and Larimer, J. (1994a), Spatial resolution, grey-scale and error diffusion trade-offs: impact on display system design, *Proc. International Display Research Conf.*, 381–385.

Gille, J., Samadani, R., Martin, R. and Larimer, J. (1994b), Grey-scale/Resolution tradeoff, *Proc. SPIE*, **2179**, 47–59.

Jacobsen, A.R. (1990), Determination of the optimum grey-scale luminance ramp function for anti-aliasing, *Proc. SPIE: Human Vision and Electronic Imaging: Models, Methods, and Applications*, **1249**, 202–213.

Larimer, J., Berreman, D., den Boer, W., Samadani, R., Lanham, J., Loomis, D., Marks, B., Silverstein, L.D., Gille, J., Lubin, J., Morrissey, J., Peterson, R., Pica, A. and Martin, R. (1994), A video display engineering and optimisation system: ViDEOS, *SID Digest of Technical Papers*, 197–200.

Larimer, J., Gille, J., Martin, R. and Lubin, J. (1995), Visual effects of the black matrix in tessellated displays, *SID Digest of Technical Papers*, 49–52.

Lubin, J. (1993), The use of psychophysical data and models in the analysis of display system performance, in A. B. Watson (ed.), *Digital Images and Human Vision*, MIT Press, Cambridge, MA, 163–178.

Martin, R.A., Chuang, H., Steemers, H., Allen, R., Fulks, R., Stuber, D., Lee, D., Young, M., Ho, J., Nguyen, M., Meuli, W., Fiske, T., Bruce, R., Thompson, M., Tilton, M. and Silverstein, L.D. (1993), A 6.3 million pixel AM-LCD, *SID Technical Digest*, 704–707.

Naiman, A.C. and Makous, W. (1991), Information transmission for grey-scale edges, *SID Digest of Technical Papers*, 109–112.

Rogowitz, B.E. (1988) The psychophysics of spatial sampling, *Proc. SPIE/SPSE: Image Processing, Analysis, Measurement and Quality*, **901**, 130–138.

Ruelberg, K.D. and Zander, S. (1993), Colour triple arrangement of liquid crystal displays (LCD), *Displays*, **14**, 166–173.

Samadani, R., Lanham, J., Loomis, D., Silverstein, L.D. and Larimer, J. (1994), Periodic plane tilings: application to pixel layout simulations for colour flat-panel displays, *J. Soc. Inf. Disp.*, **2**, 95–104.

Silverstein, L.D. and Fiske, T.G. (1993), Colourimetric and photometric modelling of liquid crystal displays, *Proc. First IS&T/SID colour Imaging Conf.: Transforms and Transportability of colour*, 149–156.

Silverstein, L.D. and Merrifield, R.M. (1985), The Development and Evaluation of colour Display Systems for Airborne Applications: Phase I–Fundamental Visual, Perceptual, and Display System Considerations, Technical Report DOT/FAA/PM-85-19, US Department of Transportation.

Silverstein, L.D., Krantz, J.H., Gomer, F.E., Yeh, Y. and Monty, R.W. (1990), The effects of spatial sampling and luminance quantisation on the image quality of colour matrix displays, *J. Opt. Soc. Amer. A*, **7**, 1955–1968.

Snyder, H.L. (1973), Image quality and observer performance, in L.M. Biberman (ed.), *Perception of Displayed Information*, Plenum Press, New York, 87–188.

PART 2

Technology

What can current displays deliver?

Contents

8

Matching display technology to the application

Anthony Lowe

8.1   INTRODUCTION

Many parameters influence the choice of a display technology for a particular application. Price may well dominate; an example of this is the widespread use of colour STN displays in notebook computers and other portable products despite their obvious disadvantages in performance compared to colour active matrix LCD (AMLCD) technology. However, it is not the intention of this chapter to dwell extensively on the subject of price, which is determined as much by market forces as by the intrinsic cost of materials and manufacture. This view is supported by the significant reduction in the price of AMLCDs up to 10.4″ diagonal which has occurred during 1995, which must be assumed to be due to an excess in manufacturing capacity over demand and not to a sudden decrease in manufacturing costs.

This still leaves us with a multidimensional problem to address. It is not the author's objection to catalogue all the relevant properties of every display technology against each application but rather to discuss in detail a few examples of applications with widely differing requirements, with a focus on techniques by which the most important attributes of a set of technologies may be compared and evaluated.

Technical details of those technologies which are discussed in subsequent chapters will be discussed here only to the extent required for clarity.

Display Systems, Edited by L.W. MacDonald and A.C. Lowe. © 1997 John Wiley & Sons Ltd.

8.2 COMPARING TECHNOLOGIES AND VISUALISING COMPARISONS

In Figure 8.1, display applications are divided into four broad groups and are mapped on to the display size, pixel content (D, N) plane. Note that, in order to present the space occupied by head-mounted displays (HMDs) in sufficient detail, logarithmic scales have been used for both axes. Figure 8.1 is intended to depict only the general area which each application occupies in this parameter space, rather than to define their precise boundaries. Only three of the four groups shown will be discussed: HMDs (retinal projection), direct view, and either front or rear projection on to a screen. The subject of display technologies for electronic advertising boards is interesting in its own right but falls outside the scope of this volume.

Print on paper has been included as a reference since it is the still the medium on which most visual information is presented. Moreover, it sets the standards of spatial and contrast resolution by which displays are judged. The boundaries of size and resolution have been chosen to represent the range of paper sizes commonly in use, A5 to A4 (which is similar to US letter size), from low (160 µm pitch, 150 dpi) to high (40 µm pitch, 600 dpi) print quality.

The properties of all display technologies vary with D and N. A method which can help to visualise comparisons between technologies in some circumstances is to plot a chosen property orthogonal to the (D, N) plane. This method can be particularly useful if

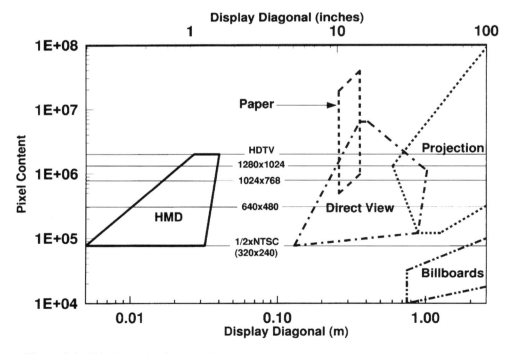

Figure 8.1 Display technology application requirements in terms of diagonal (D) and pixel content (N)

the display attribute under consideration shows significant variation with D and N for a given technology, or between technologies.

8.3   HEAD-MOUNTED DISPLAYS

8.3.1   General considerations

Head-mounted displays which use one or two CRTs located at the side of the wearer's head have been available for some years. An image is projected on to one or both eyes by an optical system consisting of lenses and mirrors. These HMDs were developed primarily for military applications and are bulky and relatively heavy. The first HMDs for non-military applications, such as virtual reality, were also based on this technology.

However, the style of HMD which will be discussed here is one that will be worn by the user more as a pair of spectacles than as a helmet. Applications for such displays will extend beyond totally immersive virtual reality to augmented reality, in which the display image is superimposed on to the normal visual field rather than replacing it. Augmented reality applications include, e.g., computer-aided manufacture and repair, and medicine, especially surgery.

HMDs must be able to deliver a sufficiently bright, magnified image of the display to the eye. This requirement will vary considerably with application, with higher luminosity typically being required by augmented than by virtual reality. Resolution must be sufficient to match the visual resolving power of a user with 20:20 vision. Moreover, since the weight of such HMDs will be borne by the user's ears and nose, these displays must be very light in weight to avoid discomfort and fatigue.

For designs in which the display cells are placed directly in front of the eyes, the dimensions of the human head place an additional constraint on size. The average interocular separation of 60–75 mm will restrict the maximum diagonal of the display module (including the peripheral space required for the cell seal and the attachment of drive circuits and electrical connections) to about 40 mm. For fully portable systems there is an additional requirement that the total system power should be sufficiently low to allow several hours of operation between battery charges. Finally, the reluctance of civilian, if not of military, users to have displays operating at several kilovolts close to their head must be recognised. These will be influential factors in determining which are the most suitable display technologies for the HMD application and they will now be discussed in more detail. (*See also* chapter 4.)

8.3.2   Pixel size

Figure 8.2 depicts the range of display sizes in terms of the diagonal dimension of the actual pixel area for 10 candidate technologies. The lower boundary for each technology has been selected either on the basis of published results, for which references are included below, or of predictions supported by experiment. The upper boundary has been chosen as a line connecting either the point where the display diagonal reaches the maximum of 40 mm, or where presently achievable pixel dimensions reach the maximum resolution considered here of 1280 × 1024 pixels and a somewhat arbitrary lower limit which represents, in the author's view, the maximum practical size for a display of 320 × 240 pixels.

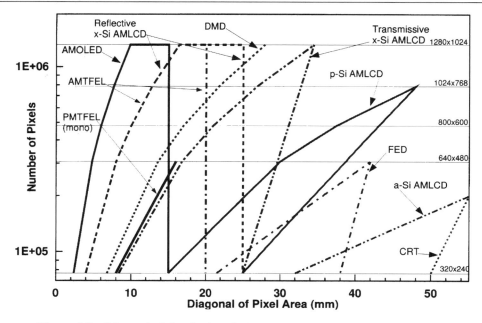

Figure 8.2   Diagonal of the display pixel area for candidate HMD technologies

In all cases, the term 'pixel' is used to describe a full colour pixel, an RGB triad for all but the Digital Micro-mirror Device (DMD) technology which uses a field sequential technique to display colour.

We shall consider three transmissive and two reflective light modulating technologies (all active matrix), two passive matrix and two active matrix self-luminous flat panel technologies and a miniature CRT. All acronyms of display names will be defined on first use in either the figure captions or the text.

From Figure 8.2 it can be seen that some technologies are extendable to considerably smaller pixel sizes than others. In some cases, e.g., amorphous silicon (α-Si) AMLCD (Active Matrix Liquid Crystal Display), and crystalline silicon (x-Si) AMTFEL (Active Matrix Thin Film Electroluminescence) and AMOLED (Active Matrix Organic Light Emitting Diode), the active matrix technology itself will be the limit. For polycrystalline and crystalline silicon (p-Si) and x-Si AMLCDs, it is the fringing field spread in the LC layer which will limit the ultimate pixel density. For CRTs it is the electron beam spot size.

The CRT is included in Figure 8.2 only to demonstrate its unsuitability for this application. This particular example (Vancil, 1994) was chosen because it probably represents the highest resolution, i.e., the smallest pixel size, available in colour CRT technology. Nevertheless, the CRT cannot reach acceptable resolution at an acceptable diagonal dimension.

Transmissive α-Si active matrix arrays suffer significant reduction in aperture ratio at pixel sizes below 80 μm. The limited mobility of α-Si of 1–2 cm^2/Vs makes it impractical to integrate the drive circuits on to the active matrix, so the display module dimensions have been increased by the space required to attach the drive circuits outside the display seal area. We have used an optimistic value of 2 mm per side.

Field Emission Displays, FEDs, also suffer from the same disadvantage of the need to attach discrete driver chips to the display. The emitter arrays of FEDs operate at switching voltages between 5 and 50 V (Gray, 1994; Meyer, 1990). The high anode voltage needs to be switched only if a frame-sequential colour scheme is used (Lévy & Meyer, 1991) and then only once per frame, so the space required for driver chips will be similar to that in α-Si AMLCDs. However, FEDs are also limited by the minimum pixel size achievable. This is because, in the normal triode emitter structure, the electron beam is not focused but spreads with a half-angle of about 15 degrees, with the result that the phosphor associated with pixels adjacent to the driven one will also be partially energised. This reduces the range of contrast and colour saturation which can be achieved. This problem can be overcome either by making the emitter area smaller than the pixel (which may either limit the luminous output or increase the drive voltage required for a given luminous output), or by using a tetrode structure with an additional focusing grid (see references in Budin, 1997). The latter alternative is more complex to fabricate and will be less power efficient than the triode, but, by allowing an increase in the emitter–phosphor separation, it does allow the use of high voltage phosphors which produce much higher luminous efficiencies than phosphors which operate at 500 V or less (Palevsky *et al.*, 1994). With such emitter structures, pixel sizes below the limits of transmissive α-Si technology are, in principle, possible provided that no spacers are used between the emitter and phosphor substrates within the display area. However, the requirement for discrete driver circuits will still make FEDs unsuitable for this application.

From the above discussion we may conclude that any display technology which requires discrete driver circuits will be unsuitable for the HMD application. This view is supported by considering the case of PMTFEL (Passive Matrix Thin Film Electroluminescence). 20 μm pixel dimensions can be achieved (Tsuchiya *et al.*, 1993) with this technology, but the extensive fan-out required to attach 200 V drive circuits to such a display will cause its size and weight to approach that of a 250 μm pitch α-Si AMLCD, so achievable pixel size is only one consideration. It is the minimum achievable overall module dimension which is ultimately important.

The remaining six technologies to be considered all have integrated drive circuitry, which can be situated under the display seal, enabling a reduction in module size of 3–4 mm per side to be achieved.

A recent development in x-Si technology is the silicon-on-insulator (SOI) transfer process developed by Kopin (Salerno, 1994), which enables transmissive AMLCDs to be based, for the first time, on x-Si. It offers very high AMLCD pixel density at large aperture ratios. Aperture ratio at the minimum pixel size is similar, at about 40 percent, to that achievable in p-Si based displays.

Turning now to reflective display technologies, in reflective x-Si AMLCDs, the pixel size for an RGB triad will be limited by the fringing field in the LC which causes the switched area to be greater than the dimension of the pixel electrode by an amount similar to the thickness of the LC layer, or about 3 μm. For the DMD, colours are produced frame sequentially, so each pixel switches all three colours. It is unclear what the lower limit of the pixel dimension will be for this technology, but since it is a mechanical device in which each pixel is a mirror which must be rotated through an angle of several degrees, it is probable that the limit will be greater than that for the reflective AMLCD. Since a pixel dimension of 17×17 μm has been used in recent publications on this technology (Sampsell, 1993), this single value has been used in Figure 8.2.

The advantages of self-luminous technologies will become more apparent once we discuss display module weight in the next section, but it is clear from Figure 8.2 that these technologies can achieve pixel sizes equal to or less than those achievable by any of the LC-based technologies under consideration or DMD. By integrating TFEL on to an SOI active matrix, pixel dimensions equal to those of reflective AMLCDs can be achieved, with the lower limit being determined by the maximum circuit density achievable at operating voltages up to 180 V (Khormaei et al., 1994).

The last technology we shall consider here is organic LEDs (OLEDs). OLEDs are divided into two main classes. Those based on monomeric materials, in general tri-hydroxyquinoline complexes of aluminium, have been the subject of study for more than a decade (Vincett et al., 1982). However, activity in this field has recently increased as a result of the discovery of light emission from polyphenylene–vinylene polymer materials (Burroughes et al., 1990). This last class of materials is at a very early stage of development and substantial improvements in life and luminous efficiency will be needed if they are to find application in HMDs. The light emitting layer in OLEDs, like that in TFEL, is extremely thin, so resolution is expected to be limited only by the AM technology and not by the display medium. The reduced pixel size predicted for OLEDs over AMTFEL is due to their low operating voltage and the consequent densification of the active matrix.

It should be mentioned why a discussion of polymer dispersed liquid crystal (NCAP and PDLC) (Drzaic, 1986; Doane et al., 1988) and polymer stabilised cholesteric texture (PSCT) (Yang et al., 1991) technologies, which switch between a transparent and a scattering state, has not been included in this section. Whilst these technologies have found some success in conventional projection systems, the increased cell thickness required over TN to achieve adequate scattering power would limit the smallest pixel size achievable to about 25 μm. In addition, it was considered unlikely that Schlieren optical systems with adequate performance could be constructed within the severe dimensional constraints of this application.

8.3.3   Display module weight

Having eliminated the CRT and those technologies which require discrete drive circuits, we shall now consider the advantages and disadvantages of the remaining six technologies in terms of display module weight. This comparison, whilst internally consistent, must necessarily be approximate since it has not been based on detailed product designs.

The following have been included: display cell (including polarisers where required), a flexible connection cable to the display adapter, backlight/diffuser (for transmissive AMLCDs), light source/light collimation and delivery system (for reflective AMLCD and DMD) and a lens system to project a magnified image of the display cell on to the retina. Plastic refractive optics have been assumed throughout, although some weight saving would be gained by the use of diffractive optics.

The weight of the remainder of the HMD system has not been included since it will be approximately constant for any of the technologies discussed. This will reduce the proportional difference in total system weight achievable between OLEDs and p-Si AMLCDs over the values shown here. However, the following comparison is still a valid one to make when considering the influence of the display technology on total system weight.

Significant differences exist between the minimum overall display weight and size which can be achieved for a given pixel size between and within the three categories of display technology under discussion. Reflective light modulating displays need to be illuminated with substantially collimated light and so must use a light delivery system which incorporates a high brightness light source and one or more lenses. The DMD (Sampsell, 1993) benefits from using unpolarised light, which reduces the lamp power, but not significantly the weight, compared to reflective AMLCDs.

By comparison, transmissive technologies can use high efficiency fluorescent sources and simple diffusers, but self luminous technologies require only a lens system, which is common to all the technologies discussed, to deliver a magnified image of the display on to the retina.

The impact of this on display module weight can be seen from Figure 8.3, which shows two different perspective views of the same data, and in which weight is plotted orthogonal to the (D, N) plane. For reasons of clarity, only data for the minimum pixel size achievable for each technology have been shown.

The advantage of the three-dimensional plots in Figure 8.3 is that technologies can be compared across a whole range of display resolutions. Such a comparison can be useful in determining which technologies might be considered strategic in that they can cover the whole range of resolution requirements.

8.3.4 Display power and operating voltage

Integrating TFEL on to a SOI active matrix results in a significant reduction of power over the PMTFEL case because the TFEL phosphor can now be driven at a duty cycle approaching 100 percent through a latching AM circuit rather than at a value of $1/R$ for the PMTFEL case (where R is the number of rows in the display) (Khormaei *et al.*, 1994). As a result, operating voltage can be reduced, and this, and the improved recovery of capacitive energy loss, both contribute to this improvement. Of course, the power consumption of self luminous displays will depend on the fraction of 'on' pixels. The power consumption for a 1280×1024 AMTFEL display with 24×24 μm pixels is reported to be 2.5 W with 15 percent of the pixels 'on' (Khormaei, 1995).

The operating power of AMLCDs and DMDs will be lower than EL. Power dissipation in the active matrix will be only a few tens of milliwatts. The power consumption of the drive circuits will be significantly lower than for a direct view display of equivalent resolution because the line resistance and capacitance will be much less in these miniature displays. The majority of the power consumption will be in the light source and its power supply. In fact the light source for both reflective and transmissive technologies may require development to reach an acceptable level of efficiency. The efficiency of fluorescent sources is known to decrease with tube length, and the smallest tungsten-halogen incandescent sources available are not small enough for this application. Calculation of the power requirements of the technologies we have discussed falls outside the scope of this chapter, not least because of the uncertainties mentioned above, but this is clearly an important area which will require attention when any low power application is being considered.

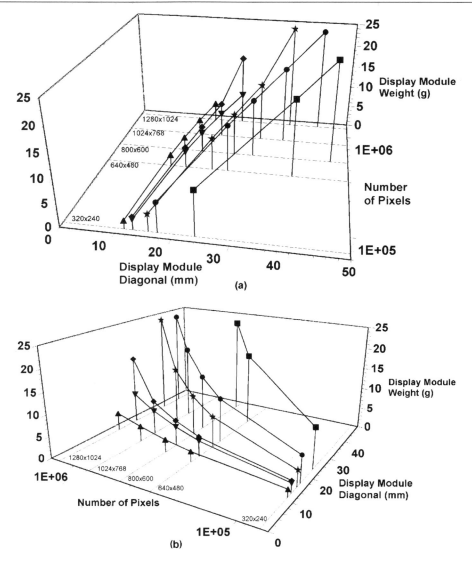

Figure 8.3 Variation of display module weight and size with pixel content for HMD technologies (shown at two different perspectives) ▲ AMOLED, ▼ AMTFEL, ♦ reflective x-Si AMLCD, ★ DMD, ● transmissive x-Si AMLCD, ■ p-Si AMLCD)

8.3.5 Summary and conclusion

The smallest, lightest and lowest-power displays for this application may, in the future, be AMOLEDs, but much development will be required before this technology could be seriously considered as product-ready, and it is unclear whether any insurmountable technical difficulties exist. Reflective technologies can achieve lower pixel dimensions than transmissive, but at the dimensions required for high resolution the weight of transmissive systems may be lower than that of reflective due to their simpler illumination optics. However, of all the systems discussed, only one is presently manufactured in volume; p-Si AMLCDs are made in large volumes for camcorder viewfinders, which typically have a resolution similar to the lowest resolution (320×240) considered here. Even though the HMD application is generally more demanding in terms of resolution, the existence of a large manufacturing base will make the economics of use of this technology attractive. When performance is the predominant requirement, AMTFEL may be the technology of choice.

However, it was not the author's intention to make technology choices because, for a comprehensive evaluation, many other attributes than those discussed here would need to be considered. The purpose of this discussion was rather to survey the issues and methods involved in technology selection, and this first example will have served to demonstrate how plotting properties in (D, N, Attribute) parameter space can help to provide a comprehensive visual comparison of alternative technologies.

8.4 DISPLAYS GREATER THAN 0.5 m DIAGONAL

CRT cost starts to increase significantly at diagonals greater than about 0.5 m. The steepness of the cost/size curve depends on resolution requirements. The fact that the CRT, which is the dominant display technology, reaches a size above which it becomes not only more costly but also much more heavy and bulky than its competitors creates an opportunity for competition from other direct view and projection technologies.

Two different market areas overlap in this space. One is the consumer market which is bounded by normal TV resolution (NTSC, PAL) at the low end and HDTV (approximately 1400×960) at the high end. The other is high pixel content workstation displays. Display technologies for the latter market have been the subject of a recent analysis (Lowe, 1993) and will not be discussed here. We have already discussed in the previous sections how not all the factors which influence the selection of a technology are technical. In the consumer TV market, it is already apparent that social factors can influence the choice of technology for large screen displays in the home. For example, house sizes vary considerably in different parts of the world. Display technologies which offer compact display systems will be at an advantage in those countries where rooms are small compared to countries such as the USA where room sizes are generally large. Thus direct view CRTs might be expected to gain greater penetration in the USA than in Europe or Asia, which might favour more compact systems such as plasma or even AMLCD or FED, with projection systems occupying the middle ground between these two extremes. Economic factors will also be very important, as has often been the case in the past when new market opportunities have appeared; the CRT was the first technology into production for the advanced TV market and will set price targets which will be difficult for any other technology to match.

Figure 8.4 shows a comparison of weight and display depth for a range of typical HDTV screen sizes. The data are shown for both 90° and 110° direct view (DV) CRTs although 90° tubes are required for full HDTV resolution (Hirashimi, 1990). It will be seen that the weight of direct view and projection CRTs increases to the point where structural

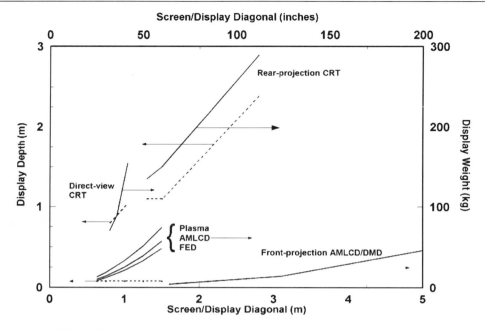

Figure 8.4 Display weight and depth vs. diagonal for HDTV resolution

reinforcement of domestic buildings might be required. In fact all displays other than flat panels become very heavy at large screen sizes. In comparing projection and direct view CRTs it will be seen that projection offers an increase in screen diagonal of about 0.33 m for a given weight and about 0.25 m for a given depth. In general a greater reduction in depth is possible with projection LCDs since an LCD target can be made smaller than a projection CRT of the same resolution. The screen size for front projectors is not fixed as is the case of rear projectors and the curve shows the diagonal achievable by typical projectors for a screen luminance ⩾100 nit at a screen gain of 1 (Candry & Derijcke, 1994; Kahn, 1993).

Power consumption may also be an important issue for these large displays, for reasons of both operating cost and heat dissipation. Plasma technology shows a strong relationship between pixel size and luminous efficiency (Yamamoto *et al.*, 1993; Deschamps, 1994). This is because the barrier technology required to separate pixels cannot easily be scaled to small pixel dimensions. An increase in cost occurs as pixel size is reduced because the low-cost screen printing techniques which are satisfactory for large pixel dimensions have to be replaced by photolithography. So, if pixel size can be maintained above about 0.5 mm, plasma appears to have some advantages over non-flat panel technologies. It will face great competition from the CRT, but this has not deterred several major Japanese companies (Fujitsu, Matsushita and NEC) from announcing major investments in colour plasma display manufacturing facilities (Associated Press, 1995; Fujitsu, 1995). The success, or not, of these ventures will influence the ability of direct view FED or AMLCD to compete in this market. It has been predicted that AMLCD will achieve the required screen size (Howard, 1994) and tip-based FED is capable, in principle, of achieving arrays of emitters over large areas if steppers are used for the single high resolution step of the manufacturing process. Each will offer better luminous efficiency than plasma (in the case of FEDs, if phosphors operating at a few kilovolts are used).

Recent developments in DMD projection technology (Sampsell, 1994; Critchley *et al.*, 1995) have demonstrated that high resolution, high luminance and flicker-free images can be produced. Despite the fact that the demonstrated systems use temporal modulation of colour and grey levels, spatial and temporal artefacts are reduced to a very low level by careful selection of the order in which the binary weighted bits are presented to the display. The fact that this technology does not require polarisers should result in projection systems with high luminous efficiency. However, the small size of the DMD target and the requirement to focus the reflected light either completely into or completely outside an aperture place some constraints on the efficiency which is achievable (Burstyn *et al.*, 1994). Consequently, published data indicate an efficiency of about 1.1 lm/W, which is actually less than the best AMLCD projection displays, which achieve better than 2.9 lm/W (Candry & Derijcke, 1994). However, DMD projection systems are at a much earlier stage of development and design studies indicate that higher efficiencies, up to 4.5 lm/W, should be possible (Burstyn *et al.*, 1994). DMD is certainly a technology to watch, with some significant alliances already announced by TI, and with more expected in the future. No data were available at the time of writing, so the author has assumed that system weight similar to front projection AMLCDs will be possible for DMD projectors.

If the HDTV market starts to grow significantly from about 1998, as is predicted for the USA, it could provide a fruitful market in which those technologies which have so far failed to penetrate either the mainstream CRT or the mobile computing market could compete. The major technical challenges of LCD projection systems and plasma seem to have been overcome, so the success of these technologies in competing with direct view and projection CRTs may be based more on successful manufacturing investment strategies than on technical considerations.

8.5 DIRECT VIEW DISPLAY TECHNOLOGIES LESS THAN 0.5m DIAGONAL

8.5.1 Introduction

Three applications will be discussed in this section:
- low power reflective displays
- applications which require wide viewing angle
- notebook computer displays

There will inevitably be some overlap between these applications, but the general requirements are sufficiently different to justify their separate discussion.

8.5.2 Low power reflective displays

A number of applications exist which require one or more of the following properties:
- sunlight readability
- maximum battery life
- high resolution monochrome or limited colour

Such applications include miniature personal computer equipment such as organisers and PDAs, portable instruments such as oscilloscopes, medical diagnostic tools, and, in the future, electronically generated and transmitted newspapers and magazines.

Here, the comparison of display visual performance with print on paper is particularly relevant. Paper of the quality used in most printers and photocopiers has a reflectivity between 70 and 80 percent. The highest reflectivity values are achieved by the use of fluorescent brighteners. Typical contrast ratios vary from 6:1 for low quality newsprint to 20:1 for high quality offset or laser print. Since uncoated matt paper is an almost Lambertian diffuser, the viewing angle is approximately ±90°. It is against this level of visual performance that reflective displays must be compared if they are to be considered as possible replacements for paper. This level of performance is exceptionally difficult to achieve with any display technology.

Displays which require polarisers

The most highly transmissive polarisers used in displays have a transmittance of approximately 45 percent for unpolarised light and 90 percent for light polarised parallel to the transmissive axis of the polariser. This means that a minimum of about 60 percent of the incident light will be absorbed by the polarisers. Reflection losses in the rear reflector and the fact that the switchable area of the pixel is less than 100 percent of the nominal pixel area add to these losses. Taking reasonable values of 0.87 for pixel reflectivity and 0.88 for the pixel fill ratio, equivalent to a 15 μm interpixel gap and a 330 μm pixel pitch, it is possible to achieve a reflectivity of only 31 percent; 20 percent is more typical.

The problem of parallax is encountered in any reflective display which uses two polarisers external to the display cell, such as the twisted nematic (TN), the supertwisted nematic (STN) and the common configuration of the ferroelectric (FLC) effects. Figure 8.5 shows a comparison between this type of cell and a cell with an internal reflector. The polarisers have not been shown for reasons of clarity. The technology does not yet exist to locate polarisers inside a liquid crystal cell, so, in Figure 8.5(a) the reflecting surface

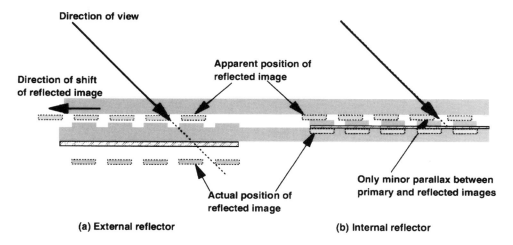

Figure 8.5   The effect of parallax in reflective displays with (a) external and (b) internal reflectors

is separated from the liquid crystal layer by a distance equal to the sum of the thickness of the rear substrate and the polariser, say 1.5 mm. Thus the reflection appears to originate from a plane double this distance, or about 3 mm, from the liquid crystal layer. This results in significant parallax between the primary image formed in the liquid crystal layer and its reflection in the external reflector when the display is viewed at an off-normal angle. As the viewing angle is increased, the reflection becomes associated with the primary image of the adjacent pixel, at which point the display becomes unusable. The problem of parallax is severe in displays with pixel dimensions of 0.33 mm (typical of a 10.4″ diagonal VGA display), and becomes increasingly severe as pixel size is reduced. Despite these limitations, all products up to now, with one exception which will be discussed below, which have used reflective displays have used displays with external reflators. Perhaps their poor visual quality is to some extent responsible for their generally low market penetration.

Although most publications on the ferroelectric smectic (FLC) effect describe cells which use two external polarisers (Matsumoto *et al.*, 1988; Surguy *et al.*, 1991), FLC displays can operate with a single polariser. Since the FLC effect relies on electrically switchable optical retardation (Dijon, 1990), all that is required is that the $\lambda/2$ retardation of a two-polariser cell is reduced to $\lambda/4$ for the one-polariser configuration. Parallax is avoided by making the rear pixel electrode reflective, which enables the inherent wide viewing angle of this technology to be exploited. This configuration is shown in Figure 8.5(b). However, although the parallax problem is avoided, the reflectivity remains low.

Displays which absorb light

Displays in this category involve the use of a dichroic dye (guest) dissolved in a nematic LC (host). If the geometry of the dye molecule is matched to that of the LC host, then the dye molecules adopt the same orientation as the LC. For optimum performance, the transition dipole associated with the absorption of light by the dye must be parallel to the geometrical long axis of the dye molecule. Thus, when the LC is aligned parallel to the display substrate, the dye absorbs light. When the LC is oriented perpendicular to the display substrate by the application of an electric field, the dye molecules absorb substantially less light. Several factors reduce the absorption of light in the absorbing state and increase absorption in the nominally non-absorbing state; the transition dipole may not be parallel to the geometric axis of the dye molecule, the alignment of the dye molecule to the LC host may not be perfect, and, because of thermal motion in the LC host, the alignment of the nematic molecules themselves will fluctuate by more than $20°$ from the notional alignment direction at room temperature. The combination of these effects is quantified by a dye order parameter, S, which was originally derived to describe the order of the liquid crystal phase itself (Maier & Saupe, 1959), the treatment of which was extended to account for the angle between the transition dipole and the geometric axis of the dye molecule (Lowe & Cox, 1980). $S = 1$ for perfect order, but $S \leqslant 0.8$ is typical of guest–host systems. This effectively limits reflectivity to 30–35 percent and contrast ratio to $\leqslant 5:1$ (Mitsui *et al.*, 1992). Higher contrast ratios than this can only be achieved by the use of a front polariser and a nematic, rather than a cholesteric LC structure (Lowe, 1980).

Displays which scatter light

If a nematic LC is dispersed as small spherical droplets in a matrix of a polymer, it is possible, by the correct choice of refractive indices for the nematic and the polymer and by using an appropriate alignment, effectively to match the refractive index of the LC to that of the polymer, creating a transparent, non-scattering dispersion. This condition can be achieved only for one direction of view, since the polymer is optically isotropic and the nematic is birefringent. When an electric field is applied to thin films of such a dispersion, the nematic in the small spherulites is reoriented, the refractive index match is destroyed, and the layer scatters light. Two distinct methods have been used to prepare such dispersions: emulsification of an immiscible mixture of monomer and LC, followed by polymerisation (Drzaic, 1986), or the polymerisation of a solution of the LC in the monomer, which causes phase separation of the polymer as it is formed (Doane *et al.*, 1988). The details of these systems are dealt with in more detail by Mosley (this volume). The guest–host effect has also been used in conjunction with NCAP materials to enhance contrast, which is generally low, because of the relatively weak scattering power of these systems.

A second class of materials in this category makes use of the fact that a cholesteric LC can be switched from a planar state, in which the chiral axis is perpendicular to the display plane (i.e., the LC molecules are parallel to the display plane) to a disordered focal conic state, which scatters light. Cholesteric LCs in the planar state reflect light by the Bragg effect (De Gennes & Prost, 1993). This will be discussed in more detail below. If the pitch of the LC is adjusted so that the planar state reflects in the infra-red, then the planar state will be transparent to visible light. This phenomenon has been known for many years (Greubel *et al.*, 1973), but it suffers from the fact that, whilst the switching time from the planar to the focal conic state is short (of the order of milliseconds), the focal conic state reverts to the planar state only slowly and may take several minutes. The discovery that, by *in situ* polymerisation of a dilute polymer network, by a technique similar to that used for PDLC, the transition from the focal conic to the planar state could be accelerated to times similar to those for the transition from the planar to the focal conic state (Yang, 1991; Doane, 1992) rekindled interest in these systems. They are significantly different from PDLCs in that only a few percent of polymer is used. This forms an open but crosslinked network throughout the display cell, with the polymer mimicking the structure of the LC in its planar state, and presumably acting as an alignment surface for the LC, stabilising the planar state. This system has been designated 'reverse mode polymer stabilised cholesteric texture' or RM-PSCT (Fung *et al.*, 1993). The existence of a well defined planar structure in the polymer network has recently been demonstrated (Held *et al*, 1996).

Because the polymer network is so dilute, RM-PSCT systems exhibit none of the off-normal scattering in the nominally transparent state which limits the usefulness of PDLC systems for wide viewing angle applications. However, they suffer from the same disadvantage as PDLC, in that the scattering power of the focal conic state is rather weak, which limits reflectivity to about 10 percent unless special techniques are used to enhance the back scatter (see below). They also have rather high switching voltages of about 2.5–3.5 V/μm, which leads to increased power consumption. Both these systems require the use of a light absorbing pixel electrode, which absorbs all light transmitted by the LC layer. Consequently, they do not suffer from parallax.

Displays in which the LC layer reflects light

These displays also use PSCT LCs, except that, in this case, the wavelength of the Bragg reflection is positioned at visible wavelengths and scattering from the focal conic state is minimised by the choice of low Δn LCs and by optimising the focal conic domain size. This class is designated 'normal mode PSCT' or NM-PSCT. Again, this effect has been known for many years in pure cholesteric systems, but two significant improvements result from the presence of a polymer network.

First, the wavelength bandwidth of the reflected light is increased over that obtained in pure LC systems. It is thought that this is due to the creation of small planar domains which are distributed at a range of angles about the notional helical axis direction. However, despite this improvement, it has not proved possible to make achromic (i.e., black/white) displays based on this effect, unless very high polymer concentrations are used, which increases the switching voltage to about 5 V/μm in cells of the order of 15 μm in thickness. Another factor to be remembered is that, although the Bragg reflectivity is very high (theoretically 100 percent at the peak wavelength), the reflected light is circularly polarised with a handedness which matches the chiral pitch sense of the cholesteric LC. Thus the maximum reflectivity for unpolarised incident illumination is only 50 percent. Two layers of opposite handedness would be required to achieve reflectivity greater than 50 percent (at λ_{max}), and this would create parallax problems similar to those discussed earlier.

The NM-PSCT effect is bistable at zero applied field, and this has important consequences. The fact that the display needs to be refreshed only when the displayed information is changed reduces power consumption significantly, despite the relatively high driving voltage of 30 V. It also means that high resolution displays with millions of pixels can be made without the need for an active matrix (Pfeiffer *et al.*, 1995). This has profound consequences on display cost, and may open up markets for this technology despite the fact that it is not achromic and that the reflected colour changes with viewing angle. Recently, it has been discovered that the properties of NM-PSCT can be reproduced by using roughened display substrates, a process which is simpler to manufacture than the *in situ* formation of a polymer network (Lu *et al.*, 1995).

Display reflectivity

If the visual performance of reflective displays is ever to compete with print on paper, significant developments will be required to maximise reflectivity whilst retaining such diffuse reflectivity characteristics that the display can be viewed over a wide range of angles. Most LC effects require that the display substrates are very smooth, or the structure of the LC will be disrupted. (This discussion relates only to those effects which employ an internal reflector. However, it has been shown (Mitsui *et al.*, 1992) that rough metal electrodes can be constructed which meet the combined requirements of not disrupting the LC structure, whilst providing diffuse reflection properties.)

Another recent development has been the creation of holographic reflectors which reflect light at an angle different from the specular reflection angle (Chen *et al.*, 1995). The hologram concentrates the reflected light over a restricted angular range and achieves reflectivity greater than that of a Lambertian reflector. However, like NM-PSCT, they cannot be made achromic and have a peak width, at half intensity, of about 100 nm. As presently demonstrated they are used externally to the display cell, and therefore suffer from the same parallax problems as conventional external reflectors.

The low backscatter from PDLC LCs has been improved significantly by placing a layer of 'brightness enhancing film' behind the display cell (Kanemoto *et al.*, 1994). This film is normally used to restrict the angular spread of the light delivered by LCD backlight systems. The ridged film refracts a portion of the forward scattered light emerging from the display and reflects it from its rear surface back through the cell. Light transmitted through the cell in its clear state emerges over a narrower range of angles and is not reflected. By this means, the reflectivity of a PDLC cell was improved from 7.9 percent to 35.5 percent. Unfortunately, as with any external reflector, parallax problems will limit the usefulness of this idea.

Summary

The development of high reflectivity, high contrast reflective displays with wide viewing angle is a difficult technical challenge, for the following reasons:

- Display effects which require the use of polarisers produce high contrast but low reflectivity. FLC does deliver very wide viewing angle which can be exploited because, unlike the TN effect, it can make use of an internal reflector, avoiding parallax.
- Displays which absorb light by using the guest–host effect are limited to about 30 percent reflectivity at contrast ratios of $\leqslant 5:1$, and they show a reduction in reflectivity and contrast as the viewing angle is increased. However, they do not suffer from parallax problems.
  Displays which scatter light do so inadequately and at present cannot achieve sufficient reflectivity without the use of layers external to the display cell to reflect a fraction of the light which has been forward scattered by the LC layer.
- PSCT displays which reflect light cannot achieve reflectivity greater than 50 percent unless a double layer cell is used. In practical terms, achievable reflectivity is much lower than this. Achromic displays based on this technology do not seem to be a realistic possibility at this time. However, they can be made bistable, and this makes low cost, high resolution displays possible.

There are no clear choices here, and much improvement is required if any of these technologies is to approach the visual quality of print on paper.

8.5.3 Light emitting direct view displays with wide viewing angle

There exist a range of applications where wide viewing angle is required, but where power consumption is less of an issue than for either of the other types of application discussed in this section. Variation in contrast ratio can be important not only for large displays observed by a single user but also for displays which are viewed by several users simultaneously. Some examples are:

- the increasing use of notebook computers as sales presentation aids
- portable medical equipment which must be viewable from any angle
- other instrument displays
- applications in which accurate colour rendition is required

Advances in manufacturing technology have enabled significant increases to be made in the maximum available size of LCDs (Kawai et al., 1993). Consequently, even when the viewer is centrally positioned in front of the display, colour and grey scale may appear visibly different between the centre and the corners of the display because of the large difference in viewing angle. The AMLCD industry is of course aware of problems associated with the viewing angle dependence of luminance and chrominance contrast and several approaches have been proposed to improve this characteristic of AMLCDs.

Table 8.1 LC technologics

Display technology	Usable viewing angle (°)	Grey levels at viewing angle limit
AMLCD; 1-domain TN	±30(H); +30, −10(V)	8
AMLCD; 2,4-domain TN	±40 (H & V)	>16
AMLCD; multidomain TN	±50 (H & V)	>16
AMLCD; 2-domain homeotropic	±50(H); ±20(V)	>8
FLC	±80 (H & V)	bistable
AFLC	±80 (H & V)	8? by subpixel halftone
CRT	±80 (H & V)	full analogue
PMTFEL	±80 (H & V)	limited, 2–4

They use two (Yang, 1991; Takatori *et al.*, 1992; Kamada *et al.*, 1992), four (Lien & John, 1994), or an arbitrarily large number (Toko *et al.*, 1993; Kobayashi *et al.*, 1994) of domains per pixel. The twist sense and/or the tilt vary from domain to domain, and with appropriate domain orientation, reduction in contrast in some domains is offset by increases in others. The same approach has also been applied to negative $\Delta\varepsilon$ nematic effects (Yang, 1991; Lien & John, 1993). Although effective in reducing contrast ratio degradation at large viewing angles, the maximum achievable contrast is also reduced by light leakage at disclination lines which are formed at domain boundaries.

Other LC technologies exist which offer wide viewing angle. These include the ferro-electric (FLC) (Ross *et al.*, 1992; Tsuboyama *et al.*, 1992), and antiferroelectric (AFLC) (Yamada *et al.*, 1992) effects. FLC and AFLC are achromic and can produce colour by the standard filter techniques. Both can be addressed by passive matrix schemes. AFLC is monostable and suitable for video-rate applications, whereas FLC is bistable. A third alternative (Yamaguchi *et al.*, 1993) uses essentially a voltage-controlled birefringence effect in a nematic LC which is aligned parallel but with opposite tilt on the two display substrates. The LC layer must be maintained in a 'bend' state, which has proved difficult to stabilise. Nevertheless, it offers the possibility of fast switching, wide viewing angle with grey scale and with no contrast loss due to disclinations. The various technologies are summarised in Table 8.1

All the self-luminous display technologies are approximately Lambertian radiators and so have very wide viewing angle. The CRT dominates this market, but there are a number of niche markets which require not only ruggedness and the ability to operate over a wide environmental range, but also compactness. A good example of a technology filling such a range of applications is PMTFEL (Haaranen *et al.*, 1992) which is used extensively in instrumentation and medical applications. By comparison to modern computer displays, these applications typically do not require very high pixel content or grey scale; nor do they require full colour. Table 8.1 shows the usable viewing angle and number of grey levels achievable for the technologies considered.

8.5.4 Notebook computer displays

This will be the last application to be discussed in this chapter. It is certainly not the least in importance as it accounts for the majority of flat panel displays, if not in number, then in the total area of displays manufactured. Two technologies dominate this market, STN and AMLCD, and this discussion will be less about comparing technologies than about discussing why this state of affairs exists.

Computer application software continues to be written for desktop systems which use CRT displays, so they make use of the full colour capabilities of that technology. It is therefore imperative that notebook computer displays have substantial colour capability. Perhaps the full 256 grey levels, or 8 bits, per colour commonly used with CRTs are not required, but certainly 64 levels, or 6 bits, per colour should be regarded as a minimum. This requirement is not static and the minimum performance level will continue to increase, with a number of companies actively developing 8-bit drivers.

The second requirement is low power. In the last few years, backlights, in which an array of fluorescent tubes were arranged behind the display, have been replaced with single tube edge lights in which the light is guided across the entire area of the display by a combination light guide and diffuser. This has resulted in a reduction of power consumption by a factor of about 3–4, whilst maintaining screen luminance at about 70 nits. Of course, this is not the whole story. Whilst AMLCD technology is capable of exceeding the colour gamut of the CRT, all manufacturers have reduced the colour gamut of their products to improve the transmittance of the colour filters, where up to 66 percent of the incident light is absorbed.

The other area where dramatic improvements have been made is in increasing the aperture ratio of the active matrix array. For some time, diode and MIM arrays were promoted as having superior aperture ratios to TFTs. This advantage has proved to be difficult to realise at the high grey scale performance now required of these displays, and several innovative new TFT designs have recently been published, e.g., in which the storage capacitor is formed as a ring around the pixel (Kim *et al.*, 1995), with a consequent increase in the aperture ratio. This subject is discussed in more detail by Lüder (this volume).

STN displays occupy the remainder of the market, with monochrome displays having a rapidly declining share. Anyone who has used modern applications, designed for colour, on a monochrome display with limited grey scale and viewing angle capability will easily understand why! Problems associated with this lack of grey scale are alleviated to a considerable extent by the use of colour STN, yet the contrast ratio and viewing angle are still inferior to AMLCD. The only reason why colour STN displays occupy their present market share is because of their low price compared to AMLCD.

This situation is not static. As AMLCDs continue to fall in price, the competition will intensify for STN, which requires flatter substrates and tighter manufacturing tolerances than AMLCD. Furthermore, state-of-the-art notebooks are now offered with displays of higher resolution than VGA, and SVGA (800×600) displays are now becoming available. This will offer an additional challenge to STN, which is already severely challenged in producing adequate viewing angle and contrast ratio at VGA resolution of 640×480 pixels. (Electrically, the display is addressed as 1280×240 pixels with dual scan driving schemes, which halves the duty ratio.)

The intense competition which exists between the two display technologies which dominate this market must be borne in mind when considering whether an alternative technology could successfully enter this market in the future. Field emitter displays have been actively promoted and have received substantial development funding over the last few years. The basis for this interest was that FEDs offer the prospect of lower manufacturing cost, lower power consumption and lighter weight than an equivalent AMLCD. The improvements in power consumption and recent reduction in AMLCD price will make these advantages more difficult to realise. There also remain two technical challenges for FEDs which must be solved if they are to achieve visual performance comparable to AMLCDs. First is the problem of phosphor ageing which leads to unacceptable burn-in of static images (such as the desktop or application icons which appear in fixed positions on the display). The use of high voltage phosphors will avoid this problem, but, because of dielectric breakdown between the emitter array and the phosphor, they can only be used with a more complex emitter structure which provides some focusing of the electron beam but which will result in increased manufacturing cost and power consumption. However, it will also solve the problem of beam spreading which has already been discussed in Section 3, and which is also discussed by Budin (this volume).

FLCs offer low power, wide viewing angle and a cost similar to STN. However, the inability of this technology to provide grey scale, except by spatial subdivision of pixels or by temporal subdivision of the frame time, both of which will increase cost and power consumption, limits the suitability of FLC technology for this application.

To summarise, AMLCD and colour STN dominate this market. STN is challenged in terms of the performance it will be able to deliver at the higher display resolutions which are now being introduced into this market, and the continually increasing level of performance which is being achieved, coupled with the intense competition between these two technologies, present a formidable challenge to any new technology.

8.6 CONCLUSION

In this chapter it has been possible to touch on only a few aspects of the complex topic of selecting the best technology for an application. The examples have been chosen to provide some perspective of the range of applications. Although CRT, AMLCD and PMLCD technologies dominate the market in terms of volume and revenue, opportunities still exist for other technologies, especially if they can be adapted to meet new requirements. The developments which have taken place in the last year or two demonstrate the enormous amount of invention and new ideas which continues to be applied in this field. The task of selecting the best technology for an application is likely to become more, rather than less, difficult in the future, because the range of available technologies will increase.

However, the existing LCD technologies are becoming mature. Display performance continues to improve and, because of yield improvements, manufacturing costs will continue to decrease. This will present a severe challenge to the ability of any new technology successfully to enter the market — just as the CRT presented, and continues to present, a challenge in those markets which it dominates. It is an encouraging sign to display technologists and to the industry that supports them that investment is now being made to manufacture some of these new technologies in large volume.

REFERENCES

Associated Press (1995), Press report, *The Associated Press*, 24 August, file: h0824081.501.
Burroughes, J.H., Bradley, D.C.C., Brown, A.R., Marks, R.N., Mackay, K., Friend, R.H., Burns, P.L. and Holmes, A.B. (1990), Light emitting diodes based on conjugated polymers, *Nature*, **347**, 539.

Burstyn, H.C., Meyerhofer, D. and Heyman, P.M. (1994), The design of high-efficiency high-resolution projectors with the digital micromirror device, *SID Int. Symp. Digest of Technical Papers*, **XXV**, 677.

Budin, J-P. (1997), Emissive displays: the relative merits of ACTFEL, plasma and FEDs, *Display Systems: Design and Applications* ed. MacDonald, L. and Lowe, A., John Wiley and Sons, Chichester.

Candry, P. and Derijcke, C. (1994), Light-value and CRT projection systems, *SID Int. Symp. Digest of Technical Papers*, **XXV**, 737.

Chen, A.G., Jelley, K.W., Valliath, G.T., Molteni, W.J., Ralli, P.J. and Wenyon, M.M. (1995), Holographic reflective liquid-crystal display, *SID Int. Symp. Digest of Technical Papers*, **XXVI**, 176.

Critchley, B.R., Blaxten, P.W., Eckersley, B., Gale, R.O. and Burton, M. (1995), Picture quality in large-screen projectors using the digital micromirror device, *SID Int. Symp. Digest of Technical Papers*, **XXVI**, 524.

De Gennes, P.G. and Prost, J. (1993), *The Physics of Liquid Crystals*, Clarendon Press, Oxford, 264.

Deschamps, J.L. (1994), Recent developments and results in colour-plasma-display technology, *SID Int. Symp. Digest of Technical Papers*, **XXV**, 315.

Dijon, J. (1990), in B. Bahadur (ed.), *Liquid Crystals — Applications and Uses*, Vol. **1**, World Scientific, London, 305.

Doane, J.W., Golemme, A., West, J.L., Whitehead, J.B. and Wu, B.G. (1988), Polymer dispersed liquid crystals for display application, *Mol. Cryst. Liq. Cryst.*, **165**, 511.

Doane, J.W., Yang, D.K. and Yaniv, Z. (1992), Front-lit flat panel display from polymer stabilised cholesteric textures *proc. 12th Int. Display Res. Conf.*, **73**.

Drzaic, P.S. (1986), Polymer dispersed nematic liquid crystals for large area displays using NCAP liquid crystals, *J. Appl. Phys.*, **60**(6), 2142.

Fujitsu (1995), Press Conference at SID Symposium, May 1995, Orlando, *Information Display*, **11**(9), 21.

Fung, Y.K., Yang, D.K., Doane, J.W. and Yaniv, Z. (1993), Projection display from polymer stabilised cholesteric texture, *Proc. Thirteenth Int. Display Research Conf.*, 157.

Gray, H.F. (1994), Electron source technology behind field emitter displays, *Int. Display Research Conf. Record*, 440.

Greubel, W., Wolff, U. and Kruger, H. (1973), *Mol. Cryst. Liq. Cryst.*, **24**, 103.

Haaranen, J., Törnqvist, R., Koponen, J., Pitkänen, T., Surma-aho, M., Barrow, W. and Laakso, C. (1992), A 9-in-diagonal high-contrast multicolour TFEL display, *SID Int. Symp. Digest of Technical Papers*, **XXIII**, 348.

Held, E.A., Kosbar, L.L., Lowe, A.C., Afzali-Ardakani, A., Schröder, U.P., Chan, K-P., Russell, T., Twieg, R.J., and Miller, R.D (1996), Relationship Between Network Structure and the Electro-Optical Properties of Polymer Stabilised Cholesteric Textures. *Proc. 16th Int. Display Res. Conf.*, **573**.

Hirashimi, T. (1990), HDTV programs in Japan, *Proc. Tenth Int. Display Research Conf.*, 22.

Howard, W.E. (1994), Limitations and prospects of a-Si:H TFTs, *Int. Display Research Conf. Record*, 6.

Kahn, F.J. (1993), Projection displays, *SID Seminar Lecture Notes*, **1**, M-4.

Kamada, T., Koike, Y., Tsuyuki, S., Takeda, A. and Okamoto, K. (1992), Wide viewing angle full-colour TFT LCDs, *Proc. Twelfth Int. Display Research Conf.*, 886.

Kanemoto, A., Matsuki, Y. and Takiguchi, Y. (1994), Back scattering enhancement in polymer dispersed liquid crystal display with prism array sheets, *Int. Display Research Conf. Record*, 183.

Kawai, K., Sakurai, M., Nagayasu, T., Kondo, N., Nakata, Y., Mizushima, S., Yano, K. and Hijiki-gawa, M. (1993), 17-in-diagonal colour TFT-LCDs for engineering workstations, *SID Int. Symp. Digest of Technical Papers*, **XXIV**, 743.

Khormaei, R., Thayer, S., Ping, K., King, C., Dolny, G., Ipri, A., Hsueh, F-L., Stewart, R., Keyser, T., Becker, G., Kagey, D. and Spitzer, M. (1994), High resolution active-matrix electroluminescent display, *SID Int. Symp. Digest of Technical Papers*, **XXV**, 137.

Kim, S.S., Moon, S.H., Kim, D.G. and Kim, N.D. (1995), High aperture ratio and fault tolerant pixel structure for TFT-LCDs, *SID Int. Symp. Digest of Technical Papers*, **XXVI**, 15.

Kobayashi, S., Iimura, Y. and Nishikawa, M. (1994), New development in alignment layers for active matrix TN-LCDs, *Int. Display Research Conf. Record*, 78.

Khormaei, R, Thayer, S., Ping, K., King, C., Dolny, G., Ipri, A., Hsueh, F-L., Stewart, R., Keyser, T., Becker, G., Kagey, D., Spitzer, M. (1994), High Resolution Active-Matrix Electroluminescent Display, *SID Int. Symp. Digest of Technical Papers*, **XXV**, 137.

Lévy, F. and Meyer, R. (1991), Phosphors for full-colour microtips fluorescent displays, *Int. Display Research Conf. Record*, 20.

Lien, A. and John, R.A. (1993), Multidomain homeotropic liquid crystal display for active matrix application, *Proc. Thirteenth Int. Display Research Conf.*, 21.

Lien, A. and John, R.A. (1994), TFT-addressed two-domain TN VGA displays fabricated using the parallel-fringe-field method, *SID Int. Symp. Digest of Technical Papers*, **XXV**, 594.

Lowe, A.C. (1980), Assessment of nematic guest–host systems for application to integrated liquid crystal displays, *Mol. Cryst. Liq. Cryst.*, **66**, 295.

Lowe, A.C. (1993), Display requirements for computer workstations of the future, *Proc. Thirteenth Int. Display Research Conf.*, 89.

Lowe, A.C. and Cox, R.J. (1980), Order parameter and the performance of nematic guest–host displays, *Mol. Cryst. Liq. Cryst.*, **66**, 309.

Lu, Z-J., St John, W.D., Huang, X-Y., Yang, D-K. and Doane, J.W. (1995), Surface modified reflective cholesteric displays, *SID Int. Symp. Digest of Technical Papers*, **XXVI**, 172.

Maier, W. and Saupe, A. (1959), *Z. Naturforsch., Teil A*, **14**, 882.

Matsumoto, S., Hatoh, H., Kamagami, S. and Murayama, A. (1988), Multiplexed ferroelectric liquid crystal display, *Ferroelectrics*, **85**, 235.

Meyer, R. (1990), 6″ Diagonal microtips fluorescent display for TV applications, *Proc. Tenth Int. Display Research Conf.*, 374.

Mitsui, S., Shimada, Y., Yamamoto, K., Takamatsu, T., Kimura, N., Kozaki, S., Ogawa, S., Morimoto, H., Matsuura, M., Ishii, M., Awane, K. and Uchida, T. (1992), Bright reflective multicolour LCDs addressed by a-Si TFTs., *SID Int. Symp. Digest of Technical Papers*, **XXIII**, 437.

Palevsky, A., Gammie, G. and Koufopoulos, P. (1994), A 10,000-fL high-efficiency field emission display, *SID Int. Symp. Digest of Technical Papers*, **XXV**, 55.

Pfeiffer, M., Yang, D.K., Doane, J.W., Bunz, R., Lüder, E., Lu, M-H., Yuan, H., Catchpole, C.E. and Yaniv, Z. (1995), High information content reflective cholesteric display, *SID Int. symp. Digest of Technical Papers*, **XXVI**, 706.

Ross, P.W., Alexander, K., Banks, L.G., Carrington, A.N., Chan, L.K.M., Gibbons, D.J., Hedgley, R.L., Lui, N., Naylor, M.J., Needham, B., Riby, N.E., Surguy, P.W.H., Vaidya, A.W. and White, J.C. (1992), Colour digital ferroelectric LCDs for laptop applications, *SID Int. Symp. Digest of Technical Papers*, **XXIII**, 217.

Salerno, J.P. (1994), Single crystal silicon AMLCDs, *Int. Display Research Conf. Record*, 39.

Sampsell, J.B. (1993), An overview of the digital micromirror device (DMD) and its application to projection displays, *SID Int. Symp. Digest of Technical Papers*, **XXIV**, 1012.

Sampsell, J.B. (1994), An overview of the performance envelope of digital micromirror device based projection systems, *SID Int. Symp. Digest of Technical Papers*, **XXV**, 669.

Surguy, P.W.H., Banks, L.G., Chan., L.K.M., Naylor, M.J., Carrington, A.N. and Riby, N.E. (1991), An 8.5-in ferroelectric video-rate colour display, *Proc. SID*, **34/2**, 375.

Takatori, K., Sumiyoshi, Hirai, Y. and Kaneko, S. (1992), A complementary TN LCD with wide-viewing-angle grayscale, *Proc. Twelfth Int. Display Research Conf.*, 591.

Toko, Y., Sugiyama, T., Katoh, K., Iimura, Y. and Kobayashi, S. (1993), TN-LCDs fabricated by non-rubbing showing wide and homogeneous viewing angular characteristics and excellent voltage holding ratio, *SID Int. Symp. Digest of Technical Papers*, **XXIV**, 622.

Tsuboyama, A., Hanyu, Y., Yoshihara, S. and Kanbe, J. (1992), Characteristics of the large size, high resolution FLCD, *Proc. Twelfth Int. Display Research Conf.*, 53.

Tsuchiya, Y., Miyamoto, S., Kuki, T., Okamoto, S., Kobayashi, K., Takahashi, S., Ishida, T. and Morokawa, S. (1993), 20 μm pixel pitch ZnS: Tb TFEL displays, *Proc. Thirteenth Int. Display Research Conf.*, 225.

Vancil, B. (1994), A moving shadow-mask colour CRT for miniature displays, *SID Int. Symp. Digest of Technical Papers*, **XXV**, 393.

Vincett, P.S., Barlow, W.A., Hann, R.A. and Roberts, G.G. (1982), Electrical conduction and low voltage blue electroluminescence in vacuum deposited organic thin films, *Thin Solid Films*, **94**, 171.

Yamada, Y., Yamamoto, N., Yamawaki, M., Kawamura, I. and Suzuki, Y. (1992), Multi-colour video-rate antiferroelectric LCDs with high contrast and wide view, *Proc. Twelfth Int. Display Research Conf.*, 57.

Yamaguchi, Y., Miyashita, T. and Uchida, T. (1993), Wide-viewing-angle display mode for the active matrix LCD using bend alignment liquid-crystal cell, *SID Int. Symp. Digest of Technical Papers*, **XXIV**, 277.

Yamamoto, T., Kuriyama, T., Seki, M., Katoh, T., Murakami, H., Shimada, K. and Ishiga, H. (1993), A 40-in-diagonal HDTV plasma display, *SID Int. Symp. Digest of Technical Papers*, **XXIV**, 165.

Yang, D.K., Chien, L-C. and Doane, J.W. (1991), Cholesteric liquid-crystal polymer gel dispersion bistable at zero field, *Int. Display Research Conf. Record*, 49.

Yang, K.H. (1991), Two-domain twisted nematic and tilted homeotropic liquid crystal displays for active matrix applications, *Int. Display Research Conf. Record*, 68.

Active matrix addressing of LCDs: merits and shortcomings

Ernst Lüder

9.1 INTRODUCTION

Active matrix addressing places an electronic switch at each pixel of an LCD thus controlling the charging of the pixel capacitor up to the voltage corresponding to the desired grey shade and then holding this voltage until the next video information is written in. The available switches are thin film transistors (TFTs) which are field effect transistors with, as a rule a-Si, poly-Si and more seldom CdSe as semiconductors or metal–insulator–metal devices (MIMs) which exhibit diode-like behaviour. Thin film diode switches, which are based on p-n junctions, will not be discussed as their performance is inferior to that of TFTs whereas their fabrication is more costly than that of MIMs. This standing of diodes between TFTs and MIMs renders them less attractive than either of the alternatives.

Passive addressing is considerably less costly as it does not require a switch at each pixel. However, in contrast to active addressing it suffers from limitations in the number of addressable lines, in the number of grey shades as well as in the time for which it is possible to hold a given grey shade, which results in flicker.

For TFTs and MIMs this chapter will outline the performance, the fabrication processes, the lowering of fabrication cost by enhancing throughput and yield, the increase of brightness of an LCD (a most crucial issue), the sensitivity to parasitic effects and the addressing of the two types of switches.

9.2   OPERATION OF TFTs AND MIMs

Figures 9.1(a) and (b) show the addressing of a pixel by TFTs and by MIMs respectively. All TFTs in the pixels of one line are made conductive by a positive gate pulse upon which the video information is charged, through the columns, simultaneously in all pixels of the line, on to the LC capacitors C_{LC} and the additional thin film capacitors C_S. The

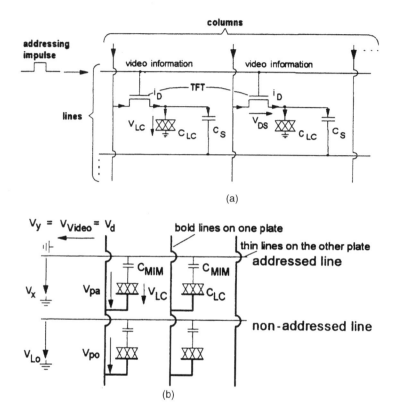

Figure 9.1   Addressing of pixels in one line by (a) TFTs and (b) MIMs

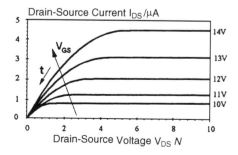

Figure 9.2   Drain–source current I_{DS} of a TFT versus drain–source voltage V_{DS}

charging of the capacitors to the voltage $V_{LC}(t)$ is governed by a non-linear differential equation as both C_{LC} and the on-resistance of the TFT are voltage dependent. As $V_{LC}(t)$ rises the voltage $V_{DS}(t)$ of the TFT drops. This results in a decrease of the drain-source current I_{DS} with time t as indicated by the arrow t in Figure 9.2.

The MIM is a capacitor with traps in the dielectric material filled with electrons. With increasing voltage, V_{MIM}, across the MIM the electric field frees trapped electrons resulting in an increase of the current, I_{MIM}, through the MIM as depicted in Figure 9.3 (Baraff *et al.*, 1981). As this effect, the Pool–Frenkl effect, is independent of the sign of V_{MIM} the characteristic in Figure 9.3 is symmetrical about the origin, unlike that of a diode. The addressing of the MIM is more complex than that of a TFT as a MIM has only two terminals. The waveforms required at the lines and columns as shown in Figure 9.1(b) are depicted in Figure 9.4(a) and (b). (Togashi, 1992; Kuijk, 1990; Knapp & Hartman, 1994). The voltage V_p in Figure 9.1(b) across the pixel is $V_p = V_x - V_d$. The voltage for the lines has four levels, namely the select voltages $+V_s$ and $-V_s$ and the holding voltages V_h and $-V_h$. With the data voltage V_d at the columns we obtain the following expression for the voltage V_{LC} across the LC cell in Figure 9.1(b) at the time V_d is applied:

$$V_{LC} = V_s - V_d - V_{MIM} \qquad\qquad 9.1$$

with

$$V_s = \tfrac{1}{2}(V_{th} + V_{sat}) + V_{thMIM} \qquad\qquad 9.2$$

where V_{th} is the threshold and V_{sat} the saturation voltage of the LC. The choice of V_s in equation 9.2 minimises V_d. With low values of V_d around 5 to 8 V the column drivers are virtually the same as for TFTs. The line drivers, however, require higher voltages with V_s around ± 15 V or higher. In the holding period the line voltage is

$$V_h = \pm\tfrac{1}{2}(V_{sat} + V_{th}) \qquad\qquad 9.3$$

where the negative sign applies for negative voltages V_d. This value of V_h minimises crosstalk from the video information of other pixels in the same column. For the four-level addressing which is symmetrical about zero voltage to work properly, the MIMs are also required to exhibit symmetric characteristics in the first and third quadrant in Figure 9.3. For 256 grey shades over a video voltage swing of 8 V this results in requirements for

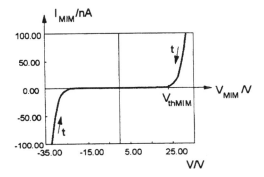

Figure 9.3   Characteristic I_{MIM}–V_{MIM} curve

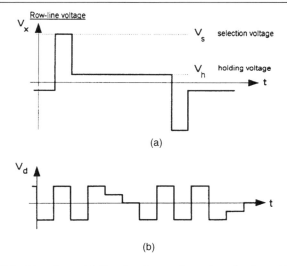

(a)

(b)

Figure 9.4   (a) MIM addressing with four-level-waveform for selection of lines; (b) waveform of video information V_d on columns for MIM addressing

MIM symmetry of better than 30 mV, which is virtually impossible to achieve. Symmetry requirements are eased if asymmetric values of V_s, V_h and V_d are chosen to compensate for the asymmetry of the MIM (Togashi, 1992) or if the five-level addressing with a reset pulse is used (Kuijk, 1990; Knapp & Hartman, 1994). However, it remains difficult to meet demand of uniform MIM characteristics over an ever-increasing display area.

A crucial difference between MIMs and TFTs is the dynamics of charging C_{LC}. With increasing V_{LC} the voltage V_{MIM} drops with time t as indicated by the arrow t in Figure 9.3. With increasing time and a similar addressing scheme to TFTs, the current quickly reaches low values which retards the further loading of C_{LC}. A deeper investigation of the non-linear differential equations which govern this behaviour reveals that V_{LC} increases during the address time as shown in Figure 9.5 (Schäpperle, 1994), where the retardation of the rise to the final value V_d is clearly visible. This retardation does not occur with TFTs, as is also shown in Figure 9.5, because the current, I_{DS}, in Figure 9.2 approaches zero with a steep slope so still provides enough current to reach the final value

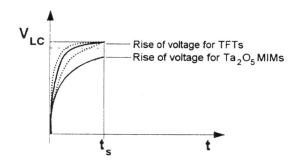

Figure 9.5   Rise of voltage V_{LC} versus time t for MIMs and TFTs

V_d. This is true even if the properties, such as the on-resistance of TFTs, fluctuate because there is still enough current available. Problems with the rise of V_{LC}, the symmetry of MIMs, and parasitic couplings, limit the number of grey shades achievable with MIMs; 34 grey shades are safely realisable, through 128 have been reported. After loading C_{LC}, the voltage must be held during the frame time which is effectively supported by an additional storage capacitor such as C_S. Contrary to TFTs, in the case of MIMs, the column lines are deposited on one glass plate and the row lines on the other one as depicted in Figure 9.1(b). Therefore an additional thin film storage capacitor in parallel to C_{LC} is not feasible, since its two terminals would be placed on different plates. To place columns and lines on one plate would, however, destroy some merits of MIMs and this will be discussed later.

In order to make the voltage $V_{MIM} \gg V_{LC}$, which results in a large charging current through the MIM if a step in V_d is applied,

$$C_{MIM}/C_{LC} \ll 1 \qquad\qquad 9.4$$

is required. Appropriate values are

$$C_{LC} \approx (3, \ldots, 10)C_{MIM}. \qquad\qquad 9.5$$

This provides a lower limit for the pixel size since C_{MIM} will reach a minimum limiting value.

Further requirements stem from the sensitivity of MIMs to parasitic couplings. The greatest degradation is caused by the capacitive coupling of steps in voltages V_{n-1} and V_{n+1} of neighbouring pixels in one line onto the voltage V_n as depicted in Figure 9.6 (Fuhrmann, 1994). One way to reduce the coupling capacitances C_{pp} is to allow for a larger gap of e.g. 6–10 μm in between the pixels. However, this also reduces the aperture ratio to 60 percent whereas 80 percent is realisable with a less conservative design (Hochholzer *et al.*, 1994). This sacrifice in aperture ratio destroys one of the merits of MIMs, namely a bright picture. Another way to ease the influence of capacitive couplings is an electronic but picture dependent compensation (Fuhrmann, 1994). The compensation of parasitic capacitive coupling between TFTs is easy to realise and has been understood for some time (Suzuki, 1987).

To summarise the conclusions we have reached so far: the currently unbeatable merits of TFTs are their capability to provide up to 256 grey shades independent of unavoidable

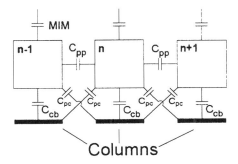

Figure 9.6   Parasitic capacitive coupling from neighbouring pixels $n - 1$ and $n + 1$ in one line onto pixel n

fluctuations of the TFT characteristics since the TFT provides enough current to reach any end value in the addressing time even at low drain-source voltages (Figure 9.2). MIMs, to the extent we have discussed them, exhibit mainly shortcomings such as their limitation to larger pixel sizes, their lack of a storage capacitor, the retardation of the rise of the pixel voltage and their sensitivity to parasitic couplings which limit the number of grey shades. The latter two effects have to be compensated by a more complex and hence more costly addressing scheme which also requires higher voltages for the line drivers. The merits of MIMs will become apparent in the next paragraphs.

9.3 FABRICATION OF TFTs AND MIMs

The fabrication of a-Si TFTs and to a lesser degree of poly-Si-TFTs, CdSe-TFTs and MIMs are mature processes. As a rule about seven masks are used to manufacture a-Si TFTs together with the row, column and the ITO pixel electrodes of an LCD. The most important issue at present is to reduce the cost of fabrication mainly by decreasing the mask count and by enhancing throughput. These two measures will now be outlined for a-Si TFTs which have by far the largest production volume.

A process with a smaller number of masks is only acceptable if the performance of the TFT does not suffer and if the process window is not narrowed so as to reduce yield. Figure 9.7 depicts and explains the process steps for a three-mask fabrication of bottom gate a-Si TFTs (the most commonly used configuraton) with storage capacitors (Glück

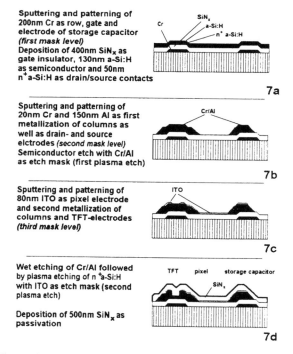

Sputtering and patterning of 200nm Cr as row, gate and electrode of storage capacitor *(first mask level)*
Deposition of 400nm SiN$_x$ as gate insulator, 130nm a-Si:H as semiconductor and 50nm n$^+$a-Si:H as drain/source contacts

7a

Sputtering and patterning of 20nm Cr and 150nm Al as first metallization of columns as well as drain- and source elctrodes *(second mask level)*
Semiconductor etch with Cr/Al as etch mask (first plasma etch)

7b

Sputtering and patterning of 80nm ITO as pixel electrode and second metallization of columns and TFT-electrodes *(third mask level)*

7c

Wet etching of Cr/Al followed by plasma etching of n$^+$a-Si:H with ITO as etch mask (second plasma etch)

Deposition of 500nm SiN$_x$ as passivation

7d

Figure 9.7   Steps of a three-mask fabrication of a Si TFTs

et al. 1993; Lüder, 1994a). The detailed description is not repeated in the text, and we shall focus only on some of the more important features of the process. For CVD processes a thermal plasma box, as shown in Figure 9.8, is used. The box is separately evacuated to ensure high cleanliness; all walls are heated resulting in a uniform temperature distribution in the box. These two features guarantee a deviation from a uniform thickness of the deposited layers of only ±1 percent on a 14″ diagonal substrate. For plasma etching through the top layers down to the i-a-Si or n^+-a-Si layers, an optical endpoint control is introduced. The 240 nm emission from CF and SiF radicals indicates when the Si layers are reached, as shown in Figure 9.9. If only small areas are etched the emission signal is weaker which necessitates the application of noise suppression in the detection system. This is avoided in a four-mask version of the fabrication (Glück *et al.* 1994; Lüder, 1994a). The a-Si layer in the three-mask process is protected by other layers until the last step resulting in excellent a-Si TFTs with a mobility of 1.2 cm²/Vs.

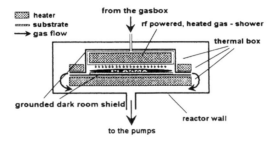

Figure 9.8 Thermal box for CVD

A two mask process for top gate TFTs was introduced by Richou *et al.* (1992); however, it cannot provide a storage capacitor. The three-mask process of Chouan *et al.* (1993) includes a storage capacitor but does not isolate the channel areas. This leads to parasitic couplings which must be compensated by a modified, more complex, addressing scheme. However, the effects associated with parasitic capacitive couplings are impossible to compensate and remain visible in the image. The simplicity of the process, which was proposed as early as 1986, is, however, admirable.

Throughput is mainly limited by the low deposition rate of PECVD which is about 80 Å/min for aSi:H films. Higher deposition rates result in particle generation and in poor

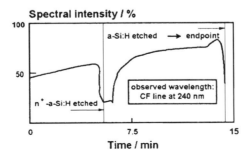

Figure 9.9 Optical emission during etching down to an a-Si layer

electrical properties of the aSi:H layers especially in reduced electron mobility. In Hayama (1994) the continuous application of rf power is replaced by a gated rf power which, as a rule, is on for 150 μs and off for 100–200 percent of the on-time. This mode produces a-Si:H films with high mobility and a low particle count but at a quadrupled deposition rate of 330 Å/min (see Figure 9.10): The reason for this effect is still under investigation, but this work demonstrates a trend in the right direction for increasing throughout and lowering cost.

Poly-Si TFTs will be discussed only briefly. At present they are produced in lower volume than a-Si TFTs. However, they might become much more attractive in the future due to their high electron mobility which is typically around 100 cm^2/Vs. This enables TFTs to be made with small channel areas down to 2 μm × 2 μm and allows for the integration of row and especially the faster column drivers in thin film technology around the periphery of the glass substrate. The capability for large currents even in TFTs with 2 μm design rules lends itself to displays with a high pixel density such as in light-valves for projectors. Shift registers, D/A-converters, clocks and buffers can be built with n-channel and p-channel poly-Si TFTs in CMOS technology. Clock frequencies of 15 MHz have been achieved for video drivers (Ohshima, 1994).

The main problem in fabricating poly-Si TFTs is the high process temperature of up to 600°C which requires expensive quartz substrates. Layers of a-Si or poly-Si with a low mobility prepared by LPCVD or PECVD, or by sputtering, are annealed by laser or in a furnace typically at 600°C for up to 100 h in order to recrystallise the material. Mobilities extend from 20 cm^2/Vs up to a peak value of 440 cm^2/Vs (Sano *et al.*, 1994), and are expected to exceed 600 cm^2/Vs in the near future. Reduction of process temperatures to below 450°C enables cheaper glass substrates, e.g., Corning 7059 glass, to be used. Such a reduced temperature process was reported by Mohri *et al.* (1992).

An attractive combination is to manufacture both the pixel and driver TFTs with the mature a-Si process and then to laser-anneal the driver TFTs (Tanaka *et al.*, 1993). A problem for all poly-Si TFTs is the non-zero hole mobility in poly-Si which causes a rise in the off-current at negative gate voltages. This rise can be suppressed by LDD techniques (Ohshima, 1994), as demonstrated in Figure 9.11.

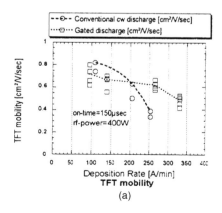

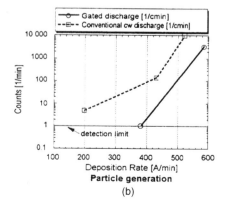

Figure 9.10 Mobility of (a) a-Si TFTs and (b) particle count versus deposition rate of a gated CVD process

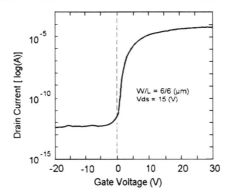

Figure 9.11 I_{DS} versus gate voltage V_G of a poly-Si TFT with LDD

A low temperature fabrication process which does not exceed 380°C is feasible for CdSe TFTs which, however, still exhibit the very high mobility of 350 cm^2/Vs (Dobler 1993). The four-mask manufacture is depicted in Figure 9.12. The glass substrates are covered by a sputtered 130 nm layer of Cr, which is subsequently etched in a solution of Ce(NH$_4$)$_2$(NO$_3$), CH$_3$OOH and water to form the gates and the row conductors (Figure 9.12(a)). The deposition of the 450 nm thick gate dielectric SiO$_2$ is done by CVD in an atmospheric pressure reactor (APCVD) using SiH$_4$, N$_2$ and O$_2$ as process gases (Figure 9.12(b)).

A viable, although more expensive, alternative is to use a double layer dielectric made of 450 nm SiN$_x$ and 50 nm SiO$_2$ deposited by PECVD. This retains the almost trapless SiO$_2$/CdSe interface but SiN$_x$ provides a higher breakthrough voltage.

SiO$_2$ is removed from the Cr lines by plasma etching (Figure 9.12(c)). Before the evaporation of CdSe the surface of the SiO$_2$ has to be cleaned. This is done by sputter etching in the load lock of the evaporation chamber. The optimum value for the sputter power is 0.25 W/cm^2 applied for 1 min. Higher power densities and sputter times lead to a degeneration of the oxide due to ion bombardment. At the same time that the sputter etching is taking place, CdSe is evaporated, e.g. against a closed shutter, thus cleaning the evaporation source. After opening the shutter, clean CdSe is evaporated onto a clean SiO$_2$ surface and a minimum number of traps is generated at the interface. This is the first crucial fabrication step (Figure 9.12(d)). Subsequent crystallisation at 390°C in vacuum for one hour produces an enhancement of mobility. The mobility is dependent both on the rate of increase in temperature and on the final temperature. A good set of values is a ramp of 18°C/min up to 390°C which produces a mobility of 250 cm^2/Vs. The CdSe is patterned into channel islands by sputter etching in Ar (Figure 9.12(f)). A first annealing at 350°C in dry air for 30 min is followed by an annealing in vacuum at 320°C.

Drain and source contacts are made by sputtering 40 nm of Cr and 120 nm of Al which are patterned by a lift-off process (Figure 9.12(h)). Al provides a low resistivity whereas Cr serves as adhesion layer.

The ITO electrodes are made by reactively sputtering 80 nm of ITO at a partial pressure of 4.5×10^{-3} mbar Ar and 1×10^{-4} mbar O$_2$, followed by a lift-off process for patterning (Figure 9.12(i)).

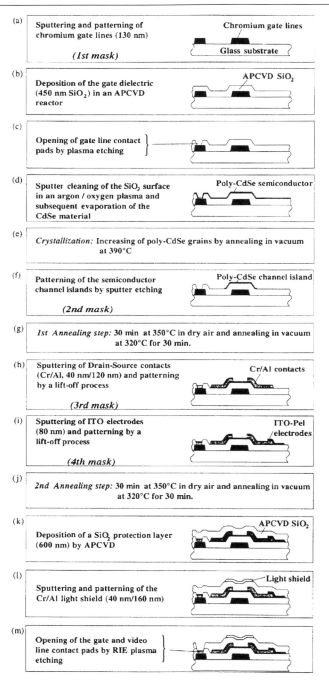

(a) Sputtering and patterning of chromium gate lines (130 nm)
(1st mask)
Chromium gate lines
Glass substrate

(b) Deposition of the gate dielectric (450 nm SiO_2) in an APCVD reactor
APCVD SiO_2

(c) Opening of gate line contact pads by plasma etching

(d) Sputter cleaning of the SiO_2 surface in an argon / oxygen plasma and subsequent evaporation of the CdSe material
Poly-CdSe semiconductor

(e) *Crystallization:* Increasing of poly-CdSe grains by annealing in vacuum at 390°C

(f) Patterning of the semiconductor channel islands by sputter etching
(2nd mask)
Poly-CdSe channel island

(g) *1st Annealing step:* 30 min at 350°C in dry air and annealing in vacuum at 320°C for 30 min.

(h) Sputtering of Drain-Source contacts (Cr/Al, 40 nm/120 nm) and patterning by a lift-off process
(3rd mask)
Cr/Al contacts

(i) Sputtering of ITO electrodes (80 nm) and patterning by a lift-off process
(4th mask)
ITO-Pel electrodes

(j) *2nd Annealing step:* 30 min at 350°C in dry air and annealing in vacuum at 320°C for 30 min.

(k) Deposition of a SiO_2 protection layer (600 nm) by APCVD
APCVD SiO_2

(l) Sputtering and patterning of the Cr/Al light shield (40 nm/160 nm)
Light shield

(m) Opening of the gate and video line contact pads by RIE plasma etching

Figure 9.12 The four-mask fabrication steps for a CdSe TFT and the pixels of a display

Uniformity and reproducibility of the transistor parameters are greatly enhanced by a second annealing step consisting of a ramp of 30°C/min up to 350°C maintained for 30 min, followed by an anneal in vacuum at 320°C. The annealing in air creates a partially oxidised material. The subsequent anneal in vacuum reduces CdO to Cd, whereas SeO_2 evaporates because of its high vapour pressure of 100 torr at 282°C. As a result the concentration of the n-doping Cd increases, which enhances I_D.

Annealing in air and the subsequent cool-down must be performed in an extremely dry environment.

A 600 nm thick SiO_2 protection layer is deposited by thermal APCVD (Figure 9.12(k)). Special care has to be taken to prevent damage to the CdSe film by the impingement of ions which could reduce mobility. The mobility reached at this stage is typically 300 cm^2/Vs. For single transistors, values as high as 460 cm^2/Vs have been measured.

Finally, if necessary, e.g., in projection systems, a 40 nm/160 nm Cr/Al light shield is sputtered and patterned (Figure 9.12(l)). Precise mask positioning is not required for this step, so this mask is not counted among the yield-determining four mask steps as listed in Figure 9.12.

The light sensitivity of CdSe is higher than that of Si. In projection systems with a powerful lamp, light shields are certainly needed to prevent an increase of the off-current due to light induced carrier generation.

The CdSe process obviously requires more steps than the a-Si process; in addition, the materials handling is more demanding, especially during annealing, which is not required for a-Si. However, since CdSe TFTs are fast enough to make integrated video drivers at a low temperature, they will play a useful role in the future, as is already being demonstrated by CdSe displays on the market (Farrell *et al.*, 1992).

MIMs are prepared with either anodised Ta_2O_5 or PECVD generated SiN_x as insulator. The geometrical structures are crossed conduction lines separated by a dielectric or an edge-type structure whose two-mask fabrication and layout is explained in Figure 9.13 (Hochholzer *et al.*, 1990). The key features are as follows. The bottom electrode is made of sputtered Ta, the upper surface of which is partly anodically oxidised, e.g., in an electrolyte containing 0.01 percent citric acid. This provides very homogeneous layers over a large area, as has been demonstrated by a 14″ 1.2 Mpixel MIM display (Hochholzer *et al.*, 1994). In order to satisfy the requirement of equation 9.5, a small MIM capacitance is realised by the self-aligned generation of the top electrode shown in Figure 9.13(b). The negative photoresist is exposed by UV light through the substrate using the non-transparent Ta electrode as a self-aligned mask. The light is scattered around the Ta edge into the resist, the penetration depth depending on the exposure time. Thus a top electrode with an overlap over the bottom electrode of only 0.3±0.03 μm is generated. Only two masks are needed because the top electrode of the MIM is made out of ITO which is patterned simultaneously with the ITO pixel electrode. For currents through the MIM in excess of 0.02 μA/μ m^2, Cr electrodes are preferable; however, they, require a third mask. Cost advantages of the MIM manufacturing process are the low mask count, the robustness of the process steps, and the use only of sputtering which is less expensive than CVD. The latter advantage is not shared by MIMs with SiN_x insulators as they require CVD for which, in addition, uniformity over large areas is harder to achieve. SiN_x MIMs on the other hand have the benefit of a lower dielectric constant of 4 instead of 24 for Ta_2O_5,

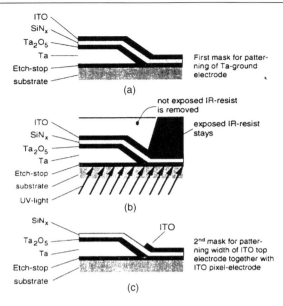

Figure 9.13 Two-mask fabrication process of Ta_2O_5 MIMs

which produces smaller MIM capacitances. Most manufacturers, however, consider the advantages of the Ta_2O_5 MIMs, especially their lack of a CVD process, to be overriding.

The pronounced merit of MIM fabrication is its lower cost compared to TFTs because of a low mask count and easier and more economic fabrication processes, especially if CVD is not used. As MIMs do not contain semiconductors, light shields, especially in projectors, are not needed.

9.4 BRIGHTNESS OF AMLCDs

The last performance issue in LCDs which requires improvement is the brightness of the display. The enhancement of brightness can be brought about by various improvements related to lamps, polarisation, colour filters and the better collimation of light (Lüder, 1994b). Here we shall only discuss the issue of aperture ratio associated with active matrix addressing. a-Si TFTs as a rule exhibit an aperture ratio around 40 percent for pixel areas of 100×100 µm meaning that 60 percent of the incoming light is lost in opaque parts of the pixels. By using a design with 3 µm gaps between the ITO and the conductors and with C_S partly on top of the lines, the aperture ratio can be increased to 60 percent as shown in the layout in Figure 9.14 (Hochholzer, 1994). An even higher aperture ratio of 70 percent was achieved by additionally placing the TFT on top of the gate bus line (Kitazawa *et al.*, 1994).

As the pixel size is reduced, the aperture ratio also decreases because the gaps and the device sizes do not shrink proportionally. The high current capability of poly-Si TFTs allows for a greater reduction in TFT size, which makes these TFTs preferable for small pixels. The relatively large aperture ratio of poly-Si TFTs versus pixel density is shown in Figure 9.15 (Ohshima, 1994). Reflective LCDs can reach aperture ratios greater than

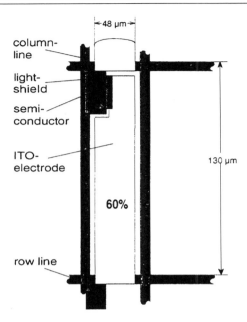

Figure 9.14   Layout of a pixel with TFT

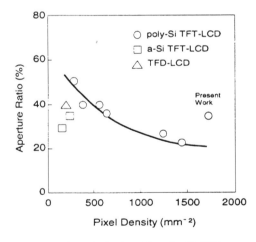

Figure 9.15   Aperture ratios of pixels with poly-Si TFTs versus pixel density

90 percent as the electronic devices and conductors are hidden beneath the pixel electrode mirror (Glück *et al.*, 1994). MIMs exhibit the largest aperture among all active matrix addressed transmissive displays, reaching at least 80 percent (Hochholzer *et al.*, 1994). The main reason for this is the fact that, in addition to the very small dimensions of the MIM devices, the video (column) lines are on a different (the front) glass plate which eliminates the gaps between the ITO electrodes and the video lines. This is demonstrated in the layout in Figure 9.16, which has the same pixel size as the TFT pixel in Figure 9.14. Hence MIM

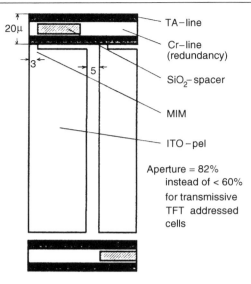

Figure 9.16 Layout of a pixel with MIM

displays are roughly twice as bright as TFT driven ones. This applies, however, only if the gap between the pixel is not kept deliberately large to minimise capacitive couplings. Electronic compensation of these couplings is acceptable because of the distinct gain in brightness.

9.5 CONCLUSIONS, APPLICATIONS AND FUTURE TRENDS

The overriding merits of a-Si TFTs are their capability to provide 256 grey shades even with slight fluctuations in the TFT characteristics, combined with a mature high yield fabrication. Addressing is straightforward and is easily able to compensate for parasitic couplings. All applications presently being manufactured are small and large area direct view displays with diagonals of up to 20″. The major shortcoming is the limited aperture ratio resulting in a reduced brightness. This grows more severe as the pixel size is reduced. Therefore a-Si TFTs do not lend themselves to high density displays such as HDTV or EWS systems or light valves in projectors.

On the other hand poly-Si TFTs are well suited for high density displays and, in addition, they have suitably high performance to realise integrated drivers including video drivers for HDTV or EWS. Their shortcoming is the high process temperature which is still required. High mobility CdSe TFTs do not share this shortcoming and will therefore remain a viable technology in spite of their more complex fabrication process. MIM driven displays are attractive due to their very low cost of fabrication especially if only sputtering and no CVD is used. They further excel in providing bright pictures unmatched by all other active matrix addressed displays. Part of their cost advantage is lost by the need for more complex addressing circuits and by the need to compensate for parasitic capacitive couplings. The line addressing ICs require higher voltages above 15 V. Compensation further increases the voltage level, resulting in more expensive circuitry, which is not yet mass-produced. MIMs are well suited for low cost displays with a high brightness but with limited pixel density and number of grey shades. They are suitable for computer displays up to XGS, displays in cars and larger size light valves for projectors with diagonals of about 4″ to 5″. Manufacturers of TFTs will be able to cope with all future demands whereas those of MIMs will need some improvements before they can address the HDTV, the EWS and the projection business, the latter with small light valves.

The mainstream technology, a-Si TFTs, will become cheaper in the future by shifting to a fabrication with a low mask count, a higher throughput by rendering CVD more economic, by realising a higher aperture ratio which, together with new low power addressing schemes, will save energy. In the poly-Si technology we shall see a decrease in process temperature to less than 450°C, displays with a high pixel density which could even allow for more economic projectors with only one light valve with colour pixels and of course integrated drivers. Low mask processes for reflective displays with TFTs underneath the mirror are also essential for projectors and direct view displays, the latter with only ambient light as a light source. Further work on MIMs must be directed towards generating more symmetric devices without annealing and with a lower voltage level; addressing has to include compensation for parasitic couplings and for video dependent distortions. In the near future light, unbreakable and bendable displays with plastic substrates require low temperature fabrication processes. ECR generated dielectrics prepared at room temperature already provide, e.g., SiO$_2$ layers with a field strength of 5 mV/cm (Dobler, 1995). For switches built at low temperatures, MIMs prepared with sputtered layers and CdSe TFTs (Lüder, 1994c), which are, without annealing, as good as a-Si TFTs, are promising candidates.

REFERENCES

Baraff, D.R., Long, J.R., MacLaurin, B.K., Miner, C.J. and Streater, R.W. (1981), The optimisation of metal — insulator — metal nonlinear devices for use in multiplied liquid crystal displays, *IEEE Trans. on Electron Devices*, ED-28, 736.

Chouan, Y., Rolland, A., Grino, J., Boutroy, J., Boisseau, G. and Szydlo, N. (1993), 3S TFT: an extension of 2S TFT for projection application, *Eurodisplay 93*, Strasbourg.

Dobler, M. (1995) Polykristalline Halbleiter und Niedertemperatur-Dielektrika zur Herstellung von Dünnschichttransistoren für flache Flüssigkristall-Bildschirme, PhD Thesis, Stuttgart.

Dobler, M., Bunz, R., Lüder, E. and Kallfass, T. (1993), Fabrication of CdSe TFTs with high mobility of 300 cm²/Vs for a 140 000 pel AMLCD, *3rd Int. CdSe Workshop 1993, Strasbourg*.

Farrell, J. *et al.* (1992), A 10″ diagonal VGA AMLCD fabrication using a high mobility, low temperature TFT process, *Japan Display 92*, 885.

Fuhrmann, J. (1994), Capacitive crosstalk between pixels in MIM-addressed LCDs (*oral communications*).

Glück, J., Lauer, H.-U., Lüder, E., Kallfass, T. and Straub, D., (1993), Improvement in light efficiency of a-Si:TFT-addressed reflective λ/4 HAN-mode light valve for colour TV, *SID 93 Digest*, 299–302.

Glück, J., Lüder, E., Kallfass, T., Lauer, H.-U., Straub, D. and Huttelmaier, S. (1994), A 14″ diagonal a-Si TFT AMLCD for PAL television, *SID 94 Digest*, 263–266.

Hayama, H. (1994), Gated rf-discharge plasma-CVD technology for a-Si:H fabrication, *186th Meeting of the Electrochemical Society, Miami, Extended Abstracts*, 732.

Hochholzer, V., Lüder, E. and Kallfass, T. and (1990), A two mask fabrication of Ta$_2$O$_5$ MIMs with adjustable threshold and gain, *SID 90 Digest*, 526–529.

Hochholzer, V., Lüder, E., Kallfass, T. and Lauer, H.-U. (1994), A full-colour 14″ MIM-LCD with improved photolithography, *SID 94 Digest*, 423.

Kitazawa, T., Asai, Y., Matsuzawa, Y., Kubo, A., Hirota, S., Higuchi, T. and Suzuki, K. (1994), A 9.5″ TFT-LCD with an ultra-high aperture ratio pixel structure, *Proc. IDRC 94, Monterey, CA, Conf. Record*, 365–368.

Knapp, A.G. and Hartman, R.A. (1994), Thin film diode technology for high quality AMLCD, *Proc. IDRC 94, Monterey, CA, Conf. Record*, 14–19.

Kuijk, K.E. (1990), D^{2}R, a versatile diode matrix liquid crystal approach, *Proc. Eurodisplay 90*.

Lüder, E. (1994a), Simplified manufacture of a-Si TFTs with four or three masks, *Chiba 94*.

Lüder, E. (1994b), Enhancement of luminance in LC-Projectors, *AMLCD '94, Shinjuku/Japan Digest of Technical Papers*, 16–19.

Lüder, E. (1994c), Fabrication of CdSe TFTs and implementation of integrated drivers with poly-crystalline TFTs, Proc. *IDRC 94, Monterey, CA, Conf. Record*, 30–38.

Mohri, M., Kakinuma, H. and Tsuruoka, T. (1992), Fabrication of TFTs using plasma CVD poly-Si at very low temperature, *IEDM 92*, 673–676.

Ohshima, H. (1994), Status and prospects of poly-Si TFT technology, *Proc. IDRC 94, Monterey, CA, Conf. Record*, 26–29.

Richou, F., Morin, F., Le Contellec, M. and Prolonge, A. (1992), The "2S" TFT Process for low cost AMLCD manufacturing, *SID 92 Digest*, 619–622.

Sano, K., Nohda, T., Aya, Y., Kuwahara, T., Iwata, H., Kuriyama, H., Takeuchi, M., Wakisaka, K., Kiyama, S., Tsuda, S. and, Yoneda, K. (1994), Excimer laser activation in ion doped poly-Si films and its application to high mobility poly-Si TFTs, *AMLCD '94, Shinjuku/Japan Digest of Technical Papers*, 104–107

Schäpperle, J. (1994), Solution of the system of non-linear differential equations for MIM addressed LC cells (*oral communications*).

Suzuki, K. (1987), Compensative addressing for switching distortion in a-Si TFT LCD, *Eurodisplay 87*, 107–110.

Tanaka, T., Asuma, H., Ogawa, K., Shinagawa, Y., Ono, K. and Konishi, N. (1993), An LCD addressed by a-Si:H TFTs with peripheral poly-Si TFT circuits, *IEDM 93*, 389–392

Togashi, S. (1992), Two terminal device addressed LCD, *Optoelectronics — Devices and Technologies*, **7**(2), 271–286.

The structure, performance and future of passive matrix LCDs

Alan Mosley

10.1 INTRODUCTION

This chapter analyses the structure, operation and manufacturing costs of passive liquid crystal displays with particular emphasis on supertwisted nematic (STN) LCDs and ferroelectric LCDs. The results of this analysis lead to an assessment of the future potential of each of these technologies, including the identification of constraints or problems affecting their growth in the marketplace.

At the present time, STN liquid crystal displays represent one of the two principal flat panel display technologies, the other being active matrix liquid crystal displays (AMLCDs). In 1993, the market value of each of these two technologies was approximately $2 billion but, because of their much lower unit cost, the volume of STN displays was about four times that of AMLCDs.

Although they were developed at the same time (1983) as supertwist LCDs, ferroelectric LCDs have still to become established in the marketplace. The present annual value of worldwide sales of ferroelectric liquid crystal displays (and optical devices) is probably <$1 million. The reason for this very slow emergence of ferroelectric LCDs is twofold. Firstly, the initial focus was on large area, video-rate flat panel displays (FPDs) which meant that ferroelectric LCDs had to compete (unsuccessfully) with more established flat panel display technologies (Mosley, 1994). Secondly, ferroelectric liquid crystal displays require a more complex liquid crystal than that used in the well-developed twisted nematic

LCDs. In comparison, supertwist and active matrix LCDs employed nematic liquid crystal mixtures and, thus, were able to make use of the infrastructure that had been established for twisted nematic LCDs.

Polymer stabilised cholesteric texture (PSCT) LCDs, formed by generating a polymer network within a cholesteric liquid crystal, were first reported in 1991 by D.K. Yang *et al.* Products based on this technology have already started to emerge (Yaniv, 1995). This rapid development is undoubtedly assisted by the infrastructure generated by products, e.g. electronic partitions, very large displays for public information, based on polymer dispersed liquid crystals (PDLC), and nematic curvilinear aligned phase (NCAP) displays. In addition, the use of a nematic liquid crystal in PSCT displays also provides an advantage to this technology relative to ferroelectric LCDs, which are based on essentially commercially unused smectic liquid crystals.

10.2 STRUCTURE AND FABRICATION

Figure 10.1 shows schematically a representative structure of both supertwist and ferroelectric monochrome LCDs. The only difference between the structures for these two displays is that the liquid crystal layer is typically 2 μm thick in the case of a ferroelectric LCD instead of the ~6 μm used for a supertwist LCD. In both cases, the uniformity of the spacing needs to be better than 0.1 μm in order to achieve uniform coloration and switching voltages.

The volume manufacture of liquid crystal displays is carried out using large area, e.g. 350×350 mm^2, indium tin oxide coated glass substrates onto which are fitted as many displays as possible. The 20 basic processing steps used in the manufacture of passive liquid crystal displays are listed in Table 10.1.

The barrier layer, which is a spin-on-glass, i.e. an organosilane which, when heated in air, forms a hard coating of silicon dioxide, is used to reduce the occurrence of short circuits between the electrodes on the two substrates that form the liquid crystal cell. The surface alignment layer, which is generally a rubbed polyimide, is extremely important,

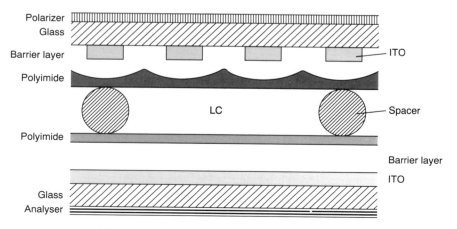

Figure 10.1   The cross-section of a passive LCD

Table 10.1   Processing steps used in the manufacture of passive LCDs

1	Clean (the ITO coated glass)
2	Coat with photoresist
3	Expose
4	Develop
5	Etch indium tin oxide pattern
6	Remove photoresist
7	Clean
8	Coat with barrier layer
9	Coat with surface alignment layer
10	Rub surface alignment layer
11	Apply edge seal
12	Apply spacers
13	Assemble two substrates into a laminate
14	Scribe and extract individual cells
15	Vacuum fill cells with liquid crystal
16	Compress cells, remove excess liquid crystal and end seal
17	Inspect
18	Clean
19	Apply polarisers
20	Pre-shipment test

particularly in the case of supertwist LCDs. This layer not only fixes the lateral orientation of the liquid crystal molecules at the surface of the substrates, but also defines the angle that the rod-shaped liquid crystal molecules make with the surface of the substrate, *i.e.*, the pre-tilt angle: see Figure 10.2.

The polyimides first used in twisted nematic LCDs achieved pre-tilt angles between $1°$ and $3°$ but supertwist LCDs require pre-tilt angles $>5°$ in order to prevent the formation of the striped domain texture which makes it impossible to multiplex the display (Scheffer & Nehring, 1994). Much work has been done by the manufacturers of polyimides in order to achieve the higher pre-tilt angles required by STN display; $6-7°$ pre-tilts are now readily achievable. Our own work has led to processes that provide stable, $12°$ pre-tilt angles. During the assembly process (step 13 in Table 10.1) it is necessary to register the electrode patterns on the two substrates to $\sim 10~\mu m$ and then, while keeping this registration, bond the two plates together using the edge seal. At this stage, all the displays are contained in the large area, e.g. $350 \times 350~mm^2$, laminate formed by the two substrates. In order to obtain the individual display cells, a microprocessor controlled scriber is used to scribe both surfaces of the laminate delineating the individual display cells, which are then obtained by cracking the two glass substrates along the scribe lines.

The vacuum filling process is one of the two areas where there is a difference between the requirements for supertwist and ferroelectric LCDs, the other being the cell spacing. The nematic liquid crystal mixture used in supertwist LCDs is a low viscosity, highly mobile liquid. On the other hand, the smectic liquid crystals used in ferroelectric LCDs are highly viscous, almost immobile fluids. This difference in viscosity occurs because smectic liquid crystals have two-dimensional order and, hence, are much closer to being

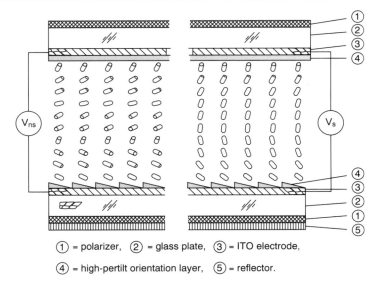

① = polarizer,   ② = glass plate,   ③ = ITO electrode,

④ = high-pertilt orientation layer,   ⑤ = reflector.

Figure 10.2   The structure of a supertwist birefringent effect LCD

a solid, which has three-dimensional order, than nematic liquid crystals, which have one-dimensional order. It is not possible to vacuum-fill a display cell with a liquid crystal in its smectic phase. To overcome this problem, the smectic liquid crystal is heated into its nematic phase or, better still, into its liquid state (which has zero-dimensional order). To achieve this, it is obviously necessary to heat both the smectic liquid crystal mixture and the display cells.

After filling with liquid crystal, the glass substrate forming the display cell may be bowed outwards and, hence, will not meet the spacing uniformity requirement of ±0.1 μm. If this is the case then, before end-sealing, the display cells are placed in some form of press in order to force the substrates onto the spacer particles. The volume manufacture of passive liquid crystal displays is now extremely efficient with a typical high volume cost of $0.15/cm^2.

The structure of PSCT displays is very similar to that shown in Figure 10.1, with the exception that they do not utilise polarisers. The cell spacing used in PSCT displays is ~5 μm.

10.3   SUPERTWIST LIQUID CRYSTAL DISPLAYS

10.3.1   Operation and performance

Scheffer and Nehring (1984) were the first to demonstrate a dot matrix supertwist display based on the birefringence of the liquid crystal material. This technology has now been adopted worldwide. The display shown by Scheffer and Nehring, which is illustrated schematically in Figure 10.2, had a 270° twist angle, a cell spacing (d)-liquid crystal birefringence (Δn) product (Δnd) of 0.75 and polarisers oriented at 30° to the orientation of the liquid crystal molecules at the surfaces of the two substrates. This structure provided a highly legible black (pixel) on yellow (background) display. (Rotation of one of the polarisers through 90° would produce a white on blue display.) Yellow/green mode supertwist displays are presently widely used in one to four line character modules.

Once supertwist technology had become established, attempts were made to remove the background colour. The first attempt resulted in the purple mode display which had a silver-white background and purple pixels. This display mode was achieved by taking a yellow mode display and using a purple polariser, i.e. one that was less absorbing in the blue and red parts of the transmission spectrum than in the green/yellow part. When this was combined with the natural yellow/green colour (of the yellow mode display), an acceptable white background was produced. Purple mode supertwist LCDs are now generally used to provide reflective or transflective graphics modules.

At the beginning of 1987, Schadt and Leenhouts reported the development of the optical-mode-interference effect, supertwist LCD which did achieve a black and white display, but the light transmission of the white state was only 10–15 percent, a limitation which rendered this display unacceptable.

The next attempt to produce a black and white supertwist LCD has proved to be highly successful. Katoh *et al.* (1987) recognised that if a second (supertwist) liquid crystal cell was placed between the supertwist LCD and one of its polarisers, then this second cell would act as an optical compensator and eliminate the natural coloration of the supertwist LCD. Although a second liquid crystal cell could provide a perfect optical compensator at all temperatures, the additional costs and weight associated with it were highly disadvantageous and there was a rapid move to the use of plastic film compensators (Ohgawara *et al.*, 1989). The high volume production by several Japanese companies of achromic supertwist LCDs with 640×480 pixels for use in laptop computers began in 1991. By the end of 1992, worldwide shipments of these displays had reached five million units per year.

Having obtained a good quality black and white LCD, the next obvious step was the development of colour supertwist LCDs. The first attempts to do this were based on displays having a duty ratio of 1/480 and resulted in unacceptably low values of contrast ratio.

The values of contrast ratio and viewing angle of a supertwist display are highly dependent on the number (N) of multiplexed rows in the display. This figure is usually known as the duty ratio ($1/N$). In the 640×480 monochrome STN displays, although there are 480 rows, the column electrodes are split across the centre of the display, leading to a duty ratio of 1/240 which, in turn, leads to a higher value for the V_{on}/V_{off} ratio, a lower battery voltage and a slightly shorter response time (see equation 10.1 and Figure 10.3, equations 10.2 and 10.3 respectively):

$$\frac{V_{on}}{V_{off}} = \sqrt{\frac{\sqrt{N}+1}{\sqrt{N}-1}} \qquad\qquad 10.1$$

(Alt & Pleshko, 1974) and

$$V_{bat} = V_{off} \left(\frac{\sqrt{N}+1}{\sqrt{2}} \right) \left(\frac{\sqrt{N}}{\sqrt{N}-1} \right)^{1/2} \qquad\qquad 10.2$$

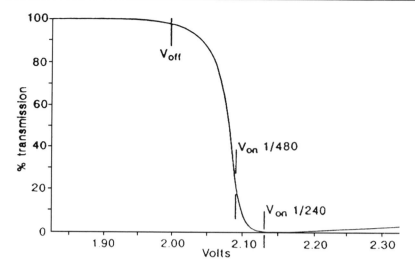

Figure 10.3 Transmission versus voltage curve for a STN display

$$t_{on}/t_{off} \approx N^{1/4} \qquad\qquad 10.3$$

The disadvantages of using split column electrodes are: (i) twice the number of column driver ICs are required, and (ii) the connection pitch is halved. Table 10.2 compares the preceding parameters for a 9.4 inch colour 640 ($\times 3$) $\times$ 480 supertwist display with duty ratios of 1/240 and 1/480, assuming a sub-pixel pitch of 0.1 mm and a V_{off} value of 2 volts.

Faced with the dilemma of the above disadvantages or low contrast, the LCD manufacturers decided to overcome the former by developing improved methods of interconnection. Today, all commercial colour VGA STN displays have a duty ratio of 1/240 and are known as dual-scan modules. A typical specification for this kind of display is shown in Table 10.3. Further improvements in connection technology have recently led to connection pitches of 80 μm, which have enabled the commercialisation of a 7.8 inch diagonal colour VGA STN display.

Table 10.2 Comparison of parameters for a 9.4 inch colour supertwist LCD

Parameter	Duty ratio	
	1/240	1/480
V_{on}/V_{off}	1.067	1.047
V_{on}-V_{off}	0.134 V	0.094 V
$V_{battery}$	24 V	33 V
Response time	150 ms	175 ms
Number of 160 output column ICs	25	12
Column connection pitch	100 μm	200 μm

Table 10.3 Typical specification for a 9.4 inch colour
VGA supertwist LCD

Total size	$243 \times 179 \times 10$ mm^3
Active area	192×144 mm^2
Pixel pitch	$(0.1 \times 3) \times 0.3$ mm
Contrast ratio	30:1
Luminance	80 cd/m^2
Response time	150 ms
Power consumption	3.4 W
Storage temperature range	$-25°$C to $+60°$C
Operating temperature range	$0°$C to $+40°$C

10.3.2 Recent developments

The most important recent development in supertwist LCD technology was the announcement in 1992 by In Focus of a method of electronic addressing of supertwist displays with response times of less than 80 ms. This technique, known as Active Addressing (a trademark of Motif Inc., USA), addresses each row of the display many times, e.g. 10 times per frame, unlike the conventional line-at-a-time addressing format in which each row is addressed only once during each frame. If the conventional addressing technique is employed in a supertwist LCD with a response time of less than 80 ms and a refresh time of 16.7 ms, which is typical for a VGA display, then the general guideline that the refresh time should be 10 percent of the response time is not observed. This leads to a reduction in the contrast ratio of the display as a result of the relaxation of the liquid crystal from its 'ON' state (see Figure 10.4).

The use of Active Addressing solves this problem. The underlying principles employed in Active Addressing (Scheffer *et al.*, 1993) are not new but their cost-effective implementation has only now been made possible by the developments in digital signal processing and multilevel integrated circuits for addressing LCDs. Commercial displays employing Active Addressing have not yet emerged but are expected to do so in the near future. Active Addressing potentially enables supertwist LCDs to provide low cost video displays, which clearly greatly extends the market opportunities for this technology.

One of the current objectives of LCD technologies is the development of a reflective colour display, thereby greatly reducing the power consumption of the LCD; 2.9 watts of the 3.4 watts quoted in Table 10.3 is due to the backlight. Recently, Sato (1994) has described the development of a 6-inch diagonal reflective colour STN with 320×240 pixels. The operation of this display is based on modulating the effective birefringence of the liquid crystal layer, i.e. changing the birefringence–cell spacing product by modulating the applied voltage. While there is still much more work to be done, *e.g.*, the present display cannot provide a black pixel, this is nevertheless an important first step.

10.3.3 Future potential

Supertwist LCD modules, ranging from one line of 16 characters to colour VGA panels, are available from several suppliers. Recently, a number of LCD manufacturers have started to provide 1/4 VGA colour panels. The uses for supertwist LCDs are also wide

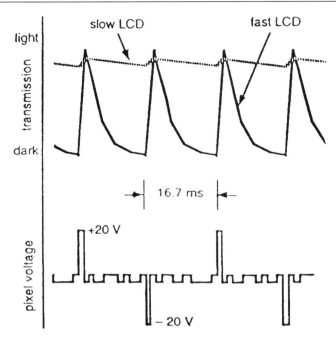

Figure 10.4   The effect of response time on the contrast ratio of a supertwist LCD driven by the conventional line-at-a-time addressing scheme

ranging, from message displays for photocopiers, through displays for marine equipment, to displays for laptop PCs. In short, the supertwist LCD is truly ubiquitous.

The two main disadvantages of the mainstream commercial, high volume supertwist LCDs are its limited viewing angle, *e.g.*, 10–30° in the vertical direction, and limited operating temperature range, *e.g.*, 0–40°. The main advantage of STN displays is their high performance-to-cost ratio resulting from their relatively low cost. However, the preceding limitations do not impact on single-user applications in office or factory environments, which are clearly very large markets.

Figure 10.5 compares the present and predicted market values of supertwist and active matrix LCDs. Even though active matrix LCDs are predicted to be the dominant product, the value of the worldwide market for STN LCDs is very high.

The future implementation of active addressing will enable supertwist displays to provide video images, which they are unable to do today. If successful, this development could open up additional large markets for this technology. The limited angle of view of supertwist displays will again limit their applications to single user products but, nevertheless, the potentially available markets are still substantial, e.g. pocket televisions, multi-media PCs, videophones and displays for in-flight entertainment systems. At the present time these markets are served by active matrix LCDs; therefore, the essential question is 'Will the cost of supertwist LCDs become low enough to compensate for the higher performance of active matrix LCDs?'. Presently, the colour VGA STN displays are approximately half the price of an equivalent active matrix LCD. If this price

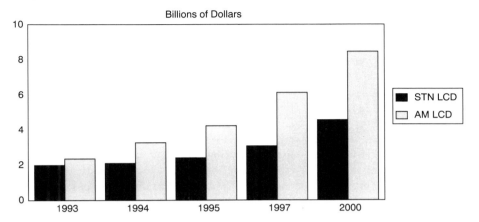

Figure 10.5   Comparison of worldwide markets for supertwist and active matrix LCDs
(source: Stanford Resources Inc., USA)

differential is maintained, then it is probable that the answer to the preceding question
will be 'yes'.

Another factor, which is exemplified by the recent developments in the 'mature' technology of cathode ray tubes, and which is in the favour of supertwist LCDs, is their very
well established infrastructure of materials, knowledge, production equipment, people and
money. This infrastructure will continue to push supertwist LCDs, and when faced with
a problem or limitation that curtails the growth of this technology, will deploy enormous
resources to overcome it. This factor, which could be called product-push, is often overlooked but can be an important factor in sustaining the growth of a technology. On the
other hand, the absence of product-push is a severe limitation to an emerging technology.

10.4   FERROELECTRIC LCDs

10.4.1   History and operating principles

The two main attributes of ferroelectric LCDs are very fast switching, typically 100 μs
per row, and bistability, which under the correct circumstances can be arranged to provide
a non-volatile display, *i.e.*, a display in which the image is maintained at zero volts. In
addition, the operating mechanism of ferroelectric LCDs leads to a very good viewing
angle, because the molecule switches in the plane of the display rather than perpendicular
to it (which is the case for supertwist and active matrix LCDs) together with the use
of a small cell spacing in order to provide a first-order λ/2 retardation. Furthermore,
the inherent bistability of ferroelectric LCDs means that the visual performance of the
display does not change as the number of row electrodes increases (*cf.* supertwist LCDs,
Table 10.2 and Figure 10.3), with the exception that the frame time is directly proportional
to the number of row electrodes.

The main impediments to the commercialisation of ferroelectric LCDs have been the
absence of grey scale and doubts about the environmental stability of ferroelectric LCDs,

i.e., limited temperature range (10–40°C) and susceptibility to mechanical shock. Although these problems can now be overcome, their previous existence has made ferroelectric LCDs less attractive than the many competing flat panel display technologies.

In 1975, R.B. Meyer *et al.* predicted, and later demonstrated, that chiral, tilted smectic liquid crystals would exhibit ferroelectricity and consequently would possess a large dipole, Ps, oriented perpendicular to the long axis of the liquid crystal molecule. The chirality required to induce ferroelectricity also promotes a helical structure which averages out the direction of the spontaneous dipole, thereby suppressing the ferroelectric behaviour. Meyer realised that making a useful device depended upon removing the helical structure. This was first done by shearing the glass substrates that enclosed the ferroelectric liquid crystal (FLC) and is now achieved by using rubbed-polymer surface alignment layers, similar to those used in supertwist LCD. In either case, the spacing between the two substrates should be about 2 μm. This spacing is also required for the FLC cell to act as a half-wave plate. (In a half-wave plate, $\Delta nd/\lambda = 0.5$, where λ is the wavelength of the light; typically, $\Delta n = 0.13$, $\lambda = 0.5$ μm, therefore $d \sim 2$ μm.)

The operation of a FLC optical device, *i.e.*, a display or an optical shutter, depends on the switching of the FLC's dipole, whose orientation depends upon the polarity of the addressing pulse (see Figure 10.6), but the FLC molecule cannot simply rotate about its

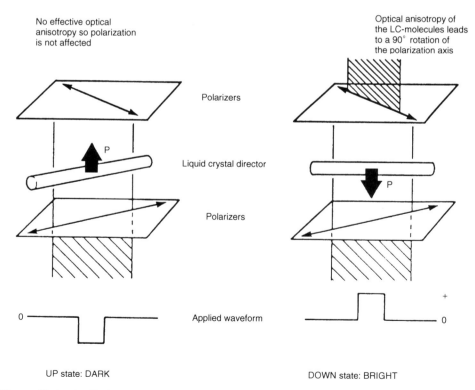

Figure 10.6 An FLCD operates by changing the orientation of the LC molecule in the plane of the display

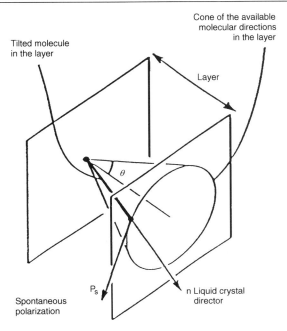

Figure 10.7 The orientation of the FLC's dipole is determined by the polarity of the addressing pulse, but the FLC molecule cannot simply rotate about its own axis. It is constrained to rotate about an imaginary cone

own axis; instead, it is constrained to rotate about an imaginary cone (see Figure 10.7). If the half-cone angle, θ, which is equal to the tilt angle of the molecules in the smectic layer, is approximately equal to 22.5°, then the change in the orientation of the FLC molecules will be 2θ, or 45°. Such an angular change produces the optimum values of transmission and contrast ratio, as shown in Figure 10.8.

Much of the pioneering work on ferroelectric LCDs was carried out by Clark and Lagerwall (1980). Between 1985 and 1987 there was a great deal of activity on ferroelectric LCDs, notably by Harada *et al.* (1985) who demonstrated a 260×162 mm^2 display with 640×400 pixels. From 1987 onwards, interest in ferroelectric LCDs waned, so much so that only a small number of groups maintained their interest in this technology. The most notable of these is Canon, which has directed huge resources to the development of large area ferroelectric LCDs for use in workstations. In September 1994, it was announced that Canon would start to produce a 15-inch diagonal colour display with 1280×1024 pixels at the rate of 5000 units per month. Shipment of these displays was planned to commence in the first quarter of 1995 in Japan and in the second half of 1995 in other countries. The selling price has been quoted to be around $7000.

By using antiferroelectric liquid crystal materials, Yamada *et al.* (1993) have developed a display with grey scale and have demonstrated high quality video images. The specification for this display is given in Table 10.4.

Antiferroelectric liquid crystals exhibit bistability but not non-volatility. At the present time there appear to be no plans to commercialise this display.

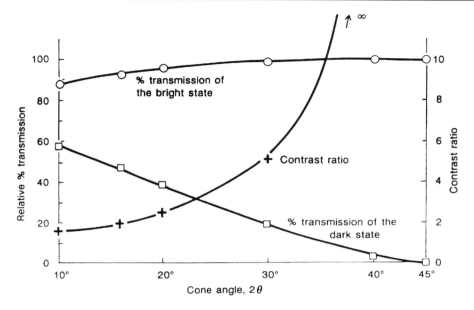

Figure 10.8   Contrast and transmission of a Ferroelectric LCD versus the switched cone angle 2θ

Table 10.4   Specification for the antiferroelectric LCD of Yamada *et al.* (1993)

Display area	125×80 mm^2
Pixels	320 ($\times$ RGB) $\times$ 220
Pixel pitch	0.13×0.4 mm
Duty ratio	1/220
Line address time	63.5 μs
Driving voltage	±38 V
Contrast ratio	30:1

Two groups, Mosley (1994) and Ross *et al.* (1994) have demonstrated simple, reflective, non-volatile ferroelectric LCDs. Figure 10.9 illustrates the iso-contrast curves for a display optimised by the former group to provide the bright background, which is advantageous to the appearance of reflective displays, at the expense of high contrast, which is less important for a reflective display. The white light transmission of the display represented in Figure 10.9 is 30 percent. Figure 10.9 also illustrates the very wide angle of view achieved with ferroelectric LCDs. It is worth noting that ferroelectric liquid crystals can also be used to provide very fast optical shutters and even more complex devices, such as optical print bars (Hedgley & de la Rossette, 1992).

10.4.2   Future potential

From the above comments, it should be clear that ferroelectric liquid crystals can provide a wide range of products, from optical shutters through non-volatile displays to large

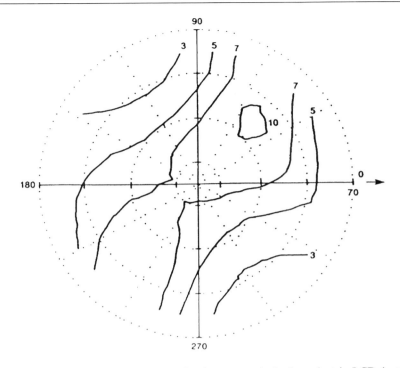

Figure 10.9 Iso-contrast curves for a reflective, non-volatile ferroelectric LCD (optimised for brightness) in the zero volts state (Mosley, 1994)

area, colour, alphagraphic displays. However, this technology has failed to penetrate the marketplace. One reason for this failure is that all the products offered by ferroelectric LCDs can be provided by other flat panel technologies: see Table 10.5.

It has been clear to the author for a number of years that the best way to introduce ferroelectric LCDs into the marketplace would be to provide products utilising the non-volatile nature of this technology, such as pagers and mobile phones. Such products would establish the infrastructure of materials, equipment, knowledge, people and revenue for

Table 10.5 Comparison of ferroelectric LCD 'products' with existing flat panel display products

Product	Ferroelectric LCD	Competing product
Large area displays	Canon's 15-inch diagonal colour display at $7000	Fujitsu's 21-inch colour plasma display at ~$7000
Small video displays	Nippondenso's anti-ferroelectric LCD, not yet available	Video, active matrix LCDs available from about 6 companies
Low power reflective displays for portable products	Hirst-LCD's non-volatile display	Kent Displays' polymer stabilised cholesteric LCD Electrochromic displays[a]

[a]Matsumoto (1990).

ferroelectric LCDs, which would in turn enable them to expand into other product areas. However, in order to establish this infrastructure, it is first necessary to identify high volume products, then to persuade a manufacturer to use this new technology in the absence of any significant infrastructure. Clearly this is not an easy task, particularly in a time of recession, but this needs to be done if ferroelectric LCDs are to become established in the marketplace. Furthermore, the present emergence of the polymer stabilised cholesteric texture (PSCT) LCD (Doane *et al.*, 1994), which is also non-volatile, poses a further threat to the future commercial development of ferroelectric LCDs.

10.5 POLYMER STABILISED CHOLESTERIC TEXTURE LCDs

10.5.1 History and operating principles

In 1985, Fergason described the nematic curvilinear aligned phase (NCAP) display formed from nematic liquid crystal encapsulated in micron size polymer capsules. In the off-state, the randomly ordered liquid crystal molecules strongly scattered light. When a voltage was applied, the liquid crystal molecules were aligned and had been chosen so that their refractive indices matched that of the polymeric encapsulant, thereby producing an optically clear state. Workers at Kent State University (Doane *et al.*, 1986) were the first to demonstrate a polymer dispersed liquid crystal (PDLC) in which the nematic liquid crystal was contained within a polymer matrix rather than capsules. These first devices contained a high proportion of polymer (~66 percent). More recently, a range of devices formed from nematic liquid crystal contained in a polymer matrix, in which the concentration of polymer is rather low (1–5 percent), have been investigated. One such device is the polymer stabilised cholesteric texture display. A far more detailed description of the historical development and structures of NCAP and PDLC displays has already been given (Doane, 1990). The first PDLC and NCAP displays had rather shallow transmission versus voltage curves and, therefore, were limited to direct or active matrix addressing. There have been several reports of active matrix addressed PDLC displays for applications in projection systems (Ginter *et al.*, 1993) where the absence of polarisers leads to brighter displays and/or lower power consumption. The main thrust of this work has been to reduce the drive voltage to <7 volts and to eliminate hysteresis in the electro-optic curve. In 1991, Yang *et al.* reported a display based on a mixture of cholesteric liquid crystal and a polymer gel which exhibited bistability at zero volts. These attributes enable the display to be multiplexed and, hence, to provide a passive matrix addressed, complex, alphagraphic display. This display is now known as the polymer stabilised cholesteric texture (PSCT) display.

The operation of the PSCT display relies on the selective reflection of light from the planar cholesteric liquid crystal texture, the stabilisation of the (slightly scattering) focal conic texture by the polymer gel, and the possibility to switch between these two states via the homeotropic texture (see Figures 10.10 and 10.11). In the planar texture, either right-handed or left-handed circular polarised light within a certain wavelength range is strongly reflected, while the remaining light is transmitted (and absorbed by the black material at the rear of the display): Figure 10.10(a). The peak wavelength (λ) of the

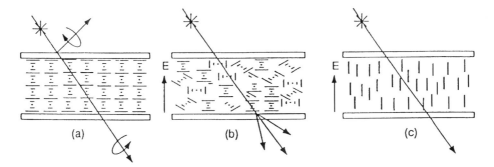

Figure 10.10 PSCT displays have three possible states or 'textures': (a) planar texture, (b) focal conic texture, and (c) homeotropic texture

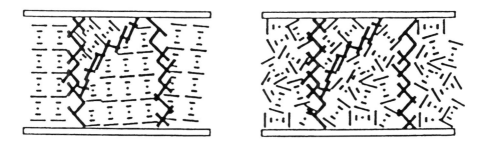

Figure 10.11 A polymer network can induce a fine-grained domain structure into a planar cholesteric liquid-crystal texture and can stabilise the focal conic texture

reflected light is given by the Bragg formula, $\lambda = n\,p$ where n is the average refractive index of the liquid crystal layer and p is the pitch of the cholesteric helix. The required value of λ is selected by varying p. The spectral width $(\Delta\lambda)$ of the reflected light is given by $\Delta\lambda = (\Delta n)\lambda/n$, where Δn is the birefringence of the cholesteric liquid crystal mixture.

Although the focal conic texture, Figure 10.10(b), is optically scattering, it is only weakly so, therefore, for the operation of the display, it is regarded as transmissive (and appears black when a black material is placed behind the display). The homeotropic texture is not used to display information but is used to switch between the planar and focal conic textures: see Figure 10.12.

Quite remarkable progress in this technology has been made since its introduction in 1991. Products, e.g. displays for public information systems, are available and a 14-inch diagonal, 1152×896 pixels display has been demonstrated (Pfeiffer *et al.*, 1995). Peak contrast ratios are typically $\sim$20:1 falling to an impressive $\sim$7:1, at 70° off axis. Clearly, one of the key features of this display technology is its ability to maintain an image at zero volts: see Figure 10.12.

Present disadvantages are relatively high drive voltages of around $\pm$40 V, i.e. 80 V peak-to-peak, and rather long row address times of several milliseconds, which can lead to frame times of several seconds (depending on the number of rows to be addressed).

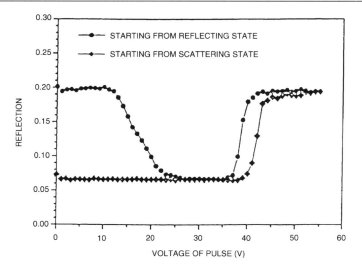

Figure 10.12   The reflectivity of a PSCT display can be changed as a function of the amplitude of an AC voltage pulse

10.5.2   Future Potential

A critical future development for PSCT display technology is the introduction of colour and grey scale. An approach to the former, by locally tuning and then fixing the pitch of the cholesteric liquid crystal, has already been reported (Chien *et al.*, 1995). Obtaining grey scale in the memory state may be more problematical. Although Figure 10.12 indicates that grey levels can be obtained by modulating the voltage between 12 and 25 volts and between 37 and 45 volts, it also suggests that these grey levels will disappear if the voltage is reduced to zero.

The rapid progress made by PSCT displays suggests that they have great potential, provided they can find applications that make the most of their advantages and are not significantly affected by their disadvantages.

10.6   CONCLUSION

Both the technical and commercial developments of supertwist LCDs have been extremely rapid; it is only about 10 years since the first STN display was demonstrated. The future of this technology appears secure, with the essential question being the precise level of positive growth. It seems probable that supertwist LCDs will be used in a wide range of products, from character modules to screens for multimedia laptop displays, while active matrix LCDs will move into the consumer TV market.

A key reason for the great success of supertwist LCDs is that the infrastructure required for their commercialisation was already in place because of the high volume production of twisted nematic LCDs. Furthermore, it could be argued that the development of the super-twist display was an example of 'product push', *i.e.*, when an established industry uses its resources to overcome a problem (in this case the inability of twisted nematic LCDs to provide complex alphagraphic displays because of their low level of multiplexability) that threatens its future.

On the other hand, ferroelectric LCDs, which were developed around the same time as supertwist LCDs, have yet to enter the marketplace and their future is not secure. While ferroelectric LCDs can offer a range of products, each one has to compete with at least one alternative technology. In the author's opinion, the best way for ferroelectric LCDs to be commercialised is through the development of non-volatile displays for portable electronic products. In this area, the competing technologies are not yet well established.

The main competitor to ferroelectric LCDs is polymer stabilised cholesteric texture displays, which are also able to provide non-volatility and wide viewing angles. The rapid introduction of this technology into the marketplace is undoubtedly due, in part, to its use of nematic liquid crystal (doped with a cholesteric liquid crystal) enabling it to utilise the infrastructure established for the mainstream LCD technologies, namely twisted nematic, supertwist and active matrix.

The difference between the rates of commercial development of supertwist, ferroelectric and polymer stabilised, cholesteric texture LCDs is a good example of the importance of an established infrastructure, or 'product push'. The benefits of product-push and the difficulties encountered without an established infrastructure should not be underestimated.

REFERENCES

Alt, P.M. and Pheshko. P. (1974), Scanning limitations of liquid crystal displays, *IEEE Trans. Electron Devices*, **21**, 146.

Chien, L.-C., Müller, U., Nabor, M.-F. and Doane, J.W. (1995), Multicolour reflective cholesteric displays, *SID Technical Digest*, **XXVI**, 169–172.

Clark, N. A. and Lagerwall, S. T. (1980), Sub-microsecond bistable electro-optic switching in liquid crystals, *Appl. Phys. Lett.*, **36**, 899.

Doane, J.W. (1990), Polymer dispersed liquid crystal displays, in B. Bahadur (ed.), *Liquid Crystals, Applications and Uses*, Vol. 1, World Scientific, London 361–395.

Doane, J.W., Vaz, N.A., Wu, B.-G. and Zumar, S. (1986), Field controlled light scattering from nematic microdroplets *Appl. Phys. Lett.*, **48**, 269–271.

Doane, J.W., St John, W.D., Lu, Z.J. and Yang, D.K. (1994), Stabilised and modified cholesteric liquid crystals for reflective displays, *Conf. Record of the 1994 IDRC*, 10–13 Oct., Monterey, CA, 65.

Fergason, J.L. (1985), Polymer encapsulated nematic liquid crystal for display and light control applications, *SID Digest of Technical Papers*, **XVI**, 68–71.

Ginter, E., Lüder E., Kallfass, T., Huttelmaier, S. *et al.* (1993), Optimised PDLCs for active matrix addressed light valves in projection systems, *Conf. Record of the 1993 IDRC*, 31 August–3 September Strasbourg, France, 105–108.

Harada, T., Taguchi, M., Iwasa, K. and Kai, M. (1985), An application of chiral smectic-C liquid crystal to a multiplexed large area display, *SID Digest of Technical Papers*, **XXI**, 131–134.

Hedgley, R.L. and de la Rossette, J. (1992), *Proceedings of Electronically Integrated Processes for Print and Intermedia*, Nashville, TN.

Katoh, K., Endo, Y., Akatsuka, M. and Ohgawara, M. (1987), Application of retardation compensation, *Japan J. Appl. Phys.*, **26**, L1784.

Matsumoto, S. (1990), *Electronic Display Devices*, John Wiley & Sons.

Meyer, R.B., Liebert, L., Strzeleckji, L. and Keller, P. (1975), Ferroelectric liquid crystals, *J. Phys. Lett.*, **36**, L69.

Mosley, A. (1994), Ferroelectric LCDs: the way to the marketplace, *Information Display*, **2**, 7–11.

Ohgawara, M., Kuwata, T., Hasebe, H., Akatsuka, M., Koh, H. and Matsuhiro, K. (1989), *SID Digest of Technical Papers*, 390–393.

Pfeiffer, M., Yang, D.-K., Doane, J.W., Bunz, R. *et al.* (1995), A high information content reflective cholesteric display, *SID Technical Digest*, **XXVI**, 706–709.

Ross, P.W., Chan, L.K.M. and Surguy, P.W. (1994), The ferroelectric LCD: simplicity and versatility, *SID Technical Digest*, **XXV**, 147–150.

Sato, A. (1994), Reflective formats for colour LCDs solve power-consumption problems, *Display Devices*, **10**, 18– 21.

Schadt, M. and Leenhouts, F. (1987), Electro-optical performance of a new black–white and highly multiplexable liquid crystal display, *Appl. Phys. Lett.*, **50**, 236.

Scheffer, T.J. and Nehring, J. (1984), A new highly multiplexable liquid crystal display, *Appl. Phys. Lett.*, **45**, 1021.

Scheffer, T.J. and Nehring, J. (1994), *Society for Information Display Seminar Lecture Notes*, **1**, M1, 1–84.

Scheffer, T.J., Clifton, B., Prince, D. and Connor, A.R. (1993), Active addressing of STN displays for high-performance video applications, *Displays*, **14**, 74– 85.

Yamada, Y., Yamamoto, N., Mori, K., Koshoubu, N., Nakamura, K., Kawamura, I. and Suzuki, Y. (1993), Multicolour video-rate antiferroelectric LCD with high contrast and wide viewing angle, *Journal of SID*, **1**(3), 289–294.

Yang, D.K., Chien, L.-C. and Doane, J.W. (1991), Cholesteric liquid crystal polymer gel dispersion bistable at zero field, *Conf. Record of the 1991 IDRC*, 15–17 Oct., San Diego, CA, 49–52.

Yaniv, Z. (1995), Reflective cholesteric displays, *Information Display*, **10**, 10–14.

Emissive displays: the relative merits of ACTFEL, plasma and FEDs

Jean-Pierre Budin

11.1 INTRODUCTION

For each of the three emissive flat-panel technologies, we shall first briefly review their operating principles. Such descriptions can easily be found in books, but not in the same chapter. Reviewing the technologies together affords the opportunity to comment on the similarities of the physics involved, and on the differences between the techniques.

The known limitations and problems will be mentioned, the latest performance data reported by the main manufacturers will be given, and the author will attempt to predict the possible future developments of each technique.

In the three cases, with the exception only of monochrome (neon orange) PDPs, light is emitted in a solid-state material, often named a 'phosphor'. The name 'phosphor' is traditionally used for the photo-luminescent (UV-excited) powdered materials used in lighting tubes. The same principle is used in colour PDPs.

The cathodo-luminescent (electron beam excited) materials which coat the back of the cathode ray tube faceplates are also called phosphors. The same principle is used in FEDs.

In ACTFEL panels, the light-emitting materials are notably different in the sense that the electrons which induce the emission of light are accelerated in the material itself. This is also the only emissive panel type in which the active material is, most often, in the form of a thin film and not a powder as in PDPs and FEDs.

Display Systems, Edited by L.W. MacDonald and A.C. Lowe. © 1997 John Wiley & Sons Ltd.

One most notable quality common to all emissive panels is the very broad 'natural' viewing angle, which the CRTs have made familiar to everyone. Also, they can all operate over a very broad temperature range (0–55°C or more).

One difficulty shared by all emissive panels is a decrease in image contrast and readability with the illumination under which the panel is being used. This is due to the diffuse scattering or specular reflection of ambient light by the very structure of the panel. To achieve adequate contrast under normal ambient conditions, this scattering, which is especially intense when the active material is in the form of a powder, must be reduced by using filters, a black matrix or other means (Budin, 1992).

Another point which deserves special attention whenever the emitting material is in the solid state (which includes the CRTs) is the image burn-in effect. This tends to make the useful life in computer applications shorter than in television applications. The decrease with time of the luminance of television panels is more or less uniform over the panel surface, so that reaching about 50 percent of the initial value may signal the end of useful life. In computer displays, part of the displayed image will very often be static, and the ageing is not uniform. The local decrease of the intrinsic local luminance for this application must definitely not exceed a few percent. A change of the light diffusivity of the display, visible under ambient illumination in the dark parts of the image, may also be objectionable, as can be seen in some CRT airport displays.

The first section of this chapter deals with alternating current electroluminescent displays (ACTFEL), and several basic properties of emissive panels are recalled based on this example. The second and third sections describe the status of plasma display panels (PDP) and field emission displays (FED), respectively. Since this is not a review paper, the list of references cited is not exhaustive, but it does contain recent review articles, and the original papers in which innovations, which are still being developed today, were first introduced.

11.2 ALTERNATING CURRENT THIN FILM ELECTROLUMINESCENT DISPLAYS (ACTFEL)

11.2.1 Operating principles, specificities and panel construction

Physical principles

Accounts of the fascinating history of electroluminescence have been given by Tannas (1985) and Vecht (1990), and several review papers on the device physics have been published (Mach & Müller, 1982; Benoit *et al.*, 1990), as well as a recent interesting 'Tentative anatomy' (Bringuier, 1994). A thorough description, in simple terms, of the mechanisms of high field electroluminescence remains difficult to find in the literature.

The only high-field electroluminescent structures currently used in display products are of the AC thin film type. The latest developments are regularly reported in the Society for Information Display Symposia, the IDRC (e.g. Müller & Mach, 1994; Barrow *et al.*, 1994), and the annual Society for Information Display Seminars (King, 1994).

The basic phenomenon is the almost loss-free (vacuum-like) acceleration of electrons in a polycrystalline thin film. It should be mentioned that this picture is now considered too simple. The non-parabolicity of the energy bands, and the effect of local space charge at high excitation levels, have been taken into account in recent models (Benoit *et al.*, 1993). The active film is usually 0.5 to 1 μm thick, and is sandwiched between two high quality insulating films of comparable thickness (Figure 11.1). The electrons originate at the film–insulator interfaces. The very sharp voltage threshold above which conduction occurs in the active film is principally due to the tunnel injection from interface states into the active layer. Since the threshold electrical field is of the order of 1.5 to 2 × 10^6 V cm^{-1}, the electrons typically acquire a kinetic energy of several electron volts in a mean path of ≈20 nm between interactions. These consist of either electron emission from traps, the direct impact excitation of activator atoms, or possibly impact ionisation of shallow levels. The electrons are eventually trapped at the (temporarily) anodic interface. During conduction, the build-up of charges establishes an internal field which opposes the externally applied voltage, so that the current terminates when the resulting field falls below threshold. Light is emitted by the excited activator atoms in the form of a pulse. Upon reversal of the external voltage polarity, the internal field effectively adds to the applied field and lowers the conduction threshold for those pixels which have just been activated.

The activators are transition metal or rare-earth atoms. Once excited, these centres can decay to the ground state through a radiative transition, and thus emit light with their specific emission spectrum.

Materials and structures

This very sketchy summary suffices to determine which critical properties are required of the materials and the structure.

The active film should support the lossless acceleration of electrons to energies of several electron volts, and the activator–host material couple should be such that the energy decay path of the excited activator atoms is mostly radiative. The best combination of properties is found in zinc sulphide films doped with about 1 weight percent of manganese. More generally, until recently only II–VI polycrystalline materials (ZnS, SrS, CaS) had demonstrated good performance, with various activators: Mn (broadband yellow), Tb (green), Eu (red), Ce (variable blue) and Pr (white). The more complex alkaline earth thiogallates are now being studied as efficient hosts for blue-emitting Ce.

Insulator films play the second critical role. The onset of conduction in the active layer is so abrupt and devoid of any self-limiting mechanism that, without an external means to impose a smooth distribution of the current density, destructive high-current channels

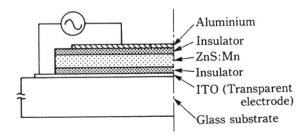

Figure 11.1   A schematic of the elementary ACTFEL structure (after Solomon & Thioulouse, 1989; courtesy Mita Press)

would form at once. The dielectric layers form capacitors which are electrically in series with the luminescent film, and effectively limit the charge density which can flow in the device (Figure 11.1). As we shall see later, this concept is exactly the same as that used in AC plasma panels. Actually, some sort of current control is required in all emissive panels. The presence of two insulating layers in the present case ensures the symmetry of the interfaces and of the injection process. It also improves the reliability, mostly because the probability of weak points occurring in both films at the same location is very small. In terms of maximum safely displaced charge density, which is equal to the product of the maximum electric field and the dielectric constant, the quality of these films is similar to that of the dielectric films used in condensers; the best values are about 5 μC cm^{-2}. Other requirements are the absence of chemical interaction with the active layer, and adequate electrical behaviour of the interfaces. This leads some laboratories to combine two or more layers with different compositions, on each side of the active layer.

The structure is completed by the electrode arrays. The front electrodes are transparent and made of indium–tin oxide (ITO). On the most current panels, they are deposited and patterned on the glass substrate as the first step of the fabrication process. The back electrodes are usually made of aluminium. One important property of the metal film is its ability for self-healing of the microscopic breakdowns which occur the first time the operating voltage is applied.

As such, this basic structure is the only one used in flat panels which is entirely solid-state and free of any vacuum enclosure.

The electrical coupling is capacitive, and the device is practically insensitive to the DC component of the applied voltage. The thickness of the active sandwich being, as stated above, of the order of 1 μm, the capacitance per unit area is high ($\approx$10 nF cm^{-2} below threshold, $\approx$20 nF cm^{-2} when the active layer conducts). This feature makes these devices very different from the plasma panels.

The fact, already mentioned above, that the threshold is lower for a reverse polarity voltage pulse for the pixels which were just lit was used to devise a clever addressing method, which was used in the first commercial ACTFEL panels offered by Sharp Company in the late 1970s, which made use of a collective 'refresh' pulse. This scheme was subsequently found to induce differential ageing effects between the top and the bottom of the panels (Flegal & King, 1988). The remedy is to use a fully symmetric drive scheme, which was proposed in 1986 and is now used in all commercial panels (Figure 11.2) (Shoji *et al.*, 1989).

Although only one light pulse instead of two is emitted by the 'on' pixels during one frame period, the luminance and the power consumption are not affected. The high capacitance per unit area, the finite resistance of the transparent column electrodes and/or the maximum current output of the drivers limit the electrical bandwidth of the panels. The use of pulses shorter than about 40–50 μs is precluded in the addressing waveforms of the larger panels. The symmetric drive does not consist of alternating the polarity of the address pulses within one row time slot, but rather every other frame (King, 1994).

Light is emitted as pulses every time the voltage exceeds the threshold, and the decay time constant of Mn in ZnS is $\approx$1 ms. For a test cell where the combined effect of the capacitance and the resistance of the access electrodes is low enough not to limit the bandwidth, the luminance is approximately proportional to the driving frequency, up to a few kilohertz.

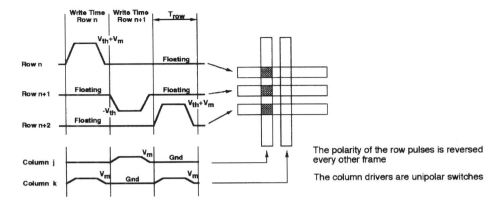

Figure 11.2 The 'symmetric drive' method for TFEL panels (after King, 1994; courtesy Society for Information Display)

The major physical factors limiting the overall efficiency of the devices are (Müller & Mach, 1994 and references therein): (a) the loss of electrons to phonons, and the fraction of electrons with insufficient energy to excite a luminescent centre (efficiency $\leqslant 0.5$), (b) the quantum efficiency of the active centres ($\geqslant 0.4$), (c) their non-radiative decay and excitation quenching ($\leqslant 0.5$, non-linear), and (d) the poor optical coupling efficiency of the emitted light out of the display (0.1).

This last factor is specific to EL panels, and is related to the fact that light is created in a solid medium, as in III–V semiconductor single crystal light-emitting diodes. The refractive index of this medium is larger than unity. For flat films, the optical efficiency is limited by the solid angle about the film normal within which light rays can escape without undergoing total internal reflection. The factor is about 10 percent for ZnS (refractive index = 2.35), if one assumes the presence of a black absorbing layer on the back side, which is obviously advantageous for a good contrast. The internally reflected light is guided within the emitting layer and the glass, and the latter may have a negative effect on the intrinsic contrast.

The largest reported overall efficiency of an experimental cell without a black layer and with a slightly diffusing active film (which increases the optical efficiency to greater than 10 percent) is about 1 percent, or an efficacy of 6 lm per watt. The practical efficacy of a cell is at most 3 lm per watt. The good contrast under illumination of commercial panels, which include a black layer or an anti-reflection filter, is largely due to the absence of optical diffusion in the emitting layer or any other layers in the display.

Panel construction

The essential steps of classical ACTFEL panel construction consist of the deposition and patterning of the transparent electrodes, the deposition of the first dielectric film, the active layer, second insulating film, the back electrode, and the protection layers. Soda-lime glass is used with an ion barrier film as the display substrate. Most classical vacuum deposition techniques (e-beam evaporation, sputtering or chemical vapour deposition) are used. One notable exception is the Atomic Layer Epitaxy (ALE) method, introduced by

Suntola *et al.* (1980) and used by Lohja Corp., now Planar International. This consists of alternately exposing the substrate in a high-temperature reactor to low-pressure chemical precursors. For instance, to deposit the ZnS:Mn active layer, the first precursor induces the chemisorption of a single atomic layer of Zn with the right proportion of Mn; the reactor is then evacuated, sulphur is introduced, then evacuated, and a new cycle begins. These surface reactions are self-limiting, so that excellent stoichiometry is achieved, as well as very good crystallinity, because of the high substrate temperature (500°C), which leads to highly efficient active layers. High-quality dielectric films, in particular the composite Al_xTi_yO, can also be grown by this method. Coverage of the substrate is conformal and very few point defects exist. The ALE deposition process is relatively slow, but is performed as a batch process.

There is no 'best choice' dielectric material, because the performance (breakdown voltage) of the film depends very much on the deposition method. SiO_xN_y is also used in commercial products. For a monochrome panel, only the electrode arrays are patterned, so that the lithography steps are reduced to a minimum.

The front transparent electrodes (we recall that the panel is usually viewed from the glass side) should have a low sheet resistance. A high capacitive current is needed to charge the columns, and the charging level should be almost exactly the same at the top and the bottom of the panel. In practical terms, a 10-inch VGA panel requires a sheet resistance of less than 7.5 ohm per square (King, 1994). The film must be much thicker than the ITO films used in LCD panels, and the step coverage by the dielectric layer which must withstand fields of more than 10^6 V cm^{-1} requires special attention. Films prepared by the ALE method meet both these requirements.

Further to this remark, the relationship which sets a limit to the information content and the size of such panels can be shown to be (for 95 percent charging) (Budin, 1993):

$$A = Nh^2 f \leqslant 0.4(R c F)^{-1} \qquad\qquad 11.1$$

where N is the number of scanned rows, h the panel height, f the frame frequency, R the sheet resistance, c the capacitance per unit area and F the vertical filling factor of the column electrode.

The technical difficulty of fabricating a panel is related to Nh^2, or the product of its surface area and the number of rows scanned in sequence. The split electrode design with 'two rows at a time' addressing divides this factor by 8 by halving N and h. It was used by Planar to realise an 18-inch diagonal (1024 × 864) panel, the largest presently available (Schmachtenberg *et al.*, 1989). Use of this technique doubles the number of column drivers and halves the number of row drivers.

Addressing and power consumption

The very steep luminance vs peak voltage curve of ACTFEL cells is quite suitable for multiplexed addressing. The slope is commonly of one luminance decade per 1.5 to 2 V peak modulation voltage. The operating points (row selection voltage, column modulation voltage) are selected for maximum efficiency, good maintenance, and conservation of power (Budin, 1993; Ono, 1993). The voltage levels used for addressing ACTFEL panels are of the order of 180 V peak for row selection (+220/180 V for the Planar symmetric drive) and 40 V for the column modulation (data) voltage. The drivers are high-voltage DMOS circuits.

The luminance depends to some extent on the panel technology, but primarily it depends on the frame rate, since one light pulse is emitted at every frame, and on the column modulation voltage. Typical values for standard commercially available ZnS:Mn panels are 50–80 cd/m^2 at 60 Hz. Much higher luminance can be obtained at higher frame frequencies and higher column modulation voltages for application to avionics (Canadian Marconi Company).

One important concern has been to reduce the power consumption. It is easily shown that the largest fraction of the power is consumed in charging the columns (Törnqvist, 1990; Budin, 1993; King, 1994). Actually King notes that the total power consumption of panels in a given technology, including the driving electronics, is proportional to A (equation 11.1). Efforts were thus made to reduce the column modulation voltage as much as possible without a loss of luminance uniformity or contrast. After a period of optimism with the objective of reducing the column modulation to 20 V, present-day values converge to 30–40 V. The column power is strongly dependent on image content, the worst case (maximum power) being a checkerboard pattern with 50 percent of the pixels lit. The 'typical' consumption which manufacturers report is just above half the maximum, and is typical of either a small ($\approx$10 percent) or a large ($\approx$90 percent) proportion of lit pixels, and of text or graphics in normal or reverse video. The methods recently introduced (King, 1994) to reduce the maximum and average power include two-step charging of the columns, which gives a theoretical power saving of 50 percent (practical $\approx$40 percent), but is naturally limited by the increase of the charging time; an inductive recovery of the reactive power; a reduction of the pixel fill factor; and a reduced contrast mode for 'worst case' patterns (reduction of column modulation with a brightness-compensating increase in row voltage). The result is that a laboratory 640 × 400 panel with a 9-inch diagonal and a luminance of 150 cd/m^2 can be made to operate with a maximum power of 6 watts (King, 1994).

Having observed that portable equipment is not presently a dominant market segment for EL panels, the main concern at Planar is more to increase luminance than to reduce power.

Memory EL panels

We shall review this field only briefly, since no product exists at this time. The considerable advantages of a bistable electro-optical effect to realise very large and complex panels are well known (Budin, 1993) and are fully exploited in AC plasma display panels. For ACTFEL, although an intrinsic memory effect can be created in ZnS:Mn cells when the Mn content and the thickness are both made larger than usual, this effect cannot be made stable with time. An extrinsic memory effect can be obtained by adding a photoconductive layer (PC) between the classical EL sandwich and the back electrode. The most recent and thorough study was performed by Thioulouse (Thioulouse, 1987; Solomon & Thioulouse, 1989). The PC layer is made of unpatterned a-Si$_{1-x}$C$_x$:H which also has the properties of a black layer (Figure 11.3). Because it is optically strongly coupled to the emitting layer, its photoconductivity can be made small enough, by adjusting the composition, x, to be insensitive to normal levels of ambient illumination.

Small demonstration panels were built and a memory margin of 28 V at 224 V and a switching time of 10 µs were obtained. The technique is based on the association of two

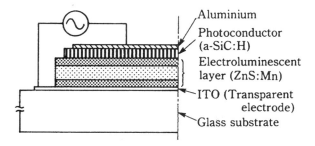

Figure 11.3   Electroluminescent display with pixel memory (PC-Memory ACTFEL). The active
EL structure of is electrically in series with a photoconducting layer. This 'photoconductor' is a
n^+ in^+ structure made of amorphous carbon–silicon (carbon proportion of about 10 percent)
(Solomon & Thioulouse, 1989; courtesy Mita Press)

mature technologies, that of ACTFEL panels and that of a-Si, familiar in active matrices
or in solar cells.

Most interesting are the predictions made by the authors for the construction of memory
PCEL panels with this technique. Contrary to the traditional belief that EL memory panels
require enormous capacitive sustain currents, the contrary is shown to hold true. The high
pixel luminance obtained as a consequence of the 1 kHz sustain voltage allows a reduction
of the pixel filling factor, and consequently of the panel capacitance. A polyphased (n-
phased) sustain voltage drastically reduces the current and the voltage drop along the
columns, and allows a writing speed of $n \times 1000$ rows/s. The capacitive sustain current
does not contain short peaks and is effectively compensated by an inductive recovery
circuit. The highest driver output voltage is 50 V. The contrast is that of a panel with
a black layer. Overall, the following reduced values are predicted, with respect to a
conventional panel: row current 1/65, column current 1/85, maximum power less than 1/4.

Finally, the presence of memory basically increases the luminance level. The method
is not linked to specific properties of ZnS:Mn, and can be used with active layers which
would otherwise not be able to provide a sufficient luminance, e.g. blue-emitting EL
structures. This work on PCEL panels remains so far entirely unexploited.

Active matrix addressing of EL panels

As seen above, the physical limits to the size and complexity of light-emitting multiplexed
panels are set by the difficulty of supplying a pixel with the required energy during one
row time slot in every frame period. Much as in memory panels, an active matrix can
increase the duty factor of the supply of power to the pixels to almost unity. The limit
set by equation 11.1 then vanishes. It can also increase the luminance to very high levels,
for the same reason. This latter objective is being pursued for helmet-mounted head-
up display applications (Khormaei *et al.*, 1994), with potential advantages compared to
backlit poly-Si AMLCDs.

Grey levels

Due to the bandwidth limitations of ACTFEL panel addressing, the pulse width modulation and the frame-sequential modulation methods, which both require higher frequency

driving waveforms (Budin, 1993) are rather limited. Commercial VGA panels can be found with 16 true levels. Dithering or patterning can also be used, at the expense of resolution. Column voltage modulation has been demonstrated on prototypes. Its practical implementation would impose very stringent requirements on the thickness uniformity of the critical layers, but above all it requires very expensive drivers. All things considered, the available grey level scale is therefore modest.

Colour

Colour is the main concern for those attempting to predict the future of the ACTFEL technology. Unfortunately, the colour of the most efficient and technically mature ZnS:Mn panels is not as such a useful primary. An extremely large number of laboratories have experimented with many materials, activators, and full-colour solutions. We suggest the reading of the complete and recent review by Ono (1993).

The first approach, which is quite common for emitters, is that of additive colour synthesis, using three juxtaposed patterned phosphors. (This approach, together with the 'patterned filter' method discussed below, suffers from a reduced spatial fill factor for each monochromatic emitter. The only way to increase this fill factor would be to stack three monochromatic fully transparent structures on a single substrate, with interposed electrode arrays and their connections, which would be entirely impractical.) The best red is obtained with Europium-doped CaS (Ono, 1993). The chromaticity is good and the luminance is not far from the required level. However, the response is slow and the efficacy rather low. Filtered ZnS:Mn provides the best overall performance in the red (nearly 1 lm/W), and is used in commercial multicolour displays (Planar). The best green is emitted by ZnS:Tb,F with an efficacy larger than 1 lm/W, and this phosphor is also used in colour products. The research on ZnS:Tb materials and structures remains active (Ohnishi & Mohri, 1992). Filtered ZnS:Mn also provides a good green.

Although only about 11 percent of the total white areal luminance should be composed of the blue primary, this colour remains the most difficult to produce. For several years, research focused on SrS:Ce, a hygroscopic material which emits an unsaturated greenish blue with a relatively good (unfiltered) efficacy of 1.4 lm/W (Velthaus et $al.$, 1994). Filtering to an acceptable blue lowers the efficacy to 0.16 lm/W. The best blue emitters available today are Ce-doped calcium or strontium thiogallates $CaGa_2S_4$:Ce. The (unfiltered) colour coordinates are good, the maintenance is satisfactory, and the luminance, although equally modest (5–10 cd/m^2 at 60 Hz), holds good promise (Barrow et $al.$, 1993).

The second approach to full colour EL displays consists of using a single white-emitting structure with patterned colour filters. This approach can lead to a much simpler manufacturing process. Preserving the balance of colours in video applications may also be much easier than in the three-phosphors approach. This approach is especially well suited to the 'inverted structure', where the active stack is on the viewer's side of the plate (Tanaka et $al.$, 1987). The EL structure is then no more complicated than the classical non-inverted one, and low temperature organic filters can be laminated on top of the ITO at the end of the fabrication process. The set of transparent column electrodes can be supplemented by Al bus-bars to improve the panel bandwidth, whereas a refractory metal would be needed in 'bottom ITO' structures.

White phosphors are being studied by many groups. The best results to date are those of SrS:Ce,Cl/ZnS phosphor structures, in which both unsaturated colours combine into a good white (Leppänen *et al.*, 1993, Velthaus *et al.*, 1994). The luminance values are claimed to be high enough to meet the requirements for commercial applications (Haaranen *et al.*, 1995; Mauch *et al.*, 1995).

The first commercially available and proven multicolour EL display belongs to this latter category, with patterned red and green filters on top of a ZnS:Mn structure.

The classical structure was used, however, in the earlier Planar 8-colour prototype shown in Figure 11.4(a). This was much less convenient: only inorganic filters able to withstand the EL stack deposition temperature could be used. The red comes from filtered ZnS:Mn. Probably no temperature-resistant green filter was available, so that a patterned ZnS:Tb phosphor (saturated green emitter) was used for the green, and both phosphors are patterned.

A clever, although costly, hybrid solution (King *et al.*, 1987) is being developed into a full-colour (not video) commercial product at Planar (Figure 11.4(b)).

It consists in stacking and registering, from the viewer's side: (1) a first glass plate with the active structure on its far side, and transparent electrodes on both sides of a patterned ZnS:Mn (filtered to red) and ZnS:Tb (green) structure similar to that just described; and (2) a second glass plate with a fully transparent blue-emitting Ce:Ca thiogallate structure on top of the plate. On both plates, row electrodes are reinforced by a thin metal bus. Since both emitting structures are in close proximity to each other, there is no parallax. A larger filling factor for the low luminance blue phosphor would result if the blue plate were in front, with organic filters on top of the plate 1 stack.

11.2.2 Performance of ACTFEL panels, present and future

The yellow emission of ZnS:Mn is extremely pleasant in monochrome displays, and it is generally agreed that EL panels with an anti-reflection filter or a black back layer are

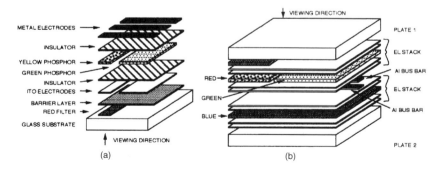

Figure 11.4 Schematic of (a) a Planar multicolour EL prototype, and (b) of the first full-(saturated) colour dual substrate EL panel. The top plate of the full-colour panel is the same as that of the panel on the left, except that ITO electrodes replace the Al row electrodes (after King, 1994; courtesy Society for Information Display)

among the most attractive flat panels available. The noted qualities are the sharp edges of the pixels, or the 'crispness' of images, the excellent contrast, typically higher than 10:1 at 400 lux, the wide 'natural' viewing angle, the fast response time, and the good durability. All EL panels have a good shock resistance (up to 100 g/4 ms) due to their simple rugged structure, a 0–55°C or larger operating range, and a MTBF of several tens of thousands of hours. The thickness and weight of ACTFEL display modules are potentially the smallest among all flat panels, due to the use of one thin glass plate and the absence of backlighting.

Most EL display modules are manufactured by only two companies: Sharp in Japan, and Planar with a base in the USA and another in Finland. Planar's catalogue is the only one to include a colour panel.

The available products include small displays (240 × 64), 10.4 inch VGA panels, with a 16-level true grey scale version available, and the larger 18 inch XGA panel already mentioned. The luminance is in the range 50–80 cd/m^2, and the typical power is 12 W for a standard 10.4 inch VGA panel, with a module efficacy of 0.4 lm/W. Although laboratory results may hold the promise of a substantial improvement of this figure in the near future, power is at present larger than that required by backlit AMLCDs.

Readily available panels are practically limited in size to about 10.4 inches, although larger units can be produced. Sharp offers both standard and high-brightness displays which utilise split-column electrodes, in sizes up to 17 inch diagonal, and a high resolution 1280 × 1024 13 inch panel.

A high contrast series is offered by Planar with a luminance approximately halved by the presence of a thin-film absorbing layer at the back of the active stack, but the resulting contrast and image crispness are still better than of standard panels with a contrast enhancement filter placed in front.

The recent progress in colour phosphors shows that the bottleneck of full colour capability may not be as narrow as predicted even recently (Friedman, 1993b).

The multicolour display in Planar's catalogue has (640 × 2) ×350 pixels at a pitch of 0.28 × 0.35 mm. It can display eight colours and requires 15 W to provide a yellow areal luminance of 15 cd/m^2 with a high contrast. A larger VGA display has been announced.

Full, saturated (i.e. two-level) colour panel prototypes have been shown by Planar since 1993. The recent models which incorporate the new blue thiogallate phosphor and two stacked plates (Figure 11.4(b)) have an excellent appearance, with high contrast, in spite of a modest luminance, due to the presence of a black layer at the back. Manufacturing of a 320 × 256 panel has been announced for 1995. This product is aimed at instrumentation applications.

No ACTFEL panel can presently be considered adequate for the rendition of full-colour video, and the limitations described above explain why ACTFEL displays are being used primarily for medical, industrial and instrumentation applications.

Their market growth rate is higher than the average growth for displays, and only second to that of LCDs. The present market size is about 0.02 percent of all displays in number of panels, and 0.5 percent in value (Stanford Resources Inc., 1994a). It can be understood why investment decisions are being delayed until the possibilities of colour and also grey scale have been fully evaluated.

11.3 PLASMA DISPLAY PANELS (PDPs)

11.3.1 Operating principles, specificities and panel construction

Physical principles

There exist only few texts on the application of gas discharges to displays, and we recommend the book chapter and the Society for Information Display Seminars written by Larry F. Weber (Weber, 1985, 1994), from whom we have borrowed much.

In monochrome plasma display panels, light is emitted by a gaseous discharge. Monochrome panels are easily recognised by the characteristic red-orange negative glow of neon which covers the cathode, the most intense line being at 640 nm.

The I–V characteristic of a plasma cell (Figure 11.5) shows a vertical branch. This feature is explained by the electron avalanche process, by which an electron ionises a Ne atom, creating a Ne ion and another electron. When this reaction becomes more probable than the loss of one electron, an exponential growth of the current results, and electrical breakdown eventually occurs. The abundance of the various species and the distribution of electrical charges then abruptly change in the cell, giving a negative differential resistance region (subnormal and normal glow regions). In this regime, the sustain voltage is lower than the breakdown voltage, so that an intrinsic memory can exist. The normal operating point is at, or slightly above, the top of the normal glow part of the curve where the cathode surface is entirely filled by the negative glow (Figure 11.6).

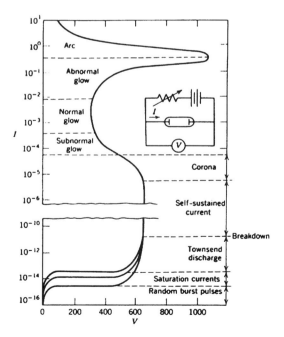

Figure 11.5   Schematic I–V characteristic of a gas discharge (after Sherr, 1993, p. 233, by permission)

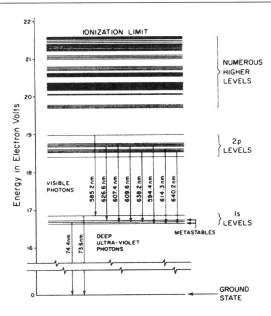

Figure 11.6   Energy-level diagram of the Ne atom (after Nighan, 1981; courtesy Society for Information Display)

Maintaining a stable current in this regime requires a current limiting element in the circuit of each conducting pixel.

The breakdown voltage is lowest if the gas is a 'Penning mixture', *i.e.*, contains a small amount of argon, whose atom can be ionised by a collision with a metastable Ne atom. The breakdown voltage is minimised, and less than 200 V, when the product of electrode spacing and gas pressure is near 50 mbar mm.

Orange light is emitted by Ne atoms when, after being excited by an electron collision to a 2p level (higher than 18.5 eV) they decay radioactively to the metastable 1s levels.

The decay from the metastable levels of rare gas atoms to the ground state is again radiative, but in the deep UV. The gas mixture can be designed to optimise this UV emission and minimise the amount of visible light. Excited Xe atoms in Ne–Xe or He–Xe mixtures emit 147 nm UV radiation efficiently. As can readily be seen in fluorescent lamps, this emission is not confined in the cathode region, but rather fills the cell. This UV emission is used to excite the photoluminescence of phosphor triads which produce the primary colours in full-colour PDPs.

The onset of the avalanche in a given cell occurs at a definite voltage. However the actual current onset and its rate of growth depend on the initial priming current, which can in practice be so low that a random delay results. The rise time proper depends on the avalanche gain, and therefore on the applied voltage. Priming is a unique and essential feature of plasma devices, and must be effectively controlled. This is accomplished by providing the cell with charged particles. These can be directly created at short range by an auxiliary pilot discharge, and they travel according to the electric field distribution and their mean free path, which is much shorter than the cell dimensions. Metastable (neutral) atoms are also effective through the Penning ionisation, and can diffuse at very short distances. UV photons can induce photo-emission of electrons at the walls, and can be active at longer range, although the absorption by the gas is strong.

After the applied voltage returns to zero, it takes time for the cell to return to rest. Charged particles and metastables persist for several microseconds. They may reduce the threshold voltage of neighbouring cells, and the next ignition of the same cell can be influenced after delays as long as one millisecond. This can be used as a memory, as we shall see below.

Materials and structures

The above summary will help in understanding the main design features of plasma panels.

The usual classification into DC and AC panels refers to the current limitation method used to avoid destructive arcs at the onset of the discharge. In DC panels, a resistor is used, or the output stage of the driver is a high-impedance current source. Because it was traditionally difficult to integrate a resistor in the panel structure, it is often connected to an outside electrode. Anyway, only one discharge can be ignited at any time along that electrode, or the current would not be equally distributed.

The sputtering of electrodes by ions limits the panel life. The addition of mercury to DC cells reduces the sputtering, but is not effective at low temperatures.

In AC panels, the current density is controlled by series capacitances, much as in ACTFEL panels: the electrodes are coated with a glass dielectric, and the pixels are AC-coupled. A consequence is that the electrodes are not in direct contact with the gas discharge, and are not subject to ion sputtering, which favours long lifetime. A MgO coating is used for its resistance to sputtering and its high secondary electron emission coefficient, which lowers the firing threshold. This coating is an important element of AC panels, and much effort has been devoted to its development.

The conduction in the gas accumulates charges on the walls, and an electric field opposing the external voltage builds up and eventually stops the current. (The accumulation of charges on the cell walls does not induce a memory effect by itself.) This description is very similar to that made for ACTFEL. The differences are, however, quite large, as we shall now see.

In order to obtain acceptable operating voltage values, the gas gap thickness must be of the order of 100 μm and the pressure of the order of 500 mbar. The glass coatings on the electrodes are fabricated by low-cost thick film techniques, and have a thickness of 10–25 μm. This leads to a specific structure capacitance of the order of 200 pF/cm^2 in the on state, and less than 10 pF/cm^2 in the off state. The charge density displaced by a voltage pulse with a similar amplitude above threshold is about 100 times lower than for an equivalent ACTFEL panel. The luminance is also proportional to the frequency of conduction pulses, and, if the efficiencies were the same, ACPDPs would require a pulse rate of several kilohertz to obtain the same luminance level as ACTFEL panels at a frame rate of 60 Hz. Since the efficiency is lower, the pixel pulse frequency for ACPDPs should be about 50 kHz. This of course is not a feasible frame frequency, but can be used for a common sustain voltage in a memory panel. We therefore arrive at the unavoidable conclusion that such an AC panel will be used in the memory mode.

The facts that the luminous volume is 'thicker' than in EL panels (50–100 μm instead of less than 1 μm) and also that the active species of the plasma diffuse over distances of a few tens of microns outside the current path allow the use of narrow metal electrodes without excessive optical blocking. The resistivity of Al is about 10^4 times lower than that of ITO. This feature of plasma cells, however, limits high resolution, and the smallest pixel triad pitch so far demonstrated is 0.4 mm (0.2 mm cell pitch). The combination of low resistance electrodes and low capacitance explains the high electrical bandwidth of the plasma panels. Short pulses (a few microseconds) and high frequencies (up to several hundred thousand hertz) can be used.

Panel construction

The construction methods of PDPs, in part because their history is longer than that of any other flat panels (30 years), but also because the minimum dimensions of a plasma glow are not of the order of microns, are quite different from those of ACTFEL displays which are 10 years younger. Screen printing the electrode patterns, sandblasting the cell structures in float glass, and coating the phosphors by methods similar to those used in CRTs, are often used. An increase in resolution introduces the need for photolithography and vacuum deposition methods for the electrodes. As has already been said, for minimum threshold the gas pressure is about one-half atmosphere and the gap between the plates about 100 μm. The spacing is kept constant either by using thick glass plates or, for large panels, by using spacers. These consist of glass ribs or pods or, more recently, of deposited glass beads as in LCD cells.

The cell and electrode structures are different for the various techniques, and will be discussed later.

Addressing and power consumption: DC panels

The extreme non-linearity of the I–V curve (4–5 decades current increase at firing) is obviously adequate for multiplexing, and is not a limiting factor, and PDPs were the first multiplexed flat panel displays ever built. The gas discharge was for many years the only transducer known to be multiplexable.

Non-memory (refreshed) DC PDPs of high information content are addressed in the classical 'one row at a time' mode to maximise the pixel duty cycle. Smaller panels are often scanned 'one column at a time', to minimise the number of data circuits. The current is limited in the date driver output stage. As for all emissive displays when the memory effect is not used, the luminance decreases with the number of scanned electrodes.

The memory effect is not used because, as already mentioned, it would require a resistor to be integrated in each pixel cell, which is technically difficult. In panels made by Matsushita, reliable firing of the cells without random delay is ensured by a short priming pulse at every refresh scan in the cell itself (Akutsu & Nakagawa, 1982) (Figure 11.7). The resulting auxiliary discharge on the portion of the cathode facing the anode is blocked from view by a black mask layer. With longer data pulses, the discharge gradually expands to the full cathode area and becomes visible. The scanning proceeds along channels parallel to the anodes, and the barriers between channels also serve as spacers. Despite the black mask layer, the priming cells emit a background glow and limit the intrinsic contrast ratio to less than about 10. The hybrid AC–DC type panel improves on this feature, as we shall see below.

The priming effect of a discharge in the neighboring volume has been used to perform the scanning with a much reduced number of drivers. The basic idea is that a given voltage

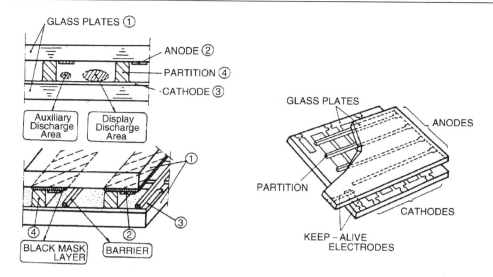

Figure 11.7 Cross-sectional view of the Matsushita display (Akutsu & Nakagawa, 1982. Courtesy Society for Information Display)

can be sufficient to switch 'on' a cell situated near an existing or just terminated discharge, but not another cell situated four or five cells away. The scanning pulses can thus be common to rows situated five, six or commonly seven spaces apart, so that only that same number of scanning drivers is needed. The scanning discharges take place in a non-visible part of the panel, and are expanded ('pulled') to the front by data 'display' anodes.

The most successful products based on this principle were the Self-Scan® displays introduced by Burroughs in the mid-seventies (Cola, 1977), and perfected along the years (Figure 11.8). The scanning speed is limited by the afterglow persistence already cited.

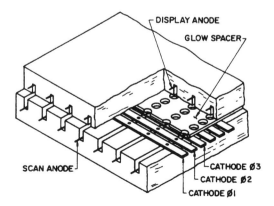

Figure 11.8 The improved Self-Scan® I display made by Burroughs (Miller *et al.*, 1981; courtesy Society for Information Display).
The design later evolved to the Self-Scan® memory display (Tannas, 1985, p. 386)

We mentioned this possibility to illustrate the capability of plasma discharges to perform logic functions. The decreased cost of driver circuits has reduced the cost savings which can be achieved by such multiple line address methods. The 'independent sustain and address' method does, however, remain of practical use (Sherr, 1993, p. 288). The most successful monochrome plasma display is of the hybrid AC–DC type (Amano *et al.*, 1982), developed by Sony Corp. and manufactured by Dixy. This success is now being shadowed by the LCDs for portable computers. The construction is very similar to that of a DC panel (Figure 11.7), but an extra electrode, parallel to the anodes, is buried under the cathodes and an insulating layer. This electrode is made positive with respect to the cathode for a very short time before the normal cathode scanning pulse. This method of priming allows a reduced data voltage, a faster ignition, and a smaller background glow. Panels with a resolution of 1024×512 at a pitch of 0.2 mm were demonstrated, and this was to be surpassed only several years later by AC PDPs.

The last DC plasma panels that we shall mention functions in the DC pulse memory mode. This technique is receiving considerable development in Japan for full-colour panels (NHK, Matsushita, Dai Nippon, TI Japan), and is discussed below with colour panels.

Addressing and power consumption: AC panels

The idea that the current-limiting function could be performed by a capacitor is due to a team at the University of Illinois (Bitzer & Slottow, 1966). The capacitor consists of dielectric layers coated onto the electrodes. Each pixel therefore has its own current limiter (actually a charge limiter), and the memory effect can be used to full advantage, so that nearly all current AC panels are memory panels. We have shown above that the panel construction is well suited to a collective sustain voltage of 50 kHz or more. With memory panels, the luminance depends neither on the number of rows nor on the panel size, and the largest flat panels in existence belong to this category (Friedman *et al.*, 1987).

Most monochrome AC PDPs are based on the simple 'opposed discharge' design introduced at Owens-Illinois (Chodil, 1976), with the electrode arrays on the opposite glass plates (Figure 11.9).

The addressing of AC panels requires a sustain generator, delivering AC pulses of 90–100 V peak with a duration of 2–10 μs. This generator provides the capacitive charge

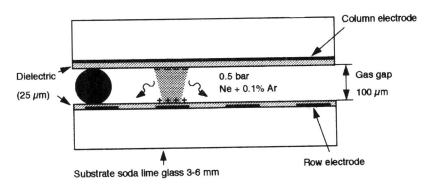

Figure 11.9   The schematic structure of a typical AC plasma display panel (after Weber, 1994; Courtesy Society for Information Display)

for the whole panel, and the discharge current for the pixels which are on. With the capacitance values already discussed, these currents are of the order of 1.2 A and 7 A, respectively, for a 10.4-inch VGA panel. About 80–90 percent of the energy can actually be recovered by an inductive circuit (Weber & Wood, 1987).

Writing of the information onto the panel is performed by address pulses of 60–70 V superimposed on the sustain pulses. The addressing can be performed in the 'one-half select' mode of multiplexing. The write/erase pulses are timed with a definite phase with respect to the sustain voltage. The duration of the writing pulses is adjusted so as to bring the wall voltage to that of the 'on' pixels, or to zero for the erasing pulses, respectively. We recall that the presence of the wall voltage reduces the firing threshold for the next pulse of polarity opposite to the last conduction. Provided that this modulation of the wall voltage is larger than the memory margin, then switching is induced.

Grey scale

Refreshed DC panels can use pulse width modulation of the data pulses. A true 256-level scale has been demonstrated.

In memory AC PDPs, if one excludes spatial modulation (dithering), the only available method is the duty cycle modulation. The normal frame period is divided into n subframes with durations graded in the sequence $1, 2, 4, \ldots, 2^{n-1}$. The panel is written n times as just described, so that the duty factor of each pixel can be adjusted from 0 to 1 with 2^n levels. The main challenge is that of speed. Blache *et al.* (1993) showed that if the frame period is T and the number of rows is L, then the row addressing time t should be such that $ntL \leqslant T$.

With $n = 8$ (256 levels), a 20 ms frame and 500 rows, t must be less than 5 µs. Fortunately, the He–Xe and Ne–Xe mixtures used in colour panels have a faster response than the Ne Penning mixture. The same group at Thomson Tubes Electroniques has succeeded in writing a row in 2.2 µs, and also in writing several rows per sustain cycle, resulting in the possibility of displaying 256 levels with 1000 rows (Deschamps, 1994).

A slightly different method is used at Fujitsu to obtain a 256-level grey scale, and is termed 'Address Display Period Separated Sub-field' (Yoshikawa *et al.*, 1992). It is said to allow lower operating voltage and lower power consumption than the conventional method.

The method of obtaining grey levels in DC pulse memory panels is based on a similar principle, as we shall see below.

Colour

The deep UV radiation (147 nm) emitted by a discharge in optimised Ne–Xe or He–Xe mixtures is used to excite the photoluminescence of phosphors. The excitation mechanism is different from that used in CRTs; the phosphors are not the same (Yamamoto *et al.*, 1993).

The construction of colour panels is much more difficult than that of monochrome units, mainly because the phosphors tend to be easily damaged by ions from the discharge, and because they tend to pollute the gas mixture. No acceptable lifetime was obtained until about 1980.

Colour purity became satisfactory when it was realised that sub-pixels should be effectively shielded from one another. The UV radiation is strongly absorbed by Xe atoms in the ground state, which are thus excited, radiate another UV photon which in turn is absorbed, and so forth many times: the photons become 'trapped' in the gas instead of directly irradiating the phosphor (Nguyen *et al.*, 1993). This has unfavourable consequences: (1) since the process is not lossless, the efficiency and the maximum luminance are limited; and (2) the photons from one sub-pixel may eventually induce UV emission near a phosphor of another colour at an adjacent pixel, not situated in direct view of the discharge. For that reason, the sub-pixel cells should be isolated by carefully designed barriers, which are found in all colour panels.

The first green-emitting panels of the DC refreshed type with a phosphor were offered by OKI in the early eighties.

The most sustained research efforts on colour panels aimed at TV applications were undertaken at NHK and at Fujitsu before 1980, and both reported spectacular results in 1993 (Kanogu, 1992 Yamamoto *et al.*, 1993; Shinoda *et al.*, 1993). Photonics Imaging, Thomson Tubes Electroniques and Plasmaco also reported remarkable achievements that same year or in 1994.

The DC pulse memory technology mentioned above was developed at NHK and used in the record 40-inch TV panel (Figure 11.10). Matsushita demonstrated a 26-inch TV panel in 1994 based on the same design.

Current limiting in 'conventional' design DC pulse memory panels is realised by using very short pulses and a discharge in the abnormal glow regime, where the differential resistance is positive, for current stability (Figure 11.5). To obtain sufficient luminance, a memory effect must be used. The sustain voltage consists in a series of positive sustain pulses on the anodes. Negative pulses are scanned on the cathodes, producing scanning discharges in vertical auxiliary (not visible) channels, which ensures fast reliable switching on by priming (Figure 11.10). The writing of images is performed in much the same way as in AC memory panels, and grey levels are also obtained by sub-fields (Tamura *et al.*,

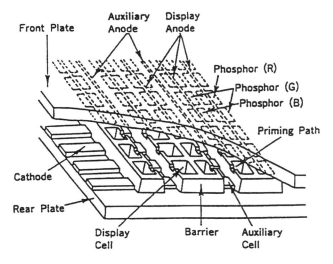

Figure 11.10   The structure of the 40-inch NHK colour DC-pulse memory PDP panel (Yamamoto *et al.*, 1993; courtesy Society for Information Display)

1994). The structure is relatively simple, and the authors claim that DC structures are simpler and cheaper to produce because, except for the phosphors, only printing is used and no vacuum deposition is required (Murakami *et al.*, 1991).

The optimisation of DC memory panels is a difficult task. Lifetime remains a concern, and the way to improvement is through a reduction of sputtering of the electrodes. Increasing the pressure is a drastic solution which has no marked effect on the luminance. However, the stable abnormal glow then sets in only at a higher (excessive) current, so that this regime can no longer be used. Rather a 'resistor in cell' is needed. The possibility of integrating a 1 MΩ current-limiting resistor in each cell was demonstrated, and lifetimes in excess of 10 000 hours were announced at a luminance level of 150 cd/m^2 and an efficacy of 0.4 lm/W (Sakai *et al.*, 1993; Takahashi *et al.*, 1994; Takano *et al.*, 1994).

The first success in an AC colour panel was obtained at Fujitsu with the 'surface discharge' configuration in the three-electrode and reflection-type structure (Shinoda *et al.*, 1981; Yoshikawa *et al.*, 1992), and this design is being used in their present colour product (Figure 11.11).

The parallel multi-layered transparent display electrodes (30 kHz sustain voltage) are formed on the front glass plate, and the phosphors on the rear plate are viewed from the same side as they receive the UV irradiation from the discharge (hence the name 'reflection type'). The auxiliary electrodes are opaque and serve to reduce the resistance. The phosphors are nearly the same as those used in the NHK panel. The gas is Ne–Xe, and the gap is 100 μm. The commercial Fujitsu 21 inch panel is available with 260 000 colours and is video-compatible. The expected lifetime is about 10 000 hours. This product is the only one being shipped to date, and it was widely publicised in the autumn of 1994 by an order for over 1000 panels from the New York Stock Exchange.

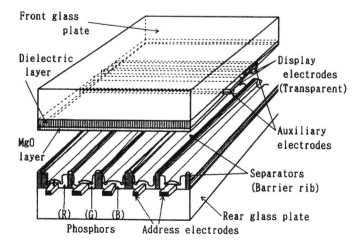

Figure 11.11   Panel structure and example image on a 21-inch diagonal full colour Fujitsu AC-PDP panel (Yoshikawa *et al.*, 1992; courtesy Society for Information Display). The highest picture resolution for colour PDPs is reported by Photonics Imaging, with a 30-inch XGA panel (Table 11.1). The structure is dual substrate with two electrodes. The efficacy was not explicitly given, and is estimated at 0.4 lm/W. The intrinsic contrast ratio is 100:1 (Friedman, 1993a)

Plasmaco, known as a supplier of monochrome AC panels (up to 21-inch 1280×1024), demonstrated a 21-inch eight colour 640×480 panel in 1994, and 3×6 bit colour has been announced for 1995 (Table 11.1). This company purchased the IBM plasma panel production plant in 1987.

The 'opposed discharge' structure is also used by Thomson Tubes Electroniques (TTE). The 13-inch VGA colour panel described by Baret *et al.* (1993) has the highest spatial resolution of any PDP with a colour pixel pitch of 0.4 mm. The phosphors are situated in an unbombarded region to ensure good luminous maintenance. The company has announced larger panels with a new triad structure, and an increased resolution ($0.3 \times$

Table 11.1 Summary of the colour plasma panel prototypes reported between 1993 and 1995. The highest performance features are outlined. The Fujitsu panel entered production in 1993. Among the 40-inch and larger panels, only that from NHK was announced before 1995

Company	Technology (*)	Diagonal (in.)	Number of cells	Pixel cells (mm)	Bits per colour	White area luminance (cd/m²)
Fujitsu	AC TSD	21 VGA	480x (3x640)	0.66x (3x0.22)	6	150-180
	AC TSD	42 TV 16/9	480x (3x852)	1.08x (3x0.30)	8	300
Matsushita	DC PM	26 TV	(2x256)x (2x448)	(2x0.65)x (2x0.65)	8	100
Mitsubishi	AC TSD	40	480x (3x640)	1.3x (3x0.42)	6	200
NEC	AC TSD	40	480x (3x840)	1.05x (3x0.35)	8	200
NHK	DC PM	40 TV 16/9	(2x400)x (2x672)	(2x0.65)x (2x0.65)	8	93
Panasonic	DC PM	40 TV 16/9	(2x400)x (2x672)	(2x0.65)x (2x0.65)	8	150
Photonics Technology	AC OD	30 XGA	768x (3x1024)	0.59x (3x0.20)	6	68-100
	AC OD	21 EWS	1024x (3x1280)	0.33x (3x0.11)	8	-
Pioneer	AC TSD	40 VGA	480x (3x640)	1.3x (3x0.42)	8	350 (1.2 lm/W)
Plasmaco	AC TSD	21 VGA	480x (3x640)	0.66x (3x0.22)	8	150
Thomson	AC OD	19 XGA	768x (3x1024)	0.38x (3x0.125)	3	50
	AC OD	22 TV	512x (3x480)	0.65x (3x0.31)	8	200-400

*Technology: AC TSD: AC three-electrode surface discharge (favourable for high resolution)
DC PM: DC pulse memory
AC OD: AC opposed discharge (favourable for highest resolution).

(3×0.13) mm) is under study. The efficacy is 0.55 lm/W, which reduces to 0.3 lm/W at the highest resolution. For TV applications, TTE has demonstrated a 22 inch $512 \times$ (3×480) panel with a pitch of $0.65 \times (3 \times 0.31)$ mm, and 3×8-bit colour (Table 11.1). The luminance decreases from 400 to 200 cd/m^2 with the proportion of on-cells (this effect is customary on CRTs). Interestingly, the contrast under illumination is specified at 28:1 under 200 lux (Deschamps, 1994).

The main panel features are summarised in Table 11.1.

11.3.2 Plasma display performance, present and future

Plasma panels have few defects, and combining the best (non-conflicting) attributes of all existing prototypes would probably yield an excellent panel for many applications. PDPs have strong supporters (Friedman, 1993b), and the funding for development is at a high level in three continents.

The useful viewing angle is naturally wide, as is typical of all emissive panels.

The 'trademark' orange colour of monochrome panels is acceptable, if not optimal. The power efficacy is at most 0.3 lm/W. However, since light is emitted in a medium with a refractive index of 1, and the scattering is small, the decrease of the contrast under the effect of ambient light is not very marked. Many suppliers offer monochrome dot matrix panels. The largest are of the AC type: Photonics Systems is offering a panel with 2048×2048 pixels and 1.5 m diagonal.

In colour panels, light is created in a powdered material, contrary to the EL situation. Since there is no light-piping effect, the coupling efficiency of light out of the display is better, but the effect of ambient light on the contrast is more severe. Back-scattering does not preserve light polarisation entirely, and circular polariser antireflection filters are not very effective. Often only intrinsic contrast values are given, and the potential user should perform independent measurements at realistic levels of ambient illumination. The goal of a 25:1 contrast under 200 lux can be attained, e.g. with 250 cd/m^2 and a diffuse reflectance of at most 15 percent which is difficult to achieve.

The colour gamut is not cited as a problem in any of the recent papers. Provided that the barriers between the sub-pixels are adequate, a performance equivalent to that of the CRT can be expected.

The overall efficacy of PDPs is higher than that obtained by the direct emission of the neon orange light, and the best figure for a commercial product is presently 0.7 lm/W (Shinoda et al., 1993). Few laboratory values are significantly higher, although sample cells have reached 0.8 lm/W. It was estimated that the physical limit, as demonstrated by fluorescent lamps, is more than 50 times higher (Weber, 1994). However, although research is being actively pursued, no breakthrough is predicted, and it is considered that it will be difficult to exceed 1 lm/W in the structure of a pixel cell. The limits of luminance and efficacy may be as high as 800 cd/m^2 and 1.5 lm/W, with optimisation of the known techniques, according to a model calculation (Uchiike et al., 1992).

The value of 1 lm/W has not been exceeded by many flat panels, except backlit TNLCDs, but this value is often cited as the threshold for portable and consumer applications. The required luminance level for computer displays and workstations is about 100–160 cd/m^2 (depending on ambient and contrast), and many colour prototypes meet this goal. For TV applications, we would set the goal at 250 cd/m^2, and only TTE panels reach that level.

In all colour panels, the memory effect is used with high frequency sustain waveforms. There is no flicker in the mid-range grey levels provided that the frame frequency is sufficiently high. The phosphors are fast enough, and the speed is perfectly adequate for video applications.

Image quality is seldom cited as an issue. However, defects which may be difficult or costly to eliminate and which are unknown to CRTs or LCDs are apparent on some prototypes. The contour noise due to random switching of the most significant bit near mid-luminance is now well understood and solutions exist. Small-range luminance heterogeneities are not tolerated as easily as the long-range luminance gradients typical of CRTs, and place difficult requirements on the fabrication tolerances.

The minimum pixel pitch is an attribute of one given technology which is not easily reduced. The smallest colour pitch for PDPs is 0.4 mm, and 0.3 mm has been announced. The latter is suitable for a 9.5-inch VGA panel. The larger pitches of many prototypes are better suited to television applications: a 1.5 m diagonal 16:9 HDTV panel would have a pitch of about 1 mm, larger than that of all recent prototypes except the NHK 40-inch panel.

Lifetime is no longer identified as a very critical issue, although solutions for DC pulse memory panels may not yet be entirely optimised.

Achieving large sizes meets no fundamental limitations with memory panels; 1.5 m monochrome panels have existed for several years.

Many authors claim that colour PDPs are easy to mass produce. However, the fabrication of very large panels faces several practical problems. The tolerance of printing techniques is adequate for display widths of about 1000 pixels, but has resolution limits towards small pixel dimensions. Glass compaction (shrinking) during the high temperature operations is also cited as a problem which may require the use of a new glass. DC panels can be made without vacuum deposition operations, whereas AC panels need at least one for the magnesia films, although it has recently been shown that this layer can also be printed.

Almost all PDP fabrication techniques are well established; however, they will have to be pushed beyond their present limits, in particular to fabricate the barrier rib structures. Screen printing machines are being developed in Japan for very large dimensions (2 × 55 inch diagonal, Noritake). These toolings for large HDTV panels will require heavy investments.

Driver and interconnection cost will heavily influence panel cost. Chips are being developed for AC and DC panels. They are fast ($\approx$100 ns) and have high impedance and high voltage capability. They will be connected to the electrode arrays by chip on glass techniques.

Can PDPs reach fabrication costs low enough for the HDTV consumer market? Except for LCD projectors, which are not really flat panels, there is no practical alternative, so that it can be assumed that the decisions to invest in production facilities will eventually be taken. The market of 19 inch and greater computer and multimedia monitors may be the first step, as shown by Fujitsu.

The present market size of PDPs is 1.1 percent of all displays in value. The production of monochrome panels has declined with the success of LCDs in portable computer applications. The commercial effects of the development of colour panels may become significant in the computer market after 1996, and subsequently in the consumer market (Stanford Resources Inc., 1994a,b).

11.4 FIELD EMISSION DISPLAYS (FEDs)

11.4.1 Operating principles, specificity and panel construction

Field emission displays (FEDs) are vacuum electron devices in which the light source is the cathodoluminescence of phosphors. These devices are fast, the slowest element being the phosphor decay. FEDs are not similar to CRTs in that there is no deflection of the electrons, but rather local modulation of the electron current by the application of suitable potentials on anodes and grids with respect to the cathodes. FEDs differ from the well-known vacuum fluorescent displays, their closest relatives, because electrons are not emitted by a cathode consisting of an oxide-coated heated filament, but by field emission from a cold cathode. This feature has given its name to the devices.

The most obvious and substantial advantage is that the heating power, which amounts to about half of the total power in VFDs, is saved. The next advantage is that the cathode can be used as an addressing electrode. In VFDs, the electron source cannot be modulated because the thermal response is slow, and would be difficult to pattern. Instead, the electron emission is permanent, is made as uniform as possible, and is modulated by a grid. In FEDs, the field-emission cathode can be patterned with a sufficient resolution, and matrix addressing can be performed with the cathodes used as one of the sets of XY electrodes. Whereas traditional VFDs must use triode structures, the diode configuration can also be used in FEDs. The main challenge is to demonstrate the feasibility of an efficient, reliable, and easily manufacturable FE cathode.

Field emission is governed to a good approximation in most cases by the Fowler–Nordheim equation, on which this discussion will be based:

$$J = A \left(\frac{E^2}{\Phi} \right) \exp \left(-B \frac{\Phi^{1.5}}{E} \right) \qquad 11.2$$

where J is the local current density, A and B are constants, E is the local electric field and Φ the cathode material work function. E is strongly enhanced in the vicinity of sharp edges or tips, where it can be many orders of magnitude larger than the average device field.

The work function is the most important parameter governing the current density. The work function of metals is ≈ 4.5 eV. It is known that the $\langle 111 \rangle$ surface of diamond has a negative electron affinity (Himpsel et al., 1979), and in 'amorphous diamond' coatings (which actually are nano-crystalline), effective work functions as low as 0.2–0.3 eV have been observed, resulting in high current densities (Kumar et al., 1994). Other possibilities exist to obtain low work functions (Curtin, 1991).

The most widely explored method to obtain useful currents at moderate macroscopic fields is to use the field enhancement induced by tips, and many fabrication techniques have been explored. The fabrication of silicon microtips using the wet etching properties of $\langle 100 \rangle$ n-doped silicon has been extensively studied (Marcus et al., 1990; Jiang & White,

1993). Silicon can be coated with a metal or a thin oxide to improve the work function or its maintenance in a less-than-perfect sealed vacuum. Many different geometries and material combinations have also been envisaged (Curtin, 1991; Busta *et al.*, 1994). Of course, the density of microtips must be sufficient to obtain a useful average current density in a display device (>1 mA/cm^2 in practice).

A quite extensive study of the application of 'Spindt cathodes' (Spindt *et al.*, 1976) to displays was performed at LETI (Meyer, 1990, 1993), and the name MFD (Microtips Fluorescent Displays) was coined. This group has developed a fabrication process for molybdenum microtip cathodes on glass. This process also provides a gate electrode with a 1.4 μm self-aligned hole around each cathode tip (Figure 11.12). Matrix addressing of a panel containing such an electron-emitting structure can be performed using cathode and gate electrodes as column and row arrays, respectively.

The gate to cathode threshold voltage is about 40 V, and the current obtained from one single tip is in the 0.11 μA range at a gate potential of 80–100 V. This current is subject to random fluctuations with time, and large differences exist between tips (Baptist, 1994). In the LETI panel, excellent uniformity is achieved by using a meshed conductive cathode covered by a resistive layer (simply shown as 'cathode' in Figure 11.12), and by having more than 1000 microtips (grouped in several tens of mesh cells) in each pixel. The tip centres in a mesh cell are typically on a 5×5 μm grid. The cathode structure therefore ensures both the current control of the tips and a pixel access resistance low enough for a good multiplexability of the device (Meyer, 1993).

The divergence of the electron microbeams must not have any detrimental effect on colour purity, contrast or resolution. This question can be addressed either by maintaining the gap at a value smaller than the pixel pitch ('proximity focusing') or by using a focus grid, which complicates the fabrication process (Kesling & Hunt, 1993; Palevsky, 1994). In the first case, the cathode to anode gap is limited at about 200 μm for a 300 μm pixel pitch. As we shall see, the switched anode design in colour displays then has great

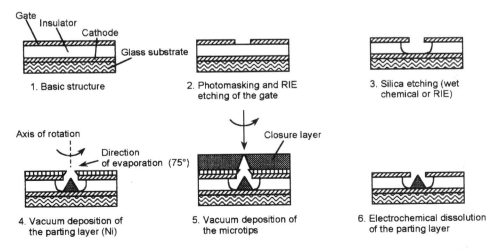

Figure 11.12   The metal microtips fabrication process used at LETI (after Baptist, 1994; courtesy Club Visu)

advantages. When using a focusing grid, the gap can be made wider and the anode voltage can be increased to the 10 kV range, yielding a very high phosphor efficacy and luminance.

Simpler and possibly cheaper structures can be fabricated using a diode configuration instead of a triode. The diamond cathode advocated by the SIDT-MCC alliance is not easily gated, so this group has proposed a diode structure (Kumar *et al.* 1994). The anode voltage must then be modulated at the row frequency for multiplexed addressing. Although the high non-linearity of the cathode emission allows the use of moderate column modulation voltages, heavy requirements are put on the row drivers (high selection voltage) and the cathode uniformity.

In proximity focusing devices, the cell gap is small and building large panels requires a spacer technique: glass spheres are used at LETI. This small gap also limits the anode voltage to less than about 500 V.

Traditional CRT phosphors working in the 20–30 kV range are insulating, and the charges are removed in part by the secondary electron emission and in part by the Al back coating. The electron penetration depth is sufficient to allow the use of this Al metallisation on the back surface of the phosphor, which also improves coupling efficiency of light out of the display. For the same reason, CRT phosphors are relatively insensitive to surface contamination. On the other hand, VFD phosphors working in the 12–50 V range must have a higher conductivity. The cleanliness of their surface is critical, since the electrons penetrate only a fraction of a nanometre. Among the latter, it was known that only ZnO:Zn has high efficiency and good maintenance.

In FEDs, below about 200 V, the situation is similar to that of 'front luminous' VFDs, i.e., with the electrons hitting the phosphors on the far side from the observer. The whitish emission of ZnO:Zn is not satisfactory for full colour, and efficient red and blue phosphors are needed. Near 200 V and above, a larger range of phosphors is available. The results obtained by Lévy at 200 V anode voltage in monochrome displays with the sulphides $Zn_xCd_{1-x}S$:Ag,Cl for red and green and with ZnS:Ag,Cl for blue yield an estimated white efficacy of 2 lm/W for full-colour displays (Lévy & Meyer, 1991). The specifications announced for the PixTech colour panel correspond to that same figure (Isnard, 1994).

The lifetime of high-voltage cathode-luminescent phosphors is often measured in C/cm^2, the total charge density received when the luminance has decreased to half of its initial value ('coulombic ageing'). For low-voltage phosphors, an average current density about 100 times higher than in CRTs must be used to obtain the same luminance, and this induced the fear of a short life. Fortunately, it was found that the ageing kinetics are entirely different here due to both the low voltage and the different deposition process. Encouraging results have been obtained at 400 V with green-emitting ZnS:Cu,Al by Meyer (1993). Intense efforts are being made by several groups (see, e.g., Toki *et al.*, 1992; Jacobsen *et al.*, 1995), which may lead to selecting new phosphor families which are more stable than the sulphides. The maintenance of panels depends on the phosphor material and on the whole fabrication process. As mentioned above, extreme cleanliness is essential for the fabrication of both phosphors and microtip cathodes.

MFD colour panels can be designed with three column (cathode) electrodes per pixel, and an unpatterned ITO anode electrode. Relatively high-resistivity RGB phosphor stripes face each column electrode triad (Figure 11.13(a)).

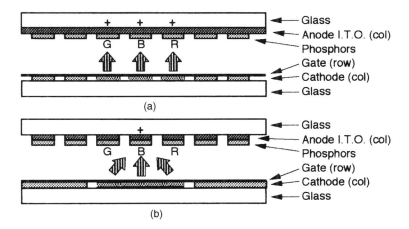

Figure 11.13   The two solutions for full colour MFD displays with a gated cathode:
(a) unswitched anode, in which the three colours are excited simultaneously; (b) switched anode,
in which the colours are excited in successive sub-frames. The blue sub-frame is being written
(Isnard, 1994; courtesy Club Visu and PixTech)

Another solution, presently favoured at PixTech, is the 'switched anode' design. The pixels have one single column electrode, but the anode is patterned in stripes (Figure 11.13(b)). The three colours are excited in successive subframes by switching the anode potential of each colour in turn.

The many advantages and few drawbacks of the switched anode mode have been summarised by Lévy and Meyer (1991). Fewer drivers (one-third as many) are required. However the capacitive current in each column is increased nine-fold (cathode area ×3, addressing speed tripled). No registration of front and back glass plates is required, contrary to the unswitched anode mode. The decisive advantage seems to be the excellent intrinsic colour purity, due to the fact that only one set of anode columns is at a positive potential at any given time. A small percentage of the electrons may hit one anode strip of the same colour on one side or the other of the one facing the pixel cathode in the selected row, slightly affecting the 'proximity contrast' or the effective pixel size, but this effect is said to be negligible in practice (Meyer, 1995).

The processing of the anode plate is more complex. The anode switching is performed at the sub-frame rate, and requires only three high-voltage switches. It is debatable whether colour break-up due to frame sequencing will be found to be a problem or not, since only a small proportion of users seem to detect its presence (Arend *et al.*, 1994).

11.4.2   Performance of FEDs, present and future

The most advanced colour MFD demonstrations to date were shown by LETI-Pixel at Eurodisplay 93, and by PixTech at SID 1994. The demonstrator was a 6-inch diagonal $(256 \times 3) \times 256$ panel with analogue column drivers, a luminance of 60 cd/m^2, and an intrinsic contrast of 60:1. The power efficacy was 1 lm/W, for the panel alone (drivers excluded). The colour purity, luminance uniformity and image quality in subdued light were judged to be good by observers. The contrast under illumination was not specified but the diffuse scattering by the phosphors is quite apparent.

The industrial development has been taken over by PixTech with several partners (Motorola Futaba, Raytheon). The first demonstrator is a CIF 6-inch $(352 \times 3) \times 288$ display. Grey levels are obtained by a combination of cathode voltage amplitude modulation (2 bits) and pulse width modulation (4 bits). The other features will be as follows: luminance 100 cd/m^2; intrinsic contrast 40/1; lifetime $>10\,000$ hours; power 1.7 W (drivers excluded). The drivers are CMOS/DMOS, and have an output of 40 V for the cathodes (column modulation) and 90 V for the gates (row selection). Engineering samples of several products in the 4–9.5-inch range have been announced for 1995, and are impatiently awaited by observers.

Other laboratories and alliances in the USA and Japan have made demonstrators with a diagonal from 1 inch to 4 inches. The funding is now at a high level in the USA, where field emitters were invented and first studied (at SRI and the NRL), and several industrial ventures have been set up (Candescent Corp., Coloray Display Corp., FED Corp., SI Diamond Technology, Inc. and MCC Corp., Micron Display Technology, Crystallume Corp.). In Japan, reports have been made by Sony, Mitsubishi, Fujitsu, Futaba and Matsushita.

There does not seem to be any severe technical difficulty in marketing MFD products, although no commercial product exists to date.

The contrast under illumination may be the most questionable point at this time. The efficacy should be increased so that filtering could bring an improvement. A black matrix is also possible. Questions raised about panel lifetime will receive independent answers when samples are made available.

An important challenge for FEDs may be that of cost. The best results are obtained with techniques which require sophisticated equipment, and are rather similar to those of the microelectronics industry (vacuum deposition, lithography). The natural competitors are ACTFEL panels and AMLCDs.

The scalability to large dimensions appears good. However, PDPs are more advanced and will probably be cheaper to produce at diagonals larger than 15 inches.

For that reason, is can be expected that FEDs will find their first applications where the combination of high resolution and full colour video rendition, good efficacy, wide angle, ruggedness, low weight, small footprint and very large temperature range, will not find any match, in sizes up to 13 inches. The military market would be a reasonable first target. The industrial market, then the automotive and portable computer markets could come next if prices could be made equivalent to that of AMLCDs.

11.5 CONCLUSION

The author's ambition has been to help the reader find his own way in appreciating the merits and the shortcomings of those emissive technologies which are thought of today as being the most promising. We have also drawn attention to the specific characteristics of each technology, and to the similarities between them. Sometimes, authors of past reviews may not have presented an entirely unbiased view of technologies which were not their own, and these comparative comments may be useful.

We have given only few personal appreciations and judgments, so as to avoid any undue prejudice. Also, every effort has been made to state clearly whether the performance data quoted concern a laboratory prototype, a sample or a commercial product.

Political and financial decisions cannot change the laws of physics, but they can exert a profound influence on the rate of progress in understanding phenomena and in developing technologies. In that sense, the future of emissive technologies, none of which has any fatal defect, will depend as much on the funding of research and the industrial investments that will soon be decided as on their intrinsic merits. Europe hosts the leader or one of the leaders in all three of these technologies, and there is extensive concern here, as well as in other Western economies, that the level of investment needed fully to commercialise these technologies may not be forthcoming.

ACKNOWLEDGEMENTS

The author acknowledges the very useful input from many colleagues, and wishes to mention Paul Benalloul from the University of Paris, Jacques Deschamps from Thomson Tubes Electroniques, Robert Meyer from LETI, Yoshimichi Takano from Nippon Hoso Kyokai and Robert Isnard from PixTech. Special thanks are due to Runar Törnqvist of Planar International, for his very extensive and stimulating comments and the communication of unpublished information.

REFERENCES

In the following list, the references to *Society for Information Display International Symposium Digest of Technical Papers* are abridged as *SID Digest*. The publisher is the Society for Information Display, Santa Ana, California, USA.

Akutsu, H. and Nakagawa, Y. (1982), A DC plasma display panel with unit with higher reliability and simpler construction, *Proc. SID*, **23**, 61–65.

Amano, Y., Yoshida, K. and Shionoya, T. (1982), High resolution DC plasma display panel, *SID Digest*, **XIII**, 160–161.

Arend, L., Lubin, J., Gille, J. and Larimer, J. (1994), Colour break-up in sequentially scanned LCDs, *SID Digest*, **XXV**, 201–204.

Baptist, R. (1994), Physique et performances des cathodes émissives, *Ecrans plats émissifs: technologie et applications, Journée d'études*, 19 Octobre 1994, Grenoble. Club Visu, Brive, France.

Baret, G., Deschamps, J., Dutin, J., Doyeux, H., Hamon, O., Salavin, S. and Zorzan, P. (1993), A 640 × 480 high-resolution colour AC plasma display, *SID Digest*, **XXIV**, 173–175.

Barrow, W.A., Coovert, R.C., Dickey, E., King, C.N., Laakso, C., Sun, S.S., Tuenge, R.T., Wentross, R. and Kane, J. (1993), A new class of blue TFEL phosphors with applications to a VGA full-colour display, *SID Digest*, **XXIV**, 761–764.

Barrow, W., Coovert, R., Dickey, E., Flegal, F., Fullman, M., King, C. and Laakso, C. (1994), A high contrast, full colour, 320.256 line TFEL display, *Conf. Record of the 1994 International Display Research Conference*, 448–451.

Benoit, J., Benalloul, P., Barthou, C., Casette, S. and Soret, J.-C. (1990), De-excitation process and efficiency in ALE ZnS: Mn thin film electroluminescent devices, *Phys. Stat. Sol. (a)*, **122**, 427.

Benoit, J., Barthou, C. and Benalloul, P. (1993), Excitation efficiency in thin-film electroluminescent devices: probe layer measurements, *J. Appl. Phys.*, **73**, 1435–1442.

Bitzer, D.L. and Slottow, H.G. (1966), The plasma display panel–A digitally addressable display with inherent memory, *1966 Fall Joint Computer Conf., Washington, DC, AFIPS Conf. Proc.*, **29**, 541.

Blache, Y., Dutin, J., Rimaud, B., Zorzan, P. and Benoit, E. (1993), Electronics for colour AC plasma panel TV display, *Eurodisplay 93 Conf. Proc.*, Club Visu, Brive, France, and Society for Information Display, Santa Ana, CA, 281–284.

Bringuier, E. (1994), Tentative anatomy of ZnS-type electroluminescence, *J. Appl. Phys.*, **75**, 4291–4312.

Budin, J.-P. (1992), Photométrie appliquée aux écrans, *Séminaries de formation générale en visualisation, VISU 92*, Club Visu, Brive, France (in French).

Budin, J.-P. (1993), The basics of flat panel displays addressing, *Seminar Lecture Notes, Eurodisplay 93*, Club Visu, Brive, France, and Society for Information Display, Santa Ana, CA.

Busta, H.H., Pogemiller, J.E. and Zimmerman, B.J. (1994), A dual-gate field emitter and its integration into a flat panel display, *J. Micromech. Microeng.*, **4**, 106–109.

Chodil, G. (1976), Gas discharge displays for flat-panel, *SID Digest*, **VII**, 14–22.

Cola, R. (1977), Gas discharge panels with internal line sequencing ("Self-Scan" displays), in B. Kazam (ed.), *Advances in Image Pick-up and Display*, 3, Academic Press, New York, 83–170.

Curtin, C. (1991), The field emission display: a new flat panel technology, *Conf. Record of the 1991 Int. Display Research Conf.*, Society for Information Display, Santa Ana, CA, 12–15.

Deschamps, J.L. (1994), Recent developments and results in colour-plasma-display technology, *SID Digest*, **XXV**, 315–317.

Flegal, R. and King, C. (1988), Differential ageing effects in ACTFEL displays, *SID Digest*, **XIX**, 177–180.

Friedman, P.S. (1993a), High-definition 30-in.-diagonal full-colour ac PDP video monitor", *SID Digest*, **XXIV**, 176–178.

Friedman, P.S. (1993b), Self-emissive colour flat panel displays: plasma vs. EL vs. field emitter, *Seminar Lecture Notes, Eurodisplay 93*, Club Visu, Brive, France, and Society for Information Display, Santa Ana, CA.

Friedman, P.S., Soper, T.J., Holloway, T.D., Reuter, C.D. and Wedding, K.W. Sr. (1987), 1.5-m-diagonal AC gas discharge display, *Proc. SID*, **28**, 365–369.

Haaranen, J., Harju, T., Heikkinen, P., Härkönen, G., Leppänen, J., Lindholm, T., Maula, J., Määttänen, J., Pakkala, A., Soininen, E., Sonninen, M., Törnqvistr R. and Vijanen, J. (1995), 512(×3)×256 RGB multicolour TFEL display based on colour by white, *SID Digest*, **XXVI**, in press.

Himpsel, F.J. *et al.* (1979), Quantum photoyield of diamond (111)–a stable negative affinity emitter, *Phys. Rev. B*, **20**, 624.

Isnard, R. (1994), Field emission displays, *Ecrans plats émissifs: technologie et applications, Journée d'études*, 19 Octobre 1994, Grenoble. Club Visu, Brive, France.

Jacobsen, S.M., Yang, S., Zhang, F.-L., Summers, C.J., Bojkov, C., Kumar, N., Fredin, L. and Schmidt, H. (1995), Improved performance of low-voltage phosphors for field-emission displays, *SID Digest*, **XXVI**, 631–633.

Jiang, J.C. and White, R.C. (1993), Electron emission from silicon tips coated with a very thin Cr film, *SID Digest*, **XXIV**, 596–598.

Kanagu, S., Kanazawa, Y., Shinoda, T., Yoshikawa, K. and Nanto, T. (1992), A 31-in.-diagonal full-colour surface-discharge ac plasma display panel, *SID Digest*, **XXIII**, 713–716.

Kesling, W.D. and Hunt, C.E. (1993), Field emission display resolution, *SID Digest*, **XXIV**, 599–602.

Khormaei, R., Thayer, S., Ping, K., King, C., Dolny, G., Ipri, A., Hsueh, F.L., Stewart, R., Keyser, T., Becker, G., Kagey, D. and Spitzer, M. (1994), High-resolution active-matrix electroluminescent display, *SID Digest*, **XXV**, 137–139.

King, C. (1994), Electroluminescent displays, *Seminar Lecture Notes*, M-9/1-38, Society for Information Display, Santa Ana, CA.

King, C.N., Coovert, R.E. and Barrow, W.A. (1987), Full Colour 320 × 240 TFEL display panel, *Eurodisplay 87, Conf. Record of the 1987 Int. Display Research Conf.*, 14–17.

Kumar, N., Schmidt, H.K., Clark, M.H., Ross, A., Lin, B., Fredin, L., Baker, B., Patterson, D., Brookover, W., Xie, C., Hilbert, C., Fink, R.L., Potter, C.N., Krishnan, A. and Eichman, D. (1994), Development of nano-crystalline diamond-based field-emission displays, *SID Digest*, **XXV**, 43–46.

Leppänen, M., Härkönen, G., Pakkala, A., Soininen, E. and Törnqvist, R. (1993), Broad band double layer phosphor for an inverted filtered RGB electroluminescent display, *Eurodisplay 93 Conf. Proc.*, Club Visu, Brive, France, and Society for Information Display, Santa Ana, CA, 229–232.

Lévy, F. and Meyer, R. (1991), Phosphors for full-colour microtips fluorescent displays, *Conf. Record of the 1991 Int. Display Research Conf.*, Society for Information Display, Santa Ana, CA, 20–23.

Mach, R. and Müller, G.O. (1982), Physical concepts of high-field, thin-film electroluminescent devices, *Phys. Stat. Sol.* (a), **69**, 11–66.

Marcus, R., *et al.* (1990), Formation of silicon tips with <1 nm radius, *Appl. Phys. Lett.*, **56**, 236.

Mauch, R.H., Velthaus, K.O., Troppenz, U., Hüttl, B. and Herrmann, R. (1995), Improved SrS:Ce, Cl TFEL device by ZnS Co-doping, *SID Digest*, **XXVI**, in press.

Meyer, R. (1990), 6-in. diagonal microtips fluorescent display for TV applications, *Eurodisplay 90 Conf. Proc.*, Society for Information Display, Santa Ana, CA, 374.

Meyer, R. (1993), Colour field emission display: state of the art and prospects, *Eurodisplay 93 Conf. Proc.*, Club Visu, Brive, France, and Society for Information Display, Santa Ana, CA, 189–192.

Meyer, R. (1995), private communication.

Miller, D.E., Ogle, J., Cola, R.A., Caras, B. and Maloney, T. (1981), An improved performance self-scan I panel design, *Proc. SID*, **22**, 159–163.

Müller, G.O. and Mach, R. (1994), The efficiency of TFEL devices: revisited, *SID Digest*, **XXV**, 554–557.

Murakami, H. *et al.* (1991), A 33-in.-diagonal HDTV display using gas discharge pulse memory technology, *SID Digest*, **XXII**, 713–716.

Nguyen, N.T., Nomura, T., Igarashi, K. and Mikoshiba, S. (1993), Monte Carlo simulation of luminance saturation and optical crosstalk due to trapping of Xe VUV photons in colour PDPs, *SID Digest*, **XXIV**, 169–172.

Nighan, W.L. (1981), Basic kinetic processes in neon gas discharge displays, *Proc. SID*, **22**, 199–204.

Ohnishi, H. and Mohri, M. (1992), Efficient green-emitting TFEL with sputtered ZnS:TbOF, *SID Digest*, **XXIII**, 363–366.

Ono, Y.A. (1993), Electroluminescent displays, *Seminar Lecture Notes*, F-1/1-30, Society for Information Display, Santa Ana, CA.

Sakai, T., Motoyama, Y. and Ushirozawa, M. (1993), A method for extending the life of a DC gas-discharge colour memory panel, *Eurodisplay 93 Conf. Proc.*, Club Visu, Brive, France, and Society for Information Display, Santa Ana, CA, 289–292.

Schmachtenberg, R., Jenness, T., Ziuchkovski, M. and Flegal, T. (1989), A large area 1024 × 864 line ACTFEL display, *SID Digest*, **XX**, 58–61.

Sherr, S. (1993), *Electronic Displays*, 2nd Edition, John Wiley & Sons, New York.

Shinoda, T., Miyashita, Y., Sugimoto, Y. and Yoshikawa, K. (1981), Characteristics of surface-discharge colour ac-plasma display panels, *SID Digest*, **XII**, 164–165.

Shinoda, T., Wakitani, M., Nanto, T., Yoshikawa, K., Ohtsuka, A., Hirose, T. and (1993), Development of technologies for large-area colour ac-plasma displays, *SID Digest*, **XXIV**, 161–164.

Shoji, K., Ohba, T., Kishishita, H. and Uede, H. (1989), Bi-directional push — pull symmetric driving method of thin film electroluminescent display, in S. Shionoya and H. Kobayashi (eds)., *Electroluminescence*, Springer Proceedings in Physics, **38**, Springer-Verlag, Berlin, 324–330.

Solomon, I. and Thioulouse, P. (1989), Electroluminescent memory display using amorphous silicon–carbon alloys, *Optoelectronics–Devices and Technologies*, **4**, 295–316.

Spindt C.A., *et al.* (1976), Physical properties of thin film field emission cathodes with molybdenum cones, *J. Appl. Phys.*, **47**, 5248.

Stanford Resources, Inc. (1994a), Market update, *Electronic Display World*, **14**(7), 3; **14**(3), 9.

Stanford Resources, Inc. (1994b), Market spotlight, *Electronic Display World*, **14**(8), 2–8.

Suntola, T., Antson, J., Pakkala, A. and Lindfors, S. (1980), Atomic layer epitaxy for producing EL thin films, *SID Digest*, **XI**, 108–111.

Takahashi, K., Sasaoka, Y., Atsumi, T., Isobe, N., Sakamoto, F., Kosugi, N., Wani, K., Murakami, H. and Sakai, T. (1994), A long life 26-in. dc pulse-memory colour PDP with resistor-in-cell structure, *SID Digest*, **XXV**, 715–718.

Takano, Y., Murakami, H., Sakai, T., Kuriyama, T. and Takahashi, K. (1994), A 40-in. DC-PDP with new pulse-memory drive scheme, *SID Digest*, **XXV**, 731–734.

Tamura, T., Sato, T., Hongo, T., Okumura, Y., Ohuchi, T., Morioka, K., Nakamura, Y. and Watanabe, K. (1994), Development of colour dc plasma display driver ICs for pulse-memory driving method, *SID Digest*, **XXV**, 723–726.

Tanaka, S., Mikami, Y., Nishiura, J., Ohshio, S., Yoshiyama, H., and Kobayashi, H. (1987), A full-colour thin-film electroluminescent device with two stacked Subtrates and colour filters, *SID Digest*, **XVIII**, 234–237.

Tannas, L.E. (1985), Electroluminescent displays, in L.E. Tannas (ed.), *Flat Panels and CRTs*, Van Nostrand Reinhold, New York, 237–288.

Thioulouse, P. (1987), Etude d'un dispositif d'affichage électroluminescent à mémoire, *Thesis*, Ecole Nationale Supérieure des Télécommunications, Paris.

Toki, T., Kataoka, H. and Itoh, S. (1992), $ZnGa_2O_4$:Mn green cathodoluminescent phosphor for VFDs, *Japan Display '92 Proc.*, 421–423.

Törnqvist, R. (1990), Aspects on thin film electroluminescence, *Acta Polytechnica Scandinavica*, 5th International Workshop on Electroluminescence, Appl. Phys. Series No. 170, 1–4.

Uchiike, H., Fukuda, M., Manabe, A., Hirata, T. and Komaki, T. (1992), Reflective phosphor deposition on the barrier electrode structure of an ac plasma display results in high brightness and high luminous efficiency, *SID Digest*, **XXIII**, 543–546.

Vecht, A. (1990), AC and DC electroluminescent displays, *Seminar Lecture Notes*, F-2/1-48, Society for Information Display, Santa Ana, CA.

Velthaus, K.-O., Troppenz, U., Hüttl, B., Herrmann, R. and Mauch, R.H. (1994), High luminance ZnS:Mn/SrS:Ce TFEL devices, *Conf. Record of the 1994 Int. Display Research Conf.*, Society for Information Display, Santa Ana, CA., 346–349.

Weber, L.F. (1985), Plasma displays, in L.E. Tannas (ed.), *Flat Panels and CRTs*, Van Nostrand Reinhold, New York, 332–414.

Weber, L.F. (1994), Plasma displays, *Seminar Lecture Notes*, M-8/1-36, Society for Information Display, Santa Ana, CA.

Weber L.F. and Wood, M.B. (1987), Energy recovery sustain circuit for the AC plasma display, *SID Digest*, **XVIII**, 92–95.

Yamamoto, T., Kuriyama, T., Seki, M., Katoh, T., Murakami, H., Shimada, K. and Ishiga, H. (1993), A 40-in.-diagonal HDTV plasma display, *SID Digest*, **XXIV**, 165–168.

Yoshikawa, K., Kanazawa, Y., Wakitani, M., Shinoda, T. and Ohtsuka, A. (1992), A full colour AC plasma display with 256 grey scale, *Japan Display '92 Proc.*, Society for Information Display, Santa Ana, CA, 605–608.

The CRT as the display
of the future

Seyno Sluyterman

12.1 INTRODUCTION

At present several trends seem to be driving the development of CRT displays. First the use of computer terminals has taken such a dominant position in today's workplace that shortcomings in the ergonomics of the display are no longer acceptable. Second, we anticipate a merger of typical computer applications and TV-like applications, indicated by 'multimedia', a term as yet undefined but which will certainly include Full Motion Video. This means that the display must be capable of representing more than a static printed page. A third trend is Power Management, where the power dissipation of the display is controlled when it is in use and in standby mode. A fourth trend is the development of new flat and thin display technologies like LCD and Plasma.

These trends raise the question of the future role of the CRT. First, we shall give a short overview of the construction of the CRT. Then we shall discuss the most significant components in more detail, and explain how they contribute to the ergonomics of the display, how they relate to the application of the display and what trends exist. As we shall see later, this leads to some interesting conclusions.

Display Systems, Edited by L.W. MacDonald and A.C. Lowe. © 1997 John Wiley & Sons Ltd.

12.2   CRT BASICS

A CRT consists of an evacuated glass envelope containing a number of components. At the back of the tube we find the electron gun for the generation of a single electron beam for monochrome CRTs or a triple gun for the generation of three electron beams for a colour CRT. These electron beams pass through the magnetic fields generated by a deflection yoke. The deflection is arranged in such a way that the electron spots scan the screen line by line, similar to the way in which lines are organised in a book. For a colour CRT, special care has to be taken in the design of the yoke to ensure that all three beams are deflected towards the same point on the screen (Figure 12.1). The three beams then pass through holes in the shadowmask in such a way that each beam strikes only its own phosphor (red, green or blue) as shown in Figure 12.2. On striking the phosphor, the energy of the electrons is converted into light which then passes through the screen and is seen by the user. We next discuss the components in more detail.

12.3   THE ELECTRON GUN

The primary function of the electron gun is to generate an electron beam and accelerate it by means of a high anode potential. The power of an electron beam is the product of the anode voltage and the beam current. The great advantage of a CRT is that, since it is an analogue device, the beam current can be varied continuously. This is important for making realistic images and is not always easy to achieve in other display types. With the introduction of multimedia, this property is important not only for television but also for computer displays with moving images.

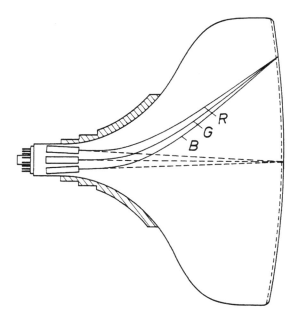

Figure 12.1   The elementary CRT

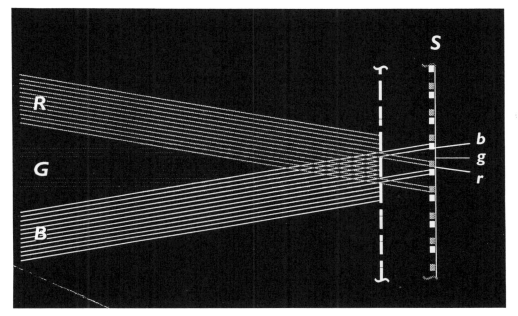

Figure 12.2 The shadowmask function

For the purposes of storage or manipulation on a computer, images are often digitised. When errors are made in the quantisation and reproduction of an image, or when an insufficient number of quantisation levels is used, contouring effects occur. These are especially visible in images where a gradual change in luminance or colour is to be reproduced. An example of such effects is given in Figure 12.3.

When luminance values of the three colours are quantised, 10 bits per colour are needed to guarantee a good image under all circumstances (Weston, 1975). The CRT, however, is unique in requiring fewer bits due to the fact that we do not digitise the luminance of the CRT but the drive voltage of the gun which has a non-linear relationship with the luminance. The luminance of the CRT is proportional to the beam power P_b which is the product of the anode voltage V_a of the CRT and the beam current I_b. The value of the beam current is controlled by a drive voltage V_d of the gun, according to:

$$I_b \approx V_d^{\gamma} \qquad\qquad 12.1$$

in which γ has a value between 2.2. and 3.0. This non-linearity is most important when grey-scales have to be reproduced. However, signal sources such as broadcast TV and PhotoCD are pre-compensated or γ-corrected. For computer-generated images, γ correction can also be achieved by the colour look-up table in the graphics controller (see Chapter 17).

The result of this non-linearity of the gun is that fewer bits per pixel are needed (Weston, 1975; Devereux, 1971). For CRTs it has been found that 8 bits per colour i.e. 24 bits per picture element (pixel), are usually adequate to approach analogue image quality.

Figure 12.3   Unintended contouring effects due to insufficient quantisation

One finds that the drive requirement of 24 bits per picture element is also used as a target for plasma and LC displays, although their transfer functions are diferent from CRTs. For LCDs, which are analogue devices, these problems can be overcome. For Plasma displays, however, luminance levels are created by varying the length of the light pulse omitted by each pixel. In this case, increasing the number of bits requires a reduction of the shortest pulse time which creates additional timing problems. It is also possible to increase the number of bits per pixel by lowering the refresh rate of the display, but at the expense of motion artifacts as will be shown later. For commercially available plasma displays even 8 bits per colour has not yet been achieved, which means that the image quality of the plasma display cannot currently approach that of the CRT.

This inherent advantage of the CRT is not widely appreciated because most currently used video-cards are unable to generate 24 bits per pixel. It will become even more apparent as soon as the peak brightness of monitor displays is increased to enable a pleasing display of video images.

Another important function of the electron gun is to focus all the electrons of one beam into one small spot and then to maintain the spot size over the entire scan. To do this, the application of so-called 'fixed focus' is usually sufficient, but for more demanding applications, for example in large screen monitors, dynamic focus voltage corrections are needed. In a self-converging colour CRT (see next section) dynamic focus is always combined with dynamic astigmatism, and guns in which both actions are achieved with the same voltage variations are called DAF guns (Ashizaki *et al.*, 1988). Such dynamic focus techniques are employed whenever performance demands are such that the higher costs associated with dynamic focus are appropriate.

The smaller the details to be resolved or the size of the characters to be displayed on the screen, the smaller the spot has to be. From the point of view of ergonomics, there is a minimum satisfactory size for characters. This has been defined in an official standard: ISO 9241 Part 3 (ISO, 1992), where it is indicated that the character height should be 20 minutes of arc (or 2.9 mm at 50 cm viewing distance). This standard was not written for Chinese characters, which on the one hand are more complex than Roman characters but on the other hand can be larger as they represent complete words, so fewer characters are required to convey a given amount of information.

When the spot is small enough to display the specified minimum sized characters clearly, there is little sense in making the spots even smaller; it may even be counterproductive if this results in spots that are so small that one can see dark gaps between the scanned lines. For this reason small size CRTs with a screen diagonal less than 17″ can be used without dynamic focus. For 21″ CRTs, dynamic focus is used because in this case the spots have to be (relatively) smaller. For even larger TV tubes, however, dynamic focus is not commonly used, because of the reduced performance requirements, larger viewing distances and larger minimum size of resolvable characters (for instance Teletext characters). Currently, much effort is being directed towards increasing beam current to increase brightness whilst maintaining a sufficiently small spot.

Although visual ergonomics prescribes a minimum character size, it does not prescribe a maximum number of pixels, because there is no maximum limit to the number of pixels that can be used in describing a character. By increasing the number of pixels per character, the characters can be given a more natural shape, like the characters in a book. One is therefore free to address 2000 by 1500 pixels on a 14″ display, as long as this high density of addressable pixels is not misused to write characters less than 20 minutes of arc in height.

With the increased line density one could reduce the size of the spot and gain some benefit from this when using fine character sets. It is still, of course, necessary to avoid the occurrence of visible dark areas between the lines. This so-called 'flat-field' requirement demands a spot with a 50 percent width equal to or greater than the line distance.

Another reason for using more pixels than needed to write the smallest allowable characters is to prevent the occurrence of the so-called staircase effect in graphic applications: diagonal lines that look like a staircase. The attraction of a CRT is that it is possible to eliminate this staircase effect, or to give characters a more natural shape, by increasing the number of addressable pixels without reducing the spot size. A similar reasoning holds for the pitch of the shadowmask, to which we will come later.

12.4 THE YOKE

The function of the yoke is to deflect the beams horizontally and vertically. In TV systems, the so-called 'interlaced scan' is used. In interlaced systems, each complete image, called a frame, is divided into two incomplete images, called fields. Each field writes only half the number of lines (every other line) needed for a complete picture. The first field writes only the odd lines, the second field only the even lines, so it takes two fields for one complete picture or frame. As a result, the field frequency of an interlaced system is always twice the frame frequency. For instance for European TV systems, the field frequency is 50 Hz while the frame frequency is 25 Hz. In the USA, the field frequency is 60 Hz and the frame frequency 30 Hz. The reason why interlacing is applied in TV systems is that it reduces the video bandwidth needed for transmissions by a factor of 2, and, for broadcasting, adequate bandwidth has always been a problem.

In computer applications, where the images are generated locally, bandwidth limitations are of a different nature. Here they are a compromise between technical difficulties, costs and picture performance. Interlaced systems are not used with monitors because they can produce oscillating vertical luminance transitions when those transitions are too sharp. Called line jitter, these oscillations are particularly noticeable in a monitor because of the close viewing distance. Monitors use non-interlaced scan, also called 'progressive scan'. With non-interlaced scan all the lines of one image (or frame) are written directly one after the other. In such scan systems, there is no distinction between frames and fields; each field contains all the lines. For monitor applications the field frequency is usually between 60 and 85 Hz.

The value of the field frequency, which can be chosen freely in monitor applications as the signals are generated locally, is determined by the desire to avoid perceived flicker. The exact frequency at which flicker can be observed varies somewhat between individuals, but depends upon the brightness and size of the screen, the lighting conditions of the room, the age of the viewer and whether or not the image is formed in the periphery of the visual field. Some TVs have 100 Hz field frequency, which might be slightly higher than needed from the visual point of view, but is a consequence of the need to derive the images from a 50 Hz source.

One could argue that the phenomenon of field flicker is a disadvantage of a CRT compared with other display types in which the image is kept on screen until it is updated. However the truth is that the CRT actually has an advantage here when it comes to displaying moving images (Fernando & Parker, 1990). The basis of this advantage is that when the eye follows a moving object, it is better for the images to appear only in pulses rather than remaining on screen between updates. Otherwise the movement of the eye causes smearing, as is illustrated in Figure 12.4. The smearing of an image always seems to lag behind the motion.

Smearing is related to the displacement s and time t by:

$$\text{smearing} = \frac{\mathrm{d}s}{\mathrm{d}t} \times \tau_{\text{hold}} \qquad\qquad 12.2$$

where τ_{hold} is the time that the image remains on screen after it is formed.

The shorter the hold time, the less smearing occurs. In a CRT the phosphor decay time is around half a millisecond which, in turn, requires the field frequency to be high enough that this is not perceived as flicker.

This fundamental smearing effect is worse in LCD displays, in which the hold time is almost equal to the refresh time. The problem can be reduced in LCDs by increasing the refresh frequency above the rate required to avoid flicker using new video information each frame. See Chapter 18 for further discussion.

For plasma displays, where the 'hold time' is determined by the required luminance, an additional problem occurs. On the one hand, the hold time is never as long as in

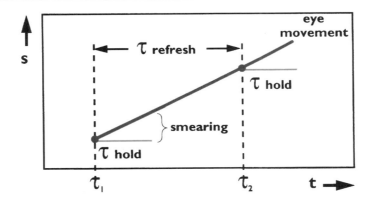

Figure 12.4 Image smearing at movement caused by long image hold times

an LCD and one might expect less smearing for a Plasma display than for an LCD. However, because the hold time varies with luminance, it is usually different for the three colours of one pixel. The result is that the smearing effects can be quite different for the three colours, and this leads to apparent convergence errors in moving images. This convergence effect is normally associated only with CRTs.

For plasma displays these problems can also be reduced by increasing the refresh rate of the display, but this will conflict with the desire to increase the number of bits per pixel (to avoid the quantisation errors) as mentioned earlier.

A very important feature of the yoke of a colour CRT is its self convergence, i.e. the property of deflecting all beams towards the same point on the screen. A deflection yoke can only provide self convergence when the three beams of the CRT are in-line, meaning that the middle one of the three beams lies between the two outer beams. This excludes delta gun configurations. At present nearly all CRTs, regardless of their shadowmask structures, have the in-line gun configuration. Most of the development effort of yokes is dedicated to improvement of convergence performance. In this there are two opposing trends. One is to improve convergence by means of electronic corrections (Jamar *et al.*, 1992); the other is to avoid electronic corrections for price reasons by further refinements of the yoke (Penninga, 1989) and the yoke matching process.

Another important feature of the yoke is its ability to handle high scanning frequencies. For a given field frequency the line frequency follows directly from the number of lines that are scanned within one field (including the lines scanned during the flyback time of the field-deflection and which are blanked). Higher line densities result in higher scanning frequencies. Furthermore, the number of lines increases with the height of the display. So in monitors the line scanning frequency usually increases with the size of the display.

Factors that set a maximum limit to the applicable scanning frequency are the temperature rise of the yoke (and ultimately its maximum operating temperature) and a set of cost/performance issues involving the cost and reliability of the video system, the horizontal deflection and high-voltage circuits, and the cost and availability of video RAM. Increasing the maximum applicable scanning frequencies is one of the present trends in CRT displays.

A slightly conflicting trend is the desire to reduce the power involved in deflection. At this point it is worth noting that although energy is stored in the magnetic deflection fields, magnetic deflection itself does not require any power. It is a challenge to the CRT and circuit designer to improve the deflection efficiency to enable deflection energy to be moved back and forth between the circuit and the yoke at the line scan frequencies with minimum losses. Naturally, reducing the energy involved in deflection (by reducing the anode voltage of the tube or by reducing the diameter of the yoke) helps, but only if this reduction is not achieved at the expense of the deflection efficiency of the yoke.

The last aspect of the yoke we shall discuss is that the fields it produces extend over a distance greater than the yoke geometry. This means that the fields (though attenuated by the third power of distance) will also be present outside the monitor. Although there is no evidence that these fields are harmful to the human body, it has become a marketing issue to reduce these fields to the level of MPR (MPR, 1990). By choosing the proper yoke concept (i.e. not using toroidal field coils) and additional attention during the design process, it is possible to keep the external fields below the specified MPR values. If needed, additional attenuation of the external fields can be obtained by using compensation coils connected in series with the line or field coils (Sluyterman, 1988).

12.5 THE SHADOWMASK

Regardless of their commercial names, more than 99.9% of all colour CRTs used in homes and offices use shadow masks. The colour selection is based on the ability of the shadow mask to transmit electrons from a particular gun only to specific areas of the screen. Only those areas are coated with the particular phosphor required for that gun. The remainder of the screen is in shadow from the mask. Electrons from a particular gun directed towards these areas are adsorbed by the shadow mask and are unable to excite the phosphors associated with either of the other two electron guns. To first order, shadow mask CRTs differ only in the structure of the shadow masks, and of the associated phosphor patterns. Basically, there are two different structures in use: a hexagonal and a line structure (see Figs 12.5 and 12.6). Hexagonal-structure masks (also called dot masks) have more inherent rigidity, whilst the line-structure masks must derive their rigidity either from bridges between the lines (this configuration is also known as a slot mask) or by placing the mask under mechanical tension in the vertical direction, combined with one or more horizontal damping wires (the Trinitron mask).

Line structures have the advantage over hexagonal structures that there is no colour selection in the vertical direction, resulting in easier manufacturability. This is why for TV applications, line-structure masks are nowadays nearly always used. Advantages of the hexagonal-structure are that for the same specified pitch value, the structure is less visible and that the equivalent horizontal pitch is only $\sqrt{3}/2$ times the specified pitch value. We therefore find for monitors, where the viewing distance is much less than for TV applications, manufacturers often still choose hexagonal structures.

A specific point of attention during the design of the CRT and monitor is the possible occurrence of moiré interference effects, which are caused by an interaction between the mask structure and the image as it is scanned on the screen. Moiré can be divided into scan-moiré, caused by the scan line structure, and video-moiré caused by the video information. Scan-moiré is avoided by taking care that the vertical dimension of the

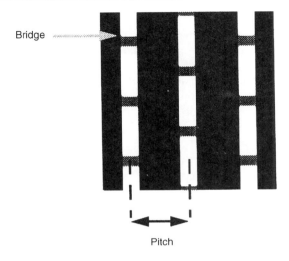

Figure 12.5   A line-structure mask

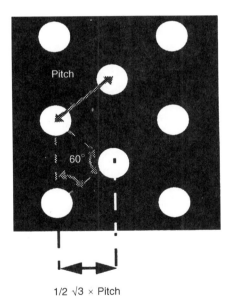

Figure 12.6   A hexagonal-structure mask

spot is large enough to satisfy the 'flat field' condition (Ramberg, 1952). Video-moiré is caused by two sets of conditions. The most frequent condition occurs when image details (a character 1 for instance) have a width equal or almost equal to the horizontal pitch of the screen. When displaying that detail, its visual clarity depends on its relative position. Because the CRT's scanning process is not correlated to the screen structure, the exact relative position of a small detail can never be predicted. The resulting video-moiré appears as a random variation in the visual clarity of small details.

There are three ways to avoid the occurrence of video moiré:

- by making the horizontal pitch of the tube smaller than the smallest detail to be displayed. This is the reason why many tube manufacturers prefer a hexagonal (= dot) mask structure;
- by increasing the minimum size to be displayed by band-limiting the video information. TV transmissions are an example of this;
- by increasing the horizontal size of the spot, which does, however, lead to some loss in perceived sharpness.

Another condition for moiré arises when we want to display a periodic structure whose spatial frequency is (or whose higher harmonics are) almost the same as that of screen structure (or its higher harmonics). An example occurs in the patterns designed to create grey levels on a binary display. Descriptions of these phenomena in CRTs are given by Barten (1969). This appearance of moiré can be avoided not only by the three methods mentioned above, but also by simply not using the critical periodic patterns. They can either be omitted because nowadays most displays allow grey scales, or be replaced by any pattern that is just different enough to avoid this moiré.

In this respect, LCD and plasma displays have the advantage that there is a one-to-one coupling between the pixels in the display and the pixels of the video card of the monitor. The CRT is, however, more flexible in its application. For example, a CRT can be used in multistandard monitors.

For getting the best resolution from a CRT display, one can address many more pixels on the CRT than there are triplets on the screen. This can be used to reduce the staircase effect as mentioned earlier (in the gun section) and illustrated in Figure 12.7. One of the reasons why increasing the number of addressable pixels reduces the staircase effect lies in the fact that the CRT is not pixellated like a flat panel display. Therefore, it is possible to write a white pixel by exciting each phosphor within a particular triplet. The beam can then be advanced by one third of the triplet pitch, deactivating e.g., the red phosphor of the first triplet and activating instead the red phosphor of the next triplet. By this means, we can display shifts of one third of the pixel pitch without having to use an anti-aliasing algorithm. An anti-aliasing algorithm achieves a similar effect by modulating the intensity of two adjacent pixels to trick the eye into seeing a single smooth intensity transition at a point within the boundary of the two pixels but at a point depending on their relative intensities. Anti-aliasing does cause a loss of sharpness and therefore has inferior visual performance to increasing the addressability of the CRT. This loss of sharpness can be understood because in the example above, two pixels are required to simulate a single pixel, so resolution is halved in one direction. Of course, this loss of sharpness will not be seen if the angle of subtense of the pixels exceeds the resolution limit of the eye, and anti-aliasing techniques work best (and are designed for) this regime. However, at present most applications are based on pixel densities which can still be resolved by the eye.

Another reason why increasing the number of addressable pixels reduces the staircase effect lies in the fact that we can have luminance variation within each phosphor dot of a triplet, a feature that will never exist in LCD or plasma displays. This feature has relevance when the screen structure is big enough to be resolved by the eye.

The elimination of staircase effects does not, therefore, require a further reduction of the pitch for CRTs. For CRTs it is sufficient that the pitch is small enough to display

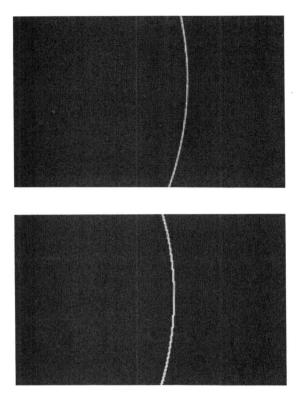

Figure 12.7 The reduction of staircase effect by increasing the number of addressable pixels far beyond the number of triplets

the smallest and most difficult character (m, for example) whilst satisfying the ergonomic requirements as laid down in ISO 9241, Part 3.

12.6 THE PHOSPHORS

The phosphor on the screen transforms the energy of the impinging electrons into light. Typical luminous efficiencies for the three colours red, green and blue are respectively 17, 66 and 9 lumens per watt. The reason why these efficiencies differ so much is that they strongly depend upon the eye's sensitivity to the various colours. In particular for the blue phosphor, one finds that the efficiency increases dramatically when the colour coordinates are moved towards white (for instance in the CIE chromaticity diagram). Nowadays, however, it is a trend for monitor tube phosphors to have the same colour coordinates as TV tube phosphors (EBU colour points) in order to be able to give good colour reproduction of images. To comply with EBU, therefore, it is not possible to increase, the luminous efficiency of the blue phosphor by moving it towards white. For plasma displays, the right colour for blue has not yet been obtained. This should be kept in mind when comparing the luminous efficiency of various display types. Another pitfall of comparing the efficiency of display types is that sometimes they are expressed in lumens per watt and at other times they are expressed in peak-lumens per average-watt.

This is both ergonomically sound and aesthetically pleasing. Angular dependency of the luminance is, however, less important than the fact that the angular distribution does not depend upon the relative intensity of the light, (i.e. on the grey level) and therefore the perceived colour is independent of the viewing angle. In LCDs the angular distribution does depend upon the grey level. So for any three colours with differing grey levels the perceived colour depends strongly on the viewing angle, which is undesirable from an ergonomic point of view. So while the primary colours of LCDs can be made to match the EBU colour points, the actual colour points as they appear in use may deviate from that because of this viewing angle dependence luminance. Naturally techniques are being developed to improve the viewing angle performance of LCDs. These improvements might, however, come at the expense of the maximum contrast and therefore might reduce the saturation of the primary colours.

Nowadays, colour filters are integrated into the phosphors (pigmented phosphors). These filters reduce the amount of reflected light, thus making the tube look darker. This allows for an increase in the light transmission of the screen and so in a higher overall tube efficiency. Investigations are currently in progress to determine whether these filters could better be replaced by separate filter layers between the phosphors and the screen glass, which could lead to a further increase in brightness. However, at this moment it is still too early to consider this as a trend.

Another property of phosphors is their decay time, typically the order of half a millisecond. In the early days of monochrome data terminals that were often based on scanning sequences derived from television, long-persistence phosphors were used to suppress field flicker or even line jitter. Such long-decay phosphors have now been abandoned because they caused smearing of the characters when scrolling texts or moving pictures. The flicker phenomenon has now been solved by increasing the scanning frequencies, and long-persistence phosphors are no longer needed. This has made the CRT even better in its capability to display moving images, a feature which will become even more important with multimedia.

12.7 THE SCREEN GLASS

Finally, the light emitted by the phosphor must be transmitted by the front screen of the CRT towards the viewer. The transmittance of the glass and its coatings is deliberately reduced to about 50%. This is done to reduce the effect of diffuse reflectance which is caused by ambient light being scattered and reflected by the phosphor particles and from the phosphor/screen glass and the phosphor/rear metallic coating interfaces. The diffuse reflected intensity adds to both the dark and the bright states of the CRT and reduces the contrast ratio of the displayed image. Although the brightness of the CRT is roughly halved by this technique, the reflected ambient light must pass twice through the glass and is reduced in itensity by a factor of four. The reader is invited to keep this fact of a 50% transmissive front screen in mind when comparing the light outputs of various display types.

A current trend is to replace the light absorbing screen glass with a light absorbing coating. Such coatings produce more uniform transmission because their thickness is more easily controlled than that of the glass screen. Such coatings can also incorporate filter to remove light of wavelengths that are not present in the emission from the phosphors. This further reduces the effects of diffuse reflections. A further trend is to incorporate a conductive component into the coating, thus eliminating variation of the potential of the screen and avoiding potential variations due to switching the terminal on and off. Limits on electric fields arising from these potential variations are for instance set by TCO (TCO, 1991), and are again regarded as marketing requirements. An undisputed benefit of this conductive component is that the screen collects less dust.

The main purpose of screen coating is, however, to reduce specular reflection. Like diffuse reflections, specular reflections also reduce the contrast ratio of the display, but the main problem associated with them is that unless they are almost completely eliminated, they are often so distracting to the user that they make the display difficult to use. Unlike diffuse reflections, specular reflections can be avoided by careful positioning of the display and the user, but this is not a satisfactory solution to the problem. Specular reflections can be reduced by reducing the sharpness of the reflected image, which is done by some form of screen roughening. In fact this treatment, called an anti-glare treatment, transforms the specular reflection into an additional diffuse reflection. Disadvantages of anti-glare treatments are loss of sharpness and increase of diffuse reflections. Another, better, approach is to reduce the amplitude of the specular reflections by applying $1/4\lambda$ layers. (See also the discussions in Section 20.4.1.). Whilst these are more efficient, they are prone to marking by e.g., fingerprints, which detracts from their appearance. Often the best results are obtained by using a combination of both types of treatment.

Figure 12.8   The effect of a screen coating, on the right-hand side, on specular reflections

Summarising, nowadays coatings can have the following functions simultaneously: light absorption, charge-conduction, anti-glare and anti-reflection. An example of what can be obtained by an optical coating (van den Eeden *et al.*, 1994) is given in Figure 12.8.

Another trend is the move towards flatter screens. In contrast to what is sometimes advertised, the flatness of the screen does not reduce the amount of reflection from the screen. When the screen is flatter, the angle of incoming light contributing to the reflections is indeed reduced; however, the amplitude of the remaining contributors is increased. Also contrary to some advertising, flatter screens do not necessarily have less distorted reflections. Flatter screens are nevertheless a current trend dictated by fashion, which can be seen, for instance, in the gradual replacement of 14″ monitor tubes by flatter 15″ monitor tubes.

12.8 CONCLUSION

In environments that do not particularly require thin and lightweight displays, CRTs will continue to play an important role in the future and not only because of their high performance–cost ratio. Other specific features of the CRT that will become more important in the future and cannot be taken for granted in other display types are the unlimited number of colour and luminance shades, EBU colour coordinates, large viewing angle and excellent representation of moving images, all present simultaneously in one and the same device. These properties are important from the ergonomic point of view and they are especially important in the era of multimedia. Trends in the design of CRTs include suppression of the reflected light, increase in brightness, increase in scanning frequencies, flatter screens and power reduction.

REFERENCES

Ashizaki, S. *et al.* (1988), A 43″ direct view colour CRT, *Proc. SID*, **29**(1), 47–51.
Barten, P.G.J. (1969), Theorie des Moire bei Shattenmasken-Farbbildrohren, *Valvo Berichte*, **15**, 79–108.
Devereusc, V.G. (1971), Pulse code modulation of video signals: subjective study of coding parameters, *BBC Research Department Report*, **1971/40**.
Fernando, G.M.X. and Parker, D.W. (1990), Display processing for HD-MAC, *Colloquium Proc. Fourth Int. Coll. on Advanced Television Systems*, 3B.6.1–3B.6.15.
ISO (1992), ISO/DIS 9241-3 Visual display terminals used for office tasks–Ergonomic requirements, Part 3: Visual Display Requirements.
Jamar, J.H.T., Still, L. and van der Voort, A. (1992), A 21-in. flat square colour CRT for CAD/CAM applications, *SID Digest of Technical Papers*, **XXIII**, 898–900.
MPR 1990:8 (1-12-1990), Test methods for visual display units–Visual ergonomics and emission characteristics, National Board for Measurement and Testing, Sweden.
Penninga, J. (1993), Computer simulation of double-mussel deflection-coil winding, *Journal SID*, **1**(1), 11–14.
Ramberg, E.G. (1952), Elimination of moiré effects in tri-colour kinescopes, *Proc. IRE*, **40**(8), 916.
Sluyterman, A.A.S. (1988), The radiating fields of magnetic deflection systems and their compensation, *Proc. SID*, **29**(3), 207–211.
TCO (1991), Screen facts — an information summary of the TCO screen checker, 15–19.
van den Eeden, A.L.G., Compen, J.M.A. and Nuijs, A.M. (1994), Improved-reflection improved-sharpness (IRIS) coatings for CRTs by an all-sol-gel processing, *SID Digest of Technical Papers*, **XXV**, 819–821.
Weston, M. (1975), Pulse code modulation of video signals: visibility of level quantising effects in processing channels, BBC Research Department, BBC RD 1975/31.

13

Projection systems

Patrick Candry

13.1 LIGHT VALVE PROJECTOR SYSTEM DESIGN

The system design of a light valve projector depends very much on the light valve technology. Nevertheless, the basic system concepts have many similarities. The main elements are the light source and illumination system, colour separator and combiner, light valves, projection optics, electronic subsystems and the screen.

A light valve colour projection display can be based on a single-light-valve or on a three-light-valve system by using transmissive or reflective light valves. There are basically two single-light-valve approaches: colour field sequential light valve and RGB sub-pixels light valve. In combination with an overhead transparency projector (OHP), laptop size (e.g. 10.4″ or 8.4″ diagonal) transmissive micro colour filter passive matrix or active matrix LCD panels form the simplest LC projection system.

Self-contained portable single panel front projectors based on laptop size LCD panels can be realised with incandescent or metal-halide light sources.

Much better chromaticity and efficiency are possible with three-light-valve systems. Such projection systems based on transmissive or reflective light valves are available.

Different optical layouts for the colour separation and recombination are possible (Shikama *et al.*, 1993; van den Brandt *et al.*, 1991; Candry *et al.*, 1993). Depending on the light valve technology, reflective systems use polarising beam splitters or TIR (total internal reflection) prisms.

Display Systems, Edited by L.W. MacDonald and A.C. Lowe. © 1997 John Wiley & Sons Ltd.

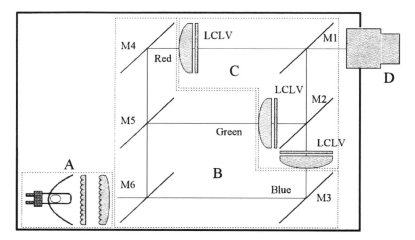

Figure 13.1   Optical path, showing four units (indicated by dashed lines). A: Illumination system; B: colour separator; C: light valves and dichroic recombiners; D: projection lens

A typical layout for transmissive light valves is shown in Figure 13.1. The opto-mechanical system consists of four units attached on a common frame. The first unit is the illumination system, the second unit is the colour separator, the third unit consists of the LC light modulators and the dichroic combiners. The fourth unit is the projection lens. The intensities of the red, green and blue light beams are each modulated by transmissive 'monochrome' TN-LC active matrix light valves. These red, green and blue light beams are produced by separating the white light beam by mirror M5 and mirror M6. Mirrors M3 and M4 are folding mirrors. M1 and M2 are the dichroic recombiners (Wierer, 1992, 1994; Clarke, 1988a). One projection lens is used to form the image of the three light valves on the screen.

In general the light source is a short arc metal-halide or a xenon short arc lamp which is placed in a parabolic or ellipsoidal cold light reflector. The illumination system must collect as much light as possible from the light source and illuminate the light valve uniformly. Several types of illumination optics are possible, e.g. Koehler-type or optical integrator. The optical path length from the light source to the light modulators must be equal for the three colours.

13.2   CRT PROJECTOR SYSTEM DESIGN

CRT-based projectors use three small (typically 5″ [7″], 5.75″ [8″], 7″ [9″] usable phosphor diagonal [tube diagonal]) monochrome red, green and blue CRTs and are in general three-lens systems (Figure 13.2). The main elements of a CRT projection system are the CRTs, the projection lenses, the electronic subsystems and the screen. The light flux and the image are generated on the phosphor layer by the impact of a small electron-spot. A real image of the phosphor layers is formed on the screen. The red, green and blue images are superimposed on the screen.

The CRTs must be driven hard in order to obtain enough luminance of the projected image (with magnification between 8 and 40). The phosphors of CRT projection tubes can

Figure 13.2 CRT projector configuration

produce linear light output over a larger current density range compared with direct-view CRTs. The high voltage for the CRTs is in general >30 kV because high beam power and good focusing of the beam are required (Gorog, 1994). Since the average value of the electron beam current is limited (by an electronic circuit), the peak value of the electron beam current strongly depends on the percentage of the phosphor layer area (picture content) excited by the electron beam. For an average value of beam current limited to 1 mA, the peak beam current can reach a value of 5 mA when a maximum of 20 percent of the area of the phosphor layer is producing light. This results in a high luminance for images with a low average picture content, e.g. video-images (Candry & Derijcke, 1994) (see Figure 13.3).

An important advantage of a CRT projection system is its adaptability to different scanning rates (horizontal scan frequency 15–130 kHz) and to different screen shapes (flat, cylindrical, parabolic, etc.) because the electromagnetic deflection system allows pre-distortion of the image on the phosphor screen. Different projection angles are also possible if the Scheimpflug condition (Kingslake, 1983) is met for the phosphor layer, the screen and the optical axis of the projection lens. Higher electron beam currents produce a larger light spot (spot size) on the phosphor layer and this results in a lower optical resolution of the image. Better optical resolution (spot performance) can be achieved with

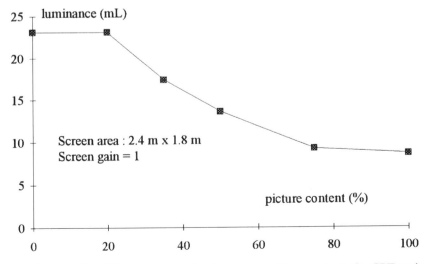

Figure 13.3 Trade-off between screen luminance and picture content of a CRT projector

larger phosphor screens and by applying static and dynamic electromagnetic focusing combined with static and dynamic astigmatism correction.

There are two main types of screens: front-screen and rear-screen. Special rear screens can be used for enhancing the contrast ratio and the brightness. These are complex optical structures and have in general a Fresnel element and a lenticular element. Colour shading is minimised by the development of special screen profiles. A screen gain between 3 and 6 is achievable by reducing the vertical viewing angle ($\pm 15°$ to $\pm 7°$) and the horizontal viewing angle ($\pm 45°$ to $\pm 30°$) where the viewing angle is defined at 50 percent luminance level. There exist single element and double element screens. The contrast ratio can be improved by applying a colour dye and by applying (vertical) black stripes on the front lenticular element. The pitch (1.5 to 0.5 mm) of these black stripes depends on the resolution of the projected image and the size of the screen. Some of the important specifications of these screens are gain, relative illumination, black stripe pitch, reflection coefficient, colour of the elements, horizontal and vertical viewing angle and colour shading.

13.3 LIGHT VALVE TECHNOLOGIES

Although many different light valve technologies for projection applications have been developed, the transmissive mode active matrix twisted nematic LC light valves is today's mainstream technology. This technology is based on the same technology as the well known active matrix twisted nematic LC technologies for direct view and camcorder applications. Because the electro-optical effect is polarisation rotation, this technology requires a polariser and an analyser. The addressing mode is electrical and requires a switching device (non-linear element) for each individual pixel in order to obtain a high contrast for a high information content light valve. This switching device can be a two-terminal device (MIM, PIN-diode, or TFD-R) or a three-terminal device (thin film transistor, TFT). Thin film transistors made in hydrogenated amorphous silicon (α-Si:H) on glass or in high temperature polysilicon (HT p-Si) on quartz are most frequently used (Wu, 1994). Each switching device technology has its advantages and drawbacks (Lüder, 1995). The two-terminal switches are easier to manufacture (no crossovers are required and the process requires fewer mask steps) but some aspects of the performance of the TFT display can be better. An overview of current technologies is given in Table 13.1.

Table 13.1 Overview of transmissive active matrix LC light-valves with different switch technologies

Technology	Manufacturer	Diagonal (inches)	No. of pixels	AR (%)	Ref.
α-Si pin diodes D²R	FPD	5.8	756×556	43	Hartman et al. (1991)
TFD-R	FPD	2.8	640×480	45	Knapp et al. (1993)
α-Si:H TFT	NEC	4.2	1280×1024	35	Takahashi et al. (1993)
HT p-Si TFT colour	Seiko Epson	1.3	$640 \times 3 \times 480$	41	Ohshima (1994)
HT p-Si TFT	Sony	1.35 (HDTV)	1068×480	40	Maekawa et al. (1994)
HT p-Si TFT	Sharp	2 (HDTV)	1280×1024	27	Yamashita et al. (1994)
HT p-Si TFT	HDTEC	3.7 (HDTV)	1440×1024	70	Matsueda et al. (1993)
HT p-Si TFT	Toshiba	3.3 (HDTV)	1840×1035	36	Kobayashi et al. (1994)
p-Si TFT PDLC	Mitsubishi	2.8	720×480	51.2	Nakanishi et al. (1994)

Thin Film Diode + Reset (TFD-R) active matrix LC light valves have a thin film diode as switching device and a four-voltage level row drive scheme (also called reset drive scheme). This switching device is a metal–semiconductor–metal sandwich which has a low photosensitivity. The purpose of the reset drive scheme is to eliminate the non-uniformities. The active plate requires only three mask steps and the TFD occupies only 1 percent of the pixel area, resulting in a large aperture ratio (Knapp *et al.*, 1993, 1994; van Mourik *et al.*, 1995). Another approach of two-terminal switches is the so-called Double Diode plus Reset (D^2R) method (Hartman *et al.*, 1991). Two α-Si pin diodes per pixel, together with a five-voltage-level row drive scheme, result in an easy to manufacture (only three mask steps) light valve with a high quality (Kuijk, 1990). In general light valves with two-terminal switches have a non-uniform transmission of the light valve due to the spread of the forward voltage of the switch. The special driving schemes for the TFD-R and the D^2R two-terminal switch technologies eliminate this non-uniformity. The result is a light valve with a good uniformity for 256 grey scales and a contrast ratio in excess of 200:1. The electron field-effect mobility of α-Si is low (0.2–1 cm^2/V s). Because the hole mobility is even lower, all α-Si thin film transistors are n-channel type (Kuijk, 1993). The common structure for the α-Si thin film transistors is the inverse-staggered structure (the gate is at the bottom). This technology requires six to eight mask steps and crossovers. A forward staggered (or top gate) structure is also possible in α-Si TFT technology (Ugai *et al.*, 1984; Arai, 1992). A top gate three-mask TFT technology for projection applications (called 3S) has been derived from the so-called 2S-TFT technology. The 3S α-Si:H TFT structure is basically a 2S TFT with an additional light shield underneath the TFT (Chouan *et al.*, 1993). High temperature (HT) (600–1000°C) p-Si thin film transistors can be fabricated on quartz substrates. High temperature p-Si TFTs have a self-aligned structure and a high field-effect mobility (>50 cm^2/V s). Integrated HT p-Si row and column drivers are possible because of this high field effect mobility. This is a very important advantage because it significantly reduces the number of interconnections, increases the reliability and reduces the module dimensions. Two drawbacks of high temperature p-Si are the high price of the quartz substrates and the incompatibility of the process with large substrates. In order to avoid light induced carrier generation in the α-Si or p-Si switches (i.e. leakage of the switch caused by the photocurrent generated by the irradiation of the light valve) a black mask is introduced avoiding direct illumination of the switch. The illumination on the light valve can reach 1 megalux after polarisation. A second function of the black mask is to avoid transmission of those areas of the light valve for which the light transmission cannot be modulated (interpixel gaps). The aperture ratio (AR) is the ratio between the area of the light valve that can transmit (and modulate) light to the total active area. Depending on the technology, number of pixels and light valve size, the aperture ratio can vary between 35 percent (Takahashi *et al.*, 1993) and 70 percent (Matsueda *et al.*, 1993).

The contrast ratio that can be obtained depends on the performance of the light valve, the polarisers and the construction of the optical system. The projection lens can accept light rays within a certain solid angle from each pixel. The contrast ratio depends on the diameter of the entrance pupil and the direction defined by the position of the pixel and the centre of the entrance pupil of the projection lens. Because, in a projection system, these angles are defined by the design of the optical system, it is possible to obtain a very high and uniform contrast ratio (e.g. 300:1) by optimising the light valve for these directions. The direction for optimum contrast is in general not perpendicular to the light valve. Active matrix TN light valves are able to produce images with more than 100 grey shades per colour. Analogue and 8-bit digital column driver ICs in combination with α-Si light valves are possible. p-Si light valves have analogue integrated column drivers. It is possible to use identical light valves for the red, green and blue light beams, because the twisted nematic effect is relatively insensitive to the wavelength of the light in the visible spectrum. This light valve technology is also relatively insensitive to temperature gradients and can operate over a large temperature range (10°C to 70°C) without very special precautions. The overall transmission of an active matrix light valve ($T_{\text{light valve}}$) (including the polariser and analyser) depends on the aperture ratio ($AR_{\text{light valve}}$) of the light valve, the transmission and reflection characteristics for polarised and non-polarised light (T_{pol} and T_{ana}) of the sheet polarisers, and the reflection of the glass–air interfaces ($R_{\text{air–glass}}$):

$$T_{\text{light valve}} = T_{\text{pol}} \cdot T_{\text{ana}} \cdot \left(1 - R_{\text{air–glass}}\right)^2 \cdot AR_{\text{light valve}} \qquad 13.1$$

The overall transmission, $T_{\text{light valve}}$, is only $\approx$10.5 percent for an active matrix light valve with an aperture ratio of 35 percent. In general, commercially available active matrix LC light valves have a 4:3 aspect ratio, VGA resolution or higher and in-line or delta pixel arrangement. High resolution active matrix light valve examples are the 4.2 inch diagonal α-Si TFT light valve with 1280×1024 pixels (Takahashi *et al.*, 1993) and the 3.3 inch HD-TV format HT p-Si TFT light valve with 1840×1035 pixels (Kobayashi *et al.*, 1994).

In a projection system the effective aperture ratio of the light valve can be increased by a planar structure of micro lenses (Hamada *et al.*, 1992). A colour LC projector with a planar micro lens array on a single monochrome TFT light valve in combination with non-parallel stacked dichroic mirrors has also been developed (Hamada *et al.*, 1994).

Many research activities are focused on the development of novel smaller transmissive and reflective light valve technologies with high transmittance. Silicon-on-quartz (SOQ) (Sarma *et al.*, 1994), device transferred single crystal silicon (Salerno *et al.*, 1992; Salerno, 1994) and low temperature (recrystallised) polysilicon (Ohshima *et al.*, 1993) are three technologies under development for high resolution transmissive light valves with the possibility of integrated row and column drivers.

Much attention is also being paid to reflective light valves because a higher aperture ratio can be achieved with this type of light valve (the addressing structure is hidden under the mirror elements). Examples of reflective light valves are the CRT addressed (photo-activated) liquid crystal light valve with perpendicular mode nematic LC (Sterling *et al.*, 1990), and the active matrix liquid crystal light valve operating in the hybrid aligned nematic mode (Glück *et al.*, 1992).

A reflective type of non-liquid-crystal light valve is the digital micro mirror device (DMD) which is based on the emerging micro-mechanical technology. High resolution DMD light valves of 0.7 inch diagonal with 768×576 pixels and 1.6 inch diagonal with 2048×1152 pixels have been demonstrated (Younse, 1993; Sampsell, 1994).

Reflective and transmissive light valves can also be based on polymer dispersed liquid crystal technology, referred to as PDLC, LCPC (Liquid Crystal Polymer Composite) or NCAP (Nematic Curvilinear Aligned Phase). These active matrix light scattering light valves have the following basic advantages: no alignment layer, high transmission because they do not need polarisers, and easy processability. The achievable contrast ratio of projectors based on PDLC light valves is rather low and depends on the scattering characteristics of the light valve, the illumination optics and the projection optics (Jones *et al.*, 1991; Tomita, 1993; Bouteiller *et al.*, 1993; Nakanishi *et al.*, 1994).

Twisted nematic LC light valves require a polariser and an analyser for modulation of the light intensity. The polariser and the analyser are crossed (i.e. orthogonal transmission axes) when the transmissive light valve is used in the normally white mode and is usually a dichroic sheet polariser. Reflective perpendicular mode nematic LC (homeotropic nematic-type) light valves use polarising beam splitters (e.g. MacNeille type). This type of polariser does not absorb the light which is rejected. The performance of the polarisers is a major determinant in determining the contrast ratio of the projected image.

Sheet polarisers are made of stretched polymeric plastic films in which one of the two orthogonal polarisations is subject to strong absorption while the other polarisation is not. The advantages of these sheet polarisers are large apertures, high extinction ratio, large acceptance angle, and simplicity of mounting. Because the polarisation of light is based on absorption, these polarisers cannot be used for very high power densities. We can distinguish two types of sheet polarisers: iodine type and dichroic dye type. The iodine type has a high extinction ratio and low durability, while the dye type has a higher durability and lower extinction ratio. In most cases the sheet polarisers have an acrylic adhesive layer and a protective plastic layer.

The transmission of a pair of polarisers (polariser and analyser) is given by the law of Malus (Jenkins & White, 1957):

$$T_{\text{pair}} = t_{90°} + (t_{0°} - t_{90°})\cos^2\theta \qquad\qquad 13.2$$

where θ is the angle between the transmission axis of the polariser and the analyser, $t_{90°}$ is the transmittance of two crossed polarisers and is called the extinction ratio, and $t_{0°}$ is the transmittance of two parallel polarisers (see Figure 13.4). A normally white twisted nematic light valve is sandwiched between two crossed polarisers. On the assumption that the light valves act as a perfect 90° rotator in the on-state and a perfect 0° rotator in the off-state, then the extinction ratio, open transmittance and angle θ between the polariser and the analyser will determine the achievable contrast ratio. For a value of the extinction

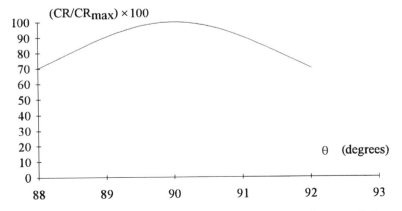

Figure 13.4 $(\text{CR}/\text{CR}_{\text{max}}) \times 100$ as a function of the angle between the transmission axis of the polariser and the analyser

ratio of 0.001 and an off-state transmittance of 0.35 the contrast ratio is 350 for perfectly 90° crossed polarisers. The contrast ratio drops to a value which is 30 percent lower than the maximum level for an error of $\pm 2°$ in the angle between the polariser and the analyser.

Another way to specify the performance of a polariser is the so-called polarising efficiency P. This specification has the following relationship with the extinction ratio and the open transmittance:

$$P = \sqrt{\frac{t_{0°} - t_{90°}}{t_{0°} + t_{90°}}}$$ 13.3

13.4   CRT TECHNOLOGY

Projection CRTs exist in sizes $5''$ [$7''$], $5.75''$ [$8''$], $7''$ [$9''$] and $12''$ [$10.5''$] usable phosphor diagonal [tube diagonal] and they have deflection angles of 70° to 90°. A tube diagonal of $12''$ is uncommon but is used in high end projectors. The deflection is electromagnetic. The CRT generates the image as well as the light flux. The electron beam focusing is either an electrostatic or a combined electrostatic–electromagnetic system. The phosphor surface is in general flat (for industrial high resolution type) or convex curved (for consumer type), and the resolution is mainly determined by the current density of the electron beam at the phosphor surface and the phosphor layer itself. The light emitted from the phosphor surface has Lambertain radiating properties which makes it difficult for efficient light collection by the projection lens.

CRT technology is a mature technology, but improvement of projection CRTs is still going on. Spot size has been reduced by some 75 percent over the last decade by improved focusing systems, electron guns and thinner, densely packed phosphor layers. Brightness has been increased by developing new phosphor mixers and smaller electron beam spot size (Yamazaki, 1993). The spot size (and MTF) increases with increasing anode current. For a $7''$ electromagnetically focused CRT the spot size increases from 0.17 mm at 0.25 mA to 0.25 mm at 6 mA (Ohmae *et al.*, 1995).

The saturation of the blue phosphor at high beam current densities is still a problem. To avoid this saturation effect the blue beam is sometimes defocused at high beam currents.

A lot of heat is generated at the phosphor layer because in a CRT only a fraction of the electrical energy is converted to light. A cooling system is therefore necessary in order to reduce thermal stress and phosphor degradation. Coupling of the faceplate to a heat sink by a liquid coolant is necessary.

Phosphor lifetime and thermal stress limit the maximum power density on the phosphor screen. The maximum power density on the phosphor screen depends on the tube construction and the cooling system. In some projectors it is limited to about 2.5–3 mW/mm^2. Because of this limitation higher light output (and resolution) is possible, for instance, by increasing the phosphor screen area, from $5''$ to $7''$ diagonals of the usable (Shirai *et al.*, 1995). The luminance level can reach a value of 35×10^3 nit (for green light) at a beam current density of 10 µA/cm^2 and an anode voltage of 34 kV. In order to improve the light collection efficiency and the colorimetry a convex curved faceplate (spherical or aspherical) with a dielectric multilayer interference filter can be used (Clarke, 1988b). Cost and limited lifetime of the interference filter ('filter-browning') remain problems to be solved.

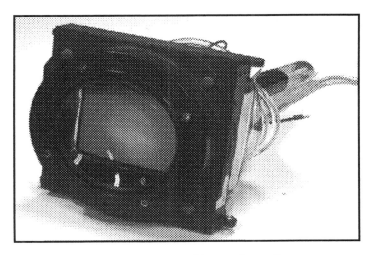

Figure 13.5 CRT with optical coupling

Phosphor life is critical for the CRT life. For home use TV under normal operating conditions a lifetime of 10 000 hours with a luminance maintenance of 70 percent is possible because the average beam current is moderate. A faster degradation of the luminous output occurs in data graphic applications because the average current is generally higher. The cathode emission life characteristics for impregnated cathodes are better than for oxide cathodes.

The chromaticity of the projected image depends on the spectral characteristics of the light produced by the red, green and blue CRTs. The spectral characteristics can get used by using colour filters on the projection lens or in the liquid for liquid-cooled tubes. New phosphor mixtures are also resulting in a better colour gamut.

Small-area contrast is reduced by light reflected from the faceplate–air transition (halation) in the air-coupled projection lens. This can be reduced by an index-matched liquid coupling between the CRT and the projection lens. This is often used for rear screen projectors, and the liquid coupling is also useful in cooling the faceplate. Because of the oblique incidence on the screen the raster is electronically predistorted on the phosphor screen in order to obtain a rectangular picture on the viewing screen. Figure 13.5 shows a CRT with optical coupling.

13.5 LIGHT SOURCE AND ILLUMINATION SYSTEM FOR LIGHT VALVE PROJECTORS

The function of the illumination system is to transfer energy from the light source to the entrance pupil of the projection lens and to illuminate the light valve uniformly. Special attention to the matching between the illumination optics and the projection optics is necessary (Stroomer, 1993; Rykowski *et al.*, 1995). The efficiency of this energy transfer depends on the characteristics of the light source, the illumination optics, and the polarising system. We can express this efficiency, $\eta_{\text{light flux}}$, as the ratio of the lumen output of the projector, Φ_{output}, to the total light flux generated by the light source, $\Phi_{light\ source}$. For commercially available LC projectors the efficiency, $\eta_{light\ flux}$, has a value between 1 percent and 3.5 percent.

$$\eta_{light\ flux} = \frac{\Phi_{output}}{\Phi_{light\ source}} \qquad\qquad 13.4$$

The efficacy η, of the projection system is the ratio of the lumen output, Φ_{output}, to the lamp power, P_{lamp}.

$$\eta = \frac{\Phi_{output}}{P_{lamp}} \qquad (lm/W) \qquad\qquad 13.5$$

In order to obtain a high projection system efficiency xenon or metal-halide arc lamps are used. The efficacy, the spectral power density, the useful lifetime and the geometrical extent (also called the *étendue*) are important characteristics of the arc lamp. A point light source placed at the focal point of a parabolic reflector provides a collimated light beam. However, real light sources have finite dimensions. A possible model for the radiating surface of a metal-halide arc lamp is a cylinder with length L (equal to the electrode gap) and radius R. The finite dimensions of the light source will result in a deviation angle at the output aperture of a parabolic reflector. The étendue (or geometrical extent) of any optical system is defined as the product of the area A of the light beam normal to the direction of propagation and the solid angle Ω over which the beam extends. For metal-halide arc lamps corresponding with the previous model the étendue of the light source, $E_{light\ source}$, has been modelled (Nicolas *et al.*, 1993). Depending on the angular emission diagram we find:

$$E_{light\ source} = kRL \qquad (mm^2\ sr) \qquad\qquad 13.6$$

where k is a dimensionless constant which depends on the angular emission characteristics of the arc lamp and has a value between 16 and 19. The étendue is an invariant property of an optical system when no light is lost geometrically, i.e. the brightness of an image cannot be greater than the brightness of its source. This invariant property can be derived from the Helmholtz–Lagrange theorem (also called the Smith–Helmholtz invariant) (Smith, 1966). For an optical system with an input aperture A_1 and an output aperture A_2, the étendue is conserved when the following relationship is valid:

$$A_1\Omega_1 n_1 = A_2\Omega_2 n_2 \qquad\qquad 13.7$$

where n_1 is the index of refraction at the input aperture, and n_2 is the index of refraction at the output aperture. A substantial amount of light will be lost when the light passes through an optical subsystem (e.g. light valve or projection lens) with a lower étendue than the étendue of the previous subsystem. It is important to note that the invariant is two-dimensional. There exists a separate invariant in two perpendicular planes both containing the axis of the system. For a one-dimensional system and a two-dimensional rotational–symmetric system we can express the étendue conservation respectively as follows:

$$D_1 \sin\theta_1 \cdot n_1 = D_2 \sin\theta_2 \cdot n_2 \qquad\qquad 13.8$$

$$(D_1 \sin\theta_1 \cdot n_1)^2 = (D_2 \sin\theta_2 \cdot n_2)^2 \qquad\qquad 13.9$$

where D_1 and D_2 are the diameters of the input and output apertures (see Figure 13.6).

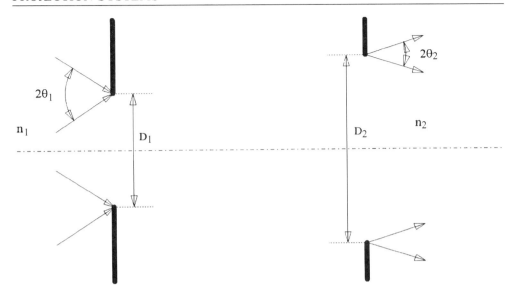

Figure 13.6   Conservation of the étendue when light is passing through an optical system
without geometrical losses

The étendue of the optical subsystem, consisting of the light valve and the projection
lens, is the area A_2 of the light valve multiplied by the solid angle Ω_2 subtended by the
entrance aperture of the projection lens:

$$E_{\text{light valve}} = A_2 \Omega_2 \qquad\qquad 13.10$$

The entrance aperture diameter of the projection lens is limited by the target value of the
contrast ratio and the cost of the projection optics. No light will be lost geometrically if
the étendue defined by the light valve and the projection lens is matched to the étendue
of the light source:

$$E_{\text{light valve}} = E_{\text{light source}} \qquad\qquad 13.11$$

In practice this means that the light sources for LCD projection systems must be a short arc
metal-halide or xenon lamp. A projection system with smaller light valves requires a light
source with a smaller radiating surface in order to obtain the étendue matching. Xenon
arc lamps have a shorter arc length compared to metal-halide lamps, but the efficacy
of metal-halide lamps ($\approx$85 lm/W) is much higher than for xenon lamps ($\approx$35 lm/W).
In the Barco Data 5000/5100 and 8000/8100 metal-halide lamps are used which have
nominal power of 575 W and 650 W respectively and an arc length of 7 mm (Candry
et al., 1993). For the Barco Data 3100 projector a 575 W/4 mm arc lamp is used. These
are single ended arc lamps with an outer glass envelope to protect the inner clear quartz
bulb from atmospheric influence (see Figure 13.7). The light produced by these lamps
has a correlated colour temperature of 5600 K and the luminous efficiency is 85 lm/W.
The lamp normally operates in a horizontal position, but it is possible to operate the lamp
in the vertical position or at any angle in between.

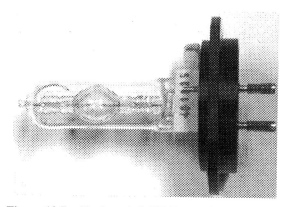

Figure 13.7   Single ended 575 W metal-halide arc lamp

Unlike the compact source xenon lamps, the fill pressure of this type of lamp, when cold, is approximately atmospheric pressure, making it safe to handle. A problem with metal-halide lamps is devitrification of the inner quartz bulb due to contact with the compounds of the filling gas. This devitrification has no influence on the luminous flux produced by the lamp, but the collection efficiency of the illumination system will decrease due to a gradual increase of the light source dimensions. The radiating surface is no longer the arc but the quartz bulb which has a much larger étendue. The result is a mismatch between $E_{\text{light source}}$ and $E_{\text{light valve}}$ resulting in substantial geometrical losses. It is possible to minimise this effect by using efficient cooling and an optimised design of the lamp and the lamp power supply. Table 13.2 compares metal-halide and xenon arc lamp specifications.

For the 575 W metal-halide lamps in the BD5000/5100 we obtained a good screen lumen maintenance during a time span of 750 hours. We specify the lifetime of the lamp as the cumulative on-time of the lamp, under switching conditions of 2 hours on and 0.5 hour off, for which the lumen output of the projector is > 90 percent of the initial lumen output (see Figure 13.8).

The arc lamp is surrounded by a parabolic reflector. A glass reflector with dielectric multilayer coating is used in order to obtain a high reflectance for visual light and to

Table 13.2   Comparison of the key specifications of a
metal-halide and a xenon arc lamp

	Metal-halide arc lamp	Xenon arc lamp
Type	BA 575 SE HR	XBO 1600 W
Source size (mm)	4.6×7	1.4×4.0
Luminous flux (lm)	49 000	60 000
Power (W)	575	1600
Efficiency (lm/W)	85	38
Lifetime (hours)	750	2000
Cost	moderate	high

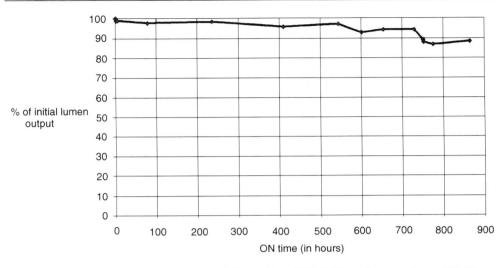

Figure 13.8   Relative lumen output of Barco Data 5100 LCD projector, using a 575 W
metal-halide lamp (duty cycle: 2 hours on, 0.5 hour off)

keep the infra-red radiation out of the light beam. An additional filter for the infra-red
and ultra-violet radiation is inserted in the beam to minimise the infra-red and ultra-
violet radiation on the light valves. In order to obtain a high collection efficiency together
with very uniform illumination, an optical integrator is used. This optical integrator also
transforms the circular cross-section of the light beam emerging from the reflector to the
rectangular shape of the light valve. For a 4:3 aspect ratio the fill factor of a beam with
circular cross section is only 61 percent, and this transformation results in a substantial
improvement of the efficiency. An improvement of the fill factor can also be obtained
by using reflectors with a rectangular 4:3 output aperture (Duwaer, 1989). The efficiency
of the LC projection system can be improved further by using a polarisation converter.
The function of the polarisation converter is to transform unpolarised light into linear
polarised light, thereby avoiding the large losses in the sheet polarisers. Several types
of polarisation converters have been proposed and can be realised by a polarising beam
splitter based on interference filters (Imai *et al.*, 1993), an oriented layer of birefringent
material (De Vaan *et al.*, 1993) or cholesteric liquid crystal filters (Schadt *et al.*, 1990).
These polarising beam splitters must have a large acceptance angle and the extinction
ratio must be high over the entire visible spectrum. The polarisation converter doubles
the étendue of the light source, therefore the efficiency will only be improved if the other
optical subsystems are matched to this larger étendue (Stroomer, 1993).

13.6   PROJECTION OPTICS FOR LIGHT VALVE AND CRT PROJECTION

Projection optics for CRT and light valve projectors are very different. The projection
lenses developed for light valve projection applications can be classified in the following

types: fixed focal length lenses, zoom lenses and anamorphic lenses. The function of the projection lens is to form the image of the light valve on a flat or curved screen. In a light valve projection system the projection lens must be matched to the characteristics of the light valve and the illumination system. These projection lenses can be realised in glass elements only or a combination of glass and plastic elements (Howe & Welham, 1979; Bohache, 1995). In order to provide space for the dichroic recombiner these projection lenses must have a long back focal length (the distance from the rear lens vertex to the focal point). The throw ratio (TR) of a projection lens is, in the case of a flat screen, the ratio of the projection distance (PD) to the screen width (SW) (see Figure 13.9):

$$TR = \frac{PD}{SW} \qquad\qquad 13.12$$

The throw ratio can be approximated by:

$$TR \approx \frac{(M + 1) \cdot EFL}{M \cdot 0.8 \cdot d} \qquad\qquad 13.13$$

where M is the image magnification, EFL is the equivalent focal length and d is the diagonal of the light valve (with 4:3 aspect ratio, SW/SH = 1.333).

A first-order (or Gaussian) model for a projection lens is shown in Figure 13.10. The active area of the light valve is the object with height h. The image of the light valve has a height h'. H and H' are the principal points. The projection lens has a limiting diameter (aperture) for the light rays; the stop which determines the cross-section of the image-forming rays is called the aperture stop. The entrance pupil is the image of this aperture stop on the object side, and the image of the aperture stop on the image side is called the exit pupil. The entrance pupil defines the diameter of the largest bundle of

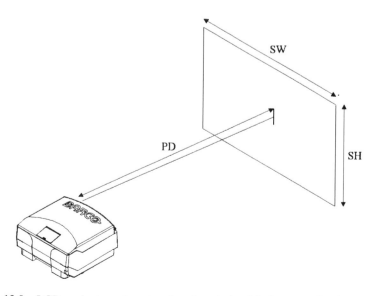

Figure 13.9   LCD projector setup showing the relationship between the throw ratio TR, projection distance PD and screen width SW

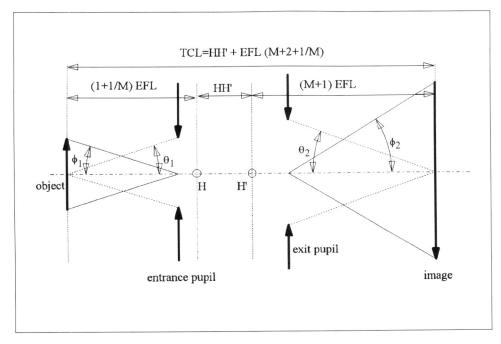

Figure 13.10   First-order (or Gaussian) model of projection lens. The magnification is defined as h'/h, H and H' are the principal points, $2\theta_1$ is the angular aperture on the object side, $2\theta_2$ is the angular aperture on the image side $2\phi_1$ is the field angle or angular field of view, $2\phi_2$ is the image field angle

parallel rays that can pass through the projection lens; the exit pupil is similarly defined by looking through the system from the other direction (Kingslake, 1978). All types of projection lenses for a specific LCD projector must have the same entrance pupil diameter and location for optimum light gathering. For objects at a great distance the f-number (generally designated as f/# and also called relative aperture) is used as a measure for the light-gathering power of a lens. This number is the ratio of the equivalent focal length to the diameter of the clear aperture. For LCD projection systems the image is usually at a large distance from the projection lens; therefore the relative aperture or f-number is defined as:

$$\text{f-number} = \frac{\text{EFL}}{\text{exit pupil diameter}} \qquad\qquad 13.14$$

Projection lenses for LCD projection generally have an f-number ≈ 4.5.

The depth of focus of a projection lens is proportional to the square of the f-number:

$$\text{depth of focus} \propto (\text{f}/\#)^2 \qquad\qquad 13.15$$

For an f/4.5 projection lens, the depth of focus is rather large, which is in practice an important feature because it allows a relatively large tolerance on the projection distance without defocusing of the image and it also allows projection on slightly curved screens without defocusing. The total conjugate length (TCL) is the distance between the light valve and its image. The total conjugate length is related to the magnification M and the equivalent focal length (EFL) of the projection lens by:

$$TCL = HH' + EFL \cdot \frac{(M+1)^2}{M}$$ 13.16

where HH' is the distance between the principal planes of the projection lens.

Real projection lenses show geometrical distortion. To be free of distortion a projection lens must have a uniform lateral magnification over its entire field. We use the radial distortion specification for the geometrical distortion specification.

The radial distortion for an arbitrary point of the image is defined as the deviation percentage of the length of paraxial image of a radial vector (Howe & Welham, 1979):

$$\text{radial distortion} = \frac{\Delta r}{r} \cdot 100$$ 13.17

Point **a** is the position of the paraxial image of a certain object point, and **b** is the position of the real image of that same object point (see Figure 13.11). The radial distortion depends on the position of the image point, and in general reaches its maximum in the corner points. Therefore the magnitude of the geometrical distortion is generally specified as a percentage of the image height at the corners of the image (the corners of the image correspond to the largest field angles). The image shows barrel distortion when the magnification decreases towards the corners (edge of the field), and pincushion distortion when the magnification increases towards the corners. The resolution of a projection lens is an important specification and is expressed in terms of the modulation transfer function (MTF). The maximum spatial frequency of the active matrix light valve is defined by

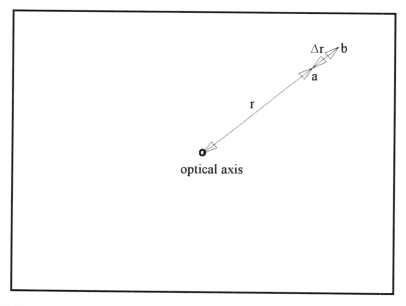

Figure 13.11   The paraxial image **a** of a point on the object; **b** is the position of the real image of the same point

the pixel pitch. The MTF value of a projection lens should be optimised at or below the maximum spatial frequency of the light modulator.

For a zoom lens the equivalent focal length is a continuous variable over a certain interval. The zoom ratio is the ratio between the maximum focal length and the minimum focal length. A zoom lens will therefore allow a continuous range of screen widths for a given projection distance, which is a very attractive feature for rental applications. These zoom lenses are complex optical subsystems (Bohache, 1995) and are therefore rather expensive. Two zoom lenses have been designed for the BD5000/5100 and BD8000/8100 LCD projectors. The focal length ranges are 170 to 350 mm (equivalent to a throw ratio range of 1.5 to 3) and 350 mm to 612 mm (equivalent to a throw ratio range of 3 to 5.2). Anamorphic projection lenses allow the light valve aspect ratio to be transformed into a different aspect ratio. We applied this solution to make the 4:3 aspect ratio light valve projector compatible with the 16:9 (or 5.333:3) aspect ratio of the high definition standard. One anamorphic projection lens has been designed for the BD8100 and BD5100 projectors because these projectors are also electronically compatible with the HDTV format. 'Ordinary' projection lenses are designed for a flat second conjugate plane. Some simulator applications require a spherical second conjugate plane. Such a projection lens with a focal length of 59 mm has been designed for the BD8100 LCD projector.

Projection lenses for CRT projectors are multi-element lenses with both glass and (aspheric) plastic lens elements which are liquid-coupled or air-coupled to the phosphor layer (Moskovich *et al.*, 1991).

For efficient light collection, projection lenses with a relative aperture of around f/1 are required. The following approximation shows that the ratio of the light flux on the screen to the light flux produced by the phosphor layer is only approximately 18 percent for f/1 projection optics, with 80 percent transmission (T). This is mainly caused by the Lambertian angular distribution of the light emitted by the phosphor layer.

$$\eta \approx \frac{m^2 T}{4 f_\#^2 (1 + m)^2} \qquad\qquad 13.18$$

where m is the magnification which varies typically between 8 and 40. Because the red, green and blue channels each have their own projection lens, colour correction can sometimes be ignored. However, high resolution applications require colour-corrected projection lenses for the green CRT because of the rather broad spectral composition of the light generated by the green phosphor (red and blue side bands).

Rear projectors require a small cabinet; this means short focal length projection lenses.

Transmission of these projection lenses varies between 89 percent for three-element lenses to 78 percent for six-element lenses.

13.7 CONCLUSION

The strength and the weakness of each projection technology depend on the type of application. The winning technology is the one that best fits the customer's requirements. A trade-off must be made between a wide variety of characteristics: portability (weight and size), performance for video and datagraphic images (contrast, brightness, chromaticity), ease of setup, compatibility with different image formats, resolution, etc. Institutional (industrial and business) applications can have very different requirements compared to consumer (home use) applications.

CRT rear projectors for consumer applications have a very good price–performance ratio. This is by far the largest (in units) projection application (US Precision Lens, 1995). For this type of application the screen diagonal is typically in the range from 40″ to 62″. The progress made in black matrix rear screens, short focal length f/1 projection lenses (<75 mm) and liquid coupled CRTs results in a small cabinet depth (~22″ for a 46″ screen), a good contrast ratio (100:1) and a high brightness for small areas of ~400 fL (for a 46″ diagonal screen) (Stupp *et al.*, 1993; Ando, 1994). Because of the limited light output and the separate screen and projector, CRT front projectors are less popular for consumer applications. These projection systems have a long lifetime (typically more than 10 000 hours).

Further incremental performance improvements are expected while the manufacturing cost continues to decrease (Ando, 1994; US Precision Lens, 1995).

CRT rear projectors for institutional use have basically the same system architecture but the screen diagonal is typically larger (67″ to 82″) and the projector can be compatible with video, data and high resolution graphics formats. These projectors have a fine pitch (black stripe) rear screen which is necessary for high resolution images. CRT front and rear projectors are popular for institutional applications. Typical applications are presentation, simulation, command and control, and entertainment. The absence of a pixel structure and the adaptability to different pixel formats and scanning frequencies are strong points for the CRT technology. This is an important advantage over all the matrix addressed technologies. The rather complex setup (convergence on the screen and geometry alignment), the trade-off between luminance and spot-size (resolution) and the trade-off between light output and picture content are drawbacks of CRT technology.

Because of the great variety of light valve technologies a comparison of the different technologies is complex.

Projectors with CRT-addressed reflective light valves combine the advantages of CRT projectors (flexibility for different pixel formats) and light valve projectors (potential for high light output). High light output (>2000 lumens) and high resolution (1280 × 1024 pixels) systems have been proposed. The absence of the matrix pixel structure is an advantage. Three-lens and single-lens systems are possible with different throw ratios. High power short arc xenon lamps (1500 to 2500 W) are used in the high light output models. The efficacy (≈1.5 lm/W) is rather low in spite of the high aperture ratio of the optically addressed light valve. These projection systems are rather bulky (as an example, the weight of a 2000 lumen projector is ~163 kg (Hughes-JVC, 1995)) and require a relative long setup time.

A wide range of products are based on three light valve transmissive active matrix TN light valves. The size of the light valve is typically ~3″ diagonal for α-Si TFT light valves and ~1.3″ diagonal for p-Si TFT light valves. Several new models based on the 1.3″ p-Si panels have recently been introduced. These video and data-graphics projectors have a single projection lens (zoom lens or fixed focal length lens) and are easy to set up. Portability is an important feature for the models based on p-Si technology. The power of the light source ranges from 120 to 250 W for low end projectors to 650 W for high end models. A high resolution 1280 × 1024 pixels projector using 4.2″ transmissive LC light valves has been developed by NEC. A light output of 2000 screen lumens with an efficacy of $\sim$3 lm/W has been achieved in the BarcoData 8100 model. Very crisp images can be produced because the pixel contrast ratio can approximate the large area contrast ratio very closely. A stripe or delta pixel arrangement is possible. The pixel multirate scan-conversion technology can adapt an arbitrary image pixel format to the pixel matrix of the light valve. Almost all commercial models so far are front projectors. Rear projection, using Fresnel lenticular sheets, is possible but moiré patterns and speckle are possible problems (Schmitz, 1995). Polarising front screens can significantly increase the contrast ratio. High resolution light valves with high aperture ratio are expected in the future.

LCD overhead projector plates and single panel projectors typically based on colour (micro colour filters) active matrix LCDs are popular tools for education and business presentations. They have the advantage of a low cost, compact design and intrinsic convergence. Portability and ease of setup are important characteristics of these projectors. These colour panels are often used in combination with incandescent light sources, which result in a poor colour performance. The light output of these projectors is rather low because of the low transmission of the LCD panels with micro colour filters and the mismatch between the spectrum of the light source and the transmission spectrum of the colour filters. Because these products are based on spin-offs of the LCD laptop displays, they closely follow the evolution to higher resolution (1024 $\times$ 768 pixels), higher transmission and more grey scales.

In order to achieve a higher transmission, micro lenses can also be applied in combination with micro colour filters. An approach with higher efficiency uses dielectric dichroic mirrors in combination with a monochrome light valve with micro lenses. The light valve needs three times the number of pixels for a given resolution.

Other single panel projectors based on colour field sequential systems have been proposed. Such a system needs a high speed light valve and a device for colour separation (e.g. rotating colour wheel, switchable colour filter or spinning prism). Prototype projectors based on a digital micro mirror device in combination with a colour wheel have been proposed (Sampsell, 1993). An inventive system based on a spinning prism in combination with a transmissive active matrix light valve has also been reported (Janssens, 1993). With the exception of the spinning prism approach, each of these colour separators can use only one third of the lamp spectrum at a time.

In order to improve the efficacy, prototype projectors based on novel reflective light valves have been developed. A first example is the projector based on three VGA NCAP/MOS 1.4″ diagonal light valves. The light valve has an aperture ratio of 91 percent and a reflection of 58 percent. The reported light output is 334 lm using a 150 W metal halide lamp (efficacy = 2.22 lm/W) (Nagae *et al.*, 1995).

A second example is a 1500 lumen colour prototype projector based on three digital micro mirror devices. This system uses a 1 kW/2 mm Xenon lamp (efficacy = 1.5 lm/W) (Sextro *et al.*, 1995). High efficiency light sources with a small geometrical extent are necessary in order to use the full potential of these small light valve technologies.

All projection light valve technologies are still struggling with the limited lifetime of the light source. For consumer applications a lifetime of the projector of 10 000 hours is required.

Several technologies for projection systems can coexist because projection systems are used in a wide variety of applications, and each application has its own specific requirements. The success of several new technologies will also depend on improvements in, e.g., light source and screen technologies.

REFERENCES

Ando, K. (1994), Projection technologies–CRT vs. LCD, *Proc. First Int. Display Workshops*, October, Hamamatsu, Japan, 7–10.

Arai, S. (1992), CRT-comparable performance makes TFT LCD's suitable for workstations, *Display Devices '92*, 20–23.

Bohache, J. (1995), Innovative zoom lenses for LCD projection, *SID'95 Digest*, 137–140.

Bouteiller, L. *et al.* (1994), Liquid crystal polymer composites for display applications, *Revue Technique Thomson–CSF*, **26**(1), 115–140.

Candry, P. and Derijcke, C. (1994), Light-valve and CRT projection systems, *SID'94 Digest*, 737–739.

Candry, P., Henry, K., Verniest, B. and Schorpion, W. (1993), A high light-output active matrix TN liquid crystal projector for video and data-graphics applications, *SID'93 Digest*, 291–294.

Chouan, Y. *et al.* (1993), 3 S TFT: an extension of 2S TFT for projection application, *13th Int. Display Research Conf.*, Strasbourg, France, 207–210.

Clarke, J.A. (1988a), Current trends in optics for projection TV, *Optical Engineering*, **27**(1), 16–22.

Clarke, J.A. (1988b), Optical aspects of the interference filter projection CRT, *SID'88 Digest*, 218–221.

De Vaan, A. *et al.* (1993), Polarisation conversion system LCD projection, *13th Int. Display Research Conf.*, Strasbourg, France, 253–256.

Duwaer, A.L. (1989), European patent application, publication number 0 322 069.

Glück, J. *et al.* (1992), Color-TV projection with fast switching reflective HAN-mode light valves, *SID'92 Digest*, 277–280.

Gorog, I. (1994), Displays for HDTV: direct-view CRT's and projection systems, *Proc. IEEE*, April, 520–536.

Hamada, H. *et al.* (1992), Brightness enhancement of an LCD projector by a planar microlens array, *SID'92 Digest*, 269–272.

Hamada, H. *et al.* (1994), A new bright single panel LC-projection system without a mosaic colour filter, *Int. Display Research Conf.*, Monterey, CA, 422–423.

Hartman, R.A. *et al.* (1991), High performance 5.8 inch display in a-Si double diode + reset technology, *SID'91 Digest*, 240–243.

Howe, R. and Welham, B. (1979), Developments in plastic optics for projection television systems, *IEEE Chicago Fall Conf. on Consumer Electronics*, 13 November 1979.

Hughes-JVC (1995), datasheet.

Imai, M. *et al.* (1993), A novel polarisation converter for high-brightness liquid crystal light valve projector, *13th Int. Display Research Conf.*, Strasbourg, France, 257–260.

Janssens, P. (1993), A novel light valve high brightness HD colour projector, *13th Int. Display Research Conf.*, Strasbourg, France, 249–251.

Jenkins, F.A. and White, H.E. (1957), *Fundamentals of Optics*, 3rd Edition, McGraw-Hill, Kogakusha, Ltd.

Jones, P. *et al.* (1991), Performance of NCAP projection display, *SPIE/SPSE Conf.*, San Jose, CA, 6–14.

Kingslake, R. (1978), *Lens Design Fundamentals*, Academic Press, New York.

Kingslake, R. (1983), *Optical System Design*, Academic Press, New York.

Knapp, A.G. *et al.* (1993), High-quality TFD-R video displays, *SID'93 Digest*, 379–382.

Knapp A.G. *et al.* (1994), Thin film diode technology for high quality AMLCD, *Int. Display Research Conf.*, Monterey, CA, 14–19.

Kobayashi, M. *et al.* (1994), High-mobility poly-Si TFTs with tungsten-polycide gate for 1.9 Mpixel HDTV LCD projector, *SID'94 Digest*, 75–78.

Kuijk, K.E. (1990), D^{2}R, a versatile diode matrix liquid crystal approach, *10th Int. Display Conf. (Eurodisplay '90)*, 174–177.

Kuijk, K.E. (1993), System aspects of a diode-matrix liquid-crystal television display, PhD thesis, Technische Universiteit Delft.

Lüder, E. (1995), Active matrix addressing of LCD's: merits and shortcomings, *Proc. 'Getting The Best from State-of-the-Art Display Systems'*, London, February 1995.

Maekawa, T. *et al.* (1994), A 1.35 inch diagonal wide aspect ratio poly-Si TFT-LCD with 513k pixels, *Int. Display Research Conf.*, Monterey, CA, 414–417.

Matsueda, Y. *et al.* (1993), HDTV poly-Si TFT-LCD light valve with 70 percent aperture ratio, *13th Int. Display Research Conf.*, Strasbourg, France, 601–604.

Moskovich, J. *et al.* (1991), CRT projection optics, *Seminar Lecture Notes, SID'91 Seminar*, M7/1–M7/41.

Nagae, Y. *et al.* (1995), Compact liquid-crystal projectors with high optical efficiency, *SID'95 Digest*, 223–226.

Nakanishi, K. *et al.* (1994), A 45-in high-brightness rear projector using a 350 k-pixel PDLC panel, *SID'94 Digest*, 749–752.

Nicolas, C., Loiseaux, B. and Huignard, J.P. (1993), Analysis of the optical components in liquid crystal projector by their geometrical extent, *13th Int. Display Research Conf.*, Strasbourg, France, 537–539.

Ohmae, H. *et al.* (1995), Wide range projection CRT's from TVs to computer graphics, *SID'95 Digest*, 63–65.

Ohshima, H. (1994), Status and prospects of poly-Si TFT technology, *Int. Display Research Conf.*, Monterey, CA, 26–29.

Ohshima, H. *et al.* (1993), Full-colour LCDs with completely integrated drivers utilising low-temperature poly-Si TFTs, *SID'93 Digest*, 387–390.

Rykowski, R. *et al.* (1995), Matching illumination system with projection optics, *IS&T/SPIE Symp. on Electronic Imaging Science and Technology 1995, Tech. Conf.*, 2407.

Salerno, J.P. (1994), Single-crystal silicon AMLCDs, *Int. Display Research Conf.*, Monterey, CA, 39–44.

Salerno, J.P. *et al.* (1992), Single-crystal silicon transmissive AMLCD, *SID'92 Digest*, 63–66.

Sampsell, J.B. (1993), An overview of the digital micromirror device (DMD) and its application to projection displays, *SID'93 Digest*, 1012–1015.

Sampsell, J.B. (1994), An overview of the performance envelope of digital-micromirror-device-based projection display systems, *SID'94 Digest*, 669–672.

Sarma, K.R. *et al.* (1994), Silicon-on-quartz (SOQ) for high-resolution liquid-crystal light valves, *SID'94 Digest*, 419–422.

Schadt, M. *et al.* (1990), New liquid crystal polarised colour projection principle, *Japanese J. Appl. Phys.*, October, 1974–1984.

Schmitz, J.H.A. (1995), Rear-projection screens, *SID'95 Digest*, 141–143.

Sextro, G. *et al.* (1995), High-definition projection system using DMD display technology, *SID'95 Digest*, 70–73.

Shikama, K. *et al.* (1993), A compact LCD rear projector using a new bent-lens optical system, *SID'93 Digest*, 295–298.

Shirai, S. *et al.* (1995), CRT projection display system, *SID'95 Digest*, 59–62.

Smith, W.J. (1966), *Modern Optical Engineering*, McGraw-Hill.

Sterling, R.D. *et al.* (1990), Video-rate liquid crystal light-valve using an amorphous silicon photo-conductor *SID'90 Digest*, 327–329.

Stroomer, M.V.C. (1993), LC projection, *13th Int. Display Research Conf.*, Strasbourg, France, 243–246.

Stupp, E.H. *et al.* (1993), LCD rear-projection television for consumer applications, *SID'93 Digest*, 283–286.

Takahashi, N. *et al.* (1993), A high-aperture-ratio pixel structure for high-density a-Si TFT liquid-crystal light valves, *SID'93 Digest*, 610–613.

Tomita, A. (1993), Status of projection-type polymer-dispersed LCD's, *SID'93 Digest*, 865–868.

Ugai, Y. *et al.* (1984), A 7.23 inch diagonal colour LCD addressed by a-Si TFT's, *SID'84 Digest*, 308–311.

US Precision Lens (1995), *Projection Television Past and Future*, 13th edition.

van den Brandt, A.H.J. *et al.* (1991), New plusfactors in an LCD-projector, *Int. Display Research Conf. 1991*, San Diego, CA, 151–154.

van Mourik, J.G.R. *et al.* (1995), Realisation of a high aperture ratio in a novel 2.8-inch diagonal VGA TFD-R projection display, *IS&T/SPIE Symp. on Electronic Imaging Science and Technology 1995, Tech. Conf.*, 2407.

Wierer, P.G. (1992, 1994), Dichroic coatings for LCLV projectors, *SID Applications Notes*, 83–86, Boston, 1992; Lichtventil-Projektoren als Herausforderung für die Dünnschichtindustrie, *Fernseh- und Kino-Technik*, **48**(4), 164–168.

Wu, I.-W. (1994), High-definition displays and technology trends in TFT-LCDs, *Journal of the SID*, **2**(1), 1–14.

Yamashita, T. *et al.* (1994), A very small poly-Si TFT-LCD for HDTV projectors, *SID'94 Digest*, 83–86.

Yamazaki, E. (1993), CRT projection, *SID'93 Digest*, 201–204.

Younse, J.M. (1993), Mirrors on a chip, *IEEE Spectrum*, November, 27–31.

PART 3

Metrology

How can display performance be evaluated?

Contents

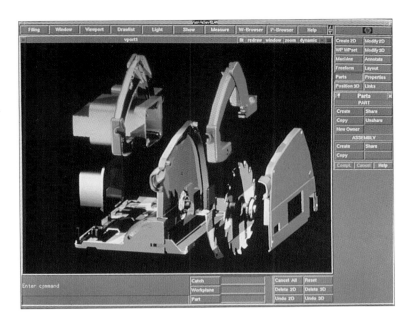

Plate 1 (Figure 1.1) CAD rendering of design for a power saw.

Plate 2 (Figure 1.2) 'Glass cockpit' of an advanced flight simulator.

Plate 3 (Figure 3.4) A colour sequence specified in device RGB coordinates (*left*) and in perceptually uniform coordinates (*right*), showing the smoother colour gradations resulting from the perceptually specified sequence.

Plate 4 (Figure 3.5) A graphical representation of the perceptual colour gamut of a CRT display, using 3D wire-frame and 2D cross-sections through the gamut. The vertical axis is the lightness axis, the radial axis colour saturation, and the hue varies angularly around the lightness axis. Cross-sections of constant (opposing) hue containing the lightness axis, and of constant lightness, are shown.

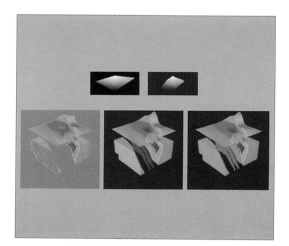

Plate 5 (Figure 3.7) *Upper left and right*: cross-sections through colour monitor and laser printer (CLC500) gamuts respectively, illustrating the substantial differences between the devices. *Lower left*: geological image with out-of-gamut points highlighted in pink. *Lower centre*: out-of-gamut points returned to the gamut along a line of constant lightness. *Lower right*: out-of-gamut points returned to the gamut along a line to the midpoint of the grey axis.

Plate 6 (Figure 3.8) The results of applying chromatic expansion on a delineated region of an image, based on a 'spectral magnifying glass' approach.

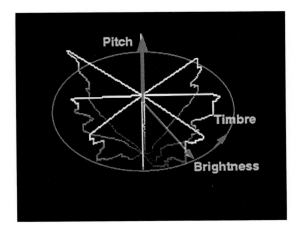

Plate 7 (Figure 3.9) The gamut of an auditory display within a perceptually linearized brightness–pitch–timbre (BPT) space.

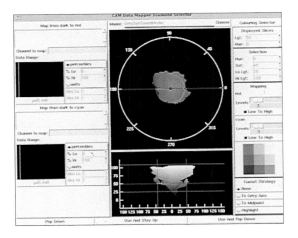

Plate 8 (Figure 3.10) Mapping bivariate data into the BPT perceptual space to portray positive and negative data correlations in pitch and brightness.

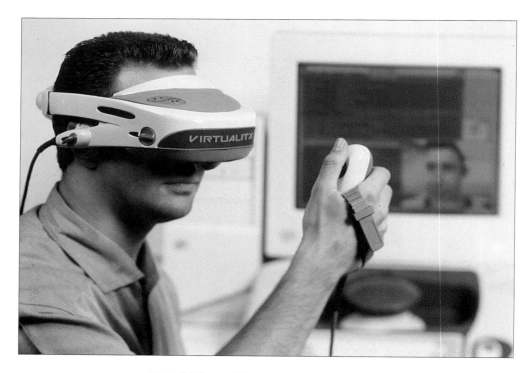

Plate 9 (Figure 4.2)   Helmet-mounted display.

Plate 10 (Figure 4.3)   Virtual Reality game scene.

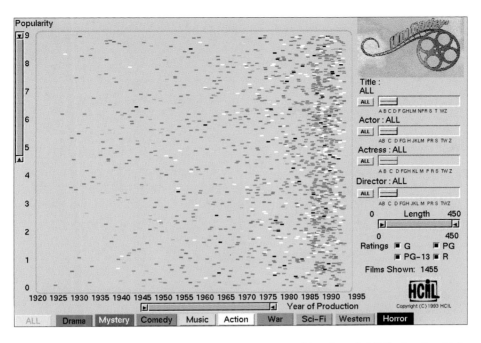

Plate 11 (Figure 5.2) Films in *FilmFinder* are represented in a 'star-field' display, in which the *X*-axis is year of production and the *Y*-axis is popularity.

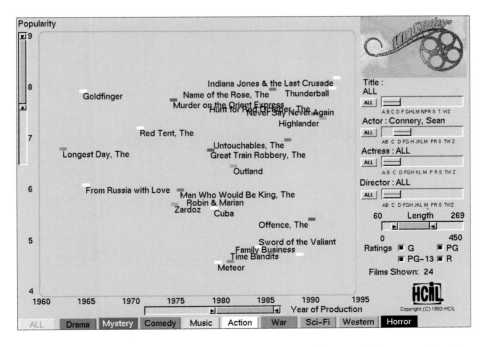

Plate 12 (Figure 5.3) Zooming into a selected region of the time–popularity space, showing films starring Sean Connery.

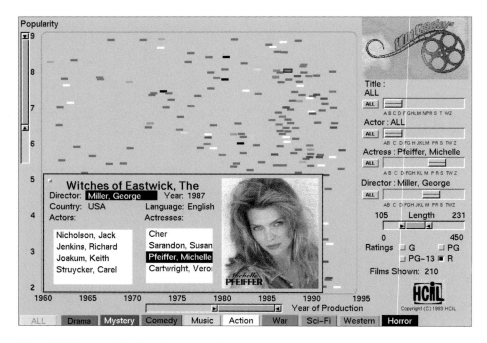

Plate 13 (Figure 5.4) Display of an information card showing attributes of selected film, including actors, actresses, director and language.

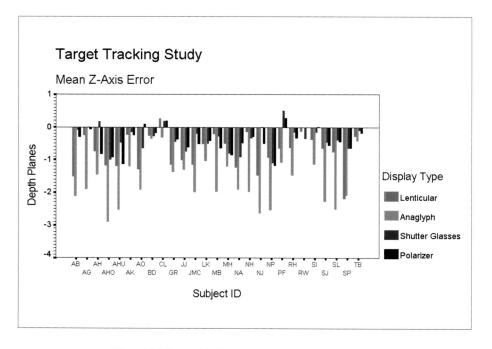

Plate 14 (Figure 19.10) Mean Z-axis tracking errors.

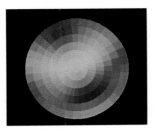

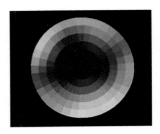

Plate 15 (Figure 15.10) Bright state colourplot of 1/4 VGA colour FSTN, calibrated.

Plate 16 (Figure 15.11) Dark state colourplot of 1/4 VGA colour FSTN, calibrated.

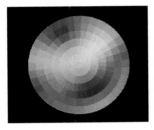

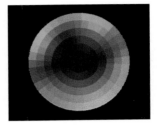

Plate 17 (Figure 15.12) Bright state colourplot of 1/4 VGA colour FSTN, non-calibrated.

Plate 18 (Figure 15.13) Dark state colourplot of 1/4 VGA colour FSTN, non-calibrated.

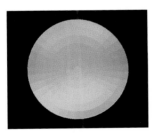

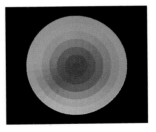

Plate 19 (Figure 15.14) Bright state colourplot of STN with yellow-green LED backlight, non-calibrated.

Plate 20 (Figure 15.15) Dark state colourplot of STN with yellow-green LED backlight, non-calibrated.

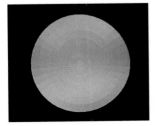

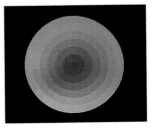

Plate 21 (Figure 15.16) Bright state colourplot of STN with yellow-green LED backlight, calibrated.

Plate 22 (Figure 15.17) Dark state colourplot of STN with yellow-green LED backlight, calibrated.

Plate 23 (Figure 20.4) Bad practice in workstation ergonomics.

Plate 24 (Figure 20.5) Good practice in workstation ergonomics.

Principles of display measurement and calibration

Jean Glasser

14.1 INTRODUCTION

'Measuring a display' is a phrase that hides a multitude of problems. The concept of measurement only applies to well-determined physical quantities. Even if measuring some of these quantities sometimes presents the greatest of difficulties, they are of an objective and physical nature in the normal sense. However, 'measuring displays' is simply another way of saying 'measuring' human beings. In truth, a display is a device exclusively intended for use by a human viewer. Measuring a display therefore involves a very ambitious plan: to model human vision so as to replace the viewer with an instrument.

It is therefore essential when dealing with display measurements and their interpretation to refer always to the properties of the human vision system. It is clear that current knowledge of this system is still imperfect. However, this certainly does not prevent meaningful measurements being taken of displays. But it is essential to know that there are still two ways of evaluating the visual performance characteristics of displays:

(1) A *subjective* approach, based on a panel of human 'guinea pigs' in a particular display usage situation. This approach is obviously complex: amongst other things it requires much testing time, control of trial conditions, separation of 'low level' visual processing effects (initial 'stages' of the vision system) from higher level cognitive phenomena, and finally a statistical approach to suit the problem. In short,

the subjective approach is expensive, cannot be used by non-specialists and is very difficult; so it is out of the question in an industrial testing or production context.

(2)   An *objective* approach, to which this paper is devoted, based on knowledge obtained subjectively on vision in general and on vision on displays in particular. Determination of objective methods involves interpreting the results obtained by subjective methods, and therefore constructing vision models. Ideally, the objective approach involves opto-electronic devices that are easy to use (but supported by associated instruments and software that may be quite complex) and therefore better suited to an industrial context.

Eventually, the subjective approach should therefore disappear, but today it is still essential. This has also been recognised in ISO standard 9241/3 on displays, the annexe to which proposes a subjective alternative to the objective methods forming the body of the standard. At the time of writing, this annexe has not been ratified and can therefore not be used, which clearly illustrates some of the difficulties that subjective methods entail.

These difficulties are quite simply linked to the complexity of the functions performed by the human visual system. Measuring a display today is still a complicated, expensive task. However, automated instruments that are just beginning to appear make it possible seriously to envisage a simpler approach in the future. But in all events, assessing the performance of a display involves a significant number of parameters. To construct an overall representation, it is important to classify these parameters logically with respect to visual functions.

Another vital question is: 'What are the objectives of measurement?' The fundamental objective is obviously to compare the measured characteristics with a particular specification. Even in a research and development environment, for example when attempting to improve a process, the measurement results are compared with earlier results, which are a type of specification. But in this context as well, the ultimate objective is to conform to a specification. Standards are an essential category of specification and are vital in display metrology as in other areas. This will be discussed later. But first it must be said that the natural interface role of displays *is* covered in the current versions of the display-related standards. There are two main international bodies dealing with display standards, the International Electrotechnical Commission (IEC) and the International Standards Organisation (ISO). In simple terms, displays are dealt with by the IEC as electronic components and by the ISO as display systems. This chapter provides an insight into the contribution of the standards of these two bodies, amongst others, in the implementation of display metrology.

14.2   OVERVIEW OF DISPLAY CHARACTERISATION PARAMETERS

It must first be realised that the display is not the only element involved in a practical viewing situation. There are normally three main items apart from the display: the viewer, the lighting environment and what may concisely be referred to as the 'image source', as shown in Figure 14.1. The viewer is taken into account implicitly in the vision model

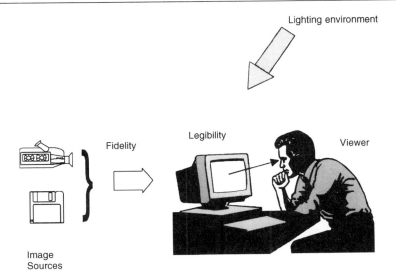

Figure 14.1 A display situation showing the different elements involved and the two basic functions of a display: fidelity and legibility

that underlies the measurement. Lighting environment is also an essential element. The image source consists of hardware and software which interact to generate the display on the screen.

In the context shown in Figure 14.1, an examination of the basic role of the display highlights a first level of separation of its functions.

(1) A display is primarily a transfer device; it must therefore be faithful ('what you want is what you get'). The concept of transfer function involves the entire image chain. Display fidelity is the essential characteristic linked to the concept of calibration. Calibration means precisely that the display must reproduce as exactly as possible the attributes of the image in the input signal applied to it. The fidelity parameters will therefore be those which characterise the input image. But the coded image applied to the display input, for example in RGB form, does not define all the attributes of the image displayed, for example it does not define luminance. The second task of the display must therefore be introduced through the concept of legibility.

(2) The display must render the image readable ('what you need is what you get'). It is necessary, for example, that in the conditions of the application, luminance and contrast are sufficient. Interaction with the light environment (lighting and background) here is fundamental and parameters such as diffuse and specular reflection factors are essential. Legibility parameters will therefore be linked to luminance, contrast and chromaticity as a function of the ambient lighting.

From a very general point of view, an 'image source' tries to represent a visual signal varying in space and time. This representation depends on the coding of the image signal; this may be, for example, a 'standardised video' signal (PAL/SECAM, NTSC) or the content of a computer's bitmap memory.

The fundamental role of a display is to produce a signal that may be referred to as a 'visual stimulus'. This visual stimulus can be characterised, for example, by its luminance and its chromaticity (the CIE 1931 system). The question of representation of the visual stimulus will be discussed later. The visual stimulus produced by the display will therefore vary in space and in time to reproduce the image as faithfully as possible. But since the display is immersed in an illuminated environment, the visual stimulus will also vary as a function of the ambient illuminance. In addition, because of technological imperatives, the stimulus produced by the display may also vary as a function of the viewing direction. These four fundamental dimensions of variation of the stimulus can be represented in a three-structured diagram such as Figure 14.2. A number of specific parameters can be associated with each fundamental dimension and these will be the characterisation parameters of a display. Each parameter and the associated methods will be described later. On the diagram the 'electro-optical response' represents the luminance/chromaticity variation as a function of image signal level for a point in the multidimensional space represented here. In other words, it is the luminance/chromaticity variation for a particular source image element (and therefore determinant in time and space), in a particular viewing direction and for a fixed ambient illuminance.

The diagram can also be used to show the distinction made earlier between fidelity and legibility. It shows that in the space and time dimensions, the parameters are those

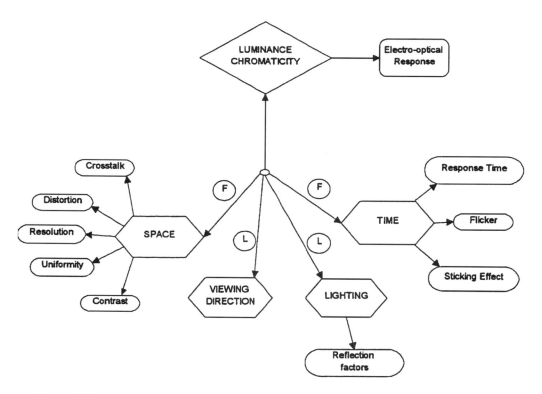

Figure 14.2 An overall view of the parameters characterising the performance of a display device. The letters F and L relate to the distinction between fidelity and legibility

of fidelity, whereas with respect to the environment, they are legibility parameters. Of course, the separation is not absolute, since for example a variation in chromaticity due to the ambient illuminance will impair the fidelity of the reproduction.

14.3 STANDARD CHARACTERISATION METHODS

14.3.1 Function and benefit of the standards

The author's firm opinion is that standards are criticised by those who are not familiar with them, whereas they are appreciated by those who know them well. Beyond this somewhat polemical aspect, standards have enormous industrial, commercial, political and legal implications which will not be discussed here (Greeson, 1990, 1991, 1994; Cone, 1993). To return to more fundamental matters, what is the basic objective of standards?

> 'The objective of standardisation is to provide *reference documents* incorporating *solutions to technical* and commercial *problems* concerning products, goods and services that are repeatedly posed in *relations between* economic, scientific, technical and social *partners*'.

This clear definition highlights the benefits of using standards:

- not to reinvent the wheel
- to use reliable, proven methods
- to use the same methods as other people.

Standards are therefore essential elements in dialogue between customer and supplier (with customer and supplier taken in a very wide sense).

14.3.2 The players in display measurement standards and the current state-of-the-art

Two main institutions deal with displays:

(1) The International Electrotechnical Commission (IEC), which deals with standards concerning electronic and electrotechnical products; displays are part of these and in this context are regarded as individual components of a monitor, for example. The European equivalent of the IEC for components is the CECC (Cenelec European Component Committee) whose work has historically been the main source of IEC documents.

(2) The International Standards Organisation (ISO) which deals with standards other than electrotechnical and electronic. Since displays are incorporated in information systems, they are naturally covered by the ISO. In this context, they are chiefly considered from the point of view of human-machine interface ergonomics.

The fact that display standards are covered by two different bodies is explained precisely by the interface role that the display plays between machine and human being. This could appear to be a source of complication in practice. In fact, the officially stated concern of the ISO and the IEC is to avoid duplication of work. With this objective, the Secretariats of the respective Technical Committees must provide each other with information on their current work. The reasons for beginning a new project must receive international approval ('New Work Item Proposal'). Mutual recognition procedures have recently been established between the bodies and this should mean that documents that are more advanced in one group can be accelerated in another. These rules must be applied by the experts in the respective Working Groups in the display area which are:

- SC47C/WG2 for the IEC: 'Liquid Crystal and Solid State Display Devices', the European CECC equivalent of which is WG20B
- TC159/SC4/WG2 for the ISO: 'Ergonomic Requirements for Office Work with Visual Display Terminals'.

The work of these groups will now briefly be examined.

The IEC Working Group SC47C/WG2 has been in operation since 1985 and is focusing mainly for the moment on Liquid Crystal flat panel Displays (LCD). It should be remembered that measurement methods are only one element of the IEC standards system, which also incorporates quality assurance and terminology as main components. The first document the group drafted was on the very subject of measurement methods. For various reasons, in particular the difficulty in achieving consensus on certain technical points, the document on measurement methods is only now on the point of being published. For LCDs, the group has also drafted a generic specification, visual inspection methods, climatic and mechanical environment tests, terminology and essential characteristics. Most of these documents should soon appear as international standards. Future work will extend the current work on bare LCD cells to colour displays and LCD modules. The reader should note that an IEC/CIE vocabulary, which will precisely define the terms 'bare LCD cell', 'colour display' and 'LCD module' is in preparation at the time of publication. The term 'LCD module' denotes an LCD cell, or display, and its drive electronics.

The CECC WG20B group was established in 1984 and has already published the 20 000 series documents on measurement methods and visual inspection and a Blank Detail Specification (BDS) for LCDs. Its current work concerns the extension of measurement methods of colour, crosstalk, uniformity and sticking effect. Overall, therefore, it is ahead of its IEC counterpart. The CECC documents have also been used as a basis by the IEC Working Group SC47C/WG2.

At the beginning of the 1980s, ISO Working Group TC159/SC4/WG2 began the work on ergonomics for office automation systems incorporating visual displays. The first to be published was document 9241/3 (in Europe 29241/3) concerning requirements relating to cathode ray tube (CRT) displays. It contains the performance levels required for all parameters deemed important and the associated measurement methods. From 1992, it was decided to draft an equivalent document for other 'flat panel' display technologies, the reference for which is 13406. This document is more complete than ISO 9241/3. ISO 9241/7, currently being drafted, is specially devoted to the role of the ambient illumination environment.

To take an overall view of the respective work of these groups, it may be considered that:

(1) The ISO attempts to find simple, sometimes rudimentary, routes to a definition of the minimum performance levels required under a general philosophy of 'health and safety at work' in an office automation environment.

(2) The IEC and the CECC propose more sophisticated methods with as wide a range of applications as possible but no associated performance level. The necessary

performance level depends greatly on the application and can be covered by various organisations (for example the ISO for Office Automation). The methods must enable the actual performance level of the device to be determined irrespective of the application. The objective of the CECC is to complement the methods that exist in the IEC by using a more flexible and less cumbersome structure, bearing in mind that Europe has an overall lead in LCD standards.

The bases for characterising the visual stimulus, which involves photo-colorimetric techniques, fall within the scope of the Commission Internationale de l'Éclairage (CIE) (International Lighting Commission). This body deals with all problems linked to illumination and naturally to vision. It too has published recommendations on display performance levels, in parallel with those of the ISO. However, there is no ambiguity in their respective roles, with the ISO and the IEC referring to the CIE for all basic photo-colorimetric methods.

In addition, other international organisations (which are not standardisation bodies as such), have worked on the visual performance of displays in their particular fields, such as the EBU (European Broadcasting Union) for studio monitors, or its world equivalent CCIR (International Radio Consultative Committee). Historically it was television, well before office automation, that was concerned with display performance. Although often limited in their scope, their work can serve as a source of useful inspiration, as can that of several national bodies, including DIN (Deutsche Industrie Normen), EIA (Electronic Industries Association) and ASTM (American Society for Testing and Materials). Indeed, when a national standard is acceptable, it generally serves as a basis of the equivalent international standards.

Table 14.1 provides an overview of existing or soon-to-be-issued standards on measuring visual display performance. To avoid complicating the table, only the standards of supranational bodies have been included (except for remarks) since they alone have any real future.

14.4 CHARACTERISING THE VISUAL STIMULUS: PHOTO-COLORIMETRIC MEASURING INSTRUMENTS AND THEIR PRACTICAL USE

There are two main aspects to measuring the characteristics of a display device:

- choosing a photo-colorimetric measuring instrument of a quality that matches requirements;
- carrying out the measurement properly to avoid spurious effects and to control the validity of the photo-colorimetric data that the instrument obtains.

14.4.1 Using measuring instruments to obtain photo-colorimetric data

Characterising the visual stimulus

First a basic problem should be stated: 'how can a visual stimulus be characterised?' Photometry and, to a greater extent colorimetry, may appear impenetrable jungles, because of the existence of several parallel standardised systems such as CIE 1931, CIELAB or CIELUV (not to mention the others). It is clear today that none of these systems is

Table 14.1 Current international standards, published or in draft, on measuring display performance, EBU = European Broadcasting Union, ASTM = American Society for Testing and Materials, EIA = Electronic Industries Association (USA), CD = Committee Draft, CO = Central Office (to appear shortly), FPD = Flat Panel Displays. The data are accurate to December 1995

Parameters	Standard or WG reference	Current status	Technology	Remark
Visual stimulus characterisation				
Luminance/chromaticity	CIE 18,15.2	published	All	see also ASTM E 1336-91
	CECC 20000/A3	published	LCD	colour in draft (WG20B)
	EBU Tech 3273	published	CRT	
	ISO 9241/3	published	CRT	no chromaticity measurement
	ISO 13406 (CD)	in draft	FPD	
	IEC 47(CO)16	in draft	LCD	no chromaticity measurement
Electro-optical transfer	EBU Tech 3273	published	CRT	for CRT - see also EIA TEP 105.17
Spatial parameters				
Resolution	CECC 11000			
Luminance/chromaticity uniformity	ISO 9241/3	published	CRT	luminance only
	ISO 13406 (CD)	in draft	FPD	luminance and chromaticity
	CECC WG20B	in draft	LCD	ditto - more complete
	EBU Tech 3273	published	CRT	
Crosstalk	CECC WG20B	in draft	LCD	will apply to FPD
	ISO 13406 (CD)	in draft	FPD	
Distortion	ISO 9241/3	published	CRT	

Temporal parameters				
Flicker	ISO 9241/3	published	TRC	*informative* annexe only
	ISO 13406 (CD)	in draft	FPD	*informative* annexe only
Response time	CECC 20000A3	published	LCD	
	IEC 47(CO)16	in draft	LCD	
	ISO 13406 (CD)	in draft	FPD	
Sticking effect	CECC WG20B	in draft	LCD	will apply to FPD
Ambient illuminance parameters				
Diffuse and specular reflection factors	CECC 20000A3	published	LCD	diffuse reflection factor only
	IEC 47(CO)16	in draft	LCD	diffuse reflection factor only
	ISO 9241/7	in draft	CRT	
	ISO 13406 (CD)	in draft	FPD	
Viewing direction parameters				
Luminance/chromaticity	CECC 20000A3	published	LCD	luminance only
	IEC 47(CO)16	in draft	LCD	luminance only
	ISO 13406 (CD)	in draft	FPD	luminance and chromaticity

really acceptable for characterising visual sensation. However, to characterise a *visual stimulus*, they are perfectly usable. The CIE representation systems guarantee that two visual stimuli perceived as identical will have the same CIE characteristics. If they are perceived as different, current CIE systems will often be defective. What can be derived from the point of view of visual sensation, in other words interpretation of the results, is another type of problem which would take too long to expand on here. It is the vision modelling concept. Certain aspects of this will be discussed later. It may be said that current CIE systems provide a sound characterisation of the basic stages of the visual system but not of the higher stages. Strictly from the point of view of acquiring visual stimulus data, that is not a problem.

To sum up, the basic requirement of a photo-colorimetric measuring instrument is that it should assess as faithfully as possible the CIE characteristics of the visual stimulus. From these characteristics, it is always possible to calculate other visual characteristics that can be used to interpret the data provided by the instrument.

Types of instrument

Characterising a visual stimulus boils down to imitating human vision, in other words evaluating the intensity distribution of an optical signal in the three spectral bands defined by the CIE. This can be done in two ways:

- using filters ('broadband' instruments)
- measuring the spectrum and calculating the intensity distribution ('narrowband' instruments).

The two types of instrument have been compared exhaustively (Berns *et al.*, 1993a,b) and are also described in Sections 16.5 and 16.6.

Table 14.2 summarises the potential advantages and disadvantages of the two types of instrument. Of course in practice the quality of manufacture of the instruments greatly affects actual performance. A filter instrument is intrinsically simple but requires high quality filter manufacture in conjunction with spectral sensitivity of the photon detector. It is more sensitive because it divides the spectrum of the stimulus into wide bands, and therefore its detector receives a proportionally large number of photons. There are instruments with sensitivity limits as low as 10^{-2} cd/m^2.

The main difficulty of a spectrophotometer is that it requires a precision wavelength monochromator (0.1 to 0.5 nm) in conjunction with a detector (motorised grating) or a set of detectors (fixed grating). The narrower the individual waveband, the more sensitive the detectors must be. In practice, spectrophotometers are currently limited to illuminance

Table 14.2   Comparison of the characteristics of the two main types of photo-colorimeter

	Filter instruments	Spectrophotometers
Precision	average to excellent	good to very good
Dynamic range	good to excellent	average
Measurement time	short	long in low light
Uses other than photo-colorimetry	none	wide
Cost	potentially low	high

levels greater than approximately 1 cd/m^2. This is sometimes inadequate, for example when measuring the luminance ratio of an LCD in darkness, which can reach 300 for a white pattern with luminance of 100 cd/m^2, therefore involving black-level luminances of 0.3 cd/m^2. In addition, the low quantity of light received involves the use of cooled (and therefore more expensive) detectors and a significant measurement time (several seconds) in low light. Some of these instruments are therefore unable to measure display response time. However, a spectrophotometer is capable of applications other than strict photocolorimetry, for example investigations into the spectral transmittance of optical components for displays. To end this overview of the characteristics of photo-colorimetric measuring instruments, it should be noted that non-synchronisation of the measurement with respect to display refresh can affect precision (Berns *et al.*, 1993a,b).

Future developments

The vast majority of current instruments take only local measurements, in that they analyze only one area of the display at a time. In other words, the instruments have no intrinsic spatial resolution. Would it not be more logical, since the objective is to imitate the human visual system, to use a camera as a photo-colorimeter (Ghilczy *et al.*, 1993)? This would offer a major advantage, for all types of measurement as a function of space, since it would be possible to evaluate the performance of several display areas at the same time. The reason that there are currently so few products of this type on the market is due to the following problems.

Photo-colorimetric response   Like any photo-colorimeter, the camera must have a stable, linear, geometrically distortion-free response in accordance with CIE standards over the widest possible dynamic range. Through solid-state sensors, in particular CCDs, this is now becoming possible. However, it is necessary to cool the sensor and to have good electronic control of the camera. Contrary to what may be thought, it is a long way from simple video to photo-colorimetric metrology.

It should become increasingly possible to resolve these problems in the near future. Since it still seems impossible to produce camera spectrophotometers, current camera photo-colorimeters use a single sensor and a set of filters. Consideration could be given to using a conventional colour sensor, incorporating on-chip mosaic filters. But it does not yet seem possible to convince image sensor manufacturers to make custom devices of photo-colorimetric quality. The requirements of response dispersion from sensor to sensor mean that the sensor must be carefully matched to its filters. In reality, it is worth noting that it is sufficient for filter responses to be a linear combination of CIE colour matching functions, which any good image sensor should theoretically achieve.

Spatial resolution   The imaging system (image sensor with its optics) must have a resolution significantly greater than the spatial resolution limit required. It is essential to avoid the subsampling and moiré phenomena which may occur because of the discrete structure of the photoelements of the camera and of the display pixels.

Intra-image dynamic range   If the image on the display has high levels of contrast, this can prove a difficulty because in this case it is not possible to act directly on the integration time of the sensor (except by performing several acquisitions). Therefore sensors with a wide dynamic range must be used.

In short, camera photo-colorimeters, a logical and attractive response to faithful simulation of the visual system, are difficult to implement. Such systems will be more and more available in the future, but they will require extremely careful manufacture.

Taking the measurement

Display photometry and colorimetry are not generally simple to implement. The accuracy and significance of the results depend on general precautions applicable to any optical measurements and specific features linked to the sources (i.e., the displays) to be assessed. See also Chapters 15, 16 and 17.

General precautions

Control of the lighting and thermal environment   It is essential to control the display illuminance conditions. This involves having a dark room or enclosure. 'Dark' means that the luminance measured in the absence of the display must be less than 0.01 cd/m^2 typically. So, within this facility, it is necessary to mask unwanted sources (for example instrument indicators) which may disturb the luminance of the display by reflecting or diffusing unwanted light into the photo-colorimeter.

The light from the display itself can interfere with the measurement by producing unwanted light in the photo-colorimeter. When measuring black areas on a white background, it is highly advisable to mask the light from the light areas using a blind with an aperture sufficient to avoid masking the measurement area.

For measurements of the effect of the lighting environment, lighting devices with properly characterised and controlled illuminance must be used. A typical example of such a device is the integrating sphere. This will be discussed later.

In an enclosure containing heat-generating devices, the temperature can rise quickly, so it must be controlled as far as possible. It is quite possible to control the temperature of a flat panel display by immersing it in optically neutral dielectric coolant which also makes it possible to vary the temperature of the display within a wide range ($-20°$C to $+80°$C in the device used in the author's laboratory).

Control of the mechanical positioning of the display   In all cases, the orientation and positioning of the area to be measured on the display with respect to the photo-colorimetric measuring instrument must be accurately controlled. For displays with parameters varying greatly with the viewing direction (such as LCDs), this must typically be controlled to within $±1°$. Taking into account the time and accuracy required by photo-colorimetric measurements, the position of the display and/or the photo-colorimeter often have to be very stable and remotely controllable by computer.

Specific precautions

Conditioning and initial adjustments of the display   This is a critical stage in the measurement process which requires the care and attention of the operator.

Depending on the display technology, certain precautions must be taken before the measurement, such as for example adjusting the backlighting voltage for an LCD module or degaussing for a CRT. The initial adjustment of the display in reproducible, stable conditions is also a crucial stage. The adjustments required, such as determining the electro-optical operating range and adjustment of the reference white, must be done with great care. For most display technologies, these adjustments involve determining electrical offset and gain parameters in conjunction with initial photo-colorimetric measurements.

Display warm-up time prior to the measurement and any drift in characteristics during the measurement must also be absolutely controlled by an extremely careful preparatory investigation. Examples are backlit LCD modules, for which the cell temperature can change during at least the first hour of use. Since the characteristics of an LCD vary greatly with temperature, it is particularly critical for this technology to ensure that the temperature is maintained typically at $\pm 2°$C.

Optical measurement conditions   The measurement area of the photo-colorimetric measuring instrument must be precisely defined and maintained in terms of dimension and position on the display surface (see Chapter 15). This area must also be stable irrespective of the display orientation with respect to the photo-colorimeter viewing direction. This is particularly critical when measuring parameters as a function of LCD viewing direction. This requirement assumes a fine opto-mechanical adjustment of the display positioning device and the photo-colorimeter. The measurement area depends on the characteristics of the photo-colorimeter and the distance from the display.

For parameters which depend on the viewing direction, the aperture of the photo-colorimeter must be matched to anticipated variations of the parameters. The term 'aperture' here means the solid angle at which the photo-colorimeter's optics see the measurement area. If the photo-colorimeter is too close to the display, its optics will integrate the photo-colorimetric variations as a function of viewing direction and therefore the effective angular resolution of the measurement will fall significantly. For example for a typical LCD, it is desirable to take readings at the very minimum every 5° to achieve adequate angular resolution. It is therefore necessary for the angle at which a small area of the display is seen by the photo-colorimeter to be less than 5°. For example, if the optics of the photo-colorimeter have an input diameter of 50 mm, it must be at least about 600 mm away from the display.

14.4.2   Electro-optical transfer

Purpose of the measurement

As shown in Figure 14.1, a display is a transfer device in which the photo-colorimetric fidelity must be characterised. This will first determine the response of the display to a given input image signal and conversely determine the image signal to be applied to obtain a given *luminance/chromaticity*. This involves modelling the display. Because of the number of individual devices (digital/analogue converters, drivers, transducers, for example) between the image signal input and the physical display of the stimulus on a screen, it will be realised that such a model has to be complex. This chapter examines only a number of individual considerations; for further details, readers should refer, for example, to Berns *et al.* (1993a,b) and Post (1992).

General considerations

Electro-optical transfer responses of most display devices are not linear. In particular, the luminance L of a CRT depends on the input voltage V in the following form:

$$L = a + bV^{\gamma}$$
14.1

The exponent γ is called the gamma factor which is therefore very important in everything to do with the transfer function of a CRT (in three-gun CRTs, the gamma factors of each gun can differ slightly). In the early stages of television, to avoid installing a correction device in each TV set, the image signal was pre-corrected. This means that normally the response of a CRT to an encoded image signal is quasi-linear. But for other technologies, there is no reason why the response should look like that of a CRT, as shown in Figure 14.3. This can be a major source of colour errors for all display technologies (Berns *et al.*, 1993a,b).

Measuring methods

From the photo-colorimetric response of each type of subpixel measured as a function of the input signal, it is normally possible to predict the response of the display to any signal. However, several causes of variability or error must be considered. The main ones are:

- temporal instability (drift or jitter)
- spatial non-uniformity
- crosstalk between guns (CRT) or between subpixels (LCD)
- memory effects
- variations in luminance/chromaticity with the size of the test pattern (CRT)
- variations in luminance/chromaticity with the viewing direction (LCD).

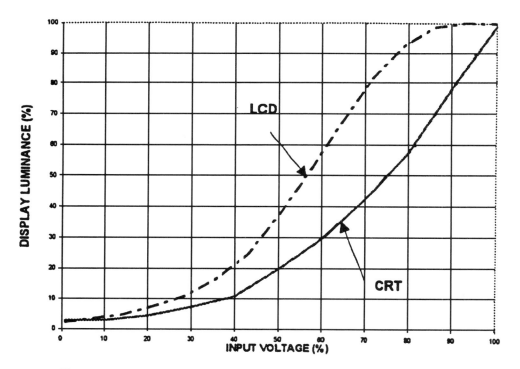

Figure 14.3 Typical measured electro-optical responses of a CRT and an LCD

The cumulative effect of these phenomena makes measuring the electro-optical transfer difficult and it must therefore be done under controlled conditions and with great care. An example of a practical measurement procedure can be found in EBU technical standard 3273 for studio monitors. Instead of measuring the transfer response for the whole range of input voltages, it is possible as a first approach to measure a limited number of carefully chosen colour samples. The colour errors for these samples can give an initial idea of the fidelity of the display. In addition, current ISO standards make no explicit provision for measuring electro-optical response, because there is no fidelity requirement. Only the default colours are checked to ensure that they are visually quite distinct.

14.5 CHARACTERISATION PARAMETERS

For an exhaustive description of the methods of determining characterisation parameters, readers are referred to the standards listed in Table 14.1. In the necessarily limited context of this work, only general principles will be discussed here, together with particular points if necessary and aspects that either are not covered or are imperfectly covered by the standards. The fundamental guide for each parameter category is of course the corresponding visual performance. The basic principles and the limits of current methods will therefore be mentioned briefly, if necessary to determine the context the basic principles and the limits of current methods.

14.5.1 Spatial parameters

Resolution

Purpose of the measurement   To assess the size of the smallest feature reproducible by the display, or the minimum distance that must separate two image features so that they can be perceived as separate.

General considerations and method   The question of effective resolution is a serious one only for CRT displays. Conventionally the question is dealt with using the Modulation Transfer Function approach. On this subject, readers are referred to Barten (1990). The Modulation Transfer Function concept strictly applies only to linear, translation-invariant systems; this is not so with a colour cathode ray tube which is not linear in voltage (but may be in current) and is not translation-invariant, because of the fixed position of the subpixels. Using the MTF concept is therefore inappropriate and the formalism certainly requires revision, as Blanc (1994) has done for discrete photo-element image analyzers, which pose a very similar problem. It seems to the author that using an approach such as that in Blanc and Glasser (1994), where the role of the display is regarded as that of an integral sampler, would enable the problem to be treated more rigorously and would also enable matrix flat panel displays to be included. This work is yet to be done.

Uniformity

Purpose of the measurement   This measurement involves evaluating luminance and chromaticity variations on the surface of the screen. Variations can first of all be aesthetically unsatisfactory and in some cases may affect legibility. An extreme case

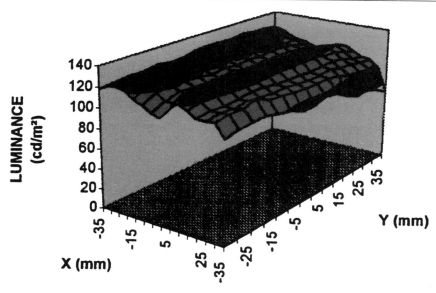

Figure 14.4 2D Luminance scan of a backlit LCD along vertical and horizontal coordinates on the display surface. Luminance variations can be at relatively high spatial frequencies and will not be detected by measuring at a limited number of points

can be imagined in which defective addressing of the screen would display a structure of permanently visible columns.

General considerations An example of measured non-uniformity is given in Figure 14.4. It shows the significant variations in luminance that can occur on a backlit LCD because of non-uniformity of the backlighting.

Current standards (ISO 9241/3 and EBU technical standard 3213), based on the CRT, refer only to slow variations in display luminance. They specify a luminance measurement at a limited number of points on the display (5 or 9) but this principle does not take into account variations at higher spatial frequencies, such as those illustrated in Figure 14.4. Flat panel displays, which do not have a centralised addressing system like the cathode ray tube, are more likely to exhibit non-uniformity defects caused for example by differences between electrical characteristics in the driving circuits or backlight non-uniformity.

Sensitivity of the visual system to luminance and colour variations depends heavily on the spatial frequency (Barten, 1990). Strictly speaking, it would be necessary to carry out a two-dimensional Fourier analysis of luminance and chromaticity variations as a function of the coordinates and compare the data obtained with the legibility thresholds provided by Barten (1990) for example. The spatial frequencies must in this case be translated into angular units (cycles/degree), because this is the appropriate unit for vision. The size of the measurement area on the display surface must be adapted according to the spatial frequency domain to be covered and the measurement distance. A small measurement area associated with a fine offset pitch enables a wide range of spatial frequencies to be covered but the measurements take a long time (except with a camera, see above).

With a larger measurement area and a limited number of measurement points only slow variations in luminance or chromaticity can be detected, but the measurements will be much faster.

Measurement principles The CECC draft standard proposes a more global approach to measuring non-uniformity. It lists three scales:

(1) Subpixel scale, which typically represents a viewing angle of 1' or less for a viewing distance of 70 cm. The size of the measurement area must be significantly smaller than a subpixel.

(2) 'Multipixel' scale, representing for direct viewing 10° or more at 70 cm. The size of the measurement area must then cover 10×10 pixels or more.

(3) 'Multicharacter' scale which is used by the standards listed above, with a measurement area of about 50×50 pixels.

The measurement pitch must of course be adapted to the size of the measurement area. In other words, the pitch must be of the same order of magnitude as the size of the measurement area to avoid under- or oversampling the signal.

The choice of scale depends largely on the aims of the measurement and on the expected luminance or chromaticity variations. In practice, a preliminary measurement on the multipixel scale over the whole display is essential to assess whether to scan at a finer pitch. Then it is simply a matter of measuring over a limited number of lines or columns or even on a 'multicharacter' scale. The subpixel scale can be used for research purposes or for projection displays, for example.

Crosstalk

Purpose of the measurement The 'crosstalk' effect consists of unwanted variations of luminance/chromaticity due to coupling effects when addressing dark areas on a light background, for example. Grey areas appear at the top, bottom, left and right of a black area, whereas they should retain the same luminance as the display background. This phenomenon is illustrated in Figure 14.5. It is common on current LCDs.

General considerations and method There is no published standard on the method, but two drafts are in hand (see Table 14.1). The measurement principle consists in displaying a dark square on a light background, a light square on a dark background and a uniform test pattern. The crosstalk coefficient is obtained by statistically measuring the luminance deviations at the same measurement point in the different configurations. Refer to the CECC and ISO draft standards for details (the ISO version uses a more rudimentary approach than the CECC).

Geometric distortion and spatial jitter

Purpose of the measurement To measure geometric distortion of the displayed image.

General considerations and method For CRTs, the form of the image and its position on the display depend on scanning of the electron beam. This does not apply for dot matrix flat panel displays where the position of the pixels and subpixels is fixed. In practice, with the technologies used for flat panel displays, geometric distortion induced

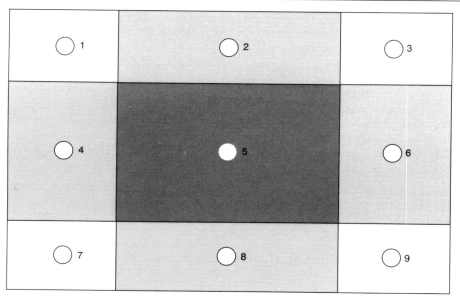

Figure 14.5 Crosstalk effect highlighted by grey bands around the central dark square. The numbers refer to the measurement areas specified in the draft standards

during manufacture is negligible. On the other hand, for CRTs, two causes of geometric distortion can be considered. Scanning can induce positional distortions of the beam. These distortions can also vary in time, since the beam is sensitive to electromagnetic interference. This is the main cause of distortion. For colour tubes, the subpixel deposition technique can in some cases lead to intrinsic distortion in the position of the subpixels. To evaluate geometric distortion it is usual to make a distinction between linearity and orthogonality (see ISO 9241/3).

For linearity,

(1) Large scale: the difference in the lengths of lines or columns must not exceed a percentage (2 percent for ISO 9241/3) of the length of these lines or columns.
(2) Small scale: the difference in relative position, horizontally or vertically, of adjacent characters must not exceed a percentage (5 percent for ISO 9241/3) of the respective dimension (width or height) of these characters.

For orthogonality, the general form of a uniform test pattern is assessed by measuring the differences in length of the outside edges and diagonals of the image compared to their respective averages.

All these measurements of geometric distortion must be taken using a mobile microscope and are more complex than a straight forward photometric measurement.

Spatial jitter   is dependent on both space and time. The geometric position of a feature of the image is measured as a function of time. ISO standard 9241/3 requires that this jitter be less than 0.0002 times the viewing distance.

14.5.2 Temporal parameters

Response time

Purpose of the measurement To assess the display's temporal response fidelity. This involves measuring the temporal luminance/chromaticity variation after applying a pulse input signal.

Method The method involves measuring the luminance rise or fall time between two stable states, for respective luminances L_1 and L_2. ISO draft standard 13406 gives an elegant formulation. For further information, the reader should refer to the relevant National Standards Committee which corresponds with the ISO.

For luminance transitions from one stable state to another (L_1 to L_2 and L_2 to L_1), the luminance is recorded as a function of time. Then, using these records, the times needed to reach 10 percent, then 90 percent, of the luminance difference are determined. The resulting four values are used to measure the response times. There is an ambiguity of terminology here: the notation t_{on} and t_{off} is often seen but, to avoid any confusion, the concepts of luminance rise time (t_r) and fall time (t_f) should be used. For LCDs, unwanted oscillations can appear on the recorded signal and interfere with the measurement, so measurements should be made on signals that are free of oscillations.

Flicker

Purpose of the measurement To assess the impairment caused by any blinking of the image. This blinking, called flicker, is due to the display refresh cycle and greatly depends on the display technology.

General considerations and measurement principle The flicker sensitivity threshold of the visual system subject to a light stimulus variable in time depends mainly on:

- the frequency variation of the stimulus
- the luminance of the stimulus
- the angular size of the stimulus.

The sensitivity threshold varies with individuals and their general state, but models can be established that quantify the sensation for a large percentage of subjects under normal conditions. This type of model is used in the annexes to ISO standard 9241 and draft standard 13406. These are only informative annexes and there is so far no consensus on measuring display flicker.

The principle consists of recording the photo-colorimeter signal as a function of time. The instrument must therefore have a short response time (typically less than 1 ms). A Fourier analysis of the signal is then carried out and the intensity of the components compared with an analytic model, obviously taking into account the luminance and size of the display. If one of the components exceeds the threshold, flicker will be visible. The specific feature of flat panel displays is that the form of the temporal signal is not known *a priori* as for a CRT, for which the Fourier analysis is therefore simplified.

Sticking effect

Purpose of the measurement To assess the spurious memory effect of a display when a given image has been displayed for a certain time. This parameter is particularly important for LCDs (but the effect can also occur for CRT displays). A DC component of the addressing voltage of an LCD cell causes movement of ions which may affect the electro-optical response. Although the drive electronics are designed to eliminate the DC component, it is generally not completely reduced to zero and therefore produces a 'ghost' effect on the display.

Measurement principle   This is similar to the crosstalk situation. A dark area, for example, is displayed on screen for a certain time (around one hour) and immediately after replacing this dark area with a light area, the variation in luminance of the light area as a function of time is measured. The sticking effect measurement is currently covered only by a draft CECC standard and is to be validated in the future.

14.5.3   Parameters depending on ambient illuminance

Diffuse and specular reflection factors

Purpose of the measurement and general considerations   The purpose of this type of measurement is to evaluate the luminance and chromaticity variations of the display as a function of the level and spatial distribution of ambient illuminance. Diffuse reflection causes an unwanted increase in luminance and a change of chromaticity over the entire screen surface. Because of this, the so-called veiling luminance in general decreases the contrast. Specular reflection, in other words the pseudo-mirror effect of the display surface, also causes a spurious increase in luminance and a change of chromaticity. This change is located on a limited zone of the display surface and can have two harmful effects. The first is similar to that of diffuse reflection-impaired contrast. The second is that the image of a source on the display which is obviously not the same distance from the viewer as the display itself, can generate a reflex accommodation of the viewer which can be uncomfortable.

In addition, it must be pointed out that the spatial distribution of the lighting used for the specular reflection measurement has a significant effect on results. For LCDs in particular, the spatial distribution of the lighting is a critical point that will be discussed in greater detail in the next section.

The diffuse and specular reflection factors of a display are therefore extremely important parameters in practice, and ones that are not generally given sufficient consideration. Display specifications often contain contrast values which are meaningless if the level and type of illuminance (see below) are not specified. It would be far more justifiable technically to consider illuminance ranges within which a display is readable or not, as suggested in Cone (1993).

Measurement method   It is essential to realise that this type of measurement is extremely difficult, and that the most comprehensive method currently published has not yet been ratified (Cone, 1993). The statement of the problem depends on the type of display, emissive (CRT) or backlit (LCD). Refer to ISO draft standard 9241/7 for CRTs for further details. To avoid complicating the issue, we shall describe only the principle and then go on to discuss related problems. The principle is as follows:

(1)   The luminance of the display (if it is emissive) is measured in darkness.

(2)   Under diffuse lighting conditions, eliminating specular reflection as much as possible, the luminance of the display and the incident illuminance are measured. Taking into

account the display operating mode (for example CRT or LCD), a diffuse reflection factor can then be deduced, which is typically of the order of 0.05.

(3) The luminances of two sources are then measured, one an extended area and the other a small area, by reflection on the display. Taking into account the previous stage, since the reflection source also generates diffuse reflection, specular reflection factors can be deduced for a small area and an extended area source. These two quantities can vary by a factor of as much as 4 for typical values of 0.01–0.05.

There are several types of difficulty in this measurement:

(1) The spatial distribution of diffuse illuminance plays an important role. In Cone (1993), light boxes are proposed that are economic to construct, but in the opinion of the author, an integrating sphere which is now widely used for measurements on LCDs, and which is not excessively expensive, would be a more reliable and reproducible source.

(2) Measuring reflection is difficult, if the surface is highly diffusive. Screen surfaces must be thoroughly cleaned.

These techniques have not yet been ratified for LCDs.

In conclusion, measuring diffuse and specular reflection factors, parameters that are extremely important in practice, requires further development and validation in the future.

Influence of the distribution of ambient illuminance

The role of the spatial distribution of ambient illuminance is vital for LCDs in which the contrast values can vary considerably according to whether illuminance is diffuse or directional. Figure 14.6 illustrates the two possible methods of illuminance and the differences obtained, in value and trend, on the contrast of an LCD. In Glasser and Rolland (1989), it was shown that only diffuse lighting enabled LCDs to be measured acceptably. This is increasingly being accepted by the displays community, where diffuse lighting systems are now widely used. Diffuse lighting is the only method accepted by the European standards, whereas CIE standards accept both approaches. What was said above concerning the measurement of reflection factors reinforces the case for using integrating spheres. The origin of these peculiarities of LCDs lies in the fact that the characteristics of the LCD cells depend on the viewing direction. A simple model takes this clearly into account (Glasser & Rolland, 1989). The role of the viewing direction is examined in the next section.

14.5.4 Parameters depending on the viewing direction

All the parameters of an LCD can vary with the viewing direction. This leads to consideration of methods for characterising luminance/chromaticity from which all other parameters can be deduced. See also Chapter 15.

Luminance/chromaticity variations

Purpose of the measurement The characteristics of directional non-homogeneity with respect to the incident light of LCD cells necessitates the measurement of luminance and chromaticity as a function of viewing direction. This involves significant complications and raises questions on the tolerance of the visual system to changes in characteristics as a function of viewing direction. This subject is discussed further below.

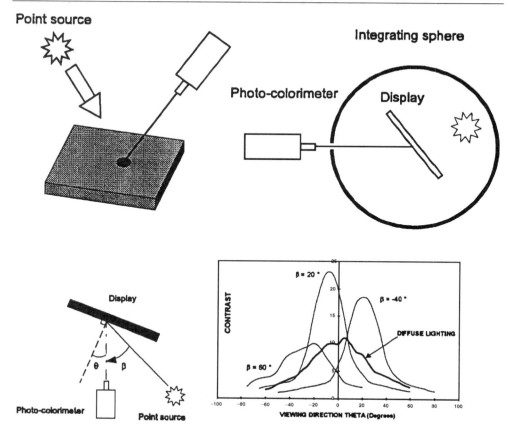

Figure 14.6 Influence of the type of illuminance, directional (top left) or diffuse (top right), on measuring the contrast of an LCD as a function of the viewing direction in a vertical plane (Glasser & Rolland, 1989). The contrast values obtained with directional lighting (bottom left) depend on the direction of the source (angle β), which is not acceptable from a metrological point of view nor in terms of practical application. Only diffuse lighting from an integrating sphere (or half sphere) is accepted in the CECC European standards

Measurement methods The method most widely used up to now is the *goniometric method* which consists simply in measuring the display from many different angles by moving it with respect to the photometer, as shown in Figure 14.7.

This method has the advantage that any photo-colorimeter can be used and provides considerable freedom in use of the display. It is possible (and in general necessary for the reasons indicated above) to place the display at a certain distance from the photo-colorimeter, for example to attach a display temperature control device. However, the display/photo-colorimeter assembly must be arranged so that the measured area on the display does not vary with the viewing direction, which requires precise adjustment. In addition, measurements over a wide range of angles generally take a long time (half an hour for scanning in a half-aperture cone of 60°) and, in practice, precise motorised display rotation mountings are required.

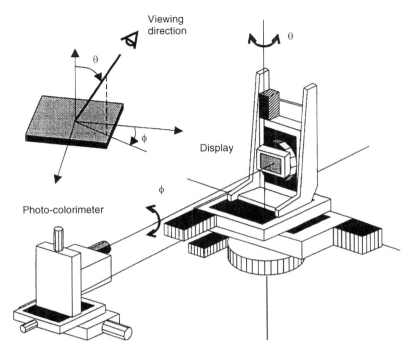

Figure 14.7   Principle of the goniometric method and typical implementation. Although it is possible to move the photo-colorimeter with respect to the fixed-mount display, it is generally preferred to move the display

The *conoscopic method* uses a special optical arrangement illustrated in Figure 14.8. This principle has long been used in crystallography and for the development of LCD cells (Berreman, 1976). However, it is only recently that devices applying the conoscopic method have been improved (Fritsch *et al.*, 1989) and made commercially available (Leroux, 1993). It was necessary to be able to achieve a large aperture optical arrangement in conjunction with a camera and powerful acquisition and processing software. The illuminance obtained in the conoscopic optical plane therefore represents directly the directional distribution of the light flux. A camera is used to analyze the illuminance and therefore to obtain conographs without calculating anything but the physical mapping between a photoelement from the camera and the viewing direction analyzed. The mapping depends only on the characteristics of the conoscope optics and the conoscope image enlargement optics. The main advantage of this is that it can be used to obtain results in approximately 20 seconds, which is a saving of a factor of around 30 to 100 (depending on the step sizes) compared with the goniometric method. Table 14.3 summarises the advantages and disadvantages of the two methods.

In addition, it is not necessary to make fine adjustments of the display with respect to the instrument, and savings can be made on the rotational positioning systems. However, in view of the short distance required (approximately 1 cm) between the display and the optics to achieve accurate results, the lighting and temperature control of the display

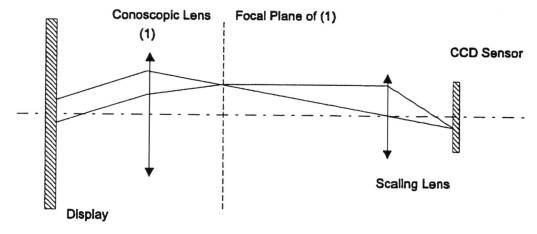

Figure 14.8 Principle of the conoscopic method. The light rays from the display in a given direction go to a given point in the focal plane of the conoscopic optics. A conoscopic lens is basically a very wide angle lens. The image of the angular distribution of the light rays is reduced by the scaling lens and is then analyzed by an image sensor. The scaling lens includes a stop which prevents the conoscopic lens from providing a normal image of the measurement zone

Table 14.3 Comparison of performance of the two methods of determining visual performance of LCDs as a function of viewing direction

	Goniometric	Conoscopic
Accuracy	linked to the photo-colorimeter and the mechanical setup	linked to the conoscopic optics itself
Measurement time	long	short
Measurement cone	no limit	$\pm 60°$ typical
Ease of use	average	very good
Use in production control	difficult	quite easy
Changing the size of the measurement area	easy	possible but requires uniform display
Screen lighting/temperature setting facilities	good	low to average
Cost	photo-colorimeter + mechanics	Conoscopic optics + camera

are difficult to implement. It is possible to position the display further away but then different areas of the display are analyzed. If the display is sufficiently homogeneous, the measurement should give reasonable results.

Instruments using the conoscopic method have not yet been validated by many laboratories and comprehensive data on comparisons with results obtained by goniophotometric methods are not yet available. If conoscopic instruments live up to their current promise, they will bring about a revolution in measuring LCDs, because of the considerable time they save. This time saving will enable far more tests to be carried out and/or enable LCDs to be evaluated in much greater depth.

As Table 14.3 shows, the conoscopic method cannot totally replace the goniophotometric method. But as they incorporate photo-colorimetric cameras, they could also be used as conventional photo-colorimeters in a goniophotometric system, by deliberately replacing the conoscopic optics with normal optics. It would then be possible in theory to have a truly universal instrument, opening up wide prospects of fast automated measurement.

Isovalue representation

Measurements obtained using the methods illustrated above are conventionally represented in isovalues, in a pseudo-polar representation in which the inclination angle θ is the vector radius and the azimuth angle ϕ is the polar angle. Any quantity derived from the luminance, contrast or chromaticity can be represented in this way. However, the practical significance from the point of view of the visual sensation of such isovalues is not immediate. It is here that the problem of visual modelling re-emerges. It is necessary to attempt to link the visual impression, absolute values and variations in luminance, contrast and chromaticity, of a user viewing a display from different directions, to measurement plots. It is obviously desirable that these plots should represent as closely as possible the visual sensation so that displays can be compared validly with each other or against a specification.

It is with this in mind that Hatoh *et al.* (1994) conducted comparisons on different types of LCD between the judgements of the viewers and the representations of various photometric magnitudes. The main conclusions are listed below.

Luminance isocontrast For isocontrasts, viewers are more sensitive to the regularity of curves and to the contrast gradient than to absolute values. It should be noted in passing that visual performance in acuity is more closely linked to the modulation contrast C_m than to the contrast ratio C_R:

$$C_m = (L_{max} - L_{min})/(L_{max} + L_{min}) \qquad 14.2$$

$$C_R = (L_{max}/L_{min}) \qquad 14.3$$

These are linked by the equations

$$C_R = (1 + C_m)/(1 - C_m) \qquad 14.4$$

$$C_m = (C_R - 1)/(C_R + 1) \qquad 14.5$$

It can be seen from these equations that a contrast ratio C_R of 50 gives a modulation contrast, C_m, of 0.96 (96 percent) while a value of 200 (measurable on LCDs in darkness) represents 99 percent, which changes little from the visual point of view. Returning to the very example given in Hatoh *et al.* (1994), a contrast ratio of 10 gives a value for C_m 82 percent while 5 gives 67 percent which does not necessarily make a great difference from the visual comfort point of view, since it is still above the legibility threshold. It would perhaps be judicious (but it is only an unconfirmed suggestion of the author) to represent modulation isovalues rather than contrast ratio isovalues. Another way could be to consider brightness rather than luminance. A problem not currently dealt with is that of isovalues representing grey levels, from which inversions may appear at certain angles. It is difficult to determine any viewer tolerance to such phenomena.

Colour isovalues Hatoh *et al.* (1994) find that CIE hue isovalues are correlated better to subjective impressions. This provides good confirmation of what is normally said

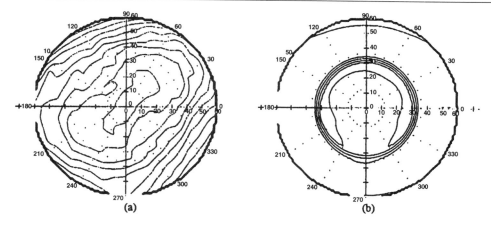

Figure 14.9 Isohues for two displays: in (a) a display with relatively little hue variation, the isohue pitch is 10°; in (b) the pitch is 50° and the variations are very rapid; these diagrams are in good correlation with the subjective impression given by these displays

concerning colour vision, that a viewer is much more sensitive to variations in hue than in saturation. Comparing display chromaticity performance should therefore be best conducted on isohues. The question of tolerance to hue differences obviously arises. By way of illustration, Figure 14.9 gives examples of isohues for two displays, one presenting a moderate hue variation, the other a strong variation. One way of representing colour variations qualitatively is proposed in Chapter 15, where the measured colours are plotted directly in a polar diagram. Although non-quantitative in the strict sense of the term, such a representation is effective for comparing displays.

14.6 CONCLUSION

Measuring displays is as varied and difficult as the complexity of vision itself. It is important to make a rational classification of the different relevant measurement parameters to obtain a clear view of the objectives sought in a particular evaluation context. In the multi-faceted field of display measurement, standards represent the beacons of knowledge and play an important role. However, certain problems remain which will only be soluble with advances in knowledge on modelling vision and in photocolorimetry.

ACKNOWLEDGEMENTS

The author would like to thank his colleagues H. Blanc, C. Billard, M. Le Cun, J. Legrand and J. Mell for their help in the preparation of this chapter.

REFERENCES

Barten, P.G.J. (1990), Image quality of CRT displays, *Seminar Lecture Notes, SID, Las Vegas*, vol. 1.
Berns, R.S., Motta, R.J. and Gorzynski, M.E. (1993a), CRT colorimetry. Part I: Theory and practice, *Colour Research & Application*, **18**(5), 299–314.

Berns, R.S., Gorzynski, M.E. and Motta, R.J. (1993b), CRT colorimetry. Part II: Metrology, *Colour Research & Application*, **18**(5), 315–325.

Berreman, D.W. (1976), Electrical and optical properties of twisted nematic structures, *Non emissive electrooptic displays*, vol. 9, Plenum Press, New York.

Blanc, H. and Glasser, J. (1994), Rigorous and accurate method for measuring the spatial resolution of two-dimensional image sensors, *Current Developments in Optical Design and Optical Engineering IV, SPIE Proc.*, **2263**, 304.

Cone, J. (1993), Survey of front-of-screen requirements from VDU standards and safety requirements, *Eurodisplay '93 Seminar Lecture Notes*, A3.

Fritsch, M. *et al.* (1989), Faster contrast measurement of LCDs with improved conoscopic methods, *Proc. Japan Display Conf.*, 372.

Ghilczy, I., Hawthorne, J., Muray, K., Rety, I. and Schanda, J. (1993), Tristimulus colorimetry with CCD cameras for video display units, *Eurodisplay '93 Proc.*, 427.

Glasser, J. and Rolland, A (1989), Visual performance evaluation of LCDs: appropriate methods for measuring luminance and contrast, *Human Vision, Visual Processing and Digital Display, SPIE Proc.*, **1077**, 9.

Greeson, J.C., *Information Display*, (1990) **6**(7–8), 14; (1990) **6**(12), 26; (1991), **7**(12), 24; (1994), **10**(12), 24.

Hatoh, H., Yamamoto, T., Sato, M. and Ishikawa, M. (1994), Psychophysical evaluation of viewing angle characteristics of liquid crystal displays, *Journal of the SID*, **2(1)**, 21.

Post, D.L. (1992), Colorimetric measurement, calibration and characterisation of self-luminous displays, *Colour in Electronic Display*, Plenum Press, New York, 299.

Leaousc, T. (1993), Fost contrast vs. viewing-angle measurements for LCDs, *Eurodisplay '93, Proc.* 447.

Selhuber, L. and Parker, A. (1995), Optical characterisation of colour LCDs: pitfalls and solutions, *Getting the Best from the State-of-the Art of Display Systems*, SID Conference, London.

Optical characterisation of LCDs: pitfalls and solutions

Ludwig Selhuber and Amboise Parker

15.1 INTRODUCTION

The ultimate goal of a visual display unit (VDU), such as an LCD, is to generate adequately clear information to be interpreted by a human observer. This statement has played a major role in recent years during which the quantity of visually displayed information has been boosted, e.g., by progress in the field of telecommunications. More and more people have daily access to displays for applications such as computer networks, dynamic images on computers, video-conferencing, automotive displays, etc., not only for professional but also for personal use.

The large variety of applications, complemented by variable observation conditions and technological differences between LCD and emissive displays such as CRTs, plasma displays, electroluminescent displays or vacuum fluorescent displays, has led to the development of reproducible qualitative and quantitative characterisation methods. It is a requirement that their output must provide objective data which enable the characterisation, evaluation and improvement of displays.

The methods are based on photometric measurements, the term 'photometry' being defined as a set of measurements of optical parameters which are related to the sensitivity of the human visual system. (See Chapter 14).

Photometry is based on a combination of radiometric measurements and visual evaluations carried out on a statistically large sample of observers. This has led the Commission

Display Systems, Edited by L.W. MacDonald and A.C. Lowe. © 1997 John Wiley & Sons Ltd.

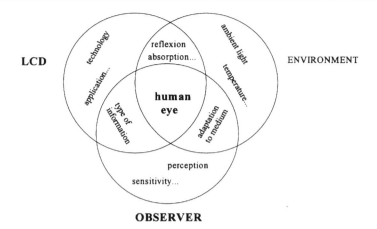

Figure 15.1   Visual Display System

Internationale de l'Eclairage (CIE) to establish a theoretical definition of a standard (or ideal) observer.

Hence, the technical, objective, characterisation of a display is fulfilled by using a photopic filter which optically imitates the spectral sensitivity of the human eye. In this way, the subjective evaluation of displays for certain specific parameters is made unnecessary; consequently easier qualification methods can be used and more reliable results are obtained. As this substitution is not always possible, the International Standards Organisation (ISO) is preparing a subjective evaluation method for flat panel displays in standard 13406, which is at the committee draft stage at the time of publication.

When speaking about the use of a display it is essential to keep in mind that its characteristics are influenced not only by the LCD itself, but also by both the environmental conditions and the observer who represents the final element of the display system, and all three must be taken into consideration (Figure 15.1).

From the above discussion, it is clear that we should always consider the Visual Display 'System' (VDS), rather than the Visual Display 'Unit' (VDU) because external features like the observer and the environment must also be included because of their influence on the parameters to be measured.

Among these interactions, the relation between the LCD and the observer is one of the most important because it implies off-normal viewing directions. This statement is crucial for LCDs whose characteristics depend on viewing angle. For this reason, various characterisation tools and measuring equipment which allow this dependence to be measured will be presented and analyzed in the next section.

15.2   CHARACTERISATION TOOLS

Before defining specific tools which will be useful in characterising an LCD, it is important to identify the different origins of potential causes of degradation of the display's visual characteristics. The related parameters can be grouped in the three main categories of the VDS (Figure 15.1).

First, since the position of the observer with respect to the display is variable, it is crucial to measure the angular luminance, contrast and chromaticity dependency. The required viewing cone, or range of angles over which the characteristics of the display are acceptable, can vary considerably, depending on the application.

Second, the characterisation of the display will be performed under precise control of environmental conditions such as ambient illumination and temperature. Variations of these parameters will give information about the diffusing properties of the display and of its thermal sensitivity.

Finally, the LCD itself is characterised by temporal and spatial criteria. The temporal criteria include the switching characteristics of the liquid crystal (LC), which indicate the time required to switch from one optical state to another, as well as light intensity variations for a fixed electrical driving condition (flicker and image sticking). The spatial features are determined by luminance and chromaticity uniformity measurements over the display area and by crosstalk measurements, the frequency of which depends on the information that is displayed.

The combination of all these measurements will lead to a classification related to the application of the LCD. However, we shall see that the dominant and limiting characteristic that has to be taken into account with LCDs is the variation of luminance and chromaticity with viewing direction.

In order to formalise the viewing direction the work space is described by using a polar representation. The observer's viewing orientation with respect to the LCD is described by a pair of angles: ϕ for the azimuth and θ for the inclination (Figure 15.2).

If a person is viewing a display at normal incidence, the values of the pair (θ, ϕ) are both zero, that is the pair $(\theta, \phi) = (0°, 0°)$. A display observed, for instance, at viewing direction $(\theta, \phi) = (30°, 90°)$ indicates that the observer is looking at the display from above (i.e., the 12 o'clock position) with an inclination of $30°$ with respect to the normal of the display.

Depending on the application of a display, the user will have very specific requirements regarding the viewing cone.

For example, a wide left–right viewing angle with inclinations between $\pm30°$ and $\pm40°$ will be necessary in certain automotive applications if both the driver and the passenger need to have access to the information displayed at the centre of the dashboard. An

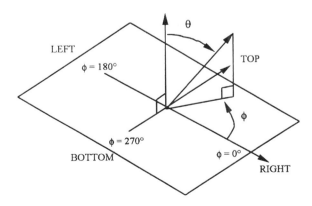

Figure 15.2 Work space

equivalent expression, describing the whole range, is commonly used and equals $60°-80°$ in this case.

On the other hand, a greater vertical viewing angle will be better suited for a laptop computer. This implies that the optical characteristics should be similar for a given inclination, independent of the azimuth.

To plot such information on the display's characteristics, synthetic graphical representations are used which can present more information than a standard graphical representation, e.g., of a two-axes curve. Their advantage is that the ability to interpret the complete data enables an objective classification of the display to be made. A complete set of specific tools used with LCDs which satisfy these requirements will now be described.

15.2.1 Luminance and contrast measurements

For a characterisation of display properties vs. viewing direction, the luminance is measured for various electrical driving conditions of the LCD: the bright state, the dark state and the required number of intermediate levels.

As shown in Figure 15.3, which is for a normally white (i.e., white at zero applied field) twisted nematic (NWTN) TFT-LCD, the measurement can be represented by a transmission vs inclination $T(\theta)$ curve for a given azimuth angle (uniaxial scanning). Figure 15.3(a) shows a horizontal, left–right, scanning and Figure 15.3(b) a vertical, bottom–top, scanning of a 6 o'clock display (the equivalent of $\phi = 270°$). In this case, the hour represents the preferential viewing direction, defined as the viewing direction at which the display has maximum contrast ratio.

The advantage of the scanning method resides in the fact that this measurement provides more complete information on the LCD's characteristics than a simple measurement at normal incidence. For instance, it indicates the preferential direction of the display. In the case of the given display, the lowest transmission of the black state ($T = 0.2\%$) is at an inclination of $\theta = 6°$ towards the bottom.

The contrast ratio CR is defined as the ratio between the bright and dark state luminance, so it is obvious that the luminance of the dark state has a greater influence on the contrast ratio than that of the bright state. Any small increase of the dark state luminance will cause a perceptible loss of contrast ratio.

The asymmetrical behaviour of the LCD about the (0,0) direction is indicative of the asymmetrical deformation of the LC layer when subjected to an electrical field, especially at intermediate grey levels. This is particularly evident with bottom–top scanning (cf. Figure 15.3).

Still, it appears that uniaxial scanning is an inadequate method for many applications, very few of which require viewing at a single azimuth angle–not even automotive applications and certainly not TV. Therefore it is necessary to use a new type of representation where all viewing directions can be represented on the same figure. Polar representations satisfy this criterion.

The first of these is the iso-luminance plot, also referred to as a luminance contour diagram. It represents all the viewing angle pairs (θ, ϕ) which correspond to a given luminance value. The inclination, θ, is represented by the radial vector and the rotation, ϕ, increases in a counter-clockwise direction.

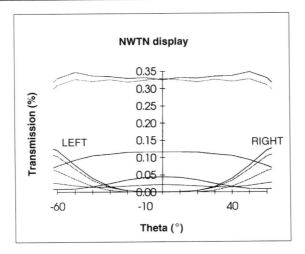

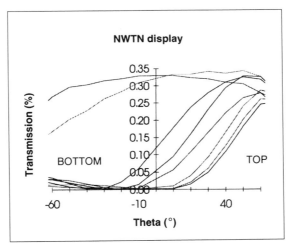

Figure 15.3 Transmission variations with viewing angle for eight grey levels of a NWTN display

The iso-contrast curve (or contrast contour diagram) is similar to the iso-luminance plot, but it represents, instead of luminance values, the contrast ratio of the display.

Figure 15.4 indicates the iso-luminance plot of a TFT-LCD dark state. Figures 15.5 and 15.6 show two different iso-contrast representations of a TFT-LCD and a passive TN display respectively. The observation directions (θ, ϕ) are indicated on Figure 15.6.

Generally speaking, the iso-contrast plot has the more widespread use, the reason being that the human eye detects data on a display by comparison rather than by absolute luminance value. For instance, to distinguish characters on a screen, the contrast ratio between the character and the background luminance should be greater than five in the case of professional applications, where displays are used for several hours a day.

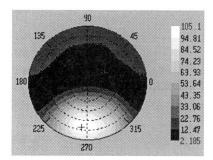

Figure 15.4 Iso-luminance plot

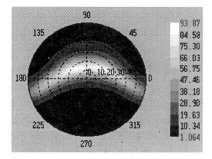

Figure 15.5 Iso-contrast plot I

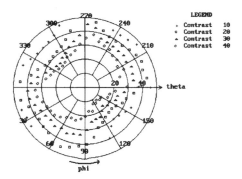

Figure 15.6 Iso-contrast plot II

The upper contrast ratio limit of our visual perception system is somewhat larger than 10, which corresponds to the limitation of visual acuity. Therefore, a contrast ratio of 10 is considered to be satisfactory for saturated, or bi-level, displays. For displays with intermediate grey levels, the contrast ratio must be greater.

The absolute lower limit is reached when the dark state becomes as luminous as or more luminous than the bright state and the contrast ratio becomes less than one. This condition is known as a contrast ratio inversion.

Although the iso-contrast plot is more common, iso-luminance plots are still useful because they make it possible to display the luminance level for a single intermediate grey level over the entire observation space and they present the data in the optimum manner to understand and hence to control the absolute luminance levels.

Iso-luminance plots also enable grey level inversion to be studied. Grey level inversion occurs when the luminance level of grey level $(n + 1)$, which is lower than that of grey level (n) at $(0,0)$, becomes greater than that of grey level (n) at a given off-normal viewing angle.

Figures 15.7(a) and 15.7(b) illustrate iso-luminance plots of two grey levels, Grey1 and Grey2. Their respective luminances at normal incidence are 2 cd/m^2 and 5 cd/m^2. Figure 15.8 represents the calculated ratio Grey2/Grey1. The black areas indicate a grey level inversion.

However, iso-contrast and iso-luminance plots, as described, provide no information about the relationships between unwanted colouring effects and viewing angle. This is a major drawback, particularly when using colour displays or intrinsically coloured LCDs such as STN displays. It has been emphasised by Becker and Neumeier (1990) that the maximum colour difference, ΔE^{ab}, on a measured display combined with the electro-optical transfer characteristics, does not coincide with the maximum luminance.

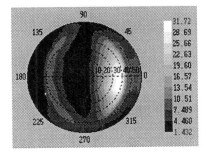

Figure 15.7(a)   Grey 1

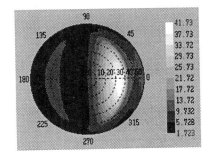

Figure 15.7(b)   Grey 2

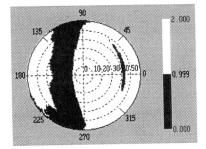

Figure 15.8   Grey level ratio

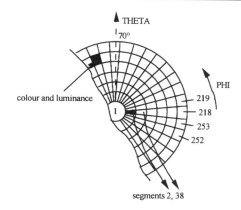

Figure 15.9 Colorplot

15.2.2 Colour measurements

To alleviate the disadvantages of iso-luminance and iso-contrast curves, colorimetric information needs to be added to some new type of representation plots.

Sato *et al.* (1994) have described an evaluation method of colour shifts of LCDs by using several parameters related to colour and comparing them with subjective results. They found that an evaluation in terms of Δh (difference in hue-angle) gave the best results. Similar plots to those described in Section 15.2.1 were used, with luminance and contrast ratio contour lines simply being replaced by iso-hue curves.

Their advantage is that they give an objective characterisation of colour changes with the viewing angle. However, it is quite difficult to interpret these plots since they only indicate an absolute hue angle difference, and it is not possible visually to determine the actual colour change from these plots.

In order to solve these shortfalls a subjective representation method, closer to the user's perception of the display, called the colourplot, can be used. It also is a polar diagram which simultaneously displays the colour and the luminance as a function of the viewing angle in 10° steps for ϕ and θ (*cf.* Figure 15.9 and Colour Plates 15–22). It is important for the reader to understand that the colourplot should be visualised on a calibrated monitor (see Section 15.4.3 and Chapter 17) for an accurate and absolute representation of the display. Nevertheless, relative comparisons between displays are possible on a non-calibrated monitor.

Contrary to the iso-contrast curves, colourplots represent a single state of the LCD for a given voltage. This allows an individual and quantitative evaluation of white, black, grey and colour states by displaying the luminance and the colouring with respect to the viewing angle. This information is very helpful for display optimisation and characterisation and also for analyzing shifts of coloration and luminance as a function of the viewing angles.

It is important to point out that the colourplot and the iso-contrast plot are complementary and that their similar styles of representation make it easy to work with them simultaneously.

As an example, we have characterised a 1/4 VGA colour FSTN (film compensated STN) display. The luminance is close to 100 cd/m^2 at normal incidence, which is

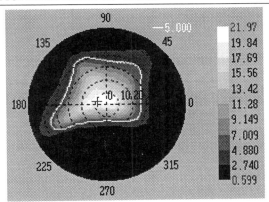

Figure 15.18   FSTN contrast ratio

considered to be good. The iso-contrast plot indicates that the viewing cone for CR > 5 is large enough for the intended application (Figure 15.18).

The user might conclude from this evaluation that the overall features of the display were satisfactory. However, if the colorimetric characteristics of the display are also measured, it will be observed that they are significantly less uniform than the luminance characteristics at off-normal viewing angles.

For an inclination $\theta > 20°$, the bright state colourplot Figure 15.10 (Colour Plate 15) shows significant variation of colouring azimuth, ϕ. The colourplot is rather homogeneous for $\theta \leqslant 20°$, but the white state has a slight bluish coloration. For $30° < \theta < 40°$, the dominant colour is blue. At larger viewing angles the colouring effects are bluish, greenish and brownish. The dark state colourplot Figure 15.11 (Colour Plate 16) shows an increase in luminance for $\theta > 20°$. This luminance increase results in dark state colouring effects (blue, green, pink and yellow).

The colourplots in Figures 15.10–15.17 (Colour Plates 15–22) show conclusively that even for displays with satisfactory iso-contrast curves, coloration effects at off-normal viewing angles cannot be neglected. Depending on the application of the display, these effects can even become limiting.

15.3 CHARACTERISATION METHODS

Two distinct measurement methods can be used to determine the intrinsic viewing direction dependence of the properties of the LCD: the goniometric and the conoscopic methods. (See also Section 14.5.4).

15.3.1 Goniometric method

The goniometric method was introduced by Barna (1976) and consists of mechanically scanning the detector through (θ, ϕ). The scanning of a viewing cone is obtained by using two rotation tables which can drive either the LCD or the optical acquisition system, or both. Commonly either the LCD is mounted on one table and the optical system on the other or the LCD is mounted on both. The latter case is shown in Figure 15.19. Each of the stepping motors drives one rotation axis of the pair (θ, ϕ) and a precise mounting system for the display is also necessary.

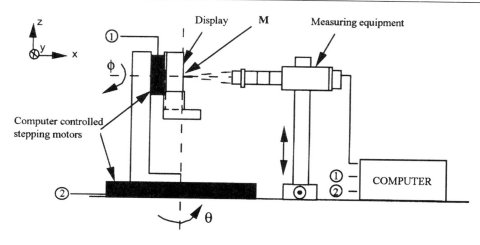

Figure 15.19   Measurement configuration bench

As the creation of a colourplot is time-consuming because of the large number of measurements required (between half an hour and several hours, depending on the optical equipment), the whole system (measurement equipment, rotation tables) is driven by a computer.

As an example, the measurement of a single state requires 217 acquisitions for an inclination up to $\theta = 60°$, with $10°$ increments in ϕ and θ. In order to plot an iso-contrast curve, more than 400 measurements are required.

The acquisition of reliable data requires that several calibrations are carried out and precautions observed. Before initiating the measurements, one has to be sure that the same area of the display is measured for all the viewing angles. The two rotation axes and the principal axis of the measurement equipment have to be adjustable so that they converge on a single point located in the LC layer of the display (point M in Figure 15.19).

The implementation is complex and exacting, but the lower limit of the size of the measured area can be reduced if the precision of the setting of the axes is increased. This is often critical when measuring areas on the display as small as one pixel and particularly when the field of the measuring equipment approaches the size of the pixel, or segment, that has to be measured.

Finally, depending on the kind of measurements that have to be carried out, the optical measuring equipment of the goniometric system can be a photometer (broadband system), a filter-colorimeter (also broadband system) or a spectrophotometer (narrowband system). This equipment must be recalibrated with respect to a reference standard at regular intervals to ensure accurate measurements.

If an iso-contrast plot is sufficient to characterise the display, as is the case for a black and white bi-level TN device where coloration at off-normal viewing angles is insignificant, a photometer is the most suitable measurement device. Its spectral sensitivity $V(\lambda)$ approximates the sensitivity of the human eye (CIE 1931, 2° observer) and provides precise luminance values in the minimum time.

In applications where colour is important, the use of a spectrophotometer or a filter colorimeter which gives luminance and colour information in various standard colour spaces such as CIE 1931, CIELUV or CIELAB, is necessary.

The filter colorimeter is a simpler device than the spectrophotometer. Because of its method of operation, the measurements are also faster by a factor of 10 to 20. The most critical feature is the fabrication of the filters. The best systems presently available use a set of four filters and have a colorimetric accuracy in the range of 0.002 for each of the chromaticity coordinates x, y, u' and v'.

The spectrophotometer combines a monochromator and a linear photodiode array detector. In general they are not as sensitive as filter colorimeters ($0.5-1$ cd/m^2 and $0.01-0.1$ cd/m^2 respectively) and they require longer integration periods to optimise the signal-to-noise ratio when measuring dark states. Consequently the filter colorimeter is better suited for colourplots.

Still, the spectrophotometer is not limited to colourplots and has wider application possibilities because of its spectral analysis capability and high accuracy. It is, for instance, better suited when measuring an emissive object whose spectrum is narrow, such as backlights, and for measuring the precise spectral transmission characteristics of, e.g., LCD colour filters.

15.3.2   Conoscopic method

The conoscopic method is based on a specific optical system which transforms the viewing angle direction of the LCD (angular distribution) into a position on the image plane (spatial distribution). In Figure 15.20, a CCD camera is located in the image plane. The first publications on such a system were by Kmetz (1978) and Penz (1978). Since then, the system has been realised and published by Leroux (1993) and by Lu and Saleh (1993).

The acquisition is done simultaneously for all (θ, ϕ) values within a viewing cone of 60° to 70° by collecting the light beams from all these viewing angles with the use of high aperture optics at the entry of the system. The image formed in its focal plane is then transformed with a second lens into a spatial distribution on the CCD camera.

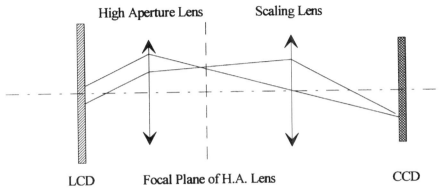

Figure 15.20   Conoscope principle

Table 15.1 Comparison of the features of optical characterisation devices

	Goniometric			Conoscopic
	Photometer	Filter Colorimeter	Spectrophotometer	Conoscope
Dark room	yes	yes	yes	no
Isoplot acquisition speed	good	average	insufficient	excellent
Spectral measurement	no	no	yes	no
Colour measurement	no	yes	yes	yes
Maximum spot size	no limit	no limit	no limit	1 mm^2
Measurement of reflective LCD	yes	yes	yes	no
Rotation tables	yes	yes	yes	no

The main advantage of this method is the reduced acquisition time which is seconds instead of hours for the goniometric method. The method does not require complicated adjustments of rotation tables as in Section 3.1. The distance between the LCD and the entrance optics is about 5 mm and under such conditions it is difficult to include an illumination system in the conoscope to measure reflective devices or to simulate a particular ambient illumination condition for reflective displays. Moreover, it is not possible to measure devices where the LC layer is more than 5 mm from the high aperture lens. The largest spot size which can be measured is also limited to about 1 mm^2 and this can be too small for a correct averaging over a spatially variable surface such as a colour filter.

Another possibility for the conoscope is to use it with a set of filters to make a conoscopic filter colorimeter. Colourplots can be plotted in less than 3 minutes. But it has to be kept in mind that this type of system has been developed only recently and is still not completely validated.

Finally, Table 15.1 compares the advantages and disadvantages of the goniometric and conoscopic methods. (See also Table 14.3). As can be seen from Table 15.1, each of the four techniques has advantages and disadvantages. For a viewing angle characterisation the high speed acquisition of the conoscopic method makes it generally the best suited one. On the other hand parameters summarised in Section 2 (response time of the liquid crystal, crosstalk, spatial and temporal uniformity, etc.) must be quantified for a complete characterisation of the LCD and this is not possible with the conoscope alone.

15.4 OBTAINING RELIABLE MEASUREMENTS

To obtain reliable results, various features of the optical acquisition systems have to be controlled. The goniometric and conoscopic systems have few common features, so each will be discussed separately.

However, one common feature between the two techniques is the sensitivity dependence of the diffraction grating of a spectrophotometer, and of the CCD camera on the conoscopic system, to the polarisation state of the light. This source of error can reach an amplitude of a few percent and might not be acceptable for absolute measurements and calibrations on LCDs, the front polariser of which transmits linearly polarised light.

Pefferkorn *et al.* (1993) have shown that when the LCD is measured at two orientations 90° apart and the results averaged, the error is reduced to <1 percent.

15.4.1   Goniometric features

The accuracy and precision of the measurements will be strongly influenced by several factors: the numerical aperture and field of view of the measuring equipment, parasitic light, and the size of the measured area of the display. Their effect, together with methods to minimise their influence, will now be discussed and comparative results will be presented.

Numerical aperture (NA) and field of view (FOV)

Both these parameters determine the angular resolution of the measurement. If the field of view is too large (Figure 15.21), the detector collects light from the points between B and C. Therefore, the measurement includes a set of points with an inclination angle $\theta \in [-\theta_{FV}, \theta_{FV}]$ and no longer corresponds to a measurement at normal incidence. So θ_{FV} must be reduced so that only light rays issued from a smaller area whose inclinations are close to the normal of the display are captured (Figure 15.22).

With a high aperture lens (Figure 15.22), the acceptance angle θ_{NA} becomes too large. The detector now collects light rays emitted, e.g., from point A with inclination angles $\theta \in [-\theta_{NA}, \theta_{NA}]$. Under such conditions, as for those of high FOV, neither does this method correspond to normal incidence.

In practice, the FOV is generally small because it is determined by the size of the diaphragm placed in front of the detector. The important point is to verify that the NA, which will depend on the lens used, remains smaller than 0.08 ($\theta_{NA} = 5°$, IEC standard 47C16).

On the other hand, too great a reduction of the NA will lead to poor signal to noise ratio. The use of an aperture angle θ_{NA} in the range 4–5° is a good compromise.

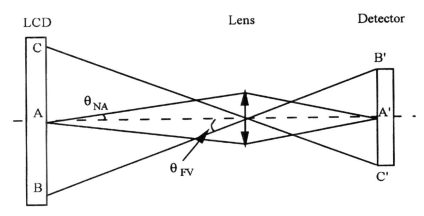

Figure 15.21   Too large a field of view

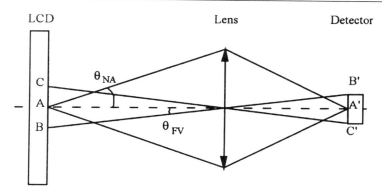

Figure 15.22   High aperture lens

Parasitic light

Any light source other than the measured spot is considered to be parasitic. As a consequence, all measurements have to be made without being affected by external light sources. Another source of parasitic light is the emission of light by the display itself from a region other than the spot under measurement, which reaches the detector after several reflections in the lens (Figure 15.23). As an example, we have taken coefficients of transmission and reflection of the lens respectively equal to 96 percent and 4 percent. In this case, the detected parasitic light represents 0.15 percent of the emission after two reflections.

In the case of a dark state measurement, the contribution of parasitic light reflected from a bright state (high luminance) area, located close to the measured spot, is very important regarding the contrast ratio (Table 15.2). The numerical example shows that in such conditions the loss in contrast is close to 30 percent, although this represents an absolute worst case with uncoated surfaces. In practice, antireflection coatings would considerably reduce parasitic reflections.

The quality of the measurement is improved by masking the surface around the spot.

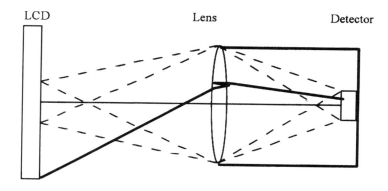

Figure 15.23   Parasitic reflections

Table 15.2 Influence of parasitic light

	Black	White	Contrast ratio
Without parasitic light	1	300	300
With parasitic bright state light (300)	1.45	300.45	207

To illustrate the examples in this section, the three representations of iso-contrast curves which follow are based on measurements made under the different conditions described above. A major influence on the results is observed.

Measurements with a large numerical aperture, NA = 0.12, and without a mask covering the area around the spot (Figure 15.24) show properties inferior to the expected behaviour of the LCD. These measurements include a significant contribution from noise (parasitic light) which reduces the contrast ratio at all observation angles.

By reducing the numerical aperture NA to 0.08 (Figure 15.25), the iso-contrast curves are clearly improved, particularly for small values of θ. The curves for different contrast

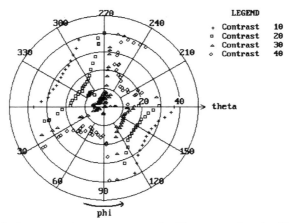

Figure 15.24 Iso-contrast curves measured without a mask and with a large NA

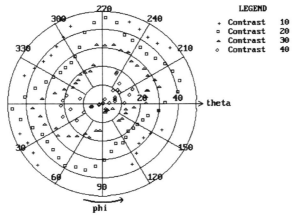

Figure 15.25 Iso-contrast curves measured with an appropriate NA but without a mask

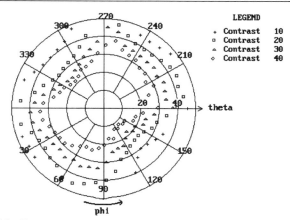

Figure 15.26   Iso-contrast curves measured with a mask and an appropriate NA

ratios no longer overlap and are extended to larger viewing angles. However, masking of the area adjacent to the measurement spot is still necessary (Figure 15.26) to obtain accurate contrast ratio measurements.

Size of the measured area

The choice of the measured area depends mainly on the requirements of the application for which the display will be used. Two situations occur in general: measurements on a very small area (i.e. one pixel) or measurements of a large area in order to have an averaging effect.

In the first case, the settings have to be extremely precise in order to keep the area measured independent of the viewing angle (see Section 15.3.1).

For a measurement on a colour filter, one might rather be interested in correlating it with the perception a human eye would have of the display. This requires measurement of a large set of pixels in order to produce an average value which includes the black matrix. As the viewing angle is varied, the translation of the measured spot, due to the imperfect alignment of the optical and rotation axes, must be negligible in comparison to the dimension of the measured area.

Table 15.3 gives an approximation of the resulting maximum colour variation ΔE^{ab} as a function of the accuracy of alignment, defined as the ratio of maximum spot translation to the spot diameter.

It appears that in order to detect a colour difference ΔE^{ab} in the range 5–10 with a maximum measurement error of 10 percent, the precision of the settings has to be better than 1 percent. This explains the high accuracy needed on the translation tables for the goniometric method.

Table 15.3   Colour variations

	1%	5%	10%
Accuracy of the settings	1%	5%	10%
Corresponding ΔE_{ab} error	1	6	12
Spot size for a 0.1 mm undesired translation (diameter in mm)	10	2	1
Approximate number of pixels	2000	400	200

15.4.2   Conoscopic features

In contrast to the goniometric method, alignment of the conoscopic system is less critical because its features (optics, CCD camera) are fixed by the manufacturer. Hence, the system is easier to use.

The main feature which must be precisely controlled by the user (close to 0.1 mm accuracy) is the distance between the display plane and the high aperture lens of the conoscope. If the display is not positioned correctly, then the position of the measuring spot on the display varies with the inclination angle θ. As the maximum spot size is only 1 mm^2, the averaging over this area is insufficient to avoid errors due to this effect, and the plot shows periodic luminance variations.

Figure 15.27 shows an iso-luminance plot of a bright state where the correct distance was set. When the positioning error increases, so does the frequency of the periodic variations. Figures 15.28 and 15.29 show the results when the positioning error is equal to 3 mm and 20 mm respectively. The best way to avoid this problem is to use the conoscope with a sighting tube with which a well-focused image of the measured area corresponds to the correct focusing of the high aperture lens.

Figure 15.27   Correct focusing

Figure 15.28   Bad focusing I

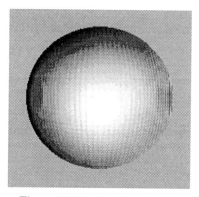

Figure 15.29 Bad focusing II

15.4.3 Monitor calibration

Finally, calibration of the colour CRT monitor is required to achieve an accurate colourplot reproduction of the measured luminance and colours. Calibration is required not only because the voltage–luminance curve (gamma function) of the CRT differs from that of an LCD, but because of differences in the luminance of the red, green and blue channels from one CRT monitor to another. (See Chapters 16 and 17).

The relation used to determine the CIE XYZ values from the RGB luminance values (Y_r, Y_g, Y_b) requires the measurement of the CIE 1931 chromaticities of the red (x_r, y_r, z_r), green (x_g, y_g, z_g) and blue (x_b, y_b, z_b) channels as well as the transfer functions from video input voltage to light output (gamma functions $f_r(Y_r), f_g(Y_g), f_b(Y_b)$):

$$\begin{bmatrix} X \\ Y \\ Z \end{bmatrix} = \underbrace{\begin{bmatrix} x_r/y_r & x_g/y_g & x_b/y_b \\ 1 & 1 & 1 \\ z_r/y_r & z_g/y_g & z_b/y_b \end{bmatrix}}_{M} \cdot \begin{bmatrix} f_r(Y_r) \\ f_g(Y_g) \\ f_b(Y_b) \end{bmatrix} \Rightarrow \begin{bmatrix} f_r(Y_r) \\ f_g(Y_g) \\ f_b(Y_b) \end{bmatrix} = M^{-1} \cdot \begin{bmatrix} X \\ Y \\ Z \end{bmatrix}$$

Assuming that CIE 1931 chromaticities, $(x_{\mathrm{CIE}}, y_{\mathrm{CIE}})$ and luminance (Y) values are used to display a colourplot, two types of measurements on large surfaces are necessary:

- CIE 1931 chromaticities x_{CIE} and y_{CIE} on red, green and blue patterns to determine the three-by-three colour transformation matrix M^{-1};
- luminance of all the intermediate levels, measured separately on red, green and blue patterns, to determine the gamma functions.

A comparison of various mathematical functions used to approximate the radiance characteristics of the monitor has been made by Bodrogi *et al.* (1995), who also proposed a new function which reduces the differences between the predicted and the measured monitor colours. These measurements are important as the quality of the displayed images will be based on this calibration. The precautions that need to be taken to obtain reliable results are the same as for the LCD characterisation with a filter-colorimeter or a spectrophotometer (see Section 4.1).

We have shown a comparison between the calibrated colourplots presented in Section 15.2.2 Figures 15.10 and 15.11 (in Colour Plates 15 and 16) and the colourplots of the same display (1/4 VGA colour FSTN) but represented on a non-calibrated colour CRT monitor Figures 15.12 and 15.13 (in Colour Plates 17 and 18). The uncalibrated bright and dark states show a reddish colouring. This is explained by a different distribution between the red, green and blue CRT channels. In this example the red tube is more efficient than the one on the calibrated monitor.

Another example of an STN device combined with a yellow-green LED (light emitting diode) backlight is shown in Figures 15.14–15.17 (Colour Plates 19–22). The bright and dark states displayed on the same non-calibrated monitor as above Figures 15.14–15.15 (in Colour Plates 19 and 20) show different colours at a given viewing angle than the calibrated monitor Figures 15.16–15.17 (in Colour Plates 21 and 22). The colour shifts towards a yellowish green is also explained by the more efficient red tube in the uncalibrated CRT. Nevertheless, the luminance variations at off-normal viewing angles are calibration independent.

As can be seen, the colourplots are very useful for relative and absolute comparisons of different LCD technologies and backlight types. They also clearly illustrate the viewing angle dependency of colour and luminance on a LCD driven at any electrical state.

15.5 CONCLUSION

In the visual display system (VDS), the interactions between the observer and the LCD are predominant and explain the importance of characterisation as a function of viewing angle and azimuth in LCD technologies.

Several types of polar plots appear to be the best graphical, synthetic representation methods for luminance, contrast and colour measurements as functions of the viewing angle. Iso-luminance plots, iso-contrast plots and colourplots are complementary tools which fulfil this function. A calibrated colour CRT monitor is essential in order to achieve a faithful representation of the colouring effects of LCDs at off-normal viewing angles.

Finally, of the various techniques presented for the characterisation of LCDs, the conoscopic method is the best suited for viewing angle measurements, its fast acquisition times and ease of use giving reliable results. Nevertheless, photometer, filter-colorimeter and spectrophotometer goniometric systems are also required for a complete characterisation of the relevant features of LCDs.

REFERENCES

Barna, G.A. (1976), Apparatus for optical characterisation of displays, *Rev. Sci. Instr.*, **47**, (10), 1258.

Becker, M.E. and Neumeier, J. (1990), Measurement of electro-optic properties of LCDs, *Proc. SID*, **31** (4).

Bodrogi, P., Muray, K., Scanda, J. and Kranicz, B. (1995), Accurate colourimetric calibration of CRT monitors, *SID Digest*, 455.

International Electronic Commission, Draft International Standard 47C16.

Kmetz, A. (1978), Characterisation and optimisation of twisted nematic displays for multiplexing, *SID Digest*, 70.

Leroux, T. (1993), Fast contrast vs. viewing angle measurements for LCDs, *Eurodisplay Conf. Proc.*, 447.

Lu, K. and Saleh, B.E.A. (1993), Fast design tools for LCD viewing-angle optimisation, *SID Digest*, 630.

Pefferkorn, S., Vienot, F., Chiron, A. and Brettel, H. (1993), Problem of spectroradiometric calibration of polarised displays, *Eurodisplay Conf. Proc.*, 443.

Penz, P.A. (1978), A figure of merit characterising the anisotropic viewing properties of TN-LCDs, *SID Digest*, 68.

Sato, M., Ishikawa, M., Hisatake, Y. and Hatoh, H. (1994), Viewing-angle evaluation method of colour shift for LCDs with gray-scale image, *SID Digest*, 333.

Measurement and standardisation in the colorimetry of CRT displays

Andrew Hanson

16.1 INTRODUCTION

This chapter deals with the colorimetric calibration of cathode ray tube (CRT) displays. The distinction should be made at the outset between the words 'calibration' and 'characterisation'. Here calibration implies the ascription of a value to a device for a set of conditions. A calibration is only true when the exact set of conditions is precisely repeated. Characterisation, on the other hand, uses a model to predict the behaviour of a device under a wide range of conditions. It is possible to write a characterisation model for a CRT, and then use calibration to provide parameters for the model.

The colorimetry of visual displays requires many considerations in addition to the general practices of colorimetry, which are summarised elsewhere (CIE, 1986; Hunt, 1991). Although this chapter concentrates on specific topics relating to a particular display technology, many of the principles can be extended to other emissive display technologies such as plasma discharge systems.

Broadly speaking, the areas pertinent to the measurement of the colour of CRTs are as follows:

- A CRT conveys information by emission of light rather than by reflection of incident light. Measurements made of the colour are traceable to a radiance scale, which is an absolute scale, in contrast to a reflectance scale, which is a relative scale. The scales

Display Systems, Edited by L.W. MacDonald and A.C. Lowe. © Crown copyright

of different instruments must be unified in order for their results to be compatible, and therefore of any use.

- The image on a CRT is highly dynamic and the colour and position of image elements change continuously. The properties to be measured are the end result of a complex system, not of a single piece of material.
- The technologies for generating the emitted light give rise to measurement hazards in the spectral, spatial and temporal domains.
- Measurement of light emitted from a CRT may be significantly affected by ambient light, manifested in the form of glare or reduced contrast ratio.

16.2 COLOUR SPECIFICATION

The basics of colorimetry have been established and published by the CIE (CIE, 1986), and this system of colour specification is widely used. The essence of the system is that any colour can be specified by a minimum of three numbers (the number three because human colour vision is afforded by three classes of cone detector in the retina). An instrument designed to measure the colour of a source using the CIE 1931 standard colorimetric system will integrate the spectral power distribution of the source with the three colour matching functions $x(\lambda)$, $y(\lambda)$ and $z(\lambda)$:

$$X = k\Sigma[P(\lambda)\bar{x}(\lambda)]$$

$$Y = k\Sigma[P(\lambda)\bar{y}(\lambda)] \qquad\qquad 16.1$$

$$Z = k\Sigma[P(\lambda)\bar{z}(\lambda)]$$

The $\bar{y}(\lambda)$ function is actually the spectral luminous sensitivity of the human eye. The constant k is chosen so that Y will give values as units of candela per square metre. For convenience, these numbers are condensed to give chromaticity coordinates which are calculated using equations 16.2:

$$x = X/(X + Y + Z)$$

$$y = Y/(X + Y + Z) \qquad\qquad 16.2$$

$$z = Z/(X + Y + Z)$$

$$x + y + z = 1$$

x and y, which may be thought of as proportions of redness and greenness respectively, can be plotted on a chromaticity chart as shown in Figure 16.1. The two chromaticity coordinates, along with luminance Y, are sufficient to specify uniquely the colour and luminance of the source.

Other systems such as CIELUV and CIELAB are also in common use. These also use three numbers to specify colour in a form more closely allied to human perception, and are derived from X, Y and Z. Their calculation and application are described in the literature (CIE, 1986; Hunt, 1991).

The units of light cannot be defined in the arbitrary manner which is used for, say, length. The scale must be related to human visual performance. Work has not ceased in

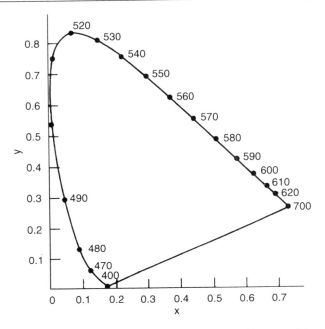

Figure 16.1   CIE 1931 chromaticity diagram with spectral locus

the definition of units, and experiments continue to define new scales describing various visual task scenarios (Taylor *et al.*, 1994).

16.3   COLOUR CRT TECHNOLOGY OVERVIEW

Colour CRT displays are dominated by the 'shadowmask' technology, whose working principles are illustrated in Figure 16.2. The shadowmask CRT is an additive colour system in which a range of colours can be obtained by mixing light from the red, green and blue primaries, each primary being under independent control. See also Chapter 12.

Three electron guns inclined at a small angle to each other are aimed at the same point on the screen. Behind the screen, at a distance of about 10 mm, is a perforated metal foil (the shadowmask) with a fine regular pattern of holes. The guns are mutually inclined in order that any one mask hole will give three displaced projection target locations at the screen. If three different phosphor types are placed at the three target positions then any one gun can land electrons on only one phosphor type. If this shadow action can be maintained as each of the beams is swept together over the screen then modulation of the electron guns will give independent control of light emission from the three phosphor types. This is no trivial task when we consider that mask-shadow to phosphor patch registration has to be maintained within a few tens of micrometres over screen distances of a few hundred millimetres.

The colorimetrist needs to be aware of the factors in the total environment of the display which can induce colour variability leading to non-repeatable measurements or measurements which are not valid for the conditions in which the display is to be used.

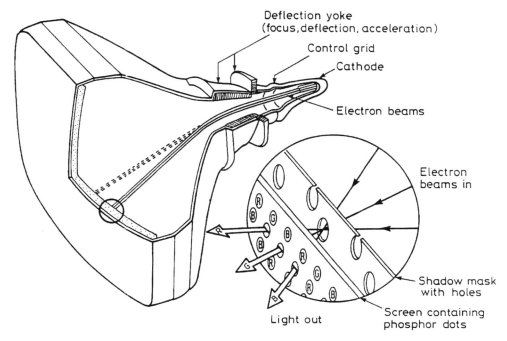

Figure 16.2 Working principle of a shadowmask CRT

The shadowmask action is the main candidate for introducing variability, because of the precise registration needed between mask-hole shadow and phosphor patch. Very small misregistration is accommodated by a guard band in the design and has no effect on the colour, but if the misregistration exceeds the guard band the light emission starts to reduce. With severe misregistration the emission magnitude falls further and also the beam may start to impinge on the wrong colour patch of phosphor, resulting in colour purity errors.

Misregistration can arise from:

- Departure from ideal internal geometry during manufacture process, yielding registration differences across the screen.
- Thermal distortion of the shadowmask due to electron beam loading and environment temperature. The effects of thermal distortion will vary across the screen and will depend on the pattern of the electron beam loading.
- Some shadowmask designs incorporate thermal compensators but the compensation can lag in time behind the error.
- Mask movement due to imposed vibration.
- Magnetic fields (even terrestrial fields) can distort the electron beam paths and give rise to misregistration.
- The CRT and/or the drive electronics have fine adjustments for registration. Sometimes these are accessible to the user and provide an opportunity for misadjustment.

Other sources of colour variability are as follows.

Phosphor contamination

A patch of, say, blue phosphor could contain a few particles of red or green phosphor.

Secondary emission

Beam electrons intercepted by the mask will yield some secondary electron emission from the hole edges. These will land on the phosphors in a diffuse manner and tend to excite all the phosphors.

Phosphor non-linearity

There is often a significant degree of non-linearity between phosphor excitation and the resultant light output. Non-linearities may be different for the red, green and blue phosphors.

Electron gun non-linearity

There is a highly non-linear relation between drive voltage and beam current (the so-called gamma function), coupled with time and temperature drift of the point from which drive voltage is defined. This has to be accommodated by complex electronic design and careful adjustment, particularly for avionic and marine applications where there may be a need to dim the display over a 5000:1 range.

Setting of white and black points

Colour errors will arise if both the white points and black levels are not set according to a well-defined procedure.

Electron gun interaction

There may be interaction between the strengths of the three electron beams. For example, the amount of red light emitted for a given digital value may change as the amount of blue and green is varied. This can be checked by displaying a series of colours and comparing the predicted with the measured colours (Cowan & Rowell, 1986).

16.4 POTENTIAL SOURCES OF MEASUREMENT ERROR FOR CRTs

16.4.1 Spatial colour variability

At the scale of the individual phosphor dot, the colour of a CRT varies dramatically. It is important that a colour measuring device takes the mean colour of several phosphor dot triads. This can be achieved either by ensuring that exactly the same number of red, green and blue dots are included in the sample, or (more practically) that an area containing at least 100 dot triads is measured, i.e. that the aperture of the measuring instrument is at least 10 times the phosphor dot pitch.

On a larger spatial scale there will be significant colour variability over the screen, due to a variety of physical and operational factors. It is important to realise that a calibration will only be valid for the particular area being measured and will not necessarily be valid elsewhere. An illustration of the variability in CIE x, y and Y over the area of a typical

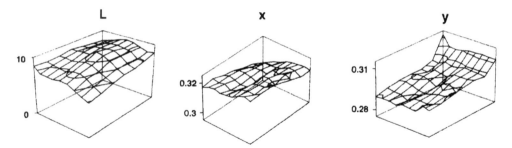

Figure 16.3 Colour variability (in CIE 1931 colour space) over the screen area of a typical CRT set to display white

CRT monitor is shown in Figure 16.3. When quoting a result it is essential to specify the position, size and shape of the area being measured.

16.4.2   Short term temporal factors

The total and relative spectral quantities of light emanating from a CRT vary considerably with time. The most dramatic is the screen refresh procedure, in which the electron beam is swept over the entire screen area at typical rates of 60 to 80 times per second in order to maintain the excitation level of the phosphors. The display is designed in such a way that these changes are (hopefully) not immediately visible to the human eye.

A colour measurement device, however, may well detect flicker and other temporal changes and these can affect the measurement results. The light output from any single point on a CRT will be in the form of a pulse, typically every 20 ms, taking approximately 1–5 ms to decay to 100th of the peak value. Most of the energy therefore is emitted in a short part of the display refresh cycle. The exact decay time will depend on the persistence of the phosphor being used. It is often the case that phosphors are mixtures of compounds with different persistence times, so that the colour within any area may vary considerably with time.

16.4.3   Changes over longer periods of time

The colour and luminance of a monitor will change considerably during the first hour of operation as components expand and warm up. Figure 16.4 shows how the spectral power distribution of a typical CRT changes over the first 100 minutes of operation. In the longer term, a CRT will permanently age as the efficacy of phosphors diminishes with use. For an example of this, recall the 'burnt in' marks of the most frequently displayed text information on a bank cash-dispenser display.

16.4.4   Spectral power distribution

The most common spectral power distributions for phosphors are broadband for blue and green, but narrow spikes for the reds as shown in Figure 16.4. Two instruments measuring with different wavelength intervals for sampling (for example, 5 nm and 10 nm) may give

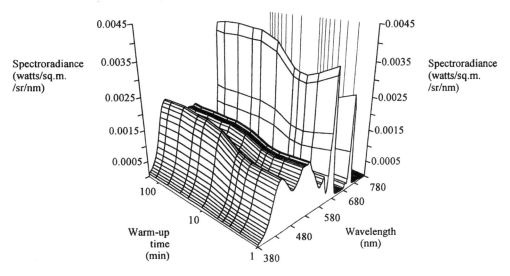

Figure 16.4 Changes in spectral power distribution of a CRT with time

different results as they will perform the colorimetric integration using different values. For accurate measurement of the red phosphor spectral power distribution, an instrument with 1 nm wavelength interval should ideally be used.

16.4.5   Black and white point settings

A CRT's contrast and brightness settings will be optimised for best visibility in a particular working environment. These settings will often leave the black point (red = blue = green = minimum) with a measurable (non-zero) luminance and colour. There are no standards published for this colour and it would probably be an impossible task to adjust a display to satisfy such a requirement. Also it is difficult to measure accurately at very low levels of emitted light from the display (less than 1 cd/m^2) because of the poor sensitivity (i.e. signal-to-noise performance) at low light levels of most commercially available instruments, and also because of the interference caused by ambient light (see below).

Standards do exist for the colour of the white point (red = blue = green = maximum) of the display. When a monitor is set up it will often be adjusted so that the white point is that preferred for a particular environment or application. The computer graphics industry has typically used a white with a colour temperature (CIE, 1986) of 9300 K, whereas the EBU broadcast television standard stipulates 6500 K, while within the graphic arts community 5000 K is the usual colour temperature for print viewing.

16.4.6   Ambient light

Without a diffuser, the specular component of light reflected off the front surface of a glass CRT will be of the order of 4 percent. A diffuse reflectance as high as 18 percent has been measured on a CRT. In a normal operating environment ambient light will affect the visibility of the display. This will be apparent as glare from specular reflectance and reduced image contrast from diffuse reflectance off the monitor, which raises the effective luminance of the black level. Even in a notionally dark laboratory there may be light originating from the display, reflected from either the measurement apparatus or the walls or even the operator. This stray light can be assessed by placing a small white opaque reflector directly in front of the display, with the display set to a high luminance, and measuring the light level on the reflector.

16.4.7 Non-additivity of primaries

Many models characterising CRT performance assume that the display primaries work independently so that, for example, the luminance of white will be the sum of the luminances of the constituent red, green and blue components, were they to be displayed separately. However, this is rarely the case on two points. An electron beam intended for one phosphor dot may partially fall on an adjacent dot of another colour. This is referred to as cross-excitation. The second factor is that one electron beam current may be affected by the other two. Figure 16.5 shows the measured maximum luminances of the primaries, secondaries and white of a low-quality CRT. Observe how the maximum luminance achievable for white is actually less than that possible for cyan. Fortunately, not all CRTs suffer from luminance additivity failures as large as those shown in Figure 16.5.

16.4.8 Environmental factors

A CRT will be affected by transport vibration and by the presence of magnetic (including terrestrial) fields. The simple act of rotating a monitor may affect its colours. These facts imply that a CRT should be calibrated at its intended operating place, and conversely that if it is subjected to vibration or movement during use, it should be regularly recalibrated.

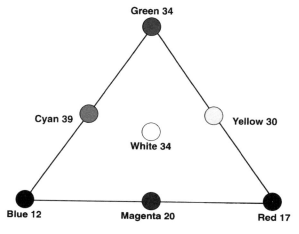

Figure 16.5 Measured maximum luminances of CRT colours

16.5 THE SPECTRORADIOMETER

The spectroradiometer measures the radiometric output of an optical source as a function of wavelength and minimally contains a dispersing element (diffraction grating) and a detector. Polychromatic light falls onto the diffraction grating in the monochromator and is dispersed at an angle determined by its wavelength. A slit-width sets the bandwidth of light exiting from the system to a detector. The position of the slit (usually the slit is kept fixed while the diffraction grating rotates) determines the wavelength of light selected. Most scanning spectroradiometers employ a stop–start method where the monochromator selects a wavelength, a measurement is taken and the monochromator then moves onto the next wavelength.

Spectroradiometers can be configured to measure either spectral irradiance or, by use of a limiting aperture and imaging system, spectral radiance. Once values of spectral radiance have been found, these data are integrated with the colour matching functions $\bar{x}(l)$, $\bar{y}(l)$ and $\bar{z}(l)$ to give tristimulus values (as shown in equations 16.1). Commercial instruments designed with the measurement of displays in mind will incorporate appropriate collection optics which usually include an alignment eyepiece.

16.5.1 Critical design factors

The most critical factors of spectroradiometer design are wavelength range, spectral band-width, wavelength sampling increment, dynamic range and measurement area.

Wavelength range

For colour measurement, the appropriate wavelength range is limited to that of the eye's sensitivity — approximately 360 to 780 nm. However, it may not be necessary to measure over this complete range provided that data are collected *well beyond* the limits of the emission spikes of the display phosphors. If it has been established that over certain wavelength regions there is no significant emission from a source, these wavelengths may be omitted during repeat measurements.

Spectral bandwidth

Choosing the optimum spectral bandwidth is a compromise between signal (a wider bandwidth gives higher signal, and thus better signal-to-noise ratio) and spectral resolution. Wider bandwidths may lead to errors in the calculation of tristimulus values. Ideally the wavelength sampling increment should be identical to the bandwidth to avoid over- or under-sampling. The trade-off between bandwidth and wavelength sampling interval depends on the required measurement resolution of the spectral profile; higher resolution will inevitably lead to more accurate results, but at the expense of longer time required to take the readings.

When the display emission contains narrow spectral lines, as is typical of red phos-phors, the radiance associated with each line can be in error if there is not a proper relationship between the monochromator band pass shape and the wavelength sampling interval. Ideally the bandwidth should be an integer multiple of the sampling interval.

For a monochromator with a triangular band-pass function (which is common), the full width at half maximum should be an integer multiple of the wavelength recording interval.

Failure to observe such a relationship can result in spectral lines being under-recorded or over-recorded, yielding significant chromaticity and luminance errors. However, this assumes that the function is perfectly triangular. Due to this problem and difficulty in matching the bandwidth to the step interval, the most accurate technique is to continuously scan through the wavelengths and integrate results over desired intervals. Using this method, the shape of the band-pass function becomes irrelevant. It is suggested that for good colorimetric calculation, wavelength intervals no wider than 5 nm should be used.

In some instruments this proper relationship between bandwidth and measurement wavelength is taken care of by the instrument manufacturer and is transparent to the instrument user. However, other instruments may, in the interests of application flexibility, allow the instrument user independent access to bandwidth and sampling interval.

Dynamic range

The dynamic range will be limited between the peak spectral radiance that can be handled by the detector and the noise floor of the system. The actual dynamic range available varies enormously between instrument designs. The errors arising from the noise floor (or a non-linearity at the bottom of the radiance scale) will be more significant for a line-spectrum emission than for a broadband emission. Ideally the detection system should have a linear response over the entire dynamic range.

It is important to note that displays like CRTs are highly variable in output over a refresh cycle (see Chapter 9). The light level can vary by a factor of 1000:1 over one refresh cycle (typically 60 Hz). A detector such as a photomultiplier tube will have very fast response and will 'track' this output well. When the signal is later processed by the electronics, it becomes time filtered and the sharp sawtooth wave becomes a ripple. Care should be taken that the detector is not saturating at the pulse peaks. A suitable test to determine whether the system is operating within its linear range is to view a display through a series of optical filters with known transmittance. These filters should cover optical transmittances over a wide range: typically 100 percent (no filter) to 0.01 percent.

Measurement area

It is important to ensure that the aperture of the measuring instrument is fully filled. The spectroradiometer sensitivity is unlikely to be uniform over the input aperture and so it is not possible simply to apply a detector 'fill factor' correction if it is not fully filled.

Often a fibre optic bundle or a transmitting diffuser is used as a spatial 'scrambler'. This scrambler can also depolarise incident light which might otherwise result in errors due to the polarisation sensitive diffraction grating. The efficiency of the randomising element can be investigated by checking that there is no image of the source at the plane of the detector. The depolarisation effect can be checked by rotating a polariser between the instrument and light source to see if there is any significant variation in signal level with polarisation orientation.

16.5.2 Scanning spectroradiometer

Figure 16.6 is a schematic of a scanning spectroradiometer, for which the light from the display is collected via an optical telescope. The light dispersing element is a diffraction grating contained within a monochromator, and the angular position of the grating (which

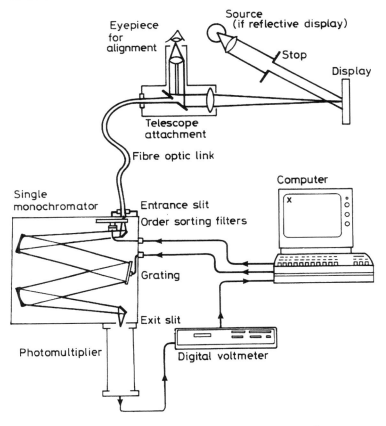

Figure 16.6   Schematic of a scanning telespectroradiometer

is computer controlled) determines the wavelength of light leaving the exit slit. The width of the slit determines the spectral bandwidth. Computer controlled order-sorting filters may be included to reduce stray light (see below). The signal from a photomultiplier tube is processed through a low-pass temporal filter to produce a time-averaged value and monitored by computer using a digital voltmeter. A complete scan through the full wavelength range may take several minutes to complete, especially if a small wavelength sampling interval is selected, and requires the source to be stable for the duration of the measurement.

16.5.3   Multi-channel spectroradiometer

This class of instrument (also known as a spectrometer) measures the entire wavelength range simultaneously, thereby considerably reducing the measurement time. The instrument has an array of detectors, which may be photodiodes or charge-coupled devices (CCDs), at the monochromator exit with each detector associated with a narrow wavelength range. Thus there is no mechanical scanning motion and the settling/averaging process can take place simultaneously at all wavelengths, providing parallel rather than serial operation. Complete measurements can be made on the time scale of a few tens of milliseconds to a few seconds, making these instruments quicker and more convenient to use. In addition the absence of precision mechanical motion can lead to a more compact design and hence a lower cost instrument.

16.5.4 Sources of error for spectroradiometers

Stray light

White light falling on a perfect diffraction grating is diffracted at an angle dependent only on wavelength, with the exception of the zero-order which is a specular polychromatic reflection (Lothian, 1975). However, as real gratings are not perfect, there occurs an additional scattering of white light at all angles which adds to the diffracted radiation. This so-called heterochromatic stray light can be reduced, for a scanning spectroradiometer, by sending the light exiting from the monochromator through a second monochromator tuned to the same wavelength. The portion of heterochromatic stray light exiting the second monochromator will be significantly less than from the first, although the overall light level will also be reduced.

The amount of heterochromatic stray light may be found using blocking filters. A selective filter (such as an interference filter) is placed between source and detector. The change in level of light measured should be proportional to the spectral transmittance of the filter. Any major deviation suggests that there is significant heterochromatic stray light present in the original system.

A second type of stray light can be caused by higher-order spectra generated by the diffraction grating reaching the detector. Both heterochromatic and higher-order stray light may be reduced by using filters. For a scanning spectroradiometer selective filters are placed at the entrance of the monochromator, whereas for multi-channel devices filters are usually placed in front of the detectors. A trap for the unwary, however, is that a filter may fluoresce and thus introduce more stray light.

Sampling time

As mentioned previously, the colour and intensity of a CRT display vary considerably over its duty cycle. The spectroradiometer will have its own sampling period which may 'beat' with the display frequency and yield errors. Figure 16.7 shows an example of different values obtained using a diode array spectroradiometer measuring a white displayed on a CRT.

The options to reduce the effect of sampling errors are threefold:

(1) Sample over a long time period–preferably 100 or more display refresh cycles.
(2) Introduce a low-pass temporal filter into the detector system, reducing the sharp sawtooth wave function of the signal to a smooth ripple. When used with a scanning instrument this method will require the system to rest after moving from one wavelength to the next to give the detector time to settle.
(3) Synchronise the measurement frequency to the display frequency. This means sampling the light emitted from the display for a time period that is an exact integer multiple of the display period. Figure 16.7 shows how effective this technique can be when used within a CCD array device.

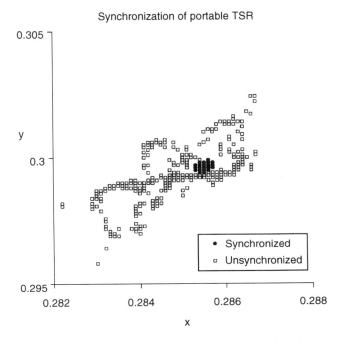

Figure 16.7   Measured chromaticities of a CRT, showing how synchronising sampling period of the detector to the display can reduce variability

16.5.5   Traceability for the scales of spectroradiometers

The two scales employed in a spectroradiometer are those of wavelength and spectral sensitivity. It is important to realise that the process of tracing a scale of the instrument to a standard is a calibration, and that it is therefore true only for the exact set of conditions under which the measurement took place, for example the temperature, aperture size, step interval and wavelength range.

Checking the wavelength scale of a spectroradiometer is crucial. A study on the effects of wavelength errors in spectroradiometers when measuring displays (Berns, 1993a,b) showed that a wavelength shift of ±0.5 nm over the whole measurement range can result in a change of $1.8\Delta E^*_{ab}$ units (equating to about twice the just noticeable difference expressed as a Euclidean distance in CIELAB colour space) for the blue phosphor of a CRT. For the red and green phosphors the change values were 0.3 and 1.1 respectively.

The dispersing element in a monochromator–a diffraction grating–is rotated to select the part of the spectrum entering the detector. If the rotation mechanics are not linear then wavelength inaccuracies may occur over part of the available range. The wavelength accuracy should be checked at several wavelengths across the range, typically using sources with spectral line output. Low pressure discharge lamps such as mercury, neon, or mercury–cadmium mixes are good for this purpose. Values for the wavelength and intensity of these spectral lines are well known (MIT, 1969) and following these checks a suitable correction can be made to the wavelength scale.

Calibrating the spectral sensitivity of a spectroradiometer requires a reference light source. The calibration of this reference light source itself is normally traceable to the National Standard (see Section 16.7 below).

A detector will generate a noise signal–called a dark current–which is usually independent of wavelength. Additionally the whole spectroradiometer system will have a sensitivity that varies with wavelength. The dark current is converted to a voltage (V_{dark}^L) which is recorded as the signal with the instrument aperture blocked. The sensitivity as a function of wavelength, sens(λ), can be found by measuring a 'standard lamp' whose spectral power density has been calibrated, $L(\lambda)$, and comparing the measured signal in detector volts, $V_{sig}^L(\lambda)$, to the known spectroradiometric value (in mW/m^2/nm):

$$\text{sens}(\lambda) = L(\lambda)/[V_{sig}^L(\lambda) - V_{dark}^L] \qquad \text{for the standard lamp} \qquad 16.3$$

Having established the sensitivity of the system, measurements may now be made of any source and the results reported in useful units:

$$\text{value }(\lambda) = \text{sens}(\lambda) \times [V_{sig}^D(\lambda) - V_{dark}^D] \qquad \text{for a display} \qquad 16.4$$

Ideally the calibration source should have a comparable spectral power distribution to the display but be much more stable. Such sources are not currently available. Sources traditionally used for the calibration of spectroradiometric scales are tungsten lamps powered by stable DC power supplies. Accurate measurement of the spectral power relies on the linearity scale of the spectroradiometer because of the difference between the radiance levels of calibration source and display.

In order to measure a self-luminous surface, a uniform luminous reference of area comparable with that to be measured on the display is required. This can be achieved by using a lamp to illuminate a plane diffuser (usually a white tile) at normal incidence, with the detector viewing the diffuser at 45°. Alternatively, the lamp may be placed within–or adjacent to–an integrating sphere. The interior wall of the sphere is diffusely reflecting. A port on the sphere wall provides an area of uniform luminance and is viewed by the detector. The integrating sphere method has the added bonus of assuring that the reference source is randomly polarised.

16.6   THE COLORIMETER

Colorimeter design is based on the assumption that any colour may be uniquely described using only three numbers. The instrument contains either three detectors, each with a filter to make them sensitive to blue, green and red wavelength ranges respectively, or a single detector with the three filters mounted in a spinning filter wheel. For a tristimulus colorimeter, the filter plus detector sensitivities should closely match the CIE colour matching functions $\bar{x}(\lambda)$, $\bar{y}(\lambda)$ and $\bar{z}(\lambda)$. The lobe of the long wavelength function $\bar{x}(\lambda)$ in the blue region is sometimes generated by a fourth channel but more usually is derived from the output of the detector used for the function $\bar{z}(\lambda)$. Another range of colorimeters, not necessarily yielding CIE values, are known as colour TV analysers.

The value of these instruments lies not in their accuracy over large ranges, but in their stability and portability. They are very useful for examining small colour differences on a display, or for checking a display's stability. If the user can be assured that nothing has changed in the light-generating part of the display, a colorimeter can be used to compare the sample display against a known good display so long as the good display has an identical spectral power distribution. Depending on the particular instrument used, this can be done either by using the instrument readings as arbitrary parameters or by using it in 'colour difference' mode, where the instrument memorises the results from a known good display and presents the divergence.

16.6.1 Major sources of error for colorimeters

Real filters that exactly match the CIE 1931 colour matching functions have yet to be manufactured, and the magnitude of the mismatch errors varies from instrument to instrument. The error versus wavelength functions of the filters are designed such that with typical continuum spectra the errors average out to a low value. However, with a line spectrum test subject no such averaging occurs and significantly larger errors in colour measurement can arise. An example of one manufacturer's attempts to match the CIE 1931 colour matching functions appears in Figure 16.8. Different sensitivities are found in different brands of colorimeter, and even instruments of identical model may perform differently for this reason.

Stray light has been found to be a problem in some designs of colorimeter. LED indicators mounted within the colorimeter which are viewed through the eyepiece can leak into the detector and increase dark signal, a significant problem when measuring low level sources.

The colorimeter may have a sampling time that beats with the CRT refresh cycle in a similar manner to the spectroradiometer. This can be checked by varying the frequency of the display and noting the repeatability of the measurement values.

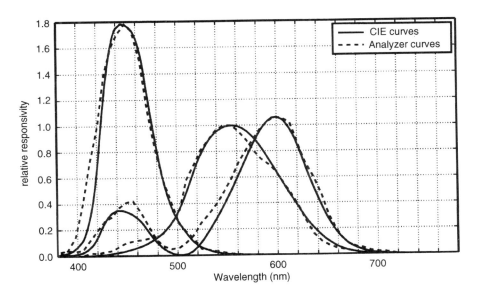

Figure 16.8 Spectral sensitivities of the three channels of a colorimeter

Different colorimeters use various methods of light collection. With some, light from the display is conveyed down a fibre optic bundle to the three (or four) detectors. The choice of which detector an individual fibre delivers light to bears a completely random relationship to the position on the display–therefore in effect the detector head can be thought of as an array of many 'micro-detectors'. A second approach is to have the three detectors looking at the same area using a beam-splitter system. A third method has the detectors looking at a diffuser placed over the display. It is worth mentioning that the third method can lead to problems. In an extreme case, light may fall on only two of the detectors but not the third, due to spatial non-uniformity on a CRT. Smaller scale non-uniformities may lead to smaller but still noticeable errors, which can be demonstrated by repeating a measurement with the colorimeter rotated by 180°.

It is important to note that a badly designed colorimeter may be sensitive to UV or IR radiation, leading to significant measurement errors.

16.6.2   Calibration of a colorimeter

If the detectors of a tristimulus colorimeter gave exact matches of the CIE colour matching functions, calibration would be necessary only to anchor the luminance scale and to ensure that the system is stable. Given that additional error sources had been taken care of, such an instrument would give the correct answer for every possible spectral power distribution, thus any calibration source could be used. However, this is not the case in practice. The spectral responses of the detectors are only approximations to the CIE functions, so that the resulting chromaticities and luminances generally contain a significant systematic error.

It would be possible to generate look-up tables to convert colorimeter values to more accurate spectroradiometer values by measuring a display with both the reference and test devices and noting the systematic difference between results. However, such tables would be valid only for that particular display. Systematic errors arise from the spectral power distribution of the display being measured. Another source would have a different spectral power distribution and would thus produce different systematic errors requiring another look-up table. Thus a colorimeter calibrated for use on one display could not in general be used to measure another. (see also Chapter 17).

16.7   TRACEABILITY TO NATIONAL STANDARDS

16.7.1   The national measurement system (NMS)

The NMS is a mechanism through which measurement scales are harmonised throughout the UK. It ensures that a bolt made in Cornwall will fit a nut manufactured in Strathclyde since the scales of the length measuring equipment used in each case are related to a common scale. At the top of the NMS is the National Physical Laboratory (NPL) which is responsible for maintaining and disseminating physical scales such as length, time, temperature and spectral radiance using primary standards and scales. The UK's NMS is harmonised with that of other countries around the world via inter-comparison, so that goods can be traded on an international basis.

16.7.2   Spectral radiance and spectroradiometric scales

A spectral radiance scale is maintained in the UK at the National Physical Laboratory using the NPL Reference Spectroradiometer, which contains a double monochromator and uses the continuous scanning technique. A linear transducer attached to the sine drive of the grating assembly gives a wavelength measurement to 0.01 nm. The detector signal and a stable reference signal are continuously integrated, using voltage to frequency converters and counters over a series of contiguous wavebands 0.2 nm wide. Fluctuations in the source are corrected for using a separate broadband detector placed next to the source. The reference signal is used to correct for changes in the scan speed–the final reading for each band is found by dividing the signal count by the reference count, then subtracting a dark current reading. The integration process ensures that no part of the spectrum is omitted or measured twice.

The spectroradiometric scale is ultimately traceable to a primary standard cryogenic radiometer. This instrument is an electrically calibrated absolute radiometer in which the heating effect of absorbed radiant power is determined by substitution with an equivalent amount of electrical power. A temperature sensor is used to establish equality between radiant and electrical heating. The cryogenic radiometer operates at liquid helium temperatures and has a measurement uncertainty of 5 parts in 10^5, a significant improvement in uncertainty over earlier room temperature radiometers. It provides an absolute radiometric scale at the wavelength of suitable intensity stabilised laser lines. These lasers may then be used to calibrate transfer standards in the form of detectors, which in turn are used to calibrate the output of lamps.

Members of the industrial and scientific community can achieve traceability from NPL spectroradiometric and luminance scales by using transfer standards (lamps or detectors), or by having a sample of their own product calibrated. This calibrated artefact can then be used as the reference to calibrate their own equipment.

16.7.3   Reflectance and transmittance scales

These scales are relevant to the characteristics of display components and LCDs. Reflectance and transmittance scales are not SI based, but are ratio measurements. National standards for reflectance and transmittance are determined at NPL using the Reference Spectrophotometer and the Reference Reflectometer. The performance of these instruments is very accurately known and they are checked against similar instruments throughout the world to achieve international compatibility in measurement.

NPL's Reference Spectrophotometer is used annually to determine the UK's transmittance scale at a series of wavelengths. The scale is held on a series of metal-on-silica filters and is transferred to the high quality commercial instruments which are used to calibrate customers' standards. The uncertainties are thus those calculated from measurements on the reference instrument summed in quadrature with those from the commercial instrument.

In order to estimate unknown systematic errors and to ensure international acceptability, inter-comparisons are made with other national laboratories, e.g. NIST (USA) and PTB (Germany) (Eckerle, 1990). These inter-comparisons show differences larger than the uncertainties quoted by each laboratory because of imperfections in the filters used for the comparisons, such as spatial non-uniformity, ageing and diffuse transmittance, and also because of the different test methods of the participants. The uncertainty quoted for NPL's final values is increased to include the differences so that a filter measured at NPL will have the same transmittance as it would have if measured at NIST or PTB within the combined uncertainties.

The scale of diffuse reflectance is based on an international mean. Absolute diffuse reflectance is a difficult parameter to measure and this partially accounts for the larger uncertainties associated with diffuse reflectance measurements than with transmittance measurement.

16.7.4   Colour

Colour may be seen as a quantity derived from spectral power distributions of a source, and as such, colour scales are direct transformations — using CIE functions — of spectral data, be it radiance or reflectance. The colour of luminous or reflective media can be related to the national standard by tracing their spectral power distribution, or spectral reflectance with illuminant to the appropriate scale and applying the standard CIE calculation. The CIE publishes the arrays of colour matching functions and illuminants on computer disk for those who wish to perform their own colorimetric calculations. In the UK the disk is available from CIBSE.

16.7.5   Measurement of colour of displays

NPL has designed and built a facility for the measurement of the colour and luminance of displays. This facility compares the spectral radiance of a customer's display with that of an NPL in-house standard lamp. The comparison can then be used to calculate the true spectral radiance of the display:

$$D_a(\lambda) = S_a(\lambda) \times \frac{D_m(\lambda)}{S_m(\lambda)} \qquad\qquad 16.5$$

where:
   $D_a(\lambda) =$ true spectral radiance of display
   $S_a(\lambda) =$ true spectral radiance of standard lamp
   $D_m(\lambda) =$ measured spectral radiance of display
   $S_m(\lambda) =$ measured spectral radiance of standard lamp

Using the standard set of CIE equations this spectral radiance data can be transformed to CIE chromaticity coordinates.

There are two instruments used at NPL to disseminate traceable spectroradiometric and colorimetric measurement of displays. One is a telespectroradiometer scanning at 5 nm intervals. The instrument has a single monochromator with order sorting filters. The detector is a photomultiplier tube. The current from the tube is converted to voltage and time-smoothed using a low pass filter. The voltage is read by a digital voltmeter. The voltmeter, filter wheel motor and grating drive are controlled by a computer which also performs colorimetric calculations. An in-house transfer standard lamp is measured at the start and end of session so the instrument is effectively calibrated every time it is used. The second instrument used for measurement of displays is a diode array telespectroradiometer. This is slightly less accurate than the former instrument but is highly portable. It is regularly calibrated using an in-house standard lamp. Laboratories with their own spectroradiometers can obtain calibrated lamps from NPL to calibrate their own instruments.

Most types of display are unstable and are affected by electromagnetic fields and physical shock. When the colour of a display is calibrated at NPL, obtaining values NPL[x, y, Y], the recommendation is to take an additional measurement of the calibrated area on the display using a tristimulus colorimeter, C[x, y, Y] (Hanson & Verrill, 1991). Note that due to systematic errors within the colorimeter, C[x, y, Y] will probably not be identical to NPL[x, y, Y]. When the display is returned to the customer's laboratory, its calibration may have drifted during transit but can be reset to show the 'certified colours' by tweaking the gun voltages until the colorimeter gives C[x, y, Y], implying that the display is showing NPL[x, y, Y]. Note that the use of colorimeters for this high accuracy purpose relies on the fact that the generation of a particular colour on a CRT has a unique solution (depending on specific proportions of the red, green and blue primaries); it would not be valid for the colorimeter to be used to measure the colours of another display which uses different primaries.

It is also possible to characterise detector performance at NPL. A regularly used service characterises the performance of tristimulus colorimeters by comparing the colour of a display as measured using the spectroradiometer with the results of similar measurements using the colorimeter. A look-up table converting colorimeter values to traceable values can be established using the results. The table is only valid for the particular display being measured, as the systematic errors of the colorimeter depend on the spectral power distribution of the display.

REFERENCES

Berns, R.S., Motta, R.J. and Gorzynski, M.E. (1993a), CRT colorimetry. Part I: Theory and practice, *Colour Research & Application*, **18**, 299–314.

Berns, R.S., Gorzynski, M.E. and Motta, R.J. (1993b), CRT colorimetry. Part II: Metrology, *Colour Research & Application*, **18**, 315–325.

CIE (1986), *Colorimetry*, Publication 15.2, CIE Central Bureau, Vienna.

Cowan, W.B. and Rowell, N. (1986), On the gun independence and phosphor constancy of colour video monitors, *Colour Research & Application*, **11**, Supplement, s35–s38.

Hanson, A.R. and Verrill, J.F. (1991), Standardisation in the measurement of the colour of self luminous displays, *Proc. 22 Session CIE*, Melbourne, **1**, 87–88.

Hunt, R.W.G. (1991), *Measuring Colour*, 2nd Edition, Ellis Horwood, Chichester, UK.

Lothian, G.F. (1975), *Optics and Its Uses*, Van Nostrand Reinhold, New York, Chapter 7.

MIT Wavelength Tables, MIT Press, MIT (1969), Cambridge, MA.

Taylor, J.A.F. *et al.* (1994), An investigation into the human visual system in the mesopic region using both a classical optical instrument and a visual display unit, *Proc. CIE Symposium*, Vienna.

Techniques for high-quality, low-cost colour measurement of CRTs

Tom Lianza

17.1 THE CHALLENGES OF EMBEDDED MONITOR CONTROL

The display system used in current computer applications provides a number of unique challenges to the colour metrology process. The combination of these challenges with the market requirements for embedded measurement leads to the following criteria for a successful product:

- Cost per station should be low.
- Measurement time should be less than 1 minute.
- Measurements should be made without significant change to environmental conditions.
- The measurement process should be automated.
- The measurement data should be fed back to various colour management systems.
- The measurements must be accurate and precise.

These challenges are further influenced by the fact that the individual who is required to make the measurements is not normally an engineer or scientist, and is neither expected nor trained to interpret the measurements. As a result, the software to control the measuring instrument must be easy to use, automatically interpret measurement errors and adapt to a wide range of measurement scenarios. In addition the measurement software must interface, either directly or by a file exchange process, with software to manage colour peripherals on the system.

This chapter will focus on the following aspects:

(1) The sensor architecture and selection process.
(2) Characteristics of the commercial monitor.
(3) Calibration issues related to the light sensing process.
(4) Processing measured data from the monitor and managing errors.
(5) The direct computer control of monitors.
(6) Matching monitors for simultaneous display.
(7) The measurement of ambient illumination.

17.1.1 The sensor architecture and selection process

Embedded monitor control systems place particular emphasis on low-cost and high speed acquisition of colorimetric data. These factors are dictated by the consumer nature of the product. The link to pre-existing colour management systems demands that the colour measurement system be capable of returning accurate information in a CIE based colorimetric notation. The measurement of the monitor colorimetry requires that the sensing mechanism be capable of synchronising with the display refresh rate. Table 17.1 lists five sensor families across seven specification areas with a rating for each.

17.1.2 Product cost

The final cost of a consumer oriented product depends on a very complex series of factors. Depending upon the marketing and distribution techniques and the prevailing market conditions, the raw component cost will often represent less than one-sixth of the suggested retail price excluding tax, shipping and import duty fees. The mark-up of 6× demands that the design engineer of the embedded monitor control system must carefully select components and architecture. Modern engineering practices dictate the use of plastics, for example, which have the advantage of lower cost to manufacture but the disadvantage of high tooling costs, which must be amortised over a large number of units. Because of cost constraints, the use of carefully designed optical glass filters and careful individual selection and measurement of sensors is not practical. The designer of products such as these is constantly faced with the need to make compromises, without sacrificing the basic requirements of other parts of the process that use the calibrator and its data. These issues will be dealt with in greater detail in the discussion of calibration.

17.1.3 Factors affecting measurement speed

Measurement speed is determined by the time it takes to make a single measurement and the total number of measurements required to complete a full measurement suite. The fundamental limitation of speed in all systems is dictated by the need to synchronise to the refresh rate of the display system, because no system can make single measurements

Table 17.1 Sensor family selection matrix

Sensor family	Speed	Cost	CIE capability	Electrical complexity	Power reqts.	Time-sync. complexity	Ambient rejection
Single element (broadband)	medium	very low	fair	low	very low	low	good
Single element (photometric)	low–medium	moderate	fair	low	very low	low	good
Tricolour (arbitrary sensitivity)	high	low	good–excellent	moderate	low	low	good
Trichromatic colorimeter	medium–high	moderate–high	excellent	moderate	low	low	good
Spectral measurement	low	high	excellent	high	moderate	high	?

in less than one field cycle (Berns *et al.*, 1993a,b). Single element sensing systems cannot measure the independent levels of combined colours and hence must measure individual phosphor contributions. This implies that for measurement of grey on the display, a minimum of three measurements for the red, green and blue phosphor intensities must be made. A device in which the photopic sensitivity is achieved by filtration generally requires some degree of signal averaging to improve signal-to-noise ratios. This requires an even greater number of samples, and hence it is classed as a low–medium speed system. Tricolorimeters can make simultaneous measurements of combinations of the three colour guns, which gives them a clear advantage in the area of speed. Once again, the imposition of colorimetric response by filtering lowers signal level and requires a larger number of samples to achieve the equivalent signal-to-noise ratio.

Full spectral measurement of monitors at high speed provides the greatest challenge. If the device uses a scanning mechanism, the need for temporal synchronisation dictates that the sensor dwell time at each wavelength interval must be an integral number of video field times. The narrow bandwidth of the spectral measurement and the relatively low power output of the CRT display combine to force integration times of tens of video fields. For spectral devices that use solid state sensors such as CCDs and/or photodiode arrays, the problem is lessened to the degree that the entire spectral signature can be captured in a single integration period, the length of which is dictated by the signal-to-noise ratio and the requirement to sample an integral number of fields. From the standpoint of speed, the trichromatic sensing technologies provide an excellent compromise.

17.1.4 Minimising environmental constraints

Colour researchers invariably conduct the measurement process in carefully controlled environments in order to eliminate artifacts introduced by the surround illumination. Embedded monitor calibrators must provide shielding of ambient illumination in order to perform the task of measurement without interfering with the normal working conditions of the user. The normal method of attaching the measurement device to the monitor is through use of an opaque suction cup. While this approach appears simple, the actual implementation can be quite tricky. The designer must select materials which have the elastic characteristics required to maintain suction throughout the duration of the measurement cycle, but still have sufficient structural stiffness to allow the screen-to-sensor distance to be accurately maintained. The device also needs to be removed, so the user must be provided with an easy way to remove the device after the measurement has been made. The fact that the sensor system is attached to the display in this fashion dictates that the entire measuring head must be lightweight, yet robust enough not to be damaged if dropped accidentally. The suction cup must also be large enough to shield against the internal reflections from ambient light falling onto the monitor surface. One manufacturer of these devices specifies that the chromaticity of a measurement of D50 white on the screen shall not deviate by more than ±0.002 in x and y from the target value, when the screen ambient illumination varies over the range 0 to 500 lux.

17.2 SPECTRAL EMISSION OF THE MONITOR

Because the class of object being measured is well defined, i.e. a monitor with a known set of phosphors operating at a known frequency, the design criteria can be chosen to minimise cost with very little compromise in measurement accuracy. In the next sections, the relationship between the spectral characteristics of the phosphors, the interaction with the CIE colour matching functions and trade-offs in instrument response will be discussed. These are design areas where significant cost savings may be realised if the limitations of the detection process are kept in mind.

Monitor phosphor characteristics can be described by either a family designation or an organisational standard. For instance, a phosphor identified as P22 can actually be

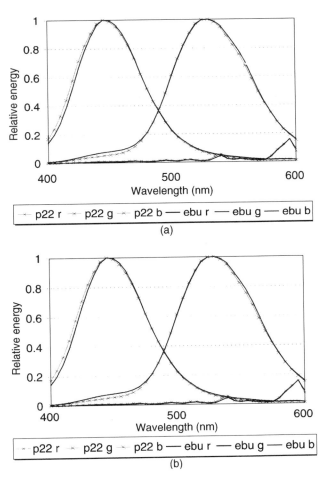

Figure 17.1 Relative spectral power distribution of two phosphor families

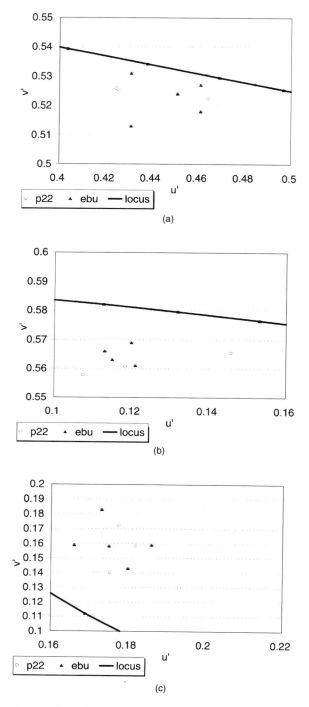

Figure 17.2   Comparison of chromaticities of phosphors

a member of a family of five distinct chemically compatible groups which have the same name but are characterised by different chromaticity coordinates (Widdel & Post, 1992). A phosphor family which is described by an organisation such as the European Broadcasting Union (EBU), will generally be specified by the specific chromaticities of the phosphors. The relative spectral differences between two physical phosphor sets are shown in Figure 17.1(a) and (b). These data were measured by a Photo Research PR650 Spectral Colorimeter. Two monitors were selected; the manufacturer of the first monitor identified the set of phosphors as P22 and the second manufacturer identified the set as EBU. From these figures, it may be seen that although the differences appear relatively small, there are nonetheless differences. We make the following observations:

- The red P22 phosphor has higher energy output at the red peak at 705 nm.
- The green P22 phosphor has slightly lower energy in the wavelength region around 450 nm.
- The blue P22 phosphor has slightly higher energy in the shorter wavelengths, but the peak wavelength of both blue phosphors is very near 450 nm.

These subtle but real differences manifest themselves as changes in chromaticity coordinates. Figure 17.2 shows the differences between the chromaticities of the P22 and EBU families of phosphors. Remember that the EBU specification relates to a chromaticity and an allowable deviation from that chromaticity, whereas the P22 designation describes a family of chemically different phosphors. From Figure 17.2(a), (b) and (c) it can be seen that there is significant overlap between the families, because the phosphors tend to have similar behaviour although they differ at the detail level.

A review of commercially available monitor phosphor sets was performed at Sequel Imaging to determine the extent and variability of phosphors found in high volume, commercial monitors. The result of this study showed that the highest degree of variability in the phosphor spectra was in the red region of the spectrum and consisted primarily in changes in the relative energy at 705 nm. Figure 17.3 shows a comparison of the range of phosphor variability for six different monitors from four different manufacturers.

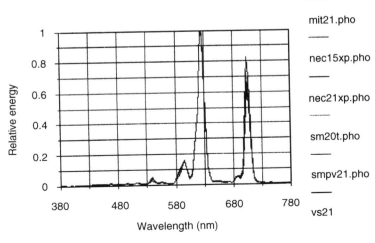

Figure 17.3 Comparison of the red phosphor spectra for six different monitors

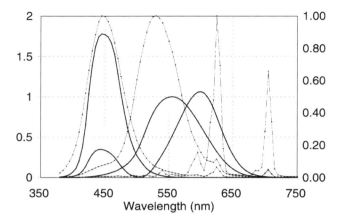

Figure 17.4 Comparison of the typical phosphor spectra and the CIE colour matching functions

Although the variance of the spectra appears quite large at 705 nm, the variance of the chromaticities is relatively small, within ± 0.002 in x and y. Figure 17.4 shows a comparison of a typical phosphor set against the CIE colour matching functions. Note that the CMFs have very reduced response in the area of the 705 nm peak, which accounts for the low chromaticity differences in the red.

17.3 SPECTRAL RESPONSE OF THE INSTRUMENT

The general requirements for colour matching function response in a colorimeter may actually inhibit, rather than enhance, instrument performance in monitor measurement applications. This arises as a consequence of signal-to-noise characteristics and the practical difficulties in constructing perfect filters. A colorimeter samples the colour through a number of filters. It is assumed that these filters can be made to 'fit' the colour matching function response by a process called matrixing. This process can be accomplished by using the spectral characteristics of the filter/detector combination to compute a linear fit to the colour matching functions. Mathematically, this appears as follows:

$$
\begin{vmatrix} x_0(\lambda) & x_1(\lambda) & \dots & x_n(\lambda) \\ y_0(\lambda) & y_1(\lambda) & \dots & y_n(\lambda) \\ z_0(\lambda) & z_1(\lambda) & \dots & z_n(\lambda) \end{vmatrix} = \begin{vmatrix} a_{00} & a_{01} & a_{02} \\ a_{10} & a_{11} & a_{12} \\ a_{20} & a_{21} & a_{22} \end{vmatrix} \times \begin{vmatrix} R_0(\lambda) & R_1(\lambda) & \dots & R_n(\lambda) \\ G_0(\lambda) & G_1(\lambda) & \dots & G_n(\lambda) \\ B_0(\lambda) & B_1(\lambda) & \dots & B_n(\lambda) \end{vmatrix} \quad 17.1
$$

The colour matching functions are fitted to an arbitrary response curve using linear matrix techniques (Hardis, 1994). The accuracy of fit is determined by the construction of the filters represented by the R, G and B vectors in equation 17.1.

For a better understanding of the effect that the phosphor has on the chromaticity measurement, it is necessary to examine the spectral power distribution of the phosphor with respect to the colour matching functions. A further examination of Figure 17.4 shows that the red phosphor's contribution to the Z component of the tristimulus calculation is essentially zero, because there is almost no energy in the region covered by the z colour matching function. The importance of this physical characteristic on the measurement

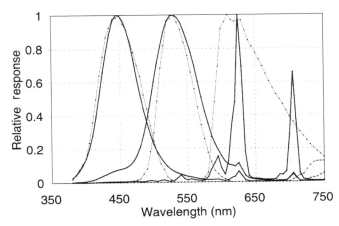

Figure 17.5 Comparison of spectral content of EBU phosphor and spectral sensitivity of typical
Sequel Imaging monitor calibrator

process will be dealt with in detail in a later section. The other two phosphors have a
significant contribution in all three colour matching functions.

Construction of filters and selection of detectors which result in linear combinations
of the colour matching functions is tedious and expensive. The construction of filters for
this application generally requires multiple glass types and sophisticated manufacturing
techniques (Ritzel & Sojourni, 1993). Such an approach is not feasible for low-cost
colorimeters.

If we ignore the requirements for colour matching function response, and assume
that we know the phosphor, a different set of response functions can be designed to
maximise signal-to-noise ratio, as shown in Figure 17.5 where the spectral response has
been designed to utilise as much of the spectral output of the source as possible. This
maximises the signal passed to the detector and minimises the effects of noise.

The problem with ignoring the colour matching function response is that the calibration
is then valid for only one phosphor type. This might result in serious measurement errors
unless some care is taken to calibrate the device properly.

17.4 DEVICE CALIBRATION AND SOURCES OF ERROR

17.4.1 Spectral response functions

The selection of arbitrary response functions based upon signal processing requirements
rather than colorimetric requirements will have an effect on the accuracy of the device.
The magnitude of the error is dependent upon the method used to calibrate the device
and the degree of spectral differences between phosphor types. Using equation 17.1 to
synthesise the colour matching function response via a matrix derived using least-squares
techniques, produces the functions shown in Figure 17.6.

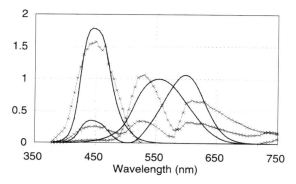

Figure 17.6 Comparison of CIE colour matching functions (solid lines) and synthesised colour matching functions (crossed lines)

The lack of fit between the real and synthetic colour matching functions is serious and if a colorimeter were calibrated in this fashion, the errors in measurement of a known phosphor would be significant. Thus the calibration process described by equation 17.1 leads to very disappointing results, because the process attempted to 'fit' arbitrary filter responses to the visual colour matching function curves. If we modify that process by simultaneously measuring the monitor with a calibrated reference device and an uncalibrated instrument, then fit the raw data to the measured data, we can use a similar least-squares method for the process:

$$\begin{vmatrix} X_0 & X_1 & \dots & X_n \\ Y_0 & Y_1 & \dots & Y_n \\ Z_0 & Z_1 & \dots & Z_n \end{vmatrix} = \begin{vmatrix} a_{00} & a_{01} & a_{02} \\ a_{10} & a_{11} & a_{12} \\ a_{20} & a_{21} & a_{22} \end{vmatrix} \times \begin{vmatrix} R_0 & R_1 & \dots & R_n \\ G_0 & G_1 & \dots & G_n \\ B_0 & B_1 & \dots & B_n \end{vmatrix} \qquad 17.2$$

In this case, the *XYZ* data represent the trichromatic CIE coordinates of the colour and the *RGB* data represent the measured data from the instrument. If both instruments are linear and noise free, and the source is additive, the resultant errors will by definition be *zero* for the given phosphor set under measurement. This departure from standard colorimetric procedures results in significant increase in accuracy and precision for substantial decreases in cost and complexity in the manufacturing process. It is a procedure used by many vendors because of the high degree of uncertainty in the manufacturing of filters that yield an exact colour matching response.

The phosphor-relative calibration process described above is good for one phosphor type. The question now becomes what happens if a different phosphor is selected. There should be some error, because the filter functions are not linearly related to the colour matching functions. To explore this problem a mathematical model of the calibrator was constructed, based upon the instrument's spectral response (Figure 17.5). Measured spectral data from the previously described EBU and P22 monitors were used to calculate hypothetical RGB responses for a number of colour mixtures. These responses and the calculated *XYZ* data of the mixtures were used to derive the matrices for each phosphor by solving equation 17.2 for the **a** matrix. The RGB response values for each phosphor were then substituted back into equation 17.2 and an 'incorrect' set of *XYZ* data values was calculated. The resultant errors in $\pm x, y$ (chromaticity coordinates) are shown in Figure 17.7.

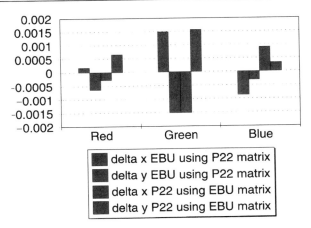

Figure 17.7   Errors due to selecting the wrong matrix to perform the measurement of the display primaries

In all cases, the errors were less than ±0.0018 in both x and y. This arises as a direct result of the small, but real, differences between the two phosphor types. The minimum error occurred in the red and the maximum error occurred in the green, which was as expected and is explained by the general discussion in Section 17.2. The red differences are in a region of the spectrum that is insignificant relative to the CMF responses and the other two colours make large contributions to both the x and y values. It should be noted that in most measurement situations the red phosphor yields the largest errors. The reason for this will be explained in a later section.

17.4.2   Electrical and photo-optical noise

If the spectral error due to phosphor variability were the only source of error, monitor calibrators could be favourably compared to the best colorimetric devices made, but in practice other factors dominate the error budget. There are numerous ways to deal statistically with noise in measurements. One widely used practice is defined by the ASTM, which is aimed directly at users of colorimetric data and describes the practices of using statistical means and standard deviations 'to allow an unambiguous decision as to whether or not the mean results are within tolerance'. Within the standard, there is a note which specifically references the underlying assumption:

'This practice assumes that all measurements are subject to the central limit theorem of mathematical statistics so that as the number of replicated or repeat measurements becomes large, the distribution of values is described by the standard normal distribution.'

The nature and distribution of noise in a colorimeter is affected by factors such as electrical noise, source noise and (if it is digital) sampling noise. Each of these factors requires different design actions to minimise the resultant measurement error.

One unique problem with any colour measurement device that reports CIE units is the fact that the linear measurement generally passes through a non-linear transform before being reported. For instance, a user may wish to report colour data in the CIE units of L^*,

u' and v' and then specify a colour difference in ΔE^*_{uv}. For this outcome the measurement process must occur in the following order:

(1) The light emitted by the display phosphors is first transmitted through the filters in the instrument.
(2) The detectors convert the filtered illumination to a corresponding voltage or current.
(3) This signal is sampled in time and quantised by an analogue-to-digital converter (ADC).
(4) The digital data are multiplied by a linear matrix to arrive at a trichromatic representation of the colour related to a known CIE-specified colour matching response (i.e. $RGB \rightarrow XYZ$).
(5) A projective transform converts the absolute trichromatic response to a three-dimensional space which has indirect correlates to luminance, hue and saturation (i.e. $XYZ \rightarrow Yxy$).
(6) This data is then rescaled to arrive at more uniform visual representation (i.e. $Yxy \rightarrow L^*u'v'$).
(7) The result is finally converted to a differential scaling system to estimate the visual magnitude of the error between the measurement and a standard (ΔE^*_{uv}).

The projective transformation (step 5 above) used in colorimetry has the general form

$$x = X/(X + Y + Z) \hspace{3cm} 17.3$$

If there is noise associated with each variable, X, Y, Z, the resultant distribution of noise associated with x is not easily calculated, because of the non-linear effect of the division operation. If X, Y and Z are independent, the probability density function of the sum of the variables is the convolution of each of the individual probability density functions. This is well defined and tractable, but the division operation coupled with one of the variables in the numerator vastly aggravates the complexity of calculation.

A numerical model was built using the colorimetric equations 17.3 with the addition of uncorrelated noise in each of the independent channels. Numerically, this is described by

$$x = (X + \varepsilon_x(t))/((X + \varepsilon_x(t)) + (Y + \varepsilon_y(t)) + (Z + \varepsilon_z(t))) \hspace{1.5cm} 17.4$$

where the error terms are denoted by $\varepsilon_x(t)$, $\varepsilon_y(t)$ and $\varepsilon_z(t)$.

The chromaticity values were calculated in this manner for a base set of monitor colours and fixed amounts of zero-mean additive noise. It is important for the reader to note that zero-mean additive noise at the detection stage can be eliminated by averaging, but if averaging is performed after the measurements have been taken, a completely different result will occur due to the non-linearities of the data processing steps.

The noise was defined as a percentage of the maximum luminance signal when measuring white. The results of the model are presented in Figure 17.8, in which the x axis is defined as 3-sigma/maximum white signal luminance. This means that the standard deviation of the white luminance measurement was used to generate the noise for each of the other two channels. For the purpose of this model the noise is assumed to be uncorrelated, zero-mean, and with a standard deviation that is equal in all three channels. The XYZ trichromatic data were then transformed to CIE L^*, u', v'. The ΔE^*_{uv} values were then calculated for each colour and each noise level and the data were averaged as specified in ASTM E1345-90 (ASTM, 1991b).

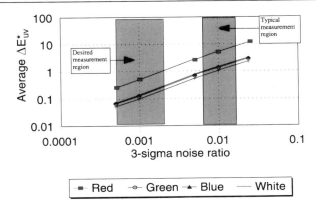

Figure 17.8 Average ΔE_{uv}^* error based upon independent noise/maximum signal level

The grey bands in Figure 17.8 represent two distinct regions of operation. The region on the right, labelled 'Typical measurement region', represents the region in which most monitor calibrators operate. This region was determined by examining the manufacturing data from thousands of embedded monitor calibrators. The noise is a combination of all the electrical noise and photo-optical noise present in the monitor detection system. The region labelled 'Desired measurement region' is indicative of where embedded monitor technology is headed in the future — an order of magnitude improvement.

Figure 17.8 can be used to determine what minimum amount of 3-sigma noise is needed to achieve an average ΔE_{uv}^* on the y axis. For instance, if it is required that the average error in the measurement of the red phosphor should be less than 1 ΔE_{uv}^*, the ratio of the 3-sigma noise to White luminance must be less than 0.002. This means that if the maximum white signal were 20 units in luminance Y, the standard deviation could not exceed $(20 \times 0.002)/3 = 0.0133$. In cases where a signal-to-noise measurement is taken to be the maximum value/standard deviation, the required signal-to-noise ratio would be in excess of 1500:1 (20/0.0133). It is interesting to note that the requirements for measuring red are much more extreme than the requirements for measuring the other colours. The reason for this was explained earlier when describing the relationship between the CIE colour matching functions and the phosphors: the red phosphor has almost no effect on the Z colour matching function, and hence random noise in Z is of the same order as the signal, thus making the chromaticity measurement far noisier than expected.

It should be noted that although noise in X, Y and Z is zero-mean, the effect upon the projective transformation data is most definitely not zero-mean. Figure 17.9 shows a relative frequency histogram of ΔE_{uv}^* which resulted from running the model with more than 2000 points. Note that the errors are not Gaussian distributed and that the spread of data is quite large, for a relatively large dynamic range white measurement (300:1).

The results of the model are independent of the instrument used, being functions only of the mathematics and physical noise in the measurement process. For normal measurement tasks, the operation of averaging data should take place in CIE XYZ space and not in any of the projective spaces. This is particularly true for monitor measurement applications. The measurement process of red primaries is especially susceptible to noise contamination and it must be undertaken with the utmost care.

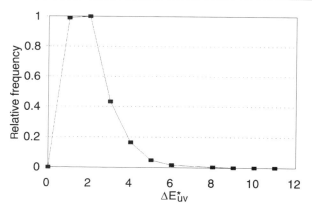

Figure 17.9   Relative frequency distribution of 2000 red measurements based upon model
parameters

17.4.3   Temporal errors in monitor measurement

The monitor is an active, time-varying and periodic source. This places an additional
set of requirements on an instrument used to measure the monitor. Nearly all monitor
calibrators mount directly onto the surface of the display CRT, in order to eliminate the
effects of ambient illumination. Because the measuring head is very near the display
surface, its field of view (FOV) is physically constrained by the mounting apparatus, but
the physical size of the screen on which it is mounted can vary over a wide range. This
means that the amount of time that the sensor is illuminated is a function of the refresh
rate of the screen, the area of the screen and the measurement field of view.

In Figure 17.10 the dwell time represents the length of time that the measurement
device is illuminated in each refresh cycle, and it can be seen that for a fixed refresh
rate the dwell time is inversely proportional to display area. If the device is to make a
measurement that correlates linearly with luminance, it must integrate the measurement
over a time which is greater than the dwell time, as illustrated in Figure 17.11.

An additional constraint is that the integration time must guarantee that an integral
number of pulses is captured. If this is not the case, significant errors will occur in the
estimate of the amplitude. Synchronisation can be accomplished by direct measurement

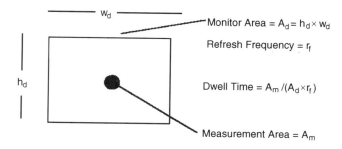

Figure 17.10   Monitor geometry and refresh rate determine the dwell time

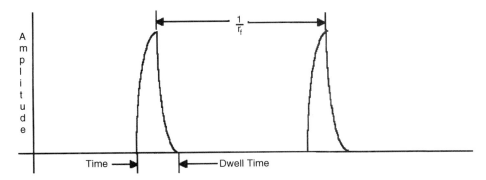

Figure 17.11   Time-varying waveform due to monitor refresh and physical measurement area

of refresh frequency using the optical sensor to characterise the time between points. In the case of a display attached to a computer system, it is often possible to determine the vertical refresh rate from the display driver parameters.

The mathematics of sampling periodic waveforms (Brigham, 1974) and estimation of the variance of the signals (Breiphohl, 1970) is well known, but quite complex. The embedded monitor calibrator allows for rapid collection of massive amounts of data and it is a good tool for investigating the effects of time domain interactions in monitor measurements. Heuristically, one would surmise that variations of integration time would lead to variations in the measured signal response. As the measurement time changes, the amount of data in the window of measurement also changes. An interesting fact is that the variance due to temporal sampling of the measured periodic waveform is itself periodic. A complete explanation of the reasons for this is beyond the scope of this chapter but the foundation can be found in an examination of Parseval's Theorem (Bogner & Constantinides, 1975), which states that the variance of the sampled time function is equal to the sum of the powers associated with the individual Fourier components of the function and that this variance is independent of phase. Figure 17.12 plots the measured variance of a single luminance level on a monitor as the integration time is increased. Each point on the graph is the resultant variance of 30 individual measurements.

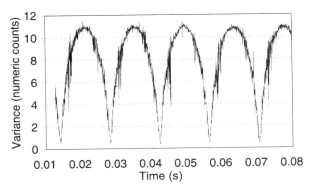

Figure 17.12   Measured variance of constant signal with variation of integration time

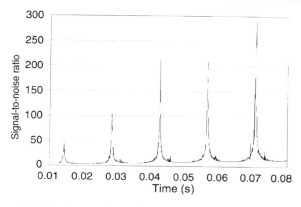

Figure 17.13   Measured signal-to-noise ratio of the measurement

The measured variance is noisy because only 30 samples were taken for each point. The minima on the plot represent the optimum sampling rate and are not zero. If the variance due to sampling is compared with the measured signal amplitude, as a function of integration time, a measure of signal-to-noise can be derived, as shown in Figure 17.13. The signal-to-noise ratio increases linearly with integration time, but there are very small bands where the signal-to-noise ratio is at a maximum. These peaks represent integration times that are precise integer multiples of the display refresh rate.

The consequences of not sampling at the proper rate are severe. If the refresh rate is not accurately determined, increasing the integration time is not guaranteed to increase the repeatability of measurement. Under these conditions, it is essential that the signal be averaged. It is worth noting that the 'reward' for sampling at the correct line rate is enormous when one considers the number of points that must be measured for an accurate sample. For example, note that the calculated signal-to-noise ratio for an integration time of 0.071 seconds was found to be approximately 300:1, whereas the signal-to-noise ratio at an integration time of 0.075 seconds is less than 25:1. In order to achieve a similar result by averaging, assuming a Gaussian distribution of the noise spectrum, approximately 140 samples (over 2 seconds) would be needed to achieve the same signal-to-noise ratio as one measurement at the 'correct' integration time. (see also Figure 16.7).

17.5   CONTROL OF THE MONITOR

17.5.1   Display adjustments

Display adjustments were originally implemented in the analogue electronic circuitry within the CRT monitor, and included brightness, contrast, focus and a range of controls for the geometry of the picture. The latest generation of colour CRT systems contain embedded digital controllers that allow for a wide range of computer-controlled adjustments. The combination of digital controls on the monitor and digital look-up tables in the computer provides the display application designer with numerous options. From the standpoint of on-line monitor control, the following adjustments are of interest:

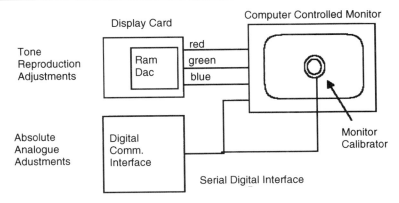

Figure 17.14 Block diagram of monitor calibration system with digital chassis and monitor calibrator

- Dark level adjustment
- Maximum white level adjustment
- Colour temperature of white
- Gamma control
- Grey balance throughout the tonal range.

The control of each of these factors is affected by the system configuration. In general, the first three items on the above list can be effectively adjusted using the controls provided by the digital monitor chassis. The partitioning of functions between the digital display card in the host computer and the digital chassis is based upon setting physical analogue limits on the monitor and using the display card to make gamma adjustments. A block diagram is shown in Figure 17.14.

The digital interface between the calibrator and the monitor is shown schematically to be bus-oriented, but some implementations have separate interfaces. A new standard interface that is emerging for monitor control is called the ACCESS bus, which allows for simultaneous control of a number of devices including keyboards, mice, calibrators and monitors. On computers manufactured by Apple Computer, the equivalent bus is called ADB (Apple Desktop Bus) and this bus is used by the Apple Macintosh to control keyboards, mice, pointing devices, computer-controlled monitors and calibrators.

17.5.2 Controlling the digital display card

The digital display card is the link between the computer and the display and it generates analogue video signals that are sent to the monitor. The control of colorimetry on the display generally requires that the display card contains mapping tables that can be used to modify the digital to analogue process. The calibrator system actively measures the display and captures the colorimetric and photometric information of the display system, which is then manipulated to generate the proper look-up tables to achieve the desired mapping function. As stated earlier, this mode of operation can be used to set the monitor to a known standard state. This can save a great deal of time in colour-managed environments because a new display profile does not have to be calculated.

One design aspect currently being debated among the manufacturers of display cards is the inclusion of digital communication interfaces on the display card itself. The VESA Display Data Channel Standard (VESA, 1995) defines a specification for the physical and architectural interface between display devices, graphic cards and other digital devices. Although the standard is quite complete, there are many issues related to the basic cost of the display card which limit the utility of these elegant communication schemes in most high volume design. The potential market acceptance of this new technology is very unclear at the present time.

One fundamental limitation to calibration of digital display systems is the ability to load the look-up table that precedes the digital-to-analogue converter (DAC) on the display card. The software interface or API (application program interface) must be defined for each different computer operating system. The Apple Macintosh operating system has always had such an interface, but most other systems do not have a standard API for this task. The introduction of Microsoft's *Windows 95* included a programming method to control the display card gamma curves, but, interestingly, *Windows NT* provided no such functionality. In the Unix world, there is a wide variety of interface capabilities with systems such as Silicon Graphics and Sun *Solaris* providing some facilities. At the present time, there is no *X-Windows* method to set a known characteristic curve on the display. The lack of a standard interface has hindered the growth of display calibration products outside the Apple marketplace.

17.5.3   Controlling the digital display chassis

The digital chassis of the modern display system allows for adjustment of the analogue 'set points' of the monitor. These controls allow for a basic setting of the colorimetry by adjustment of the individual gains of the guns in the CRT. In addition, it is possible to set the analogue brightness and contrast controls to achieve optimum adjustment for later digital calibration.

The command layer for these adjustment is specified by the ACCESS.bus specification (ACCESS.bus, 1995). Many manufacturers currently build display systems that incorporate RS-232 serial connectors to facilitate the manufacture and adjustment of the monitor. One potential problem with the standardisation of the monitor adjustments is the accidental mis-adjustment of the monitor factory settings due to a computer communications error. This has led manufacturers to develop strategies which limit the range of adjustment of the controls to 'safe' regions, but this has delayed the introduction of products into the market place.

The future of ACCESS.bus is by no means secure. Intel has recently proposed a newer high bandwidth bus called the Universal Serial Bus (USB), which is considered by many people to represent the future of digital communications in the display world, because the bus has the bandwidth to carry audio signals as well as video.

17.6   MATCHING MONITORS

In situations where multiple monitors are used to view images or data shared by a number of individuals making colour judgements, as in applications for remote collaborative working, it is often requested that each monitor should be adjusted to match a common reference standard so that they will visually match each other.

17.6.1 Limits and bounds

A number of 'hard' limits constrain the ability of one monitor to match exactly the display characteristics of another. For the purpose of this discussion, we shall call the monitor to be matched the 'reference monitor' and the monitor to be adjusted the 'working monitor'. A reference monitor is first characterised to generate a 'teaching function'. A working monitor is then 'taught' by this function and hence 'learns' from the reference monitor: *reference monitors 'teach', working monitors 'learn'.*

For an absolute match to be possible, the following conditions are necessary, but not sufficient, to ensure absolute tracking of the reference and working monitors:

(1)   The maximum luminance of the working monitor must be equal to or greater than that of the reference monitor when the white points of each are set to the same colour temperature.

(2)   The minimum luminance of the working monitor must be less than or equal to that of the reference monitor when the black points of each are set to the same colour temperature.

(3)   Given Conditions 1 and 2, the ratio of white to black (i.e. contrast range) of the working monitor will be equal to or greater than the ratio of white to black of the reference.

Conditions 1–3 can be considered the cardinal rules for monitor matching. If condition 3 is met, but condition 1 is not met, a perceptual match can still be achieved between the two displays so that perceived differences within an image on either display will be the same. If condition 2 is not met, an absolute match cannot be achieved over the entire range of adjustment. Besides these conditions, we must consider some other higher-order effects that can also impact our ability to match a reference and working monitor.

The manipulation of RGB tables in the LUTs on the display card can provide close matches in grey (achromatic tones of an image), but the extremes of the colour gamut are defined by the phosphors in the monitor. This means that coloured objects viewed on the reference and working monitors may be noticeably different, even though the grey scale response is virtually identical. Such differences can only be eliminated by a colour management system that renders an image to the display. For this process to work properly, the colour gamut of the working display must be equal to or greater than that of the reference display, i.e. there must be no colours on the reference display that the working display cannot produce (Condition 4).

If the gamma of the working monitor is much greater than that of the reference monitor, digital artifacts may be introduced into the working display through quantisation errors in the correction functions in the LUTs. A good match between two monitors is facilitated by a minimum difference between the two gammas of the monitors (see Sections 14.4.2 and 12.3). The ratio of the native gammas of the reference and working monitors should ideally be close to 1.0 (Condition 5).

17.6.2   Architectural implementation of monitor matching

An understanding of the above five conditions for achieving a match allows us to assess of two monitors to decide whether they can be matched. For the purposes of the discussions that follow, we define these terms:

- *Native Reference Response Function* The luminance–chrominance characteristics of the uncorrected reference monitor.
- *Desired Reference Response Function* The luminance–chrominance characteristics of the corrected reference monitor (i.e. the desired response of the working monitor).
- *Native Working Response Function* The luminance–chrominance characteristics of the working monitor with no correction applied.
- *Desired Response Correction Function* A set of three RGB look-up tables that correct the Native Response (Working or Reference) to the Desired Response.

This discussion is general and independent of operating system. We assume that there is some known location for reference data that we term the TEACHING FOLDER. This folder contains teaching files that describe arbitrary and absolute display mapping conditions. The term 'arbitrary' implies that the display mapping need not be either monotonic or neutral throughout the range. The term 'absolute' implies that the data in the teaching files is measured in some device-independent colour space that references absolute luminance levels. The teaching files should contain the Desired Reference Response Function, the Native Reference Response Function and the Desired Response Correction Function for the reference monitor. The teaching folder may contain many different files, but only one can be valid for a given working monitor in a given instance.

Besides the TEACHING FOLDER, there is a MONITOR DESCRIPTION FOLDER. A typical file in this folder contains the Native Working Response Function of the working monitor as well as the colorimetric model of the working monitor. The colorimetric model is usually a linear matrix that maps the device-independent colour information to an intermediate linear space that has a known correspondence to device RGB. Figure 17.15 shows a block diagram of each file.

The data required in each file are quite similar. A teaching file is a subset of a monitor description file and its data arise as the direct result of calibration of the reference monitor. The process used to achieve a match requires that the data from both files be used to calculate the final desired response function, as shown schematically in Figure 17.16.

The Desired Monitor Response Data, the Native Reference Monitor Response and the Native Working Monitor Response Data are all fed into a response comparator algorithm,

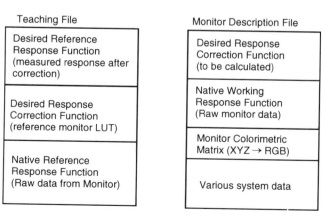

Figure 17.15 Block diagram of typical files for monitor matching function

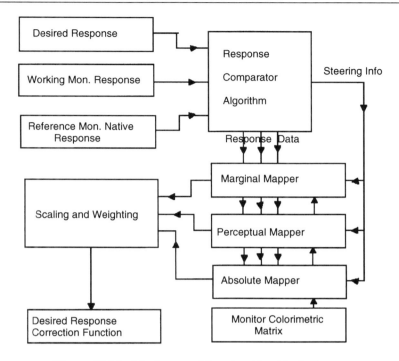

Figure 17.16 Monitor matching algorithm block diagram

which examines the functions with respect to the five basic matching conditions. The output of this algorithm steers the calculation process to one of three conditions: Marginal Mapper, Absolute Mapper and Perceptual Mapper. The Mapper functions require the Desired Monitor Response Data, the Native Working Response Function and the Working Monitor Colorimetric Matrix. The output of the Mapper function is a scaled function from which the look-up tables for the best match are achieved. The matching can be mixed–that is to say, in certain regions an absolute match can be made whilst in others the match may be perceptual or marginal. The Desired Response Correction Function can be weighted to guarantee that a minimum error mapping function can be generated.

17.6.3   Operating procedure for monitor matching

The monitor matching function should be a push-button correction. When a user selects 'Teach', he or she should be prompted to mount the calibrator device on the screen and the application should then measure the current display state. On completion it should ask the operator to name the measurement file, which will then be stored in the correct folder.

The 'Learn' function is more complicated. At the beginning of a learn function, the program should prompt the user for a file name. The file is read by the program and the user is prompted to mount the calibrator. The following actions should occur:

(1)   The working LUTs should be set to linear (output = input).

(2)   The working monitor white and black points should be measured.

(3)   These should be compared to the black and white points of the reference monitor. If they are significantly different, the user should be informed that a manual adjustment may be necessary to achieve a good match. A box-within-a-box target should be displayed with a reference area surrounding the measurement area. The user should be prompted to try to adjust the luminance to match and to ensure that the box-within-a-box target remains visible at both white and black ends of the scale. The target data should be 'manually' converted through the working monitor calibration LUT. The values displayed in the white and black targets should be calculated using a linear look-up table in the display DACs using final values of 32 and 255.

(4)   The reference white and black points are compared to the measured monitor points and calculations are performed to determine if the three cardinal matching conditions can be met. If there is no problem, skip step 5.

(5)   If there is a problem, the user should be prompted to correct the problem, normally by an analogue adjustment, or should be informed of the compromises.

(6)   The monitor transfer (gamma) function should then be measured, using at least 10 levels along the grey scale from black to white.

(7)   The mapping function will calculate the new look-up tables.

(8)   The screens should then appear the same if the environmental conditions are the same.

It should be noted that steps 5 and 6 are exactly the same as a standard calibration operation with the exception of the utilisation of an arbitrary response function.

17.7 MEASUREMENT OF AMBIENT ILLUMINATION

The monitor calibration device can also be used to measure ambient illumination if it has been designed to measure incident illumination (illuminance). The measurement of illuminance is normally performed over a full hemispherical viewing angle, accomplished by putting a hemispherical diffuser over the sensor. The purpose of this diffuser is to collect and average all the illumination striking the surface. In the monitor calibration device, the angle of collection is usually limited by the suction cup, so it is not possible to incorporate the standard hemispherical geometry. This compromise results in inaccurate measurements in viewing environments with large amounts of diffuse illumination. Fortunately, such environments are generally not conducive to comfortable viewing on CRT displays due to the large flare component introduced. Hence the monitor calibration device can give reasonable ambient measurements in most typical viewing environments.

If the device does not have a strictly designed colour matching function response, it is necessary to calibrate it for the particular illuminants to be measured. The technique is exactly like that described in Section 17.3. Identification of the lighting 'type' can be accomplished by examining the frequency and colorimetric signals generated by the source. Fluorescent tubes have a great deal of modulation due to AC line changes and it is necessary to synchronise these measurements with the line frequency to achieve accurate results, via the same technique used to measure monitor frequency. Tungsten sources, although powered by AC, exhibit minimal ripple in the amplitude due to the thermal inertia of the filament. Using these clues, the monitor calibrator can be used to select the best data collection strategy for the ambient measurement.

17.8   CONCLUSIONS

The modern embedded monitor calibration device is capable of very high quality colour measurements within the narrow context of its use. The constraints of low cost and rapid measurement speed require that careful attention be paid to signal processing techniques and calibration methodologies. The ultimate link between the device and the user is the software supplied with the device. This software must handle a robust range of potential error conditions, because the users of the device are typically neither engineers nor scientists. When attention is paid to the engineering details and the user interface software is properly designed, the embedded monitor calibration device can achieve highly accurate and precise measurements.

REFERENCES

ACCESS.bus (Sept. 1995), *Monitor Device Protocol Specification*, Section 7, ACCESS.bus Industry Group, 370 Altair Way, Suite 215, Santa Clara, CA.

ASTM (1991), *Standards on Colour and Appearance Measurement*, 3rd Edition.

ASTM (1991), Standard practice for reducing the effect of variability of colour measurement by use of multiple measurements, *ASTM E1345-90*, American Society for Testing and Materials, Philadelphia, PA.

Berns, R., Motta, R. and Gorzynski, M. (1993a), CRT colorimetry. Part I: Theory and practice, *Colour Research and Application*, **18**(5), 299–314.

Berns, R., Gorzynski, M. and Motta, R. (1993b), CRT colorimetry. Part II: Metrology, *Colour Research and Application*, **18**(5), 315–325.

Bogner, R.E. and Constantinides, A.G. (1975), *Introduction to Digital Filtering*, John Wiley & Sons, New York, 97.

Breipohl, A. (1970), *Probabilistic Systems Analysis*, John Wiley & Sons, New York, 139–160.

Brigham, E. (1974), *The Fast Fourier Transform*, Prentice-Hall, Englewood Cliffs, NJ, 87.

Hardis, J.E. (1994), *Improving Colour Measurement of Displays*, Technical Report, Radiometric Physics Division, NIST, Gaithersburg, MD.

Hunt, R.W.G. (1987), *The Reproduction of Colour in Photography, Printing and Television*, 4th Edition, Fountain Press, Tolworth, UK, 37–43.

Hunt, R.W.G. (1991), *Measuring Colour*, 2nd Edition, Ellis Horwood, Chichester, UK, 213–258.

Ritzel, J.P. and Sojourni, S. (1993), Silicon photodiodes matched to the CIE photometric curve using colour filter glass, *Optics & Photonics News*, April, 16–19.

VESA (Dec 1995), *Display Data Channel Standard*, Video Electronics Standards Association, 2150 North First Street, Suite 440, San Jose, CA 95131-2029.

Widdel, H. and Post, D.L. (1992), *Colour in Electronic Displays*, Defense Research Series Vol. 3, Plenum Press, New York, 241.

The dynamic performance of CRT and LC displays

David Parker

18.1 INTRODUCTION

This chapter deals with the situation where the light output from a display is varying with time. This can be because of a wanted effect such as the portrayal of a moving image; or an unwanted effect such as flicker. The most common types of display used for displaying moving images are those using Cathode Ray Tubes (CRT), either viewed directly or projected onto a screen, and Active Matrix Liquid Crystal Displays (AMLCD) which again can be either viewed directly or projected. The treatment compares and contrasts these two types of displays whose dynamic behaviour is quite different. As will be explained, this leads to differences in flicker levels and in the quality of the portrayal of moving images. Passive LC displays will not be considered here as their very slow response time makes them unsuitable for the display of good quality moving images.

Before describing the performance of the two display types, the subjective effects that are relevant in the comparison will be considered, and a simplified way of analyzing the portrayal of motion will be introduced.

18.2 SUBJECTIVE CONSIDERATIONS

There are three parameters to bear in mind when considering the dynamic characteristics of displays: flicker, dynamic resolution and the portrayal of motion, though of course they

Display Systems, Edited by L.W. MacDonald and A.C. Lowe. © 1997 John Wiley & Sons Ltd.

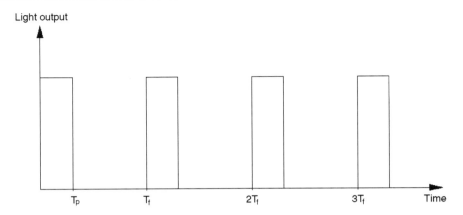

Figure 18.1   Light output from hypothetical display

are not independent of each other. Consider, first, a hypothetical raster scanned display device with a field period of T_f where the addressing time for each pixel is short compared to T_f. Let the temporal characteristics of the display be such that the temporal impulse response of a pixel can be represented by a rectangular function of time of duration T_p. Then the light output from the display for a static, uniform picture can be represented as shown in Figure 18.1.

18.2.1   Flicker

The fundamental component of the light output described by Figure 18.1 will give rise to large area flicker at a frequency F, where $F = 1/T_f$. For a given perceived display brightness, the amplitude of the fundamental increases as T_p decreases. The frequency at which flicker just becomes perceptible to the viewer varies as the logarithm of the luminance (the Ferry–Porter Law). Typical quoted threshold values are approximately 103 cd/m^2 for 50 Hz and 617 cd/m^2 for 60 Hz displays (Benson, 1985). The sensitivity of peripheral vision to flicker is higher than that of the fovea. The acceptability of a given field rate for a given application thus depends on both the brightness and the viewing angle of the display.

   In interlaced displays, the effect known as interline flicker is also present. Repeat spectra due to the interlaced sampling structure cause high static vertical frequency components in the scene to be repeated at low vertical frequencies and temporal frequencies of half the field rate (Fernando & Parker, 1986). Thus the severity of the effect is scene dependent, being worse if the signal contains high levels of high vertical frequency information. This is why for close viewing of sharp graphic or text images on CRTs, non-interlaced displays are almost always used. Natural scenes derived from television cameras tend to have less energy at high vertical frequencies and so the effect is less troublesome.

18.2.2   Dynamic resolution

It is often said that the spatial resolution of the eye is lower for moving images than for static ones. However, it is important to realise that this statement is based on experiments where the eye is fixated. In situations where the viewer is able to track the movement, very little change in perceived sharpness is observed even for quite high velocities (Westerink & Teunissen, 1990). That this is reasonable is apparent if it is realised that if the eye tracking is perfect, then the image on the retina is stationary. So, particularly for large screens and where image velocities are within the range normally used for television, it can be assumed that the viewer is able to take advantage of moving images that are as sharp as static ones (unless the imagery is so complex that eye tracking is not possible).

Now consider the way our hypothetical display will actually present a moving image. For simplicity, an image of a bright thin vertical line moving horizontally across the screen will be used as an example. This is illustrated schematically in the upper part of Figure 18.2. If this were a 'real-life' line, the light output as a function of distance, x, and time would be as shown in the lower part of the figure.

As our hypothetical display is a sampling device, its light output when displaying the moving line will be as shown in Figure 18.3. If this is compared with the 'real-life' representation of the moving line, shown by the dotted line in the figure, it can be seen that an error is introduced due to the finite width of the impulse function, T_p. Depending on the duration of T_p and assuming that the eye is tracking the image, a blurring of the moving line will be observed due to the difference, d, between the position where the eye 'expects' to see the image (that is, the position which would keep it stationary on the retina) and the position it actually occupies on the display (Shimodaira *et al.*, 1985). This effect will be considered further below.

18.2.3 Portrayal of motion

The representation of moving images on electronic displays depends on the illusion of motion produced when successive stationary images are presented to the viewer. There is considerable literature on the psychophysics of this phenomenon of 'apparent motion'; see, for example, Kolers (1972). The quality of the motion portrayal depends on the periodicity of the time sampling, T_f, the duration of each sample, T_p, the time gap between samples, $T_f - T_p$, and the velocity. A review of some of these factors as related to the portrayal of moving television images can be found in Tonge (1986). If the spatio-temporal samples

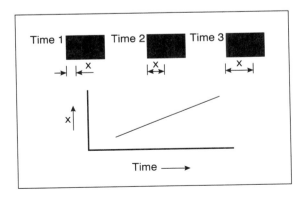

Figure 18.2 Moving line

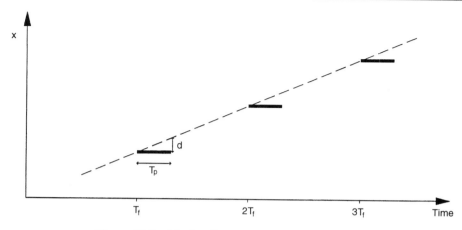

Figure 18.3 Moving line on hypothetical display

shown in Figure 18.3 are close enough both in space and time then the illusion of motion is produced of the line moving smoothly along the trajectory shown by the dotted line. For the range of velocities typically encountered in television, a field rate of a few tens of hertz is more than adequate for a smooth representation of motion (for comparision, cinema film is projected at 24 frames per second).

Where problems can arise, however, is when the image sampling is changed between the image source and the display, for example by a standards converter. Then the possibility exists of introducing image splitting or judder into the motion portrayal depending on the algorithm used to manipulate the time samples. This will be considered further in Section 18.5.

18.3 CRT DISPLAYS

The temporal impulse response of a pixel of a CRT display depends on the properties of the phosphors being used but typically has the form shown in Figure 18.4–a very rapid rise to a high peak value followed by an exponential decay. Ignoring the special case of storage tubes, most of the light will have decayed within a time of the order of a millisecond (see also Section 17.4.3).

The high amplitude and short duration of the impulse response mean that the amplitude of the fundamental component of the large area flicker frequency is high. It is difficult to be dogmatic about what flicker levels are acceptable to the viewer. For example, although the large area flicker is plainly visible, 50 Hz is generally tolerated in Europe for television even though the display brightness can be high. However, an increasing number of receivers with field rate conversion to 100 Hz are appearing on the market and finding consumer acceptance. For computer use it is usual to find field rates of at least 70 Hz which effectively eliminates large area flicker at typical monitor brightnesses.

For a given display line frequency (which largely determines complexity and cost), a choice can be made between the use of interlace at a certain field rate or a sequential scan at half that field rate. This comes down to a choice between reducing large area flicker and reducing interline flicker and the relative importance will depend on the application.

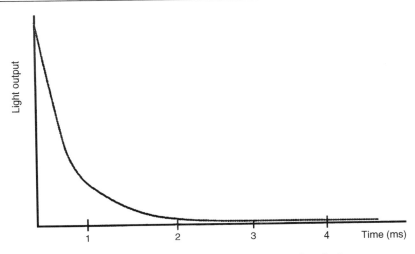

Figure 18.4 CRT temporal impulse response (typical phosphor)

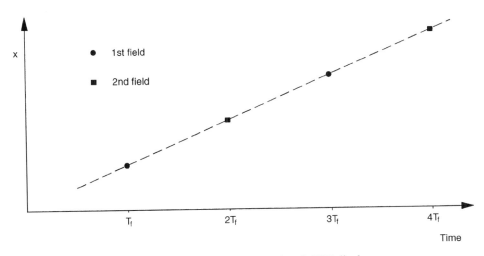

Figure 18.5 Moving line on interlaced CRT display

Because the impulse response is so short the dynamic resolution of the CRT is very good. Considering the horizontally moving vertical line of Section 18.2 again, the light output can be represented as shown in Figure 18.5 and the difference between the sampled motion and the 'true motion' is small, i.e. $d \approx 0$, and little loss of spatial resolution occurs.

18.4 AMLCD DISPLAYS

The distinguishing feature of an Active Matrix Liquid Crystal Display is that there is an active switch for each pixel such that each pixel is briefly addressed once per field and is then isolated so that it retains its value until readdressed, i.e the temporal impulse response is a rectangular function of width equal to the field period. (For the time being we will neglect the finite switching speed of the liquid crystal material.) Thus for a display showing a constant brightness, large area flicker is completely absent. In practice, the polarity of the signal applied across the LCD must be alternated at field rate or, more usually, line rate to prevent any DC across the material, and asymmetries in the LCD characteristic may lead to low levels of large area or line flicker. This is not usually a problem with a well-adjusted display.

However, this same sample and hold property that results in the absence of flicker also leads to a degradation in dynamic resolution. Consider first an interlaced LC display. The moving line diagram now becomes as shown in Figure 18.6(a). Each light sample will last for a frame period and the impression will be that the line width has been considerably broadened in the x direction (Knapp & Powell, 1989). This is the reason that AMLC displays are always operated in a non-interlaced mode. Then the moving line diagram is as shown in Figure 18.6(b) and the line broadening is halved. It can be seen, however, that it is still significant and the dynamic resolution is observed to be considerably worse than that of a CRT display (Noyori *et al.*, 1994). If a television signal is being displayed, then some form of interlace to sequential conversion is necessary. This can range from superimposing fields for small low-resolution displays, to line repetition up to more complex multidimensional interpolation systems for high quality projected pictures.

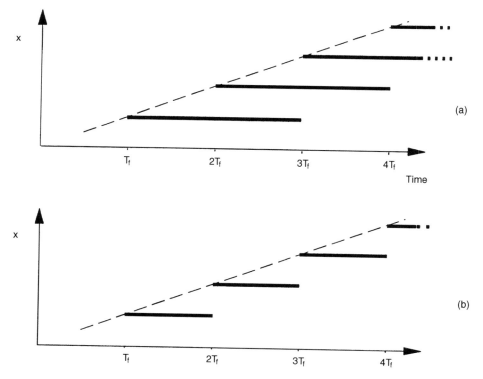

Figure 18.6   Moving line on (a) interlaced and (b) sequential LCD

The finite switching speed of the LCD has so far been ignored. There are two effects to be considered here. Depending on the properties of the liquid crystal material and the cell thickness, it will always take a certain time for the molecules to reorient themselves. Switching times as low as ~3 ms (Janssen, 1993) have been reported for special applications, but considerably longer times are more usual. The switching time will depend on the amplitude of the transition and on its direction (black to white or vice versa). This is because in one direction the molecules are driven into their new state by the applied electric field whereas in the other they relax back. The effect is due to the voltage dependent nature of the capacitance of an LC cell and this can be minimised by appropriate signal processing (Bitzakidis, 1994). See the discussion in Section 9.2.

Let the capacitance of an LC pixel be given by $C(v)$, where v is the voltage across the cell. From the black to white state this pixel capacitance can vary by a factor of about two, with a voltage dependency as shown in Figure 18.7. Consider the video signal changing such that the voltage across a cell should change from a value of v_1 in one field to v_2 in the subsequent field (Figure 18.8). The addressing time of the pixel is a small fraction of the field period and is too short a time for the capacitance of the pixel to change. If a value of v_2 is simply applied to the cell, the cell will actually settle to an incorrect value because of the subsequent change of capacitance with voltage. However, if the form of the capacitance variation is known and if the previous voltage value v_1 is stored, then a corrected value, v_{2c}, can be applied, where $v_{2c} = C(v_2) \cdot v_2 / C(v_1)$. This will ensure that the voltage across the cell will settle to the correct value of v_2. The effectiveness of this can be seen in Figure 18.9 which shows a compensated and uncompensated transition between transmission values of 50 percent and 97 percent. If this pre-correction is not applied it can take several field periods for an LC pixel to correspond to a signal change, and the blurring on the edges of sharp moving images is even worse than suggested earlier. To implement the correction, a field store is required, and for full effect an increase in the column drive voltage is necessary.

Another way to lessen the effect of the voltage dependent capacitance of the LC pixel is to add a fixed capacitance in parallel with the variable pixel capacitance. Thus the

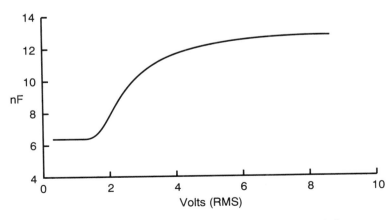

Figure 18.7 LC pixel capacitance–voltage characteristic

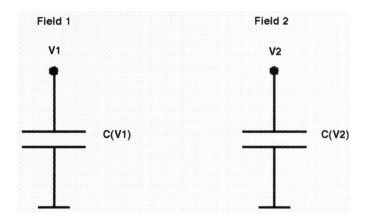

Figure 18.8   Compensation for LC voltage dependent capacitance

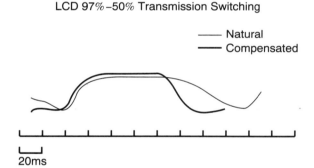

Figure 18.9   Compensated and uncompensated LC switching times

variation of the total capacitance with pixel voltage is reduced. The practicalities of doing this depend on the details of the technology used to fabricate the AMLCD.

18.5   FIELD RATE CONVERSIONS

It is sometimes necessary to change the field rate of an image between the source and the display. This can arise due to differences in TV field rates between Europe and the USA, or when a TV derived image sequence is to be shown on a computer display running at a different field rate. Another reason is for flicker reduction on bright CRT displays. A whole range of field rate conversion algorithms are available of varying complexity and performance and this section will try to briefly point out the kind of artefacts that can arise and what performance compromises are available.

The general problem is to resample an image sequence to produce intermediate temporal samples that did not exist in the original sequence. If simple temporal interpolation is used, then spatial blurring will be produced. This is illustrated in Figure 18.10 which shows that if a new '100 Hz field' is formed by averaging together the two temporally adjacent '50 Hz fields', then any moving part of the picture will be reproduced incorrectly. If, alternatively, the 'nearest' temporal sample from the original is used, then motion smoothness will be jeopardised and 'judder' or image splitting will result. The more complex television standards converters use temporal and spatial interpolation over several fields to try to achieve a good compromise between loss of sharpness and visibility of judder (Clarke & Tanton, 1984). The only way to change the field rate while preserving the spatial resolution and the motion portrayal is to use motion compensated conversion (Fernando & Parker, 1987). In this technique motion estimation is used to estimate the velocity of objects in the scene and the temporal interpolation is offset to take into account these motions. The success of the technique depends heavily on the quality of the motion estimation, but good results have been achieved in both the professional (Richards *et al.*, 1992) and consumer fields (de Haan *et al.*, 1993).

To illustrate some of the problems mentioned above, conversion from 50 Hz to 100 Hz will be considered. This is usually done to eliminate large area flicker from CRT television displays. Again using the simple example used earlier, the result of applying a simple field repetition algorithm to produce a 100 Hz signal displayed on a CRT is shown in Figure 18.11(a). As can be seen, a double image is produced and this can be observed in practice with very sharp input signals when the eye tracks the movement. The case of the 100 Hz interlaced signal being produced by perfect motion compensated interpolation is illustrated in Figure 18.11(b), again displayed on a CRT. As is to be expected this gives an undistorted image of the line moving across the screen. The subjective test results reported in Parker and Fernando (1990) suggest that observers are aware of the difference between images such as those illustrated in Figure 18.11(a) and (b) in real scenes providing that the original images are of good dynamic resolution.

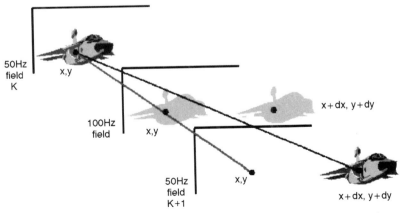

Figure 18.10   50 Hz to 100 Hz conversion by simple temporal averaging

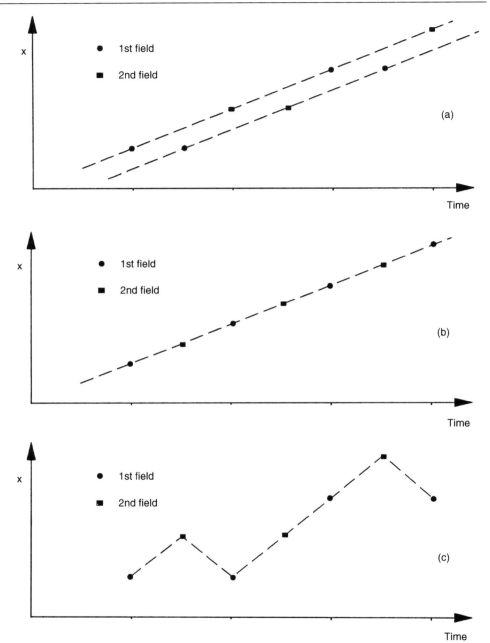

Figure 18.11   Moving line on 100 Hz CRT produced by (a) field repetition, (b) motion compensation, and (c) frame repetition

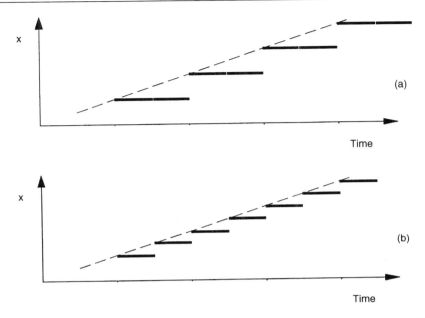

Figure 18.12 Moving line at 100 Hz on an LCD produced by (a) field repetition and (b) motion compensation

To illustrate the judder problem, now consider the conversion to 100 Hz by frame repetition. The resulting situation is illustrated in Figure 18.11(c). The eye interprets this situation as a juddery motion as indicated by the dotted line and, although this algorithm is effective at reducing interline flicker, it cannot be used for moving images.

It is interesting to look at the results of displaying 100 Hz conversions on an LCD display. The field repetition and motion compensated cases are shown in Figure 18.12(a) and (b) though in this case a sequential display is shown. In the field repetition case the result is exactly the same as the 50 Hz case. However, when motion compensation is used the line broadening is halved. Thus in the future there may be a use for motion compensated conversion to 100 Hz for LC displays, in this case not for flicker reduction but for dynamic resolution improvement.

18.6 CONCLUSIONS

The differences in the dynamic behaviour of AMLCD and CRT displays have been pointed out and their consequences have been described in terms of flicker, dynamic resolution and motion portrayal. The respective strengths and weaknesses of the two types of display should be borne in mind when considering a particular application. Most of the results presented for AMLCDs can also be applied to other types of sample and hold displays.

If the display field rate is not the same as that of the source, care must be taken in the method used for the field rate conversion if the quality of the moving pictures is not to be compromised. Again, the suitability of the method depends on the application and the viewing conditions. For the highest quality field rate conversion, motion compensation has to be used.

REFERENCES

Benson, K.B. (1985), *Television Engineering Handbook*, 21.44, McGraw-Hill, New York.

Bitzakidis, S. (1994), Improvements in the moving-image quality of AMLCDs, *Journal of the SID*, **2**(3), 149–154.

Clarke, C.K.P. and Tanton, N.E. (1984), Digital standards conversion: interpolation theory and aperture synthesis, *BBC Research Department Report*, **1984/20**.

de Haan, G., Biezen, P.W.A.C., Huijgen, H. and Ojo, O.A. (1993), True-motion estimation with 3-D recursive search block matching, *IEE Trans. Circuits and Systems for Video Technology*, **3**(5).

Fernando, G.M.X. and Parker, D.W. (1986), Improved display conversion for high definition MAC, *Proc. Eleventh Int. Broadcasting Convention 1986*, IEE Conf. Publ. 268.

Fernando, G.M.X. and Parker, D.W. (1987), Motion compensated field rate conversion for HDTV display, *Proc. Third Int. Coll. on Advanced Television Systems: HDTV '87*, Ottawa, October.

Fernando, G.M.X. and Parker, D.W. (1990), Display processing for HD-MAC, *Proc. Fourth Int. Coll. on Advanced Television Systems: HDTV '90*, Ottawa, June.

Janssen, P. (1993), A novel single light valve high brightness HD colour projector, *Proc. 13th Int. Display Research Conf.*, Strasbourg, France, September.

Knapp, A.G. and Powell, M.J. (1989), Display issues for a-Si active matrix LCTV, *Journal of the ITE*, **44**(5).

Kolers, P.A. (1972), *Aspects of Motion Perception*, Pergamon Press, 1972.

Noyori, Y., Washio, H., Shimodaira, Y., Muraoka, T., Yamamoto, K. and Ishii, Y. (1994), Subjective evaluation of quality of moving pictures on a TFT-liquid crystal display, *Proc. 1994 Int. Display Research Conf.*, Monterey, CA, October.

Richards, J.W., Keating, S.M., Saunders, N.I. and Walters, C.W. (1992), Experience with a prototype motion compensated standards converter for down-conversion of 1125/60/2:1 SMPTE-240M high definition to 625/50/2:1 video, *Proc. Int. Broadcasting Convention 1992*, IEE Conf. Publ. 358.

Shimodaira, Y., Harano, T. and Fuke, S. (1985), Blur injury caused by motion on the hold type picture display, *IEICE*, **J68-B**(12).

Tonge, G.J. (1986), Time-sampled motion portrayal, *Proc. Second Int. Conf. on Image Processing and Its Applications 1986*, IEE Conf. Publ. 265.

Westerink, J.H.D.M. and Teunissen, C. (1990), Perceived sharpness in moving images, *SPIE Proc.*, **1249**.

Evaluating stereoscopic displays for 3D imagery

Tim Bardsley and Ian Sexton

19.1 INTRODUCTION

Recent technological advances and the demands of more sophisticated methods of interaction have led to an unprecedented interest in the techniques and applications of 3D imagery. Although the head-mounted display is probably the preferred display apparatus for true (immersive) Virtual Reality systems, as described in Chapter 4, such devices are often costly and cumbersome. Because of this, and in view of rising concern regarding the health and safety issues surrounding such displays, alternative non-immersive or desktop systems are often preferable. There are also many other application areas where a stereoscopic display is desirable but where the use of head-mounted equipment is unattractive. The Imaging and Displays Research Group at De Montfort University is involved in various aspects of three-dimensional and stereoscopic display research. A theme of this research has been the development of autostereoscopic display systems, particularly display types that utilise view-selecting mechanisms in the form of parallax barriers and lenticular screens.

The use of stereoscopic and 3D displays has become well established in niche application areas where it is possible to demonstrate clearly an improvement in operator performance. This is usually achieved by comparing a particular stereoscopic system to a monoscopic counterpart (Pepper *et al.*, 1977). In areas where the use of 3D displays has become established, the evidence to support the superior performance is often

Display Systems, Edited by L.W. MacDonald and A.C. Lowe. © 1997 John Wiley & Sons Ltd.

incontrovertible but few researchers have the opportunity to make direct comparisons of different 3D systems. Because of this, the choice of display technology is often quite arbitrary.

There are many ways of producing a monoscopic display and many more ways of producing a stereoscopic system. This is to be expected as monoscopic displays are often components of stereoscopic systems. Each display type exhibits a set of artefacts, some of which are unique to the implementation. These typically include limited screen resolution (influencing depth quantisation level), crosstalk, retinal rivalry and flicker, all of which ultimately impinge upon operator performance. It is useful for both system designers and potential users of such displays to recognise these limitations in order to determine the applicability of a particular technology.

19.2 APPLICATION REQUIREMENTS

Recent developments in electronic display technology and image generation techniques have spawned many new and varied applications (Thwaites, 1991; Wichansky, 1991). The appearance of 'programmable' display media, like the CRT and flat-panel matrix displays, resulted in many new video-based televisual applications. Similarly, recent advances in computer generated imaging have served to increase the number of potential 3D applications. The distinction between *televisual* (video) and *synthetic* (computer-based) applications has become less pronounced with advent of hybrid *augmented reality systems* which offer computer enhancement of both static and real-time video imagery. Regardless of the categorisation used, there is growing evidence to suggest that the provision of a three-dimensional display capability is not only desirable, but a prerequisite for many of today's advanced imaging applications (Cole *et al.*, 1990).

19.2.1 Video imaging

Imaging applications increasingly require the facility to portray 'real-world' environments in three dimensions. This facility is particularly valuable when aspects of the environment preclude the presence of a human subject, whether for reasons of cost, severe hazard or geographical inaccessibility. Remote imaging and inspection systems, for example, allow exploration and manipulation within frequently inaccessible or hostile locations. Typical *telepresence* applications include underwater exploration, remote vehicle navigation and object manipulation within radioactive environments (Johnston *et al.*, 1950). A common feature of such systems is the provision of a live video link between the remote environment and a human *teleoperator*. Such '3D-TV' systems typically employ two adjacent video cameras, with provision for remote control of their principal operating characteristics such as focusing and convergence angle. In such a configuration, the cameras are able to generate the twin perspective views necessary for adaptive, real-time stereoscopic display.

Although two-dimensional visual feedback has proved to be quite satisfactory in situations requiring only passive observation, effective interaction with remote environments requires the provision of a stereo image (Drascic, 1991). Specific task-related studies have revealed significant improvements in teleoperator performance using systems which provide this depth-of-field visualisation (Pepper *et al.*, 1977), while in others the same facility has proved essential (Cole *et al.*, 1990). Aspects of human performance that benefit from effective 3D visualisation are an enhanced ability to perform both relative and absolute depth judgments, and improved response times when dealing with dynamic situations (Miller & Beaton, 1991). Task completion times have been reduced by up to 20 percent when using 3D visualisation techniques in dealing with remote inspection and manipulation tasks in underwater environments (Zenyuh *et al.*, 1988). There is strong evidence to suggest that subjects presented with a monoscopic view of complex visual tasks often adopt a 'trial and error' approach when performing them. Stereoscopic representation lessens this dependence on cognitive strategy and effectively reduces operator workload (Cole *et al.*, 1990).

A number of peripheral benefits may be realised when employing stereoscopic video techniques. Greater effective image quality can be achieved with stereo images, as binocular depth cues are less susceptible to the effects of low image resolution, impaired visibility, motion blur and other degrading factors. An element of visual noise may be present in the video image due to environmental factors or poor quality image reception. The human visual system is particularly adept at filtering out uncorrelated visual noise from binocular scenes to give greater picture clarity. This ability is invaluable in determining not only *where* objects are in unfamiliar or complex scenes, but frequently *what* they are (Merritt, 1983).

It has been suggested that stereo imagery can assist *visual attention localisation* (Merritt, 1991). This effect allows an observer to disregard visual clutter and concentrate on scene details having a common depth component. This property can be most beneficial in assisting the identification and disclosure of camouflaged objects. The effects of surface sheen, lustre and scintillation are perceived only by virtue of the differences in luminance and colour between two retinal images. As stereo display systems are capable of conveying this visual information, significant performance gains can be expected when they are used for surface inspection and related tasks.

The operator of a remotely navigated vehicle is heavily dependent on visual information relayed from cameras based on the vehicle itself. While the vehicle is in motion, simple monoscopic images will convey a good impression of the surrounding gradients and terrain by virtue of motion parallax cues. Unfortunately, if the vehicle is stationary, this valuable monocular cue is lost. The provision of stereopsis eliminates this shortcoming and can also enhance the sensation of forward speed when the vehicle is in motion.

The implementation of stereoscopic TV systems usually relies on the provision of two or more independent video channels. A direct consequence of this approach is the improved reliability of such systems over their monoscopic counterparts. If one video pickup fails then at least some measure of visibility is maintained by the remaining video channel, albeit monoscopic. The potential also exists for stereoscopic display systems to generate a wider field of view than their monoscopic equivalents. Alteration of camera geometry and the degree of stereo image overlap can increase the field of view by as much as 50 percent, without sacrificing horizontal display resolution.

19.2.2 Synthetic imaging

The earliest attempts at synthetic image generation began during 1939 with the introduction of perspective to simple computer generated vector graphics (Tilton, 1988). More recently the development of techniques for hidden line and surface removal, sophisticated illumination models, surface shading algorithms, and ray-traced and radiosity based rendering techniques have all contributed to unprecedented levels of photorealism. Despite this high fidelity image representation, situations frequently arise in which the objects and environments being portrayed are so abstract or complex that some additional aid to their comprehension is required. An increasing number of computer based imaging applications incorporate stereoscopic display facilities to resolve this dilemma. It is interesting to note that proposals for the stereoscopic display of synthetic images originated as early as 1942, predating suggestions for hidden line removal by five years (Tilton, 1987).

Interaction with visually complex computer generated models raises special problems of image interpretation. While computer generated representations of familiar objects may not require detailed stereoscopic rendering, abstract models of unfamiliar objects can frequently benefit from the added depth cues afforded by stereoscopy (Wichansky, 1991).

Depth ambiguity is a visualisation problem frequently associated with wire-frame graphics and this usually manifests as an apparent depth inversion, triggered by sudden head movement or blinking. Additionally, the ability to discern foreground and background detail is often compromised. Hidden line removal offers a partial solution to these problems, whereas stereoscopic display techniques provide the only correct interpretation. The computational overhead involved in generating a stereoscopic view, moreover, can be considerably less than that required for hidden line and surface removal. Consequently, applications involving real-time animation and manipulation stand to benefit from the adoption of stereo display in preference to hidden feature removal.

Somewhat paradoxically, the increased sophistication of modern image rendering techniques may actually inhibit depth discrimination. The portrayal of translucent and transparent objects on a 2D display format can introduce depth ambiguity as interposition cues become degraded. Stereoscopic display techniques can facilitate image interpretation in these difficult perceptual conditions by allowing stereopsis to supplant erroneous monocular cues.

An increasing number of scientific and engineering disciplines require the analysis of vast quantities of complex numeric information. Examples of such activity include seismological surveying, stress and thermal analysis, signal processing and the exploration of multi-dimensional statistics (Beaton *et al.*, 1987). Subsequent interpretation of the resultant complex data structures can be improved by graphical representation. Furthermore, stereoscopic presentation of inherently non-stereoscopic data can reveal hidden traits and characteristics. Such multivariate data can be presented graphically, using depth-of-field cueing to represent a key parameter. The enhanced visualisation and exploration of abstract numerical information that can be achieved in this way has been termed *Dataspace* (Thwaites, 1991).

19.2.3 Hybrid systems

Various researchers have recently been investigating the feasibility of integrating real-time stereographics with live video capture to provide a new display *hypermedium* (Drascic, 1991; Milgram *et al.*, 1990). The superimposition of animated computer graphics upon closed circuit or remotely imaged stereo video scenes is a powerful adjunct to established telepresence techniques, and is likely to be a key feature in the implementation of *predictive displays* and new multimedia applications. Predictive displays are being developed in an attempt to circumvent problems of communication lag in remote telepresence applications, in which simple televisual feedback can prove inadequate because any delay between operator input and visual confirmation of actuator response (hysteresis) can introduce positional errors. Predictive display technology enables a graphical representation of the remotely controlled mechanism to be superimposed over the video image. The position and orientation of the graphical overlay can be updated in real time to simulate the anticipated control response. Such systems are being developed for extraterrestrial telerobotics with a view to assisting off-planet construction and space exploration.

Less ambitious attempts to combine stereoscopic video and graphics can be found in a new breed of photogrammetric measuring systems. Such applications support the generation of a virtual 3D cursor within stereoscopically televised environments. Provided that the geometrical relationship between stereo cameras is known, a stereographic pointer can be accurately located within the video image to provide a 'virtual tape measure' facility. Such systems have been proposed to explore both macroscopic and microscopic environments (Milgram *et al.*, 1990), whilst similar approaches using still photography have been used to reveal object size or velocity or density information in complex underwater environments (Merritt, 1991). These photogrammetric techniques are heavily dependent on high fidelity, stereoscopic imaging to support accurate cursor positioning in three dimensions.

19.3 ASSESSMENT OF DISPLAY TYPES

This chapter presents the results of recent research concerning the evaluation of a variety of stereoscopic display systems. Emphasis is placed on four particular technologies: anaglyph display, two distinct frame sequential displays and an autostereoscopic (no glasses) system. The operation and technical limitations of the four types are discussed and an assessment methodology based upon visual search and spatial tracking tasks is presented. The limitations of the four display types are also discussed, to provide an indication of the ergonomic factors likely to contribute to display performance.

Two of the displays in this investigation are frame sequential, wherein the two views comprising the stereo pair are temporally multiplexed. One system uses active spectacles (Figure 19.1) to decode the image by means of liquid crystal shutter devices arranged in lieu of the lenses in a pair of spectacles. These shutters can selectively block an image from reaching either eye. The other system uses passive spectacles (Figure 19.2) with a large liquid crystal device (in this case a Tektronix SGS410 Stereoscopic Modulator) interposed between the monitor and the viewer. This device encodes alternate frames with either clockwise or anticlockwise polarisation, subsequently decoded by polarising spectacles worn by the viewer.

The anaglyph display barely requires explanation. The left and right views are spatially multiplexed and encoded using different colours on the display. These views are subsequently decoded by means of coloured (typically red and green) spectacles worn by the viewer (Figure 19.3).

The autostereoscopic display differs fundamentally from the others in this evaluation. The left and right views are also spatially multiplexed but the viewer is not required to wear any special spectacles. The separate images of a stereo pair reside exclusively on

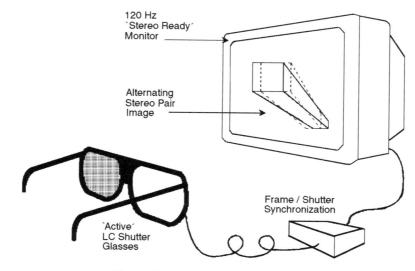

120 Hz
`Stereo Ready´
Monitor

Alternating
Stereo Pair
Image

Frame / Shutter
Synchronization

`Active´
LC Shutter
Glasses

Figure 19.1 Occluding shutter display

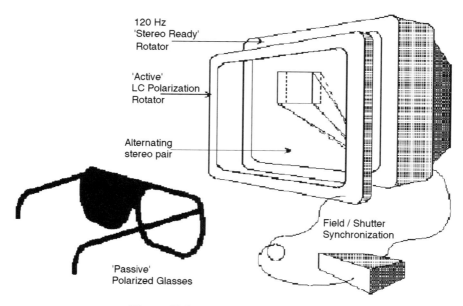

120 Hz
'Stereo Ready'
Rotator

'Active'
LC Polarization
Rotator

Alternating
stereo pair

Field / Shutter
Synchronization

'Passive'
Polarized Glasses

Figure 19.2 Polarisation rotating display

either the odd or even columns of the display. These interleaved pictures are then directed to the observer's eyes by means of a lenticular sheet at the display surface (Figure 19.4). In this case the display device is a colour (TFT) liquid crystal panel.

A variety of generic and implementation specific artefacts are expected to influence task performance when using each of these stereoscopic display techniques. The extent to

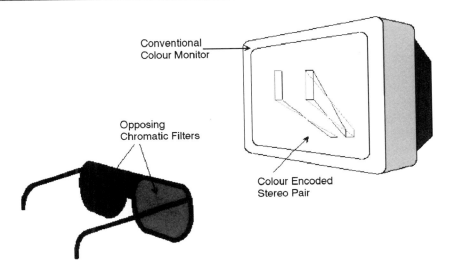

Figure 19.3   Colour anaglyph display

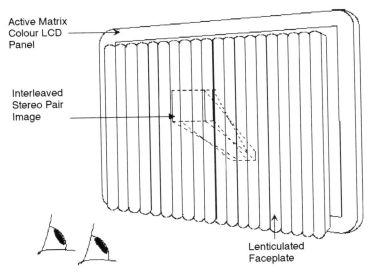

Figure 19.4   Autostereoscopic lenticular display

which individual artefacts may compromise performance is difficult to quantify; however, their nature and the opportunities for minimising their effects warrant discussion.

19.3.1   Image crosstalk

Each technology suffers to some extent from the effects of image crosstalk. Left and right views are effectively superimposed upon a single display surface and the channelling mechanisms responsible for separating or directing these views are rarely perfect. Consequently each image can be expected to intrude upon the other. This crosstalk or 'ghosting' can be irritating, and in extreme cases will make fusion of the stereoscopic image difficult (Lipton, 1982; Herman, 1971).

The solid-state shutters and polarising mechanisms used in contemporary frame sequential display systems still transmit some light while in a supposedly opaque state. The proportion of the unintended image that reaches the eye is determined primarily by the shutter extinction ratio, which in turn (for a given system) is an unalterable feature of the shutter technology.

The alternating images portrayed on frame sequential display systems take a finite length of time to decay due to CRT phosphor persistence. Crosstalk levels are increased as these 'residual images' are erroneously transmitted to each eye along with the intended view. This effect is particularly apparent at the base of the display screen where the image raster scan may coincide with the switching of the shutter mechanism. The Tektronix display incorporates a segmented shutter which alleviates this problem to some extent by horizontally subdividing the display area into sections which can be switched independently (Bos, 1991). Crosstalk can be further reduced on frame sequential systems by avoiding excessive image detail at the base of the screen, and by minimising the use of green and blue hues which tend to have a longer phosphor persistence.

Image crosstalk arises in colour anaglyph displays when the spectral characteristics of the viewing filters do not precisely match those of the colour encoded stereo pair. In such circumstances, light from a green encoded left eye view will be partially transmitted by the red filter and vice versa. This 'leakage' can be minimised by selecting filter materials with transmission characteristics that accord well with the spectral emissions of the display being used. Alternatively, the entire display colour gamut can be viewed with whatever filters are available and individual RGB levels chosen to provide optimum contrast for the left (green), right (red), and composite (yellow) views. Suppliers such as Rosco of Port Chester, New York, provide sample booklets to accompany their Supergel^{TM} filter range (Rosco, 1990). These booklets give detailed information on spectral transmittance characteristics for a comprehensive range of filters, and are a useful resource when designing appropriate anaglyph eyewear.

A series of fine semi-cylindrical lenses forms the image channelling mechanism of the autostereoscopic display. This lenticular faceplate must be manufactured with great precision and from high quality optical materials in order to maximise its directional selectivity and reduce crosstalk. In practice diffraction, lens aberration and flaws within the lens material itself all produce a degree of ghosting. In this respect, crosstalk levels on the lenticular display are fixed at the time of manufacture and there is little scope for subsequent improvement.

19.3.2 Flicker

Flicker is an artefact commonly associated with frame sequential display techniques. Left and right views comprising a stereo pair are presented in rapid succession; consequently each eye is periodically deprived of its intended view. If the images are refreshed at least 10 times each second then stereoscopic fusion is possible (Zenyuh *et al.*, 1988). Unfortunately, such a low refresh rate gives rise to an annoying and potentially distracting screen flicker. Estimates of the threshold frequency for the perception of screen flicker vary; the actual value depends on many factors like ambient lighting conditions, display intensity, scene detail and image contrast. Of the two frame sequential systems assessed in this evaluation, the Tektronix display is less susceptible to flicker by virtue of its 120 Hz field rate, and the confinement of flicker to the screen area. The system employing active glasses has a 72 Hz field rate and any flicker will be manifest over the entire field of view.

19.3.3   Binocular colour rivalry

A frequent criticism of the colour anaglyph technique is the visual discomfort that stems from viewing differently coloured images with each eye. As the brain tries to resolve the apparent conflict, each retinal image competes for dominance, a process termed *binocular colour rivalry* (Lane, 1982). The perceptual consequences of this phenomenon are that stereo images will appear first in one colour and then in the other, or may adopt some intermediate hue. Physiologically the effects can range from simple visual fatigue to headaches and even nausea during extended viewing periods.

19.3.4   Image intensity

Light attenuation is an unavoidable feature in all but the lenticular display system. In each case, light from the on-screen image must pass through one or more optical filters before finally reaching the viewer's eyes. Each stereo method varies regarding the type and number of filters it employs and this inevitably produces marked differences in image intensity.

The worst offenders in this respect are the frame sequential displays. The active LC modulator which forms the basis of the Tektronix system incorporates a linear polariser, as do the accompanying viewing spectacles. In combination these components present a formidable obstacle to the light passing through the system. The active glasses suffer in a similar way as they incorporate two orthogonally opposed linear polarisers in the LC shutter mechanism. At least 50 percent of the light emitted by the CRT is absorbed by these components so that the final image intensity is greatly reduced. Simply boosting the display brightness is not a satisfactory solution to the problem, as this can also heighten the perception of crosstalk due to corresponding increases in phosphor persistence and shutter leakage.

Although some loss is inevitable, light transmission in the anaglyph display can be optimised by careful selection of colour filters, or by 'tuning' the screen colours used to represent the independent left and right eye views.

Ambient lighting conditions can influence stereo display performance differently depending upon the technology used. Brightly lit environments tend to favour the use of *reflective* or *transmissive* devices like the LCD panel incorporated into the lenticular display system. The contrast ratio of CRTs and other *emissive* devices falls rapidly as ambient light levels increase. The Tektronix display system performs badly in this respect and is particularly prone to specular reflections from its polarising faceplate.

19.3.5   Lateral resolution

The principle behind all planar stereoscopic displays is to present separate images in which corresponding elements are separated by varying degrees of horizontal parallax.

If pixel based displays like CRT and LC devices are used for this purpose, it follows that (in the absence of suitable anti-aliasing techniques) values of horizontal parallax must be discrete. The resulting depth quantisation constrains image points to appear on specific *depth planes*. Clearly the extent of this depth quantisation is dependent upon lateral display resolution; smaller pixel separations bring about a corresponding increase in depth resolution.

The colour anaglyph and both variants of the frame sequential display technique were hosted by the same display device, a Qume 120 Hz colour monitor with a phosphor dot pitch of 0.26 mm. The smallest value of screen parallax available on this display was 0.44 mm, a limitation imposed by the graphics hardware. The lenticular display utilised a 10.4 inch diagonal active matrix colour LCD with a pixel width of 0.33 mm. The optical characteristics of this display require a lens width marginally less than twice the pixel pitch. Consequently the minimum parallax increment on the lenticular display was 0.65 mm.

Clearly the corresponding depth plane separation is somewhat coarser on the lenticular display than for the CRT based variants. Such differences in depth resolution are likely to contribute to a difference in display performances during depth correlation and spatial tracking exercises.

19.4 EVALUATION PHILOSOPHY

A revealing measure of stereoscopic display 'quality' may be obtained by determining how effectively the two images are channelled to each of the observer's eyes. Unfortunately this approach takes no account of the fundamental ergonomic differences between display types, and it was considered that more appropriate metrics should engage the concept of *fitness for purpose* whereby task-related performance could be determined. This approach is consistent with the *user performance testing* methods for proving conformance to visual display standards, as discussed in Chapter 20.

The experimental tasks and the visual stimuli used to represent them were highly simplified and not intended to be a precise replication of contemporary interactive graphical environments. All monocular cues with the exception of motion parallax, size constancy, linear perspective and object interposition were eliminated. Adopting only a subset of the available monocular cues proved to be an expedient measure to isolate the effects of binocular stereopsis while maintaining important binocular/monocular cue consistency. The nature and complexity of the tasks used during display evaluation were carefully selected to emphasise the perceptual and motor skills required for successful 3D object manipulation and graphical interaction.

Clearly this display evaluation strategy concentrates on the perceptual consequences of each display's implementation rather than addressing specific user task requirements. This *display centred* approach to display evaluation can be justified on two counts:

(1) The efficacy of each display technique is largely predetermined by its underlying stereoscopic generation technique and the technology used in its implementation. This rather precludes the use of a formative evaluation strategy, as there is little scope for iteratively refining the operation of each display system in response to user feedback.

(2) Even within the restricted domain of computer graphics, the number of 3D applications is large and increasing steadily. Evaluating the prototype in the context of every conceivable application is clearly impractical. This dilemma was overcome by abstracting a set of simple tasks and visual scenarios which are a common feature in many 3D applications. The result is a set of generic tasks and performance metrics which can be considered application independent.

19.5 EXPERIMENTAL OBJECTIVES

Objectives of the display evaluation were to determine the potential of each display technique as the basis for implementing a stereoscopic graphic display, and to establish a performance envelope for the recently developed lenticular prototype. A subsidiary goal was to identify performance metrics which might be used in future stereoscopic display assessments.

Previous investigations have suggested that some aspects of human performance are enhanced by the provision of stereopsis. Experiments originally intended to explore the superiority of stereoscopic presentation over conventional monoscopic displays have shown improvements in positioning accuracy (Beaton, 1990; Kim *et al.*, 1987; Reinhart, 1991; Takemura *et al.*, 1989), speed and accuracy during depth correlation judgements (Miller & Beaton, 1991; Reinhart *et al.*, 1990; Yeh & Silverstein, 1990; Zenyuh *et al.*, 1988), and a reduction in task completion times (Cole *et al.*, 1990). In view of these observations, it seems reasonable to assume that performance will depend upon the efficiency with which individual display types implement their stereoscopic effect.

Two separate experiments were devised to establish the capability of each display in supporting static and dynamic graphical interaction. The first experiment used real-time graphics to evaluate observer performance during a continuous tracking task. The second, a depth discrimination task, required observers to identify pairs of stimuli located at the same depth.

The target tracking task was conducted to monitor the spatial positioning error associated with the continuous pursuit of a moving visual stimulus. A measure of tracking performance was obtained from the mean Euclidean distance error during tracking operations. Additional error metrics were calculated based upon the tracking errors associated with each of the X, Y and Z display axes. The error associated with each axis was determined, and the polarity of mean tracking scores was intended to reveal any systematic bias in positional deviation.

The depth discrimination task was designed to examine the ability of each display to support three-dimensional visual search and depth correlation judgements. The measures associated with this task were response time and accuracy.

A subjective assessment of display quality and performance was obtained by interviewing participants at the end of the experiments. Subjects ranked the four displays based upon their confidence level while performing the tasks.

19.6 METHOD

An important aspect of any stereoscopic display evaluation is to ensure that participating individuals possess normal or near-normal stereoscopic ability. This is a sensible precaution in view of the fact that about 15 percent of the population suffer some degree of stereoanomalous vision (Julesz, 1977; Lipton, 1982) which might compromise the integrity of an objective display evaluation.

A variety of standard optometric tests have been utilised to measure key aspects of visual performance and provide a basis for the selection of suitable evaluation subjects (Beaton, 1990; Kost & Pastoor, 1991; Yeh & Silverstein, 1990). These tests frequently impose performance thresholds which exclude candidates on the basis of poor mono-cular vision rather than a fair assessment of their perceptual ability using the stereoscopic hardware concerned. There seems to be little merit in this approach as it may eliminate individuals who are perfectly capable of detecting even the smallest values of display parallax, and ultimately this technique will not yield a subject group which is representa-tive of the viewing population as a whole.

The absence of any extra stereoscopic (monocular) cues makes the random-dot stereo-gram (RDS) an 'unfakeable' test for stereopsis (Reinhart, 1991). The RDS was originally devised in 1959 as a research tool to facilitate investigations of human depth perception and the binocular visual system (Julesz, 1977). The RDS consists of two images (one for each eye) which contain an apparently random arrangement of small dots (Figure 19.5). When viewed individually the images give the appearance of a noisy TV picture and no depth perception results. If the images are viewed stereoscopically, however, carefully controlled parallax differences between the two images give rise to a three-dimensional depth sensation. By altering the degree of correlation between the left and right eye images, or by introducing subtle variations in binocular disparity, a valuable screening mechanism can be realised.

The latter approach was used to implement a *stereo test-card* with which to screen potential participants in the display evaluation study. A random dot stereogram was constructed containing a sequence of alphanumeric characters in a format similar to an optician's eye chart. Each character within the test-card was portrayed at a unique depth. Pixel disparities were chosen to provide visual stimuli at intervals which spanned the usable depth range of all the displays under evaluation. This strategy produced test characters with a variety of parallax values ranging from ±1 screen pixel, to values approaching the *diplopic* threshold (the limit of binocular fusion) at ±8 pixels. Although the satisfactory recognition of each character on the test-card did not necessarily imply that subjects had perfect stereopsis, it did indicate sufficient stereoscopic ability to enable them to participate usefully in the display evaluation studies. Thirty-two potential partici-pants were screened for satisfactory stereopsis using this test image. Twenty-nine subjects

Figure 19.5   The random-dot stereogram used during stereo screening (arranged for transverse viewing)

(23 male and 6 female) passed this initial screening procedure by virtue of being able to read all the characters portrayed within the test image.

All subjects were unpaid volunteers drawn from the staff and students at De Montfort University and from members of the public. Subjects were aged between 17 and 48 years old, a mean age of $25\frac{1}{2}$ characterising the group. Previous exposure to stereoscopic imaging techniques varied between subjects but none of the participants had extensive experience of any of the displays involved in the evaluation study. The experimental trials took place over a three-week period, during which time effort was made to ensure consistent environmental conditions. Ambient lighting conditions were carefully controlled to optimise the performance of all the displays involved in the experiment. Particular attention was given to the location and brightness of individual light sources to avoid introducing first- and second-order reflections from CRT faceplates and screen mounted optical components. A Spaceball™ was used as a control device for spatial tracking operations.

19.6.1 Target tracking

This task was designed to measure subject performance during the pursuit of a target symbol which moved in a random and continuous fashion in a three-dimensional viewing volume. The hypothesis under investigation was that the choice of stereo display technology significantly influences the accuracy with which subjects perform spatial tracking operations.

The tracking task comprised a green wire-frame outline of the viewing volume, a red flat-shaded target symbol and a white wire-frame full-space jack cursor. All components were rendered on a black background. These colour assignments were entirely arbitrary and–for the purpose of this experiment–the subtle influence of chromostereopsis on relative depth perception was ignored (Steenblik, 1987; Ishak *et al.*, 1969). A pictorial representation of the tracking task appears in Figure 19.6.

Although the shape of the target was fairly arbitrary it was constructed so that the 'focus' was unambiguous in all three dimensions and its size was scaled according to its depth. It might be argued that this latter precaution introduces an additional cue, but the alternative of maintaining a constant sized target gives rise to a highly disturbing 'perceptual zooming' effect when it moves in the Z direction. With the exception of depth scaling, object occlusion and linear perspective, all monocular cues were deliberately omitted to isolate the impact of stereopsis and display dependent effects.

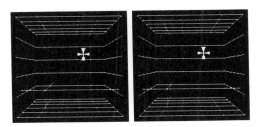

Figure 19.6 Stereogram depicting the target tracking stimulus (arranged for transverse viewing)

The target trajectory for the spatial tracking task was randomised to eliminate predictability and avoid track repetition. Target position was updated during successive animation frames at a rate of 10 Hz, and at no time was the target symbol permitted to move outside the bounds of the viewing volume.

19.6.2   Depth discrimination

The depth discrimination task was designed to reveal the influence of the various stereo display techniques on subject performance during visual search and depth correlation operations. The underlying hypothesis was that the display type affects both the speed of visual search and the accuracy of depth judgements. A sequence of static images, each containing numeric symbols scattered throughout the viewing volume, was presented to the subjects who were required to identify which of these symbols was at the same depth as a single reference symbol.

A number of factors are thought to influence the speed and accuracy of relative stereoscopic depth judgements. The number of depth planes (Reinhart, 1991), the proximity of cue and target stimuli (Reeves & Tijus, 1990; Yeh & Silverstein, 1989) and the number of distracter symbols present (Miller & Beaton, 1991) may all influence the potency of binocular cues.

Numeric symbols were used throughout the depth discrimination study to enable participants to identify their choice of stimuli quickly and unambiguously. Flat symbols were used to avoid presenting stimuli that spanned several depth planes simultaneously, and a flat 'star' symbol was used to represent the reference stimulus. All symbols appeared the same size regardless of their depth within the viewing volume. As perceptual zooming artefacts are uniquely associated with dynamic scenes, size cues could be safely eliminated from this study to increase the dependency on stereopsis for depth matching. The depth discrimination task is illustrated in Figure 19.7.

The depth axis was partitioned into 21 discrete depth planes with each plane corresponding to a unique value of screen parallax. Crossed and uncrossed disparity levels for each of the 21 depth planes ranged from −10 to +10 display pixels, the zero parallax condition coinciding with the plane of the display screen.

19.6.3   Experimental procedure

All 29 test subjects undertook an initial training period to aid familiarisation with the Spaceball input device. Subsequently, two subjects who failed to meet a minimum

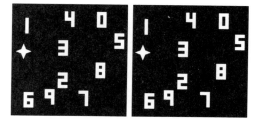

Figure 19.7   Stereogram illustrating the depth discrimination task (arranged for transverse viewing)

proficiency criterion were eliminated from the target tracking study. The remaining 27 subjects performed the tracking and discrimination tasks on each of the four displays. The order of exposure to each display was randomised between subjects to distribute the impact of learning and carry-over effects associated with task repetition.

All 29 subjects completed 20 replications of the depth discrimination task on each of the display systems. Participants were instructed to make accuracy their prime concern while remaining mindful of the fact that their response times were also being monitored. Tracking errors were calculated for X, Y and Z to establish the error associated with each display axis. Mean errors were also determined to highlight systematic bias in any particular direction.

19.7 RESULTS

Data from the target tracking and depth discrimination experiments were submitted to separate, doubly multivariate, analysis of variance procedures (MANOVA) for repeated measures. Subjective ranking scores obtained during post-experimental interview were assessed using a simple one-way analysis of variance procedure. All the results obtained were subjected to rigorous statistical analysis and the following merely presents a summary of the most significant findings. For a more detailed account the reader is referred to Bardsley (1994).

19.7.1 Target tracking performance

Table 19.1 summarises the average tracking error for each display axis as a function of display type. All values are expressed in 'world coordinates', the internal Cartesian representation of the viewing volume maintained by the graphics system. Tracking errors along the Z-axis are also given in depth planes where appropriate.

Euclidean distance tracking error

The composite measure of tracking accuracy, Euclidean distance error, was significantly influenced by the display type ($F[3,78] = 46.93$, $p < 0.001$). A clear indication of this effect can be seen in Figure 19.8 which shows the averaged Euclidean error scores for each display type.

Table 19.1 Target tracking error as a function of display type

Variable	Lenticular		Anaglyph		Shutter glasses		Polariser	
Absolute X error	9.1		11.7		8.5		8.1	
Absolute Y error	10.8		13.0		10.0		10.3	
Absolute Z error	46.0	(1.21)	71.9	(1.90)	34.8	(0.95)	36.3	(0.99)
Mean X error	0.0		−1.2		−1.4		−1.4	
Mean Y error	−1.3		−2.0		−1.3		−1.2	
Mean Z error	−30.2	(−0.75)	−61.8	(−1.61)	−13.3	(−0.34)	−16.0	(−0.41)
Euclidean error	50.8		76.3		39.9		41.3	

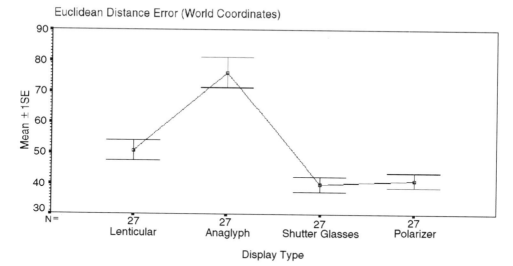

Figure 19.8   Euclidean distance tracking error

These apparent differences in display performance were investigated using a Student–Newman–Keuls multiple range test conducted at the 0.05 significance level (Devore, 1990). Results confirmed the error to be greatest for the anaglyph display, but no significant differences were found between the other display types.

Z-axis tracking error

The largest Euclidean distance errors corresponded to cursor/target displacements in the depth axis, confirming previous suggestions that performing accurate cursor positioning in depth is inherently more difficult than conventional 2D positioning (Beaton *et al.*, 1987). This observation seems to hold true regardless of the stereoscopic technique or the positioning device employed, although stereoscopic display fidelity is expected to influence the magnitude of such errors.

Figure 19.9 illustrates the average Z-axis tracking error for each display. Its similarity to Figure 19.8 suggests Z-axis deviation to be a major component of Euclidean distance error. The type of display was found to have a significant influence ($F[3,78] = 46.55$, $p < 0.001$), which confirms the anaglyph display as the worst performer with the other displays equal on merit.

An interesting trend was apparent in the Z-axis tracking errors: subjects consistently placed the cursor in front of the target stimulus. Although this bias was evident for all display types it was most pronounced in the anaglyph display followed by the lenticular display. Figure 19.10 (Colour Plate 14) illustrates the mean Z-axis error for each subject when using each of the displays. The figure provides a clear indication of each subject's tendency to underestimate target depth.

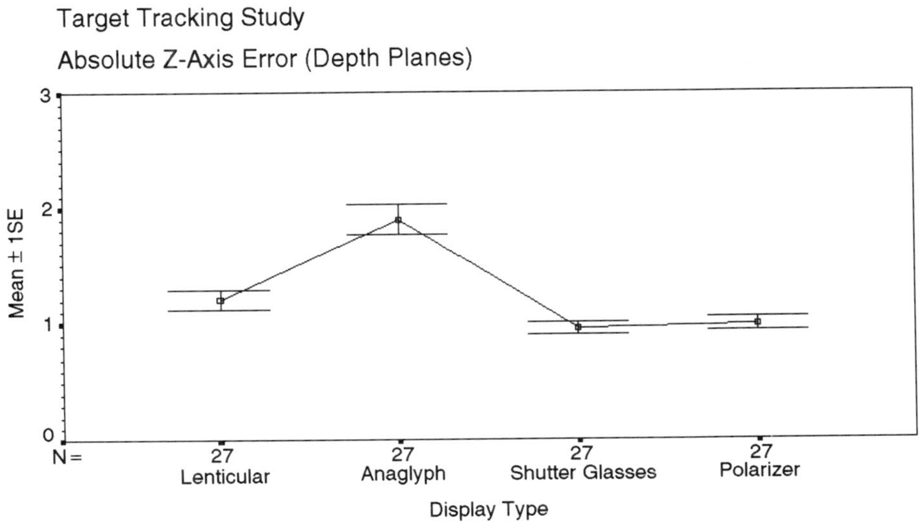

Target Tracking Study

Absolute Z-Axis Error (Depth Planes)

Figure 19.9 Average magnitude of depth axis tracking errors

19.7.2 Depth discrimination performance

Table 19.2 summarises the response measures of depth discrimination as a function of display type.

Decision response times

The observed variation in decision response times for each of the displays barely achieved statistical significance ($F[3,84]=4.05$, $p = 0.01$), and Student–Newman–Keuls tests revealed that mean response time for each display was not significantly different at the 0.05 level.

This was a disappointing result as it suggests that stereoscopic display discrimination cannot take place on the basis of accelerated assessments of task performance. However, it appears that this observation is not without precedent. During an investigation of

Table 19.2 Averaged target acquisition measures as a function of display type

Variable	Lenticular	Anaglyph	Shutter glasses	Polariser
Response time (seconds)	7.6	7.3	6.5	7.4
Percent correct	55%	36%	52%	48%
Absolute error (depth planes)	1.34	1.68	1.42	1.39
Mean error (depth planes)	0.13	0.05	0.30	0.27

monocular and binocular cue saliency levels, Reinhart *et al.* (1990) discovered that the inclusion of binocular disparity cues did not produce significantly faster response times for subjects performing simple relative depth judgements in relatively sparse graphical environments. Zenyuh *et al.* (1988) also concluded that a stereoscopic display format did not significantly improve response times during visual search and object counting operations. Unfortunately neither team of investigators offer a conclusive explanation for their observations. There is evidence to suggest that a degree of cognitive capture (acclimatisation) occurs during exposure to stereoscopic display techniques (Miller & Beaton, 1991), and this is likely to confound measurements of human performance. Response times can be expected to decrease as subjects gain proficiency during speeded depth judgements, while progressing from one display technology to the next. Such variations can mask the impact of differential display performance on decision response times. In future experiments, subjects will undergo a period of 'stereo pre-training' to exhaust such learning effects and heighten the influence of disparity cues.

Percentage of correct depth judgements

The number of search errors made by subjects when trying to identify cue and target symbols at the same depth was significantly influenced by the display type ($F[3,84] = 9.29$, $p < 0.0001$). Figure 19.11 shows the average performance or 'hit rate' attained on each display as a percentage of the total number of depth judgements performed.

Again, Student–Newman–Keuls multiple comparisons conducted at the 0.05 significance level failed to confirm any significant performance advantage for any of the four displays, suggesting that, with the possible exception of the anaglyph, all displays performed equally well.

Depth judgement error

The magnitude of errors arising from incorrect cue/target depth judgements was found to be dependent on display type ($F[3,84] = 11.11$, $p < 0.001$) and this effect is illustrated in

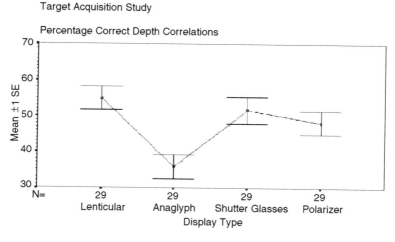

Figure 19.11   Percentage of correct depth judgements

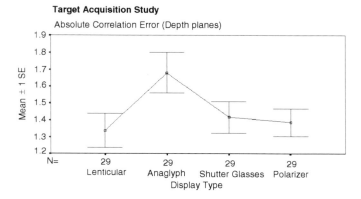

Figure 19.12 depth planes chart caption: **Figure 19.12** Average depth discrimination error

Figure 19.12. On average, depth judgement errors are between one and two depth planes in magnitude for all of the displays.

Depth judgement errors reported in previous investigations typically correspond to a single pixel disparity (Drascic, 1991). As depth planes and pixel disparities are equivalent in this context, the observed errors are within expected limits.

The comparatively poor performance of the anaglyph display was confirmed during *post hoc* analysis. However, means comparisons also concluded that error magnitudes for the other displays were not critically different. Unlike the target tracking exercise, no significant bias to either the front or the rear of the cue stimulus was detected in this experiment.

19.7.3 Subjective ranking

Subsequent to the tracking and discrimination exercises, participants produced a subjective ranking of the displays based upon their confidence level while performing the tracking

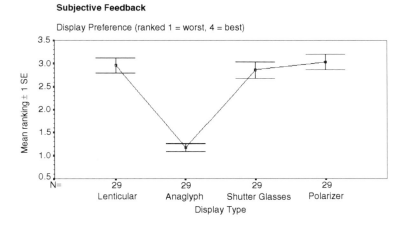

Figure 19.13 Average display ranking scores

and discrimination tasks. If subjects were unable to rank certain displays using this criterion alone, then additional considerations like viewing comfort, visual fatigue and image quality were to be taken into account. The scores 1, 2, 3 and 4 were uniquely assigned to each display in order of increasing merit.

Display type was found to have a significant effect ($F[3, 84] = 25.84$, $p < 0.001$), and this result is depicted in Figure 19.13. *Post hoc* analysis failed to detect any significant differences in mean display rankings between the lenticular, shutter glasses and polarising systems; however, the anaglyph display was clearly inferior in terms of subjective preference.

19.8 DISCUSSION

The most significant result of the study was the comparative performance of the lenticular, shutter glasses and polarising display systems, which appear to be very similar in their ability to support the tasks employed in these experiments, a verdict supported by subjective ratings of display performance. The comparatively poor performance of the anaglyph display system suggests that the evaluation strategy and response measures used were, to a limited extent, an effective tool for discriminating display performance.

The tendency for subjects to underestimate depth during the target tracking study is interesting. Drascic (1991) noted a similar phenomenon in his experiments where a small but significant foreground bias was detected during the alignment of pointers with static target stimuli. Unfortunately no explanation was offered for these observations.

A potential criticism of this investigation might be that the most important parameter to control should have been the separation between depth planes; if images are obliged to be located on discrete planes then surely the separation of these planes must influence the observer's ability to differentiate between them. Using a simplistic 2D representation of the viewing scenario and discounting any effects of screen curvature, pixel size, and non-linearities across the display surface, it is apparent from Figure 19.14 that the depth

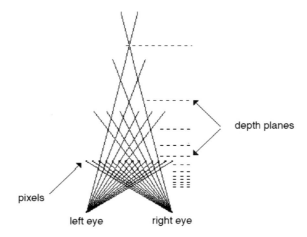

Figure 19.14 Depth plane compression

planes available from discrete pixel disparities are flat and parallel to the display surface. More importantly the foreground planes are clearly compressed in comparison to the background planes, the degree of compression being determined by a combination of interocular separation, pixel pitch and viewing distance. Although it is possible (by using an adaptation of 2D anti-aliasing techniques) to produce images which effectively fall between the otherwise discrete depth planes, the computational expense of doing so, along with the uncertainty of precisely locating images in depth, precluded this approach from our investigation.

Although the investigation was not originally designed to examine this issue, subsequent ongoing research suggests that 'foreground' depth judgements may be less reliable than 'background' judgements with similar (pixel) disparities, irrespective of display type. These observations present an interesting dilemma: because the display systems differ significantly (particularly the lenticular display) it is not practicable to arrange the same tests on all displays with equal separation of depth planes. Even if this were possible, the underlying premise of establishing task performance in terms of fitness for purpose would undoubtedly be compromised. The tasks devised for these experiments did not pay any regard to any specific display type and were considered to crudely represent 'typical' applications of a stereoscopic computer graphic display.

Ergonomic differences between the display types are potentially the most interesting aspect by which to differentiate the displays. The two frame sequential displays share common properties in that the left and right components of the stereo pair are presented sequentially; they are multiplexed in time rather than space which is the case with the lenticular and anaglyph systems. A characteristic of these displays is the necessity for the viewer to wear headgear. In the case of the Tektronix display used in this evaluation the headgear amounts to no more than a pair of 'sunglasses' whereas in the case of the shuttered spectacles the headgear comprises a pair of bulky spectacles containing liquid crystal shutters tethered to a control unit. Beyond the manufacturers and distributors of such equipment, few would argue that the latter approach is more convenient. The shuttered spectacles also suffer from a distracting peripheral flicker and both frame sequential systems are prone to temporally induced disparity errors when the displayed image moves laterally. Such errors are not accounted for in this investigation.

19.9 CONCLUSIONS

The validity of comparing dissimilar stereoscopic display implementations was initially of some concern. As all the displays in the evaluation share a common objective, namely the portrayal of a 3D spatial image, it might be argued that the manner in which this objective is achieved differs sufficiently from one display to another to preclude direct comparison.

The results obtained from this investigation indicate that stereoscopic display techniques can be differentiated on the basis of a quantitative assessment of human task performance. Unfortunately, the inability to discriminate between the lenticular, shutter glasses and polarising display systems suggests that the simple tasks adopted during the evaluation were insufficient to resolve subtle differences in performance. Extending the nature and scope of the experimental tasks is expected to yield a more decisive measure of display quality.

Simple differences in physical display attributes, such as screen resolution, for example, can have a profound influence upon display efficacy. A perverse example of this is that a lower depth resolution may apparently enhance relative depth judgements. Clearly an effective display comparison must incorporate a comprehensive range of response measures and task scenarios. Simple, isolated measures may serve to conceal critical aspects of display performance, which may be more readily apparent from a purely objective assessment.

ACKNOWLEDGEMENTS

We wish to express our appreciation to the 29 observers who took part in this investigation.

REFERENCES

Bardsley, T.N. (1994), The design and evaluation of an autostereoscopic computer graphics display, Ph.D. Thesis, De Montfort University, Leicester, UK.

Beaton, R.J. (1990), Displaying information in depth, *SID 90 Digest*, 355–358.

Beaton, R.J., DeHoff, R.J., Weiman, N. and Hildebrandt, P.W. (1987), An evaluation of input devices for 3D computer display workstations, *SPIE True 3d Imaging Techniques and Display Technologies*, **761**, 94–101.

Bos, P.J. (1991), Time sequential stereoscopic displays: the contribution of phosphor persistence to the 'ghost' image intensity, *Proc. ITEC '91 ITE Annual Convention*, **1**, 603–606.

Cole, R.E., Merritt, J.O., Fore, S. and Lester, P. (1990), Remote manipulator tasks impossible without stereo TV, *SPIE Stereoscopic Displays and Applications*, **1256**, 255–265.

Devore, J.L. (1990), *Probability and Statistics for Engineering and the Sciences*, 3rd edition, Duxbury Press, CA.

Drascic, D. (1991), Pointing accuracy of a virtual stereographic pointer in a real stereoscopic video world, *SPIE Stereoscopic Displays and Applications II*, **1457**, 623–626.

Herman, S. (1971), Principles of binocular 3D displays with applications to television, *Journal of the SMPTE*, **80**, 539–544.

Ishak, I.G.H., Said, F.S. and Abd-Elsalam, F. (1969), Colour stereoscopy, *Optica. Acta*, **16**(1), 69–74.

Johnston, H. R., Hermanson, C. A. and Hull, H. L. (1950), Stereo television in remote control, *Electrical Engineering*, 1058–1062.

Julesz, B. (1977), Recent results with random-dot stereograms, *SPIE Three-dimensional Imaging*, **120**, 30–35.

Kim, W.S., Ellis, S.R. and Tyler, M.E. (1987), Quantitative evaluation of perspective and stereoscopic displays in three axis manual tracking tasks, *IEEE Trans. on Systems, Man and Cybernetics*, **Smc-17**, 61–72.

Kost, B. and Pastoor, S. (1991), Visibility thresholds for disparity quantisation errors in stereoscopic displays, *Proc. SID*, **32**, 165–170.

Lane, B. (1982), Stereoscopic displays, *Processing and Display of Three Dimensional Data*, **367**, 20–32.

Lipton, L. (1982), Stereopsis and stereoscopy, in L. Lipton (ed.), *Foundations of the Stereoscopic Cinema: A Study in Depth*, 1st edition, Van Nostrand, Amsterdam, 53–89.

Merritt, J.O. (1983), Common problems in the evaluation of 3D displays, *SID 83 Digest*, 192–193.

Merritt, J.O. (1991), Evaluation of stereoscopic display benefits, Consultancy document prepared for Dimension Technologies Inc.

Milgram, P., Grodski, J. and Drascic, D. (1990), A virtual stereographic pointer for a real three dimensional video world, in D. Diaper *et al.* (eds), *Human–Computer Interaction–INTERACT '90*, Elsevier Science (North-Holland), Amsterdam; 695–700.

Miller, R. H. and Beaton, R. J. (1991), Some effects on depth-perception and course-prediction judgements in 2-D and 3-D displays, *SPIE Stereoscopic Displays and Applications II*, **1457**, 248–258.

Pepper, R.L., Cole, R.E. and Smith, D.C. (1977), Operator performance using conventional or stereo displays, *SPIE Three Dimensional Imaging*, **120**, 92–99.

Reeves, A. and Tijus, C.A. (1990), The pop-out effect in simple 3D visual matching task, in T. Kohonen and F. Fogel Man-Soulie (eds), *COGNITIVA'90: Proceedings of the 3rd Cognitive Symposium*, Elsevier Science (North-Holland), Amsterdam; 559–564.

Reinhart, W.F. (1991), Depth cueing for visual search and cursor positioning, *SPIE Stereoscopic Displays and Applications II*, **1457**, 221–232.

Reinhart, W.F., Beaton, R.J. and Snyder, H.L. (1990), Comparison of depth cues for relative depth judgements, *SPIE Stereoscopic Displays and Applications*, **1256**, 12–21.

Rosco (1990), 36 Bush Avenue, Port Chester, NY 10573.

Steenblik, R.A. (1987), The chromostereoscopic process: a novel single image stereoscopic process, *SPIE True 3rd Imaging Techniques and Display Technologies*, **761**.

Takemura, H., Tomono, A. and Kobayashi, Y. (1989), A study of human–computer interaction via stereoscopic display, *Proc. III Conf. on Human–Computer Interaction*, **1**, 496–503.

Thwaites, H. (1991), Three dimensional media technologies: prospects for the 1990's, *Proc. ITEC'91: Int. Symp. on 3D Images*, 591–594.

Tilton, H.B. (ed.) (1987), *The 3-D Oscilloscope–A Practical Manual and Guide*, 1st edition, Prentice-Hall, Englewood Cliffs, NJ.

Tilton, H.B. (1988), Holoform oscillography with a parallactiscope, *SID 88 Digest*, 276–277.

Wichansky, A.M. (1991), User benefits of visualisation with 3D stereoscopic displays, *SPIE Stereoscopic Displays and Applications II*, **1457**, 67–271.

Yeh, Yei-Y. and Silverstein, L.D. (1989), Depth discrimination in stereoscopic displays, *SID 89 Digest*, 372–375.

Yeh, Yei-Y. and Silverstein, L.D. (1990), Visual performance with monoscopic and stereoscopic presentations of identical three-dimensional visual tasks, *SID 90 Digest*, 359–362.

Zenyuh, J.P., Reising, J.M., Walchi, S. and Biers, D. (1988), A comparison of a stereographic 3-D display versus a 2-D display, *Proc. Human Factors Society–32nd Annual Meeting*, **1**, 53–57.

Evaluating the usability of workstation displays: a 'real-world' perspective

Nigel Heaton, Jim McKenzie and Andrew Baird

20.1 INTRODUCTION

Display technology has undoubtedly advanced a great deal in the last decade, but one may question whether attitudes to this fundamental piece of IT equipment have moved in line with the technology itself. Whilst many organisations are now beginning to consider the ergonomics issues relating to the wider aspects of the display technology they use (such as the software, the workstation, the environment, etc.), to many the display is simply a box which takes up desk space. What changes have taken place have tended to be 'knee-jerk' reactions to concerns relating to particular physical characteristics of the display (e.g. radiation, flicker, 'eyestrain', etc.). Many organisations now have a policy of buying monitors that meet MPRII (SEK, 1990) requirements, without understanding what this means and without any real concern for other, potentially more significant, aspects of the display design.

For the majority of users, it is difficult to differentiate between the display itself, the software driving that display to present information, and the situation in which they are using the display (the task and the environment). This chapter addresses all of these issues. Indeed as practising ergonomists we feel that it is pointless to discuss the 'usability' of displays in isolation. Every display is part of an IT system, which itself sits within an organisational system. Display usability can only be gauged in respect of that system, meaning that it is more beneficial to discuss how displays fit into system usability than

Display Systems, Edited by L.W. MacDonald and A.C. Lowe. © 1997 John Wiley & Sons Ltd.

to try to define a specific usability score for a display in isolation. Good ergonomics is about good systems!

A fundamental premise associated with the introduction of new technology is that it will enable users to work more efficiently, effectively and safely. However, we are all familiar with stories where the introduction of new technology has not yielded the expected benefits, or worse still where the technology (system) has actually been rejected. Technological changes have often been associated with falls in productivity, user dissatisfaction, and on a number of occasions complete system failure. The situation has become so bad that the technology often becomes the scapegoat for ill-feeling — how many ergonomists have not come across users who think that keyboards cause RSI and VDUs damage your eyes?

Experiences like those reported over the last 20 years, from Moshowitz (1976) to the DTI (1986) to Chapanis (1991), appear to demonstrate that we are still failing to learn from past mistakes. If we accept that technology *can* yield benefits to end-users why do we continue to see problems?

In our experience, by far the greatest number of problems occurs when technology is introduced that does not match the user's capabilities, does not meet the user's needs, and does not support the user in carrying out his or her task, to the extent that in some cases it can even pose a risk to the user's health. These risks to health were of such concern that the European Union introduced a Directive (90/270/EEC) in 1990 requiring all member states to implement minimum requirements from January 1993 with an absolute deadline of 1997. These minimum requirements seek to address fundamental problems associated with the use of technology, the hardware, the working environment and the software used. In the UK this Directive has been translated into the Health and Safety (Display Screen Equipment) Regulations (1992) under the Health and Safety at Work Act (1974). Attached

Figure 20.1   Display-based systems are often far from user-friendly

to the Directive was an Annex of minimum requirements, which has become a Schedule to the UK Regulations. These minimum requirements place explicit demands upon the 'Display Screen', but (quite significantly) they are not purely about display quality.

20.2 IMPACT OF STANDARDS AND LEGISLATION

Despite some reluctance from factions within both the political and business communities, legislation throughout Europe implementing the Display Screen Equipment Directive is now with us and in force. In parallel with this legal activity, a number of International (and European) Standards are being developed which will impact upon display systems. Indeed, many feel that current confusion is caused by the lack of relevant standards and are urging standards organisations to speed up the production of standards in order to clarify matters. Others, however, feel that the perennial problem with standards — that they are always out of date and lagging behind the technology — limits their relevance to a rapidly developing technology such as display systems. There is also concern over the applicability of certain tests and techniques with the traditional arguments over the validity of objective versus subjective data raging as strongly as ever.

20.2.1 The DSE regulations

Like all the recent European Health & Safety legislation, the DSE Directive is 'risk driven'. Employers must assess, reduce and monitor risks associated with workstations and their use. It is essential, therefore, to understand (and define) the risks associated with displays. So how can we tell whether a display is a source of risk? There is no simple answer to this, as it depends upon who the user is, what the display is being used for, and the working environment in which it is being used. Organisations must therefore decide on their display requirements (see below) and also carry out risk assessments to ensure that each display does not cause any problems in use (whether or not these are caused by the display itself or by workstation/environmental constraints). It is important to recognise that there is now a need to consider the 'whole workstation', i.e. the hardware, the software and the working environment together.

   Consider the following scenarios which illustrate why the 'risk driven' approach might prove more sensible than a prescriptive 'objective' standards approach:

(1)   An organisation decided to upgrade its fairly archaic DOS-based software systems by moving to a Graphical User Interface environment on the basis that this should bring improvements in ease of use, ease of learning, etc. At considerable expense, the organisation converted all its PC applications to run under *Windows*. Unfortunately, far from seeing an improvement amongst the user population, a number of users suddenly began to report headaches and eyestrain, and requests for 'screen filters' began to snowball. So what had gone wrong? The displays which had appeared 'flicker free' whilst the users worked in DOS applications in a negative presentation environment with light characters on a dark background began to cause serious problems for some users when they were 'upgraded' to positive presentation *Windows* applications with dark characters on a light background. The display was the same and the software was 'improved', but many users found themselves with headaches, eyestrain, etc. which were attributed to the 'display'. Was

this predictable? Possibly, but that assumes a level of understanding amongst the user population which simply does not exist in many organisations. What it does show is that a display may be perfectly acceptable in one situation but unacceptable in another, and it may be acceptable to one user but not to another. A glance at ISO 9241-3 would probably not have highlighted this problem to the organisation, but a proper risk assessment would have.

(2) To make purchasing easier, an organisation attempted to standardise on IT hardware. A central IT procurement section was established to deal with all hardware purchasing requirements, ranging from stockroom control systems, through word processor operators to the archive/scanning section. A decision was made, after negotiating a very favourable deal, to supply all users with 17″ displays. Based on the 'bigger is better' philosophy, this seemed a very positive step, but countless problems ensued. In the word processing environment, the display was seen as being of better quality than its predecessor, but its size was such that it was impossible to arrange the workstations effectively with current furniture. Consequently there were many complaints relating to posture and viewing distance. In the recently introduced archiving section, the problem was that the display was not big enough for users wishing to view two A4 documents side by side. As the quality of the scanned image was not high, reducing the image down to allow both pages to be viewed on the 17″ screen brought a number of visual problems and made the comparison process much slower (the previous system of two 13″ monitors had provided a better compromise). A positive action taken by this organisation backfired because IT procurement was carried out in isolation from other organisational factors (workstation and task issues).

(3) Following the release of the DSE Regulations in the UK an organisation decided to upgrade its control room operations. A decision was made that, since control room staff worked 12-hour shifts and the control room was manned 24 hours per day, extra provision was appropriate to ensure safe and efficient running of the control room. The situation was discussed with several equipment suppliers, and the suppliers suggested the use of 21″ high resolution, high refresh rate displays — at considerable expense! A subsequent analysis of the control room, however, suggested that although the displays were not in any way inefficient or hazardous they were hugely overspecified. The control room task was basically a monitoring one with the users having to respond only to alarm messages from the system. These alarms were character based and on seeing an alarm the user would briefly interrogate the system and then call on an engineer if appropriate. The task did not involve intensive interaction, and the images displayed did not require a high resolution monitor. In actual fact, there had been no visual problems reported in the control room, but back problems were rife. Money spent on these new displays would have been much better spent on high quality seating. It is unfortunately the case that despite best intentions, many organisations are woefully ignorant as to which display parameters are actually important in particular tasks or operating situations. 'MPRII' and 'Trinitron' might just as well read 'GTi' and 'Turbo' for all they mean to some managers! It is up to the display industry, and practitioners such as ergonomists, to increase understanding.

Figure 20.2   Poor seating inevitably leads to back problems for users

20.2.2   The annex of minimum requirements

As mentioned above, the EC Displays Directive has an associated annex of minimum requirements. In reference to the 'display screen' it states:

The characters on the screen shall be well-defined and clearly formed, of adequate size and with adequate spacing between the characters and lines.

The image on the screen should be stable, with no flickering or other forms of instability.

The brightness and/or contrast between the characters and the background shall be easily adjustable by the operator, and also be easily adjustable to ambient conditions.

The screen must swivel and tilt easily and freely to suit the needs of the operator.

It shall be possible to use a separate base for the screen or an adjustable table.

The screen shall be free of reflective glare and reflections liable to cause discomfort to the user.

It can be seen that not all these are related to display technology, but they are all related to the types of problem that people experience whilst using displays.

Character size on modern systems is likely to be determined more by software than by any hardware constraints, though obviously display resolution will play a part. In reality an increasingly common problem is that design improvements lead to increases in display resolution, so that small characters on the screen are clear and well defined but impossible to read from a 'normal' viewing distance. This tends to force users to lean forward to view the characters, thereby risking postural problems.

Image stability can be affected by a number of factors, but it is often a hardware problem. The general trend away from negative presentation systems to positive presentation GUI environments has served to emphasise this problem. Whilst increases in refresh rates will reduce the incidence of flicker, improvements may be gained by adjusting the brightness and contrast of the display (ambient conditions permitting) or by changing screen colours. Ease of adjustment of the image is not always the trivial matter it may appear. Too many monitors have their adjustment controls hidden away, which invariably means that they are less likely to be used.

Physical adjustment of the monitor position is important for visual comfort, postural comfort and for compensating for environmental conditions. Whilst not a 'high-tech' aspect of display design it is clear that the physical design of a display will affect user comfort. A user will not be impressed by a display, regardless of its image quality, if he or she cannot achieve a comfortable viewing angle.

The issue of reflections and glare is a contentious one. Many a 'glare guard' has been sold on the back of the Directive when the solution should have been a change in working environment or workstation orientation. Whilst surface coating of a display screen can minimise the reflection of incident light, the real solution is to control that incident light wherever possible rather than try to apply palliative measures (see Section 20.4.4).

The annex of minimum requirements addresses none of the factors that might be deemed functions of screen quality such as resolution, refresh rates, linearity, etc. It effectively says that provided the user can easily see a stable image on the screen whilst adopting a comfortable viewing angle, nothing else matters. That is absolutely true! The problem for system procurers and designers is to ensure this really is the case, particularly given that they may have no control over many of the factors that influence user comfort. Are standards the answer?

20.2.3   ISO and BS Standards

The most relevant ergonomics standards in this area are:

- ISO 9241 (EN 29241) — Ergonomic requirements for office work with visual display terminals (VDTs)
- ISO 11064 — Ergonomic design of control room centres (proposed Draft International Standard)
- BS 7179 — Ergonomics of design and use of visual display terminals (VDTs) in offices.

In the UK, BS 7179 is currently being phased out as relevant parts of ISO 9241 become available. ISO 9241 and its European equivalent EN 29241 will have most impact on displays in the next few years. ISO 9241 is a 17-part Standard, with Part 3 — Visual Display Requirements (1992) being directly applicable to display hardware. Other parts deal with reflections, colours and information presentation issues which will also impact upon IT systems.

ISO 11064 is at an early stage of development and at this stage it is difficult to comment upon the impact it may have. Work is also underway on an international standard relating to flat panel displays (DIS 13060), which will replace ISO 9241 Parts 3, 7 and 8 as they relate to flat panels only. There has been some debate as to whether the output of this work would be better incorporated into a revised ISO 9241, rather than splitting this particular technology off as a separate standard. Current predictions are that flat screens will account for about 20 percent of workplace display screens by the year 2000, although their uptake will be dictated more by price than by technical quality.

ISO 9241 Part 3 is interesting in that it proposes two methods of compliance with the Standard — a series of physical measures (the conventional 'prescriptive' approach), or a 'user performance test method' (which is not yet ratified and is currently an Informative Annex). The user performance method compares a test display to one that has already passed the physical measures (the reference display). The comparison involves a representative sample of users performing a representative task, with a predetermined margin for error. If the test display is found not to be significantly worse than the reference display, then the test display can be said to pass.

There has been some debate as to which method works better, but the answer probably depends more on an individual's background (human scientist or engineer) than on any authoritative research. Interestingly, a student project carried out at Loughborough University in 1992 found that a test display which failed some of the physical measures 'passed' the user performance test when compared against a better specified (but untested) 'reference' monitor. Engineers may well take this as proof that user performance tests are not as accurate as objective measures, but human scientists would probably take the alternative view that the physical measures chosen are inappropriate and do not predict usability or user comfort. It was clear, however, that it would require a more demanding task than character recognition (which is a fairly representative task for office work) to highlight real inadequacies in the test display.

The fundamental question is whether either test gives a true indication of a display's real-world performance and suitability for particular tasks. Indeed, one may question whether any one test could possibly prove adequate for assessing a display's suitability for the myriad of potential uses to which it might be put. The user performance test certainly appears robust enough to give a valid comparison against the physical measures — research by the HSE-funded Working Group on ISO 9241-3 proved the validity of a revised version of the test. However, it would be beneficial to see exactly how the various physical measures, both in isolation and combination, actually affect performance and comfort — not just in an abstract context but in relation to a wide variety of tasks involving text, graphics and images.

20.3 DISPLAY USABILITY — AN ERGONOMICS PERSPECTIVE

Based on the above discussion of display standards, it may be apparent why we do not believe that the application of conventional 'prescriptive' standards on their own will necessarily result in more 'usable' displays, at least from the user's perspective. It is necessary to step back from the detail of display design to look at the broader picture of how it fits into the entire working system.

We believe that the key to success in building systems is to take what is known as a 'user-centred' approach, which directs consideration towards the full range of ergonomics issues. That is not to say that users should actually design the system, but rather that the designers should consider the impact on users of every technology decision at all stages of the design and implementation process. For this approach to be successful, designers and implementers should think about users first, in terms of their characteristics, tasks, goals and working environment, before specifying or designing the system. Only by taking users fully into account can we expect to obtain the full benefit from any technological system. Thus, our aim should be to understand what we want to achieve before we specify any hardware.

A useful way of considering ergonomics in design is to think of the 'ergonomics triangle' illustrated in Figure 20.3. This splits design issues into the separate considerations of:

- user (who is involved?)
- task (doing what?)
- tool (with what?)
- environment — physical and organisational
  (where? with whom? under what constraints?)

In general terms, we should define the *users* (and their characteristics), followed by the *tasks* (which may impose particular requirements), giving consideration to the *tool* (in this case the hardware and software platform may also impose particular requirements), and also examining whether the *environment* (including workstation considerations) may limit the type of device. The following subsections address what we consider to be the most important factors influencing the usability of displays (from the user's perspective). We do discuss factors relating to the display itself, but try to place them in the context of the whole usability framework.

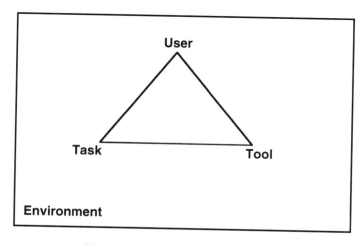

Figure 20.3   The ergonomics triangle

Figures 20.4 and 20.5 (Colour Plates 23 and 24) illustrate bad and good practice, respectively, in workstation ergonomics.

20.3.1   The user

One critical factor affecting our capability to use a display is our ability to see it! There is no evidence to indicate that looking at displays causes any permanent damage to our visual system, but there is ample evidence that intermediate visual acuity changes significantly with age. Thus the display is often the first agent of evidence about a change in our visual acuity. Hence, the change may be attributed to the display, leading to the spurious complaint that computer displays can damage your eyes! There is no doubt that working at a display can be a visually demanding task — the eye muscles are at rest when focusing at infinity, so focusing on a display at arm's length for long periods represents a significant workload for these small muscles. Add to this environmental and/or stress issues and the user's problems tend to escalate.

Using displays intensively can be associated with sore, tired, red eyes, and ultimately with headaches and migraines (Sellers, 1994). Typically, these effects are more likely to be caused by a combination of environmental factors such as low humidity, dusty environments and glare/reflections, rather than a major deficiency in the display itself (see Section 3.4).

Figure 20.6   Headaches can be caused by poor workstation layout and environmental factors rather than by the display itself

Another individual difference which is often misunderstood or overlooked is that of preferred viewing distance. Classical thinking, embodied by standards such as ISO 9241-3, suggests that users will attempt to adopt a viewing distance which produces a particular size (angle of arc) of image on the retina. However, recent research at Loughborough University by Peter Howarth (as yet unpublished) has shown that preferred viewing distance is not driven by image size (within reason) but is more influenced by preferred focal length. There appears to be a huge variation between different individuals in terms of this parameter, and the effects of not being able to achieve the preferred distance also vary significantly. Some users seem relatively untroubled by viewing distance whereas others who experience non-preferred situations demonstrate marked behavioural (postural) adaptations. Therefore small text closer to a user, or large text further away, may both afford an equal likelihood of the image being correctly recognised, but they are unlikely to be equally comfortable to work at. This research casts doubt on the appropriateness of current standards relating to VDU viewing distances.

20.3.2   Task Requirements

Particular types of task are likely to require special consideration with regard to the choice of display. This applies at both the macro- and micro-level. It is not sufficient to describe tasks simply in terms of software packages such as word processing, spreadsheets, CAD, or photo image manipulation. The design/evaluation team must understand the nature of the documents being word processed, the size and complexity of the spreadsheets, the accuracy of colour rendering required in image manipulation, etc. Now that multi-tasking is possible in desktop computers, the degree to which this is necessary should be considered.

For example at the macro-level, the task may:

- require the user to interact with the technical content of a drawing, where the response may be a mixture of text and graphics, and where detail is critical;
- expect the user to make a selection from a limited number of clearly distinct options, where a lesser quality display could be employed;
- deal with moving images, in which case refresh rate would be of more concern than if dealing with a simple character based screen;
- involve manipulating a scanned image to be printed many times, in which case any discrepancy between displayed colours and printed colours could lead to a need for costly reprints;
- be one that is performed extremely frequently, so that it may be desirable to provide a display large enough to have an area dedicated to that function;
- include applications such as video-conferencing which pose questions of both the clarity and size of the display — it becomes pointless if the detail of facial expressions and gestures is lost or if the image takes up vital space on the screen with which the user is trying to interact;
- need to accommodate the mobile user, and hence may constrain the choice of device (some types of display weigh less, are more portable and require less power than others, e.g. LCD vs CRT).

Figure 20.7 It should always be clear to the user what is expected of him by the software application

At the micro-level, there has been much empirical research to examine differences in user performance for particular user actions (e.g. speed of cursor movement, accuracy of point-and-click tasks, etc.). It is important, however, not to read too much into the results of any single study, unless, of course, it replicates the exact type of task to be performed. This is because minor variations in the task, for example the number of items to be selected from a list, or the length of the list, can greatly influence the results. Also it should be noted that although there may be a performance advantage for some tasks, the benefits may be minor and other factors may be much more important.

20.3.3   Software interface styles

Software is clearly a major factor in determining the usability of a display. The Annex to the EC Displays Directive contains mandatory minimum requirements for software. In the UK these are contained in a Schedule to the DSE Regulations, which stipulates that all software interfaces are required to comply with the minimum requirements by 1997 (unless the inherent characteristics of the task preclude it). All new workstations first put into service after 1 January 1993 must meet these minimum requirements immediately:

'In designing, selecting, commissioning and modifying software, and in designing tasks using display screen equipment, the employer shall take into account the following principles:

- Software must be suitable for the task.
- Software must be easy to use and, where appropriate, adaptable to the operator's level of knowledge or experience; no quantitative or qualitative checking facility may be used without the knowledge of the user.

- Systems must provide feedback to workers on their performance.
- Systems must display information in a format and at a pace which are adapted to operators.
- The principles of software ergonomics must be applied, in particular to human data processing.'

One of the most common usability problems with modern displays is their flexibility, which allows any user to define any display configuration. We commonly see displays with font sizes that are designed for ease of reading on paper. In other cases, we see screens that are capable of displaying tens (and sometimes tens of thousands) of colours, where all of them are being used simultaneously. In these circumstances, judicious explanation and probing of the user's (or designer's) motives and level of awareness may help to solve the problem.

The style of interface to be used will impact upon the display requirements, both in their own right and in the manner in which they are interpreted within an organisation. Many displays that work quite adequately in a DOS environment are wholly unsuited to Windows operation where flicker problems and poor legibility become evident. GUIs tend to require not only positive presentation but also relatively high resolution for definition of icons and graphics. Displays with inadequate definition will distort icons and make the

Figure 20.8   No performance checking facility may be used without the knowledge of the user

associated labels difficult to read. Once this happens, all the advantages of a graphical user interface are lost.

Although screen formatting rules have been documented for many years, probably the biggest influence on screen formatting has been the proliferation of graphic user interface style guides. These guides are typically produced by larger corporations and serve as *de facto* standards as part of their move towards the possible adoption of general *de jure* interface standards such as ISO 9241. However, it is unlikely that ISO 9241 will be able to meet the demands of all graphic user interface designers. It would be too great a task to create a document that could prescribe explicit rules for interface design in

Figure 20.9 System feedback should be helpful, appropriate to the situation and easy to understand

every conceivable application environment and, inevitably, any standard will lag behind technological innovation. It is more likely, therefore, that the software elements of ISO 9241 will become general guiding principles rather than prescriptive documents.

The benefits of a consistent 'look-and-feel' for user interfaces are well known, but application of this principle to IT hardware is relatively rare. Consistency can soon be lost if, for example, more scrolling is required or if differences in resolution or colour rendering change the appearance of key icons. Some of the earlier GUI style guides, for example IBM's Common User Access (1987), covered issues directly related to hardware and displays, such as choice of input devices, use of colour, etc. More recent style guides, however, tend to assume that the hardware issues have been largely resolved or lie outside the scope of the guidelines, and thus place much more emphasis on cognitive issues, with input devices and colour dealt with in Appendices, for example IBM's Common User Access (1991). It is clear that environmental factors as well as the quality of the display will influence its usability and consideration should be given to 'look-and-feel' issues such as the key ergonomics concerns outlined previously.

To ensure usable systems, it is essential to consider hardware issues when developing a corporate interpretation of a generic style guide such as OSF's *Motif* (1992). It is at this level that informed decisions must be made about issues such as icon design, use of colour and font size. A generic guide like *Motif* cannot provide explicit advice on these issues as they are specific to particular organisations, applications and hardware.

20.4 THE WORKING ENVIRONMENT

20.4.1 The visual environment

Complaints of eyestrain are extremely common among users of VDUs. In reality, most of these problems are the consequences of fatigue rather than any type of damage to eyes. There is a fundamental problem in that the nature of the work on many displays makes it a visually demanding task, both in terms of the muscle work required to maintain focus and the accommodation of the photoreceptors to distinguish contrasts under prevailing ambient conditions. Consequently, any shortcomings of the visual environment will tend to add to problems for the user.

The most obvious manifestation of visual problems is reflective glare on the screen. This is most commonly caused by unshielded or badly sited luminaries, or by sunlight shining through unshielded windows. Appropriate lighting design and suitable window blinds can reduce this problem to negligible proportions.

'Screen filters' must only be used as a last resort. Attempts should always be made to address problems at source. We suggest that the following types of filter be considered in exceptional circumstances:

- Mesh — an earthed mesh filter can be used for problems relating to static electricity, such as dust accumulation or skin rashes. If the problem is due to low humidity, then this must be addressed first. Mesh filters can significantly deteriorate the screen image, particularly if badly installed so that interference effects may be seen.
- Anti-reflective glass — in environments where all other remedial measures have failed to reduce glare to acceptable levels, an anti-reflective glass filter may be used.

- Polarising filter — for instances where the user reports problems with the 'image', e.g. unhappiness with green text on a black background on older systems. This would warrant a filter only if the user were experiencing serious problems such as headaches or eyestrain, and all other remedial measures (changes to lighting, humidity, etc.) had failed.

As practising ergonomists we are very concerned by some of the claims made for 'screen filters', which at times are misleading or potentially fraudulent. Many users we meet are unaware of why they have the device, but just assume because it is additional that it somehow makes the display better. These same users generally have never adjusted the brightness and contrast controls on their display! We note also that many filters affect the image, changing the colours that users see. This may cause problems if colour coding has been extensively used in the application, especially if the filter causes previously distinct colours to merge (i.e. to appear similar). If colour rendering is an important aspect of the task, then clearly any device affecting the displayed colours must be treated with caution.

Displays with a simple, polished glass surface can give good image definition, but need very carefully lit environments to avoid viewing problems. Surface treatments on displays can help to reduce the effects of glare and reflections on screen. We recommend that in relatively uncontrolled office environments etched surfaces be used as a minimum, and higher quality coatings if clarity is critical. Etching is an appropriate solution if the types of tasks undertaken are mostly office-based (e.g. word processing, spreadsheet, etc.). There can be problems in cleaning and maintaining etched screens and severe interactions between etched screens and some screen filters. However, they often represent a cost-effective procurement policy if other environmental factors cannot be adequately controlled.

20.4.2 Lighting and contrast

Problems concerning lighting in offices are often reported as a dissatisfaction with the level of light. In many cases, however, the real problem can be traced to the quality of the light (e.g. colour, glare, reflections, etc.) rather than the quantity. It is quite common to find that fluorescent tubes have been switched off or removed to reduce light which is perceived to be 'too harsh'. Removal of the tube reduces the level of light (illuminance), and this is usually perceived as an improvement with respect to display usage. The reduced light level may be below optimum (resulting in user performance below optimum) but it is generally more comfortable to work in situations of low light than in significant discomfort (e.g. due to glare).

Many lighting engineers will go to great lengths to provide an almost perfectly uniform visual environment at exactly the prescribed level. Unfortunately, such environments tend to be sterile, unfriendly and hard on the eye. Lighting variations that allow the eye to adjust can reduce fatigue, and aesthetically can add 'character'. Yet however good a lighting installation is, it will cause problems if inadequately maintained.

The ideal level of light will be dependent on both task and individual, but the basic aim must be to produce a glare-free and reflection-free environment. In the UK, BS 7179 and the Chartered Institute of Building Services Engineers (CIBSE) recommend 300–500 lux for VDU work and 500–700 lux for clerical work, but the real problems arise when people work in mixed environments, dealing with both paper and screen-based material.

Figure 20.10 Screen glare can result from inappropriate lighting design or inadequate shielding

In practice, users can work on screen-based material at ambient light levels well below 300 lux, so we recommend that overall lighting be kept relatively low with additional lighting provided locally for specific individual and tasks.

In our experience ambient light levels of 300–500 lux can often be seen as too bright for computer display users, particularly those who work at CAD stations, where light levels of less than 100 lux at the keyboard are not uncommon. Other problems with light include the choice of walls and the finish on surrounds. Grandjean (1987) provides specific guidance on the special requirements for offices with VDT workstations aimed at reducing the problematic reflections from ceiling, walls, blinds or curtains, furniture and flooring. Grandjean also provides guidelines for contrast ratios between the display and any source document. The basic recommendation is that the luminance contrast between dark screens (with bright characters) and source documents should not exceed the ratio 1:10. All other surfaces in the visual environment should have luminance levels between those of the screen and the source document.

The minimum contrast ratio for characters displayed on the screen is recommended in ISO 9241-3 as 3:1. There is some debate about whether it is better to have dark characters on a light background or light on dark. Most experts agree that dark characters on a light background are easier to view, but there are inevitable trade-offs. Users of monitors with light backgrounds are more prone to see flicker and have problems with emitted glare. Such screens are more prone to 'wash-out' caused by the ambient lighting, for example if the monitor faces a window. Also the display technology may not cope well if large white areas are displayed (Sellers, 1994). On the other hand, dark backgrounds are more prone to reflected glare which is often the major problem in an office environment. Overall, positive presentation displays (i.e. black on white) are preferred because these equate better to reading tasks and are less prone to glare.

20.4.3   Humidity

When users report visual problems the cause can frequently be traced to low humidity. In conditions of low humidity, the mucus membranes of the body begin to dry out, leading to a reduction in the protection afforded by these membranes. The most common problems relate to the drying out of the eyes and throat, with eyes beginning to feel 'sticky', 'gritty' and sore. As a general rule, low humidity (less than 40 percent) can be a significant problem. High humidity (greater than 60 percent), whilst unpleasant, is much less hazardous and as such it tends to concern engineers before users as equipment may be seriously affected. Another problem exacerbated by low humidity is static. Whilst not directly attributable to the display, high levels of static can affect the display's usability and, perhaps, its effective functioning. Static tends to attract dust and charge the air locally around the display. These factors have been associated with skin rashes and headaches.

20.4.4   Workstation constraints

The actual size of the display will influence its usability. We have seen offices where displays are so wide relative to the desks they are placed on that they have had to be bolted down in order to prevent unwary users from moving them to achieve a comfortable viewing distance and thereby sending the display crashing to the floor. Fortunately, the need to match display footprint to desk size (and vice versa) is becoming better understood but we are still seeing many cases of the viewing distance of displays being compromised

Figure 20.11   Workstation layout is frequently inappropriate for sustained keyboard and display usage

by desk size. It is sadly still common to see a display pushed into the corner of a desk, forcing the user to type with twisted wrists, back or head.

Flexibility of viewing position is the key to using displays effectively. It is important that the display is adjustable in height — through an adjustable desk, a plinth, the provision of a monitor arm, etc. Similarly, the distance between display and user must be adjustable, as must the display's swivel and tilt. The aim is to reduce problems associated with muscle and eyestrain. Displays used in combination with paper-based tasks may require monitor arms or larger desks to allow users the flexibility to perform the necessary mixture of tasks. Flexibility and adjustability are particularly important in multi-user workstations where the needs of a number of users must be met by a single workstation. Given recent trends toward 'hot-desking', this factor is likely to become increasingly significant.

20.5 ESSENTIAL DISPLAY CHARACTERISTICS

Regardless of the display technology involved, there are some fundamental issues that need to be considered when defining display characteristics (compare these with expressed user requirements in Chapter 2):

(1) Image clarity. What level of clarity is required? For text systems this relates to character definition and legibility; in GUI environments this will also relate to movement of objects; in CAD environments the accuracy with which lines can be drawn and the ease with which they can be distinguished are critical; in systems using colour, for instance when manipulating photographic images, the number of available colours (colour gamut) and accuracy of colour rendering may be the determining factors.

(2) Luminance and chromatic contrast. In addition to providing a clearly defined image, the image must be adequately contrasted from its surroundings to enable it to be seen in terms of both true luminance contrast and colour contrast (Travis, 1991). This is particularly important in multi-user offices where trade-offs in the positioning of workstations must take account of the general lighting and sources of light, as well as other environmental, task, and social issues.

(3) Image stability. The image on screen should appear stable to the human eye. The display must not flicker, jitter or smear the image. Display of movement should appear natural and smooth — there should be no 'ghosting' or 'trails' unless these are specifically required by the task (e.g. tracking the movement of objects over time). Note that flickering screens can, in very unusual circumstances, pose a physical risk to users who suffer from photo-sensitive epilepsy. In such cases expert advice may be required to deal with the problem.

(4) Uniformity. The image must appear uniform in space, time and colour. For example, a square on screen should appear square and should have the same dimensions wherever it appears on the display, and it should not vary in size or shape over time. Similarly any colours or colour combinations should appear identical at any point on the screen and over time (Travis, 1991). Applications which use colour and shape coding are reliant upon the quality of the screen and if the task is safety critical then considerations about screen quality may override more general concerns about cost.

(5) Orthogonality. Lines and columns on screen should appear parallel and orthogonal to one another to ensure that the image is not misleadingly distorted.

(6) Display adjustability. The display should provide easy user adjustment of the image. There should be easy-to-use brightness and contrast controls to allow for adjustment as ambient lighting conditions change. This is now a requirement of the Annex to the EC Directive and is critical for screens operating in an environment that has variable ambient lighting.

20.6   USABILITY EVALUATION: TECHNIQUES AND METRICS

20.6.1   Development of methods

A considerable amount of effort has been spent in determining how to evaluate usability and in creating metrics. These range from work done under European Programmes such as HUFIT (Human Factors in Information Technology) (1989) and MUSiC (Metrics for Usability in11 Context) (1993) to the production of usability checklists and general advice, e.g. Clegg *et al.* (1988), Ravden and Johnson (1989), etc. The aim of this work has been to produce an effective means of measuring usability. Ideally, such methods need to be:

- repeatable (i.e. an evaluator, evaluating the same display, will generate the same results each time the evaluation is conducted);
- reproducible (i.e. different evaluators will produce the same results when evaluating the same display under the same conditions);
- usable (i.e. the method must be efficient in terms of time and cost, easy to apply and require limited training and expertise).

HUFIT (Human Factors in Information Technology) was one of the first attempts to incorporate usability into product design. The aim was to provide designers with a simple toolset, allowing them to adopt a much more user-centred approach to design. It has been criticised for being too simplistic and not comprehensive, yet these are also HUFIT's great strengths. They allow simple steps to be taken which, whilst not producing the perfect design, do require designers to consider human factors issues throughout the design life cycle. HUFIT has been successfully applied in a number of complex designs and would provide a useful framework to any design team following a structured design methodology who wish to incorporate human factors.

MUSiC (Metrics for Usability in Context) is concerned with providing metrics that can predict the usability of a product from its specifications, to quantify the performance of the product and to assess the attitude of users to that product. The European-sponsored project generated a number of tools to aid designers in the specification of more usable products. These include comprehensive checklists, software-based evaluation tools and detailed metrics of user performance. The main strengths of the MUSiC toolset are its multi-factor approach and the recognition that usability is an ideal which is made up of many components. The main weakness relates to the need either to apply the many approaches separately or to identify which single approach is appropriate for the situation being evaluated. Parts of the MUSiC toolset continue to be developed and evaluated and are now available as commercial products.

20.6.2   Checklists and standards

Usability checklists and ideas relating to the quantifying of human factors have been around for some time. Their main strength lies in their inherent simplicity. Usability ideas can often be presented as a series of simple yes/no questions relating to specific features of the display (Does the display swivel and tilt? Are brightness and contrast easily adjustable? etc.). Checklists often work best when applied at the beginning to set design goals. By their very nature they may miss key issues, such as the complex problems arising from the interrelationship between different tasks. If used retrospectively, they may miss the point altogether. For example, if the display does not swivel and tilt, is it a problem? If so, quantify it. Thus checklists can be used to ensure that a procurement is based on good, simple ergonomic principles, but should not be seen as the sole method of incorporating usability into the display specification.

Explicit recognition that usability is a suitable theme for standardisation can be seen in the proposed ISO Standard 9241 Part 11, 'Usability Statements'. However, the complexity and problems associated with standardisation in this area are also apparent by the lack of progress made towards producing this standard. The committee draft of ISO 9241-11 provided the basis for the construction of usability statements to:

- specify usability requirements (e.g. for the development of displays, for the procurement of displays, etc.);
- describe usability (e.g. information about a product that has been developed, for which information relating to usability is available);
- determine conformance to standards (e.g. which attributes or measures are in conformance with which standards).

The draft then proposed a number of areas covered in a usability statement (context of use, usability, etc.). It will be interesting to see how this approach to creating a usability standard progresses. In the interim, it is vital when designing, procuring or using displays that those displays adhere to the minimum requirements in the Annex to the DSE Directive and ideally meet the requirements of other parts of ISO 9241 (especially Parts 3, 7 and 8).

It is difficult to identify a single approach to measuring the usability of displays that achieves all the objectives associated with production of the perfect display. Standards provide measures of display 'quality' which, although potentially valid in the laboratory, do not necessarily give any real indication of a display's usability in the real world. This is particularly true in many purchasing departments where the knowledge necessary to translate display specifications into usability criteria is completely absent. Indeed it is often assumed that if a display passes standards then it must be 'OK'. The only real answer is to ensure that relevant standards are considered alongside user-centred design methods and that companies are encouraged to consider the wider picture in terms of actual usage of displays, including the tasks that users are required to carry out and the environment in which they work.

20.6.3   Selecting monitors — a case study

We have been involved in consultancy with a number of organisations who are in the process of migrating from old-style 'dumb-terminals' to PCs connected via local area

Figure 20.12 Users may have special needs

networks (LANs). One of the more interesting projects involved the move to computer-based working for a design team and the move to server-based working for an accounts area. In selecting the displays for the two areas we were required to take into account a number of issues:

(1) Cost — a critical factor in almost every selection process!

(2) Compliance with the UK's Schedule to the DSE Regulations. A lot of companies are concerned that they might buy displays which are somehow 'illegal'. We advised the company to seek assurances from the suppliers that the displays could be configured to meet the minimum requirements laid down in the Schedule (and thus to provide some indemnity to the procurers).

(3) Usage. This is where the bulk of our involvement lay. In providing the monitor specifications we needed to understand the tasks, the environmental constraints and the users' characteristics. Clearly the CAD environment was going to require large monitors, with knock-on effects for desking, lighting and office layout. At this point assurances about the 'compliance' of the display had little meaning. The critical elements were the footprint of the monitor (it required a much bigger desk than the company's standard desk) and the ambient lighting conditions, which caused a significant amount of glare on the large display. The finance department had fewer problems, though the need to free desk space required a number of desks to be fitted with monitor arms. Our basic approach to the project was to conduct a series of usability trials with the short-listed models of display and incorporate into those trials 'generic' risk assessments, aimed at identifying potential risks and then taking steps to reduce the risks as far as possible.

(4) Implementation. At the end of the trials, we identified two monitors, two monitor arms and the requirement for a small number of wrist rests (in the finance department). The equipment was installed and the company undertook a series of DSE risk assessments, to assure themselves that the installation process had not caused any unforeseen problems and to ensure that all the users had received adequate training in the use of the equipment and the necessary adjustment to ensure safe working. The lighting problem was overcome by turning off office lights, removing some tubes and providing some of the CAD Stations with A3 document holders and good quality task lighting. The risk assessments revealed only one other problem, relating to character size on some of the CAD station software. This could be overcome either by better training in the use of the software (as character size was under user control) or by reduced usage of that part of the package.

(5) Conclusions. The project required us to work closely with a range of stakeholders in procurement, IT, finance and design. We also involved Health and Safety to ensure a robust audit trail, demonstrating how we were managing the risks associated with the equipment. At the end of the project, whilst the company did not select the cheapest displays, they certainly selected the most cost-effective and the whole process was well liked by end-users who felt not only that they had been consulted, but also that the new display equipment was more usable.

20.7 CONCLUSIONS

Displays cannot be viewed in isolation — they are part of an IT system, used within the larger work organisation. Even if the display itself meets all the relevant standards, other factors such as the way it is used or the environment in which it is used can still give rise to problems. Usability evaluation must therefore consider more than the display itself and address the wider context of the way it is used, the amount it is used, the environment, etc. One of the most critical issues to be addressed is the education of the marketplace.

Most UK organisations have now implemented risk assessment procedures in response to the new DSE Regulations. Usability problems, which are known to be causal factors in the incidence of injury associated with display use, are very amenable to identification during this sort of assessment, with fairly simple steps being necessary to reduce the risks. Any organisation using displays should certainly be conducting basic risk assessments — ideally by employees with a minimum training in ergonomics who are able to spot basic problems during the assessments. Problems reported by users should be identified, such as those associated with character size, the use of colour and screen stability. Whether assessors will be able to solve all the reported usability problems may depend upon their level of training and the characteristics of the display being assessed. Risk assessment should also aim to highlight issues to feed back into future design and procurement decisions.

Clearly, evaluating the usability of a display is more than just a simple matter of putting a tick against whether you can read the characters shown on the screen. The usability of displays depends on a combination of hardware and software factors and must take account of the end-users, their tasks and working environment. The pressure to meet both legal requirements and international standards for displays will make usability issues increasingly important in any organisation that routinely designs, procures or in any way uses displays, but one may question whether current standards provide adequate regulation. More research is required to show the effects, in both isolation and combination, of various physical parameters of the display in relation to its 'real-world' usability. In addition, much more guidance is necessary to facilitate an appropriate choice of display for a given organisation/application/environment/user.

As is so often the case, it is not the technology itself that is the problem; it is the use and understanding of the technology that is at the root of most problems.

REFERENCES

British Standards Institute BS 7179 (1990), *Ergonomics of Design and Use of Visual Display Terminals (VDTs) in Offices*, British Standards Institute, Milton Keynes, UK.

Chapanis, A. (1991), Evaluating usability, in B. Shackel and S.J. Richardson (eds), *Human Factors for Informatics Usability*, Cambridge University Press, Cambridge, UK.

Clegg, C.W., Warr, P.B., Green, T.R.G., Monk, A., Kemp, N., Allison, G. and Londsdale, M. (1988), *People and Computers: How to Evaluate Your Company's New Technology*, Ellis Horwood, Chichester, UK.

Council Directive (1990), 90/270/EEC Minimum safety and health requirements for work with display screen equipment, *Official Journal of the European Communities*, No. L156/14, 20.6.90.

DTI (1986), *Profiting from Office Automation*, Office Automation Pilots, Department of Trade and Industry, London.

Grandjean, E. (1987), *Ergonomics in Computerised Offices*, Taylor & Francis, London.

Health and Safety (Display Screen Equipment) Regulations (1992), Statutory Instruments No. 2792.

Health and Safety Executive (1992), *Display Screen Equipment Work: Guidance on Regulations*, HMSO, London.

HUFIT (1989), *HUFIT: Planning, Analysis and Specification Toolset*, ESPRIT Project 385, final report, Directorate General XIII, Brussels.

International Business Machines (1987), *Systems Application Architecture: Common User Access*, IBM Corporation.

International Business Machines (1991), *Systems Application Architecture: Common User Access, Guide to User Interface Design*, IBM Corporation.

International Standard 9241 (1992), *Ergonomic Requirements for Office Work with Visual Display Terminals (VDTs) — Part 3: Visual Display Requirements*, International organisation for Standardisation, Geneva, Switzerland.

Moshowitz, A. (1976), *The Conquest of Will: Information Processing in Human Affairs*, Addison-Wesley, Reading, MA.

MUSiC (1993), *Performance Metrics Toolkit*, ESPRIT Project 5429, final report, Directorate General XIII, Brussels.

Open Software Foundation (1992), *Motif Style Guide*, Open Software Foundation, 0-13-640491-X.

Ravden, S. and Johnson, G. (1989), *Evaluating Usability of Human–Computer Interfaces: A Practical Method*, Ellis Horwood, Chichester, UK.

SEK (Svenska Elektriska Kommissionen) (1990), *MPR 2*, Swedish National Board for Measurement and Testing.

Sellers, D. (1994), *Zap!*, Peachpit Press, Berkeley, CA.

Travis, D. (1991), *Effective Colour Displays — Theory and Practice*, Academic Press.

Index